The Future Population of the World

What Can We Assume

Revised 1996 Edition

Edited by

Wolfgang Lutz

International Institute for Applied Systems Analysis
Laxenburg, Austria

185 383 3444

The International Institute for Applied Systems Analysis

is an interdisciplinary, nongovernmental research institution founded in 1972 by lead scientific organizations in 12 countries. Situated near Vienna, in the center of Europe, IIA has been for more than two decades producing valuable scientific research on econon technological, and environmental issues.

IIASA was one of the first international institutes to systematically study global iss of environment, technology, and development. IIASA's Governing Council states t the Institute's goal is: *to conduct international and interdisciplinary scientific studie provide timely and relevant information and options, addressing critical issues of glo environmental, economic, and social change, for the benefit of the public, the scien community, and national and international institutions.* Research is organized around th central themes:

- Global Environmental Change;
- Global Economic and Technological Change;
- Systems Methods for the Analysis of Global Issues.

The Institute now has national member organizations in the following countries:

Austria
The Austrian Academy of Sciences

Bulgaria
The National Committee for Applied
Systems Analysis and Management

Canada
The Canadian Committee for IIASA

Czech Republic
The Czech Committee for IIASA

Finland
The Finnish Committee for IIASA

Germany
The Association for the Advancement
of IIASA

Hungary
The Hungarian Committee for Applied
Systems Analysis

Italy
The Italian Committee for IIASA

Japan
The Japan Committee for IIASA

Kazakstan
The National Academy of Sciences

Netherlands
The Netherlands Organization for
Scientific Research (NWO)

Poland
The Polish Academy of Sciences

Russian Federation
The Russian Academy of Sciences

Slovak Republic
The Slovak Committee for IIASA

Sweden
The Swedish Council for Planning and
Coordination of Research (FRN)

Ukraine
The Ukrainian Academy of Sciences

United States of America
The American Academy of Arts and
Sciences

The Future Population of the World

What Can We Assume Today?

International Institute
for Applied Systems Analysis

Earthscan Publications Ltd, London

Earthscan Publications Ltd
120 Pentonville Road, London N1 9JN
Tel: 0171 278 0433
Fax: 0171 278 1142
Email: earthinfo@earthscan.co.uk

A catalogue record for this book is available from the British Library

ISBN: 1 85383 349 5 paperback
         1 85383 344 4 hardback

Printed and bound in Great Britain by Biddles Limited, Guildford and
King's Lynn

Earthscan Publications Ltd is an editorially independent subsidiary of
Kogan Page Ltd and publishes in association with the International
Institute for Environment and Development and the World Wide Fund
for Nature.

Contents

List of Illustrations   viii

Foreword   xii

Preface   xiv

Introduction   xvi

Contributors   xxi

PART I: Why Another Set of Global Population
Projections?   1

1 Long-range Global Population Projections:
Lessons Learned
Tomas Frejka   3

2 Alternative Approaches to Population Projection
Wolfgang Lutz, Joshua R Goldstein, Christopher Prinz   14

PART II: Future Fertility in Developing Countries   45

3 A Regional Review of Fertility Trends in
Developing Countries: 1960 to 1995
John Cleland   47

4 Reproductive Preferences and Future Fertility in
Developing Countries
Charles F Westoff   73

5 Population Policies and Family-Planning in
Southeast Asia
Mercedes B Concepcion   88

6   Fertility in China: Past, Present, Prospects
    Griffith Feeney   102

PART III: Future Mortality in Developing Countries   131

7   Mortality Trends in Developing Countries:
    A Survey
    Birgitta Bucht   133

8   Mortality in Sub-Saharan Africa:
    Trends and Prospects
    Michel Garenne   149

9   Global Trends in AIDS Mortality
    John Bongaarts   170

10 How Many People Can Be Fed on Earth?
    Gerhard K Heilig   196

PART IV: Future Fertility and Mortality in
Industrialized Countries   251

11 Future Reproductive Behavior in
    Industrialized Countries
    Wolfgang Lutz   253

12 The Future of Mortality at Older Ages in
    Developed Countries
    James W Vaupel and Hans Lundström   278

PART V: The Future of Intercontinental Migration   297

13 Migration to and from Developing Regions:
    A Review of Past Trends
    Hania Zlotnik   299

14 Spatial and Economic Factors in Future
    South–North Migration
    Sture Öberg   336

PART VI: Projections

359

*15 **World Population Scenarios for the 21st Century**
Wolfgang Lutz, Warren Sanderson, Sergei Scherbov,
Anne Goujon

361

*16 **Probabilistic Population Projections Based on Expert Opinion**
Wolfgang Lutz, Warren Sanderson, Sergei Scherbov

397

*17 **Epilogue: Dilemmas in Population Stabilization**
Wolfgang Lutz

429

Appendix Tables

437

References

463

Index

495

Illustrations

Figures

2.1   Components of uncertainty entering population projections.   21

4.1   The nuptiality–fertility model for 216 regions.   82

6.1   Fertility decline in China compared with fertility decline in other areas in the developing world.   104

6.2   Rate of fertility decline and log population size in Asia.   108

6.3   Conventional total fertility rates in China.   110

6.4   Mean age at first marriage in China.   112

6.5   Approximate annual numbers of first marriages in China.   113

6.6   Total fertility rates calculated from period parity progression ratios in China.   118

6.7   Period parity progression ratios in China.   121

6.8   Observed and estimated total fertility rates in China.   125

8.1   Crude death rates in Dakar and Saint-Louis (Senegal).   151

8.2   Estimated mortality trends in Senegal.   156

8.3   Estimated mortality trends in Zambia.   161

8.4   Estimated mortality trends in Uganda.   162

8.5   Estimated mortality trends in Central Mozambique.   163

8.6   Estimated mortality trends in Kenya.   165

8.7   Estimated adult mortality trends in Abidjan.   165

8.8   Famine areas and locations of major wars in Africa.   166

9.1   Estimated levels of HIV seroprevalence (percentage of adults infected) for urban populations in Africa.   174

9.2   Estimated trends in HIV prevalence among adults.   177

9.3   Estimates and medium projections for incidence rates of HIV infections, AIDS cases, and AIDS deaths among adults.   180

9.4   Estimates and projections of annual number of HIV infections and AIDS cases among adults, world total.   183

9.5   Projection of deaths due to AIDS as a percentage of deaths from all causes.   187

9.6   Impact of the AIDS epidemic on the death rate and population growth rate in Rakai District, Uganda.   192

10.1   Model for analyzing the earth's carrying capacity.   200

11.1   Age-specific marriage rates for women in Sweden and USA.   256

11.2   Total divorce rates in selected European countries.   258

11.3	Total fertility rates in five selected industrialized countries.	261
11.4	Completed fertility rate for 1940–1963 birth cohorts.	262
11.5	Total fertility rates, 1965–1995, and assumptions until 2030–2035 in North America and Western Europe.	277
12.1	Force of mortality for females, ages 85, 90, and 95, Sweden.	284
12.2	Force of mortality for males, ages 85, 90, and 95, Sweden.	285
12.3	Force of mortality for females, ages 80–111, Sweden.	289
12.4	Force of mortality for males, ages 80–111, Sweden.	289
14.1	The world regions used in this book.	338
14.2	Ethnic territories and national boundaries in Africa.	343
14.3	Hard and soft push factors of migration.	346
14.4	Potential emigration areas.	348
14.5	The gap between demand for cheap labor in the North and the South.	350
15.1	Alternative projected paths of world population size.	377
15.2	Alternative paths of population size in North America.	381
15.3	World population in high-fertility/high-mortality scenario.	384
15.4	World population in low-fertility/low-mortality scenario.	385
15.5	Alternative projected trends in the proportion of population above age 60 in China and CPA.	386
15.6	Projected population size in sub-Saharan Africa.	390
16.1	Future population size in the European FSU.	408
16.2	Future population size in North America.	409
16.3	Percentage of the population in the 0–14 age group in North America and the European FSU.	414
16.4	Percentage of the population in the 60+ age group in North America and the European FSU.	415
16.5	Probability distribution of population, regions dependent and independent; fertility and mortality independent.	420
16.6	Merged distribution of the population sizes of the world.	422
16.7	Merged distribution of world population in 0–14 age group.	423
16.8	Merged distribution of world population in 60+ age group.	424
17.1	Unavoidable and avoidable world population growth to 2050.	432

Tables

1.1	Long-term global population projections.	5
2.1	Major characteristics of our projection approach.	42
3.1	Fertility trends in East and Southeast Asia.	50
3.2	Fertility trends in continental South Asia.	54
3.3	Fertility trends in Latin America.	58
3.4	Year of onset of decline and percentage decline in following decade in Latin America.	59
3.5	Fertility trends in the Arab states.	62

3.6	Fertility levels in sub-Saharan Africa.	65
3.7	Fertility trends in island states.	68
4.1	Indices of reproductive preferences of married women.	75
4.2	Forecasts of reproductive preferences, contraceptive prevalence, and fertility.	78
4.3	Linear regression equations for variables related to number of children desired by women aged 25–29.	84
6.1	Total fertility rates in China and in other major areas in the developing world.	105
6.2	Comparative data on fertility decline in Asia.	106
6.3	Total fertility rates and mean age at marriage in China.	111
6.4	Parity progression ratios for selected populations.	116
6.5	Period progression ratios and total fertility rates in China.	120
7.1	Estimated and projected life expectancy at birth.	135
7.2	Model for mortality improvement, quinquennial gains in life expectancy at birth by initial level of mortality.	142
7.3	Maximum life expectancies in UN mortality decline models.	142
7.4	Estimated and projected life expectancy at birth for less developed regions, both sexes, UN assessments.	145
7.5	Estimated and projected life expectancy at birth for less developed regions, both sexes, World Bank assessments.	145
8.1	Estimates of child mortality in sub-Saharan Africa prior to 1960, probability of dying before age 5.	152
8.2	Estimates of child mortality in sub-Saharan Africa 1960–1990, probability of dying before age 5.	153
8.3	Values of socioeconomic indicators.	158
8.4	Mean annual rates of change in socioeconomic indicators.	159
8.5	Elasticities of $q(5)$ with respect to various socioeconomic indicators, in 36 countries of continental tropical Africa.	160
9.1	Cumulative number of adults infected with HIV, cumulative AIDS deaths, number of infected adults, and percentage of adults infected by region at the end of 1994.	173
9.2	High, medium, and low variants of cumulative HIV infections, AIDS cases, and AIDS deaths among adults in 2005.	184
9.3	Projected annual number of child deaths due to AIDS, percentage of births ending in AIDS deaths, and deaths among children as a percentage of all AIDS deaths.	185
9.4	Projected annual number of AIDS deaths, percentage of all deaths due to AIDS, and AIDS death rate.	186
9.5	Birth, death, and growth rates with and without AIDS.	190
10.1	Estimates of the earth's population carrying capacity during the past 100 years.	197
10.2	Cropland in percent of land without soil constraints.	206
10.3	Lifestyle-related and nonfood agricultural production.	212

10.4	Freshwater resources and withdrawals for selected countries.	214
11.1	Marital-status above age 15 in selected European countries.	255
11.2	Evolution of nonmarital unions in Europe.	257
11.3	Total fertility rates in 30 industrialized countries.	260
11.4	Responses to question: "[In your country] today what do you think is the ideal number of children for a family like yours or the one you might have?"	263
11.5	Responses to questions on family size in Austria from women married five to eight years.	264
12.1	Average annual rates of progress in reducing mortality rates.	286
12.2	Age when remaining life expectancy is two or five years.	291
13.1	Average annual number of immigrants originating in the different developing regions and average annual net migration by country of destination and period.	306
13.2	Average annual number of asylum seekers in Europe.	316
13.3	Average annual number of migrant workers from selected countries of South Asia, East/Southeast Asia, and China.	322
13.4	Distribution of migrant workers originating in countries of East and Southeast Asia by destination.	323
13.5	Annual migration to Saudi Arabia by region of citizenship.	324
14.1	Countries of resettlement of refugees and asylum seekers.	355
15.1	Alternative fertility assumptions used in projections.	364
15.2	Alternative mortality assumptions to 2030–2035.	367
15.3	Assumed high values of annual net migration flows.	370
15.4	Projections of total population according to alternative fertility and mortality assumptions.	376
15.5	Distribution of world population by continent, according to three scenarios and under central migration.	380
15.6	Projections of percentages of the population above age 60 according to alternative fertility and mortality assumptions.	383
15.7	Proportion above age 60 and population size in China and CPA and Pacific OECD under the population-aging/fertility-feedback scenarios.	393
15.8	Most likely projections produced by the United Nations, the US Bureau of the Census, the World Bank, and IIASA.	395
16.1	Forecasts and 95 percent CI for US population around 2065.	402
16.2	Population by regions, independent case.	407
16.3	Percentage of the population in the 0–14 age group.	412
16.4	Percentage of the population in the 60+ age group.	413
16.5	Mean, median, and 95 percent CI for sub-Saharan Africa.	418
16.6	Summary of world population projections with different assumptions of the correlation between fertility and mortality both within and between regions.	418

Foreword

Forecasting is one of the oldest of demographic activities, and yet it has never been fully integrated with the main body of demographic theory and data. The fact that the public regards it as our most important task finds no reflection in our research agenda; the amount of it done is out of all proportion to the fraction of space devoted to it in professional journals. The best demographers do it, but none would stake their reputation on the agreement of their forecasts with the subsequent realization – in fact some of the most eminent demographers have been the authors of the widest departures.

Demographers do not use the departures as data for learning how to improve their skills; in fact they rarely even look back at forecasts made 10 or 20 years earlier to note what the errors have been. Anyone who expects that after a census is taken there will be a flurry of articles recalling previous forecasts and congratulating or condemning will be disappointed. Writers merely go on to forecast the next following census, usually without even a glance at their past errors.

The present volume is designed to correct this unsatisfactory condition. Its writers include some of the best-known names in the profession, as well as younger people who in due course will succeed them as leaders. They systematically go through the components of future population – births, deaths, migration – that for any individual include all the possible ways of entering or leaving the world or any country in it. The chapters explore the possibilities of bringing the best demographic methods to the improvement of our knowledge of future population. Few show any defensiveness in regard to their own earlier forecasts; the approach throughout is fresh and original.

By bringing to bear the best of demographic knowledge on an application whose importance has recently been accentuated by concern with environment, this book will provide a valuable contribution in its own right, and at the same time be a stimulus to further needed research.

Nathan Keyfitz
International Institute for
Applied Systems Analysis

Preface to the 1996 Edition

The 1990s are developing into a period of significant demographic changes in many parts of the world. The unexpected political and economic transformations in Eastern Europe brought about dramatic demographic consequences such as precipitously declining birth rates and increasing death rates, especially for men. In Russia male life expectancy has recently declined by an estimated seven years. However, at the global level, the rapid fertility declines in Southern Asia and the fact that the fertility transition in Africa finally seems to have gained momentum have had a greater influence than the changes in Eastern Europe. Also, fertility in China has further declined below replacement level. Available data indicate that fertility declined in every world region between 1990 and 1995. At the same time, AIDS and other infectious diseases have recently depressed the prospects for mortality improvements in many developing countries. The combination of decreasing fertility and higher than expected mortality means declines in world population growth. Indeed, most world population projections now call for somewhat lower growth than the forecasts presented earlier in the decade.

The population projections included in the first edition of *The Future Population of the World* were based on 1990 data and did not reflect these recent changes in the starting population. Hence, when the publisher asked us whether we wanted to include any revisions in a new edition of the book we decided to make the effort of recalculating the projections with a 1995 starting year. We also introduced a number of technical improvements, such as additional age groups at the high end (up to age 120) and adjustments in the mortality schedules. Also the definition of geographic regions was modified slightly to conform with that used by other IIASA projects. Most of the substantive background chapters in the volume were revised and updated. The chapter on AIDS in Africa was replaced by a recent paper on global AIDS mortality by the same author.

What is most important is that this volume reflects a further evolution of how to deal with uncertainty in population projections. We decided to go beyond the alternative scenario approach that was used in the first edition (and is still used in Chapter 15) and to present a fully probabilistic set of projections with confidence intervals based on expert opinion on probability distributions of fertility, mortality, and migration in the 13 world regions (as discussed in Chapters 2 and 16). To my knowledge this is the first published set of probabilistic world population projections.

Wolfgang Lutz
Leader, Population Project
Spring 1996

Introduction

Public interest in population research seems to follow a cyclical pattern of ups and downs that is not directly related to demographic trends. Whereas the 1960s and early 1970s was a period of international upsurge in public concern about population and demographic research, during the 1980s population hardly made it into the headlines. Currently, we are experiencing a new wave of public interest in world population growth which is largely fueled by ecological concerns. Population growth has been mentioned repeatedly in international fora and the media as one of the driving forces, if not the single most important factor, in global environmental change. But this time it is natural scientists rather than demographers who point at the importance of the issue.

Demographers remain conspicuously silent in the face of the attention suddenly given to an issue they have carefully studied for decades, while researchers in other disciplines attempt to occupy this territory. Demographers, who should have better knowledge of population dynamics and the determinants of fertility, mortality, and migration, tend to be embarrassed over frequent oversimplifications in the present debate, and also tend to be puzzled over how to approach the highly complex issue of population–environment interaction. Scientists from other disciplines are often less cautious in making statements about the role of population and do not always apply the same rules of scientific scrutiny to population studies that they apply to their own discipline. It is also problematic when scientific paradigms from the natural sciences and animal ecology are directly applied to complex social systems.

Without a doubt this new interest in population issues presents new challenges and opportunities for demographers and social scientists in general. Instead of retreating from this territory of increasingly interdisciplinary population analysis, the demographic community could show flexibility and directly address some of the well-justified questions asked by the outside world. These questions are discussed in Chapter 2 of this volume. One central question in this context regards possible future population trends in the face of ecological constraints and new threats to human life. An increasing number of people want to know more about possible alternative population trends than the information provided in standard population projections. Such people include scholars in energy analysis who want long-range population scenarios as inputs to their models; regional planners, politicians, and business leaders who want to develop robust strategies that hold under different possible future population patterns; and an increasing number of individuals who are simply interested in the topic. These nondemographers often want to know more about the assumptions made, their justifications, and the range of uncertainty than has been given to them up to now by demographers.

This volume has been produced because of the belief that the demographic community can do more in terms of summarizing its knowledge about future population trends than has been done in the past. In this, the book attempts to serve a dual purpose: to respond to the challenge of increased outside interest in alternative future population trends and to advance within the demographic community the discussion on the approaches and assumptions to be chosen for population projections. By summarizing essential results of demographic research and how they relate to a broad range of relevant issues, the volume may also serve as a textbook.

The volume's approach follows that of an earlier book, *Future Demographic Trends in Europe and North America: What Can We Assume Today?* (Lutz, ed., 1991, Academic Press, London, UK). The basic idea is to devote the bulk of space to substantive deliberations of experts with partly differing views about possible future trends in the three components of population change (fertility, mortality, and migration), and then translate these opinions into alternative projections. In this book the geographic focus is widened to encompass all world regions, and the treatment of uncertainty is more elaborate than in the above-mentioned book.

Part I of the volume addresses the question, Why another set of global population projections? It starts with a comprehensive survey of past long-range global population projections in Chapter 1 written by Tomas Frejka, who in the early 1970s produced the most influential set of long-range projections following Notestein's work of 1945 and introduced the concept of convergence toward replacement-level fertility. In his contribution, Frejka emphasizes the lessons learned from past projections and points at desirable features of new world population projections. In Chapter 2, Wolfgang Lutz, Joshua Goldstein, and Christopher Prinz discuss some basic questions in population projections which are rarely addressed in an explicit way. The chapter, entitled "Alternative Approaches to Population Projection," deals with such issues as who is interested in projections, what output parameters are desired, what time horizons are appropriate, and how to handle uncertainty. Chapter 2 also presents and justifies the specific approach chosen for this study.

Part II is dedicated to future fertility in today's developing countries. It consists of four chapters dealing with different aspects of this issue which will dominate the extent of future world population growth. In Chapter 3, John Cleland gives a comprehensive survey of regional fertility trends between 1960 and 1995 and the factors behind these changes. This chapter serves as an important basis for the IIASA fertility assumptions. Chapter 4, by Charles Westoff, is more explicitly oriented toward the future; it summarizes the extensive empirical evidence on reproductive preferences and discusses their implications for the future course of fertility decline. From this analysis, powerful arguments can be derived for assuming fertility declines, at least in the near future. In Chapter 5, Mercedes Concepcion looks at another important factor in determining future fertility levels, namely, the role of population policies and family-planning programs. Based on the experience from Southeast Asia, she shows that such programs can make a big difference if certain preconditions are met. In Chapter 6, Griffith Feeney gives an account of the amazing fertility changes in China. Based on the analysis of parity progression ratios, he also derives some alternative scenarios for future fertility in that country, which currently is home to one-fifth of the world's population.

Part III of the volume looks at future mortality in developing countries. It also consists of four chapters. An introductory chapter by Birgitta Bucht (Chapter 7) provides a comprehensive analysis of recent mortality trends in the different developing regions. Michel Garenne in Chapter 8 focuses on mortality in sub-Saharan Africa, the world region with the greatest uncertainties. One of the uncertainties, the mortality impact of AIDS, is explicitly addressed in Chapter 9 by John Bongaarts. Finally, Gerhard Heilig in Chapter 10 addresses a crucial question which is usually excluded from population projections, namely, Will there be enough food to feed all the people projected or is famine-related mortality likely to increase at some point? His conclusion is that, at least for the next decades, global food supplies should be sufficient under favorable political conditions.

Part IV considers fertility and mortality in today's industrialized countries. It has two chapters but, in the discussion, reference is also made to the 14 chapters included in an earlier book on that topic (Lutz, 1991). Lutz in Chapter 11 considers various arguments that would suggest further fertility declines in today's low-fertility countries as well as some arguments implying higher fertility. James Vaupel and Hans Lundström in Chapter 12 focus on the controversial issue of future old-age mortality in developed societies. For making future mortality assumptions over many decades in countries that already have female life expectancies of around 80 years, the question of an upper limit to the human life span becomes decisive.

Part V of the volume considers migration between the world regions. International migration is a weak point in most population projections because of missing data and the volatility of migration trends. For these reasons it has sometimes been omitted in population studies; this omission results in the assumption of zero net-migration. This volume makes an effort to deal with migration more explicitly than it has been dealt with in the past. In Chapter 13, Hania Zlotnik uses the best data available to present a systematic analysis of past interregional migration flows. This is complemented by a very broad consideration of possible future migration patterns by Sture Öberg in Chapter 14. Taken together, these two chapters provide a basis for making alternative assumptions on future interregional migration flows that have a status that is equal to the fertility and mortality assumptions used in the scenario calculations presented in the final section.

Part VI presents the actual population projections for 13 world regions with assumptions based on the substantive considerations given in all previous chapters. Lutz, Warren Sanderson, Sergei Scherbov, and Anne Goujon present two very different sets of population projections to 2100. The first set, described in Chapter 15, includes 27 scenarios giving all possible combinations of high, central, and low values in fertility, mortality, and migration in all world regions. It also gives a number of special scenarios assuming interactions between the components and feedbacks from the results. Chapter 16 goes further and provides a fully probabilistic projection of all world regions. To my knowledge this is the first such attempt; it is based entirely on expert assumptions about the uncertainty distributions of future fertility, mortality, and migration trends. Extensive Appendix Tables at the end of the book document the results. There is also a section comparing IIASA's projections with those of other institutions.

An epilogue by Lutz puts the results of the projection exercises back into the broader perspective of global change and international controversies surrounding population issues. It considers two necessary trade-offs which are not always recognized in the political debates – namely, that between curbing population growth and rapid population aging and that between slower growth and lower mortality. The epilogue also distinguishes between future population trends that are inevitable and those that can be influenced somewhat by human activities and changes in behavior. There still is a wide range of uncertainty and room for alternative choices that may have significant impact. This book attempts to summarize the demographic knowledge on which these choices can be based.

Wolfgang Lutz

Contributors

John Bongaarts
The Population Council
New York, New York, USA

Birgitta Bucht
Population Division
United Nations
New York, New York, USA

John Cleland
Centre for Population Studies
London School of Hygiene and
  Tropical Medicine
London, UK

Mercedes B Concepcion
The Population Institute
University of Philippines
Diliman, Quezon City, Philippines

Griffith Feeney
Program on Population
East–West Center
Honolulu, Hawaii, USA

Tomas Frejka
United Nations
Economic Commission for Europe
Geneva, Switzerland

Michel Garenne
Centre Français sur la Population
  et le Développement
Paris, France

Joshua R Goldstein
Department of Demography
University of California
Berkeley, California, USA

Anne Goujon
International Institute for
  Applied Systems Analysis
Laxenburg, Austria

Gerhard K Heilig
International Institute for
  Applied Systems Analysis
Laxenburg, Austria

Hans Lundström
Statistics Sweden
Stockholm, Sweden

Wolfgang Lutz
International Institute for
  Applied Systems Analysis
Laxenburg, Austria

Sture Öberg
Department of Social and
  Economic Geography
University of Uppsala, Sweden
and IIASA

Christopher Prinz
European Centre for Social
  Welfare Policy and Research
Vienna, Austria

Warren Sanderson
State University of New York
Stony Brook, New York, USA
and IIASA

Charles F Westoff
Office of Population Research
Princeton University
Princeton, New Jersey, USA

Sergei Scherbov
University of Groningen
Groningen, Netherlands
and IIASA

Hania Zlotnik
Population Division
United Nations
New York, New York, USA

James W Vaupel
Odense University Medical School
Odense, Denmark

Part I

Why Another Set of Global Population Projections?

The two contributions in Part I provide a framework for the substantive presentations in Parts II through V and in particular for the projections discussed in Part VI. The chapters show that the generation of new world population projections is useful provided that the approach followed (a) uses the most recent demographic data; (b) reflects the current scientific knowledge of the relevant disciplines; (c) considers several possible future trends in all three demographic components (fertility, mortality, and migration); (d) leaves room for substantive considerations of justifiable alternative future trends in the components; and (e) possibly improves the way projections deal with uncertainty or considers the interactions between the demographic variables and their socioeconomic and natural environments. The projections presented in this volume try to meet these criteria.

Users of population projections generally demand two types of information from population projections: (a) one most likely projections that can be used as a guideline and (b) information about the range of uncertainty for sensitivity analyses and for testing the robustness of certain strategies (or policies). Several users – especially environmental modelers – demand projections until the end of the 21st century.

To meet these demands the alternative assumptions defined by the group of experts are extended to the end of 21st century in Chapters 15 and 16. They provide users with one most likely path, a broad range of alternative scenarios, and a fully probabilistic projection.

Chapter 1

Long-range Global Population Projections: Lessons Learned

Tomas Frejka

Gregory King (1648–1712), the first known creator of long-range global population projections, wrote that "if the World should continue to A° Mundi [anno mundi] 20,000 [A.D. 16,052] it might then have 6,500 million" (King, 1696). In reality, the world's population will reach the number projected by King early in the next century, most likely in about 10 years from the writing of this chapter. In hindsight his projection left much to be desired. But did he provide knowledge and insights that were interesting and valuable to his contemporaries?

This chapter provides an overview of the leading long-term population projections that have been developed to date: their basic characteristics and an examination of this experience to extract the lessons learned and to attempt to formulate some general principles on what makes long-range projections interesting and useful and what kinds of circumstances justify the creation of a new set of projections. As a rule, to which there will be some exceptions, this chapter deals only with long-range population projections – i.e., those that span over a century or more.

Frejka (1981a) introduces a classification of global population projections which distinguishes between extrapolations of total numbers and global component projections. The latter are component

---

This chapter uses a significant part of the work done in Frejka (1981a).

projections in two senses: demographic components (fertility, mortality, and age structure) and country and region components that are aggregated into global projections. Progress from the former to the latter was historically the basic methodological innovation. In this chapter we briefly review other new ideas and methods as they are being applied in the preparation of long-range global population projections.

1.1 Early Global Projections: Extrapolations

The few global population projections made up to the mid-20th century tended to be long range and were based on extrapolations of total numbers (*Table 1.1*). The authors (King, 1696; Knibbs, 1928; Pearl, 1924; Pearl and Gould, 1936) based these projections on their respective observations of population growth rates and of mechanisms of population growth that were believed to regulate human population change. The reason for concern about future population growth was anxiety with regard to the world's carrying capacity. The method used by King and Knibbs was very simple. They applied the current estimated population growth rates to the estimated size of the population.

Pearl undertook extensive research which led him to believe that there is a law according to which growth of populations (not only human) takes place, that this law is in principle shaped by biological and environmental forces, and that the resulting trend can be expressed mathematically in various forms of the stretched out S-shaped logistic curve. In 1924 Pearl calculated the curve for the world population and subsequently, in 1936, together with Gould he revised the curve for the world population upward arguing that there is a "necessity for frequent revision of human population logistics as new data become available."

1.2 Modern Global Component Projections

The evolution of population theory and methods, as well as the continuously greater availability of demographic data, has provided the base for developing more sophisticated population projections.

Table 1.1. Long-term global population projections.

Author	Year	Alternative	Population (in millions)					
			To 1950	1950	1970	2000	2050	2100
King	1696		630 (B=1695)				780 (2052)	
Pearl	1924		1649 (B=1914)	1832	1901	1963	2007	2020
Knibbs	1928		1950 (B=1928)			3900 (2008)		15600 (2169)
Pearl & Gould	1936		2073 (B=1931)	2153	2305	2459	2582	2625
Notestein	1945					3300		
Frejka	1973	NRR=1.0						
		2040				6670	13025	15102
		2020				6422	10473	11169
		2000			3645(B)	5923	8172	8389
		1980				5116	6286	6417
		1970				4746	5592	5691
UN	1974	Medium			3621(B)	6406	11163	12257
Littman & Keyfitz	1977				3968 (B=1975)	5882	8188	
UN	1978	High				6509	12076	14180
		Medium			4033	6199	9775	10525
		Low			(B=1975)	5856	8004	8029
Bogue & Tsui	1979	High				5972		
		Medium			B=1975	5883	8107	
		Low				5756	7816	
World Bank	1980				4416 (B=1980)	6015		9868 (stat.)
Frejka	1980	NRR=1.0						
		plausible high				6353	11015	12348
		2040				6357	11648	13427
		2020			4412	6234	9902	10639
		2000			(B=1980)	5930	8214	8539
		1980				5333	6743	6986
		plausible low				6046	8762	9208
UN	1982	Growth			4441	6337	11690	14927
		High			4441	6337	11629	14199
		Medium			4432	6119	9513	10185
		Low			4420	5837	7687	7524
		Decline			4420 (B=1980)	5837	7667	7247
World Bank	1985				4442 (B=1980)	6147	9496	10681 (stat.)
UN	1992	High			5327	6420	12506	19156
		Medium/High			5327	6420	12495	17592
		Medium			5292	6261	10019	11186
		Medium/Low			5262	6093	7817	6415
		Low			5262 (B=1990)	6093	7813	6009

B stands for base year of projection; NRR stands for net reproduction rate.
Sources: See references.

The leading scholar who transformed the potentiality into reality was Frank Notestein. The methodology of component population projections was first applied in a study of Europe and the Soviet Union commissioned by the League of Nations in the early 1940s (Notestein *et al.*, 1944). This study was perceived as the first volume of a series of studies on world population trends and problems. Soon thereafter, Notestein (1945) presented the first modern global population projections. He reviewed past population trends of countries and continents; he discussed his understanding of the mechanisms of population change, distinguishing three main demographic types of populations corresponding to different stages of the "demographic evolution" ("incipient decline," "transitional growth," and "high growth potential"); and finally, he discussed prospects for growth and provided projections separately by continent on the basis of which he concluded that "summing the hypothetical figures for the year 2000, we have a world total of 3.3 billion people. On the assumption of general order and the spread of modern techniques of production the figure is probably conservative." Even though it spanned only over a period of half a century, Notestein's projection of the world population is discussed in this chapter because of its pioneering nature and because the applied ideas, approach, and methods provided the base for a generation of world, regional, and national projections to follow.

Notestein's projections permit the formulation of general characteristics and procedures that constitute the *basis* of long-range population projections:

- An explicit or implicit *theoretical framework* of the mechanisms of population change, which guides the formulation of assumptions about future changes in demographic trends.
- A wealth of accumulated *demographic data* which serves as the empirical base for the framework, provides the input data for the benchmark year/period of the projections, and makes possible a disaggregated approach.
- A *methodology* which usually consists of (a) a separate assessment of an initial age structure and separate projection of the two motor forces of demographic dynamics in a closed population – mortality and fertility (the combination of these elements

yields the so-called component projection of a population) – and
(b) a separate assessment and projection of national and/or regional populations, which, when aggregated, yield global projections or which provide a check on separately computed global
projections.

• Advances in any of these characteristics and procedures depend
on advances of demographic and social science research as well
as on advances in data collection.

Notestein's contribution was not only important because he applied and combined all of the above elements but also critical from a
substantive perspective. His theoretical framework is based on the
demographic transition theory labeled the "demographic evolution"
in Notestein's 1945 piece. It is the demographic transition theory
which – for the most part implicitly – is the theoretical base for
the majority of the global long-range population projections that
followed.

The sets of the United Nations population projections of the
1950s and 1960s followed Notestein's model, with refinements being
introduced as methods of demographic analysis developed and new
data became available. The time span of these projections was from
30 to 45 years. A particularly innovative set was prepared in 1957
(UN, 1958) which made considerable use of sophisticated methods in
estimating demographic parameters and in the projection computa-
tions. For these projections the UN (1955) prepared a set of model
life tables, as well as models of fertility trends. This was the first
UN projection extended to the year 2000, for which time a global
population ranging between 4.9 and 6.9 billion was projected. As we
approach the year 2000 it now appears that the UN's 1957 medium
projection will come remarkably close to what the actual figure for
the year 2000 is likely to be, 6.3 billion. The central objective of the
UN sets was defined as "an attempt to project population changes
into the future as accurately as possible with available information
to provide basic data on population size and characteristics for future planning" (UN, 1973). The focus of population projections up
to this point in time was on providing the best possible, "as accurate
as possible," projection, forecast, or even prediction.

1.3   Contemporary Long-range Projections

The first set of long-range projections to follow Notestein's work
of 1945 was developed by Frejka (1973a) in the early 1970s (the
ideas and methods applied were originally developed in a study of
the US population in Frejka, 1968). These projections were meant
to demonstrate the strength of the population growth momentum
inherent in current demographic characteristics – age structure and
levels as well as age-specific structures of fertility and mortality –
and the strength of behavioral continuities. The principal innovation
was to prepare *scenario projections* in contrast to projections that
were aimed at projecting future demographic trends as accurately
as possible. More specifically, these projections were designed:

- To map alternative scenarios of how the demographic transition
  could proceed toward an assumed low mortality–low fertility
  equilibrium expressed by a net reproduction rate of unity being
  reached at defined alternative future dates.
- To illustrate the long-range implications for population growth
  of specific demographic, mainly fertility, trends.
- To demonstrate the more likely alternatives of future population growth in the context of unrealistic/unlikely projections
  based on implausibly rapid or implausibly slow assumed trends
  of fertility decline.

The emphasis was on generating illustrative scenario projections, not on generating projections that would aim at depicting
future trends as accurately as possible. At the same time, however,
there was a clear intention to supply a good idea of likely future
trends by providing the possibility of comparing more realistic alternatives with what appeared to be clearly unrealistic options. The
projections were computed for a period of almost 200 years rather
than the customary period of between 30 and 50 years (for instance,
the UN projections).

The assumption that a low fertility–low mortality stationary
population could be achieved and possibly maintained in the long
run appeared quite plausible in light of the trends in the demographically mature countries through the late 1960s. There seemed to be
a reasonable (tacit) consensus at the time that post-demographic

transition societies would stabilize, with fertility and mortality being such that the long-term net reproduction rate average would be around unity. In hindsight, the experience of Western countries, particularly since the early 1970s, has not confirmed this assumption.

These projections provided a vivid illustration of the long-term consequences for population growth of demographic trends, mainly of fertility, of the foreseeable future, say of the 1970s and 1980s, which presumably could be modified by public policies. While the calculations of the global population for the year 2050, for example, ranged between 5.6 and 13.0 billion (see *Table 1.1*), it was argued that the alternative results yielding figures below 8 billion could be dismissed as unrealistic because the calculations were based on assumptions of unrealistically rapid fertility decline. With considerably less certainty the numbers at the upper limits of the range were cast in doubt, as historical experience seemed to indicate that fertility would be likely to decline faster than the defined assumptions for the high projection. Consequently, it was argued that the global population in the middle of the next century would probably be between 8 and 12 billion and that whether the actual population would be closer to the upper or lower limit would depend on how vigorously major factors shaping fertility decline, including public policies, would exert their impact.

During the 1970s and 1980s various institutions, in particular the UN (1975, 1981b, 1982b, 1992c) but also the World Bank (Zachariah and Vu, 1978, 1980; Vu, 1985), the US Bureau of the Census (1979), and individuals (Littman and Keyfitz, 1977; Bogue and Tsui, 1979) prepared long-range projections. To a large extent, these projections used a principle analogous to Frejka's projections, namely, that they were scenario projections aiming, sooner or later, for an eventual low mortality–low fertility equilibrium. Many did introduce additional ideas/arguments or methodological refinements.

In their projections of the early 1970s, the UN adjusted the models for the future course of fertility in both the developed and developing countries, and introduced the reverse logistic curve (a stretched-out reverse S) with specified time points at which replacement-level fertility will be reached and, beyond it, sustained.

A notable departure from the principle of aiming at eventual replacement-level fertility is contained in the UN 1992 projections where the experience of below replacement-level fertility in the Western countries is reflected. The idea of reaching and maintaining replacement-level fertility is assumed only for the medium variant and for an instant replacement-level fertility projection. Two variants assume reaching and maintaining below replacement-level fertility, two other projections assume a fertility decline that is above replacement-level fertility which when the defined level is reached it is maintained, and a fifth projection assumes constant fertility and mortality. Among the conclusions of these recent projections, the UN stresses that according to the medium projection the world population would be 11.2 billion in the year 2100 which is 1 billion, or 10 percent, larger than the UN 1982 projections. According to the UN, "upwardly revised estimated and projected average life expectancies at birth probably play the key role." Also, there is a much wider range between the lowest and highest results in the 1992 compared with the 1982 projections for the year 2100, namely, 6.0–19.2 compared with 7.2–14.9 billion. The authors emphasize "that there is a wide range of uncertainty regarding the future size of the world population."

Bogue and Tsui (1979) reached a very different conclusion, albeit over a decade earlier: "the magnitude and pace of the (1965–1975 fertility) decline is greater than many demographers had expected" and therefore

> this development makes it necessary for demographers to review and re-examine their projections for the future. We predict that by the year 2025 the world will have nearly achieved zero population growth. It is estimated that this equilibrium will be achieved with a world population of about 7.4 billion (8.1 in 2050)...primarily because of the worldwide drive by Third World countries to introduce family planning as part of their national social-development services.

In the early 1970s studies associated with the Club of Rome introduced ambitious methodological innovations. An attempt was made to link population projections more tightly to social, economic, environmental, resource consumption, and political trends. Meadows *et al.* (1972) and Mesarovic and Pestel (1974) defined global dynamic systems analysis models that contained population as one of several basic components. Projections of these systems were carried into the 21st century to demonstrate possible disastrous or harmonious long-term consequences inherent in global societal trends. According to these projections, the likely trends in population growth as well as in other societal trends will lead to a collapse of the world system. This will include an increase in mortality and a consequent rapid population decline. The studies conclude that if such a collapse is to be avoided, a rapid fertility decline, significantly faster than that of the low UN projection of that era, would have to be generated. These projections were indeed innovative in their comprehensive approach, but numerous critics doubted the validity of employed assumptions and relationships (Ridker, 1973).

1.4 A Recent Critical Review of Long-run Global Projections

A critical review of long-run population projections has recently been undertaken by Lee (1991). He takes a substantive rather than a historic approach. Lee comprehensively analyzes important aspects of population projections: demography's contribution to forecasting, theories underlying projections, the degree of uncertainty of long-run population projections, and recent long-run projections of the global population. Among the numerous insightful observations and findings, many can be applied to future work.

One observation which appears to be a central concern to Lee and which deserves particular attention in the context of this chapter is that in a number of the above-discussed global projections a sufficiently explicit and systematic theoretical framework is lacking. Two views expressed in Lee's paper warrant a brief discussion at this point.

Lee eloquently challenges a central premise applied in the long-range global projections of the 1970s and the 1980s, namely, that the end point of most of these projections are stationary populations with a net reproduction rate of unity. He claims that he could not find any explanation of this in Frejka's 1973 book (see Frejka, 1973a, which according to Lee provides the origin of this idea; actually the origin of the idea is in Frejka, 1968) and criticizes the justification given in Frejka (1981b). Admittedly, the theoretical justification of using replacement-level fertility as an end point might not have been thorough enough, however, it was clear that Frejka's work in the late 1960s and early 1970s was conducted within the demographic transition theory framework as it was understood at that time. If nowhere else this was succinctly expressed in Frejka (1973b): "The experience of history suggests that the population of the world may eventually reach a state close to non-growth, that is, all countries will be in the third stage of the demographic transition."

The second issue relates to the content and purpose of the concept of projections. A basic premise of Lee's, which he states without providing arguments or justification, is that "almost all demographic projections are in fact forecasts, in that they present the author's best guess about the future." Therefore he uses forecasts throughout his piece. As has been discussed at length above, the distinction between *forecasts* – i.e., projections that attempt to depict future trends as accurately as possible at any given moment in time – and *scenario projections* – i.e., projections which introduce elements that aim to illustrate certain developments some of which might actually be intentionally unrealistic in order to demonstrate a particular outcome – is justified. That does not exclude the purpose of *also* attempting to provide a reasonable perception of realistic future population trends through scenario projections.

1.5   Conclusions

Contemporary long-range global population projections of the past 25 years are all constructed along the lines of the Notestein model. They are based on an explicit or implicit theoretical framework, using the best available data, and they are component projections. They are usually straightforward demographic projections where the possible impacts of changes in behavioral, social, economic, or political trends are introduced via the theoretical framework. A basic innovation was added by devising and using scenario projections in contrast to projections aiming at prediction. However, even when using scenario-type projections the intention of more or less approximating likely future demographic trends is almost always present.

The various projections briefly discussed above provide examples of justifications for new projections. At the most general level, whenever a significant innovation can be introduced in any one of the elements a new projection is justified. Thus, formulating a new or different theoretical framework, the application of new data, or the development of a new or different methodology provides such a justification.

Each of the subsequent UN sets of projections used newly collected or estimated base data. Some of these sets introduced methodological advances, and in some the formulation of assumptions about demographic trends was modified based on the developments of actual trends. Bogue and Tsui (1979) based their projections on their interpretation of fertility trends between 1965 and 1975 and on their belief that policy measures in the form of strong family-planning programs could and would modify fertility trends more than experience to date indicated. Meadows *et al.* (1972) attempted to expand the theoretical framework by direct linkage to social, economic, environmental, resource consumption, and political trends and applied a large number of assumptions about trends and linkages. In addition to using new fertility and mortality data, the most recent United Nations long-range global projections (1992) assumed a variety of fertility trends: reaching and maintaining replacement-level fertility, reaching and maintaining fertility levels below and above replacement.

The purpose of long-range global population projections can be more than attempting to predict total population numbers 50, 100, or 150 years into the future. In addition, their purpose can be:

- To demonstrate shorter- and long-run implications of alternative fertility and mortality trends of the foreseeable future.
- To demonstrate what type of trends need to occur to achieve a population of a desirable size and with specific structural characteristics.
- To demonstrate various structural implications of certain fertility and mortality trends for major regions and functional age groups, for example.
- To demonstrate the consequences of intended policy interventions if they were to succeed.

Whatever the purpose of a single projection or a set of projections may be, for them to be meaningful and to provide new insights, a significant and well-justified *new* or *innovative element* has to be embedded in the projections.

Chapter 2

Alternative Approaches to Population Projection

Wolfgang Lutz, Joshua R. Goldstein, Christopher Prinz

Future demographic trends are inherently uncertain, and the further one goes into the future, the greater the uncertainty. On the other hand, few social and economic trends are as stable as population trends. No social scientist would challenge the statement that the percentage increase of the world population over the next five years can be more accurately projected than changes in unemployment rates, trade balances, or stock markets. Because of the great inertia of population trends, long term and short term mean different things for demographic and economic forecasts, but in all forecasts uncertainty is assumed to increase with the time horizon because of the greater probability of structural changes.

Summarizing the limits of population forecasting, Nathan Keyfitz (1981:583) states: "The practical conclusion, then, is that relatively short-term forecasts, say up to ten or 20 years, do tell us something, but that beyond a quarter-century or so we simply do not know what the population will be." Such a statement still seems to reflect the thinking of most demographers today, including many of the experts invited to contribute to this book, who defined assumptions only up to the year 2030. But the question of what we can know today about the future goes beyond the issue of the time horizon, which is discussed later in this chapter.

First we need to ask, What kind of knowledge of the future do we want to have? Do we want to have one single number, a certain range, or a probability distribution? Do we want total population size alone or age-structural information as well? Who is interested in these numbers and for what reason? And what is the motivation of those who prepare population projections? These questions affect the approach taken to project future population and the methods and assumptions chosen.

This chapter gives a broad and nontechnical exposition of some fundamental questions involved in choosing an approach to project future population. These kinds of questions are usually not addressed in technical scientific papers or in the publication of projection results because certain choices are taken for granted. A broader perspective is necessary, however, to answer the question which forms the title of Part I: Why another set of global population projections? Several fundamental issues in population projection are addressed in the following eight sections in this chapter. The approach taken in this book is described and justified against the background of other possible approaches. The concluding section gives a concise summary of our choice.

2.1 Who Wants Population Projections?

What motivates demographers to prepare population projections, and for whom are they preparing them? Three major groups are interested in population projections and are willing to pay demographers to do this job: other scientists, governments and international agencies, and the general public, including private industry.

A large number of natural and social scientists are increasingly demanding information about future population size and structure. The recent upsurge of environmental and global change research has further heightened this demand. A major reason for this demand lies in the fact that many of the indicators used in such studies are on a per capita basis. By definition these require a population figure in the denominator. In particular, this is the case in studies on CO_2 emissions conducted by Bartiaux and van Ypersele (1993), Birdsall (1992), and Bongaarts (1992). These studies combine future population trends with assumed future per capita CO_2 emissions. Lutz (1993) has also demonstrated that the level of regional aggregation significantly influences the results. The time horizon of these studies is typically long (at least to 2030–2050, often to 2100 and beyond) because global-warming is a long-term phenomenon.

Related to global-warming issues is the large group of energy demand models, which are probably the most numerous scientific consumers of population projection data. A few forecasters (e.g., Odell and Rosing, 1980) omit the explicit consideration of population, and instead project total energy demand. Most, however, combine scenarios of the evolution of energy demand with population forecasts (Gouse *et al.*, 1992; Leontief and Sohn, 1984; WECCC, 1983; IIASA and WEC, 1995). The time horizons of these studies range from 2020 to 2100.

Another field of studies which routinely includes population projections is the analysis of world food consumption. The Food and Agriculture Organization (FAO, 1988) has produced forecasts of demand to 2010. The approach taken by Mellor and Paulino (1986), for example, is to produce two scenarios: the first is based on present per capita calorie consumption and the second includes increased calorie consumption arising from assumed economic growth. Many more fields, such as economic forecasting, epidemiological studies, and insurance mathematics, demand population projections as input.

In the past non-demographic scientific studies requiring population forecasts tended to consider only one variant of future population trends. Recently, however, the scenario approaches in many of these disciplines have become increasingly sophisticated and allow for consideration of alternative population scenarios. There clearly is a demand not only for one best guess of the future population but also for information concerning the degree of uncertainty and more extreme scenarios for sensitivity analysis. So far demographers have not done much to satisfy this demand.

Politicians, including public administrators, need population projections largely for planning purposes. Especially in the health, education, and social-security sectors, medium- and long-term planners regard demographic variables as crucial components. Typically, politicians and administrators would like to receive one likely variant of future population size and structure that they can use in their models to determine, for example, where new hospitals and schools should be constructed and how the legal system of pension payments should be organized to accommodate changes in the age composition of the population.

Unlike the scientific community, public administrators and political planners rarely ask for alternative variants and generally have little appreciation of the methods dealing with uncertainty in population projections, despite the fact that policies should be robust and hold under varying conditions. They typically want one, most likely figure.

Despite the tradition of government planners to use only one central forecast, the design of policies that hold under uncertain future conditions should be a main concern of good politics. For instance, a restructuring of the pension scheme, as currently being done in many European countries, should by no means consider only one future mortality trend. Since national population projections tend to assume very low future mortality improvements, even a continuation of past increases in life expectancy results in a much faster increase of the old-age dependency ratio, and might bring about painful, if not disastrous, surprises in the new system. In this situation demographers have a responsibility for communicating their knowledge about uncertainty.

The third group of users of population projections is by far the largest and most heterogeneous. Many individuals, organizations, and enterprises in the general public are interested in specific population projections. Aside from individual curiosity, this interest is used in the planning of future activities and in the estimation of expected returns from such activities; the activities range from an individual's decision to buy real estate in an area with potential increases in population density to an enterprise's marketing strategy for a commercial product, such as baby food or special products for the elderly.

Generally the expectations of this group toward population projections can be assumed to be similar to that of the group of politicians and administrators. The interest tends to focus on one most likely variant. Considerations of uncertainty may play a role in corporate planning, but generally the planning horizon of companies is too short for alternative population trends to make a difference. An exception may be energy-supply companies that tend to have long time horizons.

In addition to these three major groups some specific groups explicitly use population projections for educational and illustrative purposes. The most vocal of these are environmental and family-planning groups that want to draw attention to what would happen in the distant future if policies aiming at a reduction of population growth were not implemented. Such people are not as much interested in one medium population projection as they are in the calculation of extreme alternatives to demonstrate the long-term impacts of today's choices.

Another special group are students in the social sciences who should understand the basic functioning of population dynamics. For this group, phenomena such as the momentum of population growth could best be illustrated through comparisons of alternative long-term population projections.

In summary the different groups interested in population projections are demanding two different types of results from demographers preparing such projections: one most likely variant that can be used without further consideration of the problem of uncertainty and information about less likely but still possible trends that can be used for sensitivity analysis, i.e., for understanding how the systems studied or any planned policy or individual action would perform under different possible demographic futures. Although most users of projections are satisfied with a 30- to 40-year time horizon, some clearly want a longer time horizon.

2.2   Time Horizon

Technically, it is a simple matter to continue a population projection one hundred, or even one million, years into the future. But the question is, how meaningful is such an exercise. The choice of a projection horizon, therefore, represents a compromise between the advantages of providing more information and the dangers of making inaccurate assumptions. Beyond a certain point in time, we are too unsure about the state of the family, health, and the world to specify rates of fertility, mortality, and migration. In this section we explore the possible reasons demographers have for regarding 30 to 40 years as a threshold beyond which projections become less reliable. We also address the question of whether uncertainty increases monotonically with time or whether there are thresholds and discontinuities suggesting a certain cutoff point.

The time scale of population projections is of distinctly human dimensions. This is not only because the human life span and the gap between generations have important demographic consequences, but also because forecasters' judgments about the speed of social change depend on their personal experiences.

From a psychological perspective, there may be reasons for being suspicious of projections that forecast further than 40 or 50 years into the future, a little less than two generations.[1] During our lifetimes, most of us get to know our grandparents, but not our great-grandparents. Consequently, we know first-hand the amount of social change that can occur over two generations. When we specify demographic rates beyond this, not only must we forecast the behavior of individuals whom we will probably never meet, but we must deal with individuals who are more distant, in generational terms, than anyone we have met in our own lives. In addition to this subjective reason for setting a threshold of increased uncertainty, we can point to other, less personal, justifications for a particular time horizon.

In developing countries the average age is roughly between 35 and 40. As such, this average age marks the period of time beyond which a population will consist of a majority of people not yet born. The wholly individual psychological perspective just mentioned thus also corresponds to the experience of the entire population, the timing of which might mark a rupture in social change.

In addition to uncertainty in the inputs of population projection (the demographic rates that reflect individual behavior), we must also consider the size of the population at risk. The number of births in the future is a function not only of birth rates but also of the number of potential parents in the population, itself a function of past demographic rates. This feedback property is well known in the case of the echoes of a baby boom (or bust). The time it takes for a boom to echo is approximately the mean age of childbearing, which ranges between ages 25 and 30 in almost all populations. Beyond this time horizon, therefore, we add to our uncertainty about birth rates the uncertainty of how many potential mothers will be in the population.

The number of deaths in a population is also a function of the number of past births and deaths, but since in developed countries the mean age at death (in a stationary population, equal to life expectancy) is roughly three-quarters of a century, the lagged mortality effect will be of relatively minor importance. In developing countries where mortality is still high, however, a rapid improvement in infant mortality might increase the number of potential mothers in as little as 15 to 20 years.

While not subject to uncertainties about cohort size, migration levels are subject to perhaps a more arbitrary type of change – the change in government policy. Annual migration trends are largely determined by government policy. If we were to ask, for instance, how many immigrants will Western Europe admit, most analysts would be reluctant to predict more than a few years into the future. And indeed we have seen tremendous ups and downs in migration flows in recent years. When migration plays a major role in determining the demography of a region, it would seem that 5 to 10 years might mark the point beyond which any projection would become quite speculative.

If we ask, on the other hand, why 10,000 years is too long to perform a projection, we discover a further constraint on forecast horizons. In addition to the fact that we are in no position to specify demographic rates for such a long period, the meaningfulness of the projection models used applies only to certain time scales. Assuming the case of an ageless population growing at a constant exponential rate, the only possible average growth rate in the long term that would avoid extinction or inconceivable explosion is zero.

Figure 2.1 summarizes the possible thresholds of increasing uncertainty. The times shown are in an extremely stylized form and are meant to summarize the arguments given earlier. The second wave of fertility cohort size uncertainty is added to indicate that the baby boom (bust) resulting from the cohort size uncertainty after about 25 years will have echoes in the following generation also, although of less amplitude than in the past. Cohort size is also determined by migration, so we might want to add additional uncertainty 25, 50, and 75 years after the migration uncertainty begins.

Despite its speculative nature, we can draw several lessons from *Figure 2.1*. First, no single clear threshold of uncertainty emerges.

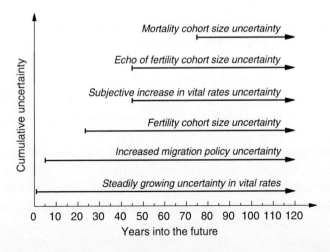

Figure 2.1. Different components of uncertainty entering the population projection over time.

Instead, there are arguments for stopping the forecast at many different times. Second, the commonly accepted threshold of a little less than half a century emerges not so much as a clear demographic threshold (which might dictate a choice closer to the mean age of childbearing), but rather from the timing of the increased subjective uncertainty in demographic rates. Last, the timing of the demographic thresholds, particularly the delayed effect of births on the future number of deaths, may vary according to the population under consideration. The average age at death in a population with high infant mortality might be considerably less than 75 years.

Equally important is perhaps what this figure leaves out, namely, the relative size of the different sources of uncertainty. For some countries, like Canada, migration levels may be the largest source of uncertainty, while for others, like many African countries, structural change in birth or death rates might play the largest role.

The risk of projecting too far into the future is the loss of legitimacy (*believability*) either because assumptions seem to lack foundation or because the projected populations violate constraints, such as an assumed carrying capacity of the globe. However, because several features of population dynamics, such as growth momentum

and echoes, persist strongly for at least one or two generations projections of less than 50 years probably do not reveal all the information already present in even today's age structure. This explanation
supports the argument for a minimum length of projection.

The reluctance of demographers to go beyond a certain time
horizon is in conflict with some of the expectations of potential
users as described in Section 2.1. Some users clearly want population figures for the year 2100 and beyond. Should the demographer
disappoint such expectations and leave it to others with less exper-
tise to produce them? The answer given in this study is no. But
as discussed below, we make a clear distinction between what we
call projections up to 2030–2050 and everything beyond that time,
which we term extensions for illustrative purposes.

2.3 Spatial Resolution and Heterogeneity

Because of the great heterogeneity of the world population it clearly
does not make sense to treat the whole world as one region in a
population projection. Users of projections want information to be
arranged by countries or at least by major world regions that group
countries by demographic, socioeconomic, and cultural characteristics. If the output parameters are to be regional, clearly the projection needs to be done on a regional basis. But even if the user is
only interested in aggregate global results, meaningful assumptions
on future fertility and mortality cannot be made for all the different
regions together for two reasons.[2]

First, different parts of the world are at very different stages of
demographic transition; in most projections this factor is the basic
underlying paradigm on which assumptions about future fertility are
based. The aggregation of these different parts obscures the picture
and makes the reasoning behind assumptions more difficult.

Second, because population growth rates are much higher in the
South than in the North, the weights of the two hemispheres will
change significantly in the future; by itself this factor leads to a
change in aggregate rates even if the rates remain constant in each
hemisphere. Lutz and Prinz (1991) have quantitatively illustrated
this by using a simple calculation. In the purely hypothetical case,

in which all vital rates are kept at their present levels, the projection carried out on the basis of six world regions yields a total population that by the end of the 21st century is 50 percent higher than the projection treating the world as one region. This amazing difference is simply due to the fact that the low-fertility regions make up a larger proportion of the world population today than they will in the future. Africa, which has by far the highest fertility, increases from 12 percent of the world population to roughly one-third under constant fertility. With this change in weights, constant fertility in the main world regions results in increasing fertility in the world total and hence in a larger total population than in the case of constant global fertility.

While the above example clearly shows that heterogeneity of the population can have a strong effect, it is not clear how much one must disaggregate to avoid this problem. Even within nations there may be subpopulations with very different demographic regimes. In some Latin American countries, such as Bolivia, national fertility rates have been stagnant at a rather high level; this may be explained by the bifurcation of society into one group that is well advanced in its demographic transition and another group, the Indian population, that has not fully entered the fertility decline and is rapidly increasing. In addition to the observable heterogeneity in a population, Vaupel and Yashin (1983) have demonstrated the significance of unobserved heterogeneity for population dynamics.

For our global population projections a basic question was, How far should one go in disaggregating the world population? Theoretically, disaggregations need not follow territorial or national boundaries but should follow the most strongly discriminating variables. In practice, however, data are most readily available by countries and groups of countries. The United Nations and the World Bank produce their population projections at the level of individual countries. In this approach the 1.2 billion Chinese receive as much attention as the 72,000 inhabitants of the Seychelles. This is due to the national constituencies of these organizations and convenience of data availability rather than to questions of demographic heterogeneity.

With more than 150 countries in the world today, however, simultaneous projections become awkward especially with respect to the migration matrix to be assumed for all these states. This perhaps explains why migration is not a major emphasis of the UN and World Bank projections. An alternative, which has been chosen for the present study, is to limit the number of populations projected simultaneously to subcontinental regions. The 13 world regions have been defined according to geographic proximity and socioeconomic criteria, as well as similar demographic and institutional aspects such as compatibility with other data sets. These 13 regions are projected simultaneously by a multistate model assuming region-specific future paths of age-specific fertility and mortality rates and full matrices of interregional migratory streams.

These regional assumptions must be considered aggregate future paths of fertility, mortality, and migration that reflect not only changing behavior within the subpopulations of the region but also the compositional effect of changing weights. This method seems to be the most pragmatic way to deal with the bothersome issue of population heterogeneity.

2.4   Expected Output Parameters

The methodology used for population projection crucially depends on the choice of relevant population characteristics. If the user is interested only in total population size, methods such as simple exponential growth models may be used; these methods, however, are not sufficient if one is also interested in the future age and sex composition of the population. But many other population characteristics, such as urban/rural residence, marital-status composition, and educational or labor-force composition, may be of considerable interest to the user of projections and require specific methodologies.

Questions about desired output parameters, together with the above-discussed issues of time horizon and of the desirability of a range of projections, need to be discussed before the question of appropriate methodologies. Introductions to population forecasting usually do not address these issues explicitly, but rather group projection methods by the statistical models on which they are based (e.g., time-series models, structural equation models) as is done in the introduction to a recent comprehensive volume on population forecasting (Ahlburg and Land, 1992). Because the evaluation of different methods requires the systematic consideration of objectives, in this section we distinguish between projections of total population size, projections of the age and sex compositions of the population, and projections of characteristics other than age and sex.

2.4.1 Projections of total population size

For projections of total population size alone a basic choice is between methods that consider the age structure of the population and those that do not. When advocates of projections of population totals through various time-series models (e.g., Pflaumer, 1992) stress that such models may be more reliable than cohort-component models, which project the population by age groups, it is important to keep in mind that this argument only concerns the aggregate totals – figures that, from a substantive point of view, have rather limited value. Most economic and social issues, for which the population variable is considered important, heavily depend on the age profile of the population, ranging from social-security considerations to marketing, from health expenditures to education, from the size of the labor force to internal migration. Even in the recent discussion on population–environment and carrying capacity, the population composition seems to make a big difference because of varying age-specific impacts (see Lutz, 1994a).

For the time being, let us assume that the number of total population size in a territory, at some point in the future, has meaning and value in itself. To derive such a figure we must choose between simple and sophisticated guesses. The most simple would be a guess of the future population size without any formal model. But this would be difficult to defend. Probably the simplest meaningful model of population growth over time is an exponential growth model with a constant rate of growth. In practice, however, growth rates have never been constant over long periods. Through the millennia of early human history, birth and death rates fluctuated widely due to weather, war, food shortages, and diseases. Typically birth rates were high when death rates were low and vice versa, resulting in even wider fluctuations in the growth rates of the population. Although during the 20th century the curve of world population growth has resembled the typical exponential growth curve, growth rates have been far from constant even if the trend is smoothed. The growth rate of the world population was about 0.5 percent during the first half of this century, increased to a peak of 2.06 percent between 1965 and 1970, and slowly declined thereafter. The appealing feature of an exponential growth model, as opposed to more sophisticated ones, is that one has to make assumptions only for one parameter – the growth rate.

Several significant deficiencies of the exponential growth model result from the fact that it does not consider the age structure of the population. The most important is that it cannot capture the momentum of population growth, a phenomenon caused by the fact that only women aged 15–49 have children, and in the case of a very young age distribution, more and more women enter this age group and hence the population would grow significantly even with fertility at replacement level. Another aspect of this deficiency relates to countries with very irregular age pyramids, such as some European countries where irregularities in births due to world wars, the baby boom, and the baby bust have resulted in great fluctuations in cohort size. Here some changes in the population growth rate are preprogrammed by the population age structures that do not reflect any change in fertility, mortality, and migration. For instance, a phenomenon such as the echo of the baby boom – the large number of babies born by the large baby-boom cohorts– could never be captured by a model that considers only total population size.

For these reasons it is generally advisable to use projection models such as the cohort-component method which explicitly considers age and sex, even if one is only interested in total population size. However, in these models one has to make assumptions on a larger number of parameters, which raise the danger of losing sight of the behavior of the total system while giving increased attention to specific issues such as period-cohort translation in fertility. In this respect the suggestion made by Pflaumer (1992), that time-series methods applied to population totals should be used as a baseline against which the results of more complex models should be assessed, is worth considering. Ideally the analyst could then identify the sources of the difference between the two approaches.

2.4.2   Projecting the age and sex composition

As mentioned above, people are interested in population projections because they want to understand population changes that go beyond projecting total population size. This knowledge is used in a variety of ways, ranging from aging and social-security considerations to labor-market questions, educational issues, and even marketing in private business. For all these considerations one needs to have estimates of the future population structure at least in broad age groups. Few users would demand projections in single-year age groups, especially in a long time horizon. Projection of five-year age groups in five-year steps of historical time has become popular, mostly for convenience.

A projection of the population by age and sex requires first the age and sex composition of the population in the starting year. Next one must assume age-specific fertility, mortality, and migration rates for each five-year period to be projected. For this age-groupwise projection of the population, the so-called cohort-component method has become standard. This method was introduced by Whelpton in 1936 and formalized by Leslie (1945). Notestein (1945) first applied it to project the world population. The basic method has not changed since then. In short, cohorts are groups of men and women born in the same time interval and representing a specific age group at any later point in time. Their sizes can only change through mortality and migration. The size of the youngest age group is determined by age-specific fertility levels applied to the corresponding female age groups. Hence the projected size and age structure of the population at any point in the future depends exclusively on the size and age structure in the starting year and on assumed age-specific fertility, mortality, and migration over the projection period.

The cohort-component method tells us what to do with assumptions on future fertility, mortality, and migration, but not how to derive them. And it is in this all-deciding question of the choice of assumptions and structuring of sets of alternative assumptions where controversy exists and continuous improvement of population projection methodologies is possible and indeed necessary. Alternative approaches to deriving assumptions on future fertility, mortality, and migration are discussed in the following sections of this chapter.

In the context of the cohort-component method, one unresolved question is whether assumptions should be made in terms of period or cohort fertility. Technically, the Leslie matrix requires age-specific period rates. But these period rates could be either assumed directly or derived from assumptions on future cohort fertility behavior. This decision essentially goes back to the rather philosophical controversy of whether the cohort approach is more appropriate in fertility analysis. In practical terms the cohort-fertility approach requires assumptions of both the level of cohort fertility and the timing of births over the reproductive life span. If the age pattern is assumed to be constant and the level is assumed to approach a certain constant value, there will be no difference between cohort and period fertility assumptions. Theoretically similar cohort-period arguments could be made for mortality and migration, but they are rarely discussed.

2.4.3   Multistate models for additional characteristics

Usually populations are defined by the a territory in which they live. But, as mentioned earlier, populations may also be defined as subgroups of the population in a given territory, such as ethnic groups, marital-status groups, or educational groups. These groups can be treated as independent populations that may interact with each other, i.e., people leave one group and join another. The traditional cohort-component method can only consider one population and needs to be expanded to simultaneously project several populations that are interacting with one another. Such expansions are called multistate models, and were developed by Rogers (1975) and others during the 1970s. The original applications of multistate models were in the field of multiregional demography and migration.

So far no global population projection has gone beyond projecting the age and sex distribution by regions or countries.[3] Highly relevant and promising from a global development perspective are multistate projections of urban/rural place of residence and educational composition. A recent set of multistate educational projections for North African countries (Yousif *et al.*, 1996) demonstrates that because of strong educational fertility differentials the changing educational composition of the population significantly effects total fertility and therefore population growth. Assumptions on fertility,

mortality, and transitions between the states must be state specific in addition to age and sex specific. This multistate approach
can be applied to any other breakdown of the population (socioeconomic, ethnic, etc.) providing that the categories are clearly defined
and sufficient empirical information on transition intensities is given.
Population projections that also provide estimates of future distributions of socioeconomic variables other than age and sex may be
useful for many users, and may become increasingly popular as more
methodologies and computer programs become available.

At the global level, however, one difficulty in applying multistate models that include not strictly demographic variables is the
availability of relevant empirical data. Hence, the projections presented in this book are based on alternative projections of only the
age and sex distribution for the 13 world regions specified.

2.5   Different Uses of Past Experience to Derive Assumptions for the Future

The real challenge in population projection is not the method itself
but the generation of one set or several sets of assumptions on age-
specific fertility and age- and sex-specific mortality and migration.
In this context there are two basic questions. The first question
relates to the way in which the past is used to derive future assumptions. The second concerns the strategy one takes to deal with
uncertainty, whether to consider a range of possible assumptions
based on some distribution or individual point scenarios. We can
distinguish three ways to draw on past experience.

- *The Future as a Continuation of the Past Trend.* This is the
  strongest possible way in which the past can enter into future
  assumptions. A simple trend extrapolation can be performed
  without any additional input about likely future conditions. It
  can be blind and mechanical after one has chosen the indicator
  to be extrapolated, the length of the period to be considered,
  and the information to be derived from the time series. It can
  take the form of simple linear trend extrapolation, other functional forms of extrapolation, or, if periodicity is assumed, a
  combined trend with superimposed cycles.

The blind continuation of past trends seems appropriate only when absolutely no information is available about likely future trends. In the context of fertility assumptions it would mean completely disregarding considerations derived from demographic transition theories, information about desired family size, and surveys on family-planning demands. But even this simple method does not save the forecaster from making choices. The indicator, the length of the past period, and the structure of the process must be defined.

- *Only Variance from History.* If one is willing to incorporate into one's assumptions external substantive information about likely future trends, one possibility of combining this with information from the past is to determine the average level from external expert knowledge but still take the variance from past time series. The idea behind such a procedure is that the level cannot be derived by extrapolation but that the past can tell us something about the variability of the process, i.e., by how much fertility tends to change (in any direction) over a five-year period. Along these lines Goldstein *et al.* (1994) have proposed a probabilistic model by which the upper and lower bounds of a random walk of fertility are externally assumed while the stepsize of change is resampled from the past. Also the work by Keyfitz (1981) and Stoto (1983) falls into this category; they estimated future errors in population projections from past errors.

- *Structure and Understanding from History.* Under this approach it is not the past time series itself which is used to derive assumptions on future evolution, but the substantive knowledge about the process and its structure. Taking mortality as an example, this approach goes beyond the analysis of past trends in integrating knowledge from medicine and biology and addressing questions such as that of a genetically determined limit to human life. Naturally this understanding is also informed by the analysis of past trends but goes further, by integrating outside knowledge derived from other sources. In this approach historical information enters only indirectly into the formulation of assumptions about the future. This third approach is the one chosen for our study. For this reason large parts of this volume consist of substantive papers about our understanding of the processes of fertility, mortality, and migration in the different world regions. Experts were asked to write about alternative future paths of fertility, mortality, and migration and to produce assumptions of a most likely central value as well as high and low extreme values for the various indicators by the year 2030, based on their substantive understanding of the processes. For the probabilistic world population projections presented in Chapter 16, these three points were assumed to define a subjective probability distribution with 90 percent of all cases between the high and low values. The approach chosen for this book is described in more detail in Section 2.9.

The evolution of the future population of the world will almost surely differ from the central scenario as described in this volume. This is unavoidable, for there is inherent uncertainty in the future. Wars will break out; some societies will modernize more quickly than we expect while others will develop more slowly; new diseases may break out, old ones may be cured; childbearing may become more fashionable in the developed world, or, quite the contrary, less so; the industrialized countries may close themselves to immigration, or might even become more open. All these factors are crucial to the demographic future, but they are also uncertain.

What does a forecaster do in the face of such uncertainty? A first approach is to freeze all demographic rates at their current level. Rates will almost certainly not remain unchanged as the future unfolds, but this approach enables the forecaster to avoid making statements about the direction of demographic trends and, at the same time, makes absolutely clear the hypothetical nature of the projection. This approach was followed by early demographic forecasters in the 1920s, 1930s, and 1940s.

A second approach is to create extreme case scenarios in addition to a most likely scenario. This enables one to make statements about how far off future population projections could be from the most likely expected evolution. It is also useful for sensitivity analysis. However, there is a danger that the range between the high and low scenarios might be so large that it is uninformative. On the other hand, when the alternative scenarios include conditions that are more probable, one automatically begins to ask about the likelihood of a given scenario. Alternative scenarios or variants without any information about their likelihood somehow remain unsatisfactory to the user.

The third approach, explicit quantification of uncertainty, is therefore designed to explicitly incorporate information about the degree of uncertainty. It is evident that both forecasters and users would like to know how much confidence to place in different projections, but as yet no single technique is available to do this unambiguously. Sanderson (1995) shows that it is impossible to produce "objective" confidence ranges for future population projections. Subjective confidence intervals are the best we can ever attain because assumptions are always involved. As a recent US Bureau of the Census (1989) forecast notes: "Many problems remain before a method can be developed for placing reliable confidence intervals around population projections." This failure to solve the problem is not for want of trying, but occurs because it is impossible to derive any "objective" confidence interval. In the following two sections we discuss in more detail the second approach (i.e., variants and scenarios) and the third approach (i.e., probabilistic population projections).

2.6   Non-probabilistic Approaches: Single Projections, Variants, Scenarios

In practice, both national statistics departments and international agencies have taken non-probabilistic approaches to forecasting. Until recently, some agencies still offered only one set of rate trajectories. Thus, it was possible to speak of *the* future population. Today, however, there is increasing concern about the uncertainties of future population growth, and it is rare to find a projection without at least one alternative set of assumptions.

Both "variants" and "scenarios" offer alternative sets of assumptions. The difference between the two is, to some extent, only a difference in detail, but this difference is also reflected in the intended use. The variant approach usually offers three alternatives: high, medium, and low. The high and low scenarios are typically defined by the resulting population size, and not by their components. Therefore, the large population in the high alternative can come from increased migration, low mortality, high fertility, or a combination of any of these.

The *World Population Prospects* produced by the United Nations Population Division (UN, 1995), the most commonly used set of world projections, currently offers four projections to 2050: high, medium, and low variants and a constant fertility projection which is called scenario. Fertility is allowed to vary, but only one set of mortality and migration assumptions are used throughout.

In their recently published long-range world population projections, the UN (1992c) gives projections to 2150 for nine world regions. Seven different fertility extensions are considered, but again mortality and migration assumptions remain invariant. The World Bank (1992b) offers only one central set of projections. Birdsall (1992), however, offers a set of alternative projections resulting from faster than expected fertility decline in the developing world.

Sometimes the selection of inputs for high and low variants is directly influenced by the interests of the agency producing the forecasts. For example, the US Social Security Administration, whose principal interest lies in the age structure of the population, combines high fertility and high mortality for its high variant and low fertility and low mortality for its low variant, giving the two most extreme values for the old-age dependency ratio. The US Bureau of the Census, however, combines low fertility and high mortality and vice versa to arrive at the most extreme values for the total population size.

Recently an increasing number of authors (Ahlburg and Vaupel, 1990; Lutz, 1991; Cliquet, 1993) and agencies (EUROSTAT, UN) have chosen to speak of population scenarios instead of, or in addition to, the traditional variants. Originally the word "scenario" comes from the theater. The *Oxford English Dictionary* (1982 supplement) defines it as, "A sketch, outline, or description of an imagined situation or sequence of events." During the 1970s and 1980s the word "scenario" became popular in the social sciences, especially in the context of computer models (Lutz, 1995a). In the realm of population projections the notion is being used in two somewhat different meanings: 1. in the sense of purely hypothetical assumptions, e.g., a "constant fertility scenario"; and 2. in the sense of a consistent story in which fertility, mortality, and migration assumptions are embedded to provide a comprehensive picture of what the future might be. While the second usage is certainly closer to the original meaning in terms of a consistent picture, the first has gained great popularity; it seems futile to try to change the common usage, especially since there is no readily acceptable alternative word for the first meaning. Hence, it remains with the authors of a projection to define what they mean by a scenario.

The meaning the user chooses not only influences the conceptual design of the scenario, but also implies differences in the setting of parameters. In the first case the three components of change (fertility, mortality, and migration) may be assumed to be independent, whereas in the second case they should be dependent. Chapter 15 of this book gives examples of both approaches. In the systematic permutations of scenario assumptions the components are assumed to be independent in the first part of the chapter; in the special long-term scenarios, specific consistent stories are described such as fertility responses to aging or mortality responses to excessive growth.

2.7   Different Probabilistic Approaches to Deal with Uncertainty

How can the future population size differ from that which is projected? The compendium of possible mistakes is long (Keilman, 1990), but we can categorize the sources of error into three types:

1. *Measurement and calculation errors.* These can take the form of mistaken input data (for example, starting the projection with a population based on an incorrect census count), imprecise algorithms, or a simple calculation mistake.
2. *Incorrect specification of trends in vital rates and migration.* One can predict that life expectancy will continue to rise at the rate that it has over the past 20 years, but instead it might well increase at twice that rate. Fertility may reverse its declining trend, or less spectacularly, the seemingly random "natural" variation (see Brillinger, 1986) might cause fertility, mortality, and migration rates to vary from year to year.
3. *Unexpected events.* The unexpected could cause large structural changes: the outbreak of war, a sudden cure for AIDS, an economic boom in Africa. Any number of ruptures with current

trends is imaginable, any of which might render extrapolated visions of the future irrelevant.

We can call these, respectively, measurement error, parameter specification error, and model specification error. To these model specification errors we could also add significant errors resulting from aggregation of heterogeneous groups. The sum of all forms of error is called total error.

At first glance, only the second source of error – the variation in vital rates – seems a likely candidate for the application of probabilistic thinking, and most attempts to incorporate randomness into population forecasting have used this as the focus. Before examining these techniques, however, one technique for quantifying the total error deserves mention. The empirical evaluation of the successes and failures of past forecasts, developed by Keyfitz and Stoto in the early 1980s, consists simply of gathering a large number of past forecasts and evaluating the average error. The most noteworthy conclusion of these studies, both of which focused only on error in total population size, was that the traditional high and low variants offered by population projections corresponded to approximately a two-thirds confidence interval. In other words, the population grew at rates outside those predicted by the high and low variants about one-third of the time (Keyfitz, 1981; Stoto, 1983).

This empirical method of estimating uncertainty clearly takes into account all three types of error.[4] To apply it to current forecasts, however, a strong assumption must be made: the errors in future forecasts are assumed to be of the same magnitude as those in the past. This assumption is of particular concern since the sample of past forecasts tends to be biased toward the older ones for which the accuracy can be checked. This is problematic because not only do the methods of choosing high, low, and medium variants change, but the potential variability of vital rates also changes. Unless both the variability of vital rates and the methodology of projection, together with the degree of care used in making the assumptions, stay the same, it is unclear how good an indicator past errors are of future uncertainty.

While an application of the results from Keyfitz and Stoto to future population projections is one way of determining uncertainty estimates, the direct analysis of population trends themselves offers a distinct alternative. It is here that time-series analysts have plied their trade. Work on time-series analysis began with Lee (1974), which studied US fertility rates, and analyses continue today. Time-series methods aim to assign structure to the process of changing rates, for example, a random walk with drift or an Auto-Regressive Integrated Moving Average (ARIMA) model. Time-series methods produce not only a central forecast, but also the entire probability distribution, showing where fertility and mortality rates are likely to be at any future specified date contingent on a normal distribution of errors.

The principal drawback of time-series methods has been the dependence of the results on the choice of a model structure – particularly for fertility, the demographic component that not only has the largest effect on the evolution of populations but also is the more variable one (Lee, 1974; Ahlburg and Land, 1992) when migration is left out, as is often done. Assuming a constant model structure is particularly problematic in the case of countries that are in the midst of the process of fertility transition and where we know that the model is likely to change toward the end of the transition process. Mortality appears to hold more promise in forecasting, at least in the most developed countries. In particular, both the Lee–Carter (1992) and McNown–Rogers (1989) methods offer means of producing trends based on large matrices of age-specific mortality rates. These techniques have large data requirements and have been criticized for producing overly narrow confidence intervals. Nevertheless, they are clear in their aim, which is to provide estimates of parameter variation, providing minimum error ranges.

An alternative method for obtaining probability distributions is to simulate the evolution of demographic rates using Monte Carlo simulation methods. Random draws of past levels (for example, see Keyfitz, 1985 and 1989) or of past variations (Goldstein *et al.*, 1994) are made and applied to the evolving population. A large number, for instance 10,000, of sample populations are projected forward, and the resulting empirical distribution of population size and age structure is used to estimate the theoretical probability range. These simulations allow users to analyze the combined effect of uncertainty in mortality, fertility, and migration; the last component, mortality, has usually not been included in time-series models.

Both the history-based simulation and the time-series techniques are means to address only the second type of parameter uncertainty. They do not deal with the possibility of structural change. Questions, such as will there be another baby boom in Western Europe, when will sub-Saharan Africa experience a fertility transition, what are the chances of a new deadly virus or of a war or revolution, cannot be addressed without probability models of the likelihood for each unexpected event. The scenario approach, based on assumptions of experts, offers the possibility of seeing the hypothesized impact of unpredictable events, and seems to be the best means for analyzing structural change in addition to parameter uncertainty. With this approach experts can step back from recent experience and consider possible alternative stories that might happen in the future. These stories may include unlikely and unexpected events that can then be translated into specific parameter assumptions.

Based on such expert knowledge it is also possible to define specific scenarios that describe not only one path out of countless possible paths but also a whole range of possible future paths. Viewing scenarios as just specific lines in the spectrum of possible future trends, one can also attempt to define the full predictive probability distribution (see Lutz *et al.*, 1995). Such an approach takes neither the trend nor the variance directly from past time series. The predictive probability distribution is entirely based on the subjective judgment of the expert who is equipped with an analysis of past trends, knows about fertility, mortality, and migration determinants, and is able to make informed guesses about possible future changes in those determinants. Such projections based on subjective probability distributions are not unusual in other disciplines, but they have not received much attention in demographic research although the approach was discussed by Muhsam (1956) and Keyfitz (1977). In practice the expert can choose one statistical distribution (e.g., normal or uniform) and then define only certain fractiles (e.g., median and upper and lower 5 percent). Combining the subjective probability distributions of a number of experts to form one joint predictive probability distribution diminishes the danger of individual bias. *However, there can never be a population projection without personal judgment. Even models largely based on past time series are subject to a serious judgmental issue of whether to assume structural continuity or any alternative structure.*

This approach to probabilistic projections based on the subjective distributions of a number of experts is applied in Chapter 16 of this volume. The chapter presents what we call "probabilistic world population projections based on expert opinion." It significantly adds to the scenario projections in Chapter 15 by giving users a better understanding of the likelihood of certain scenarios. It is important for users to know the probability of the scenario (or variant) they are considering. For example, a high-fertility scenario (or variant) with a 20 percent probability should be taken more serious in policy considerations than one with only 2 percent probability.

The reason for choosing the probabilistic approach, which is based on subjective distributions provided by a group of experts, rather than a time-series approach lies in our belief that in both the near and distant future structural changes and unexpected events are likely to happen in many parts of the world which makes alternative expert-based assumptions the only meaningful way to capture future uncertainty. Time-series analysts could be among the experts giving their subjective views, but at the global level their models could never be applied simply because the necessary data are not available.

As to the relationship between fertility, mortality, and migration, these simulations can assume either independence or certain correlations. Examples for both are given in Chapter 16. Another important issue is, whether regional demographic trends should be considered independent or follow a uniform pattern (such as high fertility in all regions) as is traditionally assumed in uncertainty variants of population projection. There is, however, no particular substantive reason why, for example, unexpectedly high fertility in China should coincide with unexpectedly high fertility in Africa. If regions are considered independent at the global level, much of the variation will be canceled out. Chapter 16 considers both regional dependence and regional independence.

2.8 Interactions among Components and Possible Feedbacks from Results

It is essential to determine whether the assumptions made for fertility, mortality, and migration are unrelated or have some form of interaction. Yet this question is rarely discussed explicitly in the description of existing population projections. The problem lies in the fact that, even when some dependency is suspected, it is very difficult to quantitatively capture and specify the nature of such interactions. One can distinguish at least three different levels of interaction:

1. Correlation between trends of demographic components.
2. Feedbacks from demographic variables resulting from projections, in particular population size or age structure.
3. Feedbacks from non-demographic variables, such as economic development, education, or environmental factors, which in turn depend on population factors.

Correlation between demographic components is incorporated relatively easily. For example, one can assume that in countries in the process of demographic transition the declines in fertility and mortality are positively correlated.

Feedbacks from other demographic variables, such as population size or age structure, are more controversial and hence more difficult to include. There is full consensus that the world population cannot grow indefinitely, but no agreement exists on the levels at which some sort of collapse might happen. The land-carrying capacity concept is accepted in the natural sciences, but less so among social scientists. Collapses, if they happen at all, will probably occur suddenly and with large regional differences. As to possible reactions of fertility, mortality, or migration to negative effects of population aging, little agreement has been reached. Rapid aging will certainly create problems, in particular when countries are not well prepared, for example, with regard to social security. But, as is shown by the example of today's industrialized world, populations can adapt to gradual changes in the age structure. Because of the possible discrepancy between individual desired family sizes and societal goals, it is unclear whether, for example, extreme aging will result in higher fertility. Examples of possible feedbacks of this kind are given in Chapter 15.

Feedbacks from non-demographic variables work indirectly via such complex matters as levels of education, status of health care, economic development, or environmental pollution. Only a comprehensive, multisector system would be able to track such feedbacks. However, the strength – and sometimes even the direction – of such multifarious feedbacks is largely unknown, or at least highly uncertain. Consequently, multisector-systems models tend to create dependencies and future paths that are far different from reality, a world in itself driven by feedback loops based often on shaky empirical or theoretical grounds.

A well-known example of such a multisector system is the World3 model – an economic, demographic, and environmental model of the world taken as a whole – developed by the Forrester–Meadows group during the 1970s (Forrester, 1971; Meadows *et al.*, 1972, 1974, 1992b; Meadows and Meadows, 1973). The crude death rate decreases with increasing food intake and improvements in the material standard of living, and increases with increasing pollution and (to a much lesser extent) population crowding.

The Bariloche model (Bariloche Group, 1976; Herrera *et al.*, 1976) is also noteworthy since it includes a relatively large number of feedbacks to the population submodel. For example, among other things, the crude birth rate is influenced by school enrollment, calorie intake, housing availability, and the life expectancy at birth (Herrera *et al.*, 1976:51).

A different approach was recently developed for a study on population–development–environment interactions in a specific setting (Lutz, 1994a).[5] A main feature of this PDE model is that it is extraordinarily flexible. Since the nature and the strength of most of the feedbacks included in previous models are subject to much debate among scientists, most of those feedbacks are not hard-wired in the model. These feedbacks must be defined by the scenario maker using the model software.

Conceptually such multisector models are desirable, but they are usually not suited for the purpose of population projections. Inclusion of multiple feedbacks from non-demographic variables in such models increases the potential for introducing more errors than one resolves.

2.9 Summary: The Approach We Chose

In this chapter we have addressed the following questions: Why another set of global population projections? Who wants projections and for what reasons? What should the time horizon and spatial resolution be? What output parameters are expected? Which alternative approaches address the issue of uncertainty in population projections? We have contrasted our approach to that of others. Issues have been identified in which progress is possible and desirable, and where alternative new strategies promise new insights. The left-hand side of *Table 2.1* summarizes some of the key issues in population projection, and the right-hand side specifies the approachs we have chosen.

There is little disagreement on the projection methodology to be used for (global) population projections. Our projections are carried out using a multiregional cohort-component model, with five-year age groups. In contrast to global projections produced by the UN and the World Bank, which are based on individual country estimates, we have disaggregated the globe into 13 major world regions. By doing so, much of the world's heterogeneity is taken into account, and we need not bother with national particularities, especially with respect to migration.

The crucial difference with respect to existing global population projections lies in the specification, justification, and combination of alternative scenario assumptions (Chapter 15) and in the definition of the first probabilistic world population projections (Chapter 16).

The approach chosen involves a number of steps. First, selected experts with different backgrounds in the fields of fertility, mortality, and migration analysis are asked to think about the future of the three demographic components. If necessary, different experts are invited for different regions. The experts are asked to suggest possible high and low assumptions for future fertility, mortality, and migration levels up to the year 2030 and discuss them in a group setting. The experts must argue their points substantively and justify their views. These elements are documented in Chapters 3 to 14.

Table 2.1. Major characteristics of our projection approach.

Issue	Our choice
Projection methodology	Multiregional cohort-component model with five-year age-groups and five-year projection intervals.
Spatial resolution	13 major world regions.
Time horizon	Experts define assumptions until 2030–2035; extensions until 2100.
Variability of components	Fertility, mortality, and migration are given equal importance; high and low values and the arithmetic mean for each component specified.
Basis of assumptions	Judgment of an interacting group of experts based on understanding of the underlying processes plus outside knowledge.
Justification of assumptions	Scientific chapters by experts in the fields of fertility, mortality, and migration; for developed and developing areas.
Uncertainty	Chapter 15: Alternative scenarios combining extreme fertility, mortality, and migration assumptions. Chapter 16: Probabilistic projections by simulations based on expert-defined probability distributions for all three components.
Interactions between the components	Independence of components in systematic permutation scenarios and probabilistic projections. Correlation between fertility and mortality in subset of probabilistic projections.
Feedbacks from results	Special scenarios assuming a food crisis in certain high-fertility regions (feedback from population size on mortality) and a social crisis in certain low-fertility regions (feedback from population aging on fertility). No feedbacks of multi-sectoral context explicitly assumed.
Correlations of regional demographic trends	The consequences of both regional correlation and independence are demonstrated.

Next, those alternative views expressed on future levels of fertility, mortality, and migration, which are sometimes only of a qualitative nature, are transformed into alternative quantitative assumptions on different future paths in each region considered. The high and low assumptions are assumed to correspond roughly to a 90 percent confidence interval of a subjective probability distribution. In other words, on each side only about 5 percent of all possible cases should lie outside the values considered. Assuming a normal distribution as representing the intuitive subjective probability distribution, the assumed central value is both the most likely case and the mean of the high and low values.

The specific process by which these subjective probability distributions were defined and combined in practical terms is described in detail in Lutz *et al.* (1995) and summarized in Chapters 15 and 16 of this book.

Acknowledgments

We would like to thank Gustav Feichtinger and Warren Sanderson for their valuable comments and discussions on this chapter.

Notes

[1] The word projection, of course, carries psychological connotations. *Webster's* defines the word as follows: "projection. 6b: the attribution of one's own ideas, feelings, or attitudes to other people or to objects ... 8: an estimate of future possibilities based on a current trend" *(Webster's New Collegiate Dictionary,* 1974). These two meanings are not wholly separable, for in imagining individual behavior in the future, we cannot but include our own perspectives.

[2] Birg (1995) presents a large set of simulations to assess the impact of alternative fertility and mortality trends on world population size. However, these calculations consider the whole world one region.

[3] The UN Population Division regularly publishes urban/rural projections for all countries by multiplying the projected population by assumed urban proportions.

[4] The possibility does exist that mistaken counts of the achieved population would give false estimates of empirical error. These could result in either overestimates or underestimates of error size.

[5] The past two decades produced a lively and rapidly growing literature on the interrelationships between economic, demographic, and environmental variables, but the development of simulation models that included these three factors almost came to a complete halt after the burst of activity in the early 1970s.

Part II

Future Fertility in Developing Countries

The material presented in Part II shows that fertility has started to decline in virtually all countries of the world. Even countries that until recently showed very high fertility levels seem to have entered the fertility transition toward low average fertility. The majority of developing countries are in the middle of this transition process, but some have nearly completed it. The China and Centrally Planned Asia (CPA) region is the most advanced in the transition process, followed by the regions of Latin America and Southeast Asia. Africa is least advanced in this process, but the most recent information shows that fertility is declining in this region as well. Survey research on preferred family sizes suggests further fertility declines in developing regions, and in many countries government family-planning policies have already had some success in lowering fertility levels.

Fertility is assumed to decline further in the future in all regions except in China and CPA, where fertility has already reached such a low level that one could even infer a slight increase if the one-child policy is relaxed in the future. In all other developing regions, differences between high- and low-fertility scenarios mostly reflect different assumed speeds of decline. But the question of what the ultimate fertility level will be at the end of the demographic transition process remains unanswered. There seems to be little substantive justification to assume that eventually fertility will stay at replacement level, which is defined as two surviving children per woman. Accordingly the low-fertility scenarios assume below-replacement fertility by 2030–2035 in all regions, while the high-fertility scenarios assume a retardation of the fertility decline.

A more detailed justification of the numerical assumptions is given in Chapter 15.

Chapter 3

A Regional Review of Fertility Trends in Developing Countries: 1960 to 1995

John Cleland

This chapter contains a review of fertility trends in developing countries over the period 1960 to 1995. The choice of the starting date is simple to justify. Before 1960, fertility decline was very rare in developing countries. Indeed, there is evidence that levels of childbearing in many countries increased in the 15 years following World War II. In this period, substantial improvements in life expectancy were achieved and thus rates of growth of Third World populations accelerated. Concerns about the effects of rapid population growth arose, and the 1960s saw the first examples of a unique and new form of social engineering: state-sponsored family-planning programs. These programs originated in Asia before spreading to other regions. As we shall see, any account of fertility trends has to address the centrally important issue of the contribution made to fertility decline by government interventions.

A broad-ranging review such as that contained in this chapter has to make explicit choices about the framework within which to present the demographic data. The goal is to choose a framework that will clarify the underlying forces of change. In this instance, a regional grouping of data has been chosen, rather than one based on development indicators. There are several reasons for this choice.

First, one clear lesson from the past 30 years is that simple mono-causal explanations of fertility decline totally fail to capture the complex interplay of factors that influence the onset and speed of fertility decline. Thus fertility trends cannot be illuminated adequately by a straightforward ordering of nations in terms of their stage of socioeconomic development. This is not to deny that development, particularly in the social sector, has an influence on childbearing. Rather it is to assert that this influence is strongly conditioned by cultural factors and government policies.

A second reason for choosing a regional framework is the existence of a pronounced regional imprint on fertility transition. The clearest example is the European fertility transition that was distinct in its timing from that in other regions. As demonstrated in this chapter, there is also an undeniable element of synchronicity in the onset of fertility transition in other major regions, such as Latin America and East Asia.

The importance of a region lies less in the implied geographical contiguity of constituent states than in the fact that it represents a surrogate for shared cultural values and features of social organization. A major advance in our understanding of fertility transition has been the realization that cultural factors, as denoted by religious, ethnic, or linguistic markers, may have a decisive impact on fertility, independent of economic and other types of influence.

The statistical underpinning for this review is the fertility rates collated and published by the United Nations Population Division. Specifically, the 1994 revision of *World Population Prospects* is the source of information on trends since the quinquennium 1960 to 1965 (UN, 1995). For some countries, UN fertility estimates are little more than guesswork; in other cases, they are based on poor data and may be incorrect and for the most recent period are based partly on projections. Nevertheless they represent the most carefully compiled and adjusted set of figures in existence and carry a corresponding authority. In the account that follows, major uncertainties about the rates for specific important countries are noted, but no attempt is made to amend UN estimates.

Throughout the chapter, levels of fertility are represented in the form of period total fertility rates (TFRs): the single most useful and widely used indicator. As is well known, period fertility rates are sensitive to variations in the tempo of childbearing as well as to the numbers of births that any cohort will achieve. Thus a period TFR can provide misleading impressions of the underlying level of cohort fertility. With the main exception of China, however, there is little evidence that TFRs in developing countries have been heavily influenced by large, reversible changes in the speed of childbearing. Insofar as this assertion is correct, period TFRs provide a valid indication of what age-specific fertility rates in a particular calendar period imply in terms of ultimate family size.

With these introductory remarks, the groundwork has been laid for the main part of the chapter: an essentially descriptive review of the course of fertility in the main regions of the developing world. Following this, an attempt is made to distill the main lessons that have been learned and what may lie ahead.

3.1 The Course of Fertility in Major Regions

3.1.1 East and Southeast Asia

East and Southeast Asia, excluding Japan, accounts for nearly one-third of the world's population, with China alone comprising about one-fifth of the total. Global population trends are thus largely determined by the course of events in this region. In contrast to South Asia, economic growth has been rapid: China, Indonesia, Thailand, Malaysia, Republic of Korea, Taiwan, Hong Kong, and Singapore have all achieved annual rates of growth in GDP per head between 1965 and 1988 of 4 percent or more. (The equivalent figure for India is 2.5 percent.) As a consequence, an increasing number of states in the region are now classified as upper-middle or high income countries; they are included in this review only because incomes per head were low at the start of the 35-year period.

As shown in *Table 3.1*, several countries (China, South Korea, Hong Kong, and Singapore) now have period fertility that is below replacement level. In all cases, decline started in the late 1950s or 1960s in response to rising age at marriage as well as increasing use of birth control. Careful analyses of South Korea (Park, 1992) and of Taiwan (Feeney, 1991) suggest that current period fertility

Table 3.1. Fertility trends in East and Southeast Asia.

	1960–65	1965–70	1970–75	1975–80	1980–85	1985–90	1990–95
Laos	6.15	6.15	6.15	6.69	6.69	6.69	6.69
Cambodia	6.29	6.22	5.53	4.10	5.06	5.25	5.25
Myanmar	6.00	6.00	5.75	5.30	4.90	4.50	4.16
Philippines	6.61	6.04	5.50	4.96	4.74	4.30	3.93
Vietnam	6.05	5.94	5.85	5.59	4.69	4.22	3.87
Malaysia	6.72	5.94	5.15	4.16	4.24	4.00	3.62
Indonesia	5.42	5.57	5.10	4.68	4.06	3.31	2.90
North Korea	5.75	7.00	5.70	3.46	2.77	2.50	2.37
Thailand	6.42	6.14	5.01	4.27	2.96	2.57	2.10
China	5.61	5.94	4.76	3.26	2.50	2.41	1.95
South Korea	5.40	4.52	4.11	2.80	2.40	1.73	1.73
Singapore	4.93	3.46	2.62	1.87	1.69	1.71	1.73
Hong Kong	5.31	4.02	2.89	2.32	1.80	1.31	1.21

Source: UN, 1995.

may be depressed by postponement of marriage and births and that
the underlying cohort level may be slightly above two births. This
interpretation is of considerable importance with regard to policy
because there is growing concern among several governments about
the implications of very low fertility. Singapore has already adopted
explicitly pronatalist policies, and it is possible that Taiwan and
South Korea will follow this lead, unless they can be reassured that
period rates are likely to rise.

Two other countries may join the below-replacement group before the end of the century: Thailand and North Korea. Thailand's
decline started in the late 1960s and has proceeded rapidly ever
since. Fertility is approaching replacement level with little sign thus
far of stabilization. Much less is known about the demography of
North Korea, and the government, unlike that of South Korea, has
been hostile or indifferent to the promotion of family planning. Nevertheless, there is evidence that fertility has fallen steeply: a vivid
demonstration that transition is not necessarily dependent on strong
government support. Another country of the region, Myanmar, appears also to have experienced fertility decline, despite government
indifference to family planning and isolation from the rest of the
world.

Fertility trends in urban China closely parallel those in the city states of Hong Kong and Singapore. Decline started in the early 1960s from a level of about 5.0 births. By 1980, fertility in all three settings had fallen below or close to replacement level. A major mechanism was increased birth control within marriage; age at marriage for women also rose sharply from about 20 years in 1960 to about 25 years in the early 1980s.

Of course, fertility in China as a whole is determined by rural trends. As in India, traditional fertility levels in China appear to have been modest, within the range of five to six births. Also like India, there is some evidence that natural fertility increased initially under the impact of modernization. Marital fertility rates in the mid-1950s appear to have been about 15 percent higher than rates recorded in the 1930s (Coale and Freedman, 1993). The first major destabilization of rural fertility was the disastrous Great Leap Forward in the late 1950s. Mortality rose sharply and period fertility plummeted to a little above three births before rebounding to over seven in 1963. There followed a period of vacillation in fertility rates during the Cultural Revolution. The dramatic decline in rural fertility started in about 1970, coinciding with the introduction of a forceful family-planning program. Between 1970 and 1980, the TFR for the whole country fell from about 6.0 to 2.4 births. This decline of nearly 60 percent in 10 years represents the single most important contribution to the fall in global fertility over the past 30 years. However, the emergence of pronounced regional variations during this period is often overlooked (Peng, 1981). By the end of the decade, TFRs in remote provinces of China, such as Tibet, Guizhou, and Ningxia, were still over 4.0.

In 1979, the Chinese government announced the one-child policy, and in the following year passed a marriage law that was widely interpreted as a relaxation of the previous strong discouragement of early marriage. Both measures had profound but partially offsetting effects on the course of fertility in the 1980s. The one-child policy was enforced with considerable success in urban areas. By 1985–1987, urban fertility was well below 2.0 in all provinces of China. Indeed in most of the larger cities, second- and higher-order births almost disappeared. In the rural areas, however, the policy encountered strong resistance. The majority was not prepared to sign the one-child pledge, and period fertility in nearly all provinces remained well above 2.0.

For the whole country, the period TFR fluctuated throughout the 1980s around a level of 2.4 births per woman, with no clear evidence of a continuation of the decline of the 1970s. Many commentators assumed that the economic reforms of the 1980s made it increasingly difficult for central and local officials to enforce an unpopular policy. However, in 1989 population policy was again strengthened and responsibility for enforcement was transferred to local civilian authorities. Analyses of results from a 1992 survey conducted by the State Family Planning Commission suggest that fertility fell sharply in the period 1989 to 1992 (Feeney and Yuan, 1994).

Fertility transition in Indonesia shares several characteristics with that in China. In both countries, levels of socioeconomic development were low at the onset of decline and, in both cases, couples were subjected to strong official pressure to adopt birth control. The Indonesian government initially focused its attention on densely settled Java, which comprises just 6 percent of the country's land area but over 60 percent of the population. Fertility started to decline there (and in Bali) in the early 1970s. By 1976, fertility in Java was actually lower among the least-educated rural population than among the urban, more-educated sectors: a highly unusual situation that undoubtedly reflected the impact of the government program (Freedman *et al.*, 1981).

Between the late 1960s and the early 1990s, fertility in the whole country fell from 5.7 to 2.9 births, a decline of over 40 percent. In Java, the current level is well below 3.0 births per woman but in Sumatra, the second most populous island, fertility remains much higher.

The neighboring countries of the Philippines and Malaysia contrast in numerous and fascinating ways with Indonesia. In the 1960s, economic and educational standards were higher than in Indonesia and fertility began to decline earlier. But the pace of decline has been much more gradual. Total fertility rates in Malaysia and the Philippines – estimated by the UN to be 3.6 and 3.9 over the period 1990–1995 – are now markedly higher than in Indonesia.

The stalling of fertility decline in Malaysia dates from the late 1970s and appears to originate with a resurgence in Islamic values and shifts in government policy. While fertility among the Chinese and Indian minorities continued to decline, and is now little above replacement level, that of the majority Malay population actually rose in the 1980s, in response to a decline in the use of contraception (Leete and Tan, 1993). In 1984, the government announced a new population policy which set a target of 70 million inhabitants by the year 2100. It was widely perceived to be a pronatalist measure, and a national survey conducted shortly afterward indicated that a significant fraction of Malay women had revised their family-size expectations upward in response (Arshat *et al.*, 1988).

In the Philippines, there was no radical change in population policy but official support for family planning has always been relatively weak because of the opposition of the Roman Catholic Church. Although President Marcos created, in 1969, a Commission on Population to coordinate family-planning activities, it failed to secure consensus support or widespread coverage of services. Support further weakened during the Aquino era. Between 1978 and 1993, the level of modern contraceptive practice among married women rose only from 17 to 25 percent.

In summary, the fertility transition in East and Southeast Asia is varied and complex. Variability is evident in the starting level of fertility; the timing of the onset of decline and level of socioeconomic development at the time; the speed of decline; and the role of government policy. Anyone who still believes that the level of reproduction is a predictable outcome of education, urbanization, and living standards should pause to ponder the difference in fertility transition between Indonesia and Thailand, on the one hand, and Malaysia and the Philippines, on the other.

3.1.2   South Asia

For present purposes, this region is defined as the Indian subcontinent, extending west to include Iran. It accounts for about 20 percent of the world's population and represents the largest numerical concentration of poverty. Bangladesh and Nepal, with GDPs per head of US$170–$180, are among the poorest countries of the

Table 3.2. Fertility trends in continental South Asia.

	1960–65	1965–70	1970–75	1975–80	1980–85	1985–90	1990–95
Afghanistan	7.01	7.13	7.14	7.21	6.90	6.90	6.90
Pakistan	7.00	7.00	7.00	7.00	7.00	6.75	6.17
Bhutan	5.92	5.92	5.92	5.92	5.86	5.86	5.86
Nepal	5.68	5.78	6.26	6.54	6.35	5.90	5.42
Iran	7.26	6.97	6.54	6.50	6.80	6.00	5.00
Bangladesh	6.68	6.91	7.02	6.66	6.15	4.80	4.35
India	5.81	5.69	5.43	4.83	4.47	4.07	3.75

Source: UN, 1995.

world, while India and Pakistan, with per caput GDPs of $350, rank twenty-second and twenty-third in the world of poverty.

In the region as a whole, fertility has declined modestly from a level of about 6.0 in the early 1960s to a little over 4.0 births in the early 1990s, a fall of some 30 percent. However, there is considerable uncertainty about South Asian demographic trends. For three countries – Iran, Afghanistan, and Bhutan – recent fertility trends are essentially unknown. For three other countries (Bangladesh, Pakistan, and Nepal) they are a matter of controversy, leaving only India for which vital rates are clearly established.

United Nations estimates for Afghanistan and Bhutan show high fertility rates in the 1960s of about seven births per woman and very modest declines in the past 20 years (*Table 3.2*). For Afghanistan, a verdict of unchanging high fertility seems entirely reasonable, though the military disruptions of recent years may well have caused a temporary drop. The UN scenario for Iran is also doubtful. Before the revolution, the country had a vigorous family-planning program that made a considerable impact. After the fall of the Shah, the program was discredited, but in recent years the government has reaffirmed the need to moderate the population growth rate and is again promoting family planning. The degree of success achieved remains uncertain; fertility has declined, although perhaps not at the rapid pace suggested by the UN.

By contrast, Bangladesh, Pakistan, and Nepal generate a relative abundance of demographic data. All three countries have conducted regular censuses; all have conducted a number of detailed fertility surveys, supplemented by contraceptive prevalence surveys; and Bangladesh and Pakistan have prospective systems that publish vital rates. Yet demographic trends remain in dispute. The reason for this uncertainty lies in the poor quality of the data. Surveys, in particular, tend to suffer from the pernicious problem of backward displacement of dates of recent births, leading to an underestimation of the current level of fertility. Claims of fertility decline are often made but these are equally often shown to be false by the next survey.

Accordingly, the results of the 1991 Demographic and Health Survey (DHS) in Pakistan, which indicates a big decline in fertility to about 5.5 births, should be regarded with great skepticism. Reliance on the prospective system, run by the Federal Bureau of Statistics in Karachi, is more prudent. This system portrays a constant total fertility of about 7.0 births until 1988, when a drop to 6.5 is recorded. The results for the early 1990s show levels of about 6.2. Falls in lower-order birth rates tend to be more pronounced than in higher-order births; thus it remains unclear whether marital fertility decline (which normally affects higher-order births at the initial stages) has really started. Certainly the level of contraceptive practice reported in the 1991 DHS (12 percent) is too low to make an appreciable impact on fertility. To conclude, the level of fertility in Pakistan remained high and constant until the late 1980s but has probably fallen slightly in the period 1988–1990. The UN estimates in *Table 3.2* are essentially correct.

In Nepal, evidence of decline is more secure than in Pakistan. The 1991 Fertility, Family Planning, and Health Survey yielded an unadjusted TFR of 5.1. The level of contraceptive use rose from 5 percent in 1976 to 23 percent in 1991, and age at marriage for women also increased over this period. Thus fertility transition in Nepal has almost certainly started.

In Bangladesh the pace of change is more rapid and pronounced than in Pakistan and Nepal. It is increasingly apparent that fertility decline started in the late 1970s and gathered pace in the 1980s. Between 1975 and 1990, the TFR fell from about 7.0 to about 4.5. Evidence for these assertions comes largely from 1989 and 1994 fertility surveys and from two contraceptive prevalence surveys in 1989 and 1991, both of which collected truncated birth histories. The consistency of these data sets is striking, although the unadjusted estimate from the more recent survey is implausibly low. Detailed analysis of the 1989 fertility survey shows that the main change has taken the form of a reduction in higher-order births; for instance, the percentage decline in age-order specific rates (cumulated to age 40) between the period 1974–1978 and 1984–1986 was 10 percent for second births but 38 percent for fifth births. This evidence of increasing marital fertility control is confirmed by the rising level of reported contraceptive use, from 7 percent in 1975 to 45 percent in 1994. Age at marriage for women has also increased but the anti-natal effect is modest and offset by a decline in widowhood and in the length of the first-birth interval.

In broad terms, the remarkable transition in Bangladesh, the fifth poorest country in the world, has affected all socioeconomic strata equally. Thus fertility decline is as pronounced among illiterate, landless laborers as among the slightly more affluent cultivators. The experience of Bangladesh proves beyond a doubt that extreme poverty and low literacy do not represent absolute barriers to fertility decline.

Like Nepal, but in contrast to its Islamic neighbors, the traditional level of fertility in India was low, fluctuating between five and six births per woman between 1880 and 1960 (Bhat, 1989). One possible reason for the slow pace of fertility decline in India is that modernization acted to increase natural fertility through changes in lactational and sexual behavior. There is evidence that marital fertility in the rural areas of many states actually increased during the 1960s, despite the existence of a family-planning program and a gradual rise in reported contraceptive practice (Srinivasan, 1989). The onset of decline in total fertility occurred in the late 1960s and continued for almost a decade; it then stalled before resuming its downward path in the mid-1980s. The most obvious explanation for this sequence concerns the politics of population control. In the 1960s under Indira Ghandi, the family-planning program became increasingly coercive and, when she fell from power in 1977, its credibility also fell and recovered only gradually. Over the entire period from the early 1960s to the early 1990s, total fertility in India fell by 36 percent, from 5.8 to 3.7 births. Various decompositions (e.g., Chaudhry, 1989; Srikantan and Balasubramanian, 1989) indicate that one-fifth of this decline is attributable to rising age at marriage and the rest to marital fertility.

Some of the reasons for the slow pace of change in India – the possible relaxation of traditional restraints on fertility and the checkered history of the family-planning program – have already been mentioned. However, no account of Indian transition can fail to note the immense cultural and economic diversity of the country and its relevance to demographic trends. Transition is most advanced in the southern states, notably Kerala and Tamil Nadu with TFRs of 2.0 and 2.5, respectively, according to the recent results of the 1993 National Family Health Survey. In most of the northern states such as Rajasthan, Uttar Pradesh, and Bihar, fertility and childhood mortality remain high with TFRs ranging between 3.6 and 4.8. Many (e.g., Dyson and Moore, 1983) attribute this north–south divide to fundamental cultural differences that affect the status of women. In Kerala, for instance, 87 percent of women are literate, compared with 20–30 percent in the high-fertility, northern states.

3.1.3 Latin America

Latin America is defined here to include all states of continental South America and Central America, except Guyana and Surinam. In contrast to other major developing regions, Latin America experienced large-scale and permanent settlement of European populations, and this legacy is evident in certain features of the economy and fertility transition. Two countries, Argentina and Uruguay, were once among the wealthiest in the world and are still ranked in the upper-middle income category. Both had completed their fertility transition by 1950, with TFRs of 3.2 and 2.7, respectively, at that time. In the past 40 years, fertility in both countries has changed little, remaining well above replacement level (*Table 3.3*). This stabilization at levels ranging between 2.3 and 3.5 births per woman appears to be characteristic of the region. In Chile, as in Argentina and Uruguay, the era of rapid decline is over but period fertility remains within this range. However, there is no good reason for believing that Latin American culture possesses features that will sustain moderate fertility indefinitely. The majorities of the populations of these three countries are of Spanish and Italian extraction. Fertility levels in the countries of origin, Spain and Italy, are now among the lowest in the world. If Latin America experiences the socioeconomic transformation – particularly with regard

Table 3.3. Fertility trends in Latin America.

	1960–65	1965–70	1970–75	1975–80	1980–85	1985–90	1990–95
Guatemala	6.85	6.60	6.45	6.40	6.12	5.77	5.36
Nicaragua	7.37	7.17	6.79	6.40	6.00	5.55	5.04
Honduras	7.42	7.42	7.05	6.60	6.00	5.37	4.92
Bolivia	6.63	6.56	6.50	5.80	5.30	5.00	4.80
Paraguay	6.80	6.40	5.65	4.88	4.79	4.70	4.31
El Salvador	6.85	6.62	6.10	5.70	5.00	4.52	4.04
Ecuador	6.70	6.50	6.00	5.40	4.70	4.00	3.52
Peru	6.85	6.56	6.00	5.38	4.65	3.83	3.40
Venezuela	6.66	5.90	4.94	4.47	3.96	3.65	3.29
Mexico	6.75	6.70	6.37	5.03	4.30	3.70	3.21
Costa Rica	6.95	5.80	4.33	3.89	3.50	3.36	3.14
Brazil	6.15	5.31	4.70	4.21	3.65	3.15	2.88
Panama	5.91	5.62	4.93	4.05	3.51	3.20	2.88
Argentina	3.09	3.05	3.15	3.44	3.15	3.00	2.77
Colombia	6.76	6.28	4.66	4.14	3.51	2.90	2.67
Chile	5.28	4.44	3.63	2.95	2.66	2.65	2.54
Uruguay	2.90	2.80	3.00	2.89	2.57	2.43	2.33

Source: UN, 1995.

to the position of women in society – that has characterized Southern Europe, it is probable that Latin American fertility will fall to replacement level or below.

From speculations about the future, let us return to a consideration of the past. Because the demography of Latin America is rather well documented, it is possible to extend the historical description of fertility trends back to the 1950s. Between the early 1950s and the early 1960s, there is little evidence of any fertility decline. Indeed, in some countries such as Costa Rica, El Salvador, and Panama, a slight increase is registered, perhaps in response to declines in widowhood (Dyson and Murphy, 1985). In this regard, Latin America is very different from Asia, where rising age at marriage for women heralded and then accompanied declines in marital fertility. For most countries, the early 1960s represent the last quinquennium prior to the fertility transition. TFRs are typically close to seven births per woman, though lower in Brazil, Chile, Panama, and Venezuela.

Table 3.4. Year of onset of decline and percentage decline in following decade in Latin America.

	Year	Percentage decline
Brazil	1960	8.3
Guatemala	1960	9.6
Venezuela	1960	15.6
Costa Rica	1961	37.5
Colombia	1962	34.3
Chile	1962	28.7
El Salvador	1962	10.8
Nicaragua	1962	8.5
Panama	1962	20.0
Paraguay	1963	19.7
Ecuador	1965	20.0
Peru	1965	16.8
Honduras	1966	11.5
Bolivia	1972	13.8
Mexico	1972	36.4

Source: Guzman, 1994.

The synchronicity of the onset of fertility decline in Latin America is its most remarkable feature. Leaving aside Argentina and Uruguay, which belong to the earlier European transition, all but two countries (Mexico and Bolivia) started their declines in the 1960s. However, the speed of change varied widely. Guzman's (1994) calculations of the year of onset of decline and the percentage decline in the following decade are shown in *Table 3.4*. Declines of over 30 percent are registered on Colombia, Costa Rica, and Mexico. At the other extreme are Brazil, Guatemala, and Nicaragua which experienced declines of less than 10 percent. Interpretation of these figures is difficult, because of the somewhat arbitrary definition of the onset of decline. For instance, it is perfectly correct to characterize the transition in Mexico as both late to start but extremely rapid once under way; but it would be misleading to claim that fertility decline in Brazil has been slow but steady. Over the whole period from 1960 to 1990, the pace of change in Brazil has been as great as in Costa Rica and Colombia.

In terms of their current situation, Latin American states fall into four groups. The first group consists of Argentina, Chile, and Uruguay where fertility is low and relatively stable. A large second group follows. In this group total fertility is now in the range of 2.7 to 3.3 births, and this group shows some sign of incipient stabilization, particularly in Costa Rica. The three most populous countries of the region – Brazil, Mexico, and Colombia – fall into this group. It should be noted that fertility in Colombia is now slightly lower than in Argentina. The third group comprises four countries which are in the midst of transition with recent fertility rates of 3.5 to 4.5 births per woman. Finally, there is a cluster of four high-fertility countries, three of which are in Central America.

While the simultaneity of the onset of decline is the most remarkable feature of Latin American transition, a further distinguishing feature is the emergence of very pronounced but temporary urban–rural, socioeconomic, and regional differentials during the period of decline. In most countries of the region, decline started among the better-educated and metropolitan sectors and spread gradually to poorly educated, rural sectors. The typical process is well illustrated by Rodriguez and Hobcraft (1984) in an analysis of Colombian data. They were able to identify the beginnings of decline in the 1960s for women with complete primary or higher education, in the late 1960s for women with incomplete primary schooling, and in the late 1970s for those with no formal schooling. Furthermore, they demonstrated that, within each educational stratum, decline was initially restricted to a reduction in higher-order births and only subsequently affected earlier stages of family formation.

This sequence suggests strongly that fertility decline in Colombia has taken the form of social diffusion of a new form of behavior, birth control. An analysis by Rodriguez and Aravena (1991) supports this view. They examined subgroup changes in fertility behavior, using World Fertility Survey (WFS) and DHS data for 15 surveys including five from Latin America. Remarkable regularities were observed in the spacing and limitation components of marital fertility. Specifically, the strata with the least evidence of fertility control at the start tended to experience the greatest proportional change. Within strata, transition followed a self-sustaining course that is consistent with a basic diffusion process. To the extent that Rodriguez's analysis and interpretation are correct, it is inevitable that fertility in all strata will converge at a modest level. Thus the prospects for a continuation of fertility decline in the region as a whole appear good.

3.1.4 The Arab states

The Arab states constitute a linguistic and cultural rather than a compact geographical entity. Most have small populations: Egypt, with over 50 million inhabitants, followed by Sudan, Morocco, and Algeria, with about 25 million each, are the main exceptions. There is a very wide spread in living standards. At one extreme are the United Arab Emirates, Kuwait, and Saudi Arabia, classified as high-income countries. At the other end of the spectrum are Sudan, Mauritania, and Yemen with per caput GDPs of less than $500.

Information on the demography of the Arab world is patchy. For Libya, Lebanon, Syria, and some of the Gulf states, there is little recent evidence concerning fertility levels. In other countries of the region – for instance, Sudan and Mauritania – recent survey information is available, but as in South Asia, data quality is poor and the estimation of trends is correspondingly difficult.

Nevertheless, several features of Arab fertility have clearly been established. At the start of the period under discussion, the early 1960s, levels of fertility were universally very high, with TFRs ranging between 6.5 and 8.0. This exceptionally high level is the result of an unusual combination of early marriage ages, relatively short periods of breast-feeding, and limited practice of birth control. It is clear from *Table 3.5* that fertility remains high in this region. Only three countries, Lebanon, Kuwait, and Tunisia, record rates decisively below 4.0.

For the entire region, total fertility has fallen from about 7.0 in the early 1960s to about 4.5 in the early 1990s, a drop of 35 percent. This average conceals very large differences in trends and current levels and an equally large divergence in government policies toward population and family planning. Apart from Lebanon, whose ethnic and religious diversity sets it apart from the rest of the Arab world, the Egyptian and Tunisian governments were the first to provide public sector family-planning services and associated publicity, and were among the few Arab states to experience fertility decline in the 1960s. Tunisian fertility dropped steadily, and this country now records one of the lowest TFRs in the region with 3.2 births per

Table 3.5. Fertility trends in the Arab states.

	1960–65	1965–70	1970–75	1975–80	1980–85	1985–90	1990–95
Yemen	7.61	7.61	7.61	7.61	7.60	7.60	7.60
Oman	7.20	7.20	7.20	7.20	7.20	7.20	7.20
Libya	7.17	7.48	7.58	7.38	7.17	6.87	6.39
Saudi Arabia	7.26	7.26	7.30	7.28	7.28	6.80	6.37
Syria	7.46	7.79	7.69	7.44	7.38	6.66	5.90
Sudan	6.67	6.67	6.67	6.67	6.42	6.10	5.74
Iraq	7.17	7.17	7.11	6.56	6.35	6.15	5.70
Jordan	7.99	7.99	7.79	7.38	6.76	6.00	5.57
Mauritania	6.50	6.50	6.50	6.50	6.10	5.70	5.40
Qatar	6.97	6.97	6.76	6.11	5.45	4.70	4.33
UAE	6.87	6.76	6.35	5.66	5.23	4.60	4.24
Egypt	7.07	6.56	5.53	5.27	5.06	4.58	3.88
Algeria	7.38	7.48	7.38	7.17	6.35	4.97	3.85
Bahrain	7.17	6.97	5.94	5.23	4.63	4.08	3.75
Morocco	7.15	7.09	6.89	5.90	5.10	4.40	3.75
Tunisia	7.17	6.83	6.15	5.66	4.88	3.94	3.15
Kuwait	7.31	7.41	6.90	5.89	4.87	3.94	3.10
Lebanon	6.35	6.05	4.92	4.30	3.79	3.42	3.09

Source: UN, 1995.

woman. For reasons that are not fully understood, Egyptian fertility plateaued in the 1970s, before resuming a downward path in the 1980s to reach a TFR of 3.9 in the period from 1990 to 1995.

In the 1970s, declines in fertility became more widespread with well-documented falls in Jordan, Morocco, and a number of the small Gulf states. By the late 1980s, fertility decline had started throughout most of the Arab world, though the change was often modest. The main exceptions include two of the poorest countries, Yemen and Mauritania, but may also include some of the richest states, such as Libya, and Oman. Little is known about fertility in Libya, but it is thought that any decline is recent and modest. In Oman, fertility in 1987 was estimated from the Gulf Child Health Survey to be 7.8 with only 9 percent of currently married women reporting use of contraception. According to the results of the Gulf Child Health Survey, fertility in the late 1980s also remained high in several other Gulf states: 6.5 among the indigenous populations of Kuwait and Saudi Arabia, 5.9 in the United Arab Emirates, and

5.3 in Iraq (Farid, 1993). However, fertility had fallen more steeply in Bahrain and Qatar.

Fertility transition in this region shares some features of both the Asian and the Latin American transitions. As in Asia, rising age at marriage for women has made an important contribution to fertility decline, and as in Latin America, huge differences in fertility have arisen between urban and rural strata and between educational strata. This differentiation, in both Latin America and the Arab states, may reflect the rather weak nature or nonexistence of many government family-planning services; under such circumstances, the poor and less-educated have limited access to modern birth control.

In general, levels of Arab fertility remain much higher than might be expected from consideration of living standards and urbanization. This resilience is sometimes attributed to low levels of female autonomy and education. While it is true that female labor-force participation remains low, educational standards for women are rising rapidly in many Arab countries. But even among educated women, fertility is remarkably high. For instance, the 1990 Jordanian Demographic and Health Survey records the following TFRs by educational status of women: no schooling, 6.92; primary, 6.00; secondary, 5.39; and postsecondary, 4.10. There are few highly urbanized countries with reasonable access to family-planning services where fertility levels, even among educated couples, remain as buoyant as in Jordan. It seems reasonable to conclude that replacement-level fertility is a more distant prospect for the Arab world than for some other regions.

3.1.5 Sub-Saharan Africa

Sub-Saharan Africa comprises only 10 percent of the population of the Third World but accounts for a disproportionately large number of the least developed countries. The economic plight of the region deteriorated further in the 1980s, with declines in income per head in many countries. Although it possesses more cultural diversity than most of the other regions considered in this chapter, sub-Saharan Africa exhibits features of social organization and cultural values that distinguish it from other major regions: traditions of postnatal abstinence, polygyny, and the importance of lineage are the best known of these.

The first comprehensive account of Africa's demography had little direct information on fertility at its disposal and had to rely heavily on stable population analysis (Brass *et al.*, 1968). Since this report, data availability has improved steadily. Large sums were invested in censuses, and in the 1970s an increasing number of countries undertook more specialized demographic surveys. The World Fertility Survey represented the next step forward with the participation of 10 African countries. Under the successor to this program (the Demographic and Health Survey project) national surveys have been conducted in a further 12 countries.

Despite this improvement, knowledge of fertility levels in Africa remains uneven. Out of 35 continental states with a population of 1 million or more, direct information on fertility in the period 1985 to 1990 is available for only 17. Moreover, the reliability of estimates is lower than in South Asia. Hence *Table 3.6* is restricted to current levels and no attempt has been made to depict trends as has been done for other regions.

However, the evidence strongly suggests that, prior to 1980, fertility in Africa remained constant at a high level and increases were even recorded in some countries. Between the early 1960s and the 1980s, UN statistics show increases of 0.5 births or more for Rwanda, Angola, Zaire, Central African Republic, Gabon, and Guinea-Bissau. In some cases, the most plausible explanation is a decline in pathological sterility. In other cases, it may be attributed to an attenuation of traditional birth-spacing mechanisms. Indeed it is probable that, prior to 1960, fertility increase was more widespread. Feeney's analysis of Kenyan census data, for instance, suggests that fertility rose substantially prior to 1960 (for details see Feeney, 1988b). Unfortunately few countries have a record of census taking as good as Kenya's to allow a similar historical depth of analysis.

The persistence of high fertility in Africa gave rise to a prevailing view that this situation would continue for some time. It was argued that Africa possessed unique cultural and economic characteristics that would render reproductive behavior unusually impervious to the forces of change (e.g., Caldwell and Caldwell, 1990). The high desired family sizes reported in surveys further strengthened this prognosis.

Table 3.6. Fertility levels in sub-Saharan Africa: 1985–1990 and 1990–1995.

	1985–90	1990–95		1985–90	1990–95
East Africa			*Southern Africa*		
Uganda	7.30	7.30	Namibia	5.60	5.25
Malawi	7.40	7.20	Lesotho	5.45	5.20
Ethiopia	7.00	7.00	Swaziland	5.25	4.86
Somalia	7.00	7.00	Botswana	5.24	4.85
Burundi	6.80	6.80	South Africa	4.38	4.09
Rwanda	7.00	6.55			
Mozambique	6.50	6.50			
Kenya	6.80	6.28			
Zambia	6.50	5.98	*West Africa*		
Tanzania	6.36	5.90	Côte d'Ivoire	7.41	7.41
Djibouti	6.24	5.80	Niger	7.71	7.40
Eritrea	6.00	5.80	Mali	7.10	7.10
Zimbabwe	5.50	5.01	Benin	7.10	7.10
			Guinea	7.00	7.00
Central Africa			Liberia	6.80	6.80
Angola	7.20	7.20	Togo	6.58	6.58
Zaire	6.70	6.70	Sierra Leone	6.50	6.50
Congo	6.29	6.29	Burkina Faso	6.50	6.50
Chad	5.89	5.89	Nigeria	6.45	6.45
Eq. Guinea	5.89	5.89	Senegal	6.50	6.06
Cameroon	6.10	5.70	Ghana	6.39	5.96
Central Africa	5.69	5.69	Guinea-Bissau	5.79	5.79
Gabon	4.99	5.34	Gambia	6.20	5.60

Source: UN, 1995.

Events of the last decade have transformed perceptions about the stability of African reproductive regimes. First, an appreciable shift in population policies has occurred, with governments increasingly expressing concern about population growth and support for family-planning services. According to Mauldin and Ross (1991), sub-Saharan Africa recorded greater increases in the strength of family-planning programs than any other region. There are also signs of change in reproductive behavior. Nearly all Demographic and Health Surveys have recorded appreciable increases in median ages at first birth. For instance, the differences between cohorts aged 30 to 34 and 20 to 24 amount to 1.0, 0.9, 0.8, and 0.8 years in Kenya, Zambia, Burundi, and Togo, respectively. Improvements in the educational attainment of young African women may be one reason for this change. It is also possible that economic stress has acted to delay the formation of stable partnerships and the onset of childbearing.

Postponement of childbearing may be a temporary phenomenon. But there is evidence in an increasing number of East and Southern African states that fertility decline, fueled by contraceptive use, has started. Such a trend is much more likely to mark the onset of a sustained transition than to represent a transitory response to economic hardship. At the forefront of this movement is the Republic of South Africa. By the late 1980s, the level of contraceptive practice among the black population was estimated to be about 50 percent and total fertility at about 4.5 births (Mostert, 1991). Moderate levels of use among married women have also been recorded in Zimbabwe (48 percent), Botswana (33 percent), Kenya (33 percent), Namibia (23 percent), and Swaziland (21 percent). In all these countries there is parallel evidence of declining fertility. In South Africa, Zimbabwe, and Kenya the decline has amounted to about 2.5 births, in Botswana to about 1.5 births, and in Namibia and Swaziland to less than 1.0 birth per woman.

Successive surveys in Kenya show how rapidly the climate of reproductive opinion and behavior can change. The Kenya Fertility Survey of 1977–1978 portrayed a very pronatalist society. Total fertility was about 8.0; desired family size averaged 7.2 children; only 7 percent of couples reported contraceptive use; and only 16 percent of women said that they wanted no more children. There was little ground for believing that fertility transition was about to start. Yet a mere decade later, desired family size had dropped to 4.4 children, 49 percent of women expressed a wish to have no more children, contraceptive use had risen to 27 percent, and fertility had fallen to 6.5 births. In the early 1990s, fertility was well below six births and the mean desired family size was 3.7 births. This radical change had affected women of all educational backgrounds and ages.

This impression of change in the subregion should be balanced by data from other countries. Recent Demographic and Health Surveys provide no convincing evidence of appreciable decline in Burundi, Uganda, Zambia, or Tanzania. Nor is it reasonable to expect any decline in Angola or Mozambique because of prolonged civil unrest.

In West and Central Africa, fertility shows fewer signs of actual or incipient decline, though it is probable that fertility decline has started among young women in Senegal and in Southwest and Southeast Nigeria (Cleland *et al.*, 1994). Elsewhere, however, there is no strong evidence of fertility decline. This stability is particularly puzzling in a country such as Ghana. Ghana has long had a rather well-educated and urbanized population, where women possess considerable autonomy and indeed dominate trading. Moreover, there has been some attempt, since the late 1960s, to promote family planning, albeit on a limited scale. Despite the severe economic recession of the late 1970s and early 1980s which threatened living standards of the urban middle classes, fertility remained rather constant until the late 1980s (Onuoha and Timæus, 1995). However, the 1993 Ghana Demographic and Health Survey suggests that fertility decline has now started. The experience suggests that Ghanaian society and perhaps other West African societies present obstacles to fertility decline and mass adoption of contraception that are absent in East and Southern Africa. While the prospects are good for widespread fertility decline in the East and South, the prognosis for West and Central Africa is uncertain.

3.1.6 Island states

To complete this geographic account of fertility trends, *Table 3.7* provides data for the main islands and island groups. Their contribution to global population trends is minimal; yet the demography of islands is of special interest, and several have been at the forefront of fertility transition. In the 1960s, Fiji, Mauritius, and Sri Lanka were among the few developing countries to have started fertility transition. This evidence supported speculations that Malthusian constraints on population growth may take a particularly visible form in islands where territorial expansion is precluded.

Table 3.7 shows that such simple generalizations are unjustified. In the period 1985 to 1990, fertility in island states ranged from close to replacement level in Mauritius to about to seven births per woman in Comoros and the Maldives.

Table 3.7. Fertility trends in island states.

	1960–65	1965–70	1970–75	1975–80	1980–85	1985–90	1990–95
Comoros	6.91	7.05	7.05	7.05	7.05	7.05	7.05
Maldives	7.00	7.00	7.00	7.00	6.80	6.80	6.80
Madagascar	6.60	6.60	6.60	6.60	6.60	6.60	6.10
Melanesia	6.25	6.01	5.78	5.51	5.23	5.04	4.68
Micronesia	6.98	6.47	5.90	5.33	4.87	4.61	4.36
Cape Verde	7.00	7.00	7.00	6.70	6.29	4.70	4.26
Polynesia	7.64	7.09	6.18	5.31	4.69	4.19	3.74
Caribbean	5.46	4.99	4.37	3.49	3.10	2.88	2.76
Sri Lanka	5.16	4.68	4.00	3.83	3.25	2.67	2.48
Mauritius	5.72	4.24	3.25	3.06	2.45	2.17	2.35
Réunion	5.65	4.82	3.93	3.28	2.90	2.54	2.32

Source: UN, 1995.

3.2   Synthesis and Implications for the Future

Several lessons can be drawn from this regional review of fertility trends in the period 1960 to 1990. The first provides grounds for optimism about the economic and environmental future of the planet. During the past 30 years, fertility transition has spread throughout the developing world with a speed that has dazzled demographers and confounded many experts. It is easy to forget the profound pessimism about the prospects for fertility decline that prevailed in the 1960s and much of the 1970s. In particular, it was doubted that the mere promotion of birth-control services could have an impact on the birth rate of largely agricultural, low income, and poorly educated nations. As a consequence, there was intense interest in so-called beyond family-planning measures that included, *inter alia*, the use of financial payments to induce couples to accept contraception or to have fewer children.

The turning point in popular perceptions came in the mid-1970s with convincing signs that fertility decline was under way in Thailand and Indonesia, both largely agricultural countries with low incomes at that time. Hitherto, fertility decline had been confined to countries with atypically favorable conditions: rapid economic transformation in the case of Taiwan and South Korea; a metropolitan environment as in Hong Kong and Singapore; and the idiosyncrasies of an insular status such as Fiji, Mauritius, and parts of the Caribbean.

As we have seen, sustained fertility decline in the Third World is now the norm rather than the exception. In Asia, the main exceptions are Pakistan, Afghanistan, and some of the small countries of Indochina. In Central and South America, fertility decline is already completed or under way in all countries. Among the Arab states of North Africa and the Middle East, most countries have experienced falls in fertility though decline is not yet ubiquitous. Finally in sub-Saharan Africa, fertility transition is clearly starting in East and Southern Africa, leaving Central and West Africa as the main areas where fertility remains largely unchanged. Such widespread transformations of reproductive behavior have come as a surprise and their existence is not yet fully appreciated outside the specialist domain of demography. The rates of population growth in most developing countries remain high because of the continued decline in mortality and because crude birth rates are buoyed by increases in the relative and absolute numbers of couples in the reproductive ages. Thus, the impact of declining fertility is offset by these other demographic forces and, in many countries, will not be felt until the next century.

A major generalization of demographic transition theory is that once fertility decline, fueled by birth control within marriage, is under way, the trend is irreversible and sustained until fertility reaches replacement level or thereabouts. Like most simple generalizations, this one must be qualified. Reversals have occurred, most notably the post–World War II baby boom in Western Europe and North America. More commonly, fertility may plateau before resuming a downward path, as has been the case in Egypt and Malaysia. Moreover, the speed of decline has varied from the near-precipitous drops in China and Mexico to a slow pace of change, as in the Philippines or Jordan. A much more profound uncertainty exists about the proposition that fertility will continue to fall until the replacement level of a little over two births per woman is reached. In the aggregate, there is a logic in this ultimate destination for levels of human reproduction because it implies long-term stability of population sizes and, in the very long term, no animal population can continue to grow or decline indefinitely. But, at the level of families and individuals, such aggregate considerations may hold little force. It has already been noted that family sizes appear to have stabilized in some Latin American countries at a level that is well above replacement. In other regions, most notably sub-Saharan Africa and the Arab states, it is difficult to imagine the achievement of replacement-level fertility under existing socioeconomic and cultural conditions. Fertility aspirations, as recorded in surveys, remain much higher. In Zimbabwe, for instance, which is at the forefront of fertility transition in Africa, the 1988 Demographic and Health Survey indicates a mean ideal family size of 5.4 children among currently married women; and nearly half of women who already have 4 or more living children want additional children.

Of course, societal conditions do not remain stable. Indeed one of the biggest mistakes of demographers has been to underestimate the rapidity with which societies change. Nevertheless, the prospects for the attainment of replacement-level fertility within the next 40 years remain doubtful in some parts of the developing world.

The second major lesson from this review concerns the need for humility on the part of scientists. Despite a huge volume of new empirical evidence concerning fertility transition that has accumulated in the past 30 years, our understanding of the underlying causes remains rudimentary. Nor is there any sign of a growing consensus among population scientists regarding fertility theories or the relative importance of specific causes. The gulf remains wide between the two dominant schools of thought – one emphasizing economic determinism and the other, culture and the diffusion of ideas.

At the start of this chapter, the inadequacy of simple monocausal explanations of fertility decline was noted. This point is vividly illustrated by recent reviews of the socioeconomic status of Asian and Latin American countries at the onset of fertility decline (Casterline, 1994; Guzman, 1994). For every indicator (life expectancy, infant mortality, urbanization, adult literacy, income per head, percentage engaged in agriculture), there was a very wide spread among countries. To take but two examples from Latin America, infant mortality ranged from 62 per 1,000 births in Paraguay to 151 in Bolivia, and adult literacy from 84 percent in Costa Rica to 34 percent in Guatemala. This huge disparity in the stage of socioeconomic development reinforces similar conclusions from studies of the European transition, where birth control spread across a region with little regard for socioeconomic differences between counties, bringing lower fertility in its wake.

With the steady increase in the number of countries where fertility transition has already started, research priorities will shift from the study of the determinants of the onset of decline to the study of factors that influence speed of decline and point of stabilization. Here again, though, it is unlikely that very strong links will be found between speed of transition and socioeconomic indicators. The earlier comparison between Indonesia, Malaysia, and the Philippines is a pertinent example. Even more striking is the rapid fertility decline that has taken place in Bangladesh, one of the poorest countries in the world.

The reason for this complexity is that both culture and government policies exert strong independent influences on fertility. It is appropriate to end this chapter with a brief consideration of one of these factors (government policies) because of its practical relevance. To the extent that state-sponsored initiatives to promote birth control and the acceptability of smaller families can be effective, the future course of human fertility depends, at least in part, on government policies and the availability of funds to implement them. Conversely, if the influence of such interventions is minor, then future fertility trends will be determined by broader forces of cultural and socioeconomic change that are less amenable to governmental and international decisions.

The effectiveness of family-planning programs has been high on the demographic research agenda for the past 20 years. The most influential body of work comprises statistical estimations of the relationship between the strength of family-planning programs and the demographic outcomes such as level of fertility, percentage decline in fertility, and contraceptive use, using countries as units of analysis (e.g., Mauldin and Berelson, 1978; Mauldin and Ross, 1991). The general finding is that strong programs do reduce fertility, though this effect is conditioned by, and subordinate to, the effect of socioeconomic development. It is also clear from these analyses that the creation of family-planning programs cannot be divorced easily from general development. Few of the least developed countries have birth-control services, education, and publicity that are rated as strong. Conversely, few of the more developed countries have programs that are rated as nonexistent or weak. This correlation obviously complicates the task of isolating the effect of programs from effects of broader development.

A major limitation of this type of study is that program strength is taken as an exogenous factor. The analytic design is vulnerable to the criticism that serious programs are most likely to arise in response to spontaneous expressions of need and prior fertility decline, and only grow in strength (i.e., political commitment and resource allocation) when success is already visible. Programs can thus be seen as a consequence as well as a potential cause of demographic change. This weakness severely limits the validity of results.

A more convincing approach to an assessment of program impact would be to compare fertility trends in countries that are broadly similar in cultural characteristics and stage of development but where population policies have diverged, perhaps because of the convictions of political leadership. Algeria and Tunisia, Pakistan and Bangladesh, Mexico and Colombia, North Korea and South Korea, Zambia and Zimbabwe are possible candidates for such a study. In each pair, the first country was much slower than the second country to adopt and implement policies and programs to reduce fertility. And in each case, the timing of the start of fertility decline appears to reflect the policy divergence. Thus it is hard to resist the inference that Mexico's very late fertility transition is connected to the government's hostility to provision of family-planning services until the dramatic change in 1972. Similarly, the persistence of high fertility in Algeria until the early 1980s is surely related to the low priority attached to birth control, which shifted only in the 1980s.

Such a comparative case study approach shows that government policies can have and have had appreciable demographic impacts by changing reproductive attitudes, by legitimizing birth control, and by enhancing access to family-planning services. To the extent that this verdict is valid, the future course of fertility in regions where it is still high depends to some extent on political leadership. As a consequence, demographic forecasting becomes more uncertain but the politics of population and birth control become more important and exciting.

Chapter 4

Reproductive Preferences and Future Fertility in Developing Countries

Charles F. Westoff

The classical paradigm of the demographic transition features a decline in the rate of reproduction from the conditions of natural fertility at high levels to a regimen in which fertility is highly controlled and has declined to replacement or lower levels. In many of the developing countries that have entered this transitional stage, increases in age at marriage have played an important role. But the principal mechanism driving this transition is birth control, mainly in the form of contraception, though abortion has made significant impacts at different times and in different places.

In Asia and in Latin America, the use of contraception has typically been adopted at higher parities after couples have achieved the number of children desired; its use at lower parities for the regulation of spacing has appeared later in the fertility transition. In contrast, in Africa, especially in sub-Saharan Africa, a demand for spacing evidently has emerged before a demand for limiting fertility. Currently, in the nine sub-Saharan African countries included in the first phase of the Demographic and Health Surveys (1986-1990), the average percentage of married women using contraception for spacing purposes was 10 percent compared with 8 percent for limiting fertility. In the 16 other developing countries (including those in

North Africa), the corresponding percentages were 12 and 36 percent, respectively, a dramatically different ratio (calculated from data presented in Westoff and Ochoa, 1991:7).

Whether contraception is employed for purposes of spacing or for purposes of limiting fertility, it reduces the likelihood of pregnancy and thus has an impact on the period rate of fertility. There is evidence that contraceptive failure rates are greater when methods are used for spacing rather than for limiting births, but, even with such higher failure rates, fertility is reduced far below that implied in the natural fertility model (especially considering the higher fecundability at the younger ages, where spacing behavior is more common). In any event, a full appraisal of the subject of reproductive preferences should ideally include both preferences to postpone the next birth and preferences to terminate fertility. Data on spacing preferences are not as widely available, however, as data on preferences to terminate fertility. The World Fertility Survey included no direct questions on the subject, and the DHS-I questionnaire did not include the questions necessary to estimate preferred lengths of birth intervals for all women. Therefore, the emphasis in this chapter is on the number of children desired and the intention to terminate fertility. These measures are particularly relevant for Asian and Latin American populations where the contraceptive prevalence level is determined largely by such limiting practice. As noted above, the use of contraception for birth spacing dominates in the sub-Saharan African countries and thus makes more of a contribution to the prediction of fertility in that part of the world.

4.1   Desired Number of Children

The most common measure of reproductive preferences is the number of children desired. The basic question included in all DHS interviews was "If you could go back to the time you did not have any children and could choose exactly the number of children to have in your whole life, how many would that be?"

The mean number of children desired is shown in the first column of *Table 4.1* for currently married women in all of the countries included in DHS-I. The range of these preferences varies widely, from

Table 4.1. Indices of reproductive preferences of currently married women.

	Mean desired number of children	% with more than desired number	TFR	DTFR	% wanting no more children
Sub-Saharan Africa					
Botswana	5.4	14	5.0	4.1	38
Burundi	5.5	12	6.7	5.7	24
Ghana	5.5	13	6.4	5.3	23
Kenya	4.8	30	6.4	4.5	49
Liberia	6.5	6	6.9	6.3	17
Mali	6.9	5	7.6	7.1	16
Ondo State	6.1	5	6.1	5.8	23
Senegal	7.2	9	6.6	5.6	19
Sudan	5.9	8	5.0	4.2	25
Togo	5.6	18	6.6	5.1	25
Uganda	6.8	9	7.5	6.5	23
Zimbabwe	5.4	15	5.2	4.3	33
North Africa					
Egypt	2.9	37	4.4	2.8	60
Morocco	3.7	27	4.6	3.3	47
Tunisia	3.5	34	4.1	2.9	58
Asia					
Indonesia	3.2	19	2.9	2.4	51
Sri Lanka	3.1	21	2.6	2.2	64
Thailand	2.8	21	2.2	1.8	66
Latin America					
Bolivia	2.8	42	5.1	2.8	68
Brazil	3.0	35	3.3	2.2	64
Colombia	3.0	31	3.1	2.1	69
Dominican Rep.	3.7	28	3.6	2.6	63
Ecuador	3.4	30	4.3	2.9	65
Guatemala	4.2	18	5.5	4.5	47
Mexico	3.3	29	4.0	2.9	65
Peru	2.9	44	4.0	2.3	75
Trinidad/Tobago	3.1	24	3.0	2.2	54

as high as seven children in a few countries in sub-Saharan Africa to under three children in a few countries elsewhere.

One well-known difficulty with this measure is that it is influenced by the number of children already born (and surviving), some of whom may not have been wanted at the time. The second column of *Table 4.1* shows, for each country, the percent of currently married women whose number of living children exceeds their desired number. Even considering the likely tendency for women to rationalize unwanted births as wanted, this statistic indicates significant proportions of women who prefer fewer children than they have. In sub-Saharan Africa, this measure shows the lowest levels of excess fertility, ranging between 5 and 18 percent except in Kenya, where 30 percent of women are classified as preferring fewer children than they have. The percentages with unwanted fertility are much higher elsewhere, involving roughly between one-fifth and two-fifths of married women. It is clear, even from this simple measure, that fertility is significantly higher in many countries of the Third World than it would be if women's preferences prevailed.

What do these levels of unwanted births imply for the rates of reproduction? In column 3 of *Table 4.1*, the total fertility rate (TFR) is shown for each country. These rates have been calculated from the birth histories of all women based on person-months of experience up to 24 months before the survey. A desired total fertility rate (DTFR) has been derived by confining the numerator for each age-specific category to those births classified as desired or, conversely, by deleting those births in excess of the number preferred. The DTFR (in column 4) is intended as an estimate of what the TFR would be if only wanted births prevailed.

In sub-Saharan Africa (including Sudan), the DTFR averages about 15 percent below the TFR. The greatest differences are in North Africa and in Latin America, where the DTFR averages 31 percent and 32 percent, respectively, below their TFRs. The levels of fertility implied by women's preferences are quite low. The lowest level is for Thailand, where the DTFR reaches 1.8, some 18 percent below the TFR of 2.2. The values of the DTFR in all of the Latin American countries except Guatemala fall below three births per woman.

In sum, the evidence implies a potential for further major declines in fertility in North Africa and in most of Latin America; for moderate further declines approaching replacement levels in Thailand, Sri Lanka, and Indonesia; and for smaller declines in sub-Saharan Africa. Section 4.2 presents some short-term forecasts of the TFR and evaluates the extent to which the DTFRs are likely to be approximated.

4.2   Fertility Forecasts

The TFR can be forecast (with considerable accuracy, judging from eight DHS-II surveys recently completed) by taking advantage of the strong interrelationships among fertility, reproductive intentions, and contraceptive prevalence. We know (Westoff, 1990; Mauldin and Segal, 1988) that there is a very high correlation between the TFR and the percentage of married women currently practicing contraception – an R^2 of 0.91, based on a large number (84) of national fertility surveys. We also now know that contraceptive prevalence has a strong association with reproductive intentions, i.e., the percentage of married women who want no more births. In a recent analysis (Westoff, 1990) of data from these same countries, the R^2 between these two variables was estimated at 0.78. We also know that the same strong associations exist not only across countries at a given time but also between successive surveys in the same countries observed at five-year intervals. In developing forecasts based on these associations, we relied upon the association between reproductive intentions and contraceptive prevalence measured in those countries where surveys have been repeated. The procedure first estimated the future proportion of women who want no more births based on the regression equation connecting this variable at two points in time. The predicted value for each country is then included in a second equation to forecast the contraceptive prevalence. To improve this fit, the regression is expanded to include the earlier contraceptive prevalence. Finally, the TFR is forecast from the predicted prevalence and, to improve the fit, from the earlier TFR. In short, the model relies upon estimates of the regressions between t_1 and t_2 to predict the values at t_3, incorporating an additional predictor at each stage (Westoff, 1991b). The results are shown in *Table 4.2*.

Let us examine the end product first – the forecasts of the TFR – and then return to the foundation of reproductive intentions. The forecasts of the TFR indicate an average decline over the next five years or so of close to 10 percent in sub-Saharan African and range

Table 4.2. Forecasts of reproductive preferences, contraceptive prevalence, and fertility.

	% wanting no more		Contraceptive prevalence		TFR		
	Current	Fore-cast	Current	Fore-cast	Current	Fore-cast	DTFR
Sub-Saharan Africa							
Botswana	38	45	33	37	5.0	4.5	4.1
Burundi	24	34	9	14	6.7	6.1	5.7
Ghana	23	33	13	18	6.4	5.8	5.3
Kenya	49	54	27	34	6.4	5.3	4.5
Liberia	17	28	7	11	6.9	6.3	6.3
Mali	16	27	5	10	7.6	6.8	7.1
Ondo State	23	33	6	12	6.1	5.7	5.8
Senegal	19	30	11	15	6.6	6.0	5.6
Sudan	25	35	9	15	5.0	4.8	4.2
Togo	25	34	12	17	6.6	6.0	5.1
Uganda	23	33	5	11	7.5	6.7	6.5
Zimbabwe	33	41	43	45	5.2	4.5	4.3
North Africa							
Egypt	60	63	38	45	4.4	3.9	2.8
Morocco	47	52	36	41	4.6	4.1	3.3
Tunisia	58	61	50	55	4.1	3.5	2.9
Asia							
Indonesia	51	55	48	52	2.9	2.7	2.4
Sri Lanka	64	66	62	66	2.6	2.3	2.2
Thailand	66	67	66	70	2.2	1.9	1.8
Latin America							
Bolivia	68	69	30	39	5.1	4.5	2.8
Brazil	64	66	66	69	3.3	2.7	2.2
Colombia	69	70	63	68	3.1	2.6	2.1
Dominican Rep.	63	65	50	55	3.6	3.2	2.6
Ecuador	65	67	44	51	4.3	3.7	2.9
Guatemala	47	52	23	30	5.5	5.0	4.5
Mexico	65	67	53	58	4.0	3.4	2.9
Peru	75	75	46	54	4.0	3.5	2.3
Trinidad/Tobago	54	58	53	57	3.0	2.7	2.2

to an average of 13 percent in Latin America. How close are these forecasts to the DTFR? A comparison of the values in the last two columns of *Table 4.2* reveals considerable variation across these countries. In most of the sub-Saharan African countries, the DTFR is modestly lower than the forecasts. Kenya and Togo show the largest differences, indicating that women's reproductive preferences are declining more rapidly than the likelihood of such preferences being realized. In a few countries, there is hardly any difference – Liberia, Ondo State in Nigeria, and Uganda. Zimbabwe is also in this category, with a forecast TFR of 4.5 and a DTFR, for example, of 4.3.

The differences between these rates are much greater in North Africa, with the DTFR considerably lower than the expected TFR. In Egypt, the forecast shows a TFR of 3.9 with the DTFR at 2.8. The three Asian countries have already gone through most of the fertility transition; although the forecast TFRs show some continued decline, they are very close to the DTFRs. In contrast, Latin America is more like the three countries in North Africa. Wide differences remain between the forecast values and the desired levels, especially in Bolivia and Peru, where the DTFR is around one-third lower than the TFR forecast. In the other seven Latin American countries, the DTFR is an average of one-sixth below the average forecast value.

One of the intrinsically unsatisfactory features of the forecasting procedure described here is its essential bootstrap nature, in particular, the initial forecast of the proportion of (married) women wanting no more children from the regression equation connecting this variable at two points in time. It is not unlike forecasting tomorrow's weather from today's weather in an area of the country that typically sends its weather systems in one direction. The underlying theory in this case is a knowledge of the prevailing wind direction and the pace of its movement. Our procedure is even less theoretically grounded. It recognizes that a population's reproductive preferences at t_1 are highly correlated with those at t_2 and that the sign of the regression coefficient indicates a decline.[1] It then uses this relationship to predict the proportion wanting no more births at t_3. The next step, which relies upon the regression of contraceptive prevalence on reproductive intentions, is less unsatisfactory because it identifies a causal antecedent in substantive terms,[2] whereas the forecast of reproductive intentions relies only on the association between these intentions over time.

The actual forecasts of reproductive intentions (columns 1 and 2 of *Table 4.2*) appear reasonable enough. The forecast for the sub-Saharan African populations show a rise from an average of 27 percent to an average of 36 percent of women who want no more children. The projected increases elsewhere in the percentage of women who want no more are less dramatic: in North Africa from 55 to 59 percent; in Asia from 60 to 63 percent; and in Latin America from 63 to 65 percent.

4.3   Determinants of Reproductive Preferences

The main reason that the forecast of reproductive intentions relies on the same variable at an earlier time is simply that we have little else to use. In a broad sense, the determinants of reproductive intentions or preferences in developing countries cover the whole range of social changes included in the concept of modernization. These determinants are only partially represented in the WFS and DHS; e.g., economic status is inadequately measured. We do know that the desired number of children has been declining in many, probably in most, developing countries. The mechanics of this process are less well known. The conventional explanations focus on the changes in the economic value of children; recent speculation minimizes the importance of structural economic changes and emphasizes the role of Western or modern ideas about the control of reproduction and small family norms (Cleland and Wilson, 1987). There is probably a time lag in the process of change in reproductive norms. The most likely process is one that first witnesses an increase in the proportion of women who want no more children without a commensurate decline in ideal or desired family size. In turn, this leads to a demand for and the use of contraception and an ensuing decline in fertility. Eventually the number of children desired begins its decline as smaller family norms develop. The urban and middle-class populations typically lead the transition.

In sub-Saharan Africa, the marital fertility transition may follow a different path. As noted earlier, the primary stage may be the adoption of fertility control to increase birth intervals, a motivation derived from health rather than from socioeconomic considerations.

Kenya is a major exception to this generalization; over the decade from 1978 to 1988, the proportion of women wanting no more children increased from 17 to 49 percent.

Analysis of the determinants of reproductive preferences can be approached at two levels: the macro-demographic level, in which the statistical units of observations are the provinces or regions of countries, and the micro or individual woman level.

4.4   Regional-level Analysis

Analysis of the determinants of reproductive preferences at the provincial or regional level focuses on the question of what characteristics of these areas are associated with the mean number of children desired or the proportion of married women who want no more children. The areas assembled for this purpose are the 302 provinces or regions of the 51 countries that participated in the WFS or in the first stage of the DHS. Although this is a relatively large number of areas for analysis, it should be kept in mind that it is not a representative sample of the developing world; China and India, for example, are not included.

Since the object of interest is the number of children desired rather than fertility and because there is some tendency to rationalize as desired children that may have been unwanted at the time of conception, we have tried to eliminate the life-cycle effects by singling out a particular age group. Women aged 25–29 were selected because most would be married by that age (removing the censoring by age at marriage) and the experience of unwanted fertility would be still largely in the future, thus minimizing the factor of rationalization. The mean number of children desired for this age group across the 302 regions is 4.6, with a range from 2.3 to 8.5. For the proportion of women who want no more children a similar logic was followed by confining the analysis to married women with four or five children. The mean percentage of women at this parity who want no more children is 58.0, with a range from 0 to 98.1. Because there is a high correlation between these two measures (-0.92), the same covariates are observed. Areas with women wanting no more children or desiring smaller families are those with high proportions of their population classified as urban, high proportions of husbands

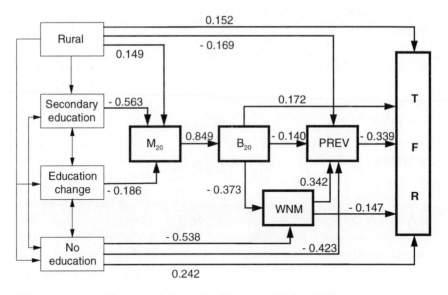

Figure 4.1. The nuptiality–fertility model for 216 regions.

in professional occupations, low proportions of women with no education, lower proportions of women 15–19 currently married, lower proportions having a birth before age 20, and are areas with lower rates of infant mortality. This constellation of correlates is a familiar package of variables associated with development. There is considerable overlap in these predictors that collectively account for 60 to 70 percent of the variance of reproductive preferences across regions. The unexplained variance is partly error of measurement, but also reflects the absence of other relevant explanatory variables, perhaps measures of income or wealth.

The complete picture of the paths through which reproductive intentions affect fertility and are determined by different variables is shown in *Figure 4.1*. In this analysis, which shows imputed causal directions and the path (standardized) regression coefficients, the role of reproductive intentions is interconnected in various ways. (The analysis is confined to a subset of 216 regions for which information on all variables is available.) The variable WNM is the proportion of married women with 4–5 children who report that they want no more children. This variable is directly influenced by the percentage of women with no education and is indirectly influenced by the proportion who have had a birth by exact age 20

(B_{20}). In turn, the latter variable is determined by the proportions first married by age 20 (M_{20}), which is seen to be a function of residence (the rural percentage), the proportion that attended secondary school, and a measure of educational change that reflects the generational decline in the proportion of women with no education. The influence of reproductive intentions on the TFR, in turn, is seen to operate indirectly through the prevalence of contraception and directly, presumably through unmeasured non-contraceptive paths such as abortion.

4.5   Individual-level Analysis

We have also explored the determinants of reproductive preferences at the level of individual women in several countries, partly to validate the aggregate analysis but also to exploit some economic and media exposure data that have not been collected by many of the surveys included in the regional-level analysis. Several countries were selected from different areas that represent various stages in the fertility transition: Colombia, Ghana, Kenya, Guatemala, Peru, Thailand, Tunisia, and Indonesia. The surveys in these countries were all part of the DHS-I project.

   In none of these countries are we able to account for much of the individual variance of the desired number of children. The regression equations for each country are shown in *Table 4.3*; the R^2s range in value from only 0.065 to 0.314. We have confined the examination to women 25–29 years of age as a life-cycle control, and our multivariate exploration has excluded measures of fertility that would add to the explained variance. We have concentrated instead on social and economic measures and have added only age at marriage and/or age at first birth in order to parallel the aggregate analysis.

   A similar set of determinants of reproductive norms operates across these countries. Several variables stand out prominently in all six countries. One is the importance of region of residence. In all of these countries, region exerts a strong influence on the number of children desired. It is a surrogate for many other variables: region frequently reflects language, ethnic origin, or religion as well as the stage of economic development. In principle, region could be further disaggregated to seek explanations at these compositional levels.

Table 4.3. Linear regression equations for variables related to number of children desired[a] by women 25–29 years of age.

	Regression coefficients[b]							
	Colombia	Ghana	Guatemala	Indonesia	Kenya	Peru	Thailand	Tunisia
Urban–rural[c]			0.586		0.692		0.237	0.462
Region[d]								
1			-1.170	-1.100			-0.246	-0.604
2	-0.365		-0.989		-0.457			-0.834
3					0.892	-0.240		-1.020
4					-0.758		0.346	
5			-0.538	-0.890				-0.360
6			-0.651	-1.159				
7								
8		3.176						
Ethnicity[e]			-1.224					
Education (wife)[f]		-0.895	-0.431	-0.209	-0.531		-0.124	-0.175
Education (husband)[f]		-0.443	-0.476	-0.169		-0.266		
Age at marriage[g]				-0.065	-0.052	-0.030	-0.045	-0.053
Age at first birth[g]	-0.050							
Watch TV[h]	-0.669			-0.340		-0.266	-0.154	-0.473
Listen to radio[h]				-0.234	-0.299			
Electricity[i]	-0.607		-0.733				-0.199	
Constant	4.835	6.655	8.016	6.247	5.317	4.000	3.495	4.970
R^2	0.123	0.314	0.223	0.108	0.146	0.065	0.085	0.164
Number of women[j]	566	745	781	2448	1126	546	1252	836
Mean number desired	2.74	5.73	5.36	3.61	4.74	2.69	2.54	3.51
Standard deviation	1.38	2.66	3.56	2.16	1.99	1.21	1.08	1.52

[a]Non-numeric responses of the type "as many as God sends" or "as many as come" were usually recoded in category 12+ or with the highest numerical response if less than 12.

[b]All of the regression coefficients shown in the table were significant at least at the 0.05 level, mostly $p < 0.001$.

[c]Urban–rural residence scored as 0 and 1.

[d]Regions were defined as dummy variables. Those with the highest significant coefficients recorded here are Pacifica in Colombia; Volta, Ashanti, and upper and northern regions in Ghana; Guatemala City, Central, Norte, and Norte Oriental in Guatemala; Java–Bali in Indonesia; central, coast, and eastern regions in Kenya; Selva in Peru; north and south in Thailand; and Tunis, north-east, north-west, and Sahel in Tunisia.

[e]Ethnicity in Guatemala is coded as Indigina or Ladino.

[f]Education of wife and husband are coded here in terms of the categories: no education, primary, secondary, higher. Single years of schooling were not used because of significant numbers of missing cases.

[g]Age at first marriage and age at first birth were coded in units of single years.

[h]Watching TV and listening to the radio coded as 0 for no and 1 for yes.

[i]Electricity coded as 0 for no and 1 for yes.

[j]These are the unweighted numbers. Missing information cases are assigned to the modal frequency category.

Where such requisite data are available, the variable still retains its power, although sometimes it obliterates rural–urban differences as well. Of course, the importance of region in the study of differences in fertility has been underscored in many other studies, including the well-known 19th-century European fertility study (Coale and Watkins, 1986). Urban–rural residence also features in half of the countries in the multivariate analysis.

One variable that holds up consistently is education of women, which is inversely related to preferences for fewer children, a pattern that persists in the presence of all other variables. In a few countries, the husband's education makes a similar and additive contribution (in Peru, it overshadows women's education). Education has been demonstrated to be probably the most dependable and predictable determinant of fertility and fertility regulation behavior among all of the socioeconomic measures examined in hundreds of studies.

Several other determinants operate in some countries but not in others. Age at marriage or age at first birth is a factor in all of these countries except Ghana and Guatemala: the later the age of the event, the fewer the number of children desired. How often the woman reports listening to the radio or watching television has an effect in all but these two countries as well. In all likelihood, the mass media transmit outside values and ideas. In other research, we have demonstrated a powerful association with reproductive attitudes and behavior of media messages on family planning, including soap operas that extol the advantages of smaller families (Westoff and Rodríguez, forthcoming).

One of the more surprising findings is a negative one, *viz.*, that various measures of economic status either singly or in combination fail to disclose any significant associations with the number of children desired. Admittedly, the availability of economic data in these surveys is less than ideal. Nonetheless, there is a variety of items including ownership of bicycles, cars, radios, televisions, refrigerators, kinds of toilet facilities, source of drinking water, electricity, and different country-specific information on ownership of homes, land, livestock, and so on. In only a few countries do any of these measures seem to play any direct role in the determination of reproductive preferences. Only in Colombia, Guatemala, and Thailand does one of these economic variables hold up – the presence of electricity in the household. The economic variables frequently show the expected negative associations with reproductive preferences at the zero-order level, but their influence is absorbed or dominated by the regional and educational factors. It seems implausible that economic status would be totally irrelevant to the number of children women desire. However, there is simply no empirical support from the data for the hypothesis that smaller or larger families are viewed as inconsistent with economic resources, or more precisely, that any such inconsistency persists in the presence of these other variables. One might of course reason that economic resources play an earlier role in facilitating education, but this notion is not testable with these data.

4.6   Conclusions

So what do we know about reproductive preferences and the dynamics of fertility change in the developing world? A fair summary would be as follows:

1. Whether measured by the average desired number of children or by the proportion of married women who want no more children, dramatic changes toward the small family norm are under way in Latin America, much of Asia, and North Africa, but only in a few sub-Saharan African countries (where spacing rather than limiting preferences and behavior predominate).
2. Reproductive preferences are highly correlated (in the aggregate) with the fertility rate, operating mainly, though not exclusively, through contraceptive prevalence.
3. At the regional or provincial level, the main determinants of reproductive preferences are those typically associated with modernization: residence in cities or in rural areas, education of women, occupational status of men, and age at marriage and at first birth.
4. Our knowledge of determinants at the level of the individual woman remains very limited: region, rural–urban residence, education of women, age at marriage, and exposure to mass media dominate the picture rather than individual economic variables. However, the amount of variation explained is very small.

Notes

[1] Unlike the direction of the wind in the weather analogy, the direction of reproductive preferences cannot remain pointed in the same way indefinitely. At the end of the fertility transition, reproductive preferences stabilize and may even change directions for periods of time, as has been observed in some developed countries.

[2] Operationally, it is also corrupted by this bootstrapping quality in that the actual forecasting equation adds the earlier prevalence value. The redeeming feature here is that at least it does not depend exclusively on the forecast value of intentions that is based on its own earlier values.

Chapter 5

Population Policies and Family-Planning in Southeast Asia

Mercedes B. Concepcion

Impressive gains in the control of fertility and in the reduction of population growth rates have been observed in many countries within the purview of the Economic and Social Commission for Asia and the Pacific (ESCAP). Family-planning (FP) and maternal and child health (MCH) programs have played an important role in reducing population growth, improving the quality of life, and developing human resources in the region. The success of FP and MCH programs is closely associated with the enhanced role and status of women, lower infant, child, and maternal mortality rates, better birth-spacing and breast-feeding practices, and the delivery of services by trained personnel. Nevertheless, the population as a whole continues to grow by more than 50 million yearly. Moreover, progress in lessening population growth rates has been uneven and has generally widened the gap between countries with continued high growth rates and those which have succeeded in moderating or lowering their growth rates.

In Southeast Asia, three of the region's 10 component countries are expected to grow at rates of 1.8 percent or less per annum during the 1990–1995 quinquennium while the rest are expected to increase annually by at least 2.1 percent. By the beginning of the 21st century, all but one of the countries in Southeast Asia are projected to grow no faster than 1.7 percent yearly. Total fertility rates (TFRs) during the early 1990s are also expected to range from Singapore's reported low 1.7 children to the estimated 6.4 children per woman in the Lao People's Democratic Republic. These rates are foreseen by the United Nations to drop to about 3 children or fewer at the start of the next century (UN, 1991b). The exceptions are Cambodia and the Lao People's Democratic Republic.

Governments in 5 of the 10 Southeast Asian countries perceive their current fertility levels as unsatisfactory and have ongoing programs to lower such rates. Three others – Brunei Darussalam, Lao People's Democratic Republic, and Myanmar – are satisfied with their present fertility levels. Brunei Darussalam and Myanmar do not report any direct intervention, while the Lao People's Democratic Republic is intervening to maintain current rates. Cambodia and Singapore consider their fertility rates too low. The former restricts access to contraception, while the latter has been offering tax rebates to couples having a third or fourth child.

This chapter examines the population policies and FP programs in selected Southeast Asian countries (Indonesia, Malaysia, the Philippines, Singapore, Thailand, and Vietnam) and attempts to draw from their experience the critical preconditions for family-planning program success. Such experiences have been gleaned from the country statements provided by participants of the 4th Asian and Pacific Population Conference (APPC) held in Bali, Indonesia, on 19–27 August 1992.

5.1 Demographic Situation

During the 4th APPC, which was entitled Population and Sustainable Development: Goals and Strategies into the 21st Century, the present population situation and future outlook were reviewed in the light of the 1982 APPC Asia–Pacific Call for Action on Population and Development. The participants noted that while substantial progress had been achieved by the ESCAP region in responding to the Asia–Pacific Call for Action, population issues continue to pose a most critical challenge. The conference adopted the Bali Declaration on Population and Sustainable Development, which set goals and made recommendations for population and sustainable development into the next century.

One of the population goals included in the Bali Declaration enjoined countries and areas to adopt suitable strategies to attain replacement-level fertility, equivalent to a TFR of around 2.2 children per woman, by the year 2010 or earlier. In addition, member countries were also urged to reduce the level of infant mortality to no more than 40 infant deaths per 1,000 live births during the same period. Countries and areas where maternal mortality remains high were called upon to effect a 50 percent reduction by the year 2010.

The Bali Declaration recommended that priority be given to strengthening policy development and related processes in those countries where the MCH and FP programs have not yet achieved desired objectives. Furthermore, such countries were urged to expand and streamline MCH and FP delivery systems within the primary health-care framework, adopt innovative management and multi-sectoral approaches, and encourage wider community and inter-sectoral participation in program implementation efforts. Countries which have already reduced their fertility to low or acceptable levels were prompted to devise program strategies aimed at achieving self-sustainability.

5.2 Family-planning Policies and Programs

The country statements circulated during the 4th APPC contained a section on the policy and objectives of national FP/family health and welfare programs.

5.2.1 Indonesia

The state policy guidelines, issued by the 1973 People's Consultative Assembly, declared that the objective of the national FP program during the second five-year development plan period (1974–1978) was to improve maternal and child health in order to create a small, happy, and prosperous family. The guidelines also stated that economic and social welfare development can be implemented rapidly, together with population growth control, through a properly administered national FP program. The most recent guidelines, issued in

1988, added that the Indonesian FP program should also be directed at reducing mortality rates. At the same time, the need for successful implementation without endangering future generations was emphasized. In addition, a policy to enhance support to FP acceptors through improvements in the quality of available contraceptives and services was outlined. As a general course of action, FP acceptors are encouraged to use more effective contraceptives, thus ensuring better protection against pregnancy and accelerating fertility reduction.

The Indonesian FP program has three broad objectives: expansion of contraceptive coverage in accordance with government targets; promotion of continued contraceptive use; and institutionalization of FP and small family norm concepts by shifting responsibility for FP decisions to the individual, the family, and the community.

Nine important program strategy elements have been taken into account in the Indonesian FP program: integration of an array of governmental, nongovernmental, private, and community agencies; decentralization of responsibility and authority; commitment to meet targets at every program level; provision of FP services combined with medical advice; National Family Planning Coordinating Board (BKKBN) cooperation with the Ministry of Health in health services beyond FP in order to improve FP outreach; development of a climate of community support for FP through the cooperation of community and religious leaders; support for activities which raise women's social and economic status; emphasis on reaching the rapidly increasing numbers of youth; and encouragement of self-reliance, the newest strategy element involving the private sector.

The Indonesian Country Report (1992) stated that the TFR which was 5.6 children between 1965 and 1969 fell to 3.0 by 1992. The corresponding decrease for the crude birth rate (CBR) was from 42.6 to 25.2 births per 1,000. By 1990, the crude death rate (CDR) was estimated to be 9.7 deaths, down from 21 deaths per 1,000 over the period 1961–1971. The CDR is projected to reach 8.5 deaths per 1,000 at the start of 1993, declining to around 7 per 1,000 by the year 2020. The infant mortality rate (IMR), currently estimated at 65 infant deaths per 1,000 live births, is expected to drop to 28 by the year 2020. The life expectancy at birth, now reported to be around 60 years for both sexes, is forecast to lengthen by 10 years during the next quarter of a century. Maternal mortality is predicted to fall from a level of 450 deaths per 100,000 live births in 1986 to 200 by 2020.

The Indonesians foresee a likely deceleration in the future rate of fertility decline. The reasons given in the Country Report were that the desired family size of some couples is unlikely to decrease further; those who most want to avail themselves of family planning as well as those for whom the services are most accessible have already been covered by the program; and the couples who still need to be brought into the program express larger family-size preferences and are more difficult to reach. Among these are the urban poor, those living in outlying areas, those with low educational levels as well as those who find it difficult to use contraceptives correctly. Therefore, further mortality and fertility reductions will entail considerably greater efforts. For example, the family-planning program will have to reach unprecedented numbers of contraceptive acceptors and motivate couples with high fertility preferences, people who are less likely to know about health and family-planning programs and are less disposed to seek services.

5.2.2   Malaysia

Given the rapid economic growth and the prospect of a further decline in fertility, the Malaysian government changed its official stance in 1984 and promulgated a national population policy. As expressed in the Malaysian Country Report (1992), a long-term target of 70 million people by the year 2100 is to be achieved through decelerating the TFR decline. The plan is to reduce the TFR by 0.1 point over five-year periods until a level of 2.05 children is reached in the year 2070. The TFR in peninsular Malaysia had fallen from a high 6.8 children in 1957 to about 3.3 children in 1990. At this pace, a TFR of 2.1 could be reached by 2010. The average age at marriage for females had risen from 22.1 in 1970 to 24.6 years in 1990. The IMR was recorded at 13.3 infant deaths per 1,000 live births in 1990. The life expectancy at birth of Malaysian males was lengthened from 55.8 years in 1957 to 69.1 years in 1990. The corresponding rates for females were 58.2 and 73.3 years, respectively. Given current trends, the most probable outlook during the next three decades is for small nuclear families with the couples participating actively in the labor force.

Since its inception in 1966, the Malaysian FP program has undergone several phases of development, each involving expansion in terms of the approach used, the area covered, or the number of agencies involved in the provision of contraceptive services. The spread of FP services to the rural areas as part of an integrated MCH/FP program was initiated in the early 1970s and led to FP services being integrated in the MCH services provided by the Health Ministry. The blending of FP with health and other social programs not only aided in overcoming the resource constraints but also contributed to wider FP acceptance and a heightened contraceptive prevalence rate.

In line with the national objective of improving the quality of life, a comprehensive family development program has been developed and is now being implemented. It emphasizes the improvement of family health and welfare through family-life education, parenting courses, and marriage and family counseling. The stress is now on improving infrastructure in underserved and remote areas, on enhancing coverage and quality of care in designated areas of low coverage, and on program consolidation. The implementation of the risk approach in MCH/FP care has for its ultimate objective the availability and accessibility of a range of services, including FP, to all women and families for their better health and well-being.

5.2.3 The Philippines

Since 1970, the Philippine FP program as described in the Country Report (1992) has been a social development initiative aimed at diminishing the country's fertility level for the benefit of family and national welfare. Over the course of its history, the program has adopted varying approaches and strategies to suit the changing needs and conditions of the time. There have been modest increases in contraceptive prevalence rate coupled with moderate declines in total fertility. Program efforts have contributed substantially to this decline. However, the gains made did not approximate those of neighboring countries owing to problems besetting policy and program implementation.

In response to the difficulties experienced in relying on static clinics, the Outreach Project was implemented in 1976 to expand the availability and accessibility of services. The Outreach Project viewed FP not only as a means to reduce fertility but, more importantly, as advancing family welfare. Furthermore, a closer integration of broader population concerns into the country's development plans, policies, and programs was sought. The Outreach Project also paved the way for strengthening and deepening local government involvement in, and support for, FP.

In 1987, a new population policy statement was formulated, taking into account relevant provisions of the 1987 constitution. The new policy broadened program concern beyond that of fertility reduction. Consequently, the 1989–1993 five-year population program directional plan was drawn up focusing on two components, namely, responsible parenthood/FP and population and development. The program's institutional arrangement was altered along with the policy and the program. The Department of Health was designated as the implementing agency for the FP program with jurisdiction over the activities of all FP service delivery agencies. The Commission on Population, on the other hand, remained as the overall planning, policy-making, coordinating, and monitoring body of the entire program with specific responsibility for coordinating the population and development integration thrust.

The new FP program uses a health-oriented, demand-driven approach, anchored on safe motherhood and child survival. Its primary objective is to reduce the level of unmet needs for FP, particularly among poor families. The population and development thrust is one of systematically incorporating population matters into the development efforts of concerned agencies.

Whether the program will be able to make a more significant contribution toward development goals depends on its ability to align policies and operational aspects to individual and societal needs. Some considerations include expanding and intensifying the provision of women's health and family-planning services; integrating FP in other health programs, particularly MCH; strengthening the capacity of agencies to manage the services; promoting collaboration among the governments, nongovernmental organizations (NGOs), and other private organizations and local communities to improve access to these services; and shortening the gestation period for an effective program implementation by local government units, including appropriating local funds for the program.

As stated earlier, the slow pace of decline in Philippine population growth is the consequence of a moderately decreasing fertility and a decelerating mortality decline. The CBR fell from a level of 46 births per 1,000 in 1969 to about 30 in 1990. The CDR dropped from 32 deaths per 1,000 in 1940 to around 7.2 in 1990. Further pronounced decreases are not expected as the pace of decline has slackened significantly. The IMR has fluctuated around 61 infant deaths per 1,000 live births since the 1960s. The estimate for 1990 was 57. Communicable diseases still account for the majority of morbidity and mortality cases. Since 1970, the TFR has been slowly but steadily declining and was estimated to be around 4 children per woman in 1990. This gradual descent can be attributed to four causes: the continued expansion in the number of women of reproductive age as an outcome of past high fertility; shrinkage in the prevalence and duration of breast-feeding; low-level use of the more effective contraceptive methods; and the Roman Catholic hierarchy's open and active opposition to the government's FP program, thus affecting its political support.

5.2.4 Singapore

The country's FP and population program was initiated in 1966, soon after independence. Ambitious FP targets were set for each five-year plan (1966–1970, 1971–1975, and 1976–1980), and social disincentives were introduced. The government actively promoted the two-child family norm. Contraceptives were made easily available, and abortion and sterilization were legalized. With the attainment of replacement-level fertility in 1975, the government started to emphasize child spacing as the main policy orientation. The program impact on population growth was significant. According to the Country Report, Singapore's fertility fell by almost 70 percent within a span of two decades (Ministry of Health, 1992). The TFR dropped from 4.7 children in 1965 to a historic low of 1.4 in 1986.

With the continued decline in fertility rates in the early 1980s, population projections indicated that if below-replacement fertility were to continue, the country would experience negative population growth within the next 30 years. A new population policy was promulgated in 1987 in response to the prospect of a decline in numbers. The new policy thrust encourages marriage and childbearing. A new slogan, "Have three or more if you can afford it," was adopted reflecting the new direction. Generous incentives are being provided such as income tax rebates, subsidies for child-care centers and for delivery fees, and special leave schemes. In addition, two programs – Strengthening the Marriage Program and Family Life Education Program – have been implemented.

Since the adoption of the new policy, TFRs have inched upward. The rate rose to 1.9 in 1988, but is now about 1.7 children. Since the tax incentives were announced, the number of third- and fourth-order births have gone up. However, marriage trends have not manifested significant improvements. The critical issue on population and development facing policy makers is one of ensuring replacement-level fertility to achieve the optimum population size and a balanced age structure.

5.2.5   Thailand

In 1970, the government officially launched the National Family Planning Program (NFPP) aimed at further reducing the population growth rate. According to targets set by successive five-year plans in the last two decades, the program succeeded in decreasing the growth rate through quantitative target-oriented strategies. The provision of an extensive contraceptive distribution system and the efforts to legitimize the preference for fewer children and to increase awareness of the possibility of controlling family size through effective and acceptable means contributed to the program's success. Past successes, however, do not imply that there are no longer any unmet needs or new and more difficult challenges ahead. The seventh plan (1992–1996) has renewed the emphasis on human resource development, thus posing new challenges to the health sector. The strategy for MCH/FP over the next five years will be to maintain the program momentum to raise contraceptive prevalence rates in the face of a 10 percent rise in the number of women of childbearing age; provide effective follow-up for couples who are already using contraceptives; meet more effectively the special needs of adolescents and ethnic minorities; and improve the management, training, and information systems, particularly at the regional level. Since health is a national responsibility, the strategy calls for providing MCH/FP services within a national and inter-sectoral framework.

Thailand's fairly well-developed and extensive health infrastructure has brought about a significant improvement in the health status of mothers and children. The NFPP is well integrated in the tasks of the Ministry of Public Health's Family Health Division. The NFPP has effectively utilized the wide primary health-care network to make contraceptive services available throughout the country. However, equal attention needs be given to both the quality of services and the achievement of the plan's targets. This action entails strong collaboration with other government agencies, with the private sector and with NGOs, all of whom have important roles to play in supplementing government activities.

The population growth rate decreased from 3.0–3.3 percent in the 1960s to about 1.4 percent in 1991, as stated in the Thailand Country Statement (1992). The seventh plan has targeted the reduction of the growth rate to 1.2 percent by the end of the plan period. The TFR has dropped from about 6.1 during the period 1968–1969 to less than 2.5 children per woman today. In 1990, the CDR was estimated at about 5 to 6 deaths per 1,000 population, with the IMR at approximately 34.5 infant deaths per 1,000 live births a year later. Currently, life expectancy is estimated to be 66 years for males and 71 years for females. Recently, married couples whether rural- or urban-based, lesser or better educated, have overwhelmingly expressed a desire for a family size of some two children.

5.2.6 Vietnam

As recorded in the Country Report (1992), decision number 29 of the Council of Ministers of the Socialist Republic of Vietnam, issued on 12 August 1981, contained the following objectives for the national population and FP program: married women should be prompted to have their first birth after age 22; each couple should be persuaded to have only one or two children; and a spacing of five years should be encouraged between the first and second birth.

According to the country's 1989 population census, there were 64.4 million people in Vietnam. The intercensal growth rate for the period 1979–1989 was 2.1 percent. The population in 1991 was estimated at 67.7 million. The CBR recorded for the 12-month period preceding the 1989 census was 31 births per 1,000, with urban and rural areas reporting 23 and 34 births per 1,000, respectively. The CDR was 8.4 deaths per 1,000, while the IMR was 49 infant deaths per 1,000 live births. The average life expectancy at birth was 63 years for men and 67.5 years for women.

On 18 October 1988, the Council of Ministers' Decree on Population and Family Planning Policies was promulgated (Vietnam, 1989). The stated goal is to reinforce and strengthen measures to lower population growth and to ensure that adequate family-planning methods are readily available and utilized by the population. Norms were set for the minimum age at first birth (at least 22 years for urban women, 19 for rural women), for the number of children (no more than two for most families), and for birth spacing (three to five years after the first).

A national health law passed by the National Assembly on 30 June 1989 legalized some of the above-mentioned measures. In addition, the law gives legal force to the individual's right to choose to limit births and provides for recourse to the judicial system should this right be violated (Allman *et al.*, 1991).

The population of Vietnam is projected to reach 87 million by the period 2005–2010 with a growth rate of 1.4 percent, a CBR of 22.2 births per 1,000 population, and a CDR of 7.9 deaths per 1,000. In projecting the future population, the National Committee for Population and Family Planning (NCPFP) took into account the over 17 million women currently of reproductive age who comprise nearly half of the country's total female population. Moreover, past high fertility rates are obviously affecting the replacement capacities of future generations. Starting in the year 2000, half a million women, on the average, will be added yearly to the cohort of reproductive age. This poses additional constraints on the achievement of an annual decrease in the TFR of 0.11 in the 1990s and of 0.6 in the first decade of the 21st century.

To achieve the immediate as well as long-term objectives set forth in the national population program, Vietnam will endeavor to improve the quality and effectiveness of FP activities by utilizing a network of intercommunal FP centers and communal health clinics; make a wider choice of contraceptives available; integrate FP activities in other MCH, nutrition, rural development, income generation, and women's status improvement programs; train FP staff at the grass-roots level; and support studies on impacts of FP programs and contraceptive methods as a basis for the formulation of a more effective and practical FP program.

5.3 Family-Planning Program Effectiveness

Family-planning programs have a long tradition in the Asian region, and are firmly established there. Various countries in the region have conceived novel approaches and have devised new strategies to reduce fertility. In this section an attempt is made to extract the most important factors contributing to family-planning program effectiveness from the experiences of the countries considered in this chapter.

In common with other Asian countries, Indonesia, Malaysia, the Philippines, Singapore, and Thailand boast of a relatively longer experience with intervention schemes to modify reproductive behavior. All these countries directly support family-planning programs and provide unlimited access to modern contraceptives. As a whole, the most common approaches in these countries consist of integrating family-planning services in the health-care system at the community level or in rural development schemes. Incentives and disincentives have been introduced to discourage large families.

Singapore, which achieved replacement fertility in 1975, introduced a comprehensive package of incentives and disincentives in 1969 which was further intensified in 1972 to exert pressure on couples to limit their family size. In addition, sterilization was promoted as the best contraceptive method for those who had completed their families. Abortion became available on demand for a small fee in government facilities. There were graduated charges for delivery in government hospitals, paid maternity leaves covering the first two children only, preferential treatment in choice of primary school for the first three children in a family, and no priority for public housing for large families. An additional policy which was made known to the public in 1976 was designed to encourage later marriage and wider birth spacing.

The high commitment of President Soeharto, reflected in the above-mentioned state policy guidelines, represents one of the keys to the success of the Indonesian family-planning program. This commitment is not merely a personal one but is institutionalized in the existing systems, both in the People's Consultative Assembly and in Parliament and other executive systems. The program strengthened its links with rural communities by recruiting acceptors by means of a village-based delivery system. Acceptors in the program are maintained through various measures extending beyond family planning. To enhance family planning within the framework of institutionalizing the small family-size norm, the BKKBN developed a system of nonmonetary rewards for individual or group acceptors. A system was introduced in 1989 whereby a community with high contraceptive prevalence rates receives a deep well. The reward can also be in the form of scholarships for children of low income families that have been resorting to contraception for at least a decade. Moreover, some private Indonesian firms give discount cards to certain acceptor groups in major cities for the purchase of selected items.

The success of Thailand's family-planning program, as stated in the preceding section, can be traced to both the provision of an extensive system of contraceptive distribution and the efforts to legitimize the preference for fewer children and increase awareness of the possibility of controlling family size through effective and acceptable means.

The Philippines has tried a variety of schemes intended to induce couples to have fewer children. Among these are income tax deductions limited to four dependents, abolition of paid maternity leaves after the fourth child, and payment of lower interest rates for rural bank loans by couples using contraceptives. However, the coverage of these schemes was limited and therefore of little value in motivating couples to limit their family size. Malaysia also introduced tax deductions and maternity benefits but limited them to the first three children.

In Vietnam the rewards that had been implemented since 1982 included monetary bonuses and exemption from the required month per year of corvée labor for sterilization, IUD insertion, or agreeing not to have another child (Banister, 1989). Violations of family-planning policy resulted in loss of bonuses, benefits, and family allowances. The Council of Ministers' Decree in October 1988 limited couples in cities, deltas, or lowlands to a maximum of two children. Those couples having more than the allowed number are required to pay extra for housing or land space, education, and health care. Such couples are prohibited from moving to urban areas and are required to perform more corvée work.

There is still considerable uncertainty concerning the processes and factors that motivate couples to limit the number of the children and account for the adoption of contraception in various societies at different periods of time. There is general agreement that socioeconomic development and organized family-planning programs play prominent roles in altering reproductive behavior. According to Bongaarts *et al.* (1990), socioeconomic development and family-planning programs operate synergistically, with one reinforcing the other.

The family-planning program experience of the selected Southeast Asian countries demonstrates that by making contraceptives easily available and by encouraging smaller families through a variety of measures, public and private sector family-planning programs have heightened contraceptive use. In turn, fertility and population growth rates have been reduced. The key to effective programs is to emphasize integrated high-quality outreach services and to take into account the traditional social structure and norms where the delivery system is to be introduced. Moreover, careful trial and phased development of alternative approaches to service delivery systems are critical to the success of a program. Finally, political support for family planning is often essential for the establishment of strong program effort.

Chapter 6

Fertility in China: Past, Present, Prospects

*Griffith Feeney**

Future population growth in any population is determined by the current age distribution and by future trends in fertility, mortality, and migration. The influence of the current age distribution is governed by purely formal demographic considerations that are the same for every population. The role of mortality depends crucially on its current level. Under conditions of high mortality, rapid declines are possible, and the normal interaction of mortality and age structure may lead to rapid population increase even in the face of substantial fertility decline. Once mortality has declined to the levels now observed in much of the world, however, mortality is relatively stable, largely because the features relevant to future population growth reflect biology more than social circumstance. Under current world demographic conditions, then, appropriate consideration of mortality and age distribution may be given without close attention to social structure or to policy issues that vary widely from one country to another.

The assessment of future levels and trends in fertility and migration is a different matter altogether. Circumstances influencing fertility, and even more so circumstances influencing migration, vary widely from one country to another, and all but the most superficial consideration of possible future trends requires study of particular

*With the assistance of Jianhua Yuan.

102

circumstances. International migration may be an important influence of future population growth for particular countries, large
as well as small. Immigration and emigration cancel out for the
world as a whole, however, whence a global perspective renders the
assessment of migration trends relatively unimportant.

Fertility behavior is heavily conditioned by both biology and society. Social influences may be roughly classified into the direct and
intended consequences of national government policy and all other
influences. The distinction is relevant to consideration of future fertility levels because it focuses attention in different directions: to
broad social and economic conditions thought to influence fertility
in the population at large, on the one hand, and to the minds of a
relatively small number of policy makers, on the other. It should
hardly be necessary to point out that the existence of policies to
limit fertility and/or population growth does not imply the effectiveness of such policies. This is an issue to be decided by empirical
analysis in each case.

The argument for country-specific consideration of influences on
future fertility is particularly compelling for China, which is unique
both in the nature and in the impacts of governmental population policies. This chapter aims to give a reasonably comprehensive treatment of China's fertility decline at the national level, with
emphasis on those factors relevant to a consideration of the future
trajectory of fertility. The qualifying clause is important, for there
is now such a quantity of demographic data available for China that
it is difficult to conceive, much less write in the space of one book
chapter, anything that might reasonably be called definitive.

6.1 China's Fertility Decline in International Perspective

That fertility declined rapidly in China is well known, but the speed
of the decline can be appreciated only when China's experience is
systematically compared with that of other countries. This section
compares Chinese experience with that of the rest of the developing
world. The analysis relies primarily on the historical estimates developed by the United Nations (1991a). These estimates share the

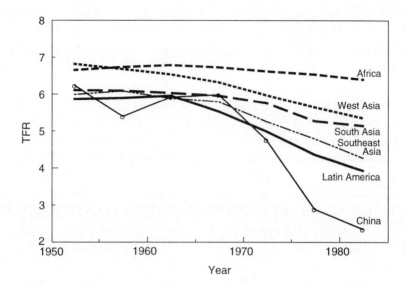

Figure 6.1. Fertility decline in China compared with fertility decline in other areas in the developing world. Source: *Table 6.1.*

weakness of all secondary compilations, most importantly the spurious impression of the uniformity of information available for various countries. An independent familiarity with demographic data sources in the various countries mitigates serious misunderstanding, however, and the United Nations estimates render a valuable service in making possible an international comparison that would otherwise be impossible.

Figure 6.1 compares fertility decline in China with fertility decline in major regions of the developing world. In each case we plot the total fertility rates for quinquennial periods from 1950 through 1985, listed in *Table 6.1*. During the 1950s and 1960s, the level of fertility in China was similar to that of the developing countries generally. Beginning in the 1970s, however, China's total fertility rate (TFR) fell from about six children per woman to slightly over two children per woman in the space of 15 years. Fertility in the rest of the developing world declined also, but at a much slower rate. Thus at the end of the period shown, total fertility for other areas ranged from a high of over six children per woman in Africa

Table 6.1. Total fertility rates in China and in other major areas in the developing world.

	1950-54	1955-59	1960-64	1965-69	1970-74	1975-79	1980-84
China	6.24	5.40	5.93	5.99	4.76	2.90	2.36
Africa	6.65	6.74	6.79	6.73	6.62	6.54	6.40
West Asia	6.82	6.68	6.54	6.32	5.97	5.64	5.35
South Asia	6.11	6.09	6.03	5.96	5.76	5.27	5.14
Southeast Asia	5.99	6.08	5.89	5.79	5.26	4.79	4.27
Latin America	5.87	5.90	5.96	5.53	4.99	4.36	3.93

Source: UN, 1991:354, 232, 262, 260, 258, 244, respectively, for the six regions.

to slightly under four children per woman in Latin America, all far above the level in China.

There may be considerable variation in fertility trends between different countries in the same region. This is particularly true within Asia, which contains many countries that have experienced rapid fertility decline, as well as a few that have experienced little or no decline. To make country comparisons it is desirable to summarize the information contained in the time series of total fertility rates, and an accepted way to do this is to calculate a rate of decline. In the case of China, for example, we see from *Figure 6.1* that the total fertility rate declined after 1970, with two rapid drops followed by a more modest fall. Consulting *Table 6.1*, we find that the total fertility rate for 1965–1969, before the decline, was 5.99 children per woman, that the two sharp drops brought it down to 2.90 children per woman for 1975–1979, and that it fell further to 2.36 children per woman for 1980–1985. To calculate a rate of decline we begin with the 5.99 children per woman in 1965–1969, the last point before the decline begins, but we may end either with the 2.90 children per women for 1975–1979, which will give a higher rate, or with the 2.36 children per woman for 1980–1984, which will give a lower rate. To make a conservative comparison, we take the latter rate. This gives a decline of 3.63 children per woman over 15 years, for a rate of decline of 0.24 children per woman per year.

Similar calculations have been made for 21 other Asian countries, yielding the results shown in *Table 6.2*.[1] The median rate of decline for the 22 populations given in *Table 6.2* is 0.10 child per woman per year, or one child per woman per decade. At this

Table 6.2. Comparative data on fertility decline in Asia.

Country	Period Begin	End	TFR Begin	End	Yrs.	Decl.	Rate
1. China	1965–69	1980–84	5.99	2.36	15	3.63	0.24
2. Taiwan	1955	1986	6.53	1.68	31	4.85	0.16
3. Hong Kong	1960–64	1980–84	5.30	1.80	20	3.50	0.18
4. Japan	1933	1953	4.42	2.26	20	2.16	0.11
5. S. Korea	1955–59	1980–84	6.07	2.40	25	3.67	0.15
6. N. Korea	1965–69	1980–84	6.97	2.76	15	4.21	0.29
7. Mongolia	1970–74	1980–84	5.80	5.25	10	0.55	0.06
8. Indonesia	1965–69	1980–84	5.57	4.05	15	1.52	0.10
9. Lao (PDR)	1970–74	1975–79	6.15	6.69	5	−0.54	−0.11
10. Malaysia	1960–64	1975–79	6.72	4.16	15	2.56	0.17
11. Myanmar	1965–69	1980–84	5.74	4.61	15	1.13	0.08
12. Philippines	1950–54	1980–84	7.29	4.74	30	2.55	0.09
13. Singapore	1955–59	1980–84	6.41	1.87	25	4.54	0.18
14. Thailand	1965–69	1980–84	6.14	3.52	15	2.62	0.17
15. Vietnam	1968–72	1983–88	5.90	3.98	15	1.92	0.13
16. Afghanistan	1975–79	1980–84	7.21	6.90	5	0.31	0.06
17. Bangladesh	1970–74	1980–84	7.02	6.15	10	0.87	0.09
18. India	1965–69	1975–79	5.69	4.83	10	0.86	0.09
19. Iran	1960–64	1980–84	7.26	5.64	20	1.62	0.08
20. Nepal	1975–79	1980–84	6.54	6.25	5	0.29	0.06
21. Pakistan	1960–65	1980–84	7.00	7.00	20	0.00	0.00
22. Sri Lanka	1950–54	1980–84	5.74	3.25	30	2.49	0.08

Stem and leaf →	0	0
(excl. Lao)	*	666888999
	1	013
Median=0.10	*	567788
	2	4
	*	9

Sources: Table 46 of UN, 1991a, for all countries except Japan and Taiwan. Data for Taiwan from *Taiwan Demographic Yearbook,* various years. Data for Japan from Feeney, 1990, time/TFR as follows: 1933.5/4.42 (Table 11), 1938.5/3.84 (Table 12), 1943.5/3.17, 1948.5/2.66, and 1953.5/2.26 (Table 13).

rate, decline from a roughly typical premodern fertility level of six children per woman to an equally roughly typical modern level of two children per woman would take 40 years. China, with a rate of decline of 0.24 children per woman per year, experienced a decline nearly this large in only 15 years.

The range of values in *Table 6.2* illustrates the difficulties encountered in international comparisons. Neither of the extreme values, for example, –0.11 for Lao People's Democratic Republic and 0.29 for Democratic People's Republic of Korea, should be given much weight. The demographic data necessary for calculating total fertility rates for Lao People's Democratic Republic over this period do not exist, and even casual scrutiny of the estimates given in the United Nations source raises suspicion that the numbers are little more than rough guesses. Little is known of data sources for Democratic People's Republic of Korea, for they are almost without exception not public, and here again scrutiny of the values shown in the source places their accuracy in doubt. For most of the other countries, however, sources are plentiful and public, and while accuracy varies from one country to another, the estimates of rate of decline may be regarded as reasonably sound.

China's rapid fertility decline is more surprising and significant for having occurred in the largest country in the world. It is more surprising because, insofar as fertility decline reflects government policy initiatives, it is a reasonable hypothesis that larger countries pose greater challenges. It is more significant because an interest in world population growth will weigh larger populations more heavily than smaller ones. The rates of fertility decline shown in *Table 6.2* are therefore displayed together with population size in *Figure 6.2*, which compares size and rate of fertility decline in China with that for 20 other Asian populations. Because of the great range in population sizes, from under 2 million for Mongolia to over 1 billion for China, we use the logarithm of population size, rather than size as such, as the indicator. Thus the vertical axis shows the logarithm of population size, and the horizontal axis the rate of decline in the total fertility rate.

We see at once how far removed China is from the experience of other countries. Only one other country in the world, Democratic People's Republic of Korea, has a rate of fertility decline exceeding

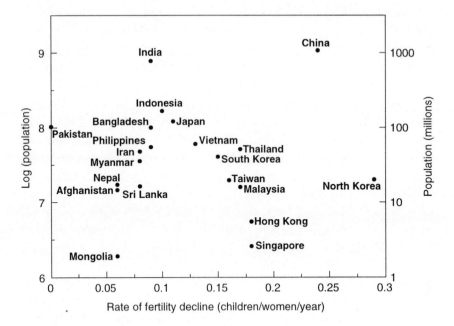

Figure 6.2. Rate of fertility decline and log population size for 21 Asian countries. Source: *Table 6.2*.

that of China, and we have just noted that these data are suspect. The highest rate of decline for all other countries is 0.18, shared by Hong Kong and Singapore. Pakistan shows no decline, though also no increase. This is the extreme low value for the populations shown in *Figure 6.2*, from which Lao People's Democratic Republic has been excluded.

It is interesting to note the level and distribution of rates of decline among countries. Until rather recently, Japan was generally considered to have experienced the most rapid fertility decline in the world. Yet the rate of decline shown here for Japan is only 0.11 children per woman per year, just over the median value for the 21 populations displayed in *Figure 6.2*. It is notable, moreover, that with the exceptions of the Philippines and Myanmar, every country in East and Southeast Asia had a rate of decline higher than Japan, and every country in South and West Asia a lower rate of decline than Japan. It is significant that the higher rates of decline are observed not only in the small city-states of Hong Kong and Singapore, but also in the large nations of Malaysia, Vietnam, and Thailand.

The inverted V pattern in the plot is particularly notable. Smaller countries tend to have either relatively high or relatively low rates of fertility decline, with a convergence toward the median as size increases. Perhaps this reflects the possibility that, in the diffusion of modernization, small countries may be bypassed altogether for a time, but may also modernize rapidly once the process begins, whereas larger countries cannot escape modernizing influences, but tend to react more slowly to them.

6.2   China's Fertility Decline: A Closer Look

Looking at total fertility rates for quinquennial periods obscures important details of China's fertility decline. In this section we examine several single-year time series to provide a more precise picture of fertility decline, a picture that may then be compared with government population policy initiatives. Incidentally, we present evidence of the accuracy of the data from which these fertility statistics are calculated. While certainly not perfect, the Chinese data are superior to those available for most countries in the world, developed as well as developing.

Figure 6.3 shows conventional total fertility rates for China from 1965 through mid-1987.[2] We are in fact looking at two different series here, shown in the first two columns in *Table 6.3*. The first, plotted with solid dots, is calculated from age-specific birth rates (ASBR) derived from the birth histories collected in the 1982 One-per-Thousand Fertility Survey conducted by the State Family Planning Commission (see China Population Information Center, 1984; Coale, 1984; Coale and Chen, 1987). The values shown are those given in Coale and Chen (1987), though these hardly differ from those reported in the first survey (China Population Information Center, 1984). These values are for calendar years.

The second series in *Figure 6.3*, plotted with small circles, is calculated from age-specific birth rates derived from birth histories reconstructed from a 10 percent sample of the 1987 One-per-Hundred

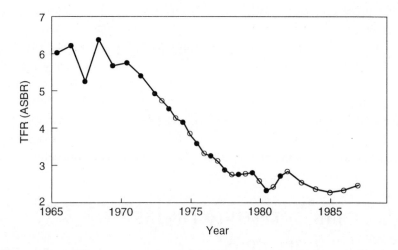

Figure 6.3. Conventional total fertility rates in China: 1965–1987. Source: *Table 6.3*, columns 1 and 2.

Survey carried out by the State Statistical Bureau. The reconstruction procedure, developed by Luther, is described in Luther and Cho (1988). An extension of the own-children method (Cho *et al.*, 1986), it begins with the "own-children histories" generated by that method and imputes deceased and non-own children to each woman based on reported numbers of children ever born and surviving and on the standard own-children estimates of age-specific birth rates.

The consistency of the two series shown in *Figure 6.3* testifies to the exceptional accuracy of these Chinese data. These two series are derived from different survey operations, conducted by different organizations, using different methods applied to different questionnaire items. Given these differences, the consistency displayed in *Figure 6.3* is most unlikely to be the result of common errors, and of course the likelihood of chance agreement over this long time series is negligible.

The total fertility rates plotted in *Figure 6.3* decline nearly linearly from 5.75 children per woman in calendar year 1970 to 2.72 children per woman for the year ending June 30, 1978. This represents a decline of 3.03 children per woman over a period of seven and one-half years for a rate of decline of 0.40 children per woman per year. This is much higher than the 0.24 children per woman

Table 6.3. Total fertility rates and mean age at marriage in China, various sources and calculations: 1965–1987.

Year	ASBR TFR (1)	ASBR TFR (2)	Mean age at marriage (3)	Mean age at marriage (4)	Mean age at marriage (5)	PPPR TFR (6)	PPPR TFR (7)	PPPR TFR (8)
1987	–	2.46	–	21.8	22.0	–	2.33	2.26
1986	–	2.33	–	21.8	21.8	–	2.17	2.11
1985	–	2.27	–	21.7	22.0	–	2.07	1.97
1984	–	2.35	–	21.7	22.1	–	2.06	1.99
1983	–	2.53	–	21.8	22.1	–	2.32	2.10
1982	–	2.83	–	22.1	21.9	–	2.63	2.58
1981	2.71	2.41	22.8	22.6	22.0	2.65	2.61	2.56
1980	2.32	2.55	23.0	22.8	22.4	2.70	2.90	2.58
1979	2.80	2.77	23.1	23.0	23.0	3.20	3.14	3.20
1978	2.75	2.72	22.8	22.8	23.2	3.16	3.14	3.16
1977	2.87	3.09	22.5	22.6	23.4	3.23	3.40	3.14
1976	3.25	3.30	22.3	22.3	23.1	3.47	3.52	3.48
1975	3.58	3.80	21.7	22.0	23.2	3.73	3.93	3.75
1974	4.15	4.24	21.4	21.5	22.8	4.14	4.33	4.33
1973	4.51	4.72	21.0	21.1	22.5	4.37	4.69	–
1972	4.92	–	20.6	20.7	22.2	4.73	4.85	–
1971	5.40	–	20.3	20.4	21.9	5.08	–	–
1970	5.75	–	20.2	20.3	21.1	5.43	–	–
1969	5.67	–	20.3	20.4	20.8	5.41	–	–
1968	6.37	–	20.1	20.2	20.6	5.68	–	–
1967	5.25	–	20.0	20.2	21.0	4.98	–	–
1966	6.21	–	19.8	–	–	5.75	–	–
1965	6.02	–	19.7	–	–	5.96	–	–

Values in columns 2 and 7 refer to years ending June 30 of each year. Other values refer to calendar years.

Sources: column 1, Coale and Chen (1987:Basic Table 1.A.); column 2, Luther *et al.* (1990:Table 4); column 3, Banister (1987:Table 6.1); column 4, unpublished computer printouts of the 1988 Two-per-Thousand Survey; column 5, Feeney and Wang (1993:Table 2); column 6, Feeney and Yu (1987:Table 1); column 7, Luther *et al.* (1990:Table 5); column 8, Feeney and Wang (1993:Table 2).

per year based on the last three points shown in *Figure 6.1*. It is also substantially higher than the rate of decline indicated in *Figure 6.1* if we leave off the last point and calculate the decline between 1965–1969 and 1975–1979, which works out to be 0.31 children per woman per year. In short, the speed and timing of China's fertility

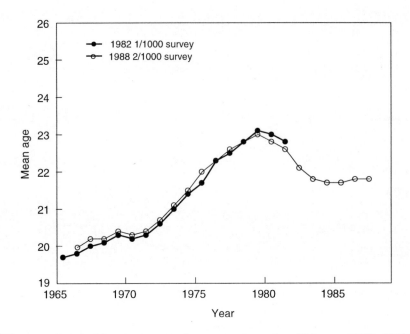

Figure 6.4. Mean age at first marriage in China: 1965–1987.
Source: *Table 6.3*, columns 3 and 4.

decline are such that the use of quinquennial periods substantially
underestimates the speed of the decline.

In reading the record of fertility change shown in *Figure 6.3*,
however, there is a confounding factor that must be taken into account. *Figure 6.4* shows mean age at marriage in China for the period in question (data from columns 3 and 4 of *Table 6.3*), defined as
the mean of all marriages occurring in each year. As in previous figures, we have statistics from two data sources, in this case the 1982
One-per-Thousand Survey and the 1988 Two-per-Thousand Survey,
both taken by the State Family Planning Commission. The consistency between the two series gives an indication of their remarkably
high accuracy.

Mean age at marriage rose rapidly during most of the 1970s.
The mean age at first marriage series shown in column 4 of *Table
6.3* rose from 20.3 years in 1970 to a high of 23.1 years in 1979, a
rate of 0.4 years per year.[3] If this rate of increase translated into
a corresponding rate of increase in mean age at childbearing, and if

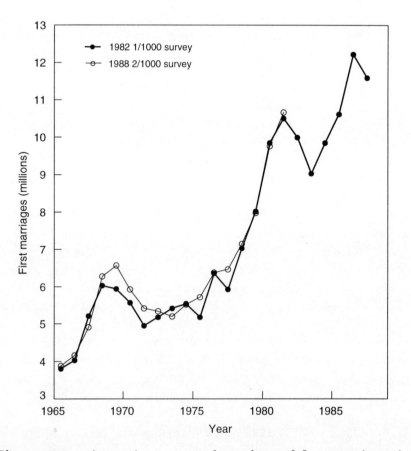

Figure 6.5. Approximate annual numbers of first marriages in China: 1965–1987. Source: Appendix *Table 6.1*.

the increase were observed over a sufficiently long period of time, it would have increased period total fertility rates by approximately 40 percent over corresponding cohort levels (Ryder, 1983:741). These conditions do not hold, and the actual effect is less than this, but it is nonetheless substantial.

Figure 6.5 shows numbers of first marriages in China during 1965–1987, based on the 1982 and 1988 surveys. Since we are looking at numbers here, there is a bias due both to mortality and to the upper age limit in the surveys.[4] The comparison of the series from the two surveys shows that this bias is not serious during the period in question.

The striking feature of *Figure 6.5* is the extraordinary rise in numbers of marriages between the late 1970s and the early 1980s. During the late 1960s and middle to late 1970s, we observe 5 to 6 million first marriages per year. During the 1980s the numbers range from slightly under 10 million in 1984 to over 12 million in 1986, fully twice the level of the 1970s.

This jump in marriages exerts a powerful upward influence on birth rates. Since virtually all Chinese women have a first birth within a few years of first marriage,[5] the increases in numbers of first marriages translate almost directly into a slightly lagged increase in numbers of first births. Thus in Appendix *Tables 6.1* and *6.2* we see that annual numbers of first births rise from about 5 million during the mid-1970s to about 10 million during the mid-1980s. This increase is due not to any change in the childbearing behavior of Chinese women, but to the rapidly increasing numbers of recently married women. If we choose to interpret the total fertility rates shown in *Figure 6.3* merely as indicators of numbers of births, these observations are irrelevant. If we wish to interpret them as indicators of childbearing behavior, however, it is necessary to recognize that they are distorted by the rapid changes in age at marriage and numbers of marriages during the period in question.

6.3   Period Parity Progression Measures of Fertility

The simplest approach to dealing with the effects of changing marriage patterns on the conventional fertility measures presented in the preceding section is to use alternative measures that are less sensitive to changing marriage patterns. Period parity progression ratios (PPPRs) calculated from birth probabilities specific for parity and birth interval provide an effective way to do this. In the calculation of probabilities of progression from marriage to first birth, for example, numbers of women marrying each year and the corresponding numbers of married women remaining in parity zero appear in the denominator of each birth probability, whence an increase in numbers of marriages from one year to the next does not imply any increase in the proportion of women progressing to first birth.

The parity progression approach to fertility measurement asks what proportions of women move from one childbearing event to the next. Of all women born, what proportion have a first birth? Of all women who have a first birth, what proportion go on (progress) to have a second, and so on? The answers may be derived from *parity progression ratios,* and like other demographic measures, they may be calculated on a period as well as on a cohort basis. (For a general discussion of period parity progression ratio measures of fertility, see Feeney and Lutz, 1991. For applications to China, see Feeney and Wang, 1993; Feeney and Yu, 1987; Feeney *et al.*, 1989; Luther *et al.*, 1990). For populations in which fertility is restricted to married couples, as in China, it is useful to break down the proportion of women ever having a first birth into two multiplicative components: the proportion of women who ever marry and the proportion of married women who ever have a first birth.

Total fertility rates may be calculated from period parity progression ratios as well as from age-specific birth rates, and the logic of the calculation is parallel. We ask what average number of children would be born to a hypothetical cohort of women that experience the parity progression ratios observed during a given time period. The formula is easily shown to be (see, for example, Feeney and Yu, 1987)

$$TFR = p_0 + p_0p_1 + p_0p_1p_2 + \dots \ .$$

A convenient approximation for use with incomplete series of parity progression ratios is given by replacing the last term in the series by itself divided by $1-p_n$, where p_n is the last available ratio.[6]

Period parity progression ratios are unusual fertility measures, even within the field of demography, and it will be useful to provide some examples of their values for different countries.[7] *Table 6.4* assembles schedules of parity progression ratios for a variety of high- and low-fertility countries. Progression to marriage and first and second births is generally high for both high- and low-fertility countries. Among the high-fertility Hutterites, some 97 percent of all married women have at least one child. In China, virtually all women married and had a first birth, both before fertility began to decline (1965) and after it had declined nearly to replacement level (1982).[8] The lowest levels of progression from marriage to first birth occur in low-fertility countries, to be sure, but even here it is

Table 6.4. Parity progression ratios for selected populations, per 1,000 women.

Population	Progression									
	B→M	M→1	0→1	1→2	2→3	3→4	4→5	5→6	6→7	7→8
Hutterites	–	971	–	988	972	968	967	953	929	905
China 1965	990	982	972	979	964	929	886	845	786	720
China 1979	994	991	985	959	700	539	431	414	322	309
Rural	997	992	989	978	759	572	448	422	328	310
Urban	981	979	960	799	259	168	131	185	44	373
Taiwan 1986	992	959	951	782	428	212	170	185	198	216
Thailand										
1960–1964	–	–	948	966	951	925	918	890	859	800
1975–1979	–	–	813	917	771	681	646	610	580	548
Japan 1982	925	916	847	856	320	137	221[a]	–	–	–
USA										
1941	–	–	779	745	628	639	651	670	666	635[a]
1960	–	–	923	922	746	645	619	650	682	689[a]
1984	–	–	802	789	488	386	382	419	439	456[a]
Canada 1985	–	–	–	793	423	301	287	370	412	430[a]
Netherlands 1985	–	–	–	835	382	298	363	483	555	562[a]
East Germany 1985	–	–	–	688	274	300	366	427	443	422[a]
Hungary 1984	–	–	–	750	242	249	377	414	470	458[a]
Yugoslavia 1982	–	–	–	815	318	416	518	567	547	464[a]
France 1976	891	939	837	645	325	267	277[a]	–	–	–
Italy 1978	926	861	797	739	345	280	287[a]	–	–	–
England										
& Wales 1977	–	829	–	855	347	267	241[a]	–	–	–

[a]Values are aggregates for progression from i-th or higher order to $(i+1)$st or higher-order births.

Sources: Cohort data for Hutterites, Eaton and Mayer (1954:Table 10). All remaining figures are period data. China, Feeney and Yu (1987:81). Thailand, Luther and Pejaranondam (1991:Tables B1 and B2). Japan, Feeney (1986:20). USA, Feeney (1988a:Table 1). Former East Germany, Feeney and Lutz (1991). Values for Canada, the Netherlands, Hungary, and former Yugoslavia estimated by the indirect procedure described in the text from time series of registered births by order from United Nations *Demographic Yearbooks*. Values for France, Italy, and England and Wales, Penhale (1984:Tables 12–14).

unusual for less than 80 percent of women who have a first birth to go on to have a second.

The difference between high- and low-fertility populations is greatest in the higher-order parity progression ratios, and most importantly in the proportion of women progressing from second to third birth. In a high-fertility population – the high-fertility Hutterites, China in 1965, and Thailand in 1960–1964 – parity progression ratios decline slowly with increasing parity, remaining in the 70 to 90 percent range even for progression from seventh to eighth birth. In a low-fertility population, however, progression from second to third birth is sharply lower than progression to first or from first to second. The values shown in *Table 6.4* range from a low of 24 percent for Hungary to a high of 75 percent for the United States near the height of the baby boom, but this last value is atypically high. The normal range for progression from second to third birth in low-fertility populations is 25 to 50 percent.

Higher-order parity progression ratios in low-fertility populations are surprisingly high – the median value for progression from seventh to ninth birth for the low-fertility countries in *Table 6.4* is 44 percent. There can be little doubt that this reflects a selection effect. In a low-fertility population, the only women who reach high parities are necessarily highly fecund, regularly exposed to the risk of conception, and either nonusers or inept users of contraception. These relatively high parity progression ratios have little effect on the overall level of fertility, however, since only a small fraction of women reach high parities.

6.4   Period Parity Progression Measures of Fertility in China

Total fertility rates calculated from period parity progression ratios are plotted in *Figure 6.6*. Here as in *Figure 6.3* we have values both from the 1982 One-per-Thousand Fertility Survey conducted by the State Family Planning Commission and from the 1987 One-per-Hundred Survey conducted by the State Statistical Bureau, and the consistency of the two series attests to their accuracy.

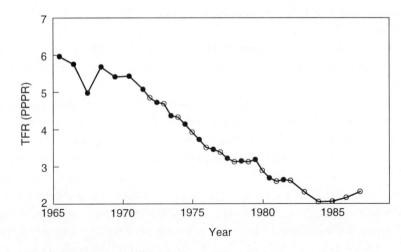

Figure 6.6. Total fertility rates calculated from period parity progression ratios in China: 1965–1987. Source: *Table 6.3*

The total fertility rates in *Figure 6.6* decline irregularly along a linear trend from 5.43 children per woman in calendar year 1970 to 2.06 children per woman in the year ending June 30, 1984. This is a decline of 3.37 children per woman in 13.5 years, for a rate of 0.25 children per woman per year – remarkably close, though only by coincidence, to the 0.24 children per woman per year indicated by the quinquennial data shown in *Figure 6.1* and *Table 6.1*.

The contrast between this picture and that shown by the conventional total fertility rates plotted in *Figure 6.3* illustrates the distorting effects of changing marriage patterns. There are two main differences. First, the rate of decline shown by the conventional total fertility rates is much more rapid, 0.40 as compared with 0.25 children per woman per year, because rapidly rising age at marriage during the 1980s caused a decline beyond that due to declining childbearing within marriage. Second, and what is more important, the conventional total fertility rates indicate a decline ending in 1978, whereas the total fertility rates calculated from period parity progression ratios continue until 1984, a full six years later.

The parity progression ratio total fertility rates show that the level of fertility implicit in the childbearing behavior of Chinese women continued to decline until the mid-1980s. Because of the tremendous surge of marriages beginning in the late 1970s, this continuing behavioral change is completely obscured by the conventional total fertility rates. The conventional total fertility rates suggest that fertility decline in China ended, at least temporarily, in 1979. This was precisely the year in which a major new policy initiative, the one-child family program, was taken. The time series of conventional total fertility rates suggest that the new policy was unsuccessful. In fact, as we see below, it achieved considerable success.

One advantage of total fertility rates calculated from period parity progression ratios is superior control over the distorting effects of changing marriage patterns. A second advantage, and one particularly important in the Chinese context, is the correspondence established with the period parity progression ratios themselves. The level of progression from first to second birth, in particular, reflects the demographic impact of the one-child family policy.

Table 6.5 and *Figure 6.7* show period parity progression ratios and the corresponding total fertility rates for the years 1967–1987 calculated from the 1988 Two-per-Thousand Fertility Survey conducted by the State Family Planning Commission (Feeney and Wang, 1993; see also Lavely, 1991). Because progression to first marriage is virtually constant at close to one throughout the period shown, *Figure 6.7* shows proportions of women progressing to first birth (B→1), the product of women progressing to first marriage (B→M) and women progressing from first marriage to first birth (M→1), rather than showing these two series separately.

Figure 6.7 shows that proportions of women ever having a first birth have been high, about 95 percent, throughout the period considered. Fertility decline has resulted entirely from declines in progression to higher-order births. Progression from first to second birth, in particular, shows the impact of the one-child family program. In 1979, the year the program was introduced, 95 percent of all women were progressing from first to second birth. By 1984, after the policy had been in effect for only five years, progression to second birth had been reduced to 63 percent. That year, however, marked a relaxation in the policy, and progression to second birth rose continuously through 1987, the last year of the series, at which point it stood at 76 percent.

Table 6.5. Period progression ratios and total fertility rates in China: 1967–1987.

| Year | Progression and progression ratio | | | | | |
	B→M	M→1	1→2	2→3	3$^+$→4$^+$	TFR
1987	995	968	765	466	384	2.26
1986	997	950	734	440	345	2.11
1985	996	944	678	423	312	1.97
1984	999	961	626	465	338	1.99
1983	997	963	695	465	339	2.10
1982	1000	979	821	571	404	2.58
1981	998	963	858	558	388	2.56
1980	999	960	886	562	340	2.58
1979	999	970	951	743	446	3.20
1978	996	963	969	710	442	3.16
1977	996	958	958	713	441	3.14
1976	983	970	964	808	508	3.48
1975	992	946	982	848	565	3.75
1974	992	958	985	883	672	4.33
1973	993	952	986	–	–	–
1972	973	941	984	–	–	–
1971	994	944	991	–	–	–
1970	999	952	984	–	–	–
1969	997	948	984	–	–	–
1968	998	961	988	–	–	–
1967	999	930	970	–	–	–

Calculated from the National Fertility and Birth Control Survey of 1988. TFR values calculated from parity progression ratio schedule extending to progression from seventh to eighth birth. Progression to fourth and higher is the aggregate of progression from third to fourth through progression from seventh to eighth. Few women reach these parities, so the difference is negligible.
Source: Feeney and Wang (1993:Tables 3, 5, 7, 9, and 16) and unpublished computer printouts for annual values in first column.

Progression to both first and second births was essentially constant through 1979, whence the great fertility decline of the 1970s was due entirely to declines in third- and higher-order births. Progression from second to third birth declined by more than half between 1974 (88 percent) and 1985 (42 percent), and progression from third- and higher-order births to fourth- and higher-order births declined from 67 to 31 percent over the same period.

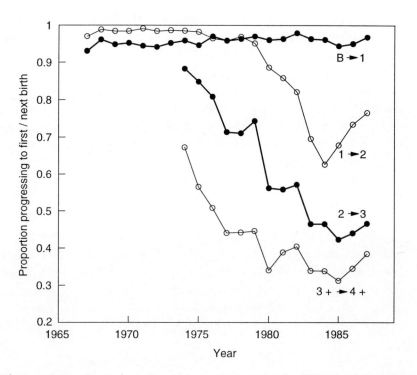

Figure 6.7. Period parity progression ratios in China: 1967–1987.
Source: *Table 6.5*.

6.5 Scenarios for Future Fertility Change

The foregoing analysis of fertility decline in China indicates that government policy and programs played a major role in these trends. (For a more detailed assessment see Feeney and Wang, 1993:92–95. On population policy in China, see Chen and Kols, 1982; Greenhalgh, 1986, 1990, 1993; Hardee-Cleaveland and Banister, 1988; Kaufman *et al.*, 1989; Tuan, 1982; and Zeng, 1989. See also the ethnographic accounts of Huang, 1989; Moser, 1983; and Potter and Potter, 1990.) The rapidity of the fall in age at marriage following the relaxation of administrative controls circa 1980 strongly suggests that the earlier rise in age at marriage was in substantial part due to explicit government policy, specifically to the later *(wan)* marriage component of the *wan-shi-shao* policy. The sudden decline in progression from first to second birth following the introduction of the one-child family program in 1979 and the subsequent rise following the relaxation of 1984 are even stronger evidence that this particular component of fertility decline was due largely to government policy.

The structure of China's birth-planning efforts and the attention and resources allocated to them make this remarkable effectiveness more plausible than it might otherwise be. Government policy was effective despite imperfect implementation. Substantial proportions of men and women married beneath the prescribed ages in the 1970s, for example, but the encouragement to marry later did result in a very substantial increase in mean age at marriage. Even at the peak of its effectiveness, the one-child family program saw well over half of all Chinese women having two or more children, but the program nonetheless had a substantial and continuing effect on fertility levels.

In considering future fertility trends, then, it makes sense to emphasize the role of government policy. The centerpiece of China's current birth-planning efforts is still the one-child family policy introduced in 1979, but this simple statement conceals a more complicated demographic reality. One-child families have been realized among most of the urban population, with progression from first to second birth in recent years between 10 and 20 percent (Feeney and Wang, 1993:Table 6.5). The one-child family remains the official population policy in rural areas as well, but numerous adaptations belie the "one-child" label, and progression from first to second birth in recent years has been around 85 percent. At the national level, progression from first to second birth in rural areas rose from a low of 63 percent in 1984 to 76 percent in 1987 (*Figure 6.7*), with a continued increase indicated.

This discussion of scenarios is limited to high and low extremes over the next two decades. A high trajectory is obtained by assuming a continued relaxation of the one-child family policy, with progression from first to second birth rising to about 95 percent, the level observed before the introduction of the policy in 1979; and with progression from second to third birth rising modestly from 47 to 62 percent, both plausible extrapolations of recent experience. This yields total fertility rates rising from 2.3 in 1987 to 2.5 in 1990, to 2.7 in 1995 and 2000, and finally to 2.8 in 2005.

A low trajectory is obtained by assuming implementation of the one-child policy in rural as well as urban areas, but assuming both a somewhat higher level of progression from first to second birth than has been achieved in cities (30 percent as opposed to about 15 percent recently) and a slower rate of decline (15 years for rural areas as compared with only four years for cities). Progression from second to third birth is assumed to decline as well, though the very low values of progression from first to second birth make this relatively unimportant. This yields total fertility rates falling from 2.3 in 1987 to 2.2 in 1990, to 1.7 in 1995, to 1.5 in 2000, and finally to 1.4 in 2005.

Between now and the beginning of the next century, we expect fertility in China not to exceed 2.7 children per woman or to fall below 1.5 children per woman.

6.6   The Scenarios Compared with Recent Evidence

The analysis and scenarios of the preceding sections are based on annual data on total fertility rates through 1987, the most recent available at the time the projections were made.[9] Detailed estimates of fertility levels from the 1990 population census became available as the chapter went to press, too late to be incorporated into the scenario analysis. At this writing we have, in addition to the census results, fertility rates through 1991 calculated from a 1992 fertility survey (Feeney and Yuan, 1994) and rates through 1995 indirectly estimated from published data on crude birth and death rates through 1995 (Yuan, 1995). How well do the scenarios of the preceding section stand up to recent evidence? Does the comparison indicate that they should they be revised?

The level of fertility rose over the period 1984–1987, and though the magnitude of the increase was small, there were grounds, at the time, for thinking that it might continue. In no large country (and almost no small country) had fertility fallen as rapidly as it did in China during the 1970s. This rapid decline was due in part to vigorous government policy measures. The one-child family policy was relaxed in the mid-1980s, partly as a result of peasant resistance, and it was conceivable that the relaxation would continue. The high scenario for future fertility change anticipated this contingency and showed fertility rising to 2.8 children per woman in 2005.

Fertility estimates from the 1990 census show, however, that 1988 was a turning point (Feeney *et al.*, 1993).[10] The total fertility rate declined between 1988 and 1990 as quickly as it had risen from 1985 to 1988. This reversal reconfirms the invalidity of simple extrapolation and makes the low scenario for future fertility change, in which fertility falls to 1.4 children per woman in 2005, seem more plausible.

The low-fertility scenario is both supported and confounded by the results of a 1992 fertility survey taken by the State Family Planning Commission. This survey shows a total fertility rate calculated from age-specific birth rates of 1.65 children per woman for 1991. Few informed observers in or outside China believe that fertility was really this low, however, and initially the survey served mainly to cast doubt not only on its own validity, but on that of previous efforts to measure fertility levels as well.

A detailed analysis of the 1992 data indicates that the survey results were not so poor as initially suspected (Feeney and Yuan, 1994). Retrospective estimates of total fertility rates for 1986–1989 from the survey agree very well with the estimates from the 1990 census and the 1990 total fertility rate is a plausible continuation of the trend. The very low value for 1991 was the result of a sharp drop from 1990, and it is likely that the 1991 figure is too low by about 10 percent, but there is little statistical evidence of more serious underreporting.

The possibility of consistent errors is discussed in detail in Feeney and Yuan (1994:391–393). While it is possible that Chinese women have consistently underreported numbers of children in all the national-level data, we conclude that it is unlikely that such consistent underreporting has biased observed fertility levels by more than a few tenths of a child per woman.

Figure 6.8 compares the 1988 TFR series given in *Table 6.5* and the high- and low-scenario TFR series (plotted with triangles) with corresponding estimates from the 1990 census (Feeney *et al.*, 1993) and age-specific total fertility rates from annual surveys conducted by the State Statistical Bureau (Yuan, 1995).[11] The last mentioned series is not strictly comparable to the others, but disparities are likely to be small, and the extension of the observed series through 1995 makes it worth including.[12]

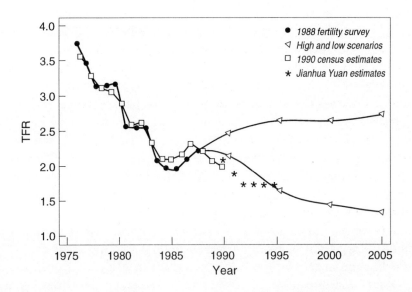

Figure 6.8. Observed and estimated total fertility rates in China: 1975–2005.

That the observed series should have fallen so quickly below the low scenario is of little consequence. We know that short-term movements can be volatile, particularly in China, and the objective of the scenarios is to capture long-term change. The pertinent question is whether the recent data change the long-term prospects. On the statistical evidence only, the answer is clearly no. The observed data from the late 1980s through 1995 track the low scenario reasonably well. Hindsight in this instance tempts us to revise the low scenario downward to fit the observed rates more comfortably inside the scenario limits. Experience of population forecasting more generally, however, suggests that the temptation should be resisted, for unexpectedly strong movements in one direction are likely to be followed by strong movements in the opposite direction.

6.7 Conclusion

It would be unwise to leave the matter at this point, however, for non-statistical considerations raise the question of whether Chinese fertility levels may not continue to defy what experience in other countries teaches. Chinese population policy over the past 25 years has been tenaciously and effectively anti-natalist. The one-child family policy has been in place for over 15 years, and though it was effectively loosened in the mid-1980s to allow a second child to many rural families, there are no serious indications that it will be abandoned. Further declines in fertility may not be in China's long-term interest, but the negative consequences are speculative and appear mostly in the very long term. It is possible that the Chinese leadership will continue to push the one-child family policy. Perception of population pressure may override anticipation of future problems and the sheer momentum of 25 years of incessant and determined efforts to lower fertility may make it difficult to change course.

Over the past 15 years various social forces have kept the one-child policy from being fully implemented. It is possible that this will change in the future. Economic liberalization and opening to the outside world have led to very rapid economic growth. This has led to great opportunity for Chinese families able to exploit the new situation, and to great uncertainty and anxiety for other families whose livelihoods are threatened. Both groups are likely to respond by having fewer children in the short run, and perhaps in the not so short run.

Could this combination of influences result in long-term fertility levels substantially below the 1.4 children per woman anticipated by the low scenario for future fertility change? My judgment is that Chinese fertility is unlikely to fall below an average level of 1.4 children per woman over the next two decades, though temporary declines below this level are possible.

There is very little basis for speculation about the extended long-term future of fertility. The only thing that can be said with any semblance of scientific support is that world demographic trends to date suggest that a plausible range is between 1.5 and 3 children per woman. It is a reasonable supposition that levels and trends of fertility over the past few decades contain information about the likely trends over the next few decades, and that is the basis of these conclusions about fertility in China through the early years of the next century. Recent levels and trends cannot plausibly be expected to contain any information about detailed levels 50 or 100 years into the future, however. Assumptions about these more distant levels must either be regarded as purely formal or be made on some basis other than a study of recent levels and trends.

Notes

[1] Since fertility decline occurs during different periods in different countries, it makes little sense to compute rates of decline for the same period for all countries. At the same time, choosing a suitable time period over which to compute a rate of decline involves an element of judgment, if not of arbitrariness. The periods shown in *Table 6.1* have been selected by examining the plot of the TFR trend in each country. Because we are interested in showing how different China is from other countries, we have chosen periods to give larger rather than smaller rates of declines for all other countries.

[2] "Conventional" total fertility rates means rates calculated from age-specific birth rates. These are to be distinguished from total fertility rates calculated from period parity progression ratios, discussed in Section 6.3.

[3] Columns 3 and 4 of *Table 6.3* show mean age at first marriage calculated directly as the mean of all first marriages occurring during the indicated year. Column 5 shows mean age at first marriage calculated from first marriage probabilities, i.e., for the period nuptiality table, for the given year. The former statistic is more readily computed and more common. The latter has the advantage of being uninfluenced by changing age distribution. All three series show a sharp rise in mean age at marriage. Comparing the plot of the nuptiality table values (not shown) with *Figure 6.4* shows sharp divergences between the two types of means. See Feeney and Wang (1993:70–71) for discussion of these differences and their significance.

[4] The 1982 survey included women less than exact age 68 years; the 1988 survey, women less than exact age 58 years.

[5] The evidence of this is given below in the form of period parity progression ratios for progression from marriage to first birth. See *Table 6.5* and the corresponding text discussion.

[6] The approximation assumes that parity progression ratios beyond p_n are identically equal to p_n. Although not in the least realistic, the approximation is very good as long as p_n is not too large, which in practice means not much over one-half. The $1-p_n$ arises from a geometric series, as a little algebra readily shows.

[7] The reasons for this are beyond the scope of the present discussion; for more information see Feeney and Lutz (1991:186–187).

[8] The value shown for the proportion of married women having a first birth is probably too high, one of the relatively few imperfections in

the data from the 1982 One-per-Thousand Survey. See Feeney and Wang (1993:71) for a discussion of evidence.

[9] The high-fertility scenario for progression from first to second birth raised the parity progression ratio to the level observed before the initiation of the one-child family policy and progression from second to third birth to the level observed circa 1980. The low-fertility scenario lowered the parity progression ratio for progression from first to second birth to the observed level of higher-order progressions during the late 1980s and the ratio for progression from second to third birth to half the level of the high-fertility scenario. The specific values are as follows:

Year	p_1		p_2	
	Low	High	Low	High
1990	0.74	0.85	0.48	0.55
1995	0.48	0.91	0.38	0.60
2000	0.34	0.93	0.32	0.62
2005	0.31	0.94	0.31	0.62

Intermediate values were obtained by cubic spline interpolation. Total fertility rates were computed as

$$TFR = p_0 + p_0 p_1 + p_0 p_1 p_2 + p_0 p_1 p_2 p_3 / (1 - p_3) \ ,$$

where p_3 denotes progression from third and higher-order births to fourth and higher-order births. The values of p_0 and p_3 were taken as fixed at their 1987 values.

[10] Total fertility rates calculated from period parity progression ratios, shown in Feeney *et al.* (1993:Table 6), are as follows:

1976	3.57	1981	2.60	1986	2.19
1977	3.30	1982	2.65	1987	2.36
1978	3.13	1983	2.36	1988	2.24
1979	3.08	1984	2.12	1989	2.11
1980	2.91	1985	2.12	1990	2.02

The one-year period for these rates begins on 1 July and ends on 30 June; for example, 1976 covers the period from 1 July 1975 to 30 June 1976.

[11] The 1992 survey estimates are based on age-parity-specific birth rates rather than on parity-duration-specific rates. Partly for this reason, and partly because including them would render the plot less readable and duplicate the analysis given in Feeney and Yuan (1993), they are not shown.

[12] The estimation procedure, described in detail in Yuan (1995:559–570), gives estimates of conventional total fertility rates calculated from age-specific fertility rates. It utilizes the single-year female age

distribution from the 1990 census in combination with vital statistics for 1990–1994 derived from the annual sample survey conducted by the State Statistical Bureau. The census age distribution is projected forward to obtain age distributions for subsequent years. A model schedule of age-specific fertility rates is then applied to the projected age distributions, multiplying the rates by a constant factor chosen to match computed and observed crude birth rates. The vital rates, given in State Statistical Bureau of China (1995:17), are as follows:

Year	Population (at year end)	CBR	CDR
1990	114,333	21.06	6.67
1991	115,823	19.68	6.70
1992	117,171	18.24	6.64
1993	118,517	18.09	6.64
1994	119,850	17.70	6.49

Appendix Table 6.1. Annual first marriages and births by order.

		Birth order							
Year	M	1	2	3	4	5	6	7	8
1987	11,605	11,951	7,283	2,619	1,022	321	145	107	55
1986	12,237	10,055	6,624	2,319	897	418	193	95	59
1985	10,624	8,937	5,416	2,151	754	298	275	143	48
1984	9,851	9,147	5,056	2,325	975	442	290	89	59
1983	9,044	9,161	5,060	2,148	923	547	348	113	59
1982	10,001	10,459	5,491	2,702	1,391	663	398	223	53
1981	10,516	9,332	4,097	2,607	1,406	842	357	285	94
1980	9,850	7,289	4,662	2,395	1,369	674	328	219	61
1979	8,036	6,923	5,365	3,564	1,874	1,080	649	266	183
1978	7,048	6,256	4,935	3,218	2,111	1,014	580	416	216
1977	5,947	5,596	4,661	3,276	1,904	1,252	676	389	234
1976	6,376	5,948	4,719	3,995	2,122	1,435	894	628	334
1975	5,191	5,117	4,975	3,785	2,594	1,650	1,156	533	365
1974	5,559	5,643	5,459	4,058	2,896	2,140	1,378	909	425
1973	5,430	5,288	5,213	4,161	3,164	2,366	1,524	1,004	510
1972	5,193	4,985	4,824	4,046	3,332	2,512	1,699	1,029	560
1971	4,964	5,193	5,383	4,151	3,832	2,609	1,616	971	530
1970	5,586	5,680	4,568	3,841	3,882	2,527	1,809	852	479
1969	5,956	5,141	4,150	4,384	3,129	2,186	1,548	826	407
1968	6,047	5,298	4,761	5,109	3,645	2,512	1,459	829	382
1967	5,226	3,781	4,020	4,030	2,592	2,077	1,001	547	191
1966	4,047	4,225	5,425	3,869	2,689	1,912	1,107	448	193
1965	3,827	4,241	4,836	3,285	2,650	1,707	821	351	143

Source: 1988 National Two-per-Thousand Fertility and Birth Control Survey.

Appendix Table 6.2. Annual first marriages and births by order.

		Birth order						
Year	M	1	2	3	4	5	6	7
1981	10,673	9,912	5,486	2,971	1,498	779	461	233
1980	9,779	7,504	4,858	2,699	1,482	690	389	222
1979	7,993	7,542	5,704	3,470	2,025	1,061	688	340
1978	7,166	6,713	5,178	3,459	1,980	1,220	671	431
1977	6,489	6,178	4,892	3,575	2,108	1,323	835	527
1976	6,399	6,004	5,224	3,837	2,468	1,565	1,058	709
1975	5,731	5,572	5,132	4,097	2,742	1,924	1,270	835
1974	5,530	5,834	5,579	4,374	3,117	2,271	1,597	1,056
1973	5,213	5,389	5,628	4,294	3,415	2,606	1,841	1,186
1972	5,350	5,500	5,488	4,195	3,702	2,914	2,119	1,356
1971	5,435	5,891	5,343	4,449	4,126	3,245	2,208	1,480
1970	5,942	6,092	5,029	4,713	4,285	3,187	2,459	1,580
1969	6,583	5,643	4,447	4,927	4,130	3,121	2,262	1,493
1968	6,293	5,618	5,319	5,586	4,400	3,276	2,522	1,729
1967	4,929	4,007	4,758	4,571	3,403	2,706	2,028	1,302
1966	4,172	4,689	5,864	4,730	3,798	3,121	2,445	1,551
1965	3,896	4,687	5,579	4,197	3,601	3,062	2,316	1,494

Source: 1982 National One-per-Thousand Population Fertility Sampling Survey.

Part III

Future Mortality in Developing Countries

The papers in this section indicate that the impressive mortality declines experienced recently in developing countries were mostly due to the decline in infectious diseases. Until recently, there was widespread optimism that these declines would continue in the future and that eventually life expectancy in all developing countries would approach the level of industrialized countries; some individual developing countries have already achieved this level. The AIDS pandemic, the return of other infectious diseases such as malaria, and increasing uncertainty about future food supply and environmental problems have significantly weakened this optimistic view. Although at the global level there should be enough food for a possible world population of 15 billion, local political crises and environmental damage as well as distributional problems may cause at least temporary famine-related excess mortality. AIDS will definitely have an effect on mortality in several regions of Africa and South Asia, but we are uncertain about how much it will impact on life expectancy. This uncertainty is reflected in the significantly diverging alternative mortality scenarios presented in Part VI. In the pessimistic case life expectancy is assumed to decline in Africa and stay constant in South Asia, whereas in the optimistic case life expectancy is assumed to gradually catch up with that in today's industrialized countries.

Chapter 7

Mortality Trends in Developing Countries: A Survey

Birgitta Bucht

In preparing population projections for low-mortality developed countries with good statistics, mortality assumptions are considered the least problematic, at least for short-term projections, because mortality rates tend to change slowly. In developing countries, assumptions about future mortality trends are much less certain, even for short-term projections, because of the inadequacy of reliable information on past levels and trends.

This chapter reviews past levels and trends of mortality in developing countries, makes assumptions about future trends made by the United Nations, compares past assumptions with actual performance, and concludes with a review of recent and possible future changes in the pace of mortality decline. Mortality assumptions made recently by the World Bank are also reviewed.

The survey of past levels and trends is based on mortality estimates prepared for the *World Population Monitoring, 1993* (UN, 1994b) as well as the latest United Nations population estimates and projections, *World Population Prospects: The 1994 Revision* (UN, 1995).

The views and opinions expressed in this paper are those of the author and do not necessarily reflect those of the United Nations.

7.1   Levels and Trends of Mortality Since 1950

Considerable progress has been made in reducing mortality in less developed regions in recent decades. Over a period of 40 years, from the early 1950s to the early 1990s, the average expectation of life at birth in less developed regions is estimated to have increased 21 years, from about 41 in 1950–1955 to 62 in 1990–1995 according to the United Nations latest world population estimates and projections (*Table 7.1*). The difference between the more and the less developed regions narrowed during this period, from 26 years in the early 1950s to 12 years in 1990–1995. Life expectancy is projected to further increase to 71 in 2020–2025, and the difference between the more and the less developed regions is expected to decline to seven years. There is a considerable degree of heterogeneity, however, at the regional and subregional levels, and differences among countries are even larger. Progress has been slowest in Africa, and life expectancy is still estimated at only about 50 years in East, Central, and West Africa. Mortality is somewhat lower in North and Southern Africa where life expectancy is estimated at 62 and 63 years, respectively, in 1990–1995. In Asia, estimates of life expectancies at birth in 1985–1990 are generally higher than those in Africa and range from 60 in South-central Asia to 70 in East Asia. (It should be noted that the latter region includes Japan, which is a developed country.) There was less regional diversity in Asia in the early 1950s, when life expectancy ranged from 39 in South-central Asia to 45 in West Asia. The estimates for the Latin American regions are still higher, on the average, than those for Asia, and fall within a narrow range: 68 years in South America and 69 years in the Caribbean and Central America. Among the developing regions of Oceania, life expectancy ranges from 59 years in Melanesia to 68 years in Micronesia and Polynesia.

It should be noted that the estimates shown in *Table 7.1* are a mixture of estimates and projections and may be revised as new data become available. The availability of data on mortality in developing countries has improved considerably over the past two decades. Vital registration is gradually becoming more complete, particularly

Table 7.1. Estimated and projected life expectancy at birth, world, major areas, and regions: 1950–2025.

Major area Region	Life expectancy (years)							
	1950-1955	1960-1965	1970-1975	1980-1985	1990-1995	2000-2005	2010-2015	2020-2025
World	46.4	52.3	57.9	61.3	64.4	67.1	69.9	72.5
More developed regions[a]	66.5	69.8	71.2	73.0	74.4	75.8	77.3	78.6
Less developed regions[b]	40.9	47.7	54.6	58.5	62.3	65.3	68.5	71.3
Africa	37.8	42.0	46.0	49.4	53.0	55.8	60.5	65.4
East Africa	36.3	40.7	44.8	46.9	49.7	51.3	57.5	64.3
Central Africa	36.0	39.6	43.9	48.1	51.3	53.7	59.0	65.1
North Africa	41.8	46.3	51.3	56.6	62.2	66.2	69.2	71.8
Southern Africa	44.2	49.3	53.4	57.6	62.6	67.1	70.5	72.9
West Africa	35.6	39.4	42.8	46.1	49.8	53.2	57.5	62.1
Asia	41.3	48.4	56.3	60.4	64.5	67.9	70.8	73.2
East Asia	42.9	51.4	64.2	67.6	69.7	72.1	73.8	75.4
South-central Asia	39.3	45.5	50.1	55.1	60.3	64.7	68.6	71.5
Southeast Asia	40.5	46.4	51.8	58.1	63.6	67.3	70.5	73.4
West Asia	45.2	52.1	57.9	62.5	66.5	69.5	72.0	74.1
Europe	66.1	69.7	70.8	71.9	72.9	74.3	76.1	77.5
Eastern Europe	65.5	69.1	69.4	69.0	68.9	70.2	72.4	74.3
North Europe	69.2	71.2	72.4	74.1	75.7	77.2	78.3	79.3
South Europe	63.3	68.6	71.5	74.0	76.2	77.7	78.9	79.9
Western Europe	67.6	70.8	71.8	74.3	76.5	77.9	79.0	80.0
Latin America[c]	51.4	56.9	61.1	65.1	68.5	71.0	73.2	75.1
Caribbean	52.0	58.4	63.1	66.4	69.2	71.4	73.3	74.9
Central America	49.3	56.7	61.5	65.8	69.9	72.3	74.2	75.7
South America	52.1	56.8	60.7	64.7	67.9	70.4	72.8	74.8
North America[d]	69.0	70.1	71.5	74.7	76.1	77.6	78.8	79.8
Oceania	60.8	64.6	66.6	70.1	72.8	74.7	76.5	78.1
Australia–New Zealand	69.5	70.9	71.7	75.0	77.3	78.5	79.6	80.5
Melanesia	37.9	45.6	50.8	55.4	59.1	62.9	66.6	69.9
Micronesia	49.4	55.3	59.4	63.7	67.7	71.0	73.3	75.2
Polynesia	45.7	53.5	59.3	64.5	68.1	70.6	73.1	75.5

[a]More developed regions comprise North America, Japan, Europe, and Australia–New Zealand.
[b]Less developed regions comprise all regions of Africa, Latin America, Asia (excluding Japan), and Melanesia, Micronesia, and Polynesia.
[c]Including Mexico.
[d]Excluding Mexico.
Source: UN, 1995:Tables A.26 and A.27.

in Latin America and East Asia. Data that permit estimation of infant and child mortality have been widely collected in censuses and surveys, in particular those conducted by the World Fertility Survey (WFS) program and more recently by the Demographic and Health Surveys (DHSs). Despite these improvements, lack of reliable data continues to be a serious handicap in the analysis of mortality in developing countries. Obviously, countries for which data on mortality are available may not necessarily be representative of other countries since mortality conditions are likely to be worse in countries lacking data. For example, there are no recent surveys or registration data in countries affected by war or civil strife. The countries without any national-level data, however, form only a small part of the total population of less developed regions, so that even large errors in the country estimates will not greatly affect regional totals.

Although the data situation has improved in Africa, it is still more problematic to estimate levels and trends there than in other less developed regions. The only countries in sub-Saharan Africa with reliable vital registration systems from which life tables can be derived are three small island countries in the Indian Ocean: Mauritius, Réunion, and the Seychelles. All three have reached low levels of mortality with life expectancies now above 70 years. Most information for mainland sub-Saharan Africa refers to child mortality. Few countries have adequate data on adult mortality.

Mortality is high throughout most of sub-Saharan Africa, but there is variation among countries in terms of both levels and trends. Child mortality has generally been most severe in West Africa, a fact attributed both to the level of socioeconomic development and to environmental factors (Blacker, 1991). Although differences with the other regions have narrowed, West Africa as a whole still has the highest child mortality on the continent. Sierra Leone, a West African country, exhibits the highest mortality ever measured in a contemporary country: a probability of dying by age 5 of 364 per 1,000 in 1971, declining to 334 per 1,000 in 1981 according to the 1974 and 1985 censuses. Gambia and Mali in West Africa and Malawi in East Africa, which had similarly high levels of child mortality in the 1970s, have experienced large improvements, but the latest estimates of mortality under the age of 5 for these countries are still above 240 per 1,000. The lowest mortality in mainland sub-Saharan Africa has been achieved by Kenya and Zimbabwe in East Africa and Botswana in Southern Africa. The low child mortality in Botswana (65 per 1,000 in 1984) may be explained, in addition to its impressive economic growth during the 1970s and 1980s, by the high proportion of women receiving prenatal care and vaccinated with tetanus toxoid, the high proportion of births delivered by trained health personnel, and the high immunization coverage of children (Lesetedi *et al.*, 1989; World Bank, 1992a). Immunization coverage and the proportions of women receiving prenatal care are also high in Kenya and Zimbabwe (Kenya, 1989; Zimbabwe, 1989).

The countries of North Africa have experienced more rapid mortality declines with an acceleration in the decline since the mid-1970s and late 1970s. In Algeria, the only country in the region with a series of life tables derived from vital registration, life expectancy increased slowly from 53 in 1970 to 57 in 1978 and then to 64 in 1985, an annual increase of one year. Life tables after 1985 are not yet available, but recent data on infants show that mortality has continued to decline. In Egypt, infant and child mortality fell by more than half between 1976 and 1986. In Tunisia, which currently has the lowest infant and child mortality rates in North Africa, the decline has been equally impressive, from an under-five mortality of 204 per 1,000 in 1968–1969 to 65 per 1,000 in 1983–1987 according to a 1968–1969 demographic survey, the 1975 census, and the 1988 DHS.

Asia presents the most varied picture among the developing regions, both in terms of levels and trends in mortality and in terms of availability and quality of data, reflecting very diverse histories and levels of development. East Asia has achieved the lowest mortality levels in the region. The main reason is obviously the remarkable progress achieved by China. Life expectancy in China was estimated at 41 in 1950–1955 and reached 67 in 1980–1985, an annual increase of almost one year. The other countries of the region with available data, Hong Kong and the Republic of Korea, have also successfully reduced their mortality levels. According to its civil registration data, Hong Kong now has the lowest mortality among all developing countries with a life expectancy in 1987–1989 of 77 years (80 for

females and 74 for males) and an infant and under-five mortality of
7 and 9 per 1,000, respectively.

Southeast Asia is characterized by a wide disparity of mortality
levels and trends. Brunei Darussalam, peninsular Malaysia, and Singapore have achieved mortality levels comparable with those of developed countries with life-expectancy estimates above 70. Progress
has also been made in other countries in the region, particularly in
Thailand where expectation of life at birth reached 66 in 1985–1986
and in the Philippines where it reached 64 in 1987–1989. However,
the region also includes areas such as East Timor, Cambodia, and
Lao People's Democratic Republic where mortality is believed to be
high and life expectancy estimated to be below 50 years.

South Asia exhibits the highest mortality levels and has experienced the slowest decline in Asia, although Sri Lanka has attained
relatively low mortality: life expectancy was 69 in 1980–1981, and is
now estimated to exceed 70. Afghanistan has the highest mortality
in the region, which is not surprising given its social and political
circumstances. Although mortality is still high in the three largest
countries of the Indian subcontinent – Bangladesh, India, and Pakistan – the levels have been declining. In Bangladesh, life expectancy
increased from 48 in the late 1970s to 56 in 1987. In India, life expectancy was estimated at 53 in 1981–1983. More recent data from
the Sample Registration System show that infant mortality has continued to decline, from 107 per 1,000 in 1981–1983 to 94 per 1,000
in 1988. The latest data for Pakistan give a life expectancy of 60 in
1984–1988, an increase from 53 in 1972–1981.

In West Asia, several countries have experienced very rapid declines, not only the small oil-producing countries of the region, but
also countries such as Jordan, the Syrian Arab Republic, and Turkey.
Cyprus and Israel have the lowest mortality in the region with life
expectancies above 75, followed by Kuwait where life expectancy was
estimated at 72 in 1984–1986. The only country with high mortality
in the region is Yemen, where infant and under-five mortality were
162 and 237 per 1,000, respectively, according to the 1979 WFS.

As mentioned earlier, Latin America has achieved lower mortality levels than Africa and Asia. The mortality decline in the
Caribbean is particularly impressive with levels of life expectancy

reaching those of developed countries despite lower levels of economic development. Life expectancy at birth is estimated to be
above 70 years on all islands except the Dominican Republic and
Haiti. In Cuba and Puerto Rico life expectancy was 75 in 1985–
1986 and 1986–1988, respectively, the highest in Latin America. To
give an example of the mortality decline that has occurred in some
of those countries, life expectancy at birth in Barbados increased
from 57 in 1950–1955 to 72 in 1980. Infant mortality declined from
132 per 1,000 in the early 1950s to 13 per 1,000 in the late 1980s,
over 90 percent. Decline has been slow in the Dominican Republic
and Haiti. Under-five mortality in Haiti was still estimated at 193
per 1,000 in 1983, higher than in many African countries.

Two countries in Central America – Costa Rica and Panama –
have also achieved very low levels of mortality with life expectancies above 70. In Mexico, the largest country in the region, life
expectancy at birth increased from 61 in 1970 to 66 in 1980 and is
now believed to be close to 70.

In South America, the lowest mortality levels are observed in
Argentina, Chile, Uruguay, and Venezuela. In Chile, life expectancy
at birth increased from 62 to 71 during the 12-year period between
1970 and 1982, and infant and child mortality declined by almost
70 percent during the same period. Recent data show a continuing
but slower decline during the 1980s. Bolivia and Peru, however,
have the highest mortality in the region but, like all South American countries, have experienced substantial mortality reductions. In
Bolivia, for example, the probability of dying by age 5 declined by
almost half between 1972 and 1988, from 254 to 130 per 1,000. In
Brazil, the largest country in the region, with half its population,
the mortality decline has been moderate. Life expectancy at birth
increased from 58 in 1970 to 62 in 1976–1980 and may be above 65
at present.

Mortality has also declined steadily in the developing countries
of Oceania, and some countries have achieved low levels of mortality.
In Guam, life expectancy was estimated at 73 in 1979–1981 and
infant mortality at 11 per 1,000 in 1985–1987. The only areas where
mortality is still high is Kiribati, a small island in Micronesia, where
under-five mortality was estimated at 123 in 1981 according to the

1985 census and Papua New Guinea, Melanesia, where under-five mortality was estimated at 96 in 1976.

The United Nations has recently completed a review of child mortality since the 1960s in developing countries with an estimated 1990 population of 1 million or more (UN, 1992b). Among the countries with adequate estimates of the probability of dying by age 5 for two points in time between 1960 and 1985, altogether 79 observations, child mortality declined by about 3 percent per annum. Asia and Latin America both experienced rates slightly above this average, whereas the rate of decline in Africa was only about 2 percent per annum. These figures may be somewhat different, however, if data for all countries were available. In sub-Saharan Africa, there are a few countries where available data show that child-mortality declines may have stalled, although the observed trend could be due to poor data quality. Data are so defective in some countries, not only in Africa, that it is not really possible to tell how mortality has evolved. In many countries outside sub-Saharan Africa with sufficient data to indicate a change in trends, child-mortality declines appear to have accelerated in the late 1970s and in the 1980s.

7.2   Assumptions about Future Trends in Mortality

The United Nations has prepared global population projections since the 1950s. The details of the projections have expanded over time with improvements in data and methods of analysis and with the utilization of computer technology. Detailed mortality assumptions by country were first made in 1968. The assumptions are formulated in terms of life expectancy at birth and age and sex patterns of probabilities of surviving, corresponding to different levels of life expectancy at birth. The age-specific survival ratios needed for the projections are derived from appropriate model life tables. For countries with reliable data on mortality by age and sex, that information is used to complement the derivation of the required survival ratios. A national life table for a given date is used as a base for the projections, and as mortality is projected to decline, it is assumed that the mortality rates of the national life table will gradually approach those of a model life table. This procedure has been referred to as the "modified method" of mortality projection (UN, 1977a). For countries without reliable mortality data by age and sex, the mortality rates are taken directly from the model life tables selected for the projections. The Coale and Demeny regional model life tables (Coale and Demeny, 1966, 1983) and, since the 1988 assessment, the United Nations model life tables for developing countries (UN, 1982a) are used in preparing the United Nations projections.

One of the roles of the United Nations projections is to produce comparable global and interregional prospects of population. To maintain comparability in the assumptions of mortality between regions and among countries within regions, a uniform procedure is used for all countries. The assumptions about life expectancy at birth are made to follow models of mortality improvement. These models have been developed using data from countries with reliable death statistics and have been revised and modified as new data have become available, reflecting the most recent observations about mortality decline. It has generally been assumed that life expectancy at birth would increase by half a year annually until life expectancy for females reaches 55, 62.5, or 65 years, followed by a slowdown in the gain thereafter. In countries where evidence suggests that the mortality decline has been faster or slower than the model implies, the assumptions have been adjusted. The most recent working model, which was developed for the 1988 assessment and is summarized in *Table 7.2*, introduces three variations in the speed of improvement and labels them fast, middle, and slow models.

In the model developed for the 1973 assessment, it was assumed that the highest female life expectancy that could be attained would be 77.5 years, the value given as maximum in the Coale–Demeny regional model life tables, and the highest male life expectancy would be 72.6 years, the value given as maximum in the first United Nations model life tables (*Table 7.3*). In the 1978 assessment, the maximum life expectancies were raised to 80 for females and 73.5 for males. In the 1982 assessment, the maxima were further raised to 82.5 years for females and 75 for males. The Coale–Demeny regional model life tables were extrapolated to incorporate survival ratios corresponding to these higher levels of life expectancies. The most recent model, developed for the 1988 assessment, represents a

Table 7.2. Working model for mortality improvement, quinquennial gains (in years) in life expectancy at birth ($^o e_o$) according to initial level of mortality.

Initial mortality level	Fast		Middle		Slow	
	Male	Female	Male	Female	Male	Female
55.0–57.5	2.5	2.5	2.5	2.5	2.0	2.0
57.5–60.0	2.5	2.5	2.5	2.5	2.0	2.0
60.0–62.5	2.5	2.5	2.3	2.5	2.0	2.0
62.5–65.0	2.3	2.5	2.0	2.5	2.0	2.0
65.0–67.5	2.0	2.5	1.5	2.3	1.5	2.0
67.5–70.0	1.5	2.3	1.2	2.0	1.0	1.5
70.0–72.5	1.2	2.0	1.0	1.5	0.8	1.2
72.5–75.0	1.0	1.5	0.8	1.2	0.5	1.0
75.0–77.5	0.8	1.2	0.5	1.0	0.3	0.8
77.5–80.0	0.5	1.0	0.4	0.8	0.3	0.5
80.0–82.5	0.5	0.8	0.4	0.5	0.3	0.3
82.5–85.0	–	0.5	–	0.4	–	0.3
85.0–87.5	–	0.5	–	0.4	–	0.3

Source: UN, 1989b:Table 1.4.

Table 7.3. Maximum life expectancies in United Nations working models of mortality decline.

Assessment year	Male	Female
1973	72.6	77.5
1978	73.5	80.0
1982	75.0	82.5
1988	82.5	87.5

Sources: UN, 1977b:11; 1981a:3; 1985b:10; and 1989b:15.

major revision in terms of long-range mortality assumptions. The highest life expectancies at birth were extended to 87.5 for females and 82.5 for males. In order to extend the model life tables to the new maximum life expectancies, working life tables with life expectancies of 87.5 for females and 82.5 for males were constructed by using the reduced values of age-specific probabilities of dying (qx) available from countries that now have the lowest mortality rates. The highest levels of survival of each of the nine model life tables

(West, North, South, and East model of the Coale and Demeny regional model life tables and General, Latin American, Chilean, Far Eastern, and South Asian model life tables of the United Nations) were linked individually with the age-specific survival ratios derived from the working life table so that survival ratios of other intermediate mortality levels could be obtained through interpolation (UN, 1989b). These survival ratios have been used in the 1988–1994 revisions of the population projections.

Several developing countries have now surpassed the maximum life expectancy for females of 77.5 assumed in 1973. Only one country, Hong Kong, is currently estimated to have a life expectancy above 80 for females, the maximum assumed in 1978, although several other countries, mainly small island countries, have reached life expectancies close to that level. Only one developed country, Japan, has reached the limit for females set in 1982, 82.5 years, but several countries have surpassed the limit assumed for males, 75 years.

The most recent United Nations projections have taken into account the effects of the acquired immunodeficiency syndrome (AIDS) pandemic in 15 high prevalence countries in sub-Saharan Africa and one country in Asia, Thailand (UN, 1995). The number of deaths related to AIDS is estimated and projected using an epidemiological model developed by the World Health Organization (Chin and Lwanga, 1991b). In applying the model, it is assumed that there are no new adult human immunodeficiency virus (HIV) infections after 2010; mother-to-child infections continue to occur after this date and AIDS deaths follow for many years thereafter due to the long latency period between HIV and AIDS. The assumption of no new adult infections after 2010 has little effect on projected AIDS mortality until after 2025. The estimates of deaths from AIDS by age and sex, for each five-year period, are then integrated into the existing (non-AIDS) model life tables, producing a set of life tables which incorporates the risk of dying from AIDS and which is used for the projections.

Recently, the World Bank has published mortality projections; the first results were published in *World Development Report 1978* (World Bank, 1978). Detailed projections have been published only

since 1984 in *World Population Projections* (various years). The
base-year mortality estimates used in the World Bank projections
were mainly obtained from the United Nations, but methods used
to prepare assumptions about future trends are different. In the
1984 to 1987–1988 assessments, life expectancy at birth was projected with a model using past patterns of relationships between
the change in life expectancy, the level of life expectancy, and the
female primary school enrollment ratio. Two different schedules of
annual increments in female life expectancy were developed: one
for countries with female primary school enrollment less than 70
percent and another for those where the enrollment is 70 percent
or more. For a given expectation of life at birth, survival ratios
for males and females were derived from the Coale and Demeny regional model life tables. In recent projections, a different procedure
has been used to project mortality (Bulatao and Bos, 1989). Life
expectancy and infant mortality are projected separately using logistic functions, taking into account past trends and socioeconomic
factors. The logistic function is determined so that life expectancy
rises most rapidly from a level of 50 years and increasingly slowly
at higher levels. Rates of change are estimated from past rates of
change and from the female secondary school enrollment ratio or,
in a few cases where data on school enrollment are not available,
from the percent urban. Maximum life expectancies were assumed
to be 90 years for females and 83.3 for males. Life tables are selected from the Coale–Demeny regional model life tables combining
different levels to give exactly the desired infant mortality rate and
life expectancy. Coale and Guo's (1989) extended model life tables
are used at low levels of mortality. The most recent World Bank
projections have also taken into account the effects of AIDS, applying an epidemiological model developed by Bulatao (1991) and Bos
et al. (1992).

The World Bank assumptions show more variation among individual countries than do those assumed by the United Nations, and
indicate, on average, slightly faster decline at lower levels of life expectancy and slower decline at higher levels. Mortality assumptions
for less developed regions according to different United Nations and
World Bank assessments are shown in *Tables 7.4* and *7.5*.

Table 7.4. Estimated and projected life expectancy at birth for less developed regions, both sexes, according to different United Nations assessments.

Year	Projection period			
estimated	1980–1985	1985–1990	1990–1995	2020–2025
1968	58.0	60.6	63.0	–
1973	56.7	58.7	60.7	–
1978	57.1	59.2	61.1	–
1980	57.0	58.9	60.7	69.6
1982	56.6	58.2	60.0	68.9
1984	57.3	59.1	60.8	69.5
1988	57.6	59.7	61.5	70.4
1990	59.4	61.4	63.3	71.6
1992	58.6	60.7	62.4	71.2
1994	58.5	60.5	62.3	71.3

Sources: UN, 1973:Table A.2.1; 1977b:Table 41; 1979; 1981a:Table A-15; 1985b:Table A-15; 1986:Table A-15; 1989b:Table 15; 1991a:Table 44; 1993a: Table A-15; and 1995:Tables A26 and A27.

Table 7.5. Estimated and projected life expectancy at birth for less developed regions, both sexes, according to different World Bank assessments.

Year	Projection period			
estimated	1980–1985	1985–1990	1990–1995	2020–2025
1984	59.5	61.2	62.8	70.7
1985	59.4	61.1	62.8	70.8
1987–1988	–	61.4	62.9	70.3
1989–1990	–	62.1	63.6	69.3
1992–1993	–	61.9	63.2	71.1

Sources: Vu, 1984, 1985; Zachariah and Vu, 1988; Bulatao *et al.*, 1990; and Bos *et al.*, 1992.

7.3 Comparison of Past Assumptions with Actual Performance

Since the United Nations has a long series of population estimates and projections, assumptions made in past projections can be compared with more recent assumptions and with actual levels. *Table 7.4* shows estimated and projected life expectancies at birth for less developed regions at different periods available from the different United Nations projections prepared between 1968 and 1994. The projected life expectancy at birth for less developed regions as a whole has turned out to be reasonably accurate in each revision carried out over a quarter of a century. In 1968, when detailed projections were first performed for each country, life expectancy at birth was projected to be 60.6 in 1985–1990 for less developed regions. In 1994, it was estimated at 60.5 for the same period. The long-range projections show a small and gradual improvement in assumed mortality levels over time. In 1980, life expectancy at birth was projected to be 69.6 in 2020–2025. In 1994, it was projected to be 71.3 in the same period.

It is remarkable that the projected life expectancy for less developed regions has changed so little despite large revisions for individual countries. Country estimates have been raised or lowered as new data have become available and with new and better methods of estimating mortality. Several countries have experienced unforeseen and almost spectacular gains in the life expectancy at birth, most notably China, the most populous country in the world. The 1968 mortality assumption for China, a life expectancy of 62 years in 1985–1990, was surpassed by five years. The mortality decline has been slower than projected in a sufficient number of countries, however, to offset the more rapid decline in others so that the regional averages have not changed much. For more developed regions, in contrast, the projected life expectancies have gradually been revised upward.

It should be noted that the sudden increase in life expectancy at birth between the 1988 and the 1990 revisions is partly the result of a new method of calculating life expectancy at the regional and global levels from country-specific figures. In the earlier revisions, regional and global life expectancies were estimated by weighing the country-specific life expectancy figures by the number of births. This method provided unbiased estimates only when countries within the region had similar age structures and similar levels of fertility. Beginning with the 1990 revision, the method was changed to exactly calculate survival ratios (and hence life expectancies) at regional and country levels by aggregating deaths and population by age and sex at the country level (UN, 1991a:91).

7.4 Possible Changes in the Pace of Future Mortality Decline

There has been some concern that the deteriorating economic conditions since the mid-1970s in many developing countries would lead to a slowdown or stagnation in the mortality decline because of a reduction in expenditures on social services implemented to cope with the economic crisis. There is no evidence yet of such a change except possibly in a few countries in sub-Saharan Africa where mortality trends are difficult to interpret. In countries with negative growth of GDP per capita from 1965–1980 or 1980–1990 (World Bank, 1992a) and with sufficient data to estimate mortality trends – for example, Senegal in sub-Saharan Africa and several countries in Latin America – mortality has continued to decline without change. However, one cannot rule out the possibility that the deterioration in economic conditions and reduced spending on health could have a delayed effect on mortality in some countries.

An important measure that is likely to have a substantial effect on mortality trends in the near future is the child survival programs that began in the 1980s by governments and international organizations. These programs have consisted mainly in making a few simple and low-cost technologies widely available, in particular immunization and oral rehydration therapy (ORT). When the World Health Organization launched its Expanded Programme on Immunization in 1974, it was estimated that less than 5 percent of children in the developing world were immunized (UNICEF, 1989). By 1985, the coverage had increased to about 30 percent for measles and 40 percent for the other diseases. Since then, many countries have sharply increased their coverage, and it is estimated that by 1990 between 79 and 90 percent of infants were vaccinated against certain diseases. Immunization of women against tetanus still lags behind, at about 56 percent (UNICEF, 1992). Awareness and use of oral rehydration therapy have also increased substantially. These efforts should have an important impact on child mortality, and favorable results have already been reported in a number of countries. However, since the programs have only recently gained momentum in many countries and since data for the late 1980s are still not available in many countries, the full impact of these programs cannot yet be measured.

Other factors that will affect child survival in the future are increasing education of women and declines in fertility, with a reduction in high-risk births. Reduced fertility is also likely to have indirect positive effects on a child's survival chances because a family with fewer children can allocate more resources per child, including parental care and attention, food, schooling, and access to health services. There is also a reduced risk of infection of children in small households. Maternal mortality, which is high in many developing countries, is also lowered with fertility declines.

In the near future, the outlook in general indicates a continuation of the mortality decline. In addition to those mentioned above, other helpful factors include further improvements in education, medical research, training of health personnel, and the spread of democracy which will enable people to put pressure on governments to improve health services.

Several developing countries have reached mortality levels comparable to those in developed countries, even in countries where the levels of economic development are far behind those of developed countries. There is no reason that the mortality declines will not continue and that other countries will not follow, barring of course wars, famines, and other catastrophes.

This does not mean that it is going to be easy to achieve continued impressive improvements. The progress in sub-Saharan Africa is likely to continue to lag behind that of the other developing regions. Apart from the droughts and famines that are plaguing substantial parts of Africa at the present time and the civil strife that exists not only in Africa but also in Asia, there are two important concerns: the AIDS epidemic and the spread of chloroquine-resistant malaria. Both are likely to have a particularly devastating effect in sub-Saharan Africa. Environmental problems of various kinds aggravated by population growth, such as water scarcity and loss of agricultural land, and cutbacks in food production could also lead to increased risks to health.

Chapter 8

Mortality in Sub-Saharan Africa: Trends and Prospects

Michel Garenne

Interest in the population growth of the Third World began after World War II, owing mostly to the growing concern for population pressure and its possible effects upon the economy, ecology, and political balance of the world. The sources of the high rate of population growth were the rapid decline of mortality and, to a lesser extent, the increase of natality. The primary concern was with Asia, in particular, China and the Indian subcontinent, and with Latin America, in particular Central America. Somewhat later, the demography of sub-Saharan Africa became a subject for research.

The first systematic studies of African populations took place in the early 1960s. A team of researchers working at Princeton University published the first comprehensive account of African demography (Brass *et al.*, 1968). At about the same time, a group of French demographers published a summary of their experiences and findings on tropical Africa, with emphasis on the sample surveys conducted by the French National Statistical Office (INSEE) since 1954 (GDA, 1967). Since this pioneer period, only a few syntheses on the population dynamics of the region have been published. Mandjale (1985) analyzed infant and child mortality. Van de Walle *et al.* (1988) reviewed the state of African demography. The collection of work edited by Feachem and Jamison (1991) focused on morbidity and mortality.

Over the past 50 years, Africa experienced minimal fluctuations in fertility, whereas its mortality rate underwent a major decline; this situation created a considerable potential for population growth. The decline in mortality has been documented only recently in a systematic way (Hill and Hill, 1988; Hill, 1991; Timæus, 1991). However, there is a growing concern that the mortality decline will not continue, and may even be reversed under new conditions such as economic crises, political turmoils, and emerging diseases such as AIDS.

This paper reviews the available evidence of mortality decline, before and since independence, and discusses the future of mortality. It focuses on the countries of sub-Saharan Africa. The small islands off the African coast, such as Cape Verde, Sao Tome and Principe, Mauritius, and the Seychelles, have been ignored in this analysis because they have very different population dynamics. Three broad periods are distinguished: prior to 1960 – that is, the colonial period for most countries; 1960–1990, the first three decades after the region achieved independence; and recent trends (when available), 1985–1994.

8.1   The Colonial Period: 1920–1959

8.1.1   Mortality trends

Data from the end of the colonial period (1920–1959) are very scarce, and there is virtually no data on tropical Africa prior to 1915. Two long-term series are available from Dakar and Saint-Louis, two cities in Senegal, where an extensive vital registration system has been maintained. The vital registration data from Saint-Louis were recently analyzed in a Ph.D. dissertation (Diop, 1990) and the data from Dakar were discussed in a recent paper (Garenne *et al.*, 1993).

For Dakar, there is clear evidence that mortality has been declining since at least 1920; the 1915–1919 period was seriously disturbed by the 1918 influenza world epidemic as well as by a local plague epidemic. For Saint-Louis, mortality has been declining steadily since 1930, the earliest date for which data were analyzed (*Figure 8.1*). In both cases, the crude death rates at the beginning of the series were among the highest recorded, and were only slightly lower

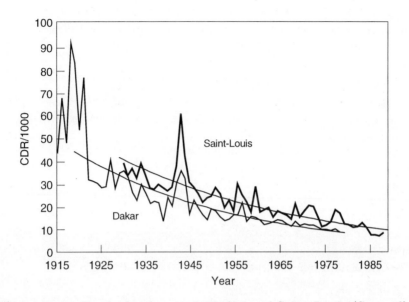

Figure 8.1. Crude death rates in Dakar and Saint-Louis (Senegal), from vital registration data. Source: Garenne *et al.*, 1993.

than the crude birth rate: CDR was 35 per 1,000 in Dakar during the 1920–1924 period, and it was 36 per 1,000 in Saint-Louis in 1930–1934.

It is reasonable to conclude that mortality began to decline dramatically during the period just following World War I. This finding is confirmed by the fact that the population increased significantly between 1920 and 1960, as shown by the series of administrative censuses in Senegal (Becker and Martin, 1983).

Other evidence is available from early censuses and from retrospective questioning of mothers (*Table 8.1*). For Ghana, the probability of dying before the fifth birthday, $q(5)$, was estimated at 380 per 1,000 in 1933, and has been declining since then with minor fluctuations. In the former Portuguese colonies, $q(5)$ was estimated at 472 per 1,000 in Angola (1935–1939), at 367 in Mozambique (1945–1949), and at 353 in Guinea Bissau (1945–1949) (Heisel, 1968). These values are very high, and they are no longer prevalent, except in special cases of severe political crisis such as the Mozambican civil war (see Section 8.3.1).

Table 8.1. Estimates of child mortality in sub-Saharan Africa prior to 1960, probability of dying before age 5, $q(5)$, per 1,000.

Country	1930–1934	1935–1939	1940–1944	1945–1949	1950–1954	1955–1959
Angola		472		438		
Benin						375
Burkina Faso				420	424	408
Centr.Afr.Rep.						345
Ghana	380	370	300	345	255	225
Congo						291
Guinea (Conakry)						383
Guinea-Bissau				353		
Mozambique				367		
Niger						365
Senegal				385	353	327

Source: Adapted from Hill, 1992, and from Brass *et al.*, 1968.

By 1960, when most countries obtained independence, major differences in infant and child mortality already existed among countries. The quotient $q(5)$ ranged from 160 per 1,000 in Zimbabwe to 400 per 1,000 in Sierra Leone (*Table 8.2*). These large differences among countries were attributed primarily to the level of development (for instance, Zimbabwe and Botswana were much wealthier than other countries in the region) and, to a certain extent, to the environment (the highland countries of East Africa were reputed to have less malaria and therefore a lower mortality rate) (Blacker, 1991). The exception to this pattern is Malawi, a country known to have a high prevalence of malnutrition and vitamin A deficiency (Feachem and Jamison, 1991).

8.1.2 Socioeconomic change

There are several reasons for the mortality decline during the 40 years following World War I. Colonial powers opened roads in most of Africa, sometimes railways, which drew most of the villages out of their isolation. One noticeable consequence of improving communications, well documented in the past in Europe and also in the 20th century in India (Davis, 1951), is the drastic reduction in the number of famines. In northern Senegal there were famines every

Table 8.2. Estimates of child mortality in sub-Saharan Africa, probability of dying before age 5, $q(5)$, per 1,000: 1960–1990.

Country	1960	1965	1970	1975	1980	1985	1990
Benin			255	240	200		
Botswana	175	160	140	120	90	53	
Burkina Faso	315	295	275	255	220	215	187
Burundi	270	240	220	220	210	152	
Cameroon		235	220	185			126
Centr.Afr.Rep.		325	295	245	245		157
Chad	310						
Congo	200	165	140				
Côte d'Ivoire		265	245	210	165	150	150
Ethiopia	235	230	225	220			
Gabon	250						
Gambia	350	345	310	275	240		
Ghana	228	208	190	173	156	155	119
Guinea (Conakry)					310	275	229
Kenya	216	186	161	139	120	89	96
Lesotho	200	195	185	175			
Liberia	280	270	255	245	235	275	
Madagascar			170	169	181	195	163
Malawi	360	345	335	320	285	246	
Mali				360	310	249	234
Mozambique		280	280	280			
Namibia					110	102	83
Niger					308	334	318
Nigeria					195	192	
Rwanda	240	220	220	245	225	176	150
Senegal	300	295	285	265	220	191	131
Sierra Leone	400	385	365				
Somalia		240	225	210			
Sudan	220	205	170	150	145	135	
Swaziland	230	220	215				
Tanzania	240	235	225	215			
Togo	300	245	220	200	180	158	
Uganda	229	201	191	178	185	180	
Zaire				235	210	200	
Zambia	220	190	180	165	152	162	190
Zimbabwe	160	155	145	140	135	75	77
Average	258	244	227	216	201	180	161

Source: Adapted from Hill, 1992, and from DHS.

three to four years in the 19th century (Chastanet, 1982). Severe
famines virtually disappeared after World War I, with a few exceptions such as in 1942 in Senegal, and although food shortages
continued to occur with the same frequency, they became far less
acute. Colonization also brought to Africa the monetary economy,
in particular cash crops (peanuts, coffee, cocoa, rubber, and so on),
which gave farmers the power to purchase what they needed.

Cities were rare and small in Africa prior to 1900. However, they developed rapidly thereafter; these cities subsequently
opened schools and provided a modern education to an elite group
of Africans. The level of modern education has been shown to
be closely associated with mortality decline throughout the world
(Caldwell, 1986).

8.1.3   Public health

In addition to improving socioeconomic conditions, considerable efforts were made to improve public health. Health programs focused
on diseases affecting the expatriate community, especially adults,
but were also directed to the whole population. Modern hospitals
were built at the turn of the century. Local dispensaries soon followed in secondary towns. Treatment of the water supply began in
cities during the same period (1928 in Dakar).

Newly developed vaccines against tuberculosis (BCG), yellow
fever, smallpox, and plague became available and widely used, even
in the remotest villages. As a consequence of vaccination and vector
control, the last three of these deadly diseases were under control
by 1960. Tuberculosis has been more difficult to control, mostly
because BCG has a low efficacy but also because the disease has a
more complex epidemiology. Major efforts were also made to control syphilis and yaws, as well as trypanosomiasis. The control of
syphilis and other infectious diseases reached a new dimension with
the marketing of antibiotics just after World War II. Synthetic antimalarial drugs became available in 1945 in most of tropical Africa.
Malaria control programs also started after World War II, and although they failed to achieve their goals, they certainly contributed
to mortality decline and perhaps to an increase in fertility.

8.2 Evolution Since Independence: 1960–1990

After 1960, a relatively large amount of data concerning mortality became available: censuses with retrospective questions, sample surveys (prospective or retrospective), maternity histories in the World Fertility Survey (WFS), and Demographic and Health Surveys (DHSs). These surveys provide levels and trends in child mortality at various points in time from which a history of mortality decline can be reconstructed (Hill, 1991). Results of this reconstruction are shown in *Table 8.2*.

Among the countries listed in *Table 8.2*, data are satisfactory in more than half the cases and roughly indicate a 40 percent decline in $q(5)$ between 1960 and 1990, from an average of 258 in 1960 to an average of 161 in 1990. This is a rapid decline in mortality. In England and Wales, it took about 80 years to achieve the same decline. A typical example of a steady mortality decline can be found in the case of Senegal, where the estimates of $q(5)$ follow quite accurately the fitted trend up to the early 1990s, which is the most recent point (*Figure 8.2*).

The speed of the mortality decline varied widely from country to country. For instance, the evolution in Ghana differed greatly from that in Kenya. Mortality levels were virtually the same in 1960 (228 and 216 per 1,000). Mortality decline was steady in Kenya from 1960 to 1985, whereas in Ghana mortality decline was slower between 1960 and 1975 and almost stopped in 1975 for about 10 years, so that by 1985 mortality was 74 percent higher than in Kenya. However, recent data show that Ghana had a rapid mortality decline between 1985 and 1993, while mortality was reversing in Kenya (see Section 8.3.1). In 1993, mortality levels in the two countries were again quite close (113 and 122), with a small excess in Kenya.

During this period, some countries failed to achieve the large mortality decline that most countries experienced. In Niger mortality was above 300 per 1,000 in the 1980–1992 period. Burkina Faso, a neighboring country, experienced this level in the 1960s; today its level is below 200 per 1,000. Another striking case is Madagascar, which experienced little change in 25 years (*Table 8.2*).

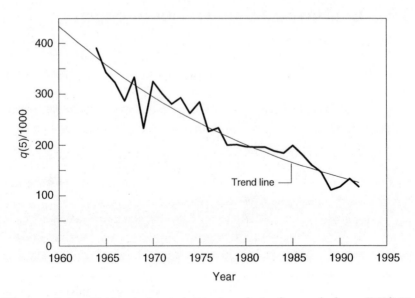

Figure 8.2. Estimated mortality trends in Senegal, from DHS-II, $q(5)$ per 1,000 live births.

8.2.1   Adult mortality

Adult mortality has also been studied, from retrospective question-naires and from direct estimates from sample surveys (Timæus, 1991). Adult mortality data are available for 21 countries, but only a few provide trends over time. Convincing evidence exists of an increase in adult survival in Benin (1967–1978), Congo (1962–1971), Cameroon (1945–1976), Sudan (1960–1974), Kenya (1955–1975), Uganda (1955–1965), Tanzania (1958–1968), Zimbabwe (1973–1979), and Swaziland (1960–1974). In these countries, life expectancy at age 15 increased by about 10 years, on average, between 1960 and 1980, from around 45 years to approximately 55 years. The only two exceptions in this study were Lesotho and Botswana, for which surprisingly no change was visible during the period studied.

8.2.2   Socioeconomic correlates

Despite the poor quality of both demographic and socioeconomic data and the numerous missing values, various socioeconomic variables appear to be significant correlates of child survival. Feachem and Jamison (1991) found a significant correlation between the level of infant and child mortality and income, measured by the GNP per capita in 1987, as well as by secondary school enrollment.

A systematic review of these correlations was undertaken by Trani (1992), using all the available evidence from socioeconomic data published by the World Bank (*Tables 8.3, 8.4,* and *8.5*). In the linear simple regressions, seven variables appear significant: two measures of income (index of GDP/capita and GNP/capita), three measures of education (literacy and enrollment in primary and secondary schools), one measure of public health (number of physicians), and one measure of nutrition (caloric consumption). Owing to the poor quality of the data, no further analysis could be done. However, these correlations indicate that the mortality decline is part of the whole development process, and that countries doing well economically and socially are also showing improvements in mortality levels. There are, however, a number of outliers in the regression analysis. Countries such as Sierra Leone, Gambia, and Malawi have higher than expected mortality, and this was also the case in 1960. Countries such as Kenya, Botswana, and Zimbabwe have lower than expected mortality; they were also among the countries with the lowest mortality in 1960 (*Table 8.2*).

8.2.3 Public health and primary health care

Modern health infrastructures developed significantly after 1960, and the number of health personnel per capita also increased. In particular, the number of physicians per capita increased by about 100 percent during the 1960–1985 period and the number of nurses per capita, by 373 percent. In Botswana, the number of physicians per capita has increased 6.2 times and the number of nurses, 70 times. Botswana has 38 times more physicians per capita than Burkina Faso. Hence, there is little wonder why Botswana has the lowest mortality levels.

Major health programs were also implemented in Africa after 1960. The interest of the health authorities and of donor agencies shifted from tropical diseases affecting adult mortality toward maternal and child health care. Efforts were made to provide new vaccines, in particular vaccines against measles and poliomyelitis. After 1978, selective primary health-care strategies were implemented

Table 8.3. Values of socioeconomic indicators: 1984–1990.

Country	Pop	Urb	GNP	FLFP	Lit	Phys	Nurse	Cal	Prim	Sec	IGDP	$q(5)$
Benin	4.741	37.7	390	47.4	74	15940	1750	2145	63	16	5.0	187
Botswana	1.254	27.5	2040	34.9	29	6900	700	2269	116	33	19.3	53
Burkina Faso	9.016	9.0	330	46.2	87	265250	1680	2061	32	6		199
Burundi	5.470	5.5	210	47.3	66	21030	4380	2253	70	4		151
Cameroon	11.941	41.2	940	33.3	44			2161	111	27	10.0	123
Centr.Afr.R.	3.036	46.7	390	45.7	60			1980	67	11		156
Chad	5.679	29.5	190	21.1	75	38360	3390	1852	51	6		223
Congo, PR	2.277	40.5	1010	38.8	37			2512			12.8	
Côte d'Ivoire	12.223	40.4	730	34.2	57			2365		19	8.2	150
Eq. Guinea	0.417	28.7	330	39.9								
Ethiopia	51.183	12.9	120	37.4	38	78770	5390	1658	36	15	1.6	216
Gabon	1.135	45.7	3220	37.3	38	2790	270	2396				
Gambia	0.875	23.2	260	40.3								206
Ghana	14.870	33.0	390	39.7	40	20460	1670	2209	73	39		153
Guinea-Bissau	0.981	19.9	180	40.8								
Kenya	24.368	23.6	370	39.9	41	10050		1973	93	23	5.2	87
Lesotho	1.771	20.3	470	43.4	26	18610		2307	112	25		165
Liberia	2.560	45.9	450	30.2	65	9350	1380	2270	35			275
Madagascar	11.620	25.0	230	39.3	33	9780		2101	97	19	3.4	195
Malawi	8.504	11.8	200	41.2	59	11340		2009	72	4	3.2	246
Mali	8.461	19.2	270	16.2	83	25390	1350	2181	23	6	2.5	248
Mauritania	1.969	46.8	500	22.2		11900	1180	2528	52	16		
Mozambique	15.784	26.8	80	47.4	62			1632	68	5		291
Namibia	1.780	27.8		23.8				1889				102
Niger	7.666	19.5	310	46.7	86	39670	460	2340	30	7		334
Nigeria	90.000	35.2	270	34.8	58	6440	900	2039	62	16	6.2	193
Rwanda	7.113	7.7	310	47.7	53	35090	3690	1786	64	6	3.0	176
Senegal	7.428	38.4	710	39.3	72		2030	1989	59	16	6.5	186
Sierra Leone	4.137	32.2	240	32.7	71	13620	1090	1806	53	18	2.6	
Somalia	6.284	36.4	150	38.7	88	16080	1530	1736				169
Sudan	25.191	22.0	520	21.9		10190	1260	1996	49	20		130
Swaziland	0.789	33.1	840	38.8								199
Tanzania	24.518	32.8	120	47.9		24980	5490	2151	66	4	2.3	199
Togo	3.638	25.7	410	36.4	59	8700	1240	2133	101	24		164
Uganda	17.358	10.4	220	41.1	43			2013	77	8		183
Zaire	35.564	39.5	230	35.5	39	12940	1800	2034	76	22		200
Zambia	8.122	49.9	480	29.0	24	7150	740	2026	97		4.3	162
Zimbabwe	9.809	27.6	640	34.6	26	6700	1000	2232	128	51	8.8	79

Pop = population (millions), Urb = percent urban, GNP = GNP/capita (US$), FLFP = female labor-force participation, Lit = percent of adults illiterate, Phys = number of people/physician, Nurse = number of people/nurse, Cal = caloric consumption/capita (cal), Prim = primary school enrollment, Sec = secondary school enrollment, IGDP = index of GDP/capita (USA=100), $q(5)$ = mortality age 0-4 per 1,000 live births. Source: Hill, 1992, and World Development Indicators.

Table 8.4. Estimates of the mean annual rates of change in socioeconomic indicators, per 1,000: 1970–1990.

Country	Pop	Urb	GNP	Phys	Nurse	Cal	Prim	Sec	q(5)
Benin	29	36	63	37	20	03	26	72	40.6
Botswana	35	59	137	73	170	06	25	104	65.7
Burkina Faso	24	23	70	−67	48	05	42	77	46.9
Burundi	25	41	54	51	27	−02	43	60	41.2
Cameroon	30	35	82			03	7	73	53.9
Centr.Afr.R.	24	21	63			−01	7	74	47.7
Chad	22	48	32	33	73	−10	17	77	27.8
Congo	32	11	71			05			
Côte d'Ivoire	40	19	49			01		50	55.1
Eq. Guinea	19	4	.						
Ethiopia	29	20	34	−6	5	−03	51	87	8.1
Gabon	41	29	79		54	12			
Gambia	32	22	47						41.6
Ghana	27	6	22	−21	42	06	2	47	33.8
Guinea-Bissau	31	14	6						
Kenya	38	41	52	15		−04	23	76	58.8
Lesotho	25	43	77	4		05	7	79	18.3
Liberia	30	28	23	16	28	03	−6		30.9
Madagascar	27	29	15	4		−05	17	37	
Malawi	32	34	60	75		−04	21	30	40.7
Mali	23	15	67	37	48	07	−1	17	29.3
Mauritania	24	61	51	59		14	60	120	
Namibia	28	20	.			00			
Mozambique	26	77	.			−02	26	22	−5.1
Niger	31	42	33	26	137	08	43	84	
Nigeria	29	28	29	80	101	−03	28	50	2.0
Rwanda	33	44	82	38	37	03	8	47	21.5
Senegal	29	07	58		10	−09	16	35	38.6
Sierra Leone	22	29	20	11	74	−04	26	55	
Somalia	28	24	25	44	50	09			38.3
Sudan	28	15	77	44	52	03	22	69	35.0
Swaziland	32	61	56						11.6
Tanzania	30	79	09	−7	−51	07	31	30	17.1
Togo	29	34	53	52	73	−04	26	68	47.4
Uganda	29	13	7			−06	6	30	22.1
Zaire	29	13	−4	52		−02	3	64	
Zambia	33	25	4	24	109	−00	26		43.8
Zimbabwe	31	25	36	9	− 1	04	6	93	48.7

Pop = population (millions), Urb = percent urban, GNP = GNP/capita (US$), Phys = number of people/physician, Nurse = number of people/nurse, Cal = caloric consumption/capita (cal), Prim = primary school enrollment, Sec = secondary school enrollment, q(5) = mortality age 0-4 per 1,000 live births.
Source: Trani, 1992, and World Development Indicators.

Table 8.5. Elasticities of $q(5)$ with respect to various socioeconomic indicators, in 36 countries of continental tropical Africa: 1980–1990.

	Standardized coefficient	P	R^2
Index of GDP/capita (US=100)	−0.745	0.002[a]	0.556
Secondary school enrollment	−0.734	0.000[a]	0.539
Primary school enrollment	−0.711	0.000[a]	0.506
% Adult illiterate	0.590	0.002[a]	0.348
GNP/Capita	−0.517	0.006[a]	0.267
Population/Physician	0.499	0.030[a]	0.249
Mean caloric consumption	−0.460	0.018[a]	0.211
Population/Nurse	0.524	0.080	0.179
Export of agricultural products	0.287	0.155	0.082
% Urban population	−0.201	0.306	0.040
Exports of fuel, minerals, and metals	−0.138	0.586	0.019
% Female in labor force	0.091	0.645	0.008

[a] $P < 0.05$.
Source: Trani, 1992.

throughout the continent. Emphasis was on the treatment of diarrhea, using oral rehydration therapy, and to a certain extent monitoring the growth of children. Recent efforts have focused on increasing vaccination coverage, on the treatment of acute respiratory infections (ARI), on the use of antibiotics and essential drugs, and on the financing and management of primary health-care systems. Thus far, little is known about the exact impact of these strategies. However, it is certain that, when well implemented, they can have a dramatic effect on a child's survival, as shown in a number of small-scale case studies (Lamb *et al.*, 1984; Garenne *et al.*, 1991).

8.3   Recent Evolution and Prospects

The global picture of general mortality decline in sub-Saharan Africa does not accurately reflect reality, even if the different levels in 1960 and the different speeds of mortality decline since 1960 are taken into account. Especially with the second and third DHSs (1990–1994), it became clear that mortality started to increase in a number of situations and for a variety of reasons. Section 8.3.1 presents examples of reversed mortality trends.

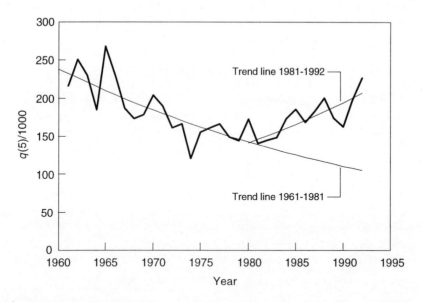

Figure 8.3. Estimated mortality trends in Zambia, from DHS-II, $q(5)$ per 1,000 live births.

8.3.1 Examples of recent reversal of mortality trends

Economic Crisis: Zambia, 1981–1992

The DHS-II conducted in Zambia in 1992 revealed an increase in mortality of children under age 5. Mortality estimates were computed by year from the original data file to reconstruct the turning points not visible in the five-year estimates published in the DHS report. In Zambia, mortality declined steadily from 1961 to 1981, with minor ups and downs which can be attributed to random fluctuations in the sample (*Figure 8.3*). Although somewhat faster than the average, the mortality decline was parallel to that of other countries, from an estimated $q(5)$ of 232 in 1961 to 141 in 1981. However, the mortality trend reversed suddenly after 1981, and by 1991 it reached 197 per 1,000, a level equivalent to that of 1968. Within only 10 years, 23 years of progress were whipped out.

During this period, Zambia went through a major economic crisis caused primarily by plummeting prices of copper, the number one export of the country (Kelly, 1991). Zambia had one of the lowest economic growth rates of all sub-Saharan African countries

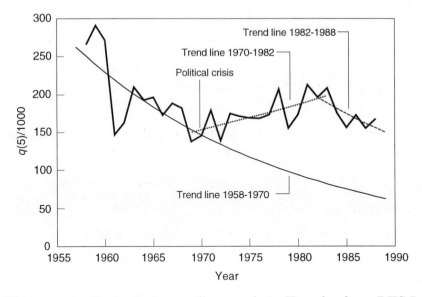

Figure 8.4. Estimated mortality trends in Uganda, from DHS-I, $q(5)$ per 1,000 live births.

from 1970 to 1990 (*Table 8.4*). The mortality crisis happened despite the fact that the country was politically stable and had made significant progresses in health services and education. Zambia is currently severely affected by AIDS, and in the future it is expected that AIDS will have a strong impact on mortality levels in Zambia. However, it is unlikely that the mortality crisis that occurred between 1981 and 1992 is due to AIDS.

Political Crisis: Uganda, 1971–1983

Uganda went through a period of political turmoil after Idi Amin seized power in 1971. The country stabilized in the mid-1980s when a new president was installed. Mortality seems to have reacted very strongly to these events (*Figure 8.4*). Under-five mortality declined from an estimated level of 227 in 1960 to 154 in 1970, on a path very similar to its neighbor, Kenya. Beginning in 1971, however, mortality increased and reached a peak in 1981–1983 (206 per 1,000). After 1983 it started to decline again. In 1988, the

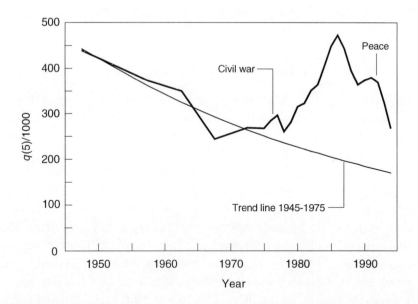

Figure 8.5. Estimated mortality trends in Central Mozambique, $q(5)$ per 1,000 live births. Source Garenne *et al.*, 1996.

last point available, mortality was 161 per 1,000, twice the level predicted, and about twice that of Kenya at that time.

Civil War: Central Mozambique, 1976–1991

A striking case of reversal of mortality trends can be found in Central Mozambique, an area severely hit by the civil war which devastated the country from 1976 to 1991. The mortality of children declined between 1945–1949, the earliest point at which data are available, and 1975, the date of independence. After this date, mortality increased dramatically and reached a peak of 475 per 1,000 in 1986, a level even higher than the earliest level, which means that 30 years of progress were whipped out within a few years (*Figure 8.5*). These data include only natural mortality and not deaths from direct war actions. Most of the deaths were due to common childhood infections, and only a few were due directly to starvation (Garenne *et al.*, 1996). One strategy of the guerrilla movement in Mozambique was, in fact, to destroy the health infrastructures and the schools.

This study clearly shows that the destruction of the health system can have a devastating impact on child mortality.

Possible Impact of AIDS on Child Mortality: Kenya, 1989–1993

After a long history of steady mortality decline, Kenya recently experienced a mortality increase. This increase is evident in the most recent DHS (*Figure 8.6*). The adjusted trend fits the mortality decline in Kenya from 1961 to 1989, when mortality reached its lowest value, 76 per 1,000. But from 1990 to 1993 mortality increased significantly above the value predicted from the previous trend. By 1993 it reached 122 per 1,000, the mortality level of 1976. This very marked mortality increase after 30 years of rapid improvements was surprising. No obvious explanation comes to mind: Kenya had political stability (despite significant domestic problems), steady economic growth, major improvements in health and education, and a remarkable decline in fertility. The recent mortality increase could be attributed to the onset of the AIDS epidemic raging in Kenya, but this interpretation would require confirmation from cause of death information.

Impact of AIDS on Adult Mortality: Abidjan, 1986–1992

AIDS is already having a strong impact on mortality of young adults in sub-Saharan Africa. A recent study in Abidjan, the capital city of Côte d'Ivoire, shows a doubling of mortality within the first seven years of the AIDS epidemics (1986–1992), after 13 years of small but regular improvements (1973–1985) (*Figure 8.7*). The demographic data are from the city's vital registration statistics, which have a high degree of reliability. From scarce cause of death information, this changing pattern has been attributed almost entirely to AIDS (Garenne *et al.*, 1995). A similar increase in adult mortality has been found in the rural areas of southwestern Uganda.

8.3.2   Socio-political factors

The complete picture of the recent evolution of mortality in sub-Saharan Africa may be optimistically biased, since the demographic situations of the most critical cases are not documented. For instance, recent reports state that famine is threatening one-third

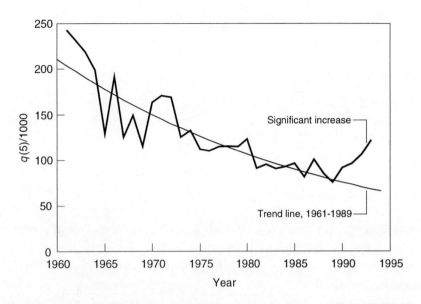

Figure 8.6. Estimated mortality trends in Kenya, from DHS-II, $q(5)$ per 1,000 live births.

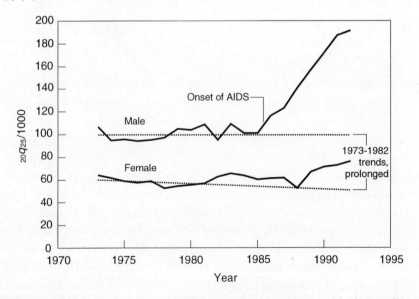

Figure 8.7. Estimated adult mortality trends in Abidjan, Côte d'Ivoire, from vital registration statistics, 20q25 (probability of dying between ages 20 and 25) per 1,000 survivors at age 25. Source: Garenne *et al.*, 1995.

Figure 8.8. Famine areas and locations of major wars in Africa.
Source: Griffiths and Binns, 1988.

of the population in Somalia. The demographic effect of the recurrent famines in Ethiopia has been poorly documented, and the
little we know leads to serious worries (Seaman, 1987). Relatively
little is known about the situation in southern Sudan, which has
been engaged in a civil war for more than three decades. The recent Sudanese data cover only the north of the country. Angola,
Mozambique, Liberia, Sierra Leone, Rwanda, and Burundi are also
involved in civil wars. Griffiths (1988) provides a striking map of
Africa: most countries experiencing political unrest and civil wars
are also experiencing famines (see *Figure 8.8*).

The future of African mortality may be divided into two categories: countries continuing their rapid trend toward low-mortality situations, and countries so politically and economically disturbed that any improvements in the mortality situation must be postponed to the unforeseeable future. International aid seems to reinforce this dichotomy rather than to diminish it. For instance, USAID, the most active agency for child-survival programs, has a list of countries for which it will not intervene. These countries are often the poorest and the most desperate. Countries that are democratic and developing rapidly receive more international support than those that are undemocratic and not developing or slowly developing.

8.3.3   Epidemiological factors

Tropical Africa is also experiencing a profound sociological and epidemiological transition. The emergence of the modern economy destroyed most of the traditional agricultural and economic system and perturbed the ecological balance between populations and resources. This change led to massive migration flows and to very rapid urbanization. In Senegal, about half of the population now lives in cities or large towns, whereas at the turn of the century 99 percent of the population was rural and no city accounted for more than 5,000 inhabitants. In Mauritania, more than half of the population became urban in less than one generation.

This pattern of migration has been favorable to the rapid spread of communicable diseases, in particular sexually transmitted diseases – as happened with syphilis at the onset of economic development in Europe, and basically for the same reasons (Shorter, 1990). The AIDS epidemic is the leading source of concern in this respect. The dynamics of the AIDS epidemic has been affected by the existence of the network of international truck drivers (along the Tanzania–Kenya–Uganda highway), by the emergence of large numbers of urban commercial sex workers, and by the appearance of large communities of single male migrants in cities, like Abidjan and Johannesburg. The spread of AIDS is probably the single most important factor propelling the mortality increase in sub-Saharan Africa. Projections made of the mortality of future generations are alarming: up to half of the population of some countries or regions may have AIDS as a cause of death. The death rates may even exceed the birth rates in extreme situations, reversing the pattern of population growth (Anderson, 1991). The AIDS epidemic has another major consequence: the disruption of families, by the death of one parent or both, exposing new orphans to risks of infection, malnutrition, and accidents. There are also increases in mortality from tuberculosis, as already shown in developed countries (Murray et al., 1990), and possibly of viral hepatitis B.

The massive implementation of modern medicine has also affected the ecology of certain diseases. This is the case for malaria, as more and more cases of strains resistant to chloroquine are documented (Bradley, 1991). Malaria has always been a leading cause of death in Africa. Resistant malaria strains may lead toward an increase in deaths attributed to this disease. There is now some limited evidence suggesting increasing malaria mortality, such as the case of Abidjan and Ouagadougou, two cities in West Africa (Garenne et al., 1995). Furthermore, the wide-scale use of antimalarial drugs may have led to a decline in natural immunity. This, in turn, may make certain populations vulnerable to major outbreaks of malaria, such as what happened in Madagascar in 1988.

Cholera came back to Africa in 1971 after an 80-year absence. The index case was brought by plane to Conakry, Guinea, an example of a new way of spreading communicable diseases. Since then, cholera has become endemic in most of tropical Africa, and seems also to have become a leading cause of death, at least in rural areas.

The vaccination coverage against yellow fever has dropped markedly in many countries. Recent outbreaks have taken place in Nigeria and will occur again in the future unless vaccination coverage increases dramatically. Although rare, plague still exists in Madagascar and occurs occasionally on the east coast of Africa.

With changing lifestyles and growing urbanization, new diseases will also emerge or reappear as a result of increasing risk factors or changing ecological conditions. Smoking has increased in Africa, with the help of massive commercial campaigns by tobacco companies. Obesity, rare in villages, has become prevalent in cities and may be linked with a probable increase in the prevalence of diabetes. Car accidents are also becoming a significant cause of death; African roads are among the most dangerous in the world. Political violence has been taking a heavy toll in the recent years; for instance, the population of Rwanda was devastated during the 1994–1995 civil war.

8.4 Discussion

The past trends of mortality in Africa have been induced by transfers of technology from the West, which have affected virtually all countries on the continent in a short period of time. Public health, nutrition, economic development, and modern education seem to have been the key determinants in mortality change. However, the future of mortality in Africa is hard to determine and even harder to quantify. There are reasons to believe that the major and quite uniform mortality decline experienced over the first 25 years of independence (1960–1985) will not be followed by a comparable decline in the next 25 years in all the countries of sub-Saharan Africa. Most likely, the principal differences that already exist between countries will prevail and may even increase. Some nations will continue along their successful routes to low mortality, and others will see their health transition stop or even reverse for some period of time. Besides the socio-political conditions, a critical factor will be the spread of the HIV virus, resistant malaria, tuberculosis, and other diseases infecting the general population.

The control that the countries have over the health of their population is also a function of their research capacity to identify new problems and to choose the most appropriate solutions in time. Essential National Health Research has recently been seen as one of the top priorities for developing countries (ENHR Report, 1990). Data information systems to identify and tackle new diseases and new health problems may be an important component of the success of health policies in the future. The AIDS epidemics could have been smaller in size if appropriate steps had been taken at its onset.

Acknowledgments

I would like to thank Jean François Trani for his contribution to the statistical analysis and Meg Tyler for editorial comments on an earlier draft.

Chapter 9

Global Trends in AIDS Mortality

John Bongaarts

The AIDS epidemic began spreading around 1980 in North America, Western Europe, and sub-Saharan Africa; since then HIV, the virus that causes AIDS, has quickly reached all corners of the globe (WHO, 1994).[1] Despite significant efforts to contain the epidemic, HIV is now spreading more rapidly than ever, resulting in an estimated 2.4 million new infections each year among adults (WHO, 1995b). Expansion is most rapid in sub-Saharan Africa and Asia, with approximately 1 million new infections annually in each continent. In addition, a growing number of infections occur through "vertical transmission" from mother to child during pregnancy, delivery, or breastfeeding. In the early 1980s AIDS was thought to be primarily a disease of homosexuals and injecting drug users, but heterosexual transmission was soon found to be common in Africa and elsewhere (Piot *et al.*, 1988). Today the large majority of infections worldwide are the result of sexual intercourse between men and women, even though this is a relatively inefficient mode of transmission (the probability of infection per heterosexual contact between an uninfected individual and an asymptomatic carrier averages less than 1 percent if the uninfected person is healthy). Transmission through transfusion with contaminated blood and blood products

Reprinted with the permission of the Population Council, from *Population and Development Review* 22(1), March 1996.

has been reduced to very low levels in countries with extensive testing, but where screening is incomplete transfusion can be a significant source of HIV infection.

The HIV/AIDS epidemic has become a serious public health problem because no cure or vaccine exists and infection almost invariably leads to death. Infection is followed by years of slow destruction of the immune system, rendering carriers increasingly vulnerable to fatal opportunistic infections such as pneumocystic pneumonia and cancers such as Kaposi's sarcoma. The median incubation period between initial infection and onset of AIDS is about a decade (Chin and Lwanga, 1991a). Carriers are typically asymptomatic for most of the incubation period and they therefore can unwittingly infect others, thus contributing to the rapid dissemination of HIV.

The World Health Organization (WHO) monitors the epidemic closely and estimates that by mid-1995 a cumulative total of about 18.5 million adults had been infected with HIV worldwide since the 1970s (WHO, 1995a). Despite the many uncertainties and limitations regarding available statistics, this global estimate and the geographic distribution of infections published by WHO are widely accepted.[2] However, the future course of the epidemic remains controversial.

During the remainder of the 1990s WHO expects 10–15 million new HIV infections among adults and 5–10 million among children (through vertical transmission), bringing the cumulative total by the year 2000 to 30–40 million HIV infections (WHO, 1994). Others expect more severe epidemics. For example Mann *et al.* (1992) project that the cumulative total of infections by 2000 could exceed 100 million. Model simulations of African epidemics by Anderson *et al.* (1991) and by Gregson *et al.* (1994) indicate that a majority of adults could become infected, leading to massive AIDS mortality and possibly even to declines in population size.

This article presents a set of projections of the epidemic from 1995 to 2005 for major world regions and assesses the corresponding effects on death rates and population growth. Estimates of the future demographic impact of AIDS for world regions have not yet been made. The United Nations (UN, 1995) and the US Bureau of the Census (Way and Stanecki, 1994) have prepared such assessments for a number of African countries especially affected by AIDS, but their findings differ substantially from each other.

9.1   Global Patterns

In the 1980s the number of AIDS cases reported to WHO was the most widely used statistic to monitor the epidemic's expansion worldwide. The exponential growth in AIDS cases then observed – a doubling annually for much of the 1980s – reflected the exceptionally rapid spread of this new disease. Unfortunately, underreporting due to limited access to health care, lack of diagnostic facilities, and reluctance of individuals, medical personnel, or governments to report the disease and/or the full extent of the epidemic has been a serious problem, especially in Africa. The cumulative number of AIDS cases reported by the beginning of 1994 is estimated to be less than a quarter of the actual number (WHO, 1994). Moreover, the number of AIDS cases, even if accurately known, does not give a complete picture of the epidemic because there are several times more individuals infected with HIV than there are AIDS cases. As a consequence, WHO now relies on the estimated cumulative number of HIV infections in major world regions as the principal statistic with which to monitor the global epidemic.

By the end of 1994 an estimated cumulative total of 17.2 million adults had been infected worldwide. Nearly 3 million of these infections have resulted in deaths from AIDS before 1995, leaving approximately 14.3 million HIV-infected individuals alive at the end of 1994 (WHO, 1995b).[3] Sub-Saharan Africa accounts for over half of this total (see *Table 9.1*). Asia and Latin America have the next largest numbers with, respectively, 3.4 and 1.7 million infected adults, and North America and Western Europe each have less than 1 million. The estimated proportion of adults infected averages 0.4 percent worldwide, ranging from a high of 2.5 percent in sub-Saharan Africa to a low of 0.2 percent in Asia and Western Europe.

These regional averages, in turn, conceal large differences in the size of the epidemic between countries. This is the case in every continent, but especially in Africa. *Figure 9.1* presents the geographic

Table 9.1. Cumulative number of adults infected with HIV, cumulative AIDS deaths, and number of infected adults (in millions), and percentage of adults infected by region at the end of 1994.

	Sub-Saharan Africa	Asia	North America	Latin America	Western Europe	World total[a]
HIV infections	9.7	3.5	1.2	2.0	0.7	17.2
AIDS deaths	1.9	0.1	0.4	0.3	0.2	2.9
Infected adults	7.8	3.4	0.8	1.7	0.5	14.3
Adults infected	2.5%	0.2%	0.4%	0.6%	0.2%	0.4%

[a]Total includes a small number of infections in the former Soviet Union, Eastern Europe, West Asia, and North Africa.
Source: WHO, 1995b.

distribution of HIV prevalence (i.e., the percent of adults infected) among low-risk urban populations in Africa circa 1993 (comparable data for rural areas are not available). Prevalence varies from more than 10 percent in parts of East and Central Africa to a fraction of 1 percent in many other countries, particularly in North Africa. Within countries, infection levels are highest in cities, in the sexually active age groups, and in groups with high-risk behaviors (e.g., prostitutes, injecting drug users, and homosexuals).

Why has the HIV/AIDS epidemic affected some regions and countries much more than others? Although there is no commonly agreed upon explanation, a number of hypotheses have been advanced. Two factors are widely accepted as at least partially responsible. First, the timing of the onset of the spread of HIV differs considerably among regions, from the late 1970s in sub-Saharan Africa, North America, and Western Europe, to the mid-1980s in Asia (Mann *et al.*, 1992). This difference no doubt contributed to large variations in the size of the epidemic in the mid-1980s because in some countries the epidemics were by then already a decade old, while in others they had just begun. Today, a majority of countries have had epidemics of at least a decade's duration, and the timing effect is therefore significantly smaller now. A second cause of differences is the nature and size of a population's "high-risk" groups. In Europe and North America homosexuals/bisexuals and injecting drug users have been the principal population groups affected by AIDS, while in sub-Saharan Africa the large majority of

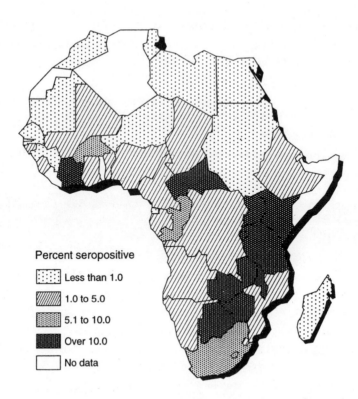

Figure 9.1. Estimated levels of HIV seroprevalence (percentage of adults infected) for urban populations in Africa: circa 1993. Estimates are based on surveys of "low-risk" groups, primarily pregnant women and blood donors. Source: US Bureau of the Census, 1994a.

HIV infections are the result of heterosexual contacts (Piot *et al.*, 1988).

But neither of these two factors explains one of the epidemic's most puzzling features: the huge differences – more than an order of magnitude – in infection levels of heterosexuals among countries where the virus has been present for some time. For example, in a few heavily affected African countries prevalence in the adult population exceeds 10 percent, while in others prevalence is below 1 percent (Berkley, 1994; Lamptey and Coates, 1994; Plummer *et al.*, 1994; Serwadda *et al.*, 1994; Way and Stanecki, 1994). Equally large differences have been observed within countries. For example, according to a 1991 survey in Rwanda, prevalence was above 25 percent in urban areas, but only 2.2 percent in rural areas (Serwadda *et al.*, 1994). In one rural area of Zaire prevalence was low and stable at 0.8 percent for a decade (Nzilambi *et al.*, 1988), while urban infection levels were about 5 percent. Low infection levels (0.17 percent) are also found among childbearing women nationwide in the United States (Centers for Disease Control and Prevention, 1994). These findings may be explained by variations in the following factors that facilitate or inhibit spread of the virus among heterosexuals:

- *Sexual behavior.* Frequent sexual contacts with individuals other than a permanent partner and frequent changes in partners are key determinants of the speed of diffusion of HIV. There is little comparative evidence on sexual behavior, but differences among countries can be substantial. According to WHO-sponsored surveys in five sub-Saharan countries, the proportion of men reporting sex with someone other than their regular partner in the past year ranged from 14 to 53 percent (Caraël *et al.*, 1992). Caldwell *et al.* (1989), Piot and Caraël (1988), and Larson (1989) discuss the social-institutional context that supports the high degree of sexual networking in sub-Saharan Africa.
- *Condom use.* African men report infrequent reliance on condoms when engaging in commercial sex (Caraël *et al.*, 1992). Condoms are more widely used in developed countries, especially in sexual contacts with one-time partners (UN, 1989a; Laumann *et al.*, 1994).
- *Sexually transmitted diseases (STDs).* The infectiousness of HIV carriers and the susceptibility of uninfected partners are apparently increased in the presence of STDs, particularly those that cause genital ulcers (e.g., chancroid, genital herpes, and syphilis) (Piot *et al.*, 1994; Cameron *et al.*, 1989; Plummer *et al.*, 1991, 1994). The prevalence of STDs is relatively high in some parts of sub-Saharan Africa (Caldwell and Caldwell, 1983).
- *Absence of male circumcision.* There is a highly significant correlation between the proportion of uncircumcised males in African ethnic groups and countries and the prevalence of HIV (Bongaarts *et al.*, 1989; Moses *et al.*, 1990; Caldwell and Caldwell, 1993). Although this association may in part be due to

confounding factors (De Vincenzi and Mertens, 1994), it is consistent with clinic-based case–control studies in which circumcised males were significantly less likely to be infected with HIV than uncircumcised controls (Cameron *et al.*, 1989; Seed *et al.*, 1995). Several biological mechanisms, including enhanced susceptibility to genital ulcer disease, may be responsible for the increased risk of HIV infection among uncircumcised males (De Vincenzi and Mertens, 1994; Over and Piot, 1993; Caldwell and Caldwell, 1994).

Lack of reliable measures prevents a quantitative assessment of the relative roles played by these factors, but it is likely that they are responsible for much of the differences in heterosexual epidemics between countries, as well as for the equally large differences between regions and demographic groups within countries.

9.2   Past Trends

9.2.1   Prevalence

HIV prevalence trends from 1980 to 1995 for five major world regions are plotted in *Figure 9.2*. Epidemics in Africa, Asia, and Latin America, although differing widely in size, continued to expand through the first half of the 1990s. Prevalence rates in North America and Western Europe also grew rapidly during the 1980s, but they apparently have leveled off in the 1990s at less than one-half percent of the adult population. These trends represent averages for regions; epidemics in countries within regions can deviate significantly from these averages not only in size but also in trend. For example, in Africa the epidemic is generally expanding rapidly, but in a few instances (e.g., in the capital cities of Bangui, Bujumbura, Kampala, and Kinshasa) the epidemic appears to be leveling off (US Bureau of the Census, 1993a, 1993b, 1994b).

The appearance of a plateau in HIV prevalence while a large proportion of a population remains uninfected is one of the epidemic's most crucial features. Although still rare in the developing world, this plateau is likely to be found eventually in all geographic areas. A stable prevalence level implies that the virus is disseminated

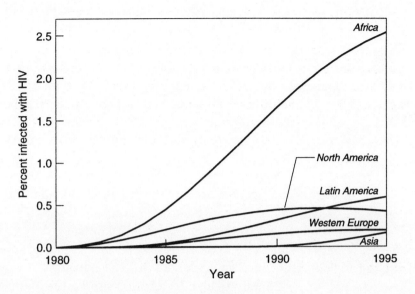

Figure 9.2. Estimated trends in HIV prevalence among adults, by region: 1980–1995. Source: WHO, 1995b.

in the population but that there is nevertheless no further expansion. An explanation for this phenomenon is that every population is a mixture of more or less frequently interacting subgroups with widely varying infection risks. In North America, for example, substantial parts of the homosexual/bisexual and injecting drug user groups are at high risk, whereas infection risks are very low for the vast majority of heterosexuals. In fact, the heterosexual epidemic in the United States is apparently not self-sustaining, and prevalence is therefore low (less than 0.2 percent) and virtually stable, despite some interaction with high-risk groups (Centers for Disease Control and Prevention, 1994).

A self-sustaining epidemic can occur in a subpopulation with a given level of infectivity per contact only if a threshold rate of sexual contact with different partners has been exceeded. This threshold is reached when the so-called basic reproductive rate of the epidemic, R, equals 1 (Anderson and May, 1988, 1992). R is the average number of new infections caused by one infected individual over his or her lifetime. The reproductive rate for a particular population is determined by its sexual behavior, the duration of infectivity, and the infectivity per contact (which in turn is affected by the presence of such cofactors as condom use, the prevalence of other sexually transmitted diseases, and the absence of male circumcision). In a population with homogeneous behavioral and biological character-istics, an epidemic will spread until nearly everyone is infected if R exceeds 1. On the other hand, if in such a population R is less than 1, a self-sustaining epidemic cannot occur. This is true even if the virus is introduced repeatedly through contacts with infected individuals outside the group.

For the sake of simplicity, this explanation for the leveling off in prevalence rates has ignored some key aspects of the epidemic, such as changes in behavior over time, the movement of individuals between risk groups, and membership in more than one group, but the main points remain valid. The virus first invades the subgroups with the highest reproductive rates, and HIV prevalence rates in these core groups rise rapidly to high levels. In contrast, the plateau in prevalence for the lowest-risk groups of heterosexuals can be at a fraction of 1 percent, as in North America and Western Europe, because the large majority of these populations do not engage in risky behavior or engage in it so infrequently that their reproduc-tive rate is well below 1, and because their interaction with high-risk groups is limited. In sub-Saharan Africa, on the other hand, the core group comprises prostitutes and their male partners; the virus can spread efficiently from these male partners to their wives and chil-dren, thus putting a large proportion of the general population at risk. An epidemic reaches a plateau when the virus has achieved maximum penetration in the vulnerable subpopulations. Because the size of the subgroups with high reproductive rates and their in-teractions with the general population vary widely among countries, the plateau levels of HIV prevalence also differ greatly, ranging from no more than a few tenths of a percent in most developed countries to more than 10 percent in a few countries in sub-Saharan Africa.

9.2.2   Incidence

The prevalence of infection at a point in time is the net result of past additions to the infected population through new infections and subtractions through deaths. Further insight into the dynam-ics of the epidemic can therefore be gained by examining trends in the annual incidence rates at which the key events – HIV infection, onset of AIDS, and death – occur. *Figure 9.3* presents WHO estimates of these incidence rates for each region up to 1995. Because the epidemics in North America and Western Europe have evolved furthest, they give the most complete picture of the phases through which other epidemics are likely to progress. In these two regions, a key turning point in the epidemic was reached in the mid-1980s when the annual rate of new infections reached a maximum, estimated, respectively, at about 0.7 and 0.3 per thousand adults per year.

The peaks in new HIV infections in sub-Saharan Africa and Latin America are estimated by WHO to have occurred in the early 1990s at, respectively, 3.6 and 0.9 infections per thousand adults per year. The incidence of infections in Asia has not yet reached its maximum, although one Asian country, Thailand, may already have passed it. In Thailand, HIV spread very rapidly in the late 1980s, and prevalence in the adult population had reached 1.5 percent in urban areas at the end of 1993. Recent analyses suggest that the incidence of HIV has been declining since 1991, in part due to vigorous public health measures implemented by the government (Hanenberg *et al.*, 1994; Tim Brown as cited in Cohen, 1994b).

Past trends in AIDS incidence are also plotted in *Figure 9.3*. Since the incubation period averages about a decade, there is a substantial delay between the rise in new infections and the corresponding increase in new AIDS cases. In all regions, the estimated AIDS incidence rose through 1994. However, in North America and Western Europe the rate of increase in AIDS incidence has slowed in the early 1990s, suggesting that a plateau is approaching. Patterns of incidence of AIDS deaths are very similar to those of AIDS; the only difference is a delay of about one year.

A comparison of *Figures 9.2* and *9.3* shows that the prevalence of HIV can continue rising for a number of years after the incidence rate has begun its decline. This is possible because individuals who are HIV-positive in a given year have become infected over a number of years in the past. For example, in the hypothetical case in which an infected individual survives exactly 10 years before dying, the number of infected individuals at any given time would equal the sum of all infections in the past 10 years regardless of whether

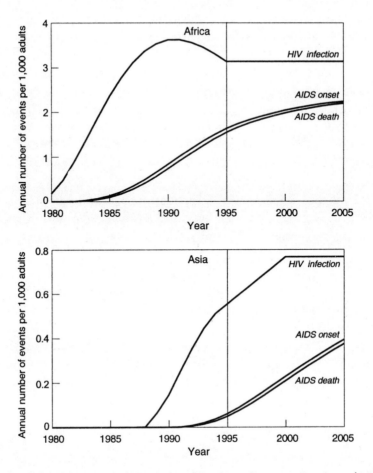

Figure 9.3. Estimates (1980–1995) and medium projections (1995–2005) for incidence rates of HIV infections, AIDS cases, and AIDS deaths among adults, by region. Sources: UN, 1995, and WHO, 1995b, for estimates; see text for projections.

the rate of new infections in those years was rising or falling. The number of infected individuals alive reaches its maximum in the year in which the (declining) number of new infections equals the (rising) number of annual deaths from AIDS. This typically occurs several years after the HIV incidence rate has peaked. As a consequence, HIV incidence rates, when available, are generally preferable to prevalence rates, because the former is a "leading indicator" of what lies ahead in the epidemic.

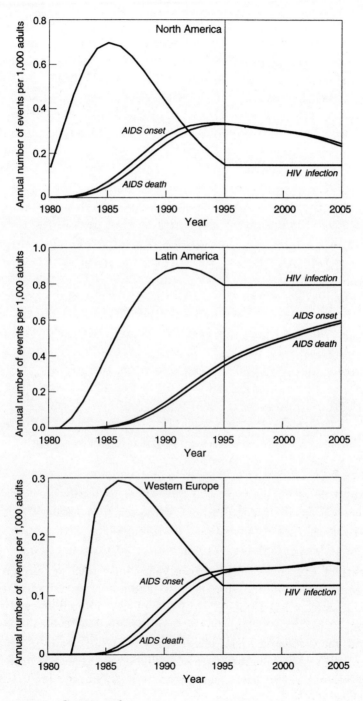

Figure 9.3. Continued.

9.3   The Coming Decade

The first step in projecting the course of regional epidemics until 2005 is to estimate plausible future trends in the variable that drives the epidemic, that is, the rate of new HIV infections among adults. Based on trends for the early 1990s, one would not expect infection rates to rise in the near future in Africa, Latin America, North America, or Europe, and they could well decline further. With little guidance from theory, it is assumed in my "medium" projection that infection rates will remain constant at 1995 levels until 2005 in each of these four regions. This may err on the high side, but, as will be shown below, trends in AIDS mortality over the next decade are rather insensitive to variations in future trends in infections. The situation in Asia is clearly different – with the infection rate still rising – and for present purposes I extrapolate the current upward trend to 2000 and assume it constant thereafter (see *Figure 9.3*). Since there is considerable uncertainty about future trends, I also present two other scenarios – a high and a low variant. These variants for each region are obtained by assuming the number of HIV infections in the year 2005 to be, respectively, 50 percent higher and 50 percent lower than the medium projection (with linear interpolation between 1995 and 2005).

Next, the projected annual number of new AIDS cases, $A(t)$, for $t = 1995$ to $t = 2005$ is calculated from the time series of annual HIV infections, $H(t)$, using a simple convolution equation:

$$A(t) = \sum D(n)H(t - n) \ ,$$

where $D(n)$ represents the distribution of the incubation period (n in years) between HIV infection and the onset of AIDS. This distribution is assumed to have a median of 9.5 years, with 90 percent of new infections progressing to AIDS after 20 years.[4] (This median is a crucial parameter in the projection. In any population where it is smaller than assumed here, the number of AIDS cases will be underestimated when the annual number of HIV infections is rising.) Once the number of AIDS cases is projected, a similar convolution procedure yields the annual number of deaths from AIDS. Median survival time from onset of AIDS to death is assumed to be 0.5 years in Africa, Asia, and Latin America, and one year in North America and Western Europe.

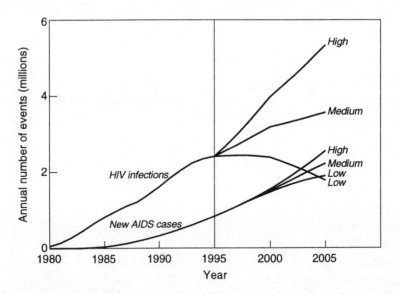

Figure 9.4. Estimates (1980–1995) and projections (1995–2005) of annual number of HIV infections and AIDS cases among adults, world total. Source: WHO, 1995b, for estimates; see text for projections.

The resulting medium projections to 2005 of annual rates of new AIDS cases and AIDS deaths among adults are shown in *Figure 9.3*, giving a broad picture of the evolution of the epidemic from its start to 2005. In North America the incidence of AIDS is expected to peak in the mid-1990s, and in Western Europe a plateau is projected starting in the late 1990s. In Asia, Latin America, and Africa the annual number of AIDS cases is projected to rise at least until 2005. By far the largest increase in AIDS cases is expected in Asia: from an annual rate of 0.06 per thousand adults in 1995 to an annual rate of 0.39 per thousand adults in 2005. In absolute terms this amounts to a change from 124,000 new AIDS cases in 1995 to 965,000 new cases in 2005.

Projections to 2005 of the absolute annual number of HIV infections and new AIDS cases among adults for the high, medium, and low variants for the world as a whole are plotted in *Figure 9.4*. For the medium variant, these totals rise between 1995 and 2005 from 2.4 to 3.6 million HIV infections and from 0.8 to 2.2 million

Table 9.2. Projected high, medium, and low variants of cumulative HIV infections, AIDS cases, and AIDS deaths (millions) among adults in 2005, by region.

	Sub-Saharan Africa	Asia	North America	Latin America	Western Europe	World total[a]
Cumulative HIV infection						
High variant	23.3	23.0	1.6	5.2	1.0	54.7
Medium variant	20.7	19.1	1.5	4.6	0.9	47.4
Low variant	18.1	15.3	1.4	4.0	0.9	40.1
Cumulative AIDS cases						
High variant	9.4	5.3	1.0	2.0	0.6	18.5
Medium variant	9.1	4.9	1.0	1.9	0.6	17.8
Low variant	8.9	4.6	1.0	1.9	0.6	17.2
Cumulative AIDS deaths						
High variant	8.9	4.8	1.0	1.9	0.5	17.2
Medium variant	8.7	4.5	1.0	1.8	0.5	16.8
Low variant	8.5	4.2	1.0	1.8	0.5	16.2

[a]Total includes a small number of infections in the former Soviet Union, Eastern Europe, West Asia, and North Africa.

new AIDS cases per year. Interestingly, the difference between the high and low variants is larger for the projected number of new HIV infections than for new AIDS cases. The same is true for the cumulative number of HIV infections and AIDS cases for each region (see *Table 9.2*). The reason for this is the long incubation period. Projected AIDS cases in 2005 are the result of HIV infections that occurred on average in the mid-1990s, when the uncertainty about the number of infections is much smaller. As a consequence, projections of AIDS cases and AIDS mortality until 2005 are subject to smaller errors than the corresponding projections of HIV incidence. Of course, future trends in AIDS mortality are highly sensitive to any errors in the WHO estimates of HIV incidence up to 1995, which provide the basis for these projections. Estimates of past levels and trends in infections are perhaps most uncertain for Africa, and the projections for this continent are therefore the least reliable.

The discussion to this point has dealt only with the epidemic among adults. A complete assessment of AIDS mortality must also include the effects of vertical transmission from mother to child. The

Table 9.3. Projected annual number of child deaths due to AIDS, percentage of births ending in AIDS deaths, and deaths among children as a percentage of all AIDS deaths, 1995, 2000, and 2005, by region, medium variant.

	Sub-Saharan Africa	Asia	North America	Latin America	Western Europe	World total[a]
Child deaths due to AIDS (thousands)						
1995	145.5	9.4	0.9	5.7	0.4	162.5
2000	191.2	33.4	0.7	7.7	0.3	234.2
2005	218.7	56.0	0.5	8.5	0.3	285.0
Percentage of births ending in AIDS deaths[b]						
1995	0.56	0.01	0.02	0.05	0.01	0.12
2000	0.68	0.04	0.02	0.06	0.01	0.17
2005	0.72	0.07	0.01	0.07	0.01	0.20
Deaths among children as a percentage of all AIDS deaths						
1995	23.5	8.7	1.3	5.4	1.0	17.2
2000	21.4	6.7	1.1	4.6	0.9	14.0
2005	19.4	5.7	0.9	3.9	0.7	11.7

[a]Total includes a small number of infections in the former Soviet Union, Eastern Europe, West Asia, and North Africa.
[b]The estimates of the total number of births are taken from UN, 1995 (medium projections).

probability that a newborn dies due to HIV infection is estimated as the product of the probability that the mother is HIV-positive, the probability of vertical transmission from an infected mother to her infant, and the probability of dying from AIDS. Prospective studies have reported vertical transmission rates from 15 to 20 percent in Europe and from 25 to 35 percent in sub-Saharan Africa (Gibb and Wara, 1994). Approximately four out of five infected newborns die by age five (Chin, 1990). *Table 9.3* presents regional projections of the annual number of AIDS deaths among children for 1995, 2000, and 2005.[5] Sub-Saharan Africa accounts for the large majority of HIV-related child deaths in the world over the next decade. This finding is attributable to Africa's relatively high birth rates, high HIV prevalence rates among pregnant women, and high risk of vertical transmission. In 2005 the fraction of all births dying from HIV infection ranges from a high of 0.72 percent in Africa to a low of

Table 9.4. Projected annual number of AIDS deaths, percentage of all deaths due to AIDS, and AIDS death rate, 1995, 2000, and 2005, medium variant.

	Sub-Saharan Africa	Asia	North America	Latin America	Western Europe	World total[a]
AIDS deaths (thousands)						
1995	619	109	64	105	36	943
2000	895	499	61	165	38	1,678
2005	1,129	976	52	217	40	2,438
AIDS deaths as a percentage of deaths from all causes[b]						
1995	7.6	0.4	2.5	3.3	0.9	1.8
2000	10.5	1.8	2.3	5.0	1.0	3.2
2005	12.9	3.5	1.9	6.2	1.0	4.5
AIDS death rate (per thousand population)						
1995	1.04	0.03	0.22	0.22	0.09	0.17
2000	1.31	0.14	0.20	0.32	0.10	0.27
2005	1.44	0.26	0.16	0.39	0.10	0.37
Low variant	1.27	0.22	0.15	0.34	0.10	0.32
High variant	1.61	0.31	0.17	0.43	0.11	0.42

[a]Total includes a small number of infections in the former Soviet Union, Eastern Europe, West Asia, and North Africa.
[b]The estimates of the total number of non-AIDS deaths and of total population size are taken from UN, 1995 (medium projections).

0.01 percent in North America and Western Europe. In sub-Saharan Africa the estimated number of AIDS deaths among children is 23.5 percent of all AIDS deaths in 1995 and 19.4 percent in 2005. These percentages in 2005 are expected to be 3.9 in Latin America, 5.7 in Asia, 0.9 in North America, and 0.7 in Western Europe.

Adding adult and child deaths yields the total annual number of AIDS deaths by region, presented in *Table 9.4*. The global total, estimated at 943,000 in 1995, is projected to more than double to 2.4 million by 2005. These numbers represent 1.8 percent of deaths from all causes in 1995 and 4.5 percent in 2005. As shown in *Figure 9.5*, regional differences are large: in 2005 AIDS deaths are expected to account for 13 percent of all deaths in Africa, compared to 1 percent in Western Europe. Differences in the AIDS death rate per thousand population projected for 2005 are similarly large (*Table 9.4*), ranging from 1.4 in sub-Saharan Africa to 0.1 in Western Europe.

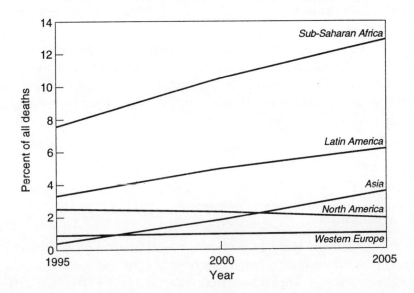

Figure 9.5. Projection of deaths due to AIDS as a percentage of deaths from all causes, by region, 1995–2005.

The high and low variants deviate from these medium projections by about 14 percent in each direction.[6]

The regional averages of AIDS mortality in *Table 9.4* conceal much variation among countries, among regions within countries, and among groups with different demographic characteristics. For example, several countries in Central and East Africa (e.g., Rwanda, Uganda, and Zambia) have much more severe epidemics and hence higher AIDS mortality than average for the continent. Within countries, above-average AIDS mortality rates are found among children under age 5 and young adults, as well as among urban residents. The death toll is highest between ages 20 and 50, when mortality is normally relatively low.

9.3.1 Comparison with other projections

Regional projections of AIDS mortality comparable to those presented in *Table 9.4* are not available from other published studies. However, the United Nations Population Division and the United States Bureau of the Census have recently updated their population projections, and these revisions include adjustments for the impact of the AIDS epidemic in sub-Saharan African countries with HIV prevalence above 1 percent in 1990 (UN, 1995; Way and Stanecki, 1994). These projections made no revisions for AIDS mortality in other African countries, even though it is recognized that these countries are not entirely free of HIV infection (accounting for perhaps 10 percent of Africa's total). Results from these studies, compared with those of the present study, are as follows:

	Average annual AIDS deaths in sub-Saharan Africa, 2000–2005
United Nations	1.07 million
US Bureau of the Census	2.16 million
Present study	1.01 million

Even though these findings are not entirely comparable, it is clear that the mortality projection from the present study is similar to the UN's but much lower than that of the US Bureau of the Census.[7] There are three potential causes for this discrepancy: differences in the HIV prevalence levels estimated at the starting point of the projections, different rates of growth in HIV infections over time, and differences in the key parameters (e.g., the duration of the incubation period and vertical transmission rates) used for calculating the AIDS mortality associated with a given level of HIV infection. Detailed further analyses will be required to quantify the role of each of these three factors in causing the differences in results.

Another comparison can be made for the global cumulative number of adult HIV infections by the year 2000. The low, medium, and high variants project, respectively, 28.1, 29.3, and 30.5 million cumulative infections. Forecasts of this same variable by Mann *et al.* (1992) have a much wider range – from 38 to 109 million by 2000. To achieve an increase from 18.5 million in 1995 to 109 million in 2000 requires more new infections each year between 1995 and 2000 than have occurred in the entire history of the epidemic until 1995. This is implausible, and the high projection of Mann *et al.* (1992) must therefore be considered unrealistic.

9.3.2 Impact of the epidemic on population growth

Table 9.5 presents estimates of the effect of AIDS mortality on annual rates of population growth by world regions in 1995 and 2005.

Birth, death, and growth rates are listed for both years with and without the epidemic. Estimates in the absence of AIDS are based on UN medium population projections,[8] which assume negligible regional migration so that the growth rate equals the difference between the birth and death rates. The estimates with AIDS are obtained by adding the AIDS death rate (from *Table 9.4*) to the death rate from other causes and by making the simplifying assumption that the birth and the non-AIDS death rates as well as the population age structure remain unaffected by the epidemic.

In sub-Saharan Africa the growth rate in 2005 is projected to be 27.7 per thousand per year in the absence of the epidemic (i.e., 38.9–11.2). AIDS mortality raises the death rate from 11.2 to 12.7 per thousand, resulting in an equivalent decline in the growth rate from 27.7 to 26.3 per thousand. If maintained over 25 years, such levels of growth would yield increases in population size of 93.4 percent with AIDS and 99.9 percent without. The epidemic has a significant moderating effect on population growth in sub-Saharan Africa, but even under the high variant AIDS projection the growth rate remains at a substantial 26.1 per thousand. In all other world regions the epidemic's impact on population growth is substantially smaller. Due to AIDS mortality, the growth rate in 2005 is expected to be 12.6 (per thousand population) instead of 12.9 in Asia, –0.5 instead of –0.4 in Western Europe, 14.4 instead of 14.8 in Latin America, and 5.1 instead of 5.2 in North America. Results for the high and low variant AIDS projections are remarkably similar.

These estimates of the effect of AIDS on population growth are approximate. The assumption that migration at the regional level is negligible is reasonable for present purposes and is also made in the standard population projections of the UN. However, the assumption that fertility and non-AIDS mortality remain invariant in the presence of the epidemic is only a first approximation. Fertility could be reduced if HIV-infected adults engage less frequently in sexual intercourse due to poor health, rely more on condoms or other contraception, or have a higher prevalence of other sexually transmitted diseases, in particular those that can cause infertility. Among uninfected adults fear of infection might also lead to lower frequency of intercourse and more condom use. Alternatively, increased fertility might result from a desire to replace dead children

Table 9.5. Projected birth, death, and growth rates[a] (per thousand population) with and without AIDS, 1995 and 2005, medium variant, by region, and projected growth rate with AIDS in 2005 for low and high variants.

	Sub-Saharan Africa	Asia	North America	Latin America	Western Europe	World total[b]
1995						
Without AIDS						
Birth rate	43.5	23.9	15.2	24.9	11.2	24.3
Death rate	13.8	8.2	8.6	6.6	10.3	9.1
Growth rate	29.7	15.7	6.6	18.3	0.9	15.3
With AIDS						
Birth rate	43.5	23.9	15.2	24.9	11.2	24.3
Death rate	14.8	8.2	8.9	6.8	10.4	9.2
Growth rate	28.7	15.7	6.3	18.1	0.9	15.1
Difference in growth rates due to AIDS	−1.0	0.0	−0.2	−0.2	−0.1	−0.2
2005						
Without AIDS						
Birth rate	38.9	20.3	13.8	21.1	10.2	21.6
Death rate	11.2	7.4	8.6	6.3	10.6	8.3
Growth rate	27.7	12.9	5.2	14.8	−0.4	13.3
With AIDS						
Birth rate	38.9	20.3	13.8	21.1	10.2	21.6
Death rate	12.7	7.7	8.8	6.7	10.7	8.7
Growth rate	26.3	12.6	5.1	14.4	−0.5	12.9
Difference in growth rates due to AIDS	−1.4	−0.3	−0.2	−0.4	−0.1	−0.4
Growth rate						
Low variant	26.5	12.6	5.1	14.5	−0.5	12.9
High variant	26.1	12.6	5.1	14.4	−0.5	12.8

[a]Discrepancies in growth rates are due to rounding.
[b]Total with AIDS includes a small number of infections in the former Soviet Union, Eastern Europe, West Asia, and North Africa.

or from a shortening of birth intervals when infant deaths interrupt postpartum amenorrhea. The epidemic's effect on non-AIDS mortality is likely to be significant in part because a large epidemic will tax already overburdened health-care systems in many countries and may draw resources from programs addressing other diseases. In addition, other diseases (e.g., tuberculosis) can become more prevalent because HIV-infected individuals are more susceptible to them. The rise in the non-AIDS death rate from these effects is counteracted by a small change in the age composition of the population caused by elevated AIDS mortality.[9] The net effect of these secondary effects on fertility and mortality cannot be assessed with available evidence, and the overall impact of an AIDS epidemic on population growth could therefore be somewhat different from the estimates presented in *Table 9.5*.

Further insight into these issues can be gained from a unique prospective study in the Rakai District of Uganda (Sewankambo *et al.*, 1994). An initial 1990 survey of 1,945 households with 5,795 adults and children collected demographic and socioeconomic information as well as blood samples. A follow-up survey of the same households in 1991 provided estimates of changes in households and of the number of births and deaths in the time between surveys. From this information, estimates were obtained of the demographic impact of the AIDS epidemic in the district. In 1990 13 percent of adults were found to be seropositive, a very high level (more than eight times the 1990 average for Africa) matched by very few other largely rural districts in Africa. The proportion of deaths attributable to HIV infection was estimated to be 28 percent among the population as a whole, 52 percent among all adults, and 87 percent among adults aged 20–39. Infant mortality among the offspring of infected mothers was nearly double that of their uninfected counterparts (210 vs. 111 per thousand births).

Despite this very high AIDS mortality, population growth declined only modestly. The main reason is that the birth rate was much higher than the death rate, and the rise in the death rate caused by the epidemic only partly reduced this difference (see *Figure 9.6*). Observed annual vital rates per thousand population were as follows: birth rate, 45.7; death rate, 28.1; and growth rate (natural), 17.6.

The authors estimated that in the absence of the epidemic the death rate would have been 20.4 per thousand. AIDS mortality therefore elevated the death rate by 7.7 per thousand. If one assumes that the birth rate remains unaltered by the epidemic, then

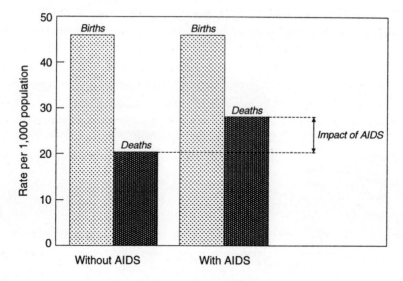

Figure 9.6. Impact of the AIDS epidemic on the death rate and population growth rate in Rakai District, Uganda. Source: Sewankambo *et al.*, 1994.

the natural growth rate is reduced by the same 7.7 per thousand (i.e., from 25.3 to 17.6 per thousand). However, the fertility of HIV-infected women was found to be slightly lower than that of uninfected women. This difference is probably due in part to the higher prevalence of other STDs among women infected with HIV; the role of HIV in reducing the birth rate therefore cannot be determined. In the absence of this difference, the birth rate would have been higher by about 1.2 per thousand (i.e., 46.9 instead of 45.7). Finally, no direct evidence for the epidemic's effect on non-AIDS mortality is available. The fact that the district's death rate without AIDS (20.4) is slightly above the average of 16.8 estimated for Uganda as a whole without AIDS (UN, 1995) is suggestive but not conclusive because Rakai is not representative of Uganda. These results indicate a need for studies that examine not only the epidemic's direct effect on mortality, but also its indirect role in affecting birth rates and non-AIDS mortality.

According to estimates of HIV prevalence in 1990 and 1992, the epidemic is no longer growing in Rakai (Wawer *et al.*, 1994). The epidemic has apparently reached an equilibrium at which HIV incidence has to remain high to offset AIDS deaths and to maintain the plateau level of prevalence in a growing population. These findings suggest that population growth will remain substantially positive in Rakai. Since Rakai is one of the districts in sub-Saharan Africa most severely affected by AIDS, it is also unlikely that population growth will drop precipitously elsewhere in the continent.[10]

9.4 Outlook

Regional trends in HIV infections over the coming decade are uncertain. The course of the epidemic depends chiefly on the behavioral responses of the affected populations, on the wider application of existing public health approaches to reduce transmissions, and on the successful development of new medical technology. A worst-case scenario would be sluggish spontaneous behavioral responses, the lack of new medical solutions for several more years, and a continuation of current, mostly weak, and uneven public-health efforts to change high-risk behaviors. In that case, the epidemic will continue largely along its natural course until all vulnerable groups (i.e., those in which R exceeds 1) are heavily infected, and HIV prevalence in the developing world will reach levels much higher than today's before eventually leveling off. This gloomiest of possible outcomes can be improved upon considerably by vigorous implementation of such public health measures as control of sexually transmitted diseases and screening of donated blood as well as behavioral interventions such as information campaigns and the distribution of condoms (Berkley, 1994; Lamptey and Coates, 1994; Philipson and Posner, 1995; Potts *et al.*, 1991). Such efforts have demonstrated their effectiveness in the past, for example, in Thailand (Hanenberg *et al.*, 1994) and among homosexuals in the United States (Centers for Disease Control and Prevention, 1991; Morris and Dean, 1994). Lack of political commitment and resources unfortunately hinders the wider application of these measures.

A large effort is now under way to develop effective HIV therapies, microbicides, and vaccines, but obstacles are many and success is probably years away (Haynes, 1993; Cohen, 1994a; Elias and

Heise, 1994; Johnston and Hoth, 1993). If and when this effort suc-
ceeds, it could end the epidemic. However, the cost of prevention
or treatment may be so high as to be out of reach for the poorest
segments of the population in Asia, Latin America, and Africa. The
epidemic would then become even more a Third World disease than
it is now.

Regardless of the long-range trends in HIV infections, the overall
course of AIDS mortality during the next decade is relatively clear.
The toll in deaths will continue to rise in much of Asia, Africa, and
Latin America, while population growth will remain high in some
regions and positive in all.

Notes

[1] This article focuses on HIV-1, which is the cause of virtually all AIDS
deaths. HIV-2, primarily found in West Africa, is less pathogenic.

[2] Estimates by Mann *et al.* (1992) put the cumulative global total of
HIV-infected adults at 17.5 million at the beginning of 1995.

[3] WHO assumes that all deaths among HIV-infected individuals are
caused by AIDS.

[4] Following WHO practice, HIV-infected individuals are assumed to be
at risk of dying from AIDS alone (see note 3). The distribution of
the incubation period is taken from Chin and Lwanga (1991a). The
projection results presented in this article are not very sensitive to
the precise shape of the distribution of the incubation period with a
given median duration.

[5] Projections assume perinatal transmission rates of 30 percent in developing regions and 17.5 percent in the developed world. The distributions of the incubation period and the survival interval after perinatal
infection are the same as those used by WHO (Chin, 1990).

[6] All variants of HIV/AIDS projections rely on the medium projections
of the UN (1995) for population estimates (including births and non-
AIDS deaths).

[7] The similarity of the results of the UN and the present study is in part
because both rely on past estimates of HIV incidence from WHO, and
their projection methodologies are similar (US Bureau of the Census
estimate: Peter Way, personal communication).

[8] Medium projections are taken from UN (1995). The projections without AIDS are obtained by subtracting estimates of AIDS deaths detailed in the same publication.

[9] Projections by the UN (1995) for African countries provide estimates of the effect of a changing age structure. In the 15 sub-Saharan countries with the most severe epidemics, the total number of deaths between 2000 and 2005 in the presence and absence of the AIDS epidemic is estimated at 19.504 and 15.169 million, respectively, giving a difference of 4.335 million. The actual number of AIDS deaths for this five-year period is projected to be 5.362 million. Non-AIDS deaths therefore decline from 15.169 to 14.142 million due to the epidemic's effect on the age structure alone.

[10] The level of HIV prevalence at which population growth becomes zero is highest in countries with the highest birth rates. Once birth rates decline, lower prevalence levels suffice to stop population growth.

Chapter 10

How Many People Can Be Fed on Earth?

Gerhard K. Heilig

Many distinguished writers have studied the question whether food is a limiting factor for population growth. Since the time when Malthus started the debate some 200 years ago (see Malthus, 1967; Ricardo, 1964) thousands of books, research papers, and study reports have been published on the subject (Boserup, 1965, 1981; Clark, 1967; Clark and Haswell, 1964; Livi Bacci, 1991).[1] Despite these intense efforts, we are still far from consensus. A screening of available literature on estimating the earth's population carrying capacity reveals surprising diversity of results (see *Table 10.1*).

In 1945 Pearson and Harper calculated that between 902 million and 2.8 billion people could be supported by the earth's agriculture. Some 20 years later Clark (1967) estimated the sustainable population maximum of the earth to range between 40 and 157 billion! However, in the 1970s Buringh *et al.* (1975) considered the world food production potential equivalent to just 5.3 billion people. In the late 1970s and early 1980s a large FAO study (Higgins *et al.*, 1983) concluded that – only on Third World soils – between 3.9 and 32.4 billion people could be fed, depending on the level of agricultural inputs. Only a decade ago, Simon's (1981) *Ultimate Resource* became a popular book. It resolutely denied any limits to (population) growth; people were considered the "ultimate resource." Today *Beyond the Limits* by Meadows *et al.* (1992a) is a best-seller.

Table 10.1. Estimates of the earth's population carrying capacity during the past 100 years.

Source	Earth's maximum population carrying capacity	Date
Ravenstein (1891)	6 billion	1891
Penck (1925)	7.7–9.5 billion	1925
Pearson and Harper (1945)	0.9–2.8 billion	1945
Baade (1960)[a]	30 billion	1960
Clark (1967)[b]	47–157 billion	1967
Revelle (1967)[a]	41 billion	1967
Mückenhausen (1973)[c]	35–40 billion	1973
Buringh et al. (1977, 1975)	2.7–6.7 billion	1975
Westing (1981), Mann (1981)	about 2 billion	1981
Simon (1981), Kahn (1982)	no meaningful limitation	1982
FAO/UNFPA/IIASA[d]	for 1975: 1.957–32.407 billion	1982
(Higgins et al., 1982)	for 2000: 3.590–33.195 billion	
Gilland (1983)[a]	7.5 million	1983
Resources for the Future (1984)	6.1 billion	1984
Marchetti (1978)	1 trillion	1978
World Hunger Program[e]	2.8–5.5 billion	1992
(Cohen, 1992)		
Ehrlich et al. (1993)	< 5.5 billion	1993

[a] Estimates are based on very low estimates of average food caloric consumption. According to Norse (1992) the three estimates of the global population carrying capacity would be much lower, if an average grain consumption of 800 kilograms per year were applied. Baade's estimate would be more than 18 billion; Revelle's would be 14 billion; and Gilland's would be 8.8 billion.

[b] "If we take world resources of agricultural land at 10.7 billion hectares of standard land equivalent, this could feed, at maximum standards, 47 billion people. ... For people living at Japanese standards of food consumption and Asian standards of timber requirements only 680 sq.m./person is required, and the world's potential agricultural and forest land could supply the needs of 157 billion people." See Clark (1967).

[c] Mückenhausen's estimate was based on a report of the US President's Science Advisory Commitee in 1967 which analyzed the world's production capacity of soils (US, 1967).

[d] The FAO/UNFPA/IIASA study estimated the global population carrying capacity for 1975 and 2000 at three agricultural input levels (low, medium, high). For details see Appendix Tables 1 and 2 in Higgins et al. (1982).

[e] "The World Hunger Program at Brown University estimated that, with present levels of food production and an equal distribution of food, the world could sustain either 5.5 billion vegetarians, 3.7 billion people who get 15 percent of their calories from animal products, ... or 2.8 billion people who derive 25 percent of their calories from animal products" (Cohen, 1992).

Among other sources the author uses a compilation on "Estimates of Arable Land: Past Studies" in Shah et al. (1985).

They argue that we have already passed the limits of sustainability and are on the way to ecological disaster. In 1992 the World Resources Institute published a wealth of data and analyses which imply that we are already approaching ecological limits in many sectors of our economies, including agriculture.

Most recently Ehrlich *et al.* (1993) analyzed the subject. According to their estimate it is "doubtful ... whether food security could be achieved indefinitely for a global population of 10 or 12 billion people." They thought it "rather likely that a sustainable population, one comfortable below Earth's nutritional capacity, will number far fewer than today's 5.5 billion people." There are many other studies, but probably the highest estimate of the globe's population carrying capacity was published by Marchetti (1978), who argued that a world population of 1 trillion people would not be impossible.

Obviously, these numbers are not much help to the student of future population trends. One reason for the large discrepancies is methodological divergences of the various approaches. Some authors deal with global averages of carrying capacity; others study small agro-ecological areas and only later aggregate the results. Some authors base their estimates on the most advanced agricultural technology or assume future innovation; others define the carrying capacity in terms of current, and in some regions rather low, levels of agricultural output.

Biologists usually explain carrying capacity as the balance between natural resources and the number of people; social scientists consider human resources the critical factor and accentuate social limits to growth. More systematically, we can identify four reasons for the conceptual confusion: dissent about the reference area, disagreement about the means of sustenance, controversy on the mode of reaction to limitations, and confusion about the time frame. We discuss some of these problems in detail in later sections of this chapter. For now we can only conclude that there are more dimensions to the problem than one would expect at first sight. It seems to be necessary to combine the various aspects of the earth's carrying capacity into a consistent theoretical framework.

10.1 Dimensions of the Earth's Carrying Capacity

To visualize the major dimensions of the problem, imagine a pipe through which the earth's food resources have to pass before they can be used for feeding people (see *Figure 10.1*). The diameter of the pipe, however, is not constant. While it is quite large on the "input" side, it is significantly smaller on the "output" end. The pipe's stepwise decreasing diameter symbolizes different kinds of restrictions to the earth's carrying capacity – technological, economic, ecological, and sociocultural.

10.1.1 The hypothetical maximum carrying capacity

On the input side of our conceptual pipe we have the theoretical maximum of the earth's food production capacity. This purely hypothetical measure is roughly equivalent to what biologists have termed the net primary production (NPP) of the earth. The measure is based on the assumption that the ultimate limitation of food production is given by the energy conversion ratio of photosynthesis. This is the basic biochemical process by which green plants transform solar radiation into biomass. Since we (roughly) know the total solar radiation input of the earth, we can calculate the globe's maximum biomass production, which quantifies the initial product of all animal and human food chains.

The NPP is only restricted by physical constants, such as the total solar radiation energy input of earth, and by natural laws that govern the biochemical processes of plant growth.[2] In its most extreme version the measure ignores not only economic, social, cultural, and political restrictions of food production, but also technical constraints and ecological feedback mechanisms. It assumes homogeneous implementation of most advanced agricultural technologies throughout the world. Authors who have adopted this rather narrow definition of carrying capacity estimate the maximum world population that can be sustained indefinitely into the future in the range of 16 to 147 billion people, depending on the specific method applied.[3] Marchetti's (1978) monstrous estimate of 1 trillion is based on a similar approach.

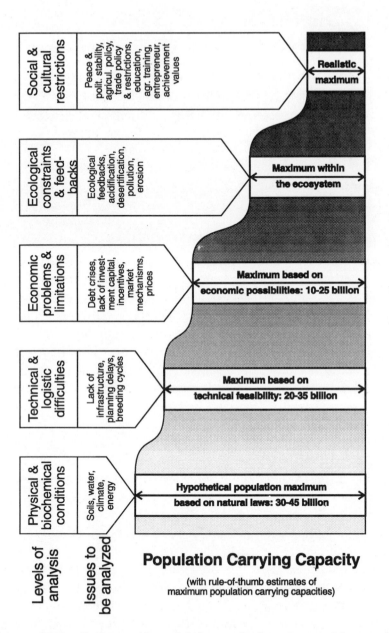

Figure 10.1. Conceptual model for analyzing the earth's population carrying capacity.

10.1.2   Technical and logistic restrictions and chances

The previous definition of carrying capacity assumes homogeneous distribution and instantaneous implementation of (advanced) food production technology. But this is impossible in reality. Even with existing agricultural technologies we would need years before we could use them throughout the world. They have to be adapted to local conditions; they must be integrated with existing food distribution channels; and they often require previous implementation of service and support schemes. The production and distribution of regionally adapted high-yield seeds, for instance, can take years or decades. Also the breeding cycles in husbandry must be considered.

In addition to the usual delays in technology transfer, we must realize that advanced agricultural methods are primarily available for good-quality soils in temperate climates and for subtropical and tropical irrigation cultures (such as Asian paddy rice crops). In the arid and semiarid zones of Africa, however, we still have traditional pastoral systems which survive quite well provided animal and human population density remains low. But since the population has doubled or tripled, the socioecological system is out of balance. The situation obviously requires new technology to increase productivity of food production. However, we cannot be sure that high-tech alternatives of animal husbandry, which could potentially boost productivity by orders of magnitude, are adaptable to the hot and dry climate. Current experiments are not too promising. It is not impossible that there simply is no high-tech alternative to traditional cattle ranging and primitive agriculture in certain parts of the world. We are just beginning to apply scientific methods to the management of arid and tropical soils, and it will probably take years or decades before we have drought-resistant, high-yield crops and livestock.

This indicates that the global carrying capacity is certainly diminished by agro-technical and logistic restrictions and delays. Some studies have tried to take this into account by defining different input levels for various agro-climatic regions. The FAO/UNDP/IIASA (1982) study, for instance, assumed three levels of agricultural input which largely correspond to levels of technology.

10.1.3   Economic barriers

Nothing in the world is free. Also the implementation of advanced
agricultural technology and the expansion of agricultural areas into
previously unused land is costly. One needs investment capital, functioning price mechanisms, adequate incentives for farmers, and a
whole set of other economic conditions and mechanisms to boost
food production for a world population of several billion. Current
estimates of a global carrying capacity usually ignore these economic
dimensions. However, in reality we find numerous economic difficulties and limitations which could further restrict global carrying
capacity. On the other hand, few spheres in human life are capable
of generating more powerful incentives and driving forces than the
economy. Recent history has shown (for instance, in China) that
agriculture can modernize within a few years and double or triple
its productivity when the economic framework is right. Only few
studies have developed agricultural models that take into account
economic mechanisms, such as prices and (international) trade. Unfortunately these models are extremely complex and their methodology and assumptions are highly debatable (Parikh *et al.*, 1988).

It is an illusion to believe that economic development is predictable for more than a few years. The fundamental changes in
global economic patterns, from the rise of the Asian Tigers (Taiwan, South Korea, Singapore, Thailand, Malaysia) and the economic boom in China to the total breakdown of former Soviet and
East European economies, should have taught us a lesson. The economic framework of agriculture is man-made and can be changed
for the better or the worse.

The earth's carrying capacity in the 21st century will be a matter of economic decisions at least to the same extent as it will be
a matter of sufficient natural resources. Three aspects are most
important: the conditions of international agricultural trade, the
dissemination of agricultural technology, and the implementation
of functioning incentive structures. We can strengthen or weaken
worldwide agricultural productivity, depending on what we do with
trade restrictions and food subsidies. We can speed up or slow down
agricultural modernization, depending on what we do with the results of agricultural research and development. We can block farmers' initiative or encourage their entrepreneurial spirit, depending on

how we arrange property rights, taxation, price mechanisms, access to modern agricultural inputs, and education. The earth's carrying capacity not only depends on natural conditions and technology; it is also a function of specific economic arrangements.

10.1.4 Ecological constraints and feedback mechanisms

Since agriculture and livestock production – as everything else – is embedded into a natural environment, we also have to take into account ecological constraints and feedback mechanisms, such as acidification, soil loss, groundwater pollution, or desertification. These consequences of intense agriculture and animal production can gradually diminish returns. Some ecologists have argued that the overutilization of arable land and forest areas in Europe and North America has already degraded the soils to such an extent that artificial fertilization and soil management techniques cannot repair the damage.

However, there is more to the ecological perspective than the necessary modification of production systems in order to minimize harmful impact on the environment. For instance, we need to reserve space for the (still remaining) fauna and flora, if we want to avoid additional termination of whole strains of evolution. Keeping biodiversity at a high level is not (only) a matter of aesthetics and respect – a large pool of plant and animal genes could be a primary resource for future bio-sciences. We must also reserve natural space for human recreation. The 10 billion world population of the 21st century, cramped into multi-million urban agglomerates, will certainly need some of the potential crop area for leisure activities, such as playing golf or riding a horse. Finally, a significant proportion of our environment cannot be utilized for agriculture or cattle ranging because it has vital functions in stabilizing the climate. Cutting down tropical rain forests for agricultural expansion would probably backfire. It would trigger or speed up climate change which could worsen agricultural conditions elsewhere and diminish overall food production. These examples show that the ecologically sustainable population maximum is certainly below a level that is determined by physical laws, technological possibilities, or optimal economic structures.

10.1.5   Social, cultural, and political conditions

Some people believe that we just have to provide land, tractors, high-yield seeds, fertilizers and pesticides, agricultural training, and free markets to make a farmer highly efficient. This technocratic approach, however, ignores the social nature of man. We must realize that probably the most serious restrictions for maximal utilization of the earth's population carrying capacity arise from social, political, and cultural conditions.

Social and cultural constraints which prevent optimal land utilization can be found not only among traditional food collectors, hunters, and cattle rangers of Africa and Asia. In many societies we have political and social conditions which hinder farmers from fully exploiting the carrying capacity of their land. In some cases these restrictions are voluntary and based on ecological considerations. For instance, a growing number of European farmers and agricultural politicians have realized that maximizing food production by means of agrochemistry and mechanization cannot be the ultimate goal of agriculture. They begin to exclude land from cultivation to make it available for natural reservations or recreational purposes. In Germany, for instance, 911,576 hectares (or 7.8 percent) of arable land was taken out of production between 1988–1989 and 1990–1991. In eastern Germany even 12.8 percent of the arable land was excluded from cultivation in 1990–1991. There are similar trends in all European countries, especially in Italy and France, where 357,922 and 113,922 hectares of land were taken out of agricultural production (Bundesministerium für Raumordnung, Bauwesen und Städtebau, 1991:62–64).

However, this noble self-restriction of agriculture (which is facilitated by substantial government subsidies) is rather untypical. Usually, there are other, more unpleasant sociocultural and political constraints. Many farmers throughout the world are working their fields amid (civil) wars, suffer from lack of technology and modern inputs, or are restricted by ridiculously low producer prices or market regulations. They are forced into collectivization by fanatical bureaucrats, and their children are deprived of adequate education and training. These kinds of sociocultural and political constraints probably restrict the carrying capacity of the earth much more than anything else.

To my knowledge there is no estimate of carrying capacity which takes into account all five kinds of restrictions. Scientists particularly shy away from addressing sociocultural and political constraints. Usually, the concept is defined in terms of natural resources available for food production at a given level of agricultural technology. This reflects widespread ignorance of key factors – economic, social, cultural, and political – that limit food production. In Section 10.2 we examine the multiple dimensions of the earth's carrying capacity in greater detail.

10.2   Natural Resources

According to our pipe concept of carrying capacity, natural conditions (such as the globe's solar radiation input) and basic biochemical processes (such as photosynthesis) ultimately determine the earth's food production potential. If we could transform the total solar energy input of the earth into biomass – and if we could eat this biomass – we could probably feed 1 trillion people. But this is just a theoretical exercise (which we discuss later). For all practical purposes we must consider real agro-climatic conditions. Four natural resources and conditions directly limit the globe's carrying capacity: land, water, climate, and fossil energy.

10.2.1   Land

Since the beginning of the debate on the globe's carrying capacity, the land factor has usually been considered a limitation for increasing food production. The world's land area is, undoubtedly, limited, and only a small proportion is suitable for agriculture (*Table 10.2*). Many physical and chemical constraints restrict the arable area – some land is too steep or too shallow, other areas have drainage or tillage problems. There are serious constraints of soil fertility, such as low nutrient retention capacity, aluminum toxicity, phosphorus fixations hazards, low potassium reserves, or excess of salts or sodium.

Both in its 1990–1991 and 1992–1993 reports on world resources, the World Resources Institute (WRI) published detailed estimates of these physical and chemical soil constraints by climatic class for major regions and on a country-by-country basis. The estimates in

Table 10.2. Cropland in percent of land without soil constraints, 23 highest and lowest: 1989.

Country	Population (1000)	Land area (1000 ha)	Cropland (1000 ha)	Land without soil Constraints (1000 ha)	Cropland in % of land without soil constraints
Lesotho	1724	3035	320	1	32000.0
Malaysia	8451	32855	4880	196	2489.8
Lao PDR	4024	23080	901	37	2435.1
Thailand	54857	51089	22126	983	2250.9
Burundi	5315	2565	1336	66	2024.2
Mauritius	1069	185	106	7	1514.3
Rwanda	6994	2467	1153	91	1267.0
Sierra Leone	4049	7162	1801	187	963.1
Syrian Arab Rep.	12085	18406	5503	643	855.8
Vietnam	65276	32549	6600	989	667.3
Uganda	18118	19955	6705	1210	554.1
Bangladesh	112548	13017	9292	1719	540.5
Benin	4493	11062	1860	360	516.7
Lebanon	2694	1023	301	59	510.2
India	835610	297319	168990	33232	508.5
Côte d'Ivoire	11552	31800	3660	730	501.4
Brazil	147283	845651	78650	17081	460.5
Togo	3424	5439	1444	319	452.7
Cambodia	8044	17652	3056	695	439.7
Nigeria	105015	91077	31335	7797	401.9
Pakistan	118476	77088	20730	5250	394.9
Cuba	10500	10982	3329	888	374.9
Cameroon	11453	46540	7008	1949	359.6
Ethiopia	47942	110100	13930	30079	46.3
Mexico	86672	190869	24710	55930	44.2
Kenya	23187	56969	2428	7342	33.1
Argentina	31914	273669	35750	111781	32.0
Botswana	1256	56673	1380	4792	28.8
Sudan	24487	237600	12510	50390	24.8
Peru	21105	128000	3730	15264	24.4
Somalia	7257	62734	1039	4519	23.0
Bolivia	7115	108439	3460	15415	22.4
Uruguay	3077	17481	1304	6100	21.4
Kuwait	1971	1782	4	31	12.9
Egypt	51186	99545	2585	24633	10.5
Chad	5539	125920	3205	34160	9.4
Niger	7492	126670	3605	41388	8.7
Namibia	1725	82329	662	9308	7.1
Mali	8938	122019	2093	40865	5.1
Libya	4382	175954	2150	54004	4.0
Saudi Arabia	13585	214969	1185	30579	3.9
Yemen, PDR	2416	33297	119	3870	3.1
Oman	1446	21246	48	3897	1.2
United Arab Emirates	1538	8360	39	3707	1.1
Albania	3186	2740	707	96958	0.7
Mauritania	1970	102522	199	58867	0.3

this discussion are from the 1992–1993 WRI report and are based on a complex methodology, which combines the Fertility Capability Classification (FCC) system developed at North Carolina State University (Sanches *et al.*, 1982), agro-climatic data from FAO's Agro-Ecological Zones project (FAO, 1978a, 1978b, 1981a, 1981b), and the FAO/UNESCO soil map of the world.

The estimates are shocking. The most seriously handicapped region is Southeast Asia: more than 93 percent of the soils have physical or chemical constraints. The situation is not much better in Southwest Asia: only 12 percent of the soils are free of inherent fertility constraints. In South America 80 percent and in Africa 82 percent of the soils have constraints. Central America is a little better: "only" 73 percent of the soils are hampered by physical or chemical restrictions (World Resources Institute/United Nations Environment Programme/United Nations Development Programme, 1990:286–287).[4] On a country-by-country basis the estimates are even more dramatic. For India, the WRI reports just 33.2 million hectares of unconstrained soils; this is equivalent to just 0.04 hectares (or 400 square meters) per person. Bangladesh's unconstrained soil resources are even less: only 0.02 hectares per person. Pakistan, the Philippines, and Indonesia would have from 0.4 to 0.6 hectares of soil without inherent physical or chemical constraints for each person.

What do these statistics indicate? The WRI reports that "the extent of land with soil constraints is an important indicator of agricultural costs, the *potential and success of future expansion* [emphasis added], and the comparative advantage of a nation's agricultural production" (World Resources Institute/United Nations Environment Programme/United Nations Development Programme, 1990:289).

The WRI further explains that "in the past 10 years, the FCC system has proven a meaningful tool for describing fertility limitations on crop yields" (*ibid*:289). Do the estimates – in other words – indicate that we are already short of fertile soils for future expansion of food production?

Not at all! First, one has to read the footnotes attached to the WRI tables. Here we find a few hints that explain what is meant by the various soil constraints. It turns out that most of the so-called constraints are just specific natural conditions that can be somewhat easily overcome with modern agricultural technology. Consider the case of soils with "low potassium reserves" which constrain crops because of potassium deficiency. There is a simple solution: throw potassium fertilizer on them! Other examples of soil constraints are "steep slopes" or "drainage problems": would one think that many of these soils can be found in the extremely productive paddy rice and wheat areas of Asia, where agriculture in some places has been practiced for more than 8000 years (as in China)? "Aluminum toxicity" is also called a constraint, but its impact turns out to be less dramatic than its name: it limits the growth of common crops, "unless lime is applied" (World Resources Institute/United Nations Environment Programme/United Nations Development Programme, 1992:284) – a practice that should not be completely impossible.

There are, of course, serious soil constraints that cannot be overcome by technology, but the WRI data do not distinguish between these and simple problems of soil management. For thousands of years farmers had to cope with soils that were less than perfect. They had to build terraces, add (natural) fertilizers, irrigate or drain the soil. But this did not hinder them from supplying some of the most prominent empires of history, such as the dynasties of China or the kingdoms of ancient Egypt.

There is a second reason why the WRI data on soil constraints are worthless as indicators of the earth's carrying capacity: they do not match with current trends in food production – to be more precise, in some cases the indicators are just absurd when compared with agricultural performance. For instance, according to the WRI the continent-size nation of India has only 33.2 million hectares of internally unconstrained soils, but FAO reports that India's farmers are cultivating some 169 million hectares of cropland – which is five times the area of "unconstrained soils" (cropland equals arable land plus land under permanent crops). In other words, according to the WRI most of India's farmers are producing on marginal land, which should limit crop yields. But just the opposite has happened during the past 30 years. Between 1961 and 1989 India's farmers increased cereal production by a spectacular 129 percent (from 87,376,000 to 199,816,000 metric tons). They also increased the cereal yields from

947 to 1,921 kg per hectare area harvested. In Thailand just 983,000
hectares are free of soil constraints, according to WRI data. Is it not
strange that the country's farmers actually cultivated 22.1 million
hectares of cropland – nearly 23 times the area of the unconstrained
soils? Only the rice area harvested was 10 times the size of the unconstrained soils area. Thailand's farmers also managed to increase
cereal production by 131 percent between 1961 and 1989. Most absurd are the estimates of soil constraints for Malaysia. According
to WRI data only 0.6 percent (or 196,000 hectares) of the country's
land area is covered by unconstrained soils. Obviously this did not
have a great effect on the country's farmers, who cultivated 4.9 million hectares of cropland in 1989 – 25 times the area of unconstrained
soils. It also did not affect their productivity, since they managed
to increase cereal production by 62 percent between 1961 and 1989.
These are only a few examples. We can find a large number of
countries where the farmers expanded cultivation far into the area
of so-called constrained soils, while at the same time substantially
increasing crop yields.

There is a third reason why WRI's soil data have limited relevance: a high percentage of unconstrained soils in a country does
not correlate with good agricultural performance. For example, according to the WRI, Chad has one of the largest areas of excellent
soils – 34.2 million hectares have no inherent physical or chemical
constraints, an opulent 6.2 hectares per person. Is it not strange
that the farmers use less than 10 percent of this area for cultivation
and that famines are notorious in a place with one of the largest per
capita resources of first-rate soils? This is not just an isolated case.
According to WRI data, nearly all typical famine countries of Africa
(Ethiopia, Sudan, Somalia, Mali) have huge areas of top-rated soils
which are many times the size of their actual cropland.

Given these examples it is obvious that factors other than soil
quality by itself are responsible for agricultural performance. There
is simply no correlation between food production and soil constraints
as reported by the WRI.

On the other hand, we have a large number of agricultural techniques available that could help to either expand the arable land and
increase yields on marginal soils or improve the overall efficiency of
crop production.

First, we could expand the area of multiple harvests. In many places farmers could use their land several times during a growing season instead of only once or twice. Modern seeds, advanced agricultural technology, artificial fertilizers, and other agricultural inputs have made these techniques of multi-cropping possible. It is a myth that we are already overutilizing the world's arable land. This is only true in some European and Asian regions. Large parts of Latin America and Africa have excellent soils which are still cultivated with most primitive agricultural technology. Crop yields are often 60 to 90 percent below the average European level. Better inputs and modern agricultural methods could substantially expand the area of multiple harvests.

Second, we could expand cultivation to marginal land. There is still plenty of dry land that could be irrigated, swamps that could be drained, steep hills which could be terraced. We could cover land with greenhouses in cold regions or use forests for multilayered cultivation. It is also possible to convert shallow seas into agricultural land. The Netherlands have demonstrated that even in an adverse climate one can produce more than enough (tropical) fruits and vegetables on artificially climatized and drained land. In most countries it was not necessary to increase arable land during the past decades, but some agricultures have demonstrated that a spectacular expansion of cultivation is still possible. Libya, for instance, has converted desert into circles of irrigated cropland; between 1961 and 1989 its area of irrigated agriculture doubled from 121,000 to 242,000 hectares (Allan, 1976). Burundi, which is already densely populated, managed to increase its arable land from 765,000 to 1,120,000 hectares and the area of irrigated agriculture from 3,000 to 72,000 hectares. Tanzania nearly doubled its arable land and increased the irrigated agriculture more than seven times. There are still spectacular land reserves in parts of Africa and Latin America. Of course, some of these expansions are rather absurd in terms of energy efficiency or economic costs; one might even consider the idea of growing wheat in the desert a form of hypocrisy. But these cases show what could be done in agriculture if money and technology were accessible and environmental concerns could be ignored.

Third, we can expand food production areas to the water bodies of our globe – lakes, rivers, and seas (Sindermann, 1982). While there is certainly a danger of exploiting the natural fish population of the sea, efforts are being made to begin exploring the potential of fish farming. There is already some fish farming on the northern coast of England, in Norwegian fjords, along the coast of Sweden, and in Chinese paddy rice fields. A significant proportion of Europe's salmon supply is produced in fish farms near the Shetland Islands. But these are still small production sites compared with the huge coastal zones of our continents. It has been argued that large-scale fish-farming schemes might disturb the natural balance of the maritime ecosystem, which, in turn, could limit its production potential (Uthoff, 1978; UNO/FAO, 1976). However, recent research has found only a minimal risk of local sea pollution caused by a discharge of nutrients in intense fish farming (Ackefors and Enell, 1990).

Fourth, we can switch from nonfood to food crops. Currently, a significant proportion of fertile land is used not for food production in a narrow sense, but to grow lifestyle-related cash crops, such as tobacco, tea, cocoa, or coffee. It is hard to estimate the areas wasted for the illegal cultivation of drugs (marijuana, coca, etc.), but it must be substantial. Farmers also spend arable land for producing natural fibers, such as jute, flax, or sisal – nonfood products for which synthetic substitutes are available. In some countries, such as Brazil, there is substantial energy-cropping (sugar cane), and some European governments encourage farmers to grow rape seed and produce bio-fuel. In some countries (Italy, Spain) large areas are used to grow wine. And – last but not least – we spend considerable amounts of land to produce hops, which is mainly used for brewing beer. According to FAO statistics, it is quite likely that some 20 percent of all arable land worldwide is used to produce nonfood or lifestyle-related products, including drugs (see *Table 10.3*).

Previously it was thought that a given plot of land can only feed a fixed number of people. Later, scientists realized that it is not only the size and natural quality of the land, but mainly the level of agricultural technology which determines the land's food production capacity. This basic understanding is still rare among today's

Table 10.3. Lifestyle-related and nonfood agricultural production.

	Area harvested (1,000 ha)		Growth (%)	In % of total arable land	
	1961	1990	1961–1990	1961	1990
Drugs (marijuana, coca)	?	?	?	?	?
Wine	?	?	?	?	?
Tobacco leaves	3,397	4,629	36.6	0.3	0.3
Hops[a]	55	79	43.6	0.0	0.0
Tea	1,318	2,442	85.3	0.1	0.2
Coffee	9,706	11,241	15.8	0.8	0.8
Cocoa beans	4,100	5,312	29.6	0.3	0.4
Sugar beets	6,917	8,656	25.1	0.6	0.6
Sugar cane	8,914	17,120	92.1	0.7	1.3
Flax fiber	2,041	1,113	−45.5	0.2	0.1
Hemp fiber	685	233	−66.0	0.1	0.0
Jute, jutelike fibers	2,629	2,218	−15.6	0.2	0.2
Linseed	7,615	4,078	−46.4	0.6	0.3
Rape seed[a]	6,277	17,588	180.2	0.5	1.3
Sunflower seed	6,667	16,913	153.7	0.5	1.3
Seed cotton[a]	31,897	32,984	3.4	2.5	2.4
Sesame seed[a]	5,051	6,336	25.4	0.4	0.5
Soybeans	23,806	56,351	136.7	1.9	4.2
Castor beans	1,233	1,657	34.4	0.1	0.1
Groundnuts	16,641	20,135	21.0	1.3	1.5
Total	138,949	209,085	50.5	11.1	15.5

[a]1961–1991.
Source: FAO, 1994.

environmental doomsayers, such as the World Resources Institute. They continue to focus their attention on the physical conditions of soils, collecting ever-more detailed inventories of soil characteristics. But they are obviously blind to the fact that these characteristics are becoming relevant. The size and quality of soils are just two variables in a multiterm equation of agricultural productivity, which is mainly determined by technological, economic, sociocultural, and political factors.

10.2.2   Water

Some experts have argued that it is not land, but water which is the critical resource for the global carrying capacity (Rivière, 1989). The most prominent Cassandra of a world water crisis is Malin Falkenmark. She has argued that "water scarcity [is] now threatening two-thirds of the African population" (Falkenmark, 1989:118). Her pessimism, however, is not shared by prominent hydrologists who have collected detailed water resource inventories for Africa. Almost three dozen water experts, assisted by five major hydrological institutes, contributed to a UN publication which concluded:

> There is almost nowhere in Africa where groundwater is not found at one depth or another.... Mineral-water and thermo-mineral springs abound in the African continent in the fracture zones. They constitute a major potential resource which has been explored and exploited in only a few places. [UN, 1988:13–14]

Other water experts have raised the argument that we should not confuse man-induced regional or local water shortages with climate-related resource scarcity (Bandyopadhyay, 1989).

Globally about 70 percent of all water withdrawal is used in agriculture (*Table 10.4*). This explains why the water situation is, in fact, important to the food production capacity of the earth. There are also some reasons for concern. Available statistics confirm that in some river basins, freshwater is being extracted for human use (including agriculture) at rates approaching those at which the supply is renewed. In particular, Egypt is probably on the brink of a water crisis. The country's renewable freshwater resources include some 58.3 km^3, of which 56.5 km^3 are from the Nile's annual flow and 1.8 km^3 from other internal renewable resources. Some 97 percent of these resources (or 56.4 km^3) are already being withdrawn. Egypt's agriculture needs 49.6 km^3 of water. Only 2.8 km^3 are used in industry, and the withdrawal for domestic purposes is about 3.9 km^3.

Libya's agriculture might also be limited by extreme water shortages. According to recent estimates the country has a renewable freshwater resource of some 0.7 km^3 per year – mostly from underground aquifers. Libya's annual withdrawal, however,

Table 10.4. Freshwater resources and withdrawals for selected countries: sorted by withdrawal in percentage of total resources.

	Annual river inflow (km³)	Annual internal renewable water resources				Annual withdrawal per capita (m³)	Annual withdrawal in % of total water resources[a]	Agricultural withdrawal in % of total withdrawal
		Total (km³)	Per capita (m³)	Per 10,000 ha of cropland[b]	Per 10,000 ha of land			
Congo	621	181	90.77	10.77	0.05	20	0	11
Zaïre	x	1019	28.31	1.30	0.04	22	0	17
Gambia	19	3	3.50	0.17	0.03	33	0	91
Cambodia	410	88.1	10.68	0.29	0.05	69	0	94
Paraguay	220	94	21.98	0.42	0.02	111	0	78
Cameroon	x	208	18.50	0.30	0.04	30	0	35
Uganda	x	66	3.58	0.10	0.03	20	0	60
Angola	x	158	15.77	197.50	0.01	43	0	76
Haiti	x	11	1.69	0.12	0.04	46	0	68
Zambia	x	96	11.35	0.18	0.01	86	0	26
Benin	x	26	5.48	0.14	0.02	26	0	58
Chad	x	38.4	6.76	0.12	0.00	35	0	82
Brazil	1760	5190	34.52	0.66	0.06	212	1	40
Uruguay	65	59	18.86	0.45	0.03	241	1	91
Ghana	x	53	3.53	0.19	0.02	35	1	52
Guatemala	x	116	12.61	0.62	0.11	139	1	74
Tanzania	x	76	2.78	0.14	0.01	36	1	74
Indonesia	x	2530	14.02	1.19	0.13	96	1	76
Niger	30	14	1.97	0.04	0.00	44	1	74
Bangladesh	1000	1357	11.74	1.46	0.94	211	1	96
Côte d'Ivoire	x	74	5.87	0.20	0.02	68	1	67
Nigeria	47	261	2.31	0.08	0.03	44	1	54
Lesotho	x	4	2.25	0.13	0.01	34	1	56
Mozambique	x	58	3.70	0.19	0.01	53	1	66
Vietnam	x	376	5.60	0.57	0.11	81	1	78
Canada	x	2901	109.37	0.63	0.03	1752	1	8
Nepal	x	170	8.88	0.64	0.12	155	2	95
Malawi	x	9	1.07	0.04	0.01	22	2	49
Ethiopia	x	110	2.35	0.08	0.01	48	2	86
Malaysia	x	456	26.30	0.93	0.14	765	2	47
Mali	x	62	6.62	0.30	0.00	159	2	97

Table 10.4. Continued.

| | Annual river inflow (km³) | Annual internal renewable water resources | | | | Annual withdrawal per capita (m³) | Annual withdrawal in % of total water resources[a] | Agricultural withdrawal in % of total withdrawal |
		Total (km³)	Per capita (m³)	Per 10,000 ha of cropland[b]	Per 10,000 ha of land			
Rwanda	x	6.3	0.87	0.05	0.02	23	2	68
Argentina	300	694	21.47	0.19	0.03	1059	3	73
Burundi	x	3.6	0.66	0.03	0.01	20	3	64
AFRICA	x	4184	6.46	0.22	0.01	244	3	88
Former Yugoslavia	115	150	6.29	0.19	0.06	393	3	12
Senegal	12	23.2	3.15	0.04	0.01	201	4	92
Swaziland	x	6.96	8.82	0.42	0.04	414	4	93
Hungary	109	6	0.57	0.01	0.01	502	5	36
Australia	0	343	20.48	0.07	0.00	1306	5	33
Zimbabwe	x	23	2.37	0.08	0.01	129	5	79
Somalia	0	11.5	1.52	0.11	0.00	167	7	97
Kenya	x	14.8	0.59	0.06	0.00	48	7	62
Former USSR	300	4384	15.22	0.19	0.02	1330	8	65
Turkey	7	196	3.52	0.07	0.03	317	8	57
WORLD	x	40673	7.69	0.28	0.03	660	8	69
Philippines	0	323	5.18	0.41	0.11	693	9	61
Syria	27.9	7.6	0.61	0.01	0.00	449	9	83
Greece	13.5	45.15	4.49	0.12	0.03	721	12	63
Romania	171	37	1.59	0.04	0.02	1144	12	59
Sudan	100	30	1.19	0.02	0.00	1089	14	99
Sri Lanka	0	43.2	2.51	0.23	0.07	503	15	96
Dominican Rep.	x	20	2.79	0.14	0.04	453	15	89
ASIA	x	10485	3.37	0.23	0.04	526	15	86
EUROPE	x	2321	4.66	0.17	0.05	726	15	33
Mexico	x	357.4	4.03	0.14	0.02	901	15	86
Peru	x	40	1.79	0.11	0.00	294	15	72
Algeria	0.2	18.9	0.75	0.02	0.00	161	16	74
Portugal	31.6	34	3.31	0.09	0.04	1062	16	48
Netherlands	80	10	0.68	0.11	0.03	1023	16	33
China	0	2800	2.47	0.29	0.03	462	16	87
South Korea	x	63	1.45	0.30	0.06	298	17	75
Thailand	69	110	1.97	0.05	0.02	599	18	90

Table 10.4. Continued.

| | Annual river inflow (km³) | Annual internal renewable water resources | | | | Annual withdrawal per capita (m³) | Annual withdrawal in % of total water resources[a] | Agricultural withdrawal in % of total withdrawal |
		Total (km³)	Per capita (m³)	Per 10,000 ha of cropland[b]	Per 10,000 ha of land			
India	235	1850	2.17	0.11	0.06	612	18	93
South Africa	x	50	1.42	0.04	0.00	404	18	67
USA	x	2478	9.94	0.13	0.03	2162	19	42
Japan	0	547	4.43	1.18	0.14	923	20	50
North Korea	x	67	2.92	0.34	0.06	1649	21	73
France	15	170	3.03	0.09	0.03	728	22	15
Oman	0	2	1.36	0.42	0.00	325	24	94
Former West Germany	82	79	1.30	0.11	0.03	668	26	20
Poland	6.8	49.4	1.29	0.03	0.02	472	30	24
Italy	7.6	179.4	3.13	0.15	0.06	983	30	59
Pakistan	170	298	2.43	0.14	0.04	2053	33	98
Morocco	0	30	1.19	0.03	0.01	501	37	91
Iran	x	117.5	2.08	0.08	0.01	1362	39	87
Spain	1	110.3	2.80	0.05	0.02	1174	41	62
Jordan	0.4	0.7	0.16	0.02	0.00	173	41	65
Iraq	66	34	1.80	0.06	0.01	4575	43	92
Afghanistan	x	50	3.02	0.06	0.01	1436	52	99
Tunisia	0.6	3.75	0.46	0.01	0.00	325	53	80
Belgium	4.1	8.4	0.85	0.10	0.03	917	72	4
Israel	0.45	1.7	0.37	0.04	0.01	447	88	79
Malta	0	0.025	0.07	0.02	0.01	68	92	16
Egypt	56.5	1.8	0.03	x	0.00	1202	97	88
Yemen, PDR	0	1.5	0.60	0.13	0.00	1167	129	93
Saudi Arabia	0	2.2	0.16	0.02	0.00	255	164	47
United Arab Emirates	0	0.3	0.19	0.08	0.00	565	299	80
Libya	0	0.7	0.15	0.00	0.00	623	404	75

[a]Total water resources include both internal renewable resources and river flows from other countries.
[b]Cropland includes arable land and land under permanent crops.
x = unknown/no data available.
Source: World Resources Institute/United Nations Environment Programme/United Nations Development Programme, 1992:328–329, 274–275.

is estimated at 2.83 km^3 – which is four times the rate of natural replacement. Some 75 percent of this unsustainable withdrawal is used in agriculture. The country's spectacular increase of grain production is obviously borrowed from future generations.

Another interesting case is Saudi Arabia. Since 1961 the desert country has increased its wheat production by a spectacular 4,706 percent, from merely 85,000 to 4,000,000 metric tons. Today, the country's farmers are not only able to provide more than 35 percent of the domestic food supply – which is a spectacular achievement in itself – but they actually produce more grain than the country needs. In 1991 Saudi Arabia's net export of wheat was 1,805,000 metric tons, as compared with a net import of 67,600 metric tons in 1974. Ecologists have argued that the bumper harvests were mainly achieved by exploiting fossil – that is, nonrenewable – water resources below the desert. They estimate that in 1988 the country withdrew some 20.5 km^3 of water, 90 percent from nonrenewable fossil groundwater aquifers. They also estimate that Saudi Arabia's agriculture needs 90 percent of the water available, with 35 percent of the agricultural water consumption being used in wheat production. According to the *Middle East Economic Digest* (Hopes dry up..., 1989:15), which cites a confidential US government agency report, at the current rate of depletion Saudi Arabia's fossil groundwater would be exhausted by 2007.

Many authors have argued that Africa is a parched continent (Pearce, 1991). The most pessimistic position maintains that by the year 2000, Tunisia, Kenya, Malawi, Burundi, and Rwanda will suffer a permanent water crisis (Falkenmark, 1989:116).

There is also much concern about the arid regions of the north China plain. According to recent calculations by the World Resources Institute, the 200 million population is already exploiting the freshwater resources to a large extent. The WRI concludes that "if present trends continue, the region will have 6 percent less water than needed by the end of the century" (World Resources Institute/United Nations Environment Programme/United Nations Development Programme, 1992:163). These examples certainly seem to confirm the conclusion that water is a critical factor for limiting global carrying capacity, but there is also empirical evidence that does not fit into the pessimistic outlook.

According to the most recent estimate the earth's total annual freshwater resource is some 40,673 km^3. The annual agricultural withdrawal is about 2,236 km^3, which is less than 6 percent of the globe's renewable water. Worldwide industrial and domestic water consumption together account for another 995 km^3, or just 2.5 percent of the total water resource (World Resources Institute/United Nations Environment Programme/United Nations Development Programme, 1992:328). It is hard to imagine that we are approaching global limits of freshwater withdrawal when more than 92 percent of the known reserves are still untouched.

If there is no scarcity at the global level, the uneven regional distribution of resources might be the problem. Africa is frequently considered an example of continentwide agricultural stagnation – triggered, or at least intensified, by water scarcity (Falkenmark, 1991). Available statistics, however, do not confirm this theory. Africa has 4,184 km^3 of annual internal renewable water resources, which was nearly 6,500 m^3 per person per year in 1990. This is almost five times the per capita freshwater availability of western Germany, which is only 1,300 m^3. Moreover, Africa's freshwater is not only located in the tropical areas, as one might suspect. There are large reserves all over the continent: famine ridden Somalia has more than twice the per capita internal freshwater resource of the Netherlands (1,520 versus 680 m^3).[5] The "arid" Chad has internal freshwater sources of 6,760 m^3 per person – more than three times the rainy UK's per capita water resource (which is only 2,110 m^3). In Angola there are 15,770 m^3 of freshwater for each person – nearly 28 times more than, for instance, in Hungary, which has just 570 m^3 available.

There is also more than enough freshwater in South America. The total resource is estimated at 10,377 km^3 which is equivalent to the combined renewable water resources of Europe, the former Soviet Union, and Africa. On average, each inhabitant of South America has potential access to 34,960 m^3 of freshwater, which is 7.5 times more than in Europe. All large South American nations have abundant per capita freshwater resources, ranging from 18,860 m^3 in Uruguay to 43,370 m^3 in Venezuela (which is many times the typical ratio for Europe, Asia, or the USA). Only Peru is somewhat "shorter" in freshwater: 1,790 m^3 per person are available –

a still abundant amount, however, if compared with the 850 m^3 of Belgium's internal renewable water resource.

The situation in North America and Central America is mixed: very large resources in Canada, more limited resources on the Caribbean Islands. However, there is no indication that freshwater resources are running out in the region. Mexico, for instance, has larger internal freshwater resources than Italy: 4,030 compared with 3,130 m^3 per person per year.

The freshwater resources of Asian countries are very different. At the national level, China has enough water – 2,470 m^3 per person per year.[6] India, Pakistan, and Thailand have a little less (2,170, 2,430, and 1,970 m^3 per person per year, respectively), but are far from critical. There is abundant freshwater in Indonesia (14,020 m^3), Bangladesh (11,740 m^3), and Malaysia (2,630 m^3).

An interesting indicator of water stress is the proportion of annual withdrawals from available resources. In 51 countries the annual withdrawals are equal to or less than 1 percent of the renewable freshwater resources – including populous nations such as Indonesia, Brazil, and Nigeria. China uses 16 percent of its annual freshwater resource; India, 18 percent; Kenya, just 7 percent. In all of Africa, including the drought-affected Sahel, only three countries extract more than 50 percent of their annual freshwater resource, namely, Egypt (90 percent), Libya (404 percent), and Tunisia (53 percent). Most African countries are extracting less than 3 percent of their resources. In South America the highest extraction is reported from Peru: a mere 15 percent. All other South American nations have not even touched their renewable water reserves – they use typically less than 2 percent. Even in Asia, where the situation is a little tighter, extraction rates typically range between 1 and 30 percent. Only Afghanistan, Israel, and Cyprus have extraction rates of more than 50 percent. For these countries the situation is certainly serious. Jordan, Algeria, and Tunisia are also critical. The real "dramatic" cases, however, are only a small number of states of the Arabian peninsula: Qatar, Saudi Arabia, United Arab Emirates, and Yemen. They are all withdrawing water at much higher rates than those at which their resource is renewed.

These statistics indicate that at the national level only a very small number of countries are facing water resources shortages. On the other hand, local or regional water shortages are well known, as well as strong seasonal variation of availability. It is also obvious that groundwater pollution is a major problem in some places, such as in very intensely used agricultural or industrial areas. Can we solve these water problems, or will they impose serious restrictions on the world's agricultural production? To answer these questions three aspects have to be taken into account.

First, with a 10 to 15 billion world population there is no alternative to the implementation of (advanced) water management and exploitation technologies. It will also be necessary to find political solutions to water conflicts. But this is nothing new. Water – as well as air – has always been a natural resource that must be managed. No one knew this better than the ancient civilizations along the Nile or in the desert. They developed highly sophisticated methods of water exploitation, storage, distribution, and conservation. We tend to forget that large irrigation systems were built in the Middle East some 4,000 to 5,000 years ago and that during the Roman Empire the capital city could flourish only because it was supplied with water through aqueducts across hundreds of miles. We have to advance these methods (Meybeck *et al.*, 1990). Most likely it will be necessary to pump freshwater to agricultural areas over long distances (such as from northern United States to southern California); we certainly will have to settle conflicts over limited water resources between neighboring countries (such as between Israel and Lebanon); some islands (such as Malta) and some densely populated agricultural regions (such as northern China) will require the implementation of advanced water conservation and recycling schemes. These methods are not impossible, and they have proved to be successful in the past.

Second, we have to understand that water use is essentially a recycling process: frequently water is just moved through biological and technical systems for cleaning or as some kind of biological catalyst. Much of the freshwater withdrawal (especially in agriculture) is not consumed, but directly returned to a river or underground aquifer. From there it can be used several times before it finally reaches the sea. We usually do not consume water in the same way we exploit fossil fuels or scarce minerals. These natural resources have a much lower recycling rate than water – they are actually destroyed or at least removed from natural cycles for a very long time through human consumption. Consumptive uses of water, such as the evaporation from industrial cooling towers and irrigation systems, make up only a small proportion of water withdrawal. The real water problem is not its natural scarcity, but the pollution we add to the returning flows and the carelessness with which we use freshwater in households, industries, and agriculture.

Finally, both industries and private households have already caused serious local or regional water contamination. Unfortunately, high-tech agriculture itself is a major polluter of groundwater and river flows (Biswas, 1993). In some intensively cultivated agricultural areas of Europe the excessive use of fertilizers has raised the nitrate concentration in groundwater to dangerously high levels. We can also observe pesticide contamination of freshwater resources in some areas of North America and Europe (Hallberg, 1989; Leistra and Boesten, 1989). An increase in food production could easily lead to further deterioration of water resources. On the other hand, this trend is not inevitable. All experts agree that there is still a huge potential for improving the efficiency of fertilizer use, irrigation, water treatment, and recycling (Biswas and Arar, 1988). Much has already been done to clean lakes and rivers in Europe. Twenty-five years ago the lakes in southern Germany frequently had to be closed to swimmers because of pollution with coli bacteria; today one could drink the water. European farmers have also realized the danger of overfertilization. Contrary to popular belief they have not increased nitrogen fertilizer application per hectare of arable land during the past 10 years.

On the basis of these considerations we cannot see water as a serious limitation for the globe's carrying capacity. No doubt, there are nations with rather limited resources. As well, local or regional shortages will require expensive water infrastructures. However, the only dramatic shortages can be found in a small number of desert states of North Africa and West Asia. Most of these countries are enormously wealthy oil exporters that could artificially "produce" water for their unconventional high-tech agriculture – in fact, this is what they are doing with the highest density of desalination plants in the world. But is the natural water scarcity of some oil billionaires really worth the concern?

10.2.3 Climate

The globe's food production potential certainly depends on the climate. The annual fluxes of precipitation and evapotranspiration which determine the potential water supply available for human exploitation (runoff) vary greatly by region. They are much higher at the equator than in the arid or semiarid regions around the latitudes of 40° north or 30° south (Baumgartner and Reichel, 1975). The vast deserts and arid lands of Asia and Africa that have emerged from these climatic conditions are certainly among the most hostile environments for agriculture on earth. The lowest precipitation and evapotranspiration, and consequently the lowest potential water supply for human exploitation, can be found at the poles.

The spatial pattern of the global water cycle not only influences the water supply for rainfed agriculture, but also determines variations in the flux of solar radiation energy, which is the fuel of photosynthesis – the basic process of plant growth. In the arid or semiarid mid-latitudes of low precipitation, cloud cover is rare or absent so that less solar radiation is absorbed or reflected. Consequently, insolation in these regions is some 20 percent higher than at the equator, where one would expect the highest solar energy flux (Stanhill, 1983). Since there is also a low level of actual evaporation in these arid zones, the solar energy input mainly heats up the ground and the air, which further increases the region's water deficit and worsens environmental conditions for agriculture.

It is not only the (absolute) shortage of water and the high temperatures in arid and semiarid regions that make agriculture difficult or impossible. There is also the interannual variation in precipitation, which is typically three or four times greater in these regions than in temperate regions. This high climatic variability explains why the desert can widen and narrow in an unpredictable temporal pattern. During the early 1970s we experienced a global redistribution of rainfall which led to the 1970–1972 Sahel drought and contributed to widespread famines in the Sahel and Ethiopia. The bioclimatic zones of the Sahel moved to the south and expanded the area of high desertification risk.

During the 1970s and 1980s many authors considered desertification – triggered by climate variation – a major cause of declining food production potential in large parts of Africa and Asia. But there is no general consensus. Other scientists reported evidence for a major anthropogenic component in the desertification process (Garcia, 1981; Rubenson, 1991; Kiros, 1991). We also have to take into account that the transformation from arid and semiarid lands to desert during the Sahel drought was (at least partially) compensated by higher precipitation north of the Sahara (Stanhill, 1989). There is still a debate over whether the total desert area really expanded or just shifted southward into densely populated and more intensely cultivated areas, causing serious famines.

There is also evidence that the climatic risk of desertification in the arid and semiarid regions of Africa is amplified by unsustainable practices of agriculture, deforestation, and cattle ranging in this region. According to some authors, human mismanagement of land resources are major factors of desertification in the African Sahel (Stanhill, 1989). Finally, climate data show that the drought was not restricted to the famine areas of the Sahel. Much higher precipitation anomalies were observed during the same period in Asia and south of the equator. The absence of serious famines in these regions indicates that factors other than climatic conditions must have caused the great African famines (Lamb, 1982).

Climate conditions are certainly important factors restricting the area of profitable agriculture, but this does not mean that we are totally dependent on them. We can grow tropical fruits in cold climates or wheat in the desert. We can heat or cool, irrigate or drain cultures. These are matters of technology, food prices, and investment capital. Of course, farmers are still restricted by natural conditions, such as soils or climates, but they have also made great steps toward reducing their dependence. Between 1961 and 1990 Finland, which certainly does not have the most favorable climate for agriculture, increased its total production of cereals from 1.94 to 4.30 million metric tons (by almost doubling average yields from 1.88 to 3.54 metric tons per hectare).

Farmers in Sweden and Norway could also achieve spectacular increases of cereal production. By comparison, climatically privileged Argentina only increased its cereal yields from 1.41 to 2.22

metric tons per hectare, and Brazil's farmers could only improve yields from 1.35 to 1.76 metric tons per hectare. Obviously, there must be important conditions other than climate (and soils) which determine agricultural output. As we discuss in Section 10.3, agricultural technology plays a major role in agricultural output.

10.2.4   Fossil energy input

Most experts agree that we could boost food production in many developing regions if we modernize agriculture. Crop yields in Africa and Latin America are frequently 70 to 80 percent below the European average. Modern agricultural inputs, such as nitrogenous fertilizers, irrigation, pesticides, and agricultural machinery, could easily double or triple the output. There is no doubt that nitrogen fertilizer production must increase substantially to meet the food demand of the rapidly growing Third World population. Recently it was estimated that, until the year 2000, world nitrogen production must increase by 15 million metric tons, which is equivalent to the output of 10 large new plants each year (Constant and Sheldrick, 1992:115). With modern technology after-harvest losses could also be reduced. These losses are substantial in many developing countries. This modernization, however, is linked to one basic factor: commercial energy. Therefore, some authors have argued that (fossil) energy is the limiting factor for the global carrying capacity.[7]

However, available statistics and research on energy consumption in agriculture give no indication that fossil energy will be a limiting factor for agricultural modernization. Modern agriculture does not consume large amounts of commercial energy. On average, just 3 percent of worldwide fossil energy consumption is used in agriculture, and less than 1 percent is needed for the production of (nitrogenous) fertilizers (Smil, 1987). Most likely it takes more fossil energy to fly the doomsayers of the global food problem to their many international conferences than it would cost to produce adequate amounts of crop nutrients, pesticides, and fungicides for the stagnating agricultures in Africa and Latin America.

Some critics have rejected agricultural modernization as an option for increasing global food production on the basis of its supposedly high consumption of fossil energy. They obviously misunderstand energy statistics which indicate that some 70 to 80 percent of all commercial energy is used in the food sector. While these numbers might certainly be correct, they only indicate the overall fossil energy consumption in human food chains. Most of this energy, however, is not spent in agriculture, but used for packaging, cleaning, transport, conservation, bottling, canning, refrigeration, and preparation of food. We spend enormous amounts of fossil energy for post-harvest processing of food and ￼or running a most energy-consuming international food distribution network (Heilig, 1993). We have accepted the preposterous situation that, for instance, French or Austrian mineral water is bottled and shipped to the USA or Australia – completely unaware of the fact that a huge amount of fossil energy is needed to produce the bottles and ship the water halfway around the globe. Most of the energy consumption in the food sector has nothing to do with agriculture, but with lifestyles, trade regulations, state subsidies, or marketing strategies. If we would discontinue only the most absurd practices in the food processing and distribution sector, we could save much more fossil energy than is needed for modernization of agricultures in developing countries.

10.2.5 Conclusion: Are the natural resources limited?

If we take into account the creative potential of man, there is no foreseeable limitation to the basic natural resources of food production, which are space, water, climate conditions, solar energy, and man-made inputs. All these resources are either unlimited or can be expanded, better utilized, or redesigned to a very large extent. This might be the reason why several experts have denied any upper limit to population growth. The notion of "physical limits to growth" is a faulty concept. It makes it easy for agricultural technocrats to deny any basic problems in boosting the world food supply. Better arguments must be found to convince people that global food production may be limited.

10.3 Technical Limitations and Chances

Technology is certainly one of the most important determinants of the earth's carrying capacity. If the human race would have failed to invent agriculture some 10,000 years ago, only a few million people could have survived on this planet as hunters and gatherers. Cut and burn agriculture, which was the next step in the evolution of human sustenance, lifted the carrying capacity to at least twice or three times the level of primitive food collectors (Pimentel, 1984:4). The invention of soil cultivation and animal husbandry in stable settlements, which was the first agricultural revolution, prepared the way for the empires at the Nile, Euphrates, and Tigris and along the great Asian rivers.

Since World War II, the second – chemo-technological – revolution of agriculture has established a new level of sustenance. We are certainly capable of producing enough food for a world population of 5 to 6 billion; in fact we are facing severe problems of overproduction. Now, the important question is whether technologies will be available that could further increase the earth's carrying capacity? And what are the restrictions on and risks for their implementation?

10.3.1   Chances

Despite nearly hysterical criticism by some scholars, only the application of modern technology to agriculture will provide the necessary tools for increasing the earth's carrying capacity. Of course, we are not talking about simple-minded high-input agriculture which – for the sake of short-term increase of yields – would degrade soils, pollute groundwater, or harm the environment in some other way. We are talking about the numerous technical options that could improve yields, while at the same time reduce the environmental impact of agriculture. In general these technical options would be targeted to improve energy and water efficiency, refertilize exhausted soils, or minimize pesticide application. They would optimize crop rotation, adapt cultivation methods to local soil conditions, or prevent adverse effects of large-scale irrigation.

10.3.2   Fertilizer application

Many people are not aware that in some developing countries there is a threat to the environment, not because of too much use of modern technology, but because of too little. A case in point is fertilizer application. Especially in less developed Africa there is the problem of excessive nutrient removal or "nutrient mining" from soils.

While farmers try to respond to the growing food demand by using better crop seeds, reducing fallow periods, and so on, they have frequently failed to prevent the constant nutrient removal which is typical for modern crops. These require an essential supply of plant nutrients (such as nitrogen, phosphorus, and potassium), because with each harvest the farmer permanently removes some 100 to 150 kg per hectare of these major plant nutrients from the field. Therefore it is imperative that (artificial) fertilizers are applied to ensure sustained productivity of the soil. However, according to recent estimates, African farmers replace only some 50 percent of the harvest-related crop nutrient loss in their soil by applying (artificial) fertilizers. They permanently degrade their soils because of a less than optimal input of fertilizers (Constant and Sheldrick, 1992:114).

10.3.3 Irrigation

One possibility for increasing the earth's food production capacity is the expansion of irrigation. However, since two-thirds of global freshwater withdrawal is already used in agriculture it would be essential to implement only those technologies that improve irrigation efficiency, reduce water loss, and prevent environmental damage in irrigation schemes. Fortunately, techniques are available that could achieve these objectives. In a study on agricultural water efficiency Xie *et al.* (1983) conclude:

> Technologically, there is great potential to improve water use efficiency in both the agriculture and urban sectors. Despite demonstrated success in water saving and favorable experience in many developing countries, advanced technologies, such as sprinkler and drip systems, are applied to less than 3 percent of the world's irrigated lands.

We cannot go into detail, but list a few options that are considered rather promising by agricultural experts (most examples are from Stanhill, 1989).

An obvious technical option is the conservation of existing water resources (rather than the exploitation of new ones). In most irrigation schemes efficiency is incredibly low – usually less than 25 percent of the applied water is consumed by plants. In the USA it was possible to double water-use efficiency by simple means, such as laser land leveling and automatic pulsed water application.

Runoff control, cleaning, and recycling of agricultural waste-water could also contribute to the conservation of existing water resources.

A modification of cropping practices could save water or increase yields with available resources. For instance, farmers could switch to crops that can be grown during seasons of lower climatic water demand – which are the cooler and more humid seasons of the year. This simple measure could increase yields per unit of water by up to 50 percent. Only by carefully timing planting dates are substantial yield increases possible.

Insufficient leaching is one of the most serious dangers in irrigation agriculture.[8] To avoid problems farmers tend to apply more water to their irrigated fields than would be necessary. This frequently results in serious soil damage and has already destroyed large irrigation areas. Agricultural science and technology could prevent this irrigation mismanagement. There are methods for calculating and applying the amount of water needed for leaching requirements, which take into account soil salinity and evaporation.

Desertification and soil loss is frequently triggered by removal of significant areas of the vegetation cover – through overgrazing, cattle trampling, or deforestation. Intelligent land-use practices which avoid phases of total vegetation removal could substantially increase the local water availability. Afforestation on water catchment areas would also help to conserve water resources.

Modern technology could reduce water evaporation losses. The three major sources of water evaporation in agriculture are water storage and conveyances, irrigation systems, and plant evapotranspiration. All three can be reduced by technical means. There are several methods for reducing plant transpiration (Stanhill, 1986), but the gains are probably not very big and negative side effects are likely. Much, however, could be done to reduce evaporation in irrigation, such as better timing of water application and trickle irrigation. The evaporation from lakes and conveyances could be reduced by removing water plants and by building deep, instead of shallow, reservoirs. It was estimated that Lake Nasser, dammed by the Aswan Dam, is losing more water by evaporation than it makes available for irrigation (Stanhill, 1989:268).

Water harvesting is also a very attractive technical option for increasing local water resources for agriculture (Reij *et al.*, 1988). For example, special kinds of fences can be used at high altitude to "milk" water out of clouds, as is being done in some places in the Andes Mountains. A very cost-efficient method is cloud seeding. Certain chemicals are used to increase the number of condensation nuclei in the atmosphere which can trigger precipitation. Recently detailed studies were undertaken to assess the possibility of water harvesting in Burkina Faso, Kenya, Niger, Somalia, Sudan, and Zimbabwe (Critchley *et al.*, 1992). Rapid development of desalination technologies has also been observed. Prices for the desalination of water are declining rapidly as larger plants with better technology are set up (Wangnick, 1990).

Finally we can exploit previously neglected sources of water. Also several great rivers are practically unused for irrigation, such as the Shari and Logone rivers in Chad (Melamed, 1989). Their combined water flow is comparable to Egypt's withdrawal from the Nile. Well-designed irrigation schemes could make the desert bloom. Many arid and semiarid countries in Africa have vast resources of fertile soils. If these countries were able to apply proper irrigation technology to their lands (such as Israel did under similar climatic conditions), they could significantly increase food production.

10.3.4 Breeding, bioengineering

Apart from irrigation there are many technological options to boost rainfed agriculture. We have just started to explore the potential of bioengineering for increasing crop yields (Gasser and Fraley, 1989) and livestock efficiency (Pursel *et al.*, 1989). In a few years or decades the *creation* of new plants by techniques of bioengineering could replace traditional breeding methods. This would speed up the process of adapting animal and plant species to marginal environments, such as arid regions or wetlands. The new techniques could also lead to high-yield food and feed crops which bind nitrogen from the air and thus require less fertilizer inputs. There is also speculation about bioengineering plants and animals that have a natural resistance against many kinds of diseases; this would reduce the consumption of pesticides and animal medicines. Most experts agree that these techniques could possibly boost food production by orders of magnitude (Holló, 1986).

Photosynthesis is the complex and still poorly understood biochemical process by which plants build up biomass. It is fueled by solar radiation energy, and needs – among other things – atmospheric carbon, plant nutrients, and water as inputs. Until today not much could be done to increase the overall efficiency of the process – other than creating artificially CO_2-enriched atmospheres in greenhouses. However, there is a chance that recent advances in biochemistry and plant genetics can somewhat improve the net efficiency of photosynthesis by reducing the respiratory losses of CO_2 (Smil, 1987:165–166). The gains will probably not be spectacular in food grain, but it is possible that animal food with very high photosynthetic efficiency can be bioengineered.

10.3.5   Food processing

Much can be done to optimize post-harvest crop processing, drying, transport, and storage. In some parts of the Third World (such as India) enormous amounts of food and feed crops are lost to mice, rats, and fungi. Improper storage and transport frequently causes after-harvest losses of up to between 40 and 50 percent.

Much can also be done to improve the processing, transport, and preparation of food. Most people are not aware that some 90 percent of fossil energy use in the food chain is linked to nonagricultural activities – only 5 to 10 percent is consumed on the farm.

Also, if we were to reduce meat consumption in Europe and North America by a few percent we could save enormous amounts of grain. Finally, we could boost the productivity of agriculture by optimizing system integration of farms, such as linking energy generation (biogas) and livestock production.

10.3.6   "Frankenfood"

Finally, there is the option of synthetic food production. Those who shiver from abhorrence about this possibility have coined the term "frankenfood"; but they should think twice about this option. We are already using considerable amounts of artificial ingredients in our food. The yeast in our beer and bread is industrially produced in bioconverters, and citric acid and hundreds of food preservatives are manufactured by the biochemical industry.[9] The taste of fruit yogurt is usually a synthetically redesigned and enforced "natural" flavor. The colors of meat sausages or fruit juices often come straight from the chemical laboratory. In the not-too-distant future it is very possible that we will produce "synthetic" meat or vegetable protein in cell cultures. If this perspective affects your appetite, it is just because you are not familiar with what is currently done in slaughterhouses or chicken farms all over the world. Actually, it might be more humane to feed a 10 or 12 billion world population on bioengineered protein than to breed and kill billions of animals or convert the last natural ecosystems into paddy rice fields.

A big step toward synthetic food production was recently made in Japan, where 12 *lettuce factories* began production. They look like high-tech electronic laboratories; the *lettuce farmers* wear white gloves and breathing masks. The production sites are so-called clean rooms – hermetically isolated and sterilized chambers which prevent introduction of fungi, insects, and crop diseases. There is no soil, rainfall, or sun. The lettuce is grown on a synthetic fiber, the roots are automatically sprayed with fertilizer-enriched water, and radiation energy (for photosynthesis) is applied by special electric lights. Lettuce output is 10 times that of natural cultivation and highly profitable. The taste of this high-tech lettuce cannot be distinguished from the naturally grown plant. Rash critics might jump to the conclusion that this high-tech production is rather energy-inefficient as compared with conventional cultivation, but this is most likely not the case. More fossil energy is used to control the production environment (heating, lighting, irrigation), but much less is needed for production of pesticides, fungicides, weed killers, and insecticides because of the sterile growing conditions.

Moreover, high-tech cultivation needs much less space and can be located close to the consumers, such as in the middle of a city. Thus, enormous amounts of fossil energy for transportation, conservation, and storage can be saved. (Usually, the fossil energy consumption needed for the production of lettuce and other vegetables is a small fraction of the energy that is spent in packaging, transportation, and storage of the product.) In some Japanese supermarkets lettuce is already produced directly on the spot and *harvested* by the sales personnel according to demand. It is very likely that the urban agglomerates of the 21st century will be supplied locally with vegetables and fruits. This is not science fiction. Large proportions of the tomatoes, cucumbers, zucchini, and eggplants consumed in Europe are already produced in a similar way in the high-tech greenhouses of the Netherlands.

10.3.7 Limitations

After reading the previous section one might have the impression that technology is the "golden key" to open the earth's unlimited resources of food, but this is not the case. Agro-science and agro-technology have limitations and dangers.

First, there are unintended side effects of agricultural technology. Especially the input-oriented large-scale technology of the 1970s and early 1980s has caused many problems, such as soil degradation, over-fertilization, salination or water logging in irrigated soils, groundwater pollution, and toxification of agricultural workers. These problems are usually caused by lack of know-how, poor management techniques, faulty maintenance of irrigation systems and agricultural machinery, or corruption and ignorance.

Second, we have consequences of agricultural modernization and expansion that were well predicted but seem to be inevitable. When farmers transform natural ecosystems into cropland or meadows, they inevitably disturb their biological balance. A new, artificial balance has to be re-established. This action requires careful planning and proper long-term management of soils, water sources, and infrastructure. One of the greatest threats to natural ecosystems – such as the tropical rain forests – is the "unconfined cut-down, plant, and move" exploitation by poorly trained, inexperienced farmers (or ignorant and cynical agribusinesses).

Third, there is the problem of education and sociocultural adaptation. Not every culture and ethnic group is flexible enough to learn new ways of food production. Chinese farmers, for instance, quickly adapted to using modern technology when the government abandoned many restrictions of the communist economy during the 1970s. Within a few years China experienced one of the most spectacular increases in nitrogenous fertilizer consumption and tractor use – and a tripling of cereal production. Compare this to Nigeria, the oil-wealthy African nation. The country has all the resources (including capital, land, water, and fossil energy for fertilizers) to make it the breadbasket of Africa, but agriculture has stagnated for the last three decades.

Finally, there are enormous costs for implementing a more efficient agricultural technology. We are not only referring to farmers who need investment capital. There is also the need for upgrading the general infrastructure. Agricultural modernization requires a steady supply of inputs (fertilizers, water for irrigation, crop sanitation products) for which working transportation and distribution systems have to be implemented. There are also significant social costs. Agricultural modernization inevitably increases the pressures on the rural labor force. Both farmers and landless agricultural workers have to adapt to new methods and conditions. They must accept retraining and technical education, and there are always groups of the population that lack the necessary flexibility for change. It is also very likely that agricultural modernization will produce rural unemployment, even if labor-intensive production methods are applied.

10.4   Ecological Limits

Ecological constraints and feedback mechanisms are frequently considered limiting factors of growing food production (Chen, 1990). Currently scientists are discussing four types of problems. First, the expansion of agricultural areas and increases in the catch of fish could destroy large ecological systems. This would lead to a reduction of biodiversity in the fauna and flora and diminish the global gene pool. Second, the increase of agricultural inputs, such as fertilizers, pesticides, fungicides, weed killers, and other chemicals, could pollute groundwater bodies, lakes, and the sea. It could change the chemistry of the soils and speed up soil erosion. Third, genetically modified plants (and animals) could be a danger to the natural environment. Finally, a significant increase in food production could even change the global climate; emissions of greenhouse gases, such as methane, could dramatically increase due to the expansion of livestock and paddy rice production. What evidence do we have that these ecological consequences are in fact unavoidable?

10.4.1 Shrinking of natural ecological systems

There is little doubt that feeding an ever-growing number of people will further diminish the living space of other species. For many kinds of wild animals we leave only small niches of natural ecosystems. This competitive race between man and other living creatures (including plants) is probably unavoidable. It seems to be an evolutionary constant. The best we can hope for is that we will be able to preserve key natural habitats in order to stop further extinction of species. The only realistic protection of the planet's natural "gene pools" and "green lungs," such as the Amazonas, is a combination of strictly managed natural parks and careful economic utilization with a minimum of environmental damage. If we want to reserve the tropical rain forests exclusively for butterfly catchers, anthropologists, and botanists in the face of millions of landless hungry farmers, we have to answer some tough questions on our moral standards.

Food production, however, is not the only activity that tends to diminish the natural ecosystem. The spread of human settlements, infrastructures, and industries must be added to a possible expansion of agricultural land. Undoubtedly, the human race is changing the surface of the earth with unprecedented speed.

10.4.2 Soil degradation (acidification, soil loss) and water pollution

Many agricultural practices can have a destructive impact on the environment. Excessive use of fertilizers can contaminate the groundwater; crop monocultures and unsuitable tillage practices can aggravate soil erosion; the use of pesticides poses health risks on farm workers; and the runoff of pesticides can pollute groundwater. There are concerns that "artificial" pest and weed control can trigger the emergence of resistant animal and plant species, which in turn would require the further increase of pesticides. In some parts of Europe we have industrial-size livestock production systems which produce enormous amounts of manure. If the manure is not properly processed and is only spread in large quantities on crop fields and meadows, it can run off into rivers and lakes, seep into the groundwater, or increase the already existing nitrogen overload of the soil. In

Africa's pastoral societies overgrazing and trampling by cattle is an enormous problem.

These environmental risks of agriculture are well known and certainly diminish the actual carrying capacity of many regions. A recent study conducted by the International Soil Reference and Information Centre in Wageningen has estimated that agricultural activities have caused moderate to extreme soil degradation of 1.2 billion hectares worldwide – which is about the size of China and India (Oldemann *et al.*, 1990). This does not mean that the soils are completely unproductive, but that their natural fertility is diminished. The impact of agriculture on the water is also well documented: some 25 percent of the population in the European Union is already drinking water with a nitrate level greater than the recommended maximum of 25 milligrams per liter (Gardner, 1990:5). Pesticides can be found in the groundwater of 34 states in the USA.

These problems of intensive crop and livestock production are serious, but there is no reason why we should not be able to solve them. With modern technology, agricultural know-how, and better agricultural policy it would be possible to expand food production, while reducing its environmental impact. A good example is Europe's agriculture. Contrary to widespread belief, the farmers did not just proceed with their practices of overfertilization and mindless use of pesticides (which they in fact had adopted during most of the 1970s and 1980s).

If the FAO statistics are correct the consumption of nitrogenous fertilizers significantly declined during the past six or seven years in most European countries, while production increased. In all of Europe the consumption of nitrogenous fertilizers fell from some 15.1 in 1983–1984 to about 13.6 million metric tons in 1990–1991 – a decline of more than 10 percent (FAO, 1992:56). In West Germany farmers consumed 1.52 million metric tons in 1985; four years later consumption was down to 1.48 million metric tons (FAO, 1994). The fertilizer input in kilograms per hectare of cropland fell from 464 to 404 between 1977–1979 and 1987–1989 (World Resources Institute/United Nations Environment Programme/United Nations Development Programme, 1992:275).

Modern methods of crop management have tried to optimize, rather than maximize, the input of crop nutrients and pesticides.

We also have to take into account that in large parts of the Third World, especially in Africa, fertilizer consumption is a small fraction of what is typical in Europe or some Asian countries. Even if these farmers doubled or tripled fertilizer consumption they would be far from the levels that are typical for high-input agriculture.

10.4.3   Risks of genetic engineering and advanced breeding practices

Previously we mentioned that genetic engineering could be a great opportunity for increasing food production, especially if we could breed drought- and pest-resistant crops, but it could also be a danger. There was much concern that genetically manipulated plants and animals could *escape* and drive out other natural species from their habitat. Also several other unintended side effects have been under discussion.   However, governments in Europe and North America have recently loosened restrictions for field experiments with genetically modified plants. They obviously consider the risks rather low as compared with possible benefits.

10.4.4   Climate change

In theory, there are two links between climate change and global food production. First, the expansion and intensification of agriculture, which is necessary for sustenance of the growing world population, could be a driving force for global warming. Emissions of methane (CH_4), which is the third most important greenhouse gas, could increase when livestock and paddy rice areas are expanded. Livestock and paddy rice areas are important sources of anthropogenic methane emission to the atmosphere (Heilig, 1994b). Agricultural mechanization could boost CO_2 emissions. The second link between climate change and agriculture works the other way: global warming could reduce (or increase) agricultural output. One of the most detailed approaches to the problem was IIASA's integrated climate impact assessment which – for the first time – analyzed not only first-order consequences of global warming to agriculture, but also second-order impacts (Parry *et al.*, 1988). This is not the place to analyze this major scientific study, but it should be pointed out that Parry and Carter (1988) are very cautious about the predictive validity of their research. In a summary of results they write:

> The estimates reported in this volume are *not predictions* of future effects. Present-day uncertainties and inaccuracies in simulating the behavior of the world's climate and in evaluating the agricultural implications of climatic change do not permit realistic predictions to be made. Furthermore, we cannot forecast what technological, economic and social developments in agriculture will occur over the next half century. The estimates should therefore be considered as measures of the *present-day sensitivity* of agriculture to climate change. [Parry and Carter, 1988:69]

No doubt, there are links between climate and agriculture, but it is also obvious that these links are not just simple one-way causations. They work through a complex system of intermediate variables, which not only can modify their strengths, but also can turn them around from positive to negative (and vice versa). The most important intermediate variables are the availability of advanced technology, the existing economic arrangements, the political situation, and the level of education and training among farmers. If farmers have no access to advanced technology, are hampered by poor education and training, or are restricted by stupid economic arrangements, a worsening of climate conditions (such as the increase of drought or unstable precipitation) can seriously diminish agricultural output. However, the climate change could also have the opposite effect: it could trigger the development of advanced agricultural methods, which in the end are even more productive. Israel's and Finland's farmers have demonstrated that high productive agriculture is possible under harsh, and diverse, agro-climatic conditions.

Our knowledge is too limited to decide whether the projected climate change would reduce global carrying capacity. However, we believe that a possible (but by no means certain) global warming would be a gradual process, which would give us enough time to adapt the socioeconomic framework of agriculture and implement new technologies in order to counterbalance its negative effects.

10.5   Social, Economic, and Political Dimensions of Carrying Capacity

For decades the scientific discussion on the food–population nexus has avoided a key issue. While scientists spent their time elaborating hypotheses with rather weak empirical evidence (such as the law of diminishing returns) or engaged in intellectual self-gratification by building all kinds of complex models of global carrying capacity, they mostly ignored the political, social, and economic dimension of food production. The news media, however, reported the facts on a day-by-day basis: in most cases it was colossal policy failure which caused widespread undernutrition and famine during the past four decades. Agricultural stagnation and food deficits were usually unrelated to a shortage of soil, water, rainfall, fossil energy, or investment capital. They were also unrelated to high population growth. Typically, food crises could be found where social, cultural, and economic conditions have prevented agricultural modernization, as in large parts of Africa.

There are so many sociocultural constraints to agricultural modernization that we could dedicate an entire chapter to this problem. Due to space limitation we mention only a few of the most important factors.

Policy failure. The most serious famines in recent times had nothing to do with population pressure, crop failure, or natural disasters. They were directly and intentionally triggered by unscrupulous regimes as a means for executing their political strategies as the Khmer Rouge did in Cambodia (Becker, 1986; Barnett *et al.*, 1980), accepted as necessary side effects of coercive development measures as in China's Great Leap Forward during the Mao Tse-Tung era (Bernstein, 1984), or simply emerged from cynical ignorance because the regimes were more interested in other political and military issues as in most civil wars of Africa from Ethiopia to Somalia (Griffith, 1988).

False economic policy and corruption. The stagnation of agricultural production in some parts of the Third World – especially in sub-Saharan Africa and in parts of Latin America – was closely related to the notorious inefficiency, massive corruption, unbelievable incompetence, and ideological blindness of political leaders and their administration. Many of these incompetent regimes in Africa simply transplanted the Soviet model of a centrally planned command economy to their preindustrial society. They eliminated traditional market mechanisms by fixing food prices at ridiculously low levels to appease urban masses (Bale, 1981). They collectivized most of the fertile land (as in Ethiopia) and forced farmers to sell their production to state-owned trade agencies for prices that were close to production costs (as in Tanzania). The ideologically legitimized lack of incentives discouraged farmers and prevented agricultural modernization (Bates, 1981). In Latin America military regimes stabilized feudalistic rural societies and prevented agricultural modernization. Very often these disasters of agricultural policy were joined by a general failure of development policy. The political and administrative elites in many developing countries of Africa and Latin America did not do much to modernize infrastructure; they neglected technical education and training and blocked industrial modernization. Huge amounts of development aid were wasted on expensive but useless prestige projects or simply vanished into bank accounts of the small ruling class. Even rich countries, such as exporters of oil and other natural resources (Nigeria), neglected the agricultural sector.

Social inequality. There is still chronic undernutrition and hunger among certain groups of the population in food surplus countries, as in India or Indonesia. However, this kind of food problem can also be found in highly developed, affluent countries, such as the USA. It is a problem of income distribution and has nothing to do with the availability of food. Lack of entitlements to acquire adequate food in the lowest classes of society is the cause of the problem. The class and cast structure of some societies also prevents adequate distribution of agricultural land.

Development of human resources (health, education). Much land in the Third World cannot be cultivated in the most efficient way because farmers are suffering from chronic diseases (malaria, river blindness) or are hampered by a lack of education and agricultural know-how. Several studies, for instance, have shown the impact of malaria among rural populations on food production (Bradley, 1991). A dramatic situation is evolving in parts of Africa and Asia (Thailand) because of AIDS. The spread of this disease among rural populations in East Africa has already made a measurable impact on food production (Norse, 1991). Is it not rather absurd that we spend considerable efforts on the collection of soil inventories to determine Africa's carrying capacity, while whole villages in Africa are wiped out by a virus infection?

Traditions.   Many traditions help people improve their sustenance. Agricultural societies have developed numerous rules, habits, taboos, and traditions to prevent food crises, maintain soil fertility, or improve the environment for the next generation. Consider the traditional rules of crop rotation or the tradition to plant a tree on certain occasions. Unfortunately some cultural values also prevent agricultural modernization and full utilization of resources. For instance, in most of Africa agriculture is considered low-prestige women's work. It is part of their household duties – in addition to cooking and caring for children. Whenever a man can afford to avoid working on a field, he will do so. This traditional disregard of food production, deeply embedded in African men, can also be found in development plans and investment decisions of African governments.

   Culture and food are closely related. A society can only develop sciences, technology, and arts when it has a highly productive system of food supply. As long as everyone is busy collecting or hunting food, no real modern development is possible. We can study this link between cultural development and food in early agricultural societies that originated in the alluvial lowlands and river floodplains of Africa and Asia. These ancient people developed complex social and economic systems, which included bureaucratic hierarchies and specialized professions. The social differentiation was necessary to solve typical problems of agriculture, such as water management or storage administration. The societies also institutionalized mechanisms of conflict resolution – for instance, to settle conflicts of water distribution and land ownership. They developed cognitive systems which helped them to understand and predict the natural cycles of floods and rainfalls. They also managed to establish a stable (if not always peaceful) relationship with their neighbors. This social and cultural framework was essential for making their agriculture prosper – and in turn, the highly productive agriculture also propelled social and cultural development. In his many books on Indonesia, Clifford Geertz (1963) has studied these dialectics of food and sociocultural development.

10.6   Discussion

From a system-analytic point of view, most studies on carrying capacity are surprisingly unrealistic in their economic and social assumptions. They usually define carrying capacity in terms of direct agricultural self-supply – as a population supporting capacity of land, given a certain level of agricultural technology. This concept might be sufficient to describe traditional rural societies, which lack a clear division of labor, international trade, political organization, science, and industry. But this concept is inadequate for today's functionally differentiated societies and economies. Here the division of labor expands from the household to the national economy and the international market. In the past, Arab nomads in the deserts of Saudi Arabia could feed their families quite well from the scarce land by selling their oil resources on the world market – for instance, to French farmers, who in turn produced a significant proportion of their meat supply.

Today, the supply of food, which once was a simple process of collecting, hunting, or self-sufficient local agriculture, has evolved into a complex international network of production activities, industrial processes, market and price mechanisms, trade arrangements, food policies, and distribution channels. At each stage of this widely expanding food chain we might find conditions that could limit the food supply of a population. It might be a shortage of fertile soils or water; it might be adverse climate conditions; or it could be a lack of fossil energy for fertilizer production. But the limitation might also arise from widespread analphabetism and a lack of agricultural know-how in a population; it could be caused by the persistence of inefficient market structures and production regulations; or it might be the consequence of international trade restrictions.

The carrying capacity of the earth depends on its natural resources or the level of technology and on the quality of our worldwide economic, social, and political arrangements. Land, water, climate, and energy are just four parameters in a more complex set of equations for calculating a measure of carrying capacity. These equations must describe the world as a system of interdependencies – a system of exchange mechanisms (food trade) and complementary production activities, which can counterbalance regional variations in the density of natural and human resources. Today, carrying capacity cannot be defined at a purely local or regional level. It cannot be calculated from the availability of natural resources. We know that the natural supporting potential of land can only be realized if there are educated and trained people who can live in peace, who have access to (world) markets, who can use modern agricultural and industrial techniques and inputs, who are not punished and unmotivated by a centrally planned command economy.

10.7   Conclusion

How many people can be fed on earth if we take into account technical, ecological, political, and social constraints? Most experts would probably agree that we could sustainably supply the current 5.5 billion world population. At the moment European governments are pressing their farmers to reduce food production; grain is cheap on international markets; and Asian countries are harvesting bumper crops year after year. The scandal of famines in Africa is not a result of agriculture approaching carrying capacity; it is mostly a consequence of massive policy failures, corruption, ethnic conflicts, ignorance, and incompetence of ruling elites. There are different and more complex reasons for widespread undernutrition in some parts of Asia, but they have nothing to do with natural limitations. Certain groups of the population lack the means to acquire food, which would be available in principle. Here we obviously have the socioeconomic and cultural problems of uneven distribution of entitlements. Latin America has vast resources of land, freshwater, and – at least in some cases – oil money. The real problem is the feudalistic distribution of land which prevents a more efficient agriculture.

But could we also feed 10 or 15 billion people? Most likely, if we can prevent (civil) wars with soldiers plundering harvests or devastating crop fields with land mines; if we can stop the stupidity of collectivization and central planning in agriculture; if we can agree on free (international) trade for agricultural products; if we redistribute agricultural land to those that actually use it for production; if we provide credits, training, and high-yield seeds to poor farmers; if we can adapt the modern high-yield agriculture to the agro-climatic and sociocultural conditions of arid regions and use it carefully to avoid environmental destruction; if we implement optimal water management and conservation practices. If we do all this during the next few decades, we would certainly be able to feed a doubled or tripled world population.

There are many "ifs" in our conclusion. Almost certainly, business as usual will not provide the conditions which are necessary for feeding the world population of the 21st century. We need fundamental political, social, and economic changes, especially in Africa, Latin America, and parts of Asia. Only a democratization in these regions will open the gates for the development of human resources, for better education and training, for private economic initiatives, and for functioning markets.

There are positive and negative signs that this change will be possible: the governments of China, India, and some other Asian countries have removed economic controls which prevented agricultural productivity; they have provided a relatively stable political environment; and they have actively supported agricultural modernization (the green revolution). Consequently, they doubled or tripled domestic food production within two or three decades. Many African governments, on the other hand, neglected the agricultural sector. They introduced rigid methods of central planning, suppressed free markets, and collectivized or coercively resettled farmers. They did not stop the devastation of agricultural areas due to civil wars, and they mostly failed in introducing modern techniques of crop production and livestock management. It is no wonder that per capita food production stagnated or declined in most parts of Africa during the past three decades.

Let us do a simple exercise: How many people can be fed in Sudan? The FAO estimated that at a low input level the country's arable land could sustain nearly 60 million people – 3.7 times the actual population of 1975 (which was 16 million); a high-input

agriculture could feed 1.036 billion Sudanese, which would be twice
the actual population of Africa. All we hear from Sudan, however, are reports of persistent famines and slow degeneration of the
agricultural system. Theoretically, Sudan could be the breadbasket of Africa; in practical terms it is one of the continent's famine
areas. On the other hand, the FAO has estimated that Algeria's
agro-climatic conditions could support only 7 million people at low
inputs and 24.6 million at medium inputs. Currently Algeria has
a population of 25 million and not much can be heard about food
shortages in this country. Given the substantial restraints and difficulties that can slow down or even prevent the theoretically almost
unlimited increase of global food production, we have to lower our
expectations. It is unlikely that the world food problem will be
solved within the next decades, despite the fact that it would be
possible in theory. There are serious social, economic, and political
limits to growth.

We should come back to the initial concept that visualizes the
problem of carrying capacity in a pipe with a declining diameter.
Using this image, we can conclude that the key for balancing people
and food is the speed with which the social, economic, cultural, and
political constraints are pushed back that hinder people to utilize
the full potential of the earth's food resources in a sustainable way.
If we can open the pipe quickly enough, if we can stop some of our
collective stupidities, we could produce more than enough food for
the people of the 21st century. The carrying capacity of the earth
is not a natural constant – it is a dynamic equilibrium, essentially
determined by human action.

10.8   The Discussion Continues

Two major books have recently been published on the issue of the
carrying capacity of the earth. These books differ from each other
in intention, methodology, empirical data base, and analytical approach, but both are important contributions to the ongoing debate on the world's carrying capacity. Do they provide any new
arguments or data which would make it necessary to revise the conclusions in this chapter? The authors of these books might see it

differently, but I consider their analyses quite similar to my conclusions. Of course, both books had access to new data, and the
authors have applied analytical techniques and models which are
far more advanced and rigorous than those I used. One can learn
a great deal from the authors' analytical insights and the wealth of
new empirical evidence and agro-economical considerations. But, in
the end, both books answer the question, How many people can be
fed on earth?, in a way which confirms my arguments.

The first book is an updated edition of the well-known FAO
study, *World Agriculture: Towards 2000* (Alexandratos, 1995). It
assesses world agricultural prospects to the year 2010; in some cases
even to 2025. An international team of highly acclaimed (mostly
agricultural and economic) experts selected, evaluated, and analyzed empirical data, mostly from the FAO's statistical system, in
order to model the world's agricultural potential and project future
trends in food supply. The book is packed with facts on (changing)
biophysical conditions of agricultural production (such as land and
water resources, crop yields, livestock productivity). Fortunately, it
is not restricted to this technical analysis of the world's agricultural
potential. There are also detailed studies of agro-economical and
socio-political factors, such as "international trade issues and policies" and "rural poverty." One of the most important sections of the
book, however, is the discussion of agricultural pressures on the environment. One chapter explicitly deals with the trade-off between
necessary agricultural development and environmental degradation.
The book carefully investigates prospects and technological requirements for putting world agriculture on a sustainable path.

It is risky to try to summarize the results of a 488-page book,
but I consider the main message of this FAO study to be that we
will be – despite numerous pressures, constraints, and risks – able
to feed the growing world population in the foreseeable future. We
have not reached, and will not reach during the next two or three
decades, insurmountable biophysical limits. The only sector where
global natural resource constraints are imminent is the sector of
fisheries (but even here we can anticipate alternatives, such as fish
farming). This optimistic outlook, however, is only possible under
certain conditions. We can improve future food security only if we
bring modern agricultural technology and management techniques

to underdeveloped agricultures and if – and only if – we eliminate
social and economic conditions (at both the national and international levels) that constrain farmers from fully utilizing their soils
and livestock. Food security also requires socioeconomic development to give the poor better access to available food supplies. In
concluding remarks the FAO team writes:

> There appear to be no insurmountable resource and technology
> constraints at the global level that would stand in the way of
> increasing world food supplies by as much as required by the
> growth of effective demand. And, on balance, there is scope for
> such growth in production to be achieved while taking measures
> to shift agriculture on to a more sustainable production path.

The second book, *How Many People Can the Earth Support*, is a
landmark study by Joel E. Cohen (1995). As a theoretical biologist,
mathematician, and demographer (to list just a few of his talents),
Cohen applies his analytical rigor to more dimensions of the problem
than most other authors. He first analyzes past long-term trends
in world population growth. This analysis is essential, because it
reminds us to consider the uniqueness of the present demographic
situation and the exceptional challenges we face. He then reviews
the methods of projecting future population change – a sobering
exercise that highlights fundamental uncertainties in demographic
projections and a few, rather irrelevant, facts we know for sure. The
main part of the book begins with a review of eight major studies
that have attempted to estimate the human carrying capacity of the
earth. It is followed by a survey that compiles estimates of carrying
capacity from 1679 to the early 1990s. Cohen reports a most striking
finding:

> There is no clear increasing or decreasing trend in the estimated
> upper bounds [of carrying capacity]. ... [In fact,] the scatter
> among the estimates seems to increase with the passage of time,
> as more and more extreme (both high and low) estimates are
> proposed, challenged and defended. [Cohen, 1995:214]

Cohen's interpretation of this growing diversity is carefully phrased:

> The increasing scatter, or at least absence of convergence, is the
> opposite of the progressive refinement and convergence that would
> ideally occur as time passes when a constant of nature like the
> speed of light or Avogadro's number is measured.

I arrive at a more drastic conclusion: This lack of scientific progress indicates that we have probably used the wrong approach to deal with the earth's carrying capacity.

My last sentence in Section 10.7 of this chapter also points to this problem: The carrying capacity of the earth is not a natural constant – it is a dynamic equilibrium, essentially determined by human action. The reason for highly diverse estimates of carrying capacity is that human choices determine, to a great extent, how many people can be fed on earth. The estimated number will vary depending on the type of food people will choose to eat and which (international) system of food distribution and trade they will implement. There will be great differences in carrying capacity depending on the technology and management farmers will apply; but carrying capacity will also vary with the level of environmental change or degradation people will tolerate. Because of these future human choices we cannot base our estimates of carrying capacity on demographic arithmetic and quantification of natural constraints alone. We must develop conditional models and projections that take into account the element of human action. All we can say at this time is that "if future choices are thus-and-so, then the human carrying capacity is likely to be so-and-so" (Cohen, 1995).

Is this the end of the story? I don't think so. This is just the end of the agro-ecological approach to the problem of determining carrying capacity. Cohen's book is a brilliant dissection of all the failed efforts to quantify the earth's carrying capacity by estimating natural constraints. It is packed with critical (and sometimes sarcastic) comments on all those gross abstractions, (unspoken) assumptions, and far-reaching *ceteris paribus* clauses which are necessary to calculate carrying capacity but ignore important economic, social, cultural, and political factors of the problem. Conditional models of carrying capacity are a last attempt to save the failing natural science approach to solving an essentially social, economic, and political problem. These models just "download" the complexity of our socioeconomic world into long arrays of rather arbitrary conditions. In the end, we are as clever as before. We have to decide which future human choices (defined as model conditions) we consider most likely. Cohen draws a similar conclusion. In his last chapter, in which he is "looking beyond the next hill," he deals with social and economic arrangements that would enable us to actually increase the earth's real carrying capacity by improving our societies and economies:

> I aim in this book not to sell any particular approaches, but to promote a view of the Earth's human carrying capacity that is more modest, more in touch with a complex reality and more likely to enable you to think through your own choices of action than many of the simpler alternative views. [Cohen, 1995:380]

The carrying capacity of our earth is a problem of political planning, education, social balance, economic restructuring, and institutional efficiency. We are far from physical or biological limits if – but only if – we use creativity, social responsibility, economic initiative, and political vision to restructure still highly inefficient agricultural and international food trade systems. Where we do not have enough fertile soils we can educate young people to design and produce computer chips (as in Malaysia) which will provide them with the means to buy food on international markets. Where we have economic arrangements that discourage farmers (as in former centrally planned command agriculture) we can introduce incentives and more efficient, decentralized planning. Where we have environmental degradation from high-input agricultural practices we can introduce legislation to ensure that pesticide or fertilizer use; we can reduce the environmental impact of industrial-type pig farming by limiting livestock per hectare of land. No natural law prevents us from changing absurd agricultural subsidies in Europe's Common Agricultural Policy; no physical constant stands in the way of social and economic reforms in India that would reduce poverty (a major factor of food insecurity today and in the future). We can establish or improve institutions, such as early warning systems and international emergency food reserves, to deal with sudden food deficits that are due to war, droughts, cyclones, and other unexpected events. And, above all, we can plan and reduce the size of families in countries where rapid population growth prevents economic and social reforms.

Notes

[1] Malthus was not the first scholar dealing with the problem, but probably the most influential.

[2] Usually the total solar radiation input of earth is seen as a (near) constant. However, at the soil level, it can certainly vary considerably with specific atmospheric conditions, such as water vapor and dust concentration in the higher atmosphere, as well as cloud cover conditions in the lower atmosphere.

[3] Clark (1967) estimated that the earth could support between 47 billion people on an American-type diet and 147 billion on a cereal-subsistence diet.

[4] These data are from the 1992–1993 WRI report. The estimates of soil constraints in the 1990–1991 report were even higher for most countries.

[5] River flows from other countries are an unreliable source of water supply, since they can be influenced by neighboring countries. Therefore we compare only "annual internal renewable water resources," such as underground aquifers.

[6] The situation within this continentlike country is, however, different. There is water scarcity in the northeastern agricultural areas.

[7] In 1974 *The Futurist* wrote that Lester Brown "refuses to own an automobile and uses public transportation, so that more energy can go into food production" (cited in Smil, 1987:100).

[8] In irrigation systems a certain proportion of the water applied is not intended for plants, but for washing out (leaching) soluble salts which are concentrated in the topsoil by evapotranspiration. Especially in arid and semiarid areas this practice is absolutely essential. Otherwise soil salinity would build up to toxic levels. Frequently farmers apply too much water for leaching, which not only is a waste of the resource, but also results in serious soil damage.

[9] This industry is highly profitable; Austria's richest man made his fortune by producing citric acid for the European food industry.

Part IV

Future Fertility and Mortality in Industrialized Countries

The nature of uncertainties in fertility and mortality in today's industrialized countries is very different from that in developing regions. For mortality the relevant questions are: What will happen to old-age mortality? Is life expectancy already approaching an upper limit? These are highly controversial issues. Medical science does not provide a convincing reason to assume that a limit will soon be reached. In our scenarios this optimistic view is translated into an assumed three-year increase in life expectancy per decade. The alternative view of stagnating improvements, due to a possible increase in adverse conditions (stress, toxification, risky behavior, etc.) is reflected in the low assumption of a general one-year improvement per decade.

The future direction of fertility change is unclear in industrialized countries. On the one hand, fertility could further decline if certain social trends such as increasing individualism and consumerism continue. On the other hand, fertility may increase to replacement level or above if certain counterforces, such as community orientation, become stronger than they are now and social services are improved to make it easier for women to combine motherhood and work. However, more factors seem to point toward lower fertility than toward higher fertility, but the issue remains unsettled. This uncertainty can be translated into possible low values of 1.3–1.4 children and high values of 2.1–2.3 children per woman depending on the specific region.

Chapter 11

Future Reproductive Behavior in Industrialized Countries

Wolfgang Lutz

For countries that have fully passed through the fertility transition from high fertility to modern family limitation, there is no convincing theory on what should happen to fertility trends in the future. This is not for lack of trying. Approaching the issue from several different disciplines, scientists have made innumerable efforts to analyze and understand past trends and to derive from these hypotheses about the future.

Economists tend to look at fertility fluctuations, trying to discover regularities in the sequence of ups and downs and associations with economic cycles. Demographers have given much attention to the comparison of period and cohort fertility rates. Sociologists and psychologists have studied myriads of survey data and developed theories of increasing individualization and changing gender roles. Family historians have pointed at the changing structure and function of the family. And the medical profession has contributed to the issue by looking at sub-fecundity and effectiveness of contraceptives. In sum, there are many interesting ideas and hypotheses that tend to refer to specific aspects of reproductive behavior, but they are of limited value for predicting the final outcome, namely, age-specific fertility rates in the years to come.

The remarks made in this chapter are based on the huge literature available on the determinants of fertility in modern industrialized countries which cannot be exhaustively summarized here (see Kiernan, 1993, for a more detailed discussion). The chapter is guided by the goal of determining reasonable and defendable assumptions about alternative high and low paths of future fertility trends in modern industrialized countries. In doing this, we first look at unambiguous empirical evidence from past years, and then list possible arguments that could be used to support alternative assumptions of either further declining fertility rates or increasing fertility levels. The final section focuses on how these alternative forces could work in a heterogeneous society and result in specific assumed fertility levels.

11.1   Recent Trends in Partnership Formation and Dissolution

Human procreation is intimately linked to the institution of marriage in virtually all historical and contemporary societies. In some populations this link has been stronger than in others, and recently, in highly industrialized countries, new forms of partnership have been spreading that directly compete with traditional marriage. With respect to fertility, this situation raises the obvious question whether such changes in living arrangements and partnership have affected and will affect the average number of children born to women and men. For this reason we must first look at changes in the marital-status composition of industrialized populations.

Over recent decades the proportion of the married adult population has declined markedly in many industrialized countries. *Table 11.1* gives these proportions for 1960 and 1985 in selected European countries. This decline was most significant in Sweden, where the proportion of married adult women declined from more than 60 percent in 1960 to only 48 percent in 1985. The decline for men was of similar magnitude. The decline is mostly attributable to increases in the never-married and divorced proportions. A similar pattern can be found in the other Scandinavian countries and in the UK. In former West Germany (FRG) the decline in the proportion married was much steeper for men than for women, which is largely explained by a significant increase in the never-married male population. Of the countries listed, Italy shows a slight increase between 1960 and 1985 which is due to the fact that the decline in marriage

Table 11.1. Marital-status distribution of the population above age 15 in selected European countries: 1960 and 1985.

Country	Women				Men			
	Never married	Mar-ried	Di-vorced	Wid-owed	Never married	Mar-ried	Di-vorced	Wid-owed
France								
1960	20.7	60.3	2.5	16.6	27.3	66.4	1.9	4.3
1985	24.5	56.6	4.6	14.3	31.5	61.9	3.6	3.1
FRG								
1960	22.7	57.7	2.6	17.0	26.8	67.9	1.5	3.9
1985	24.4	54.3	4.4	16.9	33.5	59.8	3.5	3.2
Hungary								
1960	17.3	64.4	2.6	15.7	23.7	71.5	1.4	3.4
1985	14.2	61.5	6.9	17.4	23.1	68.0	5.0	3.8
Italy								
1960	29.1	58.0	0.0	12.9	34.4	62.1	0.0	3.5
1985	24.5	61.1	0.4	14.0	30.8	65.8	0.3	3.1
Netherlands								
1960	26.9	63.0	1.3	8.8	30.7	64.9	0.8	3.6
1985	26.4	57.6	4.8	11.2	33.5	60.0	3.9	2.6
Sweden								
1960	26.2	60.7	3.0	10.1	31.6	61.9	2.3	4.3
1985	30.0	48.4	8.7	12.9	38.7	50.4	7.3	3.5
UK								
1960	21.9	63.6	0.9	13.6	25.6	70.0	0.6	3.9
1985	24.0	56.4	5.7	13.9	31.4	60.2	4.8	3.5

Source: Prinz, 1995.

rates started later in Italy than in the other countries. This table clearly shows that the proportion married is a cumulative indicator which is largely determined by past trends; therefore, it is hardly appropriate to study recent behavioral changes.

Trends in contemporary marriage behavior can be derived from age-specific marriage rates. An analysis of such rates in industrialized countries since the 1960s makes it apparent that men and women are marrying later and that the probabilities of marriage have decreased. To illustrate this pattern, *Figure 11.1* plots age-specific marriage rates of women in the USA and Sweden in 1967 and 1990/1993. In 1967, marriage rates peaked in both countries in the 20–24 age group with about 20 percent of all women in this

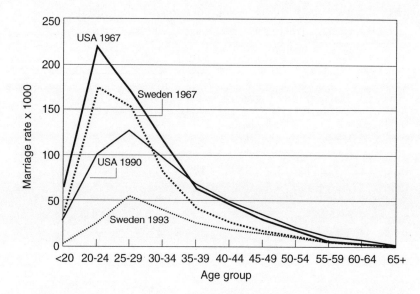

Figure 11.1. Age-specific marriage rates for women in Sweden and the USA: 1967 and 1990/1993. Source: National Statistical Yearbooks, various years.

group marrying. Some 20 years later the peak moved to the 25–29 age group with marriage intensities slightly above half of the 1967 level in the USA and only at less than one-third of the 1967 level in Sweden. The figures include remarriages which explains why rates especially in the USA are still rather high; many individuals in their late 30s and 40s are remarrying. Marriage rates among American women aged 45–49 are even higher than those for Swedish women in the traditional prime age group for marriage, 20–24. While the pattern of marriage and especially remarriage after divorce still seems to be popular in the USA, the new Swedish pattern can only be explained by a significant societal change in the role of marriage and an increase in other living arrangements.

Table 11.2 gives data on the evolution of nonmarital unions in Europe between 1960 and 1985. It shows that in Sweden, despite a 20 percent decline in proportions married, the proportion of women living in unions (marriages and consensual unions) remained virtually unchanged. Not surprisingly this trend toward nonmarital unions is strongest among younger couples. Of all women aged

Table 11.2. Evolution of nonmarital unions in Europe.

Country	Changes 1960 to 1985 in percentage points of women living in		Proportion of consensual unions among all unions by age of woman (in %) ca. 1985		
	Marriage	All unions	20–24	25–29	30–34
Austria	−3.0	1.6	25.8	8.2	3.5
Finland	−7.0	5.0	49.7	23.9	11.6
France	−4.6	4.6	35.8	14.0	10.1
Germany	−6.1	−1.5	30.0[a]	6.2[a]	6.2[a]
Hungary	−2.8	0.1	3.3	2.4	2.7
Italy	4.4	5.9	2.1	1.8	1.6
Netherlands	−9.1	−1.7	36.3	15.9	6.7
Norway	−9.8	1.1	47.0	23.0	12.0
Sweden	−20.3	−0.4	77.1	48.1	29.6
UK	−11.3	−5.4	29.0	12.8	6.8

[a]Data only given for 15–24 and 25–34 age groups.
Source: Prinz, 1995.

20–24 living with a man, only 23 percent were married. This trend toward nonmarital unions was less extreme in other European countries but still went in the same direction. In all countries a decline in proportions married was associated with an increase in nonmarital unions. Only Hungary and Italy stand out with very low proportions of women living in nonmarital unions in 1985.

The other significant trend over recent decades was the increase in divorce rates that could be observed in all industrialized countries. Crude divorce rates (the number of divorces per 1,000 inhabitants) showed an increasing trend between the 1950s and the 1990s in most industrialized countries. At every point in time between 1950 and 1990, divorce rates were the highest in the USA. Between 1965 and 1980 the rate more than doubled. Currently about every second marriage ends in divorce in the USA. In Europe this proportion ranges from about 1 out of 10 marriages in Southern Europe to 3 out of 10 in Central Europe and to about 4 out of 10 in Scandinavia and the UK (as indicated by the total divorce rates in *Figure 11.2*).

In the present context the crucial question with regard to future fertility levels is to what extent changes in the patterns of union formation and dissolution affect the number of children. The empirical evidence so far is very mixed. In Sweden the fertility of nonmarital

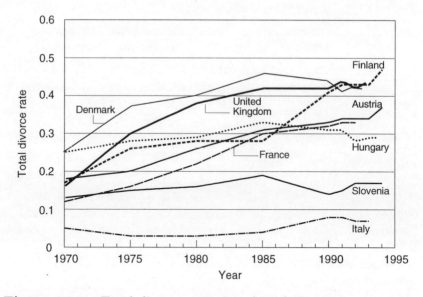

Figure 11.2. Total divorce rates in selected European countries: 1970–1994. Source: Council of Europe, 1995.

unions is not considerably different from that of married couples, although dissolution rates of the former unions are still significantly higher. In Southern and Eastern Europe fertility is still closely tied to marriage. In western Germany, despite rapidly declining proportions married, only 10 percent of all children are born out of wedlock. In the USA, this proportion recently increased to about 25 percent (Pagnini and Rindfuss, 1993). For most industrialized countries it seems likely that a possible future decline in the prevalence of marriage and marital stability will tend to decrease fertility, but the extent of this decline will largely depend on whether other countries follow the Swedish or the German pattern. This issue is discussed in Sections 11.4 and 11.5.

11.2   Recent Trends in Period and Cohort Fertility

Fertility can be measured and described with respect to different demographic dimensions, such as age, duration of marriage, birth order, period between births, and calendar year. One principal conceptual distinction is whether to consider the reproductive experience of birth cohorts of women over their life span (cohort approach) or to study the fertility of different age groups in a specific calendar year (period approach). For the purpose of population projections the number of children born in a particular year is needed as an input parameter, which is derived from the application of age-specific period fertility rates to the age structure of the female population. Hence, assumptions must be defined in terms of period fertility. If one believes, however, that cohort fertility – because it has greater stability – is the more appropriate indicator for making assumptions, assumed cohort fertility can be translated into period rates if additional assumptions about the timing of births over the course of a life are made.

Table 11.3 gives period total fertility rates, i.e., the mean number of children per woman implied by age-specific fertility rates of a year, for 30 industrialized countries over the period 1950–1995. In all countries except Malta, Japan, and countries in Eastern Europe, fertility increased during the late 1950s. This indicates the start of the postwar baby boom, which peaked in the early 1960s in most countries. Of the 30 countries listed, in 1960–1965 only Estonia and Hungary had fertility rates below two children per woman, but several countries had rates above 3.0. The 1970s were a period of fertility decline in practically every industrialized country. By 1980–1985 only Iceland, Ireland, Poland, and Slovakia had a fertility level above 2.1. For all industrialized countries together – which comprised 0.8 billion people in 1950 and 1.2 billion in 1995 (UN, 1995) – fertility declined from 2.77 in 1955–1960 to 1.91 in 1975–1980 and to 1.70 in 1990–1995.

As to regional differences in fertility trends (see *Figure 11.3* for five selected countries), there seems to be a West European pattern with a moderate baby boom and a steep decline during the 1970s. Southern Europe follows the pattern with some delay. The United States clearly falls out of the general pattern: because of an exceptionally pronounced baby boom, it reached fertility levels of 3.7 in 1955, which is above any level registered in Europe since early in this century. Japan shows a completely different pattern with a steep fertility decline during the 1950s which brought down total period

Table 11.3. Total fertility rates in 30 industrialized countries: 1950–1995.

	1950–1955	1955–1960	1960–1965	1965–1970	1970–1975	1975–1980	1980–1985	1985–1990	1990–1995
Australia	3.18	3.41	3.27	2.87	2.53	2.09	1.93	1.87	1.87
Austria	2.10	2.53	2.79	2.54	2.02	1.65	1.62	1.45	1.53
Belarus	2.60	2.72	2.68	2.37	2.24	2.09	2.06	2.03	1.65
Belgium	2.33	2.50	2.66	2.34	1.94	1.70	1.59	1.56	1.64
Bulgaria	2.48	2.27	2.18	2.15	2.17	2.18	2.01	1.92	1.50
Czech Rep.	2.69	2.35	2.21	1.94	2.21	2.32	1.99	1.92	1.83
Denmark	2.54	2.54	2.59	2.25	1.97	1.68	1.43	1.54	1.70
Estonia	2.06	1.99	1.94	2.01	2.15	2.06	2.08	2.18	1.61
Finland	2.97	2.78	2.58	2.06	1.62	1.64	1.69	1.66	1.85
France	2.73	2.71	2.85	2.61	2.31	1.86	1.87	1.80	1.74
Greece	2.29	2.27	2.20	2.38	2.32	2.32	1.96	1.53	1.40
Hungary	2.73	2.21	1.82	1.97	2.09	2.11	1.81	1.82	1.71
Iceland	3.70	4.02	3.94	3.15	2.84	2.29	2.25	2.12	2.23
Ireland	3.37	3.67	3.96	3.86	3.80	3.46	2.87	2.28	2.10
Italy	2.32	2.35	2.55	2.49	2.28	1.92	1.55	1.35	1.27
Japan	2.75	2.08	2.01	2.00	2.07	1.81	1.76	1.66	1.50
Luxembourg	1.97	2.22	2.36	2.22	1.96	1.50	1.47	1.47	1.65
Malta	4.14	3.73	3.10	2.17	2.07	2.02	1.96	2.02	2.05
Netherlands	3.06	3.09	3.12	2.73	1.97	1.58	1.51	1.56	1.61
Norway	2.60	2.84	2.90	2.72	2.25	1.81	1.69	1.80	1.93
Poland	3.62	3.29	2.65	2.27	2.25	2.26	2.33	2.15	1.88
Portugal	3.05	3.04	3.09	2.86	2.76	2.42	1.99	1.60	1.55
Russian Fed.	2.51	2.62	2.48	2.02	1.98	1.92	1.99	2.10	1.53
Slovakia	3.52	3.27	2.89	2.49	2.51	2.47	2.28	2.15	1.92
Spain	2.57	2.75	2.89	2.93	2.89	2.63	1.86	1.46	1.23
Sweden	2.21	2.23	2.33	2.12	1.89	1.65	1.64	1.91	2.10
Switzerland	2.28	2.33	2.50	2.27	1.81	1.53	1.53	1.53	1.60
Ukraine	2.51	2.30	2.08	1.95	2.04	1.98	2.00	2.01	1.64
UK	2.18	2.49	2.81	2.52	2.04	1.72	1.80	1.81	1.81
USA	3.45	3.71	3.31	2.55	2.02	1.79	1.82	1.92	2.08

Source: UN, 1995.

fertility from 3.6 in 1950 to 2.0 in 1960. An East Asian particularity is the low fertility in 1966 which is attributable to the *Hinoeuma* ("fire horse") year during which it was considered unpropitious to have a daughter (Atoh, 1989).

In many of the East European transition countries fertility rates have recently declined sharply. The most extreme case is eastern

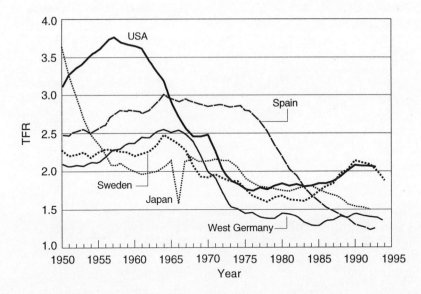

Figure 11.3. Total fertility rates in five selected industrialized countries: 1950–1995.

Germany with a TFR of 0.77 in 1994. But a number of other countries have also reached very low levels: Bulgaria, 1.46; Czech Republic, 1.44; Latvia, 1.40; Romania, 1.41; Ukraine, 1.40; Croatia, 1.52; as well as others. It is still too early to assess whether the sharp fertility declines in these countries mostly reflect a postponement of births that will be followed by a recovery of fertility rates or a transition to a different reproductive pattern.

As can be expected the completed fertility of generations (cohorts) shows a much smoother trend as plotted in *Figure 11.4*. The figure gives the average number of children born between 1940 and 1960 to women by age 45. For cohorts born after 1950, the data are partly based on estimations because the women have not yet reached age 45. There seem to be two types of countries, those that show a steadily declining trend, such as West Germany, Switzerland, Italy, and the UK, and those that do not show a steady decline, such as Sweden and Poland. The French data are particularly interesting because several years ago France saw a heated public debate over whether cohort fertility was actually still above replacement level despite of a period TFR of 1.8 (Le Bras, 1991). The most recent

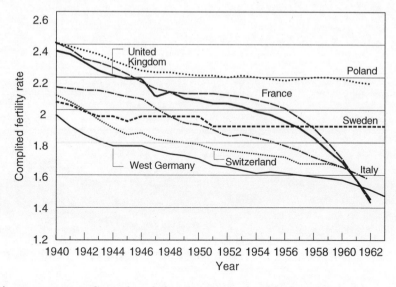

Figure 11.4. Completed fertility rate for birth cohorts born between 1940 and 1963. Source: Council of Europe, 1995.

cohort data resolve this debate by clearly showing that the fertility of French couples is below replacement level.

Under the cohort perspective, fertility declines over recent decades look less dramatic than under the period perspective. The baby boom and the following baby bust are not clearly visible because these events were largely phenomena of birth timing. However, there is little doubt that in most countries cohort fertility has also been declining significantly below replacement level.

11.3   Desired Family Size and Childlessness

Since the information derived from the analysis of past fertility trends in industrialized countries that have already completed the demographic transition does not suggest any obvious future trend, one must look at other sources of information, such as reproductive intentions as stated in interview surveys. For short-term studies, such expressed intentions are clearly a relevant piece of information although they cannot be readily translated into fertility rates because of various biases.

Table 11.4. Responses to question: "[In your country] today what do you think is the ideal number of children for a family like yours or the one you might have?" Poll taken in 1989.

| Country | Number of children (in %) | | | | | Mean |
	0	1	2	3	4 or more	
Belgium	5	18	52	21	3	2.01
Denmark	3	9	65	20	4	2.13
Germany, West	7	14	58	18	3	1.97
Greece	2	13	42	33	11	2.42
France	3	19	47	28	4	2.13
Ireland	2	9	33	30	27	2.79
Italy	2	9	61	24	4	2.20
Luxembourg	3	21	56	19	3	1.99
Netherlands	3	5	65	22	5	2.23
Portugal	3	21	55	16	4	2.01
Spain	4	22	55	15	3	1.94
UK	2	10	67	15	6	2.14
EC12	4	14	57	21	4	2.10

Source: Eurobarometer, 1991.

A recent survey with comparable data for a large number of industrialized countries was given in an annex to the Eurobarometer 1991 which asked identical questions in 12 countries of the European Community. *Table 11.4* lists the responses to the question on the ideal number of children in a family. Despite some variation across countries, the general pattern is similar: very few European men and women find a childless family ideal; the proportion is highest in West Germany with 7 percent and Belgium has the second highest proportion with 5 percent. In all countries there is a clear majority for the two-child family. In the UK, the Netherlands, and Denmark, up to two-thirds of the population thinks that two children are desirable. About one-fifth thinks that three children are ideal. The proportion preferring three children is 30 percent in Ireland and 33 percent in Greece. In the UK and Spain this proportion is as low as 15 percent. The proportion indicating four or more children as ideal is extremely small in all countries except Ireland and Greece. The ideal mean family size is lowest in Spain, West Germany, Luxembourg, Portugal, and Belgium. While these results are expected for Germany, they are surprising for Spain and Portugal because not

Table 11.5. Responses to questions on family size in Austria from women married five to eight years: 1981–1982.

Number of children	Societal ideal	Personal ideal	Desired number of children	Expected number of children	Children already born (incl. pregnancies)
Zero	0.1	2.4	2.2	2.2	10.1
One	1.4	7.3	13.8	14.1	30.7
Two	72.3	53.4	51.6	50.0	46.0
Three	24.5	28.1	24.6	25.3	10.8
Four	1.4	6.6	5.9	6.5	1.8
Five or more	0.3	2.2	1.9	1.9	0.6
Mean	2.27	2.37	2.25	2.26	1.65

Source: Gisser *et al.*, 1985.

too long ago they still had rather high fertility (in the World Fertility Survey in the late 1970s, Portugal was considered part of the high-fertility/developing country group). The low levels of stated ideal family size in these countries also support the view that the present low period fertility rates are not just a temporary phenomenon.

However, a stated ideal family size is not an actual family size, especially if the ideal refers to an abstract average family rather than one's own. An Austrian fertility survey conducted during the early 1980s asked five different questions related to family size to understand better the personal biases involved. (Similar surveys have also been conducted in other European countries.) *Table 11.5* gives the responses to questions on the societal ideal, the personal ideal, the actual desired number of children, the realistically expected number of children, and the children already born after five to eight years of marriage. The survey shows an interesting result: the respondents' support for the two-child family is much stronger at the societal level than at the personal level.

Only 2 percent of the married women expressed that they prefer to remain childless, but the data on actual fertility show that the proportion childless is much higher. Because the Austrian data come from a panel study, it was possible to determine how many women have completed their stated plans over a three- to four-year period (see Lutz, 1985). More than half of the births that were planned did not occur (pregnancies were also counted as births). On the other hand, 13 percent of the women had more children than they planned. This resulted in a significant net deficit. It also implies that if unplanned pregnancies could be avoided by better contraception, the deficit may become even larger.

The most significant case of a personal deficit, that is, having fewer children than originally intended, seems to be with the first birth. The actual number of childless women tends to be much higher than the number of women who say in their early adulthood that they prefer to remain childless. It is quite difficult to calculate the proportion of women remaining without children (and complete family-size distributions) as implied by period fertility rates because birth-order specific information is required. A recent survey article by Feeney and Lutz (1991) describes alternative methods and shows estimates of childlessness among all women by age 45 as implied by period rates in the early 1980s: 27 percent of women remain childless in the USA; 31 percent, in the Netherlands; and 28 percent, in Austria.

More accurate but less up-to-date information on childlessness is available on cohorts of women. A study of Austria, East Germany, and West Germany shows that about 30 percent of cohorts above age 70 were childless in the late 1980s (see Büttner and Lutz, 1990b). Between 15 percent and 20 percent of cohorts aged 50–70 were childless. This decline in childlessness is evidence of the disappearance of the traditional "European marriage pattern" under which high proportions of women remained unmarried. Childlessness had always been somewhat lower in East Germany than in Austria, but after the 1940 cohort the trends of childlessness completely diverge, with decreases in East Germany and increases in Austria. As discussed later, the very low levels of childlessness in East Germany are partly attributable to government policies. For West Germany the existing data for marriage cohorts after 1956 show a clear increase of childlessness over time (after 11 to 15 years of marriage) to almost 20 percent for those married in the period between 1971 and 1975. Taken together with the fact that the proportion of married women has been declining and that fertility outside marriage is very low, this implies very high levels of cohort childlessness in West Germany.

These family-size distributions, including childlessness, also have direct implications on distributional and equity issues, such as the concentration of childbearing and the division of labor for

society's reproduction among women of one generation. The rather
even distribution and low childlessness in East Germany in the late
1980s implies that 33 percent of all women had half the children
born, whereas in Austria 23 percent of all women had half the children (Lutz and Vaupel, 1987). In West Germany 29 percent of all
married women had half the children, but for all women together the
proportion should be lower than in Austria, i.e., the concentration
higher. The concentration of childbearing has many implications
which are discussed in Lutz (1989).

One relevant issue for future fertility levels is whether there will
be a trend toward some women specializing in childrearing while
the rest have few or no children. Such a pattern could result in
higher total fertility, but is very unlikely. All empirical information
shows that very few women have expressed that they want to have a
large number of children and that the overwhelming majority have
expressed the desire to have at least one child or two children. The
normative trend toward the two-child family, at least as a goal, seems
to be very strong, which implies that in the future childrearing is
unlikely to be concentrated in a certain group of women.

11.4   Arguments for Assuming Higher Fertility

In several countries period fertility has been below so-called
replacement-level fertility (i.e., a net reproduction rate of 1.0) for
more than two decades. Is this a stable and sustainable pattern of
reproduction in modern industrialized societies, or is it only a transitory state that will be followed by higher fertility? One can think
of several mechanisms that can potentially lead to higher average
fertility in these countries.

11.4.1   The homeostasis argument

The usual interpretation of the demographic transition theory is that
an initial equilibrium between high birth rates and high death rates
is disturbed by declining mortality which in turn triggers a fertility
decline that brings birth and death rates back to an equilibrium at
low levels. However, history has shown that fertility declines with all

their irregularities and national particularities generally do not stop at replacement level, but continue to decline further. The homeostasis argument would stress that this is simply an overshooting that will be reversed after some inevitable societal adjustments. Most explicitly this has recently been expressed by Vishnevsky (1991) who does not see fertility levels as the sum of individual behavior, but rather sees it as one aspect in the evolution of a system that determines behavior. He believes that the development of the demographic system is directed by a proper, inherent goal. In the process of self-organization the system aims at self-maintenance and survival. For human beings at a certain stage of evolution, a new and higher goal is assumed to appear that goes beyond pure population survival – namely, that of maintaining homeostasis in the population's reproduction, even in the face of considerable fluctuations in external conditions (see Vishnevsky, 1991:265).

It is not yet possible to empirically test this hypothesis. Trends such as the recent fertility increase in Sweden, which has been a forerunner of many other social changes, may be taken as evidence by supporters of this hypothesis. But the hypothesis is not specific enough to be tested (e.g., it does not state by how much fertility should increase over a period). Since studies have not addressed the mechanisms and motivations that induce couples to have more children, it remains largely a philosophical argument. Nevertheless, this hypothesis seems worth considering at this general level, although it is highly controversial. For example, authors such as Westoff (1991a) criticize the assumption of a "magnetic force" toward replacement.

11.4.2   Assumption of fertility cycles

Several views summarized under this heading contend that the present low level of period fertility is just the end of a cycle and that the future will bring an upward trend. These views can be grouped into arguments dealing with the timing of fertility within cohorts and those dealing with intergenerational fertility fluctuations. The first argument is based on the observation that in many countries the recent declines in total fertility were accompanied by declines in the fertility rates of younger women. Hence, one could assume that observed trends only reflect a delay in childbearing (the timing of fertility) and do not indicate a decline in the number of children a woman has over her life span (the quantum of fertility). As described earlier it is evident in all countries that declines in cohort fertility have been slower than declines in period fertility. But in most European countries, meanwhile, cohort fertility is also below 2.0, and in several countries even below 1.6.

It is difficult to evaluate the argument that women will soon begin having their delayed births, hence increasing period fertility. The slight recovery in total fertility around 1990 in several European countries may be partly attributable to this phenomenon. Studies for Sweden have also shown that current high period fertility is largely due to this timing phenomenon and was likely to decline soon (Hoem, 1990). Indeed, the most recent data indicate such decline. The timing phenomenon could only have a sizable impact on future period fertility levels if one assumes that cohort fertility tends to be substantially higher than present period rates. This may be the case in Southern Europe, where period fertility recently declined extremely fast, but generally there is no clear substantive reason to assume that a significant catch-up phenomenon will occur. For longer-term fertility trends (more than 10 years) such timing aspects are irrelevant in any case.

The second argument focuses on longer-term cycles. It assumes that the fertility level of the parents' generation is a determinant in their children's reproductive behavior. Best known in this context is Easterlin's relative income hypothesis (Easterlin, 1980). In short, it assumes that fertility is determined by income relative to aspirations, with cohort size determining income: generation one has low relative income and low fertility; generation two grows up with low aspirations for wealth but finds advantages in labor-market conditions because of few competitors, hence it has high relative income and high fertility; generation three is large and has high aspirations resulting in low relative income and low fertility. Empirically, this model fits nicely to the US baby boom in the 1960s and the subsequent fertility decline. But this is not a complete cycle. So far a new baby boom has failed to materialize. For other countries the historical long-term cycle argument is even less applicable. There are also a number of conceptual problems such as the fact that within a generation fertility is unevenly distributed among families – some families have many children, others only one (see discussion in Lutz,

1989) – and that women have children at different ages which soon smoothes out any cycles based on intergenerational dynamics. But even if this assumed mechanism is not a dominating factor for fertility trends, it may play some role.

11.4.3 Pronatalistic policies

Governments in countries with very low fertility have reason to worry about the long-term implications of subreplacement fertility together with increasing life expectancy at higher ages on the pension system and other social-security systems such as health care. Because the baby-boom generation is currently in its main productive ages, the economic dependency burden is still quite favorable. But projections indicate that in Western Europe, the proportion of the population above age 60 will increase significantly over the next few decades. This situation poses an extremely serious threat to present forms of pay-as-you-go pension schemes, where the active people pay for the pensioners. For this and other reasons, several European countries have tried to stimulate fertility through policies that make it slightly more profitable to have children. It must be stressed, however, that most countries that provide extensive child-care benefits do this for reasons of social policy rather than population policy (Höhn, 1991). But still such policies might be relevant for individual reproductive decisions.

If couples react to reproductive incentives in the way that individuals react to other incentives, then changes in the incentive structure will have an impact on fertility. Monetary incentives for having children are only one possible mechanism of government policies to increase fertility. There is very little evidence that such monetary policies actually work. For instance, Germany and Austria provide many direct and indirect child benefits while in the USA the benefits are almost nonexistent; yet fertility is much lower in Germany and Austria than it is in the USA. Also over time it is hard to link changes in fertility rates to changes in government benefits (Chesnais, 1985; Klinger, 1985). One exception is the marked fertility increase in East Germany between 1976 and 1977, which can clearly be attributed to the introduction of a package of social-policy measures (Büttner and Lutz, 1990a; Vining, 1984). But conditions in East Germany were very specific: there was a severe housing shortage, and the birth of a child was an easy way to get access to an apartment and other benefits. Since these benefits provided for basic needs that otherwise could hardly be met, the motivation for childbearing became very strong. But this already goes beyond the usual understanding of incentives, because it is associated with deprivations that are hardly acceptable in democratic, free-market societies.

Beyond material incentives, social pressure and changing attitudes as well as infrastructural arrangements for childrearing may be very important. Because no monetary transfer can realistically compensate the cost of children, including the opportunity costs of women not working because of a child, nonmaterial motivations for parenthood remain extremely important. These motivations can also be influenced by government policies that try to remove institutional and other obstacles so that women can combine motherhood with a profession. In Sweden, the universal and low-cost provision of public child-care starting at very young ages and the many opportunities for part-time work may be important factors in explaining the high level of fertility.

11.4.4   National identity and ethnic rivalry

National identity may have an important influence on individual reproductive behavior. Fears related to the ethnic composition of the population and ingroup–outgroup feelings can be powerful emotional forces that may directly influence fertility. Examples of this may be found in Israel, Northern Ireland, and the Baltic states; in these areas there is clear rivalry between two groups of the population. This rivalry may be an important reason why fertility levels are higher in these countries than in other countries under similar socioeconomic conditions. One possible hypothesis is that through international migration such rivalry may also affect other industrialized countries. But there are strong counterexamples, such as francophone Canadians, non-Hispanic Californians, or Germans living in cities with many Turks, where ethnic-linguistic rivalry is carried out by means other than reproductive behavior.

11.5   Arguments for Assuming Lower Fertility

11.5.1   Trend toward individualism

According to the sociological theories of Durkheim (1902) and Tönnies (1887) the process of "modernization" is characterized by a transition from "community" (*Gemeinschaft*) to "society" (*Gesellschaft*). While "community" refers to a living arrangement that is lasting and complete under a relatively stable structure, "society" means a mere proximity of persons who are independent of one another living within relatively open structures. In this process of transition, an increasing number of needs that were once met by the family are taken over by anonymous institutions. This means an increase in equality and personal freedom, but also an increase of individualism and a weakening of interpersonal bonds.

With respect to the future of the family, Hoffmann-Nowotny (1987) assumes that the trend of increasing differentiation as well as multiple and partial integration will continue, especially for women. From a sociological point of view, he concludes that there is little reason to believe that the family as we know it can and will survive as the mainstream model for future living patterns. This view is not too different from the notion of a "second demographic transition" put forward by Lestaeghe (1983) and van de Kaa (1987) to characterize a new phase of demographic behavior that expresses itself through lower marriage propensities, higher instability of unions, increase in extramarital fertility, and lower total fertility.

Another psychological aspect of this supposed trend toward individualism is that men and women are increasingly reluctant to make decisions that have long-term consequences and clearly limit the future freedom of choice. The decision to have a child predetermines many choices for the following two decades, and makes second thoughts impossible once the child is born. If the trend toward greater mobility in all aspects of life continues, this might well mean fewer responsible men and women daring to become parents.

There is little empirical basis to evaluate the validity of these hypotheses for the future, but they seem to be powerful arguments and plausible explanations of recent trends. In the future it might well happen that, if this trend develops to an extreme, counterforces will be mobilized to compensate some of the negative aspects of this trend. But a return to traditional patterns of "community" with their restrictions on individual freedom is very unlikely. Most of the following arguments are related to this general "continued modernization" argument.

11.5.2   Economic independence of women

One recent trend that has often been singled out as a dominating feature of societal change is the increasing economic independence of women. Female labor-force participation has been steadily increasing in virtually all industrialized countries over recent decades. The increase has been strongest in Scandinavia, where labor-force participation is almost universal among adult women below age 50, but female activity rates in North America are not much lower. In Italy, female labor-force participation increased by more than one-third in the 1980s. This fundamental change in economic activity of women is obviously connected to changing reproductive patterns. Increasing economic independence of women also tends to result in a postponement of marriage, which typically is associated with lower fertility.

One must be cautious, however, in pointing out female economic activity as a major determinant of declining fertility. It may also be that the lower desired number of children motivates women not to stay at home but rather to enter the labor force, or there may be another driving force behind both trends. This last possibility is supported by evidence from several countries that are experiencing improvements in fertility rates, despite very high and still increasing female labor-force participation. The key question in this multifaceted issue seems to be: How can women combine parenthood with participation in the labor market (see, e.g., Kiernan, 1991)? This may be a decisive question in determining future European birth rates. Nevertheless, even with flexible regulations and good child-care systems, working women, on average, will not have very large families.

11.5.3   Instability of partnership

As described above, marital stability has been declining in all industrialized countries. Part of the reason for this phenomenon clearly lies in the increasing economic independence of women. Women are no longer economically forced to stay in an unsatisfactory union if they earn an independent income. Other reasons may lie in the general increase in mobility in modern industrialized societies and in a decreasing threshold in the level of dissatisfaction necessary to attempt to change conditions. Whatever the social and psychological reasons may be, the chances of a young couple today staying together for 20 years, the minimum time required to raise a child, are slimmer than they were in the past.

Increasing evidence from empirical studies (Kiernan, 1992) shows that the separation of parents actually does more harm to children than had been assumed in the past. Such harm is measured by studying a child's social behavior, intellectual performance, and feeling of happiness and security. Thus, responsible prospective parents may decide not to have children if they have doubts about the stability of their partnership. This may be a very important factor in the decisions of couples in consensual unions, which seem to have much lower stability than marital unions (Prinz, 1995).

One possible counterargument would be that remarriage (or formation of new nonmarital unions) may actually be an incentive to have an additional child to strengthen the relationship with a new partner. Empirical analysis on data cross-classified by marital status and number of children for Finland (see Lutz, 1993a) shows that a slight effect of this kind exists, but it does not have a significant impact on total fertility.

11.5.4   Consumerism and use of time

Commentators often mention the increase in consumerism as a basic underlying cause for the recent fertility decline. The argument is that people would rather invest in pleasures for themselves than in children; they would rather buy a new car than have another child; they would rather spend their time watching TV than changing diapers. Children are considered work and not fun. As pointed out by Keyfitz (1991), in earlier times couples had to work harder

and more hours to earn a living and still found the time to have
many children. The extra leisure time couples have today is not
being spent on having children. Having children is defined as work
and therefore one talks about its opportunity cost. In the words
of Keyfitz (1991:239): "No one complains about the opportunity
cost of having sex. Thus to talk about opportunity cost of children
indeed highlights the problem of non-childbearing." He suggests
thinking of a work–fun continuum and trying to move childbearing
toward the fun end of that continuum.

Whether childbearing and, especially, childrearing will become
favored leisure-time activities of men and women will depend on
the trade-offs between fun and burden. Some European cities already have more dogs than children. Obviously in these areas the
work–fun balance is more favorable for pets, which require less of a
commitment and in the worst case can always be given away. This
argument clearly suggests that unless the burden of having children
is diminished or the rewards from children is enhanced, the balance
will continue to be negative for childbearing.

11.5.5   Improving contraception

The final argument in this series is less concerned with changing values but is at a more mechanical level. It is an empirical fact that, in
all industrialized societies, a significant number of pregnancies are
unplanned. Demographers often distinguish between timing failure
(early pregnancy) and quantum failure (unwanted pregnancy). Both
could be reduced by more efficient contraceptive use: for the latter
this would clearly imply lower fertility; for the former this would
theoretically have no effect on fertility. In practice one can assume
that a certain number of the births categorized as timing failures
may not be realized at a later point in time because of changing
living conditions, such as disruption of a union, a more demanding
job, or physiological reasons. With respect to unwanted pregnancies, Westoff *et al.* (1987) estimate that for a number of low-fertility
countries, completely efficient contraception would bring down fertility rates by somewhat less than 10 percent, as well as significantly
lower the number of abortions.

Currently, we are still far from a perfect contraceptive that requires no effort to use and has no negative side effects. An increasing

number of women report being tired of using the pill, yet sterilization is not acceptable to all men and women (especially in continental Europe) because of its irreversibility. New empirical data suggest that the number of risk-takers or couples practicing less reliable natural methods may have increased because of higher awareness of the side effects of the pill. A hypothetical perfect contraceptive without any side effects, which is taken once and then requires some reverse action for a woman to become pregnant, certainly would change the situation; this hypothetical contraceptive would clearly inhibit unplanned pregnancies which currently are still quite numerous. It will make quite a difference for future fertility levels whether one must go to the doctor to have a child or not to have a child; currently the latter is the case.

11.6 Fertility Assumptions and Population Heterogeneity

All the arguments given in Sections 11.4 and 11.5 for a tendency toward either lower or higher future fertility levels have some degree of justification. Each argument is based on assumed developments that impact on future reproductive behavior in industrialized countries, but it is unclear what the possible balance, the synergism, of these partly contradictory developments will be. For this reason we cannot provide one estimate but can only suggest alternative scenario assumptions.

A probable situation is that the synergism of these various trends will not result in a uniform pattern of childbearing in all countries and in all population groups within countries. Heterogeneity of reproductive behavior has been increasing since the postwar baby boom, and there is no indication that this heterogeneity is likely to diminish. Quite the contrary, the above-mentioned trend toward a societal structure labeled "society" rather than "community" implies lower normative pressure toward uniform behavioral patterns. There may be many subgroups and subcultures in society that have quite different reproductive behavior. On the other hand, it is often argued that mass media exert a powerful force toward standardization. But with respect to fertility the direction of this standardization is not clear. Among TV "protagonists" you find singles, childless couples, and traditional families. It seems to be the case that the plurality of lifestyles is in itself one of the key messages from the media.

Heterogeneity of the population has important impacts on demographic dynamics. In mortality, heterogeneity affects the overall dynamics of the system through selection processes resulting in changing weights of the subgroups. As to differential fertility – aside from individual biological differences – subgroups with higher fertility grow more rapidly and hence have more weight in the population structure. Empirically this can be observed for certain high fertility religious groups but also with respect to foreigners who have not fully adapted to the host country's average fertility level. In Germany, for instance, the slightly positive balance of births and deaths around 1990 was attributable to the large birth surplus of foreigners living in Germany. While only 1 in 12 inhabitants of Germany is a foreigner, 1 in 8 children born has foreign citizenship. In other words, without non-Germans the German fertility rate would be even lower than it actually is.

Such considerations of heterogeneity also entered the final numerical choice of fertility assumptions for the five industrialized regions considered in this study. At least in the long run, fertility levels should not be considered independent of migration levels just as they should not be seen as being completely independent of mortality levels in developing countries. Some of these dependencies are modeled in Chapters 15 and 16.

Figure 11.5 shows the fertility assumptions for Western Europe and North America together with recent trends in total fertility rates. The high, central, and low assumptions reflect different combinations of the trends described above. The often-assumed replacement-level fertility was not used as a benchmark because there is little substantive reason for such a "magic" level. The uncertainty range is assumed to widen quickly over the next decade. By 2030–2035 the uncertainty range is assumed to increase even further. The low value will reach 1.3 in Eastern Europe, Western Europe, Pacific OECD, and the European part of the former Soviet Union and 1.4 in North America. The assumed high values are 2.1 (which is somewhat above replacement under low-mortality conditions) in Western Europe, Pacific OECD, and Eastern Europe and

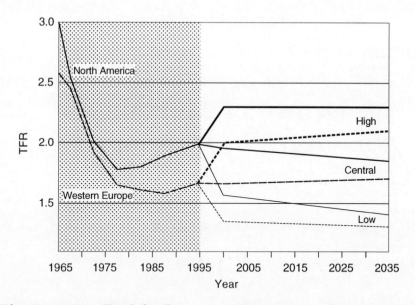

Figure 11.5. Total fertility rates, 1965–1995, and assumptions until 2030–2035 in North America and Western Europe.

2.3 in North America. The assumed central values are always the arithmetic means of the low and high values. They may be seen as the values with the greatest probability. The range between the low and the high assumptions is assumed to include roughly 90 percent of all possible future trends.

A complete description of specific fertility assumptions made for each region and a more detailed discussion of these issues are given in Chapter 15.

Chapter 12

The Future of Mortality at Older Ages in Developed Countries

James W. Vaupel and Hans Lundström

Death in developed countries usually strikes at older ages. In most developed countries the life table probability of survival to age 65 is over 75 percent for men and over 85 percent for women. Median life table life spans typically exceed 75 years for men and 80 years for women. Populations are aging, but even given current age distributions, about one-third of male deaths and half of female deaths in developed countries occur after age 80.

Not only is mortality concentrated at advanced ages in developed countries, but uncertainty about the future of mortality in these countries largely stems from uncertainty about the future of death rates among the elderly. There may be some surprises in trends at younger ages, analogous perhaps to the unanticipated epidemic of AIDS, but it seems plausible that the death rates at most ages under 65 will continue to fall at rates of perhaps 1 or 2 percent per year. In some countries for some subpopulations and in some age categories – e.g., males in their 20s – death rates may rise somewhat, at least in the short term. In the longer term, however, any such rise in mortality will produce public health responses that will probably lead to mortality improvements.

Whether or not it will be possible to continue to reduce death rates at older ages is, in contrast, an open and highly controversial question. Many gerontologists and demographers believe that death rates at advanced ages cannot be substantially reduced and that life expectancy will not increase beyond 85 years (Fries, 1980; Fries *et al.*, 1989; Olshansky *et al.*, 1990; Lohman *et al.*, 1992; Harman, 1991; Hayflick, 1977; Bourgeois-Pichat, 1978; Keyfitz, 1978; Demeny, 1984). Most deaths after age 80 are taken to be natural, senescent deaths due to intrinsic, intractable aging process. Little, then, can be done about saving lives (i.e., substantially postponing deaths) among the oldest-old. Opinions differ about whether this barrier to progress is due primarily to biological causes or to practical impediments, but the canonical view is that death rates at advanced ages in developed countries are close to limits that can only be relaxed by fundamental and currently unforeseeable breakthroughs in slowing the process of aging itself. This assumption underlies the long-term mortality forecasts published by the World Bank, the United Nations, and many national statistical offices.

Other researchers are skeptical about the existence of an upper limit to life expectancy, at least at an age as early as 85. They foresee continuing and perhaps even accelerating progress in reducing mortality rates at all ages, including the most advanced ages (Manton *et al.*, 1991). Some projections suggest that the life expectancy of the current generation of children in the United States might be 100 years or more if progress in reducing mortality rates continues over the next century (Vaupel and Gowan, 1986; Guralnik *et al.*, 1988).

If progress can be made, growth of the oldest-old population will quicken, with major economic and social consequences, including escalation of the cost of public health care and retirement programs. Progress is most important at the ages when most deaths occur; it is the weighted average of age-specific rates of mortality improvement, with weights corresponding to the product of death counts and remaining life expectancy, that determines change in life expectancy. As a rule of thumb, an average rate of improvement of 1 percent would yield an increase of one year in life expectancy per decade; an average progress rate of 2 percent would yield a two-year increase per decade (Vaupel, 1986). At current mortality levels a newborn girl in most developed countries has a life expectancy of about 80 years. If progress in reducing mortality rates could be maintained at an average of 1 percent per year, then her life expectancy would be about 90 years. Sustained 2 percent progress would imply that the typical newborn girl in developed countries will live to celebrate her 100th birthday (Vaupel and Owen, 1986; Vaupel and Gowan, 1986).

Such an increase in female life expectancy and a corresponding increase in male life expectancy would result in a radical increase in the number of persons at advanced ages. For instance, according to one projection for the United States that assumes 2 percent annual progress (Ahlburg and Vaupel, 1990), the population above age 85 could increase from 3 million in 1990 to 72 million in 2080. This figure may be contrasted with the estimate of 17 million persons in the "middle projection" of the US Bureau of the Census (Spencer, 1989), which assumes much lower rates of mortality improvement, especially after 2005.

The conjunction of these three considerations – most deaths in developed countries occur at older ages, future trends in death rates at older ages are particularly uncertain, and alternative trends have very different demographic implications – suggests that studies of the future of mortality in developed countries should pay particular attention to the future of death rates at older ages. In this chapter we therefore review the reasons for the uncertainty surrounding the future of death rates at older ages and then present some new evidence based on Swedish data.

12.1   85 or 100+?

A major biomedical uncertainty lies at the core of the disagreement between those who foresee life expectancy leveling off at about 80 or 85 years and those who predict more radical increases to a century or more. Does the force of mortality (i.e., the age-specific hazard of death) sharply and inexorably rise for the typical individual to extremely high levels around age 85 or increase after age 85 at about the same rate or even at a slower rate than before age 85, with the likelihood that the rate of progress being made in reducing the force of mortality among the very old will be of the same magnitude as the rate of progress being made among the younger old?

The first perspective implies that life spans are limited. Individuals may differ somewhat in their maximum potential life spans, with some individuals having a potential of 100 years and others a potential of 75 years. On average, however, the typical individual's longevity is unlikely to exceed the natural limit of 85 years or so that has prevailed. Most of those who adhere to this perspective believe that continued progress in reducing mortality rates up to age 75 or so is likely to be made, so that death before age 75 will become rare. Consequently, life expectancy will approach the length of the typical maximum life span, i.e., about 85 years. Eventually, some extraordinary breakthroughs may be made that permit humans to live beyond their natural life spans, but when such breakthroughs will occur, if ever, is uncertain.

This general point of view is often illustrated with diagrams showing an increasing rectangularization of survivorship curves or showing bell-shaped distributions, centered at age 85, of what Fries (1983) describes as "natural death (due to senescent frailty)." Such survivorship curves and distributions of deaths imply that little or no progress can be made in reducing death rates after age 80.

The second perspective implies that the force of mortality rises fairly smoothly to very advanced ages exceeding 100 years or more; there is no sharp increase for the typical individual around age 85, and there may even be some gradual lessening of the rate of increase after age 90 (as implied by the power function or the logistic function used instead of an exponential function in some models of mortality). Furthermore, there is no discontinuity around age 85 in the rate of progress that is likely to be made in reducing the force of mortality, so that substantial reductions in mortality rates will probably be achieved at all ages. Consequently, life expectancy will continue to gradually but steadily increase and may rise to 90, 95, or even longer by the year 2050. Major biomedical breakthroughs are likely over the course of the next century, although the exact nature and significance of these breakthroughs cannot now be foreseen: these breakthroughs may result in some acceleration in the rate of progress made in reducing the force of mortality, so that a life expectancy of well over 100 years less than 100 years from now cannot be ruled out. In contrast to the limited life-span paradigm, this might be called the mortality-reduction paradigm.

Given current knowledge, no judicious researcher can claim to know for certain which of these two paradigms is more correct – or whether some combination of them or some entirely different perspective will eventually prove to be true. Furthermore, each paradigm has numerous variants that have not yet been conclusively shown to be inconsistent with reliable empirical evidence.

Broadly speaking, the limited life-span paradigm can be associated with the stream of research done by Pearson (1897), Pearl (1923), Clarke (1950), Bourgeois-Pichat (1952, 1978), Comfort (1964), Ryder (1975), Hayflick (1977, 1980), Sacher (1977), Keyfitz (1978), Kohn (1982), and their colleagues. The most prominent advocate and popularizer of this general perspective is Fries (1980, 1983, 1984; Fries and Crapo, 1981; Fries *et al.*, 1989); useful reviews are also provided by Rosenfeld (1976) and Gavrilov and Gavrilova (1991). These researchers generally assume that there are biological barriers to longer life expectancy; in contrast, Olshansky *et al.* (1990) stress practical barriers that may effectively limit life expectancy to values less than 85. Whether the barriers are practical or genetic is, however, rarely explicitly addressed: in much of the gerontological literature it is simply accepted as a stylized fact that natural or senescent death implies that mortality rates cannot be substantially reduced at advanced ages. Harman (1991) and Lohman *et al.* (1992) provide two recent examples of the strength and persistence of this point of view.

The possibility that the mortality-reduction paradigm may be more correct is implied by most of the process models of mortality developed from Gompertz (1825) onward. This viewpoint has been cogently argued by Manton (1982; Manton and Soldo, 1985; Manton and Woodbury, 1987; Myers and Manton, 1984; Manton *et al.*, 1991), and is supported either explicitly or implicitly by Schatzkin (1980), Schneider and Brody (1983), Peto *et al.* (1986), Vaupel and Owen (1986), Vaupel and Gowan (1986), Schneider and Guralnik (1987), Poterba and Summers (1987), and Rowe and Kahn (1987).

The key reason that the controversy between the limited life-span and mortality-reduction paradigms has not been resolved is that there is relatively little reliable data on mortality rates over age, time, and sex among the oldest-old (i.e., after age 85). Indeed, it is remarkable how little is known considering the rapidly increasing population at advanced ages and the high life table probability, approaching 50 percent for females in some countries, of survival past age 85.

Very few published human life tables extend past age 85, and the population and death counts that are available for the oldest-old tend to be suspect. As reviewed by numerous demographers (including Shryock and Siegel, 1976; Mazess and Forman, 1979; Rosenwaike, 1981; Horiuchi and Coale, 1983; Spencer, 1986; Coale and Kisker, 1986, 1990; Kannisto, 1988), various kinds of gross errors are common in reported age-specific deaths and population sizes above age 85. These errors – such as age-heaping caused by rounding off ages to the nearest age divisible by five or ten, the tendency of some older people to falsify their age, the fact that relatively few errors in misclassifying younger people as very old people can swamp actual counts of very old people, or failures to remove the deceased from population registers so that the dead appear to survive eternally – may represent systematic biases across populations. Hence it may be impossible to reduce these errors by the usual statistical expedient of examining many data sets and either formally or informally averaging them. It is consequently essential that large, reliable data bases on oldest-old human mortality be assembled and analyzed.

The most reliable data on mortality rates up to the most advanced ages over a long period of time pertain to Sweden. Excellent data exist for Sweden since 1750; superlative data have been archived since 1895. The published Swedish data that are readily available are highly accurate, but even these data have some deficiencies at advanced ages. In particular, a large part of the published data has been smoothed by actuarial methods after age 90 or so, and the most widely available mortality rates are based on aggregated data on several years of age and time rather than by single years of age and time. Furthermore, the data, once published, have not been revised as new information (from censuses or cohort death counts) has become available.

Using unpublished information in the archives of Statistics Sweden, one of the authors (Hans Lundström) is in the process of meticulously verifying, correcting, and computerizing the death counts

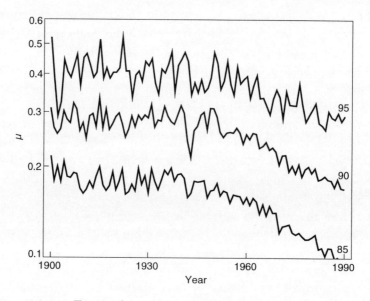

Figure 12.1. Force of mortality for females, ages 85, 90, and 95, Sweden: 1900–1990.

and population counts needed to estimate mortality rates at advanced ages in Sweden from 1750 to 1992. For this presentation, we made use of a nearly completed version of the data base for 1895 to 1990. Minor changes may be made to a few of the death and population counts in this data base, but the version used is undoubtedly extremely close to the final version.

12.2 Force of Mortality at 85, 90, and 95

Figure 12.1 plots the force of mortality for Swedish females at ages 85, 90, and 95 from 1900 through 1990. Other ages between 80 and 100 show similar patterns.

The force of mortality, also known as the hazard or intensity of death, is a measure favored by demographers to capture the level of mortality. It is defined, at age x and time y, by

$$\mu(x) = -\frac{ds(x,y)/dx}{s(x,y)} \ , \quad y = y_o + x \ ,$$

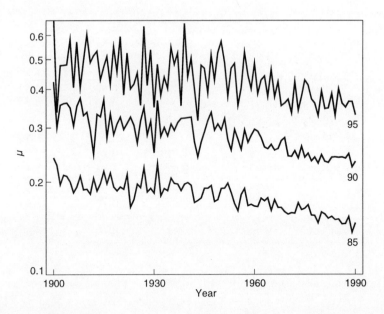

Figure 12.2. Force of mortality for males, ages 85, 90, and 95, Sweden: 1900–1990.

where $s(x, y)$ is the proportion of the cohort born x years ago that is surviving at time y and y_0 is the time the cohort was born. The Swedish data are available by single years of age and time, so a discrete approximation must be used to estimate μ. We used the standard approximation

$$\mu(x, y) = -\ln[1 - D(x, y)/N(x, y)] \ ,$$

where $D(x, y)$ represents the number of deaths among the cohort of people who were between exact ages $x - 1$ and x on January 1 of year y and $N(x, y)$ represents the number of people in this cohort on January 1. It should be noted that the members of this cohort attain exact age x (i.e., celebrate their xth birthday) over the course of year y. Also in- and out-migration is ignored: net migration is negligible in Sweden after age 80.

Population sizes are small, especially at age 95, so the trajectories in *Figure 12.1* show considerable random fluctuation. The overall trends, however, are clear. There was little progress in reducing the force of mortality at advanced ages before 1940 or 1950.

Table 12.1. Average annual rates of progress in reducing mortality rates in various age categories and over various time periods.

Sex	Age category	1900–09 to 1920–29	1920–29 to 1940–49	1940–49 to 1960–69	1960–69 to 1980–89
Males	60–69	0.50	0.44	0.28	0.62
	70–79	0.37	0.20	0.19	0.62
	80–89	0.36	0.13	0.36	0.53
	90–99	0.27	0.11	0.36	0.56
	100+	1.76	−1.07	0.97	0.18
Females	60–69	0.24	0.61	1.88	1.63
	70–79	0.18	0.22	1.25	2.08
	80–89	0.19	0.10	0.78	1.64
	90–99	0.13	0.03	0.60	0.94
	100+	0.23	0.41	0.80	0.49

Afterward, the force of mortality declined considerably, even at age 95. At age 85 the force of mortality declined from about 0.2 to about 0.1. At age 90 the decline was from a level of about 0.3 to about 0.2. An absolute decline on the order of magnitude of 0.1, from about 0.4 to about 0.3, is also apparent at age 95.

As shown in *Figure 12.2*, the trends for Swedish males are roughly similar although less dramatic. It is clear that the force of mortality for very old males in Sweden was substantially lower in 1990 than it was in 1900, although the reduction was less for males than for females and the levels of mortality were higher for males than for females. At each age, the absolute decline for males was on the order of magnitude of 0.05 in contrast to the decline of roughly 0.1 for females.

12.3   Average Annual Rates of Progress in Reducing Mortality Rates

To summarize the overall pattern of reduction, *Table 12.1* presents average annual rates of progress in reducing the force of mortality for Swedish females and males over successive 20-year time periods and for people in their 60s and 70s as well as octogenarians, nonagenarians, and centenarians.

For males and for females, the average level of the force of mortality over a decade of time and age was calculated as follows:

$$\bar{\mu}(x_o, y_o) = \frac{\sum\limits_{y=y_o}^{y_o+9} \sum\limits_{x=x_o}^{x_o+9} \tilde{N}(x)\mu(x,y)}{\sum\limits_{y=y_o}^{y_o+9} \sum\limits_{x=x_o}^{x_o+9} \tilde{N}(x)} \ .$$

In this equation $\tilde{N}$ is used to standardize the age composition of the population. We calculated $\tilde{N}$ from the population of Sweden in the 1980s:

$$\tilde{N}(x) = \sum_{y=1980}^{1989} N(x,y) \ .$$

The values of $\mu(x, y)$ were calculated as described above. If the death count equaled the population count, then the standard approximation μ equals 2 was used. Occasionally, at ages greater than 100, it was impossible to estimate μ for some specific years because no one was alive at that age and year. In such cases, the μ term was dropped from the numerator and a corresponding correction was made in the denominator. The average annual rate of progress in reducing the force of mortality was then calculated using

$$\rho(x_o, y_o) = -\left\{ \left[\frac{\bar{\mu}(x_o, y_o + 20)}{\bar{\mu}(x_o, y_o)} \right]^{0.05} - 1 \right\} \ .$$

Table 12.1 indicates that progress has been made in Sweden in reducing the force of mortality at all ages after 60 for both males and females. Estimated rates of progress fluctuate erratically for centenarian males, probably because there are so few observations in this category, but even so the general trend is toward a reduction in mortality rates. For females and for younger age categories, the picture is clear: mortality rates among the elderly are declining in Sweden and at a faster pace in recent decades than in the first decades of the century.

For males in the most recent time period, the rate of progress is roughly the same – about half a percent per year – for men in their 60s, 70s, 80s, and 90s. For females in the most recent time period, the rate of progress is about 2 percent for women in their 70s and

half as much for women in their 90s. However, the rate of progress
for women in their 80s is the same, 1.6 percent, as that for women
in their 60s.

If rates of progress in the first 20 years of the century are compared with the most recent 20-year period, it is apparent that there
has been a considerable acceleration of rates of progress. The acceleration is greater for females than for males. The acceleration is also
greater in older age categories than in younger ones, at least in the
age categories below age 100, where there are substantial numbers
of observations.

The overall acceleration in rates of progress and the greater acceleration at older ages may reflect actual changes at the individual
level: the elderly today may be healthier than in the past, and they
may be receiving better health care. A supplemental explanation
was suggested by Vaupel *et al.* (1979). Progress in reducing mortality rates at younger ages makes it more difficult to make progress
at subsequent ages if the persons whose lives are saved are frail and
vulnerable. In effect, progress in reducing cohort mortality rates at
younger ages masks the true rate of progress (controlling for compositional changes) at older ages. However, as mortality rates in an
age category decline, this effect diminishes in importance, resulting
in an apparent acceleration in rates of progress.

12.4   Lexis Maps of Force of Mortality

Another way to summarize data concerning a surface of demographic
rates over age and time is to present a Lexis map, i.e., a shaded contour map of the surface (Vaupel *et al.*, 1987). *Figure 12.3* displays
a Lexis map of the force of mortality for Swedish females at ages 80
to 111 and from 1900 through 1990. *Figure 12.4* displays a corresponding map for Swedish males.

The data available include death counts by year of birth as well
as by current age and year. Furthermore, the data include population counts of those attaining a specific age in some year (e.g., the
number of those who celebrated their 85th birthday in 1970) as well
as counts of the number of people at a given age on January 1 of a
given year. Hence it is possible to estimate the force of mortality for
triangular categories of age and time. Let $q = D/N$ be the ratio of

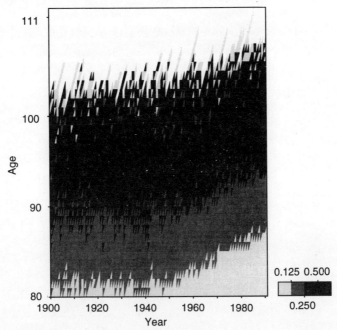

Figure 12.3. Force of mortality for females, ages 80–111, Sweden: 1900–1990.

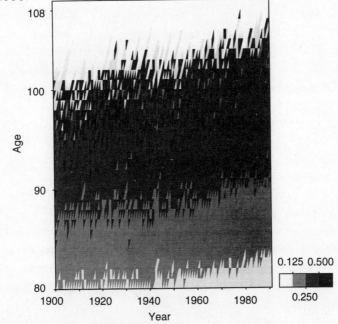

Figure 12.4. Force of mortality for males, ages 80–111, Sweden: 1900–1990.

the death count to the population at risk in one of these triangles.
To convert this to an annual probability of death, let

$$q^* = 1 - (1 - q)^2 \ .$$

Then, analogous to the formula used earlier, the force of mortality can be estimated by

$$\mu = -\ln(1 - q^*) \ .$$

The four shades of gray in *Figures 12.3* and *12.4* represent four levels of this estimated force of mortality. The light gray tones along diagonals above age 100, terminated by a black triangle, generally represent cohorts with one remaining member: the force of mortality is zero until this person dies.

Consider the age at which the force of mortality for females crosses the level of 0.125, as shown in *Figure 12.3*. Until 1945 or so, this age is around 81; by 1990 the age is up around 87. One interpretation of this is that an 87-year-old Swedish female in 1990 was as healthy (at least in terms of probability of death) as an 81-year-old Swedish female in the first four decades of the 20th century. The age at which the force of mortality for females crosses the level of 0.250 increases by about five years from a level fluctuating around 89 to a level of 94. Despite substantial statistical noise, a shift upward is also apparent at the level of 0.5, and there is also a clear increase in the maximum age attained. The record longevity is 111 years, attained by the grandmother of an employee of Statistics Sweden.

For males, as shown in *Figure 12.4*, the surface of mortality rates is higher than for females. Furthermore, the upward shift is less substantial at the 0.125, 0.25, and 0.5 levels and in the maximum age attained. Nonetheless, it is clear that there has been a definite shift on the order of three years. As noted above, this can be interpreted as the result of a downward shift in mortality curves or, alternatively, as a delay in the aging process: elderly Swedish males in 1990 can be considered to be three years *younger* (in terms of their risk of death) than Swedish males of the same age in the first part of this century.

Table 12.2. Age when remaining life expectancy is two years or five years.

Period	Two years left		Five years left	
	Males	Females	Males	Females
1900–1909	93.9	95.3	80.5	81.7
1910–1919	94.1	95.7	80.7	81.8
1920–1929	95.3	96.1	81.2	82.0
1930–1939	94.4	95.4	80.9	81.5
1940–1949	95.0	96.9	81.6	82.3
1950–1959	95.9	97.3	81.8	82.9
1960–1969	96.3	99.0	82.5	84.0
1970–1979	97.6	99.7	83.2	85.8
1980–1989	98.1	100.1	83.7	86.7

12.5 Remaining Life Expectancy

A final perspective on the decline in oldest-old mortality rates in Sweden is presented in *Table 12.2*. For the various decades from 1900 until 1990, the table gives, for males and females, the age when remaining life expectancy is two years and the age when remaining life expectancy is five years.

The numbers given are based on decennial life tables. The age-specific mortality rates, for single years of age, that form the basis of these life tables were calculated using the following formula:

$$q(x, y_o) = \frac{\sum\limits_{y=y_o}^{y_o+9} D(x, y)}{\sum\limits_{y=y_o}^{y_o+9} N(x, y)} \quad ,$$

where, unlike above, $D(x, y)$ now represents the number of deaths of people who attain exact age x in year y and $N(x, y)$ represents the number of people who attain age x in year y.

It should be noted that in *Table 12.2*, for both males and females and when remaining life expectancy is either two years or five years, there was little net change between the decade from 1900 to 1909 and the decade from 1930 to 1939. From the 1930s to the 1980s, however, the shifts were substantial. For males, the age when two years of life expectancy are left increased by almost four years, from 94.4 to 98.1. For females, the corresponding shift was close to five years, from 95.4 to 100.1. The age at which remaining life expectancy is five years increased for males by almost three years, from 80.9 to 83.7. For females, the increase was five years, from 81.5 to 86.7.

As suggested earlier, one interpretation of these shifts is that the process of aging has been slowed or delayed in Sweden such that elderly Swedish men are effectively three or four years *younger* than they used to be, and elderly Swedish females are five years younger. Caution is required because these figures are based entirely on mortality statistics, with no information about morbidity or disability. Nonetheless, treated judiciously, this perspective suggests that certainly mortality, and perhaps health more generally, is plastic even at the most advanced ages. It has been possible, at least in Sweden, to lower the force of mortality and to significantly postpone death even among the oldest-old.

12.6   Discussion

Swedish life expectancy has been among the very longest in the world for many decades. If progress can be made in Sweden in lowering mortality rates at advanced ages, then the contention that oldest-old mortality rates cannot be significantly reduced seems questionable. Using highly reliable data, we presented four perspectives on mortality changes in Sweden since 1900 among the elderly. As shown in *Figures 12.1* and *12.2*, the force of mortality at ages 85, 90, and 95 has substantially declined, especially since 1945, and more for females than for males. As shown in *Table 12.1*, rates of progress in reducing mortality rates among the elderly have accelerated over the course of the century, and from the 1960s to the 1980s ran at an average annual rate of 1 to 2 percent for females and half a percent for males. As shown in *Figures 12.3* and *12.4*, the age at which the force of mortality attains the levels of 0.125, 0.25, and 0.5 has shifted upward substantially since 1945, by about five years for females and three years for males. Finally, as shown in *Table 12.2*, the age when remaining life expectancy reaches two years or five years has also shifted upward, by about five years for females and three or four years for males. These four perspectives are consistent with each other. They indicate that the theory that oldest-old mortality rates cannot be significantly reduced is incorrect.

Other strands of evidence, reviewed by Manton *et al.* (1991), point in the same direction. Most of this evidence pertains to small special populations followed for short periods of time or is based on the results of sophisticated mathematical modeling. The evidence from Sweden is highly reliable, pertains to a sizable national population followed since 1900, and is so straightforward that it does not have to be filtered through a statistical model.

The available evidence, taken together, suggests that if historical rates of progress in reducing mortality rates continue to prevail in the future, today's newborns can expect to live about 90 years on average. If, as knowledge of health and biomedical research develops, progress accelerates so that age-specific mortality rates come down at an average rate of about 2 percent per year, then the typical newborn in developed countries will live to celebrate his or her 100th birthday.

If our children survive to become centenarians, what will their health be like during their extra life span? Will the added years be active, healthy years or years of decrepitude, disability, and misery? The answer to this question is central to forecasting the impact of population aging on health and social needs and costs, on retirement decisions and policies, and on other questions in the economics of aging, but very little is currently known about what the answer might be.

12.7 Conclusion

Let us return now to the original question: What is the future of mortality in developed countries? It has been argued that the answer to this question hinges on a narrower question: What is the future of mortality at older ages? This question in turn hinges on the question: Is it possible to substantially reduce death rates after age 80? The Swedish data, together with other data reviewed by Manton *et al.* (1991), indicate that it is possible. However, whether progress in reducing mortality rates will continue at historical levels or even accelerate is, of course, an open question.

Biomedical research may fail to continue to produce the advances needed to reduce mortality rates. Social and economic conditions may become unfavorable to further improvements. Environmental conditions may substantially deteriorate. Nuclear war may kill millions or even billions. New diseases, like AIDS, may decimate populations.

On the other hand, the acceleration of mortality improvement at older ages may continue, so that mortality rates may fall not at 1 or 2 percent per year but at 3 or 4 percent per year over the course of the 21st century. Biological, medical, and gerontological breakthroughs could lead to considerable extensions of the human life span. The life sciences may be poised at roughly the point the physical sciences were at a century ago, and biological innovations comparable to electricity, automobiles, television, rockets, and computers may be forthcoming. Fundamental advances could occur over the next few decades in genetic engineering, in the prevention and treatment of such diseases as arteriosclerosis, cancer, or diabetes, and perhaps even in understanding and controlling human aging itself.

The future is not just uncertain: it is surprisingly uncertain. As Ascher (1978), Keyfitz (1981), Stoto (1983), and others reviewed by Ahlburg and Land (1992) have demonstrated, the actual course of demographic events often leads to outcomes beyond the most extreme projections. Consequently, forecasts ought to include wide bands of uncertainty that spread outward at an accelerating pace into the more and more distant future.

Recent research by Lee (1992), Lee and Carter (1992), and Tuljapurkar (1992) provides a good starting point. Using time-series methods, Lee and Carter project life expectancy in the United States, with confidence bands. Their forecast is that life expectancy at birth in the United States in 2065 will be around 86 years with a 95 percent confidence interval of plus or minus 4 or 5 years. This projection, however, is based entirely on analysis of historical trends of US data. The future of developed countries may not be like the past of the United States: that is an important source of additional uncertainty. The results presented above for Sweden plus the research summarized by Manton *et al.* (1991) suggest that future improvements in death rates at older ages may be more rapid than in the past.

Taking those two considerations into account and using methods of subjective probability assessment (as explained, e.g., in Behn and Vaupel, 1982), a more judicious guesstimate might be that life expectancy in the typical developed country in 2065 is not 86 plus or minus 4 or 5 but perhaps the following. There is a 50/50 chance that life expectancy will be above or below 92. There is a 50 percent chance that life expectancy will be between 85 and 100 and a 50 percent chance it will be outside this range. There is a 5 percent chance that life expectancy will be below its current level of about 75 and a 5 percent chance that it will exceed the current record longevity of 120. This is speculation, as are all predictions, but it is informed speculation that takes into account our vast ignorance of what breakthroughs or catastrophes the future might bring.

Part V

The Future of Intercontinental Migration

Chapter 13 gives the most complete account of intercontinental migration that can be produced with existing data. Even without considering illegal migration, data on official or legal migration are fragmentary. In a discussion on the forces that will induce future migration, Chapter 14 shows that the traditional pull and push factors of economic disparities are often submerged by the impact of legal and logistical restrictions on international migration. Short-term political changes as well as refugee movements spurred by war or famine can significantly affect migration level. Given the experience of the past, international migration can be assumed to show great volatility in the future.

How can one derive from this information assumptions about the future? For our projections it seems reasonable to assume that in the high-migration case the future annual level assumed over the whole period will roughly equal the maximum that has been observed in the past. There is little basis for making any assumptions on possible future mass migration induced by global environmental change. Past environmental disasters, however, show that such migration mostly occurs within regions.

At the low extreme a convenient assumption is that there will be zero net-migration, namely, in-migrants will equal out-migrants. Such a scenario reflects the possibility of xenophobic policies. The central scenario then gives the average of these two extreme scenarios; it is also considered the most likely case.

Chapter 13

Migration to and from Developing Regions: A Review of Past Trends

Hania Zlotnik

At least since the "discovery" of the Americas in 1492, intercontinental migration has been a key factor influencing the demographic evolution of the developing world. During the first decades of this century, the major international flows originated in Europe and were directed mostly to the "New World," that is, to the overseas countries of permanent resettlement and certain Latin American countries. Despite the dampening effects of the two world wars and the Depression, major intercontinental flows continued to be dominated by Europeans until the early 1960s. Since then, migration from developing to developed countries has been growing and important interregional flows within the developing world have also gained prominence. This chapter provides a comprehensive view of the main migration flows either originating in or directed toward seven developing regions, namely, sub-Saharan Africa, North Africa and West Asia, South Asia, China, the rest of developing Asia (called East and Southeast Asia), Central America and the Caribbean, and South America.[1]

The task of quantifying migration to and from the regions is far from straightforward. A variety of data sources must be used to

The views and opinions expressed in this paper are those of the author and do not necessarily reflect those of the United Nations.

299

piece together the facets of the phenomenon. The lack of comparability between data sources severely constrains the types of estimates that can be derived, so that in most cases only rough indications of the magnitude of flows can be presented. On the other hand, the use of major regions as units of analysis precludes the need to consider every flow between developing countries. Most flows occurring between neighboring countries, which are often the main sources of migrants in specific countries, are excluded from the analysis.

Given the state of international migration statistics, more information is available on migration to and from developed regions than on that between developing regions. Therefore, most of the quantitative analysis presented in this chapter focuses on statistics derived from developed countries. Problems arising from lack of quantitative information on a given flow are pointed out as appropriate. Before proceeding with the presentation of migration estimates from a comparative perspective, an overview of the main data sources used and their limitations is provided.

13.1   The Statistics Used

13.1.1   The universe covered

There are basically two different sources of information on international migration: those producing data on the stock of migrants at a given time and those producing statistics on the flow of immigrants or emigrants over a given period. Clearly, the latter are the most useful in tracking the evolution of migration through time and thus providing the basis to project it. However, whereas adequate estimates of migrant stocks can be obtained from censuses that may be carried out at relatively lengthy intervals, the availability of flow statistics depends on the existence of relatively sophisticated data-collection systems that must function continuously. Only a few countries have those systems in place, and both their existence and adequacy are highly correlated with whether a country considers itself to be a recipient of immigrants or a sender of emigrants. Indeed, most countries that gather information on migration on a continuous basis do so for administrative purposes and, consequently, tend to identify migrants on the basis of administrative or regulatory principles rather than on demographic ones (Zlotnik, 1987). The USA, for instance, gathers information on immigrants defined as aliens granted the right of permanent residence. Since that right may be granted to aliens who are already present in the country under a temporary permit, the number of immigrants admitted annually by the USA is not equivalent to the number of new arrivals of aliens. In contrast, the statistics gathered on aliens granted only temporary permission to stay in the USA refer to their entries into the country. Consequently, to the extent that some such persons enter the USA several times during a year, the statistics available overestimate the number of persons involved.

Aside from data on permanent immigration to the United States, this chapter makes use of those available for the other countries of permanent resettlement, namely, Australia, Canada, and New Zealand. Information on immigration to Israel is also used, together with those available for European countries having flow statistics, namely, Belgium, Germany (the data refer only to the former West Germany), the Netherlands, Sweden, and the United Kingdom. Selected data on immigration to France are also used.

The data for Canada resemble those available for the United States, because they reflect only the number of foreigners who are granted the right of permanent residence. Australian and New Zealand statistics are gathered at the time of entry and conform better to demographic concepts. The Australian data in this chapter refer to the arrivals of persons admitted as permanent settlers and to their permanent departures. For New Zealand, the data also reflect the number of arrivals of permanent immigrants and their departures when they intend to stay away permanently. In all cases, the data are classified by place of birth. No emigration data are available for either Canada or the USA.

In the case of Israel, the data used represent the number of immigrants and the so-called potential immigrants entering the country and classified by place of birth. Although some statistics on departures are gathered by the Israeli government, they are not tabulated by place of birth, thus precluding the estimation of net migration by region of origin.

In France, l'Office National d'Immigration (ONI), which became in 1988 l'Office des Migrations Internationales (OMI), has been in charge of gathering statistics on the number of migrant workers and their families being "introduced" into the country. However, since the data are gathered through control procedures from which many migrants are exempt by law, they have generally been incomplete. In particular, after Algeria became independent in 1962, Algerians have been subject to a special immigration regime that has precluded a statistical accounting of their inflow (Tribalat and Muñoz-Pérez, 1989). Given that France is a major receiving country of citizens from the Maghreb countries (Algeria, Morocco, and Tunisia) and Turkey, statistics on both workers and family members from those countries are used as indicative of migration from North Africa and West Asia to France. The data regarding Algerians have been derived from estimates presented by Benamrane (1983) and Tapinos (1975). It must be noted that OMI statistics include both new arrivals and persons regularizing their status after being present in France for a time.

Several European countries gathering information on migration flows do so as part of the normal operation of their population registers (Belgium, Germany, the Netherlands, and Sweden). Therefore, the definition of immigrant and emigrant is derived in each case from the rules establishing who can be added to or deleted from the register. In the Netherlands a person is removed from the register when he or she intends to stay abroad for at least a year. However, Dutch citizens who have been abroad are inscribed in the register when they intend to stay in the Netherlands for at least one month and aliens are inscribed if they intend to stay for at least six months (Verhoef, 1986). Statistics on immigrants and emigrants are apparently adjusted to take into account only persons who intend to stay in the country or out of it for a year or more (Schoorl and Voets, 1990).

In Belgium, an emigrant is someone coming from abroad and intending to establish permanent residence in the country, whereas an emigrant is someone giving up permanent residence (UN, 1978). Similarly, in Germany, an immigrant is a person coming into the country to establish residence and an emigrant is a person departing and intending to give up residence in the country (UN, 1978). In both cases, "residence" is a legal concept that remains ill-defined since it is not clear under what circumstances foreigners are allowed to establish residence.

In Sweden, incoming persons must register if they intend to stay in the country for at least a year and those leaving must de-register if they intend to stay abroad for a year or more. Different definitions, however, are applied to immigrants and emigrants from Nordic countries in order to harmonize registration practices among them (Nilsson, 1990).

In the United Kingdom, information on immigration and emigration is gathered via the International Passenger Survey (IPS), a survey of travelers entering or leaving the United Kingdom by the principal air and sea routes. The IPS has been operational since 1964 and, although it gathers information on both British and foreign travelers, persons moving between the United Kingdom and Ireland are beyond its scope (Haskey *et al.*, 1989). The IPS is based on definitions of immigrant and emigrant consistent with United Nations standards, using an intended stay of over a year and an intended absence of over a year to identify each group, respectively.

It must be noted that both the systems based on population registers and the British IPS gather information on both immigration and emigration. Furthermore, similar coverage is extended to citizens and aliens. Consequently, there are major differences between the data produced by such systems and those yielded by the administrative records used by Canada, France, or the USA. Aside from the fact that the latter records lack information on emigration, both of nationals and foreigners, their statistics are only rough indicators of true population flows. Indeed, in the USA, a major problem of interpretation has arisen lately because normal immigration statistics have been artificially swollen by the regularization of undocumented aliens carried out under the provisions of the Immigration Reform and Control Act (IRCA) of 1986.

According to the IRCA, two groups of undocumented aliens could legalize their status (US Immigration and Naturalization Service, 1991). The first and larger group consisted of persons who could prove that they had been present in the USA since before 1 January 1982 and who began regularizing their status in 1989. The second group consisted of "special agricultural workers" who had to prove that they had worked in agriculture at least 90 days during each of the three years preceding 1 May 1986 and who became eligible to start adjusting their status to permanent resident on 1 December 1989. Therefore, although these two groups began appearing in the immigration statistics only in 1989, the first entry of the former group must have taken place before 1982 and that of the latter group before 1984. Since other evidence suggests that illegal immigration to the United States grew significantly during the 1970s, the data presented here have been estimated assuming that those persons regularizing their status during 1989–1992 as part of the first group entered during 1972–1981. Their entries over that period were distributed according to a linearly increasing trend. That assumption is validated, to a certain extent, by the terms of the regularization drive itself. With regard to special agricultural workers, however, assumptions about their entry and stay in the USA are less straightforward, particularly because many fraudulent applications were reportedly filed. Thus the group of migrants regularized under the special agricultural worker program is likely to include an important number of undocumented migrants who arrived in the USA after the 1 January 1982 cutoff date and even up to the time at which the IRCA was passed. It was decided, therefore, to distribute their numbers uniformly over the 1982–1986 period.

13.1.2   Problems of data classification

Regarding the criteria used to identify region of origin, data classified by country of last or next residence would appear to be the most useful for projection purposes, since they allow straightforward demographic accounting. However, aside from the misreporting problems arising from the different possible interpretations of the term "residence," data thus classified are often not available. Consequently, consideration of data classified by place of birth or citizenship becomes mandatory, though their use involves the tacit assumption that persons born in a given country who leave another are intending to return to their country of birth or that citizens of a country who leave another are intending to return to their country of citizenship (and the equivalent in terms of arrivals).

The data used in this paper as indicative of migration flows are classified by place of birth for Australia, Canada, Israel, New Zealand, and the USA; by citizenship for Belgium, France, and the Netherlands; and by country of last and next residence for Germany,

Sweden, and the United Kingdom. However, citizenship being a criterion so intrinsically linked to the international migration process, it often colors the manner in which other criteria are used. Thus, the data for Australia, Canada, Israel, and the USA include only foreigners. In addition, German data distinguish between foreigners and German citizens, thus permitting the consideration of only foreigners as originating in or leaving for developing regions. Similarly, the United Kingdom publishes data that are classified first by citizenship (Commonwealth citizens vs. other) and then by place of residence. Only the data thus classified distinguish between Commonwealth citizens originating in Central American and Caribbean countries and non-Commonwealth citizens originating mostly in South America. British data classified only by place of last or next residence make no distinction between the two regions of the Americas. Hence, the two series have been used, as appropriate, in presenting the data by regions (see *Table 13.1*).

Although the use of data classified by citizenship has been kept to a minimum, the series for the Netherlands is based on that criterion; consequently Dutch citizens from overseas Dutch territories migrating to the Netherlands cannot be identified separately. In particular, the relatively large flow of Dutch Surinamese who migrated to the Netherlands just before and after Surinam's independence in 1975 shows up as an increased inflow of Dutch citizens during the 1970s. To take this group into account in interregional migration, an annual net gain of 4,000 persons during 1970–1974 and 6,000 during 1975–1979 has been added to the estimated number of migrants to the Netherlands originating in South America (the net migration gain of Dutch citizens during the 1970s was roughly of that magnitude, whereas during earlier or later periods net gains of Dutch citizens were negative or virtually nil).

A further caveat relates to the actual classification by country of origin used by the various receiving countries in publishing flow statistics. The practice of listing separately only the countries of origin of sizable numbers of migrants and grouping the rest into a single figure often precludes an adequate calculation of regional indicators. Problems encountered fairly frequently include the practice of reporting together all persons originating in the People's Republic of China and in Taiwan; the separate listing of only a few countries in

Table 13.1. Average annual number of immigrants originating in the different developing regions and average annual net migration by country of destination and period: 1960–1991; panel 1.

Origin Sub-Saharan Africa	1960–64	1965–69	1970–74	1975–79	1980–84	1985–89	1990–91
Emigrants to							
Canada	794	2,217	5,819	5,707	3,585	6,174	–
USA	1,106	1,888	4,276	10,110	13,921	14,768	16,191
Israel	318	465	670	807	2,803	1,330	4,329
Subtotal	2,218	4,570	10,765	16,624	20,309	22,272	20,520
Australia	1,604	2,551	3,401	2,719	4,308	5,708	3,960
New Zealand	468	172	431	404	146	–	–
Belgium	7,932	7,919	7,660	5,774	3,176	4,403	–
Germany	5,355	3,829	8,695	7,644	11,672	16,106	–
Netherlands	–	–	444	1,196	1,602	5,008	–
Sweden	–	–	–	–	698	2,367	–
UK	–	25,940	34,200	27,640	20,220	23,760	–
Subtotal	15,359	40,411	54,831	45,377	41,822	57,352	3,960
Net emigration to							
Australia	1,529	2,286	3,033	2,531	4,079	5,548	3,865
New Zealand	377	52	367	322	67	–	–
Belgium	6,565	5,174	4,736	2,929	541	824	–
Germany	3,145	1,262	3,872	1,589	2,056	5,297	–
Netherlands	–	–	139	761	1,032	4,282	–
Sweden	–	–	–	–	445	2,096	–
UK	–	–6,960	–1,320	2,060	–5,520	13,160	–
Subtotal	11,616	1,814	10,827	10,192	2,700	31,207	3,865
Total emigrants	17,577	44,981	65,596	62,001	62,131	79,624	24,480
Maximum net loss	13,834	6,384	21,592	26,816	23,009	53,479	24,385

a continent thus precluding the proper identification of persons originating in the different subregions; the practice of using idiosyncratic regions (e.g., the British Commonwealth); and the use of different classifications through time which lead to spurious variations in the regional estimates. Though there is no ideal solution for any of these problems, the data on China were accepted as given (if given) and the "other Asia" category was assigned to the East and Southeast Asia region, "other Africa" was generally assigned to sub-Saharan Africa, and no general rule was followed for "other America." Because of the ensuing ambiguities in the last case, a region comprising

Table 13.1. Continued, panel 2.

Origin North Africa & West Asia	1960-64	1965-69	1970-74	1975-79	1980-84	1985-89	1990-91
Emigrants to							
Canada	3,146	6,534	4,698	6,858	4,878	9,829	–
USA	5,348	9,652	14,620	19,180	22,105	21,653	26,521
Subtotal	8,494	16,185	19,319	26,038	26,983	31,482	26,521
Australia	2,133	4,777	9,027	7,461	2,625	6,217	5,701
New Zealand	38	14	60	–	–	–	–
Belgium	5,402	3,084	3,455	7,043	6,089	4,231	–
France	40,869	48,245	79,159	32,474	43,841	22,623	–
Germany	38,721	85,143	201,123	133,466	88,874	77,084	–
Netherlands	843	9,595	16,522	18,882	15,066	16,666	–
Sweden	113	569	686	1,393	1,135	1,411	–
UK	–	–	–	7,420	13,140	15,360	–
Subtotal	88,119	151,428	310,034	208,139	170,769	143,591	5,701
Net emigration to							
Australia	2,090	4,673	8,841	7,281	2,455	6,039	5,621
New Zealand	29	4	45	–	–	–	–
Belgium	4,732	1,210	2,647	4,236	1,925	965	–
Germany	29,144	44,813	121,251	17,017	-26,939	25,304	–
Netherlands	746	6,599	13,132	14,563	8,244	10,770	–
Sweden	94	488	486	1,228	994	1,315	–
UK	–	–	–	-8,160	-9,700	260	–
Subtotal	36,835	57,787	146,403	36,164	-23,021	44,652	5,621
Total emigrants	96,613	167,613	329,349	234,177	197,752	175,073	32,222
Maximum net loss	86,198	122,218	244,881	94,675	47,802	98,757	32,142
Israel							
Immigrants from North Africa & West Asia	30,779	8,562	4,840	2,359	1,627	716	612
Immigrants from elsewhere	26,233	19,698	26,532	31,089	15,101	13,323	198,904
Total immigrants	57,012	28,260	31,373	33,448	16,727	14,039	199,516
Net loss for North Africa & West Asia	-59,965	-102,520	-218,348	-63,586	-32,701	-85,434	166,762

Discrepancies in totals and subtotals are due to rounding.

the whole of Central America, the Caribbean, and South America (denominated Americas–developing) was also considered.

Problems of classification by country of origin prevented the use of the flow statistics available for Switzerland, a fairly important

Table 13.1. Continued, panel 3.

Origin South Asia	1960–64	1965–69	1970–74	1975–79	1980–84	1985–89	1990–91
Emigrants to							
Canada	1,365	5,815	11,713	10,450	11,361	16,990	–
USA	1,387	5,393	17,335	25,739	45,271	54,540	64,553
Israel	3,007	3,014	2,194	1,647	858	1,158	162
Subtotal	5,759	14,222	31,242	37,836	57,490	72,689	64,715
Australia	1,042	2,521	4,547	1,909	2,166	5,687	8,280
New Zealand	330	276	342	–	43	–	–
Germany	4,234	3,318	4,395	7,170	10,636	21,824	–
UK	–	32,440	21,600	28,260	26,280	23,520	–
Subtotal	5,606	38,555	30,884	37,339	39,125	51,031	8,280
Net emigration to							
Australia	980	2,408	4,388	1,793	2,075	5,607	8,235
New Zealand	226	150	285	0	31	–	–
Germany	2,528	586	1,536	2,999	3,165	12,486	–
UK	–	23,880	12,560	22,520	20,800	17,020	–
Subtotal	3,734	27,024	18,769	27,312	26,071	35,113	8,235
Total emigrants	11,365	52,777	62,126	75,175	96,615	123,720	72,995
Maximum net loss	9,493	41,246	50,011	65,148	83,561	107,802	72,950

migrant-receiving country in Europe. Since most of the migrants in Switzerland originate in other European countries, exclusion of Swiss data is not likely to lead to important biases. Indeed, the data available did not identify separately a single category of migrants originating in the developing world, though a fair number of Turkish citizens and at least some Vietnamese refugees are known to have been admitted by Switzerland.

The data discussed so far have been used to derive the estimates presented in *Table 13.1*, which shows for each major region of origin the number of emigrants that have originated in that region and that have been recorded as immigrants by each receiving country discussed. In addition, whenever possible net emigration from the region of origin being considered has been presented. In general, the table makes a distinction between the receiving countries that have immigration and emigration statistics and those that have only immigration statistics by region of origin. The sum of all emigrants originating in a certain region and recorded as immigrants by the receiving countries listed in the table is presented under the label

Table 13.1. Continued, panel 4.

Origin East & Southeast Africa	1960–64	1965–69	1970–74	1975–79	1980–84	1985–89	1990–91
Emigrants to							
Canada	692	7,237	15,602	21,064	27,850	34,871	–
USA	9,156	21,783	66,070	114,762	186,948	168,707	183,552
Israel	26	23	20	19	79	21	677
Subtotal	9,874	29,043	81,692	135,845	214,877	203,599	184,229
Australia	1,010	2,071	3,910	10,661	23,059	31,759	43,069
New Zealand	391	472	496	1,080	925	–	–
Belgium	752	1,298	2,219	2,932	3,206	3,675	–
Germany	3,449	3,988	10,097	19,140	26,439	41,502	–
Netherlands	2,213	2,258	3,214	5,981	6,329	8,679	–
Sweden	–	–	–	–	3,144	12,559	–
UK	–	25,420	27,100	29,800	30,100	32,680	–
Subtotal	7,815	35,507	47,036	69,594	93,202	130,854	43,069
Net emigration to							
Australia	888	1,880	3,689	10,450	22,710	31,285	42,739
New Zealand	287	222	357	798	679	–	–
Belgium	464	849	1,250	1,552	1,655	1,778	–
Germany	2,257	1,836	6,243	10,932	9,378	22,776	–
Netherlands	1,886	1,830	1,971	4,298	4,186	6,475	–
Sweden	–796	–1,409	–2,634	–2,059	1,365	11,808	–
UK	–	6,860	5,000	4,140	6,200	6,960	–
Subtotal	4,986	12,068	15,876	30,111	46,173	81,082	42,739
Total emigrants	17,689	64,550	128,728	205,439	308,079	334,453	227,298
Maximum net loss	14,860	41,111	97,568	165,956	261,050	284,681	226,968

"Total emigrants." That number can be interpreted as representing the gross emigration from the region of origin considered.

Since net emigration figures are available for certain receiving countries, a second indicator of overall emigration is calculated by adding the data for receiving countries without emigration statistics to the net gains or losses recorded by the rest. This second indicator, denominated "maximum net loss," represents an upper limit for the number of emigrants originating in a given region or, equivalently, the maximum net gain by the developed countries listed as receiving countries of immigrants from the developing region considered.

All data are presented in terms of average annual number of emigrants or average annual net emigration for the periods indicated. Average annual numbers were used not only to make comparisons

Table 13.1. Continued, panel 5.

Origin China	1960–64	1965–69	1970–74	1975–79	1980–84	1985–89	1990–91
Emigrants to							
Canada	1,123	4,288	4,865	5,055	7,230	6,572	–
USA	4,116	13,142	16,434	21,390	26,642	26,492	30,223
Israel	10	8	6	5	9	7	29
Subtotal	5,249	17,438	21,305	26,450	33,881	33,071	30,252
Australia	694	393	376	883	1,452	4,150	4,690
New Zealand	110	103	70	–	–	–	–
Germany	108	27	53	308	1,245	2,733	–
Subtotal	912	523	499	1,191	2,697	6,883	4,690
Net emigration to							
Australia	655	342	320	832	1,406	4,062	4,615
New Zealand	81	69	50	–	–	–	–
Germany	72	5	25	123	461	1,245	–
Subtotal	808	416	396	955	1,867	5,306	4,615
Total emigrants	6,160	17,961	21,804	27,641	36,578	39,954	34,942
Maximum net loss	6,057	17,854	21,701	27,405	35,748	38,377	34,867

easier and thus facilitate the derivation of projection assumptions on the basis of such a measure, but also to obviate the problem of missing information for selected years: 1961, 1962, and 1989 in the case of Belgium; 1960 in the case of Germany; 1988 and 1989 in the case of British data for the Caribbean and South America only; and 1991 for Australia and Israel. The set of data available for the 1990s is so incomplete that it is only presented for illustrative purposes.

13.1.3   Asylum seekers

A major development in the 1980s was the sharp increase in the number of persons seeking asylum in developed countries, particularly those of the European Community. Since a large proportion of asylum seekers originates in developing countries, their numbers must be considered in this overview. However, it is difficult to decide how to use such numbers as indicators of migration since they have several shortcomings.

First, statistics on asylum seekers represent applications filed rather than persons and, at least during the 1980s, a person could

Table 13.1. Continued, panel 6.

Origin Central America & Caribbean	1960–64	1965–69	1970–74	1975–79	1980–84	1985–89	1990–91
Emigrants to							
Canada	2,381	8,947	16,490	13,244	9,822	15,176	–
USA	76,977	123,664	165,308	304,958	372,592	276,725	178,201
Israel	121	122	130	136	127	92	93
Subtotal	79,479	132,733	181,928	318,338	382,541	291,993	178,294
Australia	179	638	3,645	507	533	1,798	2,341
New Zealand	28	42	84	36	9	–	–
Belgium	–	–	–	147	283	169	–
Germany	1,245	1,591	2,120	2,217	2,912	4,730	–
Netherlands	–	–	442	6,451	6,570	5,323	–
Sweden	371	389	794	2,728	1,671	674	–
UK[a]	–	–	5,280	4,460	3,000	3,667	–
Subtotal	1,823	2,660	12,365	16,546	14,978	16,361	2,341
Net emigration to							
Australia	165	588	3,494	443	485	1,754	2,311
New Zealand	21	29	78	21	3	–	–
Belgium	–	–	–	4	9	30	–
Germany	707	375	820	526	705	1,323	–
Netherlands	–	–	187	5,599	5,201	4,454	–
Sweden	91	85	406	2,271	1,173	366	–
UK[a]	–	–	–2,000	1,280	–400	1,000	–
Subtotal	984	1,077	2,985	10,144	7,176	8,927	2,311
Total emigrants	81,302	135,393	194,293	334,884	397,519	308,354	180,635
Maximum net loss	80,463	133,810	184,913	328,482	389,717	300,920	180,605

[a]The data for the UK are classified by both citizenship and place of previous residence.

lodge asylum applications in several countries simultaneously. Second, asylum seekers are not necessarily new arrivals: some were already legal, albeit temporary, residents of the country where they filed an application. Third, it is not clear what is the overlap between asylum statistics and normal migration statistics. In countries having population registers, for instance, at what point are asylum seekers who are allowed to stay and work pending consideration of their application inscribed in the register? Clearly, if such inscription takes place at any time (which it must, at least in the case of persons granted refugee status or who are otherwise allowed to stay), asylum seekers will be counted twice. *Table 13.2* presents the

Table 13.1. Continued, panel 7.

Origin South America	1960–64	1965–69	1970–74	1975–79	1980–84	1985–89	1990–91
Emigrants to							
Canada	1,031	2,555	7,139	8,773	5,452	7,492	–
USA	20,026	23,844	22,495	37,870	44,498	44,316	46,732
Israel	1,894	1,667	2,132	2,442	1,633	1,675	2,522
Subtotal	22,951	28,066	31,766	49,085	51,583	53,483	49,254
Australia	–	–	809	3,300	1,164	2,399	1,604
New Zealand	9	7	39	102	15	–	–
Belgium	496	844	1,076	956	815	725	–
Germany	2,322	2,297	3,393	3,052	3,701	3,140	–
Netherlands	–	–	4,000	6,000	–	–	–
Sweden	–	–	–	–	1,212	3,966	–
UK[a]	–	–	1,140	1,160	1,400	1,333	–
Subtotal	2,827	3,148	10,457	14,570	8,307	11,563	1,604
Net emigration to							
Australia	–	–	797	3,167	1,002	2,265	1,529
New Zealand	5	–	36	90	3	–	–
Belgium	281	499	286	290	277	272	–
Germany	1,249	882	1,459	813	704	1,027	–
Netherlands	–	–	4,000	6,000	–	–	–
Sweden	–	–	–	–	896	3,416	–
UK[a]	–	–	–240	–560	–200	–	–
Subtotal	1,535	1,381	6,338	9,800	2,682	6,979	1,529
Total emigrants	25,778	31,214	42,223	63,655	59,890	65,046	50,858
Maximum net loss	24,486	29,447	38,104	58,885	54,265	60,462	50,783

[a]The data for the UK are classified by both citizenship and place of previous residence.

data on asylum applications lodged in European countries during 1983–1990 classified by region of citizenship of the persons involved.

13.2 Overview of the Main Interregional Migration Flows

13.2.1 Sub-Saharan Africa

Information on migration flows affecting sub-Saharan Africa since 1960 is highly asymmetric: there is more information on migration originating in the region than on that directed toward the region. Although sub-Saharan Africa attracted considerable numbers of European and Asian migrants before 1960, the decolonization process

Table 13.1. Continued, panel 8.

Origin Americas (developing)	1960–64	1965–69	1970–74	1975–79	1980–84	1985–89	1990–91
Emigrants to							
Canada	3,413	11,502	23,629	22,017	15,274	22,668	–
USA	97,003	147,508	187,804	342,828	417,090	321,041	224,933
Israel	2,014	1,789	2,262	2,578	1,759	1,767	2,615
Subtotal	102,430	160,799	213,695	367,423	434,123	345,476	227,548
Australia	179	638	4,454	3,807	1,698	4,197	3,945
New Zealand	37	49	123	139	23	–	–
Belgium	496	844	1,076	1,102	1,098	894	–
Germany	3,567	3,888	5,513	5,269	6,613	7,870	–
Netherlands	–	–	4,442	12,451	6,570	5,323	–
Sweden	371	389	794	2,728	2,883	4,640	–
UK	–	16,080	8,980	8,520	6,780	6,760	–
Subtotal	4,650	21,888	25,382	34,016	25,666	29,684	3,945
Net emigration to							
Australia	165	588	4,291	3,610	1,487	4,019	3,840
New Zealand	26	29	114	111	6	–	–
Belgium	281	499	286	294	286	302	–
Germany	1,956	1,257	2,278	1,340	1,409	2,349	–
Netherlands	–	–	4,187	11,599	5,201	4,454	–
Sweden	91	85	406	2,271	2,069	3,783	–
UK	–	5,080	–1,200	1,360	–180	420	–
Subtotal	2,519	7,538	10,363	20,585	10,278	15,327	3,840
Total emigrants	107,080	182,687	239,077	401,439	459,788	375,160	231,493
Maximum net loss	104,949	168,337	224,058	388,008	444,401	360,803	231,388

led to a reversal of the flow. Not only did the independence of certain countries trigger important repatriation flows directed mostly to European countries, but there were also cases of outright expulsion (e.g., that of British Asians from Uganda ordered by President Idi Amin in 1972).

As the first panel of *Table 13.1* indicates, the total number of immigrants originating in sub-Saharan Africa and recorded by the selected set of receiving countries considered rose significantly between 1960–1964 and 1970–1974 and remained fairly stable until the late 1980s when another increase was recorded. Although the evolution of net migration (i.e., net emigration from sub-Saharan Africa) paralleled that of gross emigration as of 1970 (it changed relatively little between 1970 and 1985, to rise sharply thereafter), during

Table 13.1. Continued, panel 9.

Origin / All regions	1960–64	1965–69	1970–74	1975–79	1980–84	1985–89	1990–91
Emigrants to							
Canada	88,008	181,976	158,857	130,127	114,056	137,910	–
USA	283,803	358,947	422,206	628,397	801,189	692,250	680,058
Israel	57,012	28,260	31,373	33,448	16,727	14,039	199,516
Subtotal	428,822	569,184	612,436	791,971	931,972	844,199	879,574
Australia	115,021	147,213	141,588	70,635	94,258	114,485	121,458
New Zealand	31,292	31,002	31,713	13,673	11,434	–	–
Belgium	69,056	65,583	64,688	58,271	47,862	48,559	–
France	174,285	203,735	192,585	70,398	78,889	36,660	–
Germany	576,211	706,144	873,051	527,483	502,179	817,754	–
Netherlands	57,746	71,009	115,425	103,571	79,419	90,567	–
Sweden	26,140	42,221	38,938	36,114	27,069	40,488	–
UK	–	215,540	205,340	186,580	186,340	232,120	–
Subtotal	1,049,752	1,482,447	1,663,329	1,066,724	1,027,449	1,380,634	121,458
Net emigration to							
Australia	106,824	128,387	112,532	54,525	81,351	103,865	115,408
New Zealand	16,281	5,439	16,921	-2,777	-4,340	–	–
Belgium	33,785	24,080	17,073	5,281	-10,801	-4,783	–
Germany	212,104	197,449	306,211	6,352	3,040	377,695	–
Netherlands	6,528	10,679	38,952	43,833	17,457	35,079	–
Sweden	15,321	27,821	11,874	18,929	8,126	27,291	–
UK	–	77,520	-50,400	-21,100	-27,580	24,160	–
Subtotal	390,844	316,335	453,163	105,042	67,254	563,307	115,408
Total emigrants	1,478,574	2,051,631	2,275,765	1,858,695	1,959,421	2,224,833	1,001,032
Maximum net loss	993,951	1,089,254	1,258,183	967,411	1,078,115	1,444,166	994,982

Discrepancies in totals and subtotals are due to rounding.

the 1960s the trend in net emigration was the opposite of that in gross emigration. The United Kingdom was mainly responsible for such contrasting trends during the 1960s because, even though it received nearly 26,000 immigrants annually from sub-Saharan Africa between 1965 and 1969, it sent out an annual average of 33,000 during the period. However, British data include both British citizens and foreigners, so that it is likely that a significant proportion of those individuals leaving for or coming from sub-Saharan Africa were British citizens.

The first panel of *Table 13.1* also indicates that, since 1960, there has been a steady rise in the number of persons from sub-Saharan Africa admitted as immigrants by the main countries of permanent resettlement. For Israel, in particular, the admission of Ethiopian Jews led to the rise registered during the 1980s. Although gross immigration from sub-Saharan Africa to European countries has also, by and large, been growing, the changes registered during the 1980s are the most significant: net emigration from the region to Europe rose from 2,700 annually during 1980–1984 to over 31,000 annually during 1985–1989, with Germany, the Netherlands, and, especially, the United Kingdom registering very substantial gains. Not surprisingly, the number of citizens from sub-Saharan African countries seeking asylum in Europe also rose dramatically: from 16,000 annually during 1983–1984 (an average that would be considerably lower if the data for the full five-year period were available) to 39,000 in 1985–1989 (see *Table 13.2*). Furthermore, preliminary data for 1990 already indicate that the number of Africans from south of the Sahara filing asylum applications in Europe rose to nearly 77,000.

In addition to the flows documented in *Tables 13.1* and *13.2*, between 500,000 and 800,000 inhabitants of the Portuguese colonies of Angola, Cape Verde, Guinea-Bissau, and Mozambique returned to Portugal during the 1970s when those countries gained independence (Ferreira de Paiva, 1983). The majority of these returnees were Portuguese citizens. However, African nationals have also emigrated to Portugal. By 1990, over 45,000 citizens of African countries, mainly from Cape Verde (over 28,000), Angola (5,000), and Guinea-Bissau (3,500), were legal residents of that country (OECD, 1991, 1992).

Table 13.2. Average annual number of asylum seekers in Europe
by region of citizenship: 1983–1990.

Region of citizenship	1983–1984	1985–1989	1990[a]
Sub-Saharan Africa	15,890	38,991	76,660
North Africa and West Asia	12,896	60,266	97,671
South Asia	26,375	58,029	65,867
East and Southeast Asia	6,071	3,971	13,671
China	0	869	1,946
Central America and Caribbean	1,097	1,318	867
South America	2,682	5,629	3,544
Total	88,024	240,876	412,889

[a]Data for 1990 are preliminary and do not necessarily refer to the whole year.

Italy has also experienced important inflows of migrants from
sub-Saharan Africa, especially during the 1980s. By the end of 1990,
75,000 citizens of countries in the region were registered as legal residents in Italy: 25,000 from Senegal, 12,000 from Ethiopia, 11,000
from Ghana, and 9,000 from Somalia. At least 17,000 of the total had been regularized in 1986 and 36,000 in 1990. However, the
increase in these figures cannot be interpreted as necessarily indicating an increase in inflows, since much depends on the stringency
of the regularization drive.

In Spain, where regularization drives were carried out in 1985
and 1991, the number of citizens from sub-Saharan African countries
who were officially registered as residents increased from about 1,000
by the end of 1980 to nearly 9,000 by the end of 1990 (Spain, 1991).
Among the 43,800 persons filing for regularization in 1985, 3,600
were Senegalese and 2,700 were Gambian (OECD, 1990). Preliminary data regarding the 1991 regularization drive are only available
for selected nationalities of applicants (OECD, 1992).

Information on inflows of migrants from other regions to sub-
Saharan Africa is mostly lacking. Indirect indications can be obtained from stock data derived from censuses, though very few countries have two censuses with comparable information. In Liberia, for
instance, the population born outside of Africa increased from 8,600
to 11,800 between 1962 and 1974, in Réunion it rose from 16,300 to
30,200 during 1974–1982, and in Swaziland it increased from 4,200 to
6,700 during 1976–1986. The population of non-African citizenship

also rose from 5,500 in 1974 to 8,300 in 1984 in the Congo and from 7,600 to 8,800 between 1963 and 1974 in Sierra Leone. A very rough estimation of net migration based on the figures spanning the 1975–1980 period would suggest that at least 2,500 persons immigrated annually to sub-Saharan Africa from other regions.

More recent data for the Republic of South Africa suggest that this country alone may have recorded even higher net migration gains. Thus, its foreign-born population rose from 426,000 to 450,000 between 1980 and 1985. Making allowance for mortality at the level of 8 per 1,000 (lower than the 11 per 1,000 estimated by the United Nations for the total population of South Africa to make some allowance for the selectivity of migration), the estimated net inflow of migrants to South Africa during 1980–1985 would have been of the order of 41,000 – that is, about 8,200 per year. However, it is likely that at least some of those migrants have already been accounted for by the emigration data of the United Kingdom.

Given the paucity of the information available, only guesses are possible regarding the possible net inflow to sub-Saharan Africa of persons originating in countries other than those listed in *Table 13.1*.

To conclude, it is worth noting that sub-Saharan Africa hosts the second largest number of refugees in the world, amounting to about 5.2 million in early 1991 (UN, 1994b). Most of the refugees, however, have found asylum in neighboring countries and have therefore remained within the region as defined here. Their movements, therefore, need not be taken into account in projecting the total sub-Saharan population.

13.2.2   North Africa and West Asia

The region comprising the northern part of Africa and the western part of Asia has been one of the most dynamic in terms of its participation in interregional migration flows, both as a region of origin and as one of destination. There have also been important intraregional flows that need not be documented here. The main sources of interregional emigration have been the Maghreb countries (Algeria, Morocco, and Tunisia) and Turkey.

Because the region encompasses many of the oil-rich countries of the developing world, particularly those having a limited work force both in general terms and, more importantly, in terms of needed skills, it has been a major destination of migrant workers, particularly those originating in countries of South, East, and Southeast Asia. The region also includes Israel, one of the few countries pursuing an active policy of permanent resettlement. Lastly, as a result of both internal and international conflict, the region has been the source of important outflows of population both to neighboring regions (South Asia) and, to a lesser extent, to the rest of the world (via, for instance, the emigration of Lebanese).

Turkey

The second panel of *Table 13.1* shows that the region has been the source of very sizable migrant outflows directed mainly to European countries, especially France and Germany. However, at least in the case of Germany, gross inflows have been considerably larger than net migration. The same may apply to France, although lack of information on emigration from that country prevents an adequate assessment of net gains. Indirect evidence suggests that net migration from the Maghreb countries to France was positive during the late 1970s but very low or possibly negative during at least part of the 1980s. Thus, the number of citizens of Algeria, Morocco, Tunisia, and Turkey enumerated by the censuses of France increased from 1,161,000 in 1975 to 1,560,000 in 1982 and only to 1,614,000 in 1990 (OECD, 1992). Whereas the number of Moroccans, Tunisians, and Turks in France grew between 1982 and 1990, that of Algerians declined sharply, passing from 805,000 in 1982 to 620,000 in 1990. Although some of that change may have been due to naturalization or better reporting of citizenship by persons of Algerian descent (many of whom have the right to French citizenship), return migration is also likely to have contributed to the change observed.

In 1990, Belgium, France, Germany, the Netherlands, and Sweden were hosting a total of 2,196,000 Turks, 951,000 Moroccans, 631,000 Algerians, and 242,000 Tunisians (OECD, 1992). Sizable Turkish populations were also present in other European countries. Thus, between 1980 and 1990, the number of Turks in Norway and Switzerland increased from 40,600 to 69,700, and the number of Turkish workers in Austria rose from 28,300 to 50,500. At least part of the increase in the Turkish population in Europe was associated with the very sizable inflows of Turkish asylum seekers. As *Table 13.1* shows, the number of asylum seekers from North Africa and West Asia rose very markedly between the early and late 1980s, and Turks accounted for much of that increase (figures not shown).

Among the other nationalities, about 2,200 Moroccans were reported to be present in Norway in 1990 and they figured prominently in the regularization drives carried out by Italy and Spain since 1985. In Italy, for instance, 146,000 persons from North Africa and 12,000 from West Asia were present in 1990, of which 78,000 were Moroccan, 41,000 Tunisian, 20,000 Egyptian, and 6,000 each Lebanese and Jordanian. Of the total 158,000 North Africans and West Asians present in 1990, 39,000 had regularized their status as a result of the 1990 drive and 18,400 during that held in 1986 (OECD, 1991).

In Spain, the register of foreigners indicates that the North African and West Asian population declined slightly from 1975 to 1980 (from 7,500 to 6,800), rose to 9,200 in 1985, and then increased sharply to reach 21,100 by the end of 1990 (Spain, 1991). This rise was partly due to the 1985 regularization drive where at least 8,000 Moroccans lodged applications for regularization (OECD, 1990). Preliminary results from the 1991 drive indicate that a further 40,000 Moroccans may be regularized (OECD, 1992).

Lastly, it must be noted that the changes taking place in the former East bloc countries have made Turkey a migrant-receiving country. Indeed, in 1989, 314,000 Bulgarians of Turkish ethnic origin moved into the country. By September of 1991 there were 358,000 Bulgarians in Turkey. Nearly two-thirds had settled permanently and virtually all had acquired Turkish citizenship (OECD, 1992).

Israel

Panel 2 of *Table 13.1* indicates that gross immigration to Israel, most of which has originated outside the region in recent years, has contributed significantly to reduce the net emigration balance of the region (see the last line of the second panel). The high levels of immigration recorded by Israel during the 1970s and again during the 1990s are associated with the arrival of Soviet Jews whose emigration during the 1970s was permitted as part of "détente" and during the 1990s as a result of the liberalization of the Soviet and now the Russian regime. In 1990 alone, 185,200 Soviet Jews immigrated to Israel, and the figure for 1991 is 147,800 (Sabatello, 1992). The 1989 census of the USSR enumerated 1.45 million ethnic Jews. Taking into account Jews registered under other "nationalities" and their non-Jewish relatives, an estimated 1.8 to 2 million persons might still be eligible for eventual admission to Israel (Sabatello, 1992).

Unfortunately, information on emigration from Israel by region of origin or region of destination could not be obtained. Available information on net migration indicates that during 1975–1979, it amounted to only 12,200 persons annually (UN, 1985a), a level far lower than the gross immigration figure of 33,400 shown in *Table 13.1*. In addition, data on the number of Israeli residents who left in a given year and had not yet returned by May 1990 indicate that, on average, 9,700 emigrated annually during 1976–1979, 12,100 did so during 1980–1984, and 22,700 during 1984–1988 (Israel, 1990). Of course, the last figure is likely to overestimate permanent emigration somewhat because the time elapsed since departure is shorter. However, such figures indicate the approximate levels of emigration that Israel has been experiencing, levels that would reduce considerably the gross gains presented in *Table 13.1*.

Oil-rich Countries

It is well known that the oil-rich countries of North Africa and West Asia have been major importers of foreign labor. Even before the dramatic rises in the price of oil during the early 1970s, several countries in the region had been resorting to foreign workers. The most complete estimates on worker migration to the region indicate that, between 1975 and 1980, the total number of foreign workers employed in Bahrain, Iraq, Jordan, Kuwait, Libya, Oman, Qatar, Saudi Arabia, the United Arab Emirates, and Yemen increased from 1.8 to 2.8 million (Birks and Sinclair, cited in UN, 1985a). The largest proportions (43 percent in 1975 and 36 percent in 1980) were employed in Saudi Arabia. Libya with 19 percent in 1980, the United Arab Emirates with 15, and Kuwait with 13 followed.

Until 1980, most foreign workers in the region also originated in countries of North Africa and West Asia: 71 percent in 1975 and 63 percent in 1980. The rest were mostly citizens of India, Iran, and Pakistan (25 percent in 1975 and 27 percent in 1980). Whereas Indians and Pakistanis worked in almost every possible receiving country, Iranians were mostly concentrated in Iraq and Kuwait.

During the late 1970s a new trend took hold. The main labor-importing countries in the region turned to migrant workers from East and Southeast Asia. *Table 13.3* shows the average annual number of persons granted permission to work abroad under temporary contractual agreements by various sending countries in both South Asia and East and Southeast Asia. The data, though probably fairly incomplete for earlier periods, indicate that by 1975–1979 an annual average of 330,000 persons were being granted permission to work abroad. During the 1980s, the equivalent figure remained above 1 million. The distribution by region of origin has changed substantially since 1975. Whereas during 1975–1979, 52 percent of all workers securing permits to go abroad originated in South Asia, by 1980–1984 their share had dropped to 43 percent, and during 1985–1989 it decreased further to 30 percent.

Care must be taken in interpreting the figures presented in *Table 13.3*. They represent generally the number of exit permits granted by government authorities to persons wishing to work abroad. Since temporary engagements are possible, multiple work permits may be issued to a single person during a given year. Furthermore, even from year to year, figures cannot be interpreted as representing new workers joining the expatriate labor force. The policy of worker rotation adopted by many receiving countries implies that foreign workers usually remain abroad for relatively short periods (one or two years) and need to return home before having their contracts renewed. Unfortunately, figures on net flows are not available. On the other hand, since workers have been known to emigrate "illegally" without obtaining the necessary permits, the figures presented may be subject to a counterbalancing negative bias. Lastly, although the oil-rich countries of West Asia have been a major destination of migrants originating in most of the countries listed in *Table 13.3*, it is by no means certain that they are the only destination. Data classified crudely by region of destination indicate that, at least for Indonesia, the Philippines, the Republic of Korea, and Thailand, the proportion of workers intending to go to the Middle East has varied substantially since 1975 (see *Table 13.4*).

Table 13.3. Average annual number of migrant workers leaving from selected countries of South Asia, East and Southeast Asia, and China: 1970–1991.

Region and country of origin	Average annual number of work permits issued (thousands)				
	1970–74	1975–79	1980–84	1985–89	1990–91
South Asia					
Bangladesh	–	13.8	53.0	78.0	125.5
India	–	53.6	236.5	139.7	–
Nepal	–	–	–	0.2	0.3
Pakistan	7.3	92.3	133.9	80.3	128.3
Sri Lanka	–	11.5	28.5	$(12.7)^a$	–
Sri Lanka (final approvals)	–	–	–	15.3	53.8
Subtotal	7.3	171.2	451.9	313.5	307.9
East and Southeast Asia					
Indonesia	–	4.7	24.4	66.3	105.5
Korea, Republic of	2.9	72.3	171.1	77.0	–
Myanmar	–	–	–	1.6	9.8
Philippines	15.5	75.9	330.9	$(460.3)^a$	$(650.3)^a$
Philippines (deployed)	–	–	$(70.2)^a$	426.0	530.6
Thailand	0.1	6.3	60.0	97.0	63.5
Vietnam	–	–	13.3	38.9	2.1
Subtotal	18.5	159.2	599.7	706.8	711.5
China	–	–	–	27.6	73.9
Total	25.8	330.4	1,051.6	1,047.9	1,093.3

^{a}Entry has not been used in calculation.

Unfortunately, data relative to the countries of destination are generally lacking. In particular, no reliable information is available regarding the size and composition of the foreign population present in the main labor-importing country of the region, Saudi Arabia. Although it has been estimated that the number of foreign workers in the member states of the Gulf Cooperation Council – Bahrain, Kuwait, Oman, Qatar, Saudi Arabia, and the United Arab Emirates – increased from 2.1 to 5.1 million between 1980 and 1985 (Russell, 1990), the bases for such estimates remain obscure. Data on entries to and departures from Saudi Arabia indicate that the country has been gaining population from regions other than North Africa and West Asia, particularly from South Asia and East and Southeast

Table 13.4. Distribution of average annual number of migrant workers originating in countries of East and Southeast Asia by destination: 1975–1988.

Country of origin and intended destination	Average annual number of work permits issued		
	1975–1979	1980–1984	1985–1988
Korea, Republic of[a]			
Total workers	97,500	171,800	96,200
Workers to Middle East	77,800	128,400	42,600
Percentage to Middle East	79.8%	74.7%	44.2%
Indonesia			
Total workers	–	24,400	61,400
Workers to Middle East	–	15,800	48,100
Percentage to Middle East	–	64.8%	78.4%
Philippines			
Total workers	75,900	330,900	433,500
Workers to Middle East	28,500	232,300	278,700
Percentage to Middle East	37.6%	70.2%	64.3%
Thailand			
Total workers	6,300	60,000	89,900
Workers to Middle East	5,100	56,400	75,600
Percentage to Middle East	81.2%	93.9%	84.1%
Total			
Total workers	179,800	587,100	681,000
Workers to Middle East	111,500	432,900	445,000
Percentage to Middle East	62.0%	73.7%	65.3%

[a]Data on Middle East destinations are available only since 1977.

Asia (see *Table 13.5*). However, the usual drawbacks of entry and departure statistics make them less than ideal indicators of long-term migration to the country.

A word must be said about the effects of the Gulf War on migration to and from West Asia. The invasion of Kuwait by Iraq led to the large outflow of expatriate workers. At least 700,000 were reported to have fled to Jordan from where they were eventually repatriated to their countries of origin. Estimates by the ILO indicate that of the 2.6 million foreigners present in Iraq and Kuwait before the invasion, only 1.4 million remained two months later. Among those departing, there were some 229,000 persons from South Asia, 49,000 from the Philippines and Thailand, and 68,000 from other

Table 13.5. Average annual migration to Saudi Arabia by region of citizenship: 1977–1984.

Region of citizenship	1977–1979	1980–1984
Southern Africa	8,998	−5,281
North Africa and West Asia	22,938	4,208
South Asia	59,144	102,894
East and Southeast Asia	51,937	37,663
China	1,865	−1,131
Rest of the world	9,076	−84,530
Total	153,958	53,823
Total from outside North Africa and West Asia	131,020	49,615

Asian countries (ILO, 1990). There is as yet no information about the resumption of labor migration after the war, but the task of reconstruction is likely to have attracted not only those who fled but other workers as well. Reports about the decision of Kuwaiti authorities to dispense with Palestinian workers suggest that workers from other countries may have to be imported to take their place.

The war also caused major dislocations in Iraq. In particular, 1.4 million Kurdish and Shiite refugees from Iraq fled to Iran between February and May 1991. Their repatriation, however, was swift. By early July, only 252,000 remained in Iran (De Almeida e Silva, 1991). Yet, continued instability in Iraq may lead to further outflows to neighboring countries.

13.2.3 South Asia

The major countries of South Asia, by virtue of having been under British colonial rule, have traditionally had close migration ties with the United Kingdom and other developed members of the British Commonwealth. As panel 3 of *Table 13.1* shows, since 1970 the region has been an important source of immigrants for the USA and Canada, and over the period considered net migration between South Asia and the United Kingdom has been positive. Important contingents of South Asians have also been recorded recently in Germany, a development that is likely to be associated with the movement of asylum seekers from the region to Europe. As *Table*

13.2 shows, the number of asylum seekers from South Asia increased from an annual average of 26,000 during 1983–1984 to 58,000 during 1985–1989. The main sources of asylum seekers in the region have been Iran and Sri Lanka.

As discussed in Section 13.2.5, South Asia has also been an important source of labor migration for the oil-rich countries of West Asia. Data on the outflow of workers from the main sending countries in South Asia are presented in *Table 13.3*. It is worth noting that, particularly for India and Sri Lanka, the number of work permits issued to those intending to work abroad is thought to underestimate true outflows. Sri Lanka's worker migration has attracted attention because of the high proportion of women it involves. Most of them work as maids in West Asian countries. Although there is no information on the country of destination of the South Asian workers who have been granted exit permits, it is safe to assume that most of them intend to work in West Asia.

Only lately have there been reports of an increasing number of South Asian workers finding employment in other Asian countries, such as Japan or Taiwan. However, most of them work illegally. Japanese statistics show that during 1985–1990, 11,600 citizens of Bangladesh, 10,700 of Pakistan, 1,000 of Sri Lanka, 700 of each Iran and India, and 400 of Nepal were deported. For each nationality, the number of deportations rose rapidly over the period considered.

South Asian workers are also finding their way to Europe. Toward the end of 1990, Italy recorded 34,100 citizens of Bangladesh, India, Pakistan, and Sri Lanka as legally residing in the country, 13,400 of whom had legalized their status during the 1990 regularization drive and 12,100 during that held in 1986 (OECD, 1990). In Spain, the number of South Asian nationals legally present by the end of 1990 amounted to nearly 8,000, a substantial increase from the 2,600 registered in 1980 (Spain, 1991).

Some of the largest population outflows have occurred within the South Asian region itself. According to statistics on the foreign-born, India was the second largest migrant-receiving country in the world in 1980. Most of the migrants thus identified had moved to India from Bangladesh or Pakistan, probably as a result of partition. In addition, the region hosts the largest refugee population originating from a single country, Afghanistan. As of early 1991 an estimated 6.2 million Afghani refugees were present in Iran and Pakistan (UN, 1994b). Furthermore, by mid-1991 Iran was still hosting 252,000 Iraqi refugees.

13.2.4   East and Southeast Asia

The East and Southeast Asia region has been a major source of migrants for both the developed countries and the labor-importing countries of West Asia. As *Table 13.1* indicates, immigrants from the region have constituted the second largest contingent admitted by the USA since 1970–1974. The close strategic, military, or even colonial ties that link several countries in the region with the USA have fostered such migration. Thus, the Philippines, the Republic of Korea, and Vietnam have been among the main sources of immigrants to the USA for over a decade. Migration from Vietnam, Cambodia, and Laos has occurred mostly within the framework of refugee resettlement. It is estimated that between 1975 and 1988 nearly 1.5 million Indo-Chinese refugees were resettled abroad, the vast majority (1.15 million) in developed countries, including 108,000 in France, 8,000 in Switzerland, and 6,000 each in Norway and Japan (UN, 1992a). The Vietnamese resettled in other developed countries are already reflected in the statistics presented in *Table 13.1*. In addition, during the 1980s China admitted 284,000 ethnic Chinese from Vietnam for resettlement.

Emigration from Vietnam has also occurred in the context of labor migration. Newly available statistics from the former German Democratic Republic indicate that by the end of 1989 there were over 60,000 Vietnamese in that country, a number that had declined to 35,000 by the end of 1990 (OECD, 1992). In the former Czech and Slovak Federal Republic 34,000 Vietnamese workers were present in 1990, but their number had declined to barely 10,000 by 1991 (OECD, 1992). Vietnamese workers are also known to have migrated to the former Soviet Union, but no information on their numbers is available. *Table 13.3*, however, indicates that during the 1980s a growing number of Vietnamese received clearance to work abroad.

At least part of the growth of the number of East and Southeast Asian immigrants recorded by the countries listed in panel 4 of *Table 13.1* is attributable to the intake of Indo-Chinese refugees after the fall of Saigon in 1975. However, especially during the 1980s, the numbers of migrants originating in countries like the Philippines, Hong Kong, or Malaysia have also been growing. Indeed, the planned devolution of Hong Kong to the People's Republic of China has fueled emigration from the Crown Colony. Countries like Australia, Canada, and the United States have established special immigration categories aimed, at least in part, at attracting affluent Hong Kong residents. Although emigration from Hong Kong has been increasing, net migration to the Colony may still be positive. Estimates of net migration for earlier periods indicate that Hong Kong gained an annual average of 11,500 persons during 1961–1971, 20,400 during 1971–1976, and 80,000 during 1976–1981 (Skeldon, 1986). The sharp rise registered in the late 1970s was due to the increased inflow of illegal migrants from China lured by the possibility of regularizing their status in Hong Kong if they managed to reach the urban areas of the Colony. The rise in illegal migration prompted British authorities to remove that possibility in 1980. The effects of such a change are noticeable in the evolution of the Hong Kong population born in China. Whereas the 1976 census of Hong Kong showed that 1.66 million Hong Kong residents were born in China and the 1981 census put that figure at 1.97 million, the 1986 census showed that the population born in China increased only to 2 million (Hong Kong, 1988). The figures imply that net Chinese migration would have amounted to an annual average of 79,000 during 1976–1981 (assuming a mortality of 10 per 1,000) and of some 25,000 during 1981–1986 under unchanging mortality conditions.

The growing variety of sources of emigration from East and Southeast Asia has been paralleled by an increasing diversification of possible destinations. During the 1980s, not only did increasing numbers of East and Southeast Asian workers secure permits to work in West Asian countries, but the proportion obtaining permits to work elsewhere rose in the Philippines, the Republic of Korea, and Thailand (see *Table 13.4*). Although many of those workers found employment in other countries of the region, such as Brunei, Hong Kong, Malaysia, Singapore, or Taiwan, others went further afield. Rising numbers of Filipinos, in particular, have been recorded in Japan (49,000 were registered aliens in 1990 compared with only 5,500 in 1980), Italy (34,000 in 1990), and Spain (where 2,500 applied for regularization in 1991). In addition, during 1985–1990, 31,400 Filipinos were deported from Japan, 72 percent of whom were women. The same proportion of women was found among the 7,100 Thai migrants deported from Japan during 1985–1990. In contrast, among the 6,600 Malaysians deported during the same period, women accounted for only 12 percent (Japan, 1990).

In conclusion, the number of citizens from East and Southeast Asia seeking asylum in Europe has remained relatively small (see *Table 13.2*). The generous resettlement opportunities granted to Indo-Chinese refugees during most of the 1980s are probably responsible for these trends. However, as conflict in Indochina subsides and a growing number of would-be refugees are denied asylum in the region, they may start seeking it elsewhere.

13.2.5   China

The fact that in 1980 over 26 million Chinese or descendants of Chinese were estimated to be living in countries other than mainland China or Taiwan (Poston and Yu, 1990) proves that Chinese emigration has been significant in modern times. However, during the first three decades of the People's Republic of China (from the late 1940s to the late 1970s), Chinese emigration from the mainland was severely restricted and only a small number of people left legally during the period. More recently, as Chinese authorities have increasingly opened the country to foreigners, emigration levels have risen somewhat (see panel 5 of *Table 13.1*) but, in general, Chinese emigration remains highly restricted.

As panel 5 of *Table 13.1* indicates, the main receivers of Chinese emigrants have been the USA and Canada. Only during the 1980s did Chinese immigration to Australia or Germany surpass the 1,000 mark. However, as already noted, Chinese emigration to neighboring countries, particularly Hong Kong, has been considerably larger. In addition, the number of Chinese registered as resident aliens in Japan has been rising in recent years, passing from 49,000 in 1975 to 75,000 in 1985 and reaching 150,000 in 1990 (Japan, 1990). It is not clear, however, whether the data refer only to mainland Chinese or also to those of Hong Kong or Taiwanese origin.

As *Table 13.2* indicates, the number of Chinese asylum seekers in Europe, though small, has been increasing. Chinese became more likely to obtain asylum after the events of Tiananmen Square in 1989. The USA passed at the time a Deferred Enforced Departure Act that allowed virtually every Chinese student in the country and his or her dependents to stay. By August 1992, a bill that would grant permanent residence to an estimated 80,000 Chinese students and dependents in the USA had been passed (FAIR, 1992).

Chinese are securing entry to developed countries not only via asylum procedures but also as needed workers. In Italy 18,700 Chinese were resident aliens by the end of 1990, 4,500 of whom had regularized their status in 1986 and a further 9,700 in 1990. A high proportion of them were registered as own-account workers. In addition, Chinese authorities themselves are promoting the export of labor. As *Table 13.3* indicates, the number of Chinese workers obtaining permits to work abroad increased markedly from an annual average of 27,600 during 1985–1989 to nearly 74,000 during 1990–1991. Given the increasing misgivings that West Asian countries are having about hiring Muslim workers from other Asian countries (Economist Intelligence Unit, 1990), resorting to Chinese labor may be a desirable option during the 1990s.

13.2.6   Central America and the Caribbean

According to the data presented in *Table 13.1*, the region identified here as Central America and the Caribbean, which includes Mexico, has been the main source of emigrants during 1960–1984. Only for the period 1985–1989 did the gross number of emigrants originating in East and Southeast Asia surpass those coming from Central America and the Caribbean. However, the data in panel 6 of *Table 13.1* include the over 2 million legalizations from Central America and the Caribbean that were registered during 1989–1992 and that have been redistributed over the period 1972–1986. As a result of such redistribution, the average annual number of admissions of permanent immigrants from Central America and the Caribbean by the USA increased from 133,000 to 165,000 in 1970–1974, from 158,000 to 305,000 in 1975–1979, from 162,000 to 373,000 in 1980–1984, and from 198,000 to 277,000 in 1985–1989. Since most of the legalizations correspond to Mexican citizens, Mexico became the main source of migrants to the USA during the late 1970s.

In fact, any attempt at incorporating undocumented migration into overall migration estimates would make Mexico a major country of emigration. Indeed, because the regularization established by the Immigration Reform and Control Act of 1986 imposed time limits on those who could have their status legalized, it did not eliminate entirely the undocumented population present in the USA. It has been estimated that, even taking into account the regularization results, by June 1988 nearly 1.9 million undocumented migrants were still in the country, 1.1 million of whom were Mexican and another half a million were from the rest of North America (Woodrow and Passel, 1990). Furthermore, some 70,000 were estimated to have entered the country during 1987–1988. However, that number of entries was not statistically significant (Woodrow and Passel, 1990).

Not only do the figures on immigration to the USA presented in panel 6 of *Table 13.1* exclude estimates of undocumented migration, they also exclude the inflow of persons from Caribbean Islands whose inhabitants are US citizens. Puerto Rico is probably the main source of such migrants. According to census figures, the number of net migrants from Puerto Rico amounted to an average annual intake by the United States of 17,700 during 1955–1960, 19,200 during 1965–1970, and 20,000 during 1975–1980 (Ortiz, 1986).

It is noteworthy that relatively few migrants from the region have found their way to overseas countries. Although migration from the English-speaking Caribbean to the United Kingdom was significant during the late 1950s and early 1960s, as the data in *Table 13.1* show, the net migration of Commonwealth citizens from the Caribbean and Belize to the United Kingdom has been relatively small or even negative since 1970. However, several Caribbean countries have been the source of emigrants to other regions. Cuba, for instance, sent both troops and workers to Angola, and it was also a source of workers for certain East bloc countries. There were, for instance, 8,000 Cubans in the former German Democratic Republic in 1989, only 3,000 of whom remained by 1990 (OECD, 1992). In the Czech and Slovak Federal Republic, 1,100 Cuban workers were present in 1990, but by 1991 only 100 remained.

Citizens from the Dominican Republic have also migrated in search of work to both regional and overseas destinations. Thus, the 1980–1981 regularization drive of Venezuela recorded 4,300

Dominicans and 1,900 persons from other countries of Central America and the Caribbean (Torrealba, 1985). In addition, by the end of 1990, 4,400 citizens from the Dominican Republic were registered as legal resident aliens in Italy, and 5,000 more applied for regularization in Spain in 1991 (OECD, 1992). Interestingly, the foreign population of Central American and Caribbean origin residing legally in Spain changed relatively little, declining from 13,700 to 10,800 between 1975 and 1985 and then rising to 14,000 by 1990 (Spain, 1991).

Although during the 1980s several countries of Central America were important sources of refugees, relatively few persons from the region have applied for asylum in Europe (see *Table 13.2*). Again in this instance, the USA and Canada have been the preferred destinations of asylum seekers from Central America and the Caribbean. During 1984–1990, US authorities adjudicated 102,000 applications for asylum filed by citizens of just three Central American countries, namely, El Salvador, Guatemala, and Nicaragua. Those applications constituted 64 percent of all the asylum cases adjudicated in the USA during the period, and the vast majority (88,000) were denied. Since most applicants remained in the USA even after their asylum request was turned down, they became undocumented aliens and were probably adequately reflected by the statistics on undocumented alien stocks reported above. However, as a result of a lawsuit by human rights advocates, US authorities granted all Salvadorans present in the country as of 19 September 1990 and all Guatemalans present on 1 October 1990 the right to new hearings on their asylum claims and the possibility of staying in the country and working until 30 June 1992 (UN, 1994b). Approximately 185,000 Salvadorans have benefited from the temporary protected status thus granted (Weintraub and Díaz-Briquets, 1992).

13.2.7 South America

Until the late 1950s, South America was a region of immigration, since countries like Argentina, Brazil, Chile, and Uruguay attracted an important number of immigrants from European countries after the end of World War II. The main sources of European migration to the Americas were Italy, Spain, Portugal, and several East European countries. By the 1960s, however, the inflow of Europeans had largely run its course. Only Venezuela was successful in attracting overseas migrants well into the 1970s. Entry and departure statistics for Venezuela indicate that during 1974–1979 the country registered, on an annual basis, a net inflow of some 10,000 European immigrants and another 1,000 from other regions (Torrealba, 1982). During 1980–1981, however, the net flow became negative and is likely to have remained so during the rest of the decade.

Census data from two of the main receiving countries in the region, Argentina and Brazil, suggest that during the 1970s net migration became negative. In Argentina the population born in Europe declined from 1.47 million in 1970 to 1.08 million in 1980, a reduction that cannot be accounted for by mortality alone. In Brazil the population of European nationality declined from 803,000 in 1970 to 638,000 in 1980. Although such a change could be the result of naturalization, return migration is likely to have also contributed to it.

As panel 7 of *Table 13.1* shows, South America has been a relatively important source of immigrants to the USA. A fair number of them remained in that country illegally because, although the numbers legalizing under IRCA were small in comparison to those of undocumented aliens from Central America and the Caribbean, the trend since 1970 has been affected by the redistribution of those legalizing during 1989–1992. In particular, without the IRCA legalizations, the average annual number of admissions of South Americans by the USA would have amounted to only 31,000 instead of 38,000 in 1975–1979, to 37,000 instead of 45,000 in 1980–1984, and to 42,000 instead of 44,000 in 1985–1989.

Emigration from South America is likely to have grown significantly during the 1980s. Part of it, however, is difficult to measure, since it involves the emigration of second- and third-generation migrants (i.e., the children and grandchildren of the original immigrants) who have been granted citizenship rights by the countries of origin of their forebears. Thus, Italy and Spain have been receiving the inflow of Italian or Spanish citizens born overseas who do not appear on statistics relative to foreigners. According to statistics on the foreign stock, there were 47,000 South American citizens in Italy at the end of 1990 (14,000 of whom were Brazilian and 13,000 Argentine citizens), and the number of South American citizens in

Spain nearly doubled, passing from 24,000 in 1975 to 30,000 in 1985 and then to 49,000 in 1990 (Spain, 1991). In addition, about 7,000 nationals of Argentina and 5,000 of Peru lodged applications for regularization during the 1991 drive carried out in Spain.

Perhaps one of the most interesting cases of return migration among the descendants of former immigrants is the migration of Brazilians and Peruvians of Japanese descent to Japan. Between 1985 and 1990, the population of South American origin in Japan increased dramatically, rising from 3,600 to 71,500. Underlying such a change was the decision of Japanese authorities to permit the establishment in Japan of persons of Japanese descent. Both Brazil and Peru host relatively sizable subpopulations of Japanese ethnic origin that may decide to go back to their roots.

The number of South American asylum seekers in Europe has remained modest. Until the 1990 change of government in Chile, citizens of that country were likely to obtain asylum in Europe, particularly in the Nordic countries. The new Chilean government is planning to facilitate the repatriation of those wishing to return.

13.3   Conclusion

This overview of migration trends to and from the main developing regions, though fairly comprehensive, is still a weak basis on which to estimate current interregional migration or derive assumptions regarding future trends. Although data on migration flows are not entirely lacking, those available are often incomplete (they do not refer to all possible long-term movements), and they are not easily comparable from one country to another. In addition, when the main countries of destination are located in the developing world, data on migration flows are often entirely lacking or cannot be readily obtained. The political sensitivity of the migration phenomenon is such that existing information is often treated as highly classified material that must be protected. Countries are often guilty of benign neglect, preferring to ignore the magnitude of flows than to measure them adequately. Despite efforts to improve the quality and availability of international migration statistics, little progress has been made. In the meantime, migration continues to increase and its complexity rises. Part of that complexity stems from the barriers that potential countries of destination are using to control or stop migration. When legal migration is highly restricted or not desired under any circumstances, different varieties of illegal or undesirable flows will arise. Such a situation makes the job of the forecaster even more difficult, since policy aims are at odds with likely outcomes.

On the other hand, consideration of any time series on migration is a sobering experience. As *Table 13.1* indicates, relatively drastic changes in trends can and have occurred over the course of the past 30 years in many developing regions. Events like the Gulf War can trigger large interregional flows over relatively short periods. Given the difficulties in forecasting such events and their likely effects on migration, population projections are often based on relatively simplistic assumptions regarding future migration trends. Perhaps the most common assumption is that migration will, in the long run, have little effect on population dynamics, so that it can be assumed to be zero. Otherwise, migration assumptions are generally made in terms of net numbers of migrants gained or lost during each of the projection quinquennia (see, for instance, Arnold, 1989). When the latter approach is taken, nonzero assumptions are typically made for a few projection periods (usually one to four, thus covering at most a span of 20 years) and from then on migration is assumed to taper off to zero or to remain constant at the last assumed level. Although undoubtedly simplistic, such practices have much to recommend them, particularly when one is dealing with large and complex regions such as the ones considered in this paper. Given the relatively large population bases of most regions, estimated net migration levels of the magnitude presented in *Table 13.1* are likely to have relatively small effects on the overall evolution of the population.

At the level of individual countries or smaller regions, however, the situation may be different. Migration is also likely to be an important component of population change when fertility has reached very low levels, especially if it remains below replacement for a certain period (see, for instance, OECD, 1991). Yet, even in countries facing such fertility prospects, projections continue to be made using the type of migration assumptions described above: total net numbers of migrants that vary minimally over time. Although the construction of more complex assumptions is technically possible, policy considerations usually dissuade technicians, who are mostly at the service of governments, from using more realistic scenarios, especially if these scenarios are likely to run counter to major policy stances. Whether the use of such scenarios would help or hinder the debate on migration, its desirability, or the degree to which it must be tolerated is a matter that needs to be considered carefully.

Note

[1] Definitions of developing regions used.

Sub-Saharan Africa. East Africa: British Indian Ocean Territory, Burundi, Comoros, Djibouti, Ethiopia, Kenya, Madagascar, Malawi, Mauritius, Mozambique, Réunion, Rwanda, Seychelles, Somalia, Uganda, Tanzania, Zambia, Zimbabwe; Central Africa: Angola, Cameroon, Central African Republic, Chad, Congo, Equatorial Guinea, Gabon, Sao Tomé & Príncipe, Zaire; Southern Africa: Botswana, Lesotho, Namibia, South Africa, Swaziland; West Africa: Benin, Burkina Faso, Cape Verde, Côte d'Ivoire, Gambia, Ghana, Guinea, Guinea-Bissau, Liberia, Mali, Mauritania, Niger, Nigeria, St. Helena, Senegal, Sierra Leone, Togo.

North Africa and West Asia. North Africa: Algeria, Egypt, Libya, Morocco, Sudan, Tunisia, West Sahara; West Asia: Bahrain, Cyprus, Gaza Strip (Palestine), Iraq, Israel, Jordan, Kuwait, Lebanon, Oman, Qatar, Saudi Arabia, Syria, Turkey, United Arab Emirates, Yemen.

South Asia. Afghanistan, Bangladesh, Bhutan, India, Iran, Maldives, Nepal, Pakistan, Sri Lanka.

East and Southeast Asia. East Asia: Hong Kong, Korea (Democratic People's Republic), Korea (Republic), Macau, Mongolia; Southeast Asia: Brunei Darussalam, Cambodia, East Timor, Indonesia, Lao People's Democratic Republic, Malaysia, Myanmar, Philippines, Singapore, Thailand, Vietnam.

China.

Central America and the Caribbean. Central America: Belize, Costa Rica, El Salvador, Guatemala, Honduras, Mexico, Nicaragua, Panama; Caribbean: Anguilla, Antigua & Barbuda, Aruba, Bahamas, Barbados, British Virgin Islands, Cayman Islands, Cuba, Dominica, Dominican Republic, Grenada, Guadeloupe, Haiti, Jamaica, Martinique, Montserrat, Netherlands Antilles, Puerto Rico, St. Kitts & Nevis, St. Lucia, St. Vincent & the Grenadines, Trinidad & Tobago, Turks & Caicos Islands, US Virgin Islands.

South America. Argentina, Bolivia, Brazil, Chile, Colombia, Ecuador, Falkland Islands (Malvinas), French Guiana, Guyana, Paraguay, Peru, Surinam, Uruguay, Venezuela.

Chapter 14

Spatial and Economic Factors in Future South–North Migration

Sture Öberg

The objective of this chapter is to estimate future migration flows between less developed countries and more developed countries. This could be an easy task, where earlier flows are used as a basis for trend projections, or an aim far too complex for the scope of this chapter.

The solution here is close to the first idea. The estimated figures are based on three factors that determine the probabilities of future migration. The first is present trends as they are measured by the UN (see Chapter 13). The second is an estimate of public attitudes toward immigrants. The assumption is that these attitudes do not change easily over time. Attitudes are also reflected in contemporary flows, so these two factors are interrelated. The third factor examines the proximity of push and pull regions, present contacts between people living in rich and poor regions, and the welfare gap between regions. This last factor is, of course, also interrelated with the other two.

There is no official prognosis on future international migration, a fact which has to do with political politeness. For a sending country it is not easy to accept in hard figures that it will not be able to organize its labor market or food production in the near future via emigration. For a receiving country, it is not easy to reveal, for example, that it will deny citizenship to refugees in the future or that it will continue to accept mostly well-educated immigrants from poor countries. Prognoses of this kind therefore have to be personal guesses made by individuals not working for UN agencies or any other official authority.

Another reason for the lack of migration prognoses is the fairly low interest in migration figures among demographers and others working with forecasts. Migration figures are small compared with other demographic changes. Every day there are 250,000 more inhabitants on the globe (UN, 1992a). Every day 25,000 children and adults die of starvation and diseases related to lack of nutrition (Durning, 1989). Compared with this, the number of net migrants from the South to the North during one day is a small number, about 5,000 each day. Per year, fewer than 1 inhabitant out of 2,000 in developing countries migrate North. This could partly explain the lack of prognoses on international migration.

The numbers are small, but the resulting political tension in both sending and receiving countries is significant. Even small streams are visible and create positive and negative changes in the industrialized world. In the long run, say after one generation, small numbers add up to large numbers and to more impressive demographic-ethnic changes. But of course, at a very aggregated level, the size of the numbers is still smaller than the numbers influenced by future changes in fertility and mortality patterns.

Before the prognosis in this chapter is presented let us define some concepts and then determine how theories from different scientific disciplines could be used to contribute to an understanding of historical and current flows which in turn would make it easier to speculate about future flows. This discussion is based on Öberg and Wils (1992).

14.1 Definitions

The *North* is synonymous with the industrialized countries where the income, on average, is roughly six times higher than in the developing countries, the *South*. The North consists of Europe, North America, Japan, and Oceania.

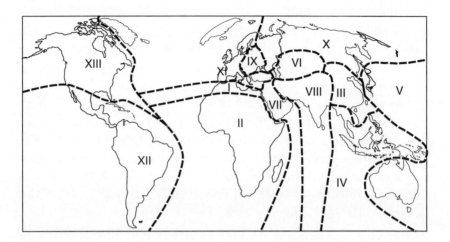

Figure 14.1. The world regions used in this book. See text and Appendix Table 1 for definition of world regions.

Europe is sometimes divided into Western Europe, which is part of the North, with around 400 million inhabitants and a high per capita income, and the rest of Europe, the former communist countries, with more than 300 million inhabitants and a much lower per capita income, thus statistically part of the South. North America consists of the USA and Canada. Oceania is dominated by Australia and New Zealand.

The regions used in this chapter are consistent with the regions defined for the projections in this book. Thus, there are 13 groups of nations forming the regions: I North Africa; II sub-Saharan Africa; III China and Centrally Planned Asia; IV Pacific Asia; V Pacific OECD; VI Central Asia; VII Middle East; VIII South Asia; IX Eastern Europe; X European part of the former Soviet Union; XI Western Europe; XII Latin America; XIII North America. The regions are presented in *Figure 14.1*.

Migration usually means "relatively permanent" changes of residence. Since we define regions as continents or groups of nations, interregional migration refers to movements across the boundaries of these regions. Permanence stands for several years, preferably a lifetime.

Of the large number of persons who enter or leave a country, only a small portion are defined as migrants. Tourists, business executives, temporary workers, and asylum seekers trying to find a new home (Rogge, 1992) are usually not defined as migrants. This definition makes it easier to make a prognosis because the accepted flows are statistically better known than the illegal and temporal ones. Most of the discussion in this chapter uses a wider definition of migrants, but the prognosis at the end of the chapter is only concerned with migrants receiving permission to stay permanently, including those who later become citizens of the new country.

Citizenship is an individual's formal membership of a state. This is a purely legal definition that serves as the basis for a number of rights and duties. The most important here is the legal right for a person to stay in the country where he or she is a citizen. There are also other aspects, like political and psychological ones, but they are not considered here (see Reinans and Hammar, 1993).

14.2 Theories on International Migration

Today, migration is understood as a process of complexity and heterogeneity. It can be analyzed from several perspectives and within different conceptual frameworks or paradigms. Migration studies can concentrate on individuals or structures, on micro or macro factors. These studies consider a wide range of historical processes and contemporary situations.

Migration concerns individuals, and thus it is a result of unique responses to an actual, potential, or perceived understanding of many processes. It is partly a voluntary and partly a forced action controlled not only by the migrant but also by others, including regulating governments. With this complexity in mind, researchers still try to find regularities which could be used for theories or prognoses. Different scientific disciplines have specialized in different aspects on regularities or prevailing ideas behind migration processes.

The basic idea in the scientific literature on migration between less developed and more developed countries, South–North migration, is that people should migrate North. This will equalize the capital per worker ratio and thus increase efficiency and hence incomes and welfare. A majority of the population in the North will gain from migration (Simon, 1993). Industrialists are happy to employ less-expensive labor. An increased supply of labor would decrease the wage level. Rich and well-educated people would also be better off if they could afford to employ housemaids and gardeners for low wages. People in possession of real estate will earn money on increased demand for housing.

Many people in the South would also gain. Migrants would be better off in their new countries. They could help new migrants settle in the North. They would probably send money home to their relatives in less developed countries. At present the remittances are about $75 billion annually, substantially more than development aid.

The first ideas on international migration that were developed into a theoretical framework are more than two centuries old. In a study by Kryger (1764), a Swedish social scientist, causes of international migration were discussed as well as how authorities could influence the size of the flows. His idea was that migration cannot be explained in simple words. Individual households could have several reasons for migrating, and the gross migration flows could have several causes. At that time the academic disciplines were broader and fewer than today, but Kryger's study could be labeled "applied economics." As Sweden at that time was a poor country, he concentrated his analysis on push factors, such as low wages in some sectors, unfair taxation, badly organized social-security systems, and lack of a well-functioning food distribution system. Several of these factors are still push factors in today's poor countries.

A little more than a century later, several researchers like Ravenstein (1885) in England and Rauchberg (1893) in Austria formulated theories on interregional migration that could be extended to international migration. A French researcher (Lavasseur, 1885) discussed, as we often do today, "the increased facilities for communication, and the multiplicity of the relations existing between the countries of emigration and immigration" as two of the main factors behind migration.

An example of a summary of present knowledge on regularities can be found in Lee (1966). He deals with a prevailing set of factors both in the sending and in the potential receiving regions. These factors could be positive, neutral, or negative. Added to them are potential barriers to migration, "intervening obstacles," such as spatial and cultural distances between regions, costs of migration, or government restrictions. Böhning (1981) provides a more general overview. A recent survey of macro determinants of international migration is given by Greenwood and McDowell (1992).

Today, economic theory is less applied than during Kryger's time and thus further from actual socioeconomic processes. It is a scientific discipline with a hard and coherent theory, based on a number of simplified assumptions about people and society. However, several economists are struggling to develop theories that can be applied to real world situations, like international migration (e.g., Lucas, 1981; MacPhee and Hassan, 1990; Blanchard *et al.*, 1991). According to economic theory we could expect not only labor to move North but also capital to move South. These activities would increase the total production of goods and services. In a hypothetical future with only economic considerations, no restrictions on international migration, and no ethnic tension or social problems, the greatest economic efficiency would be attained by a very large redistribution of the population.

In reality, economic theory cannot be used in this simplified way. Rather than calculating the flows necessary to achieve a theoretically efficient equilibrium, economic theory should be used to indicate the direction of the flows – not only migrants but also capital and trade commodities – and the marginal returns of these flows.

In geography, a more applied discipline, researchers on migration have been concerned mainly with intranational migration, including urbanization. Strong theories, like the gravitation approach from the 1940s, could then be applied to make probable prognoses on migration flows. However, South–North migration is not only dependent on factors such as distances, information flows, the size of populations, or the number of employment opportunities in different regions. Legal restrictions in the rich countries prevent many foreigners from entering. With present trends, less than 1 percent of the population in the South will probably migrate to the North before 2010.

The well-known mobility transition theory (Zelinsky, 1971), which sometimes is treated as a deterministic theory, tells us that there are historical phases, for example, the demographic transition, when movement is related to general processes of urbanization, industrialization, and modernization. It is, however, not self-evident how these ideas could be applied to South–North migration.

Political science can teach us about public institutions and public decision systems concerning, for example, the formation of immigration policies (Kelley and Schmidt, 1979). Law can explain the background and practice of immigration rules. However, neither discipline has a theory on international migration flows.

The geopolitical future of the world, studied by geographers and political scientists, is important, but there are no good theories which could help us make forecasts. We know that the lack of congruence between ethnic settlements and political borders will continue to be a problem – it is a problem in several regions. The present situation in Africa is shown in *Figure 14.2.* In Europe, a strong ethnic chauvinism not only created more than a dozen new nations in past years, but also caused "ethnic cleansing." Unwanted minorities have been either expelled from their settlements or killed in a systematic way. This type of geopolitics is currently taking place in the former Yugoslavia.

Sociology can explain some of the flows. According to one theory (Hoffman-Nowotny, 1981), some flows have to do with the distribution of power and prestige in a social system. A typical migrant would first live in a poor country with a specific status among friends and neighbors, then migrate to a rich country where he or she would work hard, accumulate savings, and finally move back to the poor country with the savings and with a higher status than before. The attractive aspect of this theory is that it fits many movements between South and North.

Demographers speculate less than other researchers. They want clear assumptions and established methods. A typical study would, for instance, assume that 20,000 migrants with a specific ethnic belonging and age and sex distribution settle permanently in Australia every year. The study would then make calculations on how this flow would change the demographic structure of the Australian population over time. Lutz and Prinz (1992), in their study on hypothetical migration flows from Eastern Europe to Western Europe, show that assimilation processes would soon reduce the number of "foreigners" in the West to very small numbers.

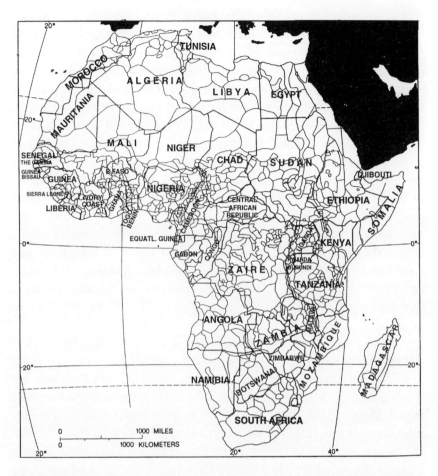

Figure 14.2. Ethnic territories and national boundaries in Africa. Present boundaries were drawn with very little consideration of ethnicity and long-lasting peaceful coexistence within and between nations. Source: Peoples and Bailey, 1991.

The dependency burden is one of the central concepts in demography, and an international gap in this burden would lead to migration flows. The discrepancy of an elderly (and wealthy) population in the more developed countries and a young (and poor) population in the less developed is repeatedly pointed out by demographers. This creates a "demographic potential" for migration.

Demographers are also concerned with feedback and return flows, as are scientists in other fields, such as geography and sociology. It is a well-known fact that small, pioneer flows of a new group of migrants into a region later generate larger flows. First a small group of new migrants is established in a new region. If the members in this group are better off there than others are at home, they can receive friends or relatives and give them a base to start from; these friends can in turn receive others, and so on. A further example of feedback effects is that a migration flow grows as agencies (formal and informal) are set up in the sending country to help potential migrants by providing them with information and practical assistance.

Another well-known fact is that migration flows in one direction will later cause counterflows. An early reference with both ideas and empirical evidence on this statement regarding international migration flows is Ravenstein (1885). For example, a large proportion of the immigrants, legal and illegal, to the USA from Mexico returns home after a work season or a few years.

History is, of course, not only an academic discipline; it is also the empirical source of all applied social science. We understand the world by observing it. By knowing more about past and present migration flows it is hoped that we will be better prepared for expected future flows. There have been many mass migration flows over long distances. In the last century, Europeans migrated to North America, South America, and Australia; Russians colonized parts of Asia; Chinese went South. The British, Ottoman, and, more recently, the Russian empires fell, resulting in large numbers of British, Turkish, and Russian settlers belonging to the ruling class migrating from conquered territories. In recent decades, the Rio Grande and the Mediterranean have become symbols of borders that are crossed by large numbers of migrants. Today, the need for foreign labor in the USA, Europe, and the oil-producing countries is resulting in large flows of labor migrants, staying for shorter or longer periods, some of them becoming citizens in their new countries.

Can these and other earlier movements tell us anything about the future? Yes, they can teach us that a few thousand net migrants per year add up to many millions over several decades. During the 1970s and 1980s about 4 percent (net) of the Mexican population migrated to the USA. History also tell us that economic booms in the North result in large labor flows in the future. Less comforting is that history also tells us that several flows were not regarded as probable before they became a fact. History, however, cannot tell us about future details; it can only provide probable patterns.

The main factors influencing historic and contemporary international migration are well known, and will continue to be important. There are many ways to label them. Economic factors include wage differences, different access to economic wealth, and material standard of living. Social factors comprise proximity to relatives and friends. Cultural factors, such as lifestyles and ethnicity, include social organizations, religion, and values. Geopolitical factors concern tension or conflict, political instability, and threats to life. Environmental factors, such as the carrying capacity of land for inhabitants with limited resources, cause large migration flows, especially when they are combined with geopolitical instability.

The causal links between these factors and the flows are generally clear. For example, if everything else is equal, most people prefer higher wages, nearness to family, and religious freedom.

Migrants from the South usually go directly to the North, but sometimes they first migrate to another developing country before continuing to an industrialized country. For example, ethnic Turks from the Balkan states often migrate to Turkey in a first move and then to Western Europe. A study of such indirect international migration to the United States was carried out by Greenwood and Trabka (1991).

14.3   Push Factors

The welfare gap between countries in the South and North, which includes factors such as a structural income gap or physical proximity, does not change easily over time. The income gap between Eastern Europe and Western Europe or between North America and South America will not disappear before the year 2020 (Öberg and Boubnova, 1993). Also even with unrealistically large investments in the South (for example, 50 percent), it may still take a long time to reduce this gap. If present policies continue, the gap could even be larger in the future than it is today. There are more dollars

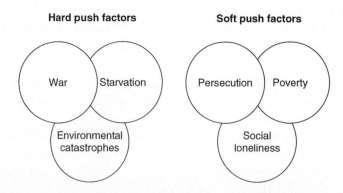

Figure 14.3. Hard and soft push factors of migration.

invested per person in the North today than the total income per person in the South.

As indicated earlier, causes of migration are sometimes divided into two groups – push factors and pull factors. The ways these factors influence South–North migration have been discussed by several authors (e.g., Golini *et al.*, 1991; Heyden, 1991). Push factors can be structural, such as the rapid global population growth with its effects on competition for food and other resources. Population growth is most severe in poor countries that are already struggling with major food problems. Another structural cause is the welfare gap between the North and the South. There are several other structural forces, but they are all somewhat internally interrelated in a causal structure.

Push factors can also be related to individual motives as shown in *Figure 14.3*. There are no indications that these factors will become less important in the future. Without being pessimistic, it is easy to believe the opposite for several reasons.

Wars between or within nation-states are usually caused by a combination of long-lasting ethnic tensions and economic inequalities. They can create large migration flows. For example, in the past migration flows occurred in many former African colonies such as Algeria, Angola, Guinea-Bissau, Mozambique, Namibia, and Zimbabwe (Rogge, 1992). Today these migration flows are taking place in former Yugoslavia, Sudan, and Sri Lanka. Usually people try to move to neighboring countries. In some cases, they may move to distant places if relatives and friends are already located there. Indonesians migrated to the Netherlands, Armenians to the USA, and Croats to Sweden. War between nations usually occurs where it has occurred before, where ethnic hate exists, and where the social systems are under too loose control (anarchy) or too strict control (dictatorship).

In some parts of Africa, the Balkan area, and Southeast Asia, the risk of war in the coming decades is high. Countries like South Africa and Israel have more tension in relations to their neighbors than Switzerland or Canada, and thus the risk for future war is higher in the former countries. However, higher risks do not forecast future outcome. Peace can come unexpectedly in some areas; and tension can rise fast in peaceful regions.

Persecution exists in many parts of the world, such as in Sudan, Myanmar, former Yugoslavia, and El Salvador. Ethnic tension leads to murder in war times and persecution in peace times. It will continue to be a problem in most parts of the world in the coming decade. Africa may see more of this problem than other parts of the world in the near future.

Starvation with high mortality is already prevalent in many countries (Dréze and Sen, 1989). In most African countries the consumption of calories has decreased in the last decade: 35 out of 47 countries were worse off in 1989 than in 1980, according to FAO statistics. The worst decline was in sub-Saharan countries like Angola, Botswana, Gabon, Mozambique, and Rwanda. Starvation in the future is more probable in poor countries with a small domestic food production or in nondemocratic nations, since "no democratic country with a relatively free press has ever experienced a major famine" (Sen, 1993). Starvation is also more probable in countries with ethnic/political tension since it is a weapon that can be used to hurt enemies, for example, in the Ukraine in the 1930s, Biafra in the 1960s, and southern Sudan in the 1990s. Areas with current low income, high debts, and low food consumption are shown in *Figure 14.4*.

Poverty is probably the largest single factor behind current and future migration flows. According to one estimation from the UN (1993b), 100 million migrants have left their home countries because of poverty. It is of course hard to define poverty gaps, but

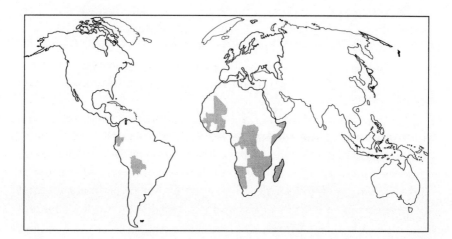

Figure 14.4. Potential emigration areas. The map shows countries with low income per capita, large debts in relation to income, and low food consumption. A quarter of a billion people live in these countries. Low income is defined as less than $1,500 per person in 1990; high debts mean more than one year's GNP; and at present low food consumption implies that the supply of food is lower than 2,300 calories per person per day. Source: UNEP and UNDP, 1992.

they certainly constitute a contemporary and a future main force behind international migration. The search for a good living standard can be combined with all the push factors mentioned earlier, such as parenthood or ethnicity. Poverty has indirect effects on migration flows in the sense that we do not find the poorest part of the population among the migrants. Large numbers of very poor in a country will increase competition for resources, add to crime and violence, and thus decrease the living standard for others, including the lower and upper middle classes. It is in these latter groups that we find most migrants.

   Environmental catastrophes are often discussed as a common future cause behind large migration flows. Nuclear power stations or factories producing atomic, biological, or chemical (ABC) weapons could pollute large areas, such as Chernobyl did in the Ukraine in 1986. A rise in sea level or more hurricanes, which are phenomena discussed as a possible scenario if global warming becomes a reality, will create floods in lowlands in many countries. With less ozone protection in the atmosphere, large areas will be uninhabitable. For the moment there are no good prognoses of where future environmental catastrophes are likely to occur. Most environmental catastrophes have occurred in developing countries. Drought, floods, soil erosion, and desertification are widespread, recurrent problems. According to a 1992 report by the International Organization for Migration, environmental migration will be caused by the following disruptions: elemental, biological, slow-onset accidents; development factors; and finally, environmental warfare. Each category covers a spectrum of disruptions ranging from mild to catastrophic. For an excellent overview of the literature on links between environmental degradation and migration see Suhrke (1993).

Social loneliness is a problem of much less general importance than others mentioned here. Furthermore, it will be a problem only for a very small minority in the South, such as some parents with children in the North. However, this small group can be a substantial proportion of the migrants going North, since they are usually allowed to move to their close relatives (Jasso and Rosenzweig, 1986).

Summarizing the short discussion of push factors is easy. They are overwhelming and will probably change the world in many ways. We may be facing an unrecognizable world in the year 2020 with migration flows of the same magnitude as during the last century when Europeans flooded other parts of the world.

The North will be affected in an unforeseeable way, especially if the future flows are determined by the supply of emigrants in the South instead of, as today, by the demand for immigrants in the North. However, a large part of these international flows will continue to be between neighboring countries in the South. A large part will also be refugees who will not be allowed to stay permanently or temporary workers; neither group is defined as migrants in this chapter.

The basic assumption in this chapter is that changes are not very spectacular. Restrictions placed by countries in the North will regulate future immigration. Future changes in restrictions are assumed to be mainly influenced by present attitudes toward strangers, attitudes that will not change during one generation.

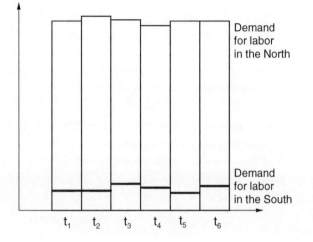

Figure 14.5. The gap between demand for cheap labor in the North and the South is so large that minor changes in the demand only influence migration flows indirectly through policy formation.

14.4   Pull Factors

The distinction between push and pull factors is usually unclear from a scientific point of view. Wealth can be a pull factor in the North, attracting migrants from less wealthy countries, but this phenomenon could also be described as a push factor, lack of wealth, in the South. With this in mind, caution must be taken when push and pull concepts are under study.

From a technical point of view, it is difficult to distinguish between the importance of push and pull factors in relation to South–North migration. The gap between indicators such as salary, security, and demand for cheap labor is usually so large between the South and the North that changes in either the push or pull factor only marginally affect it.

Also, theoretically a distinction is combined with severe problems. A larger flow of migrants during a period of low demand in poor countries could be dependent either on the low demand during the period, in which case it is a push factor, or on a delayed response to an earlier situation with a high demand in the rich countries, in which case it is a pull factor (see *Figure 14.5*). Thus, not only can data be selected in different ways, but the same information can also be interpreted in many ways. Concerning, for example, the early migration flows between Sweden and the United States, Wilkinson (1967) states that they were mainly determined by labor demand in the USA, while Thomas (1941) reports that the economic conditions in Sweden were more important. Quigley (1972) shows that conditions in both the sending country and the receiving country were important. An overview of these and other empirically based studies on patterns and dynamics of push and pull factors can be found in Greenwood and McDowell (1992). The most successful studies of international migration are theoretically weak but empirically strong.

Models of migration are specific to the relative importance of push or pull factors. Depending on which theory a researcher uses, he or she is restricted to specific mathematical tools. Each modeling technique emphasizes either push or pull factors. For example, a Markov model "pushes" migrants between time steps in the future depending on earlier trends. An overview on how different methods rely on push or pull ideas can be found in the geographic literature (Alonso, 1974).

In the literature, pull factors are expressed in terms of gaps. A high demand for labor with a corresponding high salary level is related to the wage gap between countries. Pull factors of this kind are difficult to trace in empirical figures because the gap is so enormous that it is not theoretically sound to relate marginal changes directly to migration flows.

It would be better to relate pull factors indirectly to migration flows through the formation and implementation of immigration policies in the North. According to this idea, there is always a long-lasting, large structural welfare gap between the North and the South. The average income on one side of a geographical border can be more than 2000 percent higher than on the other side – for example, along the northern Mexican border or along the eastern Finnish border. An increase in the wage level of a few percentages on either side of the border does not change the gap as such. However, in some situations, pull factors in the North, such as a shortage of labor, could make it easier for the people in the North to accept immigrants. Policies could change and migration flows could increase. This view makes the distinction between push and pull factors instrumental in studies of South–North migration.

Related to this idea is the concept of migration pressure. This commonly used expression roughly means unrealized migration desires. The migration pressure from the South thus increases either if fewer people are allowed to migrate through a more restrictive policy or if a larger proportion of the population in the South would like to move North.

Pull factors that could change migration policies are related to economic and humanitarian ideas. Economic considerations are stronger than humanitarian factors. If influential actors in the North could earn money on immigration, this would probably be the most important pull factor. A few can always gain – farmers in California or fishermen in Sicily – but they must be supported by other groups, usually more than half of the population in democracies.

Looking ahead, there are different opinions on the future demand of labor in the North. One extreme argument is that there will not be a future need for more immigrants. The demand for labor has changed structurally in recent decades. In the future few laborers will be employed in modern agriculture in the North, yet this sector will produce more food than ever. Furthermore, there will not be a future need for industrial workers in the North. This is not only because of the increasing competition from the newly industrializing countries but also because of new technologies in the production system. More investments in industry and its productivity will only decrease demand for employees. Robots and computers will run machines in some rich countries. For example, in the Netherlands, only three workers out of ten in the labor market are in farming or in industry.

A further argument for why there is no need for immigration is that even with a future demand for labor in a booming economy, many millions of homemakers in the North can enter the labor market. Today, the low labor-market participation in southern Europe, for example, functions as a reserve supply of labor.

The opposite argument is that the demand for labor in the North will increase as a function of income, not as a function of demand for labor in agriculture and industry. Service employment must also be included in the analysis. For example, many rich old people in the

North will need help in the future, but a shortage of people willing to care for them has been projected. The shortage is due partly to a new demographic situation, with a decrease in working-age groups, and partly to the fact that it is difficult to recruit people living in the North for jobs with a low status.

The humanitarian rationale for accepting refugees as immigrants has been quite strong, and will probably maintain its strength in the future. A tendency to decrease its influence on migration is the argument that more refugees could get help for the same amount of money if they did not have to migrate to the North. Temporary refugee camps in the South will probably be more common in the future. Another tendency is that attitudes toward immigration are changing slowly. Right-wing political parties tend to try to promote policies that result in fewer migrants (Vandermotten and Vanlaer, 1993; Fielding, 1993). It is hard to see how the humanitarian pull factor can change policies so that more migrants will be accepted in the future. Yet, if a change in attitudes occurs, it could influence immigration much more than changes in the labor market.

14.5 Policies

In this chapter, the most important factor for future permanent immigration flows to the developed countries is assumed to be attitudes toward foreigners within the receiving countries. These attitudes determine regulation policies in the North. Ethnicity in a broad sense plays an important part in this context. Feelings of superiority among rich majority groups in the North or of hate or fear of potential immigrant groups belonging to other ethnic groups cause decreases in future flows. Native ethnic Estonians are afraid of large flows from Russia. Ethnicity also plays an important role when internal flows in the South are determined. Muslims in Pakistan are not interested in large flows of Hindus from India.

Since there is no comparative study of this sensitive issue on feelings on ethnicity and attitudes toward other ethnic groups, the current international discussion among researchers is based on a combination of nonsystematic interviews with colleagues from different countries, official policies, and statistics on actual permissions for foreigners to obtain citizenship. According to this soft approach,

Japan, the oil-rich Muslim countries, and Australia will be hesitant to accept immigrants from other cultures; North America will welcome large streams; and Western Europe will hold a position in between these two.

Within Western Europe, current practice varies: Sweden accepted one non-European asylum seeker for every 80 inhabitants during the 1980s; Finland accepted almost no non-European immigrants. On average, there are large migration flows within Europe but very limited immigration from other parts of the world.

However, small labor flows from neighboring regions continue. For example, in Germany, Belgium, and the Netherlands, the Turkish population increased from 1.6 million to 1.8 million between 1985 and 1988. During the same period, the number of Algerians, Moroccans, and Tunisians living in those countries rose from 330,000 to 370,000 (UN, 1992a:179). The majority of the labor migrants are legal. Most of the illegal migrants are now in Italy. There are several estimates on the number of illegal migrants, but most give estimates of about 1 million (Montanari and Cortese, 1993).

In the past the immigration policy in Western Europe varied from country to country, but a more coherent policy is now emerging (Widgren, 1992). Five countries (Germany, France, the Netherlands, Belgium, and Luxembourg) have signed an agreement to harmonize immigration. This group of countries, the Schengen group, will directly or indirectly influence other countries to adjust their policies in the same direction. Europeans are very restrictive to non-European immigrants. On average, around 1 percent of the population are non-Europeans. France, the UK, Germany, Sweden, and Belgium have higher figures.

Within the former USSR, which comprises a European part (the Baltic states, Russia, Ukraine, Belarus, and Moldova) and an Asian part (including Georgia, Armenia, Azerbaijan, and Kazakhstan), there are now flows from Asia to Europe. Ethnic Russians migrate to Europe from territories where they used to belong to a ruling minority, or where they were working for high salaries as compensation for poor working conditions. The same is true for ethnic Ukrainians and Belarussians (Öberg and Boubnova, 1993).

The two countries in the North American region are of special interest in this chapter since they have traditionally accepted

Table 14.1. Principal countries[a] of resettlement of refugees and asylum seekers.

Resettlement country	1975–1990	Ratio refugees/population
Sweden	121,000	1/71
Canada	325,000	1/82
Australia	183,000	1/96
USA	1,478,000	1/171
France	200,000	1/238
Germany[b]	91,000	1/869

[a]Some countries with very small populations – Denmark, Norway, and New Zealand – have high ratios, as high as those in the USA or France.
[b]Excludes ethnic Germans from Eastern Europe. If this group is included, Germany has the same ratio as France.
Source: USCR, *World Refugee Survey*, 1992, cited in Rogge, 1992.

immigrants with different ethnic backgrounds. The United States accepts more immigrants than any other country in the world. The USA and Canada belong to the principal countries of resettlement of refugees and asylum seekers (see *Table 14.1*). Canada accepts fewer immigrants in absolute numbers but more than the USA in relative terms. The USA granted permanent resident status to nearly 6 million people and Canada to 1 million during the 1980s.

The US immigration policy legalized the stay of another 0.5 million people in 1989. For more than a decade, immigration has been increasing. About one-third of the immigrants today are admitted because they are adult children or siblings of US citizens, another third are spouses, children, and parents, and the last third are humanitarian or economic immigrants without close relatives living in the USA.

The Canadian immigration policy has always been based on humanitarian ideas and economic considerations (Green, 1976). Family reunions and protection of refugees belong to the former category; labor-market needs, to the latter. Approximately one-third of the immigrants belong to the latter group. They have desired skills or occupations or business intentions, or they are members of a family having this labor-market advantage. In recent years, labor-market needs have become more important, and there are discussions on increasing this group of immigrants still further.

The majority of the population in Oceania lives in Australia and New Zealand. Australia admitted about 0.8 million immigrants from countries outside Oceania during the 1980s. New Zealand, a country with net emigration, admitted less than half in relative terms, which is approximately one-tenth in absolute numbers. Roughly every fifth person moving to Australia was skilled and defined as a "business migrant." Every tenth (between 1986 and 1989) was a refugee or a person admitted under the Special Humanitarian Program.

Japan is a rich country with a demand for foreign labor. It is by tradition a closed society. However, its strong and successful economy has increased the demand for labor within the country to a degree where legal and illegal imports become a factor. The legal workers are mainly women entertaining Japanese men, 71,000 in 1988 (UN, 1992a). The unregistered, illegal workers are increasing in numbers but are still less than 1 percent of the labor force (Shah, 1992). Thus there are some foreigners working in Japan, but they seldom get permission to settle in the country. A reasonable guess is that present attitudes toward non-Japanese will not change within one generation. The result could then be a large number of temporary guests or guest workers employed in Japan but not allowed to be citizens.

The rich oil-producing countries, especially in West Asia, will probably use the same strategy; they will continue their policy to allow workers to stay in the country on temporary jobs but will not allow foreigners to become citizens. Today, they accept large numbers (perhaps 2 or 3 million) of foreign workers: people of Arab origin (e.g., Egyptians, Palestinians, and Jordanians), people from countries in South Asia (e.g., India, Pakistan, and Bangladesh), and people from Southeast Asia (e.g., the Philippines, Republic of Korea, and Thailand). By 1985, it was estimated that 63 percent of all workers in the six Gulf States (Bahrain, Kuwait, Oman, Qatar, Saudi Arabia, and the United Arab Emirates) were from South or Southeast Asia (Shah, 1992). Since these workers are not allowed to be citizens in West Asian countries, they are all temporary visitors and are not treated as (permanent) immigrants in this chapter. The assumption is that even in the coming decades, very few people will be allowed to become permanent immigrants to this rich part of the world.

Hong Kong, which is a part of China in this book (and will formally be a part of China as of July 1997), has an unpredictable future. Many inhabitants have already moved to other countries. The UK says that it will no longer accept the inhabitants as privileged members of the Commonwealth, except for 50,000 people with their families. China will, according to a probable scenario, become more integrated with the economy of the rest of the world in the coming decades. This event could result in larger migration flows to North America where there is a positive attitude toward immigrants from Asia. Also, Australia could be affected demographically by more intense economic cooperation with China.

The attitudes toward immigration in the rich countries are generally in favor of strong regulations and limitations on the numbers allowed to enter. The attitudes vary from a more generous North America to a restrictive Japan. Australia is similar to North America, but has clear ethnic priorities. Europe is, on average, closer to Japan, but some individual countries are exceptions.

The discussion of attitudes is mainly based on knowledge from historic and current situations. Attitudes toward future immigrants are based on attitudes toward immigrants today. These attitudes are already known indirectly through the size of contemporary migration flows. Previous migration flows between South and North, to a large extent, determine future flows. There are at least three reasons for this. First, an existing flow tells us that the receiving rich country accepts immigrants. Second, earlier immigrants, now living in the North, with social contacts to people in the South, make it easier for potential migrants to realize their wishes and thus become new immigrants. Large proportions of present immigrants are related to earlier immigrants. For example, more than one-third of the immigrant flow to the USA consists of close relatives of US citizens (spouses, children, and parents). Third, if many immigrants of one ethnic background move to a country with a democratic society, they become a political force because they have many votes, have economic power, and can organize lobbies. The Hispanic part of the US population is a good example of an immigrant group reaching the point of being able to exercise political power.

More detailed figures on assumed future migration streams between the world regions are discussed in Chapters 15 and 16.

Part VI

Projections

This concluding section translates the substantive considerations given in Parts II through V into alternative population projections. This exercise is done for 13 world regions over the 1995–2100 period.

The central scenario describes the most likely future population path under our assumptions. This scenario results in a world population of 7.88 billion in 2020, 9.87 billion in 2050, and 10.35 billion in 2100. These findings are remarkably close to the medium variant projections of the United Nations.

The systematic combinations of the three values (low, central, and high) for all three demographic components (fertility, mortality, and migration) result in 27 scenarios. These scenarios provide a broad range of possible future population trends. However, three findings hold across all scenarios:

- The world population will grow substantially.
- The world population will become older.
- The proportion of the population in today's developing countries will continue to increase.

The fully probabilistic projections contribute additional information. For example, given our assumptions there is a 64 percent chance (i.e., roughly two-thirds) that the current world population will never again double in the future – that is, it will not reach the 11.5 billion mark (which is twice the present level of 5.75 billion).

Chapter 15

World Population Scenarios for the 21st Century

Wolfgang Lutz, Warren Sanderson, Sergei Scherbov,
Anne Goujon

The previous chapters provide expert views on fertility, mortality, and migration. This chapter presents a synthesis of the expert views and, based on this synthesis, two sets of alternative scenario projections: one set in which the fertility, mortality, and migration components are assumed to be deterministic, independent of one another, and not subjected to any feedbacks; and another set in which certain consistent "stories" are defined and the components interact and react to certain outcomes of the projections such as population growth and aging. These two sets correspond to the two different meanings of "scenario" used in population projections (as discussed in Section 2.6). In Section 15.2 all possible combinations of the high, central, and low assumptions in fertility, mortality, and migration are presented. Section 15.3 provides three examples of interaction scenarios.

15.1 Synthesis of Expert Views on Future Fertility, Mortality, and Migration

A complex process led to our specifications of low, central, and high values for the three components in each of the 13 regions defined in this book. A basic outline of the process is given in Chapter 2, and more details can be found in Lutz (1995a). One feature of this exercise is that the experts only agreed to define alternative trends up to the period 2030–2035. For every world region and for each component they assumed three values: high, central, and low values. To limit the possible number of choices the central value was determined to be the mean of the high and low extremes; roughly 90 percent of all possible future cases were to be included in the range between these two extremes. Extensions of the assumptions beyond 2030–2035, as well as the specification of the exact path between the current level and the level to be reached by 2030–2035, are defined in Section 15.2. In this section we present a synthesis of the reasoning that led to the low, central, and high values assumed for 2030–2035 and listed in *Tables 15.1* to *15.3*.

15.1.1   Future fertility

Assumptions about the future course of fertility may be derived from several sources of information. First, past trends may be analyzed to assess the status of individual countries and regions in the process of demographic transition. Chapter 3 presents an assessment of this type on today's developing countries. This assessment was a major guideline in making specific assumptions for individual regions under the basic premise that the fertility transition that has started almost everywhere will essentially continue. While low values assume a rapid pace in the continuation of the fertility transition, the high values assume a much slower pace, in some cases even a stagnation, of the declining trend. In parts of Asia this even implies increasing fertility.

For the near future the intentions expressed by women in representative surveys can be taken as an additional important piece of evidence. Chapter 4 analyzes this information for a number of countries. Sub-Saharan Africa has, by far, the highest fertility levels and the lowest levels of contraceptive prevalence, but in all countries in this region the desired fertility rates, which have been derived from surveys, are clearly lower than actual levels – for example, in Kenya by almost two children. This fact, together with indications of increasing contraceptive prevalence, leads to the expectation of significant fertility declines in the next decade, even in sub-Saharan Africa which until recently has shown constant high fertility. In North

Africa the fertility transition is already much further advanced, and more than one-third of the female population uses contraceptives. Desired fertility rates in this region indicate that further significant fertility declines are to be expected unless dramatic events, such as a rise in pronatalist fundamentalism, change the pattern.

The three Asian countries considered in Chapter 4, Indonesia, Sri Lanka, and Thailand, already have total fertility levels below 3.0 with further declines expected. Latin America has an intermediate position comparable with that in North Africa. A noteworthy feature of this region is that over recent decades fertility was rather stagnant at this intermediate level, but the most recent evidence indicates further decline.

In the long run, without doubt, the general socioeconomic and cultural changes will determine fertility levels. But these trends are by no means easier to forecast than the path of fertility change itself. One more specific aspect in this context is the role of government policies and family-planning programs. As pointed out in Chapter 5, experience with such programs has shown that, over several decades, they can have an important effect if they are well integrated into other government policies and particularly if the socioeconomic development of the population has reached a point at which limitation of family size is considered advantageous and a real option by sizable segments of the population. Since many countries have been adopting such programs, they may well accelerate the fertility decline.

In terms of specific numerical assumptions, the high value in 2030–2035 was assumed to be lower than the current fertility level for all developing regions except East and Central Asia. This is due to the overwhelming evidence of a continuation of the demographic transition process in parts of the world that still have high fertility. For this reason no constant fertility scenario was specified (as done by the UN, 1994b). However, the high values do not assume a smooth fertility transition but rather an interruption or at least retardation of the process. This could be due to setbacks in socioeconomic development, cultural or religious movements such as a rise of fundamentalism, or strong heterogeneity with pre- and post-transitional populations living together in one region. The low values indicate a very rapid fertility decline that does not stop at 2.1 but

Table 15.1. Alternative fertility assumptions used in projections.

Region	TFR 1995	TFR 2030–2035 Low	TFR 2030–2035 Central	TFR 2030–2035 High
Africa				
North Africa	4.35	2.00	3.00	4.00
Sub-Saharan Africa	6.18	2.00	3.00	4.00
Asia-East				
China & CPA[a]	2.00	1.50	2.25	3.00
Pacific Asia	2.88	1.70	2.35	3.00
Pacific OECD	1.53	1.30	1.70	2.10
Asia-West				
Central Asia	3.35	2.00	3.00	4.00
Middle East	5.47	2.00	3.00	4.00
South Asia	3.77	1.70	2.35	3.00
Europe				
Eastern Europe	1.66	1.30	1.70	2.10
European FSU[b]	1.50	1.30	1.70	2.10
Western Europe	1.67	1.30	1.70	2.10
Latin America	3.10	1.70	2.35	3.00
North America	1.97	1.40	1.85	2.30

[a]Centrally Planned Asia.
[b]European part of the former Soviet Union.

continues to subreplacement fertility as it did in most industrialized countries. The resulting central values (the mean of the high and low values) lie somewhat above replacement level in most developing regions and significantly above in Africa, Central Asia, and the Middle East. The fertility assumptions for China are based on the discussion in Chapter 6, and are set at a low value of 1.5 and a high value of 3.0 in 2030–2035.[1]

The process of making assumptions for today's industrialized countries is in one way more difficult and in another way easier than for today's high-fertility countries. It is more difficult because the direction of change is unclear: Will fertility increase or decrease? It is easier because the margin of uncertainty may be assumed to be smaller. For a modern urban society with increasing female economic activity, it is unlikely that fertility will be significantly above replacement level in the future. But it seems equally unlikely that fertility will remain permanently below a very low level such as about half of replacement because, at an individual level, the desire for children seems to be deeply rooted in women and men and, at a societal level, very rapid population aging results in serious problems (see deliberations in Chapter 11).

Until a few years ago, the United Nations and other institutions preparing population forecasts assumed that fertility would increase to replacement level and that subreplacement fertility was only a transitory phenomenon. This assumption is supported by the argument of homeostasis as discussed in Chapter 11. In this view, fertility levels are not seen as the sum of individual behavior, but as one aspect of the evolution of a system in which individual behavior is a function of the status of the system (see Vishnevsky, 1991). Under such a systems approach the assumption of replacement fertility in the long run seems a defendable possibility. Therefore, we assumed a TFR between 2.1 and 2.3 in 2030–2035 as the high-fertility assumption in the five industrialized regions.

It is difficult, however, to find many researchers who support this view. Too much evidence points toward low fertility. The return to replacement fertility has been criticized as an assumed magnetic force without empirical support (Westoff, 1991). Many significant arguments support an assumption of further declining fertility levels. They range from the weakening of the family in terms of both declining marriage rates and high divorce rates, to the increasing independence and career orientation of women, and to a value change toward materialism and consumerism.

These factors, together with increasing demands and personal expectations for attention, time, and also money to be given to children, are likely to result in fewer couples having more than one or two children and an increasing number of childless women. Also, the proportion of unplanned pregnancies is still high, and future improvements in contraceptive methods are possible.

In conclusion one can say that the bulk of evidence suggests that fertility will remain low or further decline in today's industrialized societies. How far it will decline is not clear at this time. The expert group decided to settle for a TFR of 1.3 as the low value to be reached by 2030–2035. This value is below the low-fertility assumptions in some other projections, but it is far from being impossible. Actually several populations have already experienced such levels for extended periods. Taking into account the different ethnic composition in North America, the fertility range in this region was chosen to be slightly higher (1.4 to 2.3) than in Europe and Japan.

15.1.2   Future mortality

Mortality conditions at one point in time can be conveniently summarized by period life expectancy at birth, an indicator that results from a life table based on all age-specific mortality rates observed at that time. In this section, this indicator is used to define mortality assumptions.[2]

The uncertainties about future improvements or possible declines in life expectancy in today's high-mortality countries differ from those in low-mortality countries. With the exception of Eastern Europe, the latter countries have seen impressive increases in life expectancy and segments of their populations are approaching ages that were once considered a biological upper limit to the human life span. Hence assumptions about future improvements crucially depend on whether such a limit exists and will soon be reached (see Chapter 12; Manton, 1991). In regions that still have very low life expectancy, this question is irrelevant, and future mortality conditions will be determined by the efficiency of local health services, the spread of traditional (e.g., malaria) and new (AIDS) diseases, and the general level of subsistence.

Currently, life expectancy at a national level is highest in Japan: 82.5 years for women and 76.3 years for men. Only 30 years ago in 1960–1964, female life expectancy was 71.7 and male life expectancy was 66.6, implying an average increase of more than 3.5 years per decade for women. Eastern Europe, on the other hand, had the same life expectancy as Japan during the early 1960s but has had almost no improvement since then, bringing it to only 67.3 for men and 75 for women at present. During the 1980s the Soviet Union even experienced a decline in male life expectancy, and current estimates for Russia are as low as 59 years. Western Europe and North America took an intermediate position; life expectancy increased steadily by about two to three years per decade. The recent trend clearly points toward further improvements, and the analysis of age- and cause-specific mortality trends does not give any indications of improvements leveling off (Valkonen, 1991). Also studies of occupational mortality differentials in the Nordic countries – which are

Table 15.2. Alternative mortality assumptions to 2030–2035.

Region	Life expectancy 1995 Men	Women	Assumed change in years of life expectancy per decade Low	Central	High
Africa					
North Africa	62.7	65.3	0.5	2.3	4.0
Sub-Saharan Africa	50.6	53.9	−2.0	1.0	4.0
Asia-East					
China & CPA	66.4	70.1	Men 1.0	1.5	2.0
			Women 1.0	2.0	3.0
Pacific Asia	63.1	67.4	0.0	2.0	4.0
Pacific OECD	76.1	82.2	1.0	2.0	3.0
Asia-West					
Central Asia	65.1	72.5	1.0	2.0	3.0
Middle East	65.6	68.0	0.5	2.3	4.0
South Asia	59.7	59.7	Men 0.0	1.5	3.0
			Women 0.0	2.0	4.0
Europe					
Eastern Europe	67.3	75.0	1.0	2.0	3.0
European FSU	61.1	72.8	Men 0.0	2.0	4.0
			Women 1.0	2.0	3.0
Western Europe	72.1	78.1	1.0	2.0	3.0
Latin America	66.3	71.5	1.0	2.0	3.0
North America	72.3	79.1	1.0	2.0	3.0

more homogeneous than countries in many other regions – still show significant inequalities by social class (Andersen, 1991), which may be taken as an indication of the possibility of further improvements if the higher-mortality groups change their lifestyles. Vaupel and Lundström (in Chapter 12) show in the case of Sweden that at very high ages mortality also continues to decline.

These considerations in the low-mortality countries prompted us to assume future improvements that are more significant than those assumed by most other national and international population projections. As a high variant life expectancy is assumed to increase by three years per decade to 2030–2035. It is clearly not impossible since it is still below recently observed improvements in Japan and parts of Western Europe. The resulting central variant of a two-year improvement per decade also seems plausible, as supported by Mesle (1993). A broader margin was chosen for men in the European part of the former USSR because of greater uncertainties: assuming a continuation of bad conditions, the low value was set at zero years; the upper value was fixed at 4.0 because of the potential that life expectancy will greatly improve if the lifestyles in the region become similar to the Western patterns.

Health conditions in the developing regions have generally experienced very impressive improvements since World War II. Life expectancy in all developing countries has increased by more than 20 years since 1950–1955, when it was estimated to be about 40 years for both men and women. Some regions, such as East and West Asia, have experienced especially rapid increases. Latin America, which already had higher life expectancies during the 1950s, has achieved lower mortality levels than Africa and Asia. In the Caribbean, the mortality decline is particularly impressive.

These rapid improvements in mortality have led institutions that produce population projections to regularly change their assumptions. The UN raised the life expectancy limit for men from 72.6 years, assumed in 1973, in steps to 82.5 years, assumed in 1988. Similar adjustments were made for women (see Chapter 7).

Africa has the greatest mortality uncertainties of all regions. In Chapter 8, Garenne concludes his survey of African mortality by pointing out that past trends in Africa have been induced by technology transfers from the West, which affected virtually all countries in a short period of time. Public health, nutrition, economic development, and modern education were the key determinants of mortality decline. There are reasons for assuming that this declining trend of the past 30 years will not continue in Africa, and that differences between countries will prevail or even increase: one reason is that infectious diseases, especially the HIV virus, may spread further; another is that problems of basic subsistence and food supply may continue (see Chapter 10). In Chapter 9, Bongaarts presents a new calculation of the possible impact of AIDS on mortality. Translated into life expectancies and projected further into the future, his calculations result in a considerable range of uncertainties. For sub-Saharan Africa, the values for the scenario assumptions include uncertainties about AIDS as well as other uncertainties, such as possible wars and food shortages. The most optimistic case assumes further increases of four years per decade during a catching-up process with the rest of the world. The low scenario assumes declines in life expectance of two years per decade. Consequently, the central value shows only very modest improvements of one year per decade.

In the other developing regions, a general increase in life expectancy of between one and three years per decade has been assumed. In South Asia and Pacific Asia, which are also seriously affected by AIDS, the range was chosen to be greater assuming no improvements in the low case and four years per decade in the high case. In South Asia and China, where the sex differential in mortality is still unusually low because of differential treatment of girls and boys, life expectancy is assumed to increase somewhat more rapidly for women over the coming decades. For the Islamic regions of North Africa and the Middle East, a minimum increase of 0.5 years and a maximum increase of 4 years was chosen reflecting the somewhat greater potential for improvements in these regions.[3]

15.1.3 Future interregional migration

Of the three components of population change, international migration is the most difficult to examine for two reasons: less reliable and representative statistical information is available for assessing past and present migration levels; and migration patterns tend to show much less continuity. Recent immigration trends in Western Europe clearly demonstrate the volatility of migration trends. During the early 1970s West Germany had an annual net migration gain of more than 300,000; five years later this number had declined to only 6,000 and 3,000 during the early 1980s. During 1985–1989, however, the annual net gain increased sharply to 378,000, 100 times that of the previous period. Few other countries have these extreme fluctuations, but the traditional immigration countries – USA, Canada, and Australia – show remarkable ups and downs. Annual net migration to Australia declined from 112,000 in the early 1970s to 54,000 in the late 1970s. During the 1980s it increased again to over 100,000. For the United States and Canada, only immigration figures are available, which for the USA shows a steady increase from around 280,000 per year during the early 1960s to around 800,000 during the early 1980s. In 1990–1991 the figures have declined to under 700,000.

Table 15.3. Matrix of assumed high values of annual net migration flows (in thousands).

From	To North America	Western Europe	Pacific OECD	Middle East	Total
Africa					
North Africa	90	250	20	15	375
Sub-Saharan Africa	115	150	40	5	310
Asia-East					
China & CPA	270	50	50	–	370
Pacific Asia	400	50	100	10	560
Asia-West					
Central Asia	10	30	–	–	40
Middle East	15	30	10	–	55
South Asia	300	100	80	15	495
Europe					
Eastern Europe	50	100	–	–	150
European FSU	50	150	25	–	225
Latin America	700	90	25	5	820
Total	2,000	1,000	350	50	3,400

Aside from the migration streams into Western Europe, North America, and Australia/New Zealand, labor migration within Asia has been remarkable over recent decades (see Chapter 13 by Zlotnik). For instance, during the late 1980s more than 430,000 workers left the Philippines annually, with some 280,000 of them going to the Middle East. South Korea lost an average of 170,000 workers per year during the early 1980s, India lost 240,000, and Pakistan lost 130,000 during the same period. The largest proportion of these workers went to the oil-rich countries in the Middle East. During the late 1980s these migratory streams within Asia have shown significant declines.

Because of the volatility of these trends and the great role that short-term political changes play in both the receiving and sending countries, it is more difficult to speculate about the future of migratory streams than about future fertility or mortality trends. Furthermore, net migration always results from the combination of two partly independent migration streams, namely, that entering and that leaving a certain region for whatever reasons. These reasons are sometimes grouped into political (asylum seekers), economic (expected differentials in standard of living), and recently environmental factors. This last category remains rather vague because worsening environmental conditions often result in worsening economic conditions. As pointed out in Chapter 14, for all categories the potential for further increases in interregional migration is great because of better communications between the regions, cheap mass transport facilities, and the persistent gap between the North, which is not only richer but also rapidly aging and most likely in need of young labor, and the South, which has many young people with only limited opportunities in their home countries.

The actual extent of future South–North migration streams depends not only on the pull and push factors, but also on the immigration policies in the receiving countries. If the European Union, for instance, decides to enforce a policy of virtually closed borders to the outside because of popular demand within the EU, this may well result in a situation of almost no net migration. Hence in the projections, zero net migration was chosen for the low variant. This does not mean that borders are entirely closed to migrants; it only assumes that the number of in-migrants approximately equals the number of out-migrants.

For the high-migration scenarios, annual net migration gains of 2 million in North America, 1 million in Western Europe, 350,000 in the Pacific OECD region, and 50,000 in the Middle East have been assumed. The distribution of migrants from the assumed sending regions to the receiving regions and migration patterns among the less developed regions are based mostly on current migratory streams as described in Chapter 13. *Table 15.3* gives the migration matrix assumed in the high-migration case. In the low-migration case, all cells are zero; in the central scenario, values are half of those given in *Table 15.3*. The high scenario assumes an annual net migration loss of 375,000 in North Africa, 310,000 in sub-Saharan Africa, 370,000 in China and other Centrally Planned Asia, 560,000 in Pacific Asia, 495,000 in South Asia, 150,000 in Eastern Europe, and 225,000 in the European part of the former Soviet Union. Model migration schedules by Rogers and Castro (1981) were used to determine the age patterns of migrants.

It is almost certain that actual migration streams will not be constant over time. But assuming that the short-term fluctuations average around certain levels of constant annual net migration is the most practicable way to deal with this volatility.

15.2   Scenarios with Independent Fertility, Mortality, and Migration Trends

15.2.1   Specific model assumptions

In addition to the general assumptions described above, every projection must make several specific choices concerning the age patterns of fertility, mortality, and migration as well as the specific patterns of change over time and many other more technical details. The most important choices are summarized in this section.

The projections were generated using DIALOG, a software program developed by Sergei Scherbov; DIALOG is specifically designed for multistate population analysis and projection. The projections were done in five-year intervals for five-year age groups. These projections differ from most other projection models because we define separate age groups up to age 120; extending the age categories beyond the usual 80+ category helps to avoid serious biases that occur when significant proportions of the population in low-mortality regions come into the highest age group.

As described in previous chapters all countries were grouped into thirteen world regions that can be regrouped into six continents as well as into two groups of less developed and more developed regions. The population data for the starting year, 1995, were taken from the Population Reference Bureau (PRB) World Population Data Sheet 1995, which gives the most recent estimates for total population size as well as fertility and mortality levels in all countries. Since this source does not provide the full age distribution of the population, age distributions were taken from the United Nations 1994 assessment by proportionally adjusting the age groups to match the PRB total population figures in the case of discrepancies between the two sources. Age patterns of fertility and mortality in the starting year were derived using the same procedure.

As to the assumptions of fertility, mortality, and migration, the 1995 values and the alternative values chosen for 2030–2035 have been described above. A more detailed table giving the specific time path of the values and their extensions to 2100 is given in the Appendix. The values for 1995–2000 and 2000–2005 reflect the assumption of a quick opening up of the uncertainty range over the first five years followed by linear interpolation ("sausage model"). This particular decision was based on the observation that, under strictly linear interpolation, the range of uncertainty given for the first interval is far too small; therefore, between 1990 and 1995, many countries showed empirical trends that were outside the range assumed by the projections based on 1990 data.

Fertility assumptions for the second half of the 21st century are usually considered to be more art than science. Typically long-range projections assume some kind of a convergence toward the so-called replacement level. This is done for two reasons: first, it is convenient; second, no plausible alternatives seem to exist. But there is no good theory to explain how some *magic hand* should raise fertility to a level slightly above two children per woman after completion of the demographic transition. Only a vague and unproven homeostasis hypothesis would suggest such a pattern.

In this analysis we suggest another rationale. Ultimate fertility is assumed to be a function of region-specific population densities within a predefined range of ultimate TFRs. After the completion of the demographic transition, low population densities are assumed to be associated with higher fertility, and vice versa.[4] Fertility is assumed to reach a level between 1.7 and 2.1 children per woman depending on density (for the central scenario) by the year 2080. The projected density for 2030 (central scenario) is taken as a criterion. The least densely populated region – South America with 28 persons per km^2 projected for 2030 – is given the highest TFR (2.1), while beyond 300 persons per km^2 (only South Asia, with a density of 478 persons per km^2 by 2030) a TFR of 1.7 is assumed. For densities between 28 and 300, intermediate fertility levels are obtained through linear interpolation. The low-fertility (and high-fertility) assumptions are set at 0.5 children below (and above) the value obtained for the central scenario. Appendix Table 1 gives assumed fertility and mortality levels for the period 2080–2085 for each of the three scenarios. Beyond 2080–2085, levels are assumed to remain constant. Between the periods 2030–2035 and 2080–2085, levels are derived from linear interpolation.

Future age-specific fertility rates have been obtained by proportionally changing the age-specific rates of the starting year in accordance with the TFR level chosen. Extensive analysis of changing age profiles of fertility under different fertility levels has indicated that this is a reasonable approximation.

With respect to mortality, the United Nations (in the bi-annual assessments as well as in long-range projections) presents only one fixed path for each region without any uncertainty variants. Maximum life expectancy at birth is assumed to be 87.5 years for women and 82.5 years for men, and improvements in life expectancy end once the maximum figure is reached (between 2075 and 2150, depending on the region). For countries that already have very low mortality this implies very little prospects for further improvements in the future. In sharp contrast, our mortality assumptions span a very broad range in the long term, reflecting the great uncertainty about possible maximum mortality levels (see discussion in Section 15.1.2). In the low-mortality case, mortality rates continue to decline with a speed that corresponds to the past experience of the more successful countries. The high-mortality case even assumes some worsening in certain regions (see Appendix Table 1). Life-expectancy increases after 2030–2035 are generally smaller than before 2030, with constant mortality under the high-mortality assumption, a one-year increase per decade under the central-mortality assumption, and a two-year increase per decade under the low-mortality assumption. In regions with small mortality differentials by sex, future increase of the differentials has been assumed, as described in Appendix Table 1.

A Brass-type relational logits model was used to produce a new set of age-specific mortality rates at a given level of mortality. For sub-Saharan Africa and South Asia special life tables have been applied; these tables include the specific age pattern of AIDS mortality which has been used by Bongaarts (Chapter 9). For age-specific migration, the model migration schedules by Rogers and Castro (1981) have been applied.

The following sections give a summary of the most important results. The Appendix Tables provide more information on each region. A complete set of results is available from the authors and accessible on the internet (http://www.iiasa.ac.at); in this set the results are arranged by five-year age groups (age 0–120) in five-year time intervals (1995–2100) for all 13 regions and all 27 scenarios that result from the combination of the three fertility, mortality, and migration assumptions.

15.2.2 Population size by region

World Population

Table 15.4 lists the total population sizes for the six continental divisions, the two economic divisions, and the world total in 1995 and population projections for 2020, 2050, and 2100. The table comprises nine cells that present the results for all possible combinations of assumptions of low, central, and high fertility and mortality under central-migration assumptions. The Appendix provides detailed tables on the 13 regions, at additional points in time, and also under the low- and high-migration assumptions in the regions most significantly affected by migration.

Table 15.4 is different from the usual presentation of population projection results in two important ways: first, the user can freely choose any combination of the three fertility and mortality assumptions; second, the user may combine different scenarios in different continents. Hence, the user can derive the total world population resulting from high fertility and low mortality in Africa but low fertility and low mortality in Europe. Traditionally, uncertainty variants, such as the low variant in UN projections or the low-fertility/low-mortality scenario given in the 1994 edition of this book, present figures assuming lower than expected fertility in all parts of the world. This strong assumption of a perfect correlation between the regions results in the most extreme low figures for total world population. In the more likely case of no strict conformity of trends in different parts of the world, results tend be close to the central scenario because, for example, higher than expected fertility in Africa may be compensated by lower than expected fertility in East Asia. The figures given for the world in *Table 15.4* thus refer

Table 15.4. Projections of total population (in millions) according to alternative fertility and mortality assumptions (and central-migration assumptions): 2020, 2050, and 2100.

| | | Fertility | | | | | | | | |
| | | Low | | | Central | | | High | | |
	1995	2020	2050	2100	2020	2050	2100	2020	2050	2100
Mortality										
High										
Africa	720	1202	1312	707	1278	1710	1484	1355	2173	2739
Asia-East	1956	2239	1979	994	2412	2601	2308	2589	3369	4650
Asia-West	1445	2073	2210	1241	2181	2741	2432	2290	3352	4321
Europe	808	769	593	291	811	716	546	854	860	961
Latin America	477	644	687	454	686	867	927	729	1080	1700
North America	297	335	321	251	354	386	423	374	463	697
Less developed	*4451*	*6011*	*6071*	*3330*	*6404*	*7780*	*7040*	*6802*	*9810*	*13228*
More developed	*1251*	*1250*	*1032*	*607*	*1319*	*1241*	*1081*	*1388*	*1486*	*1841*
World	**5702**	**7261**	**7103**	**3937**	**7723**	**9021**	**8120**	**8191**	**11300**	**15070**
Central										
Africa	720	1252	1562	1140	1332	2040	2366	1414	2599	4349
Asia-East	1956	2268	2116	1205	2444	2760	2704	2621	3554	5348
Asia-West	1445	2117	2421	1634	2228	2995	3136	2338	3659	5508
Europe	808	782	640	342	825	766	624	868	912	1075
Latin America	477	650	722	530	693	906	1056	737	1125	1910
North America	297	339	340	283	359	406	467	378	483	757
Less developed	*4451*	*6138*	*6694*	*4433*	*6541*	*8554*	*9137*	*6946*	*10765*	*16915*
More developed	*1251*	*1270*	*1107*	*700*	*1340*	*1319*	*1216*	*1410*	*1568*	*2033*
World	**5702**	**7408**	**7802**	**5134**	**7879**	**9874**	**10350**	**8356**	**12330**	**18950**
Low										
Africa	720	1298	1799	1662	1381	2344	3348	1467	2983	6058
Asia-East	1956	2296	2257	1440	2473	2918	3090	2652	3733	5960
Asia-West	1445	2158	2624	2073	2270	3235	3847	2383	3939	6627
Europe	808	796	692	402	839	819	705	882	968	1185
Latin America	477	656	756	612	700	945	1180	743	1169	2096
North America	297	344	360	318	363	427	511	383	505	812
Less developed	*4451*	*6257*	*7301*	*5701*	*6665*	*9285*	*11325*	*7080*	*11643*	*20524*
More developed	*1251*	*1291*	*1188*	*806*	*1360*	*1402*	*1355*	*1431*	*1654*	*2214*
World	**5702**	**7547**	**8488**	**6507**	**8026**	**10690**	**12680**	**8510**	**13300**	**22740**

Discrepancies in totals are due to rounding.

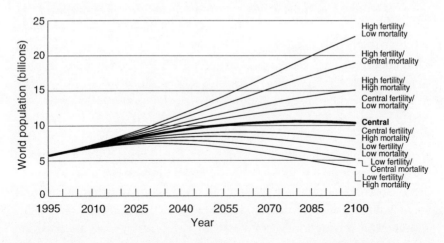

Figure 15.1. Alternative projected paths of world population size (nine scenarios, central migration).

only to the very unlikely case that all regions follow the same trends. The figures given for the two economic divisions, also assume that the same trends occur in each division.

Given the possible combinations of scenarios for different parts of the world, it is difficult to summarize the information contained in the table in a few sentences. If every region followed the central-fertility, central-mortality, and central-migration assumptions – which are assumed to be the most likely ones as seen today – world population would increase from 5.7 billion in 1995 to 7.9 billion in 2020, 9.9 billion in 2050, and 10.4 billion in 2100. This time path is plotted in *Figure 15.1* which shows that this set of assumptions implies a clear leveling off of world population growth toward the end of the 21st century. Before 2050 world population still increases by another 4 billion people. It surpasses the 10 billion mark in 2050–2055, then reaches an all-time high of 10.6 billion around 2080, and starts to decline somewhat to 10.35 billion by the end of the 21st century. In other words, the world population under the central scenario falls short of doubling from its present size of 5.75 billion (end 1995).

The most extreme case of high population growth results from the combination of high-fertility assumptions in each region with low-mortality assumptions in each region. In this highly unlikely

case, the world population would double before the middle of the
next century and reach an incredible 22.7 billion by the year 2100.
High fertility combined with high mortality – which is a more probable combination – would only result in 15.1 billion people. Hence,
given a high-fertility case, alternative mortality assumptions can
make a difference in total population size that is larger than today's
world population.

On the low-fertility side, the combination of low fertility with
high mortality yields the lowest path of world population growth. If
these rather unlikely assumptions were strictly applied to all world
regions, world population would still increase by another 30 percent
until 2030 and thereafter would enter a population decline that gains
momentum during the second half of the century and might bring
world population down to a low 3.9 billion by 2100. This would
be significantly below today's total population size. It would equal
the population in 1973–1974. Because of the significant population
aging implied by this scenario, an inverse momentum of population
growth (shrinking momentum) suggests further population decline
during the 22nd century because smaller and smaller cohorts would
enter the main reproductive ages. But aside from the incredible
population aging implied by this, this scenario cannot be called desirable because it is associated with the highest mortality and thus
a great deal of human suffering. In many parts of the world this
scenario assumes very little or no future progress in mortality reduction; in sub-Saharan Africa it even assumes declining trends in
life expectancy. The most desirable, under the criteria of a high
quality of life and low population growth, is the low-fertility/low-
mortality scenario, which results in a further increase of population
size to 8.5 billion by 2050 followed by a more moderate decline to
6.5 billion by 2100.

Table 15.4, together with *Figure 15.1*, can be used to evaluate
the relative impacts of the difference in the assumed mortality and
fertility alternatives. The nine cells in the table and the nine lines
in the figure show a clear ranking of the demographic variables,
with fertility being the dominating variable but mortality still being
highly significant. The impact of alternative mortality assumptions
on total population size is more significant in the low-fertility case
than in the high-fertility case. In the high-fertility case by 2100

the low-mortality assumptions yield a population size that is 50 percent higher than that of the high-mortality assumption; in the low-fertility case the differential is 65 percent. This differential is clearly big enough to justify the analysis of alternative mortality assumptions in addition to alternative fertility assumptions.

As stated above, *Figure 15.1* only gives the scenarios in which fertility and mortality trends in all regions follow the same pattern. Combining different assumptions in different regions results in several additional lines that all lie between the extremes given. Most are close to the central scenario; the positions of the lines depend on the degree to which trends in one region compensate for those in another. A more systematic analysis of these aspects is provided in the context of the probabilistic population projections in Chapter 16.

Regional Population Distribution

The global population growth described above results from a great diversity of different regional patterns. Under the assumptions of central fertility, mortality, and migration the population on the African continent grows the most rapidly. Its population almost triples in size over the next five decades from 720 million in 1995 to more than 2 billion in 2050. Accordingly, the share of the world population that lives in Africa increases from 13 percent to 21 percent (see *Table 15.5*). In the high-fertility/low-mortality case Africa's population more than quadruples by 2050, whereas under the low-fertility/high-mortality scenario, it does not even double. By 2100 the pessimistic mortality assumptions of this scenario lead to a population size that is smaller than today's.

The population of East Asia, which is currently home to one-third of the world's population, increases by 41 percent under the central assumptions until the year 2050. Because this growth lies well below the world average of 73 percent, the proportion of the world population living in this region declines by six percentage points to 28 percent. West Asia, on the other hand, gains five percentage points and holds 30 percent of the world population; by 2050 the population in this region more than doubles under the central assumptions. The reason for this difference lies predominantly in the fact that the fertility transition is already much further advanced in

Table 15.5. Distribution of world population (in %) by continent, according to three scenarios and under central migration: 1995 and 2050.

		Three scenarios in 2050		
	1995	Low fert. High mort.	Central fert. Central mort.	High fert. Low mort.
Africa	13	18	21	22
Asia-East	34	28	28	28
Asia-West	25	31	30	30
Europe	14	8	8	7
Latin America	8	10	9	9
North America	5	5	4	4
Less developed	*78*	*85*	*87*	*88*
More developed	*22*	*15*	*13*	*12*
World	**100**	**100**	**100**	**100**

East Asia. Latin America currently has 8 percent of the world's population; it is likely to maintain this proportion because its growth is expected to be close to that of the world average.

Europe and North America both grow below the world average under all three scenarios. The fraction of the world population living in Europe falls from the current 14 percent to 7–8 percent by 2050. Looking at economic divisions, today's more developed regions decline from 22 percent to only 12–15 percent depending on the scenario, while the less developed regions grow from 78 percent to 85–88 percent (*Table 15.5*).

Alternative migration assumptions show sizable impacts on total population size only in the low-fertility industrialized regions of Western Europe and North America. *Figure 15.2* illustrates the impacts of high- and low-migration scenarios in North America over the 21st century. As indicated above the high-immigration scenario for North America assumes average annual net migration gains of 2 million, whereas the low-migration assumption sets net migration at zero. The central scenario assumes a net migration of 1 million per year. Fertility assumptions in North America (for 2030–2035) vary from a TFR of 1.4 (low) to one of 2.3 (high). All the scenarios plotted in *Figure 15.2* are based on central-mortality assumptions and alternative fertility and migration assumptions.

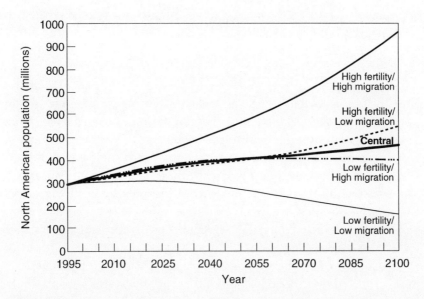

Figure 15.2. Alternative projected paths of population size in North America.

The figure shows that under all scenarios the total population size of North America increases from the present 300 million, at least for the next 30 years. After that time the combination of low fertility and low migration results in a significant decline of total population size, reaching about 160 million by the end of the 21st century. Combining the low-fertility assumption with high migration, however, results in a stable total population size of some 400 million. This difference of 240 million is due to alternative migration assumptions. Combined with high-fertility assumptions, the impact of high- and low-migration assumptions is greater in absolute terms (because the immigrants also have higher fertility) but smaller in relative terms. The combination of high fertility with low mortality is very close to the central scenario until the middle of the 21st century but then results in higher population growth later in the century. The unlikely combination of high fertility and high immigration results in significant exponential population growth in North America, coming close to 1 billion by the end of the 21st century. Government policies have more influence on immigration than on either fertility or mortality; therefore, immigration is clearly the

key policy variable for influencing the extent of population growth
in North America over the next century.

15.2.3 Population aging

Universal population aging (as measured by the mean age of the
population or the proportion of the population above age 60) is the
most consistent and dominant population trend of the next century.
In all regions, the scenario projections show an aging population.
Population aging has long been recognized as a cause of concern in
the industrialized countries, but projections clearly show that over
the coming decades it is likely to hit less developed countries even
harder than it has industrialized countries because of more rapid
fertility declines.

Table 15.6 has the same structure as *Table 15.4* but gives the
proportions above age 60 instead of total population. Currently only
9.5 percent of the world population is above age 60. Since the early
1950s this percentage has slowly increased from 8.1 percent in 1950
to 8.4 percent in 1970 and 8.8 percent in 1985. Over the coming
decades this percentage is projected to increase much more rapidly
under all possible scenarios. Under the three central assumptions
it increases to 13.2 percent in 2020, 19.6 percent in 2050, and 26.8
percent in 2100. These projected increases are much higher than
any increases that have been experienced today in industrialized
countries. Currently, Western Europe, the region with the oldest
population, has 18.6 percent of the population above age 60.

Even under the extreme high-fertility and low-mortality scenario, which results in more than 22 billion people in 2100, the
percentage of elderly increases to above 17 percent. Under the low-
fertility/low-mortality assumptions the aging figures become truly
daunting. By the end of the the 21st century, this scenario shows
that 42.5 percent of the population is above age 60. In industrialized countries half of the population is projected to be above age
60 under these assumptions, which are often called most desirable
by ecologists and the media because they result in the lowest total
population size. If mortality is high, fewer people survive to an old
age, lowering the old-age dependency ratio. But even in this case of
undesirably high mortality one-third of the population will be above
age 60 by the end of the 21st century.

Table 15.6. Projections of percentages of the population above age 60 according to alternative fertility and mortality assumptions (and central-migration assumptions): 2020, 2050, and 2100.

	1995	Fertility Low			Central			High		
		2020	2050	2100	2020	2050	2100	2020	2050	2100
Mortality										
High										
Africa	5.0	6.2	12.5	28.5	5.8	9.6	20.0	5.5	7.5	14.8
Asia-East	9.4	16.1	29.7	34.9	15.0	22.6	24.6	14.0	17.4	18.0
Asia-West	6.6	9.9	18.5	34.1	9.4	14.9	24.4	9.0	12.2	18.2
Europe	17.8	25.1	38.1	37.5	23.8	31.6	28.5	22.6	26.3	22.0
Latin America	7.6	12.4	24.4	33.1	11.6	19.4	23.8	10.9	15.5	17.8
North America	16.4	24.5	32.9	33.2	23.1	27.4	26.3	21.9	22.8	20.6
Less developed	*7.2*	*11.2*	*21.1*	*32.9*	*10.5*	*16.4*	*23.3*	*9.9*	*13.0*	*17.3*
More developed	*17.7*	*25.7*	*36.9*	*36.2*	*24.4*	*30.7*	*28.1*	*23.1*	*25.7*	*21.9*
World	**9.5**	**13.7**	**23.4**	**33.4**	**12.9**	**18.4**	**24.0**	**12.2**	**14.7**	**17.8**
Central										
Africa	5.0	6.3	13.1	30.7	6.0	10.0	21.5	5.6	7.9	15.8
Asia-East	9.4	16.6	31.9	40.1	15.4	24.5	28.4	14.3	19.0	20.9
Asia-West	6.6	10.1	19.7	37.7	9.6	16.0	27.2	9.2	13.1	20.3
Europe	17.8	25.9	41.4	44.1	24.6	34.6	34.0	23.4	29.1	26.3
Latin America	7.6	12.7	26.0	37.5	11.9	20.7	27.1	11.2	16.7	20.3
North America	16.4	25.2	35.9	39.1	23.8	30.0	31.2	22.6	25.2	24.6
Less developed	*7.2*	*11.5*	*22.2*	*36.4*	*10.8*	*17.4*	*25.9*	*10.1*	*13.8*	*19.2*
More developed	*17.7*	*26.5*	*40.2*	*42.5*	*25.1*	*33.7*	*33.4*	*23.9*	*28.4*	*26.1*
World	**9.5**	**14.0**	**24.8**	**37.2**	**13.2**	**19.6**	**26.8**	**12.5**	**15.7**	**19.9**
Low										
Africa	5.0	6.5	14.3	35.8	6.1	11.0	33.5	5.8	8.6	13.9
Asia-East	9.4	17.0	34.5	46.6	15.8	26.7	47.1	14.7	20.9	17.3
Asia-West	6.6	10.4	21.3	43.0	9.9	17.3	40.2	9.4	14.2	18.1
Europe	17.8	26.8	44.9	51.1	25.4	38.0	52.3	24.2	32.1	23.8
Latin America	7.6	13.0	27.8	42.8	12.2	22.3	41.3	11.5	18.0	17.5
North America	16.4	25.9	38.9	45.0	24.5	32.9	45.4	23.2	27.8	22.7
Less developed	*7.2*	*11.7*	*23.8*	*41.6*	*11.0*	*18.7*	*40.0*	*10.4*	*15.0*	*16.5*
More developed	*17.7*	*27.3*	*43.6*	*49.1*	*25.9*	*36.9*	*50.1*	*24.7*	*31.3*	*23.9*
World	**9.5**	**14.4**	**26.6**	**42.5**	**13.5**	**21.1**	**41.1**	**12.8**	**17.0**	**17.2**

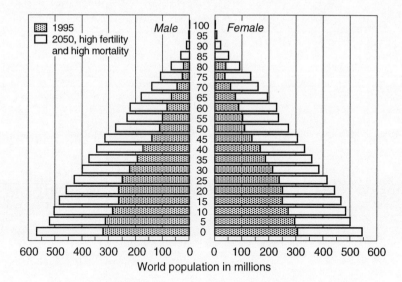

Figure 15.3. World population (in millions) under high-fertility and high-mortality scenario in all regions: 1995 and 2050.

Given the dynamics of the population age structure one can safely say that in the foreseeable future the proportion of the population above age 60 will not return to today's low level. Only major disasters affecting the elderly could bring about such a situation, and then only for a limited period. Continued exponential growth at very high rates (which would be necessary to produce a younger age structure through fertility) can be ruled out for several obvious reasons.

Figures 15.3 and *15.4* depict age pyramids for 2050 of the two extreme scenarios in terms of the resulting age structure – namely, that of high fertility combined with high mortality (*Figure 15.3*) and that of low fertility combined with low mortality in all regions (*Figure 15.4*). The shaded area gives the 1995 age pyramid for comparison. The high-fertility/low-mortality scenario (*Figure 15.3*) results in an age distribution that closely resembles the shape of the 1995 pyramid but at 2.3 times its population size (13.3 billion). Although it may not be directly visible from the graph, the population in the 2050 pyramid is clearly older than that in the 1995 pyramid both in terms of mean age and the proportion above age 60.

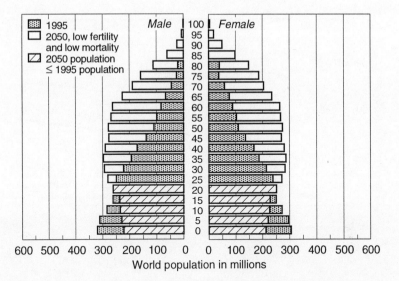

Figure 15.4. World population (in millions) under low-fertility and low-mortality scenario in all regions: 1995 and 2050.

Under the low-fertility and low-mortality assumptions (*Figure 15.4*), the 2050 age distribution no longer has a pyramid shape but resembles that of a bottle; this shape is already visible today in the age pyramid of some very low-fertility countries. *Figure 15.4* shows that, although the population in the 2050 age pyramid is 50 percent larger than the population in the 1995 pyramid, it is made up of fewer children. The proportion above age 60 consequently increases from 9.5 percent to 26.6 percent under this scenario. The pyramids graphically depict this dramatic aging within only 55 years.

Among the developing regions, China (together with Centrally Planned Asia) is certain to experience the most rapid aging because fertility has already declined dramatically. *Figure 15.5* shows the increase in the proportion of the population above age 60 under five different scenarios for this region. Currently, only 9.2 percent of the population is above age 60. This percentage is much lower in China than in all industrialized regions. But a steep increase in this proportion is already preprogrammed in the age structure of China. Over the next 15 years a moderate increase in the age structure occurs followed by a steep increase; these increases show

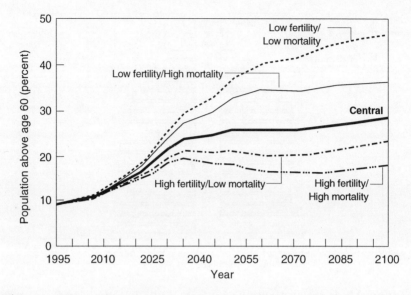

Figure 15.5. Alternative projected trends in the proportion of population above age 60 in China and CPA.

up under all alternative fertility and mortality assumptions. Only after 2035, when the large cohorts born before 1975 are over age 60, does this proportion stabilize under certain scenarios. Within less than four decades China's old-age dependency burden will be higher than North America's and about the same as that in Western Europe today. Western Europe's old-age dependency burden has built up over more than a century, so the region has been able to develop social-security schemes for the elderly. Nevertheless, Western Europe is confronted with serious problems in the pension system today and will have to deal with more problems in the future.

To avoid some of these problems China must take immediate and intensive actions. China's authorities are well aware of this issue and are considering not pushing programs to lower fertility further in order to avoid the large imbalances in the future age structure.

15.2.4   Population growth versus population aging

When comparing the information on projected aging to that on projected population growth, one very important feature becomes apparent. The scenarios that result in the highest population growth show only moderate population aging, while those showing a leveling off in population size imply very rapid population aging. Generally, very rapid population growth and very rapid aging are considered undesirable, but the scenarios described above clearly show that one cannot avoid both. An intermediate path, such as that given by the central scenario, avoids extremes but still combines substantial population growth with substantial aging at the global level. Since the problems caused by rapid growth and rapid aging are felt more at the regional level rather than at the global level, solutions to the problems must work at the former level. This issue must be discussed within a more regional context. The epilogue to this volume takes up some of the policy issues related to the aging versus population growth dilemma.

15.3 Special Interaction Scenarios for Selected Regions

So far in this chapter the fertility, mortality, and migration components have been considered independent determinants of population size and structure. When different scenario assumptions are combined to produce alternative scenarios, all combinations are given equal weight. However, certain combinations of indicators, such as very high fertility with very high mortality, are very unlikely and implausible given the analysis of past trends.

Why, then, do we present such systematic permutations of scenario assumptions without explicitly specifying likely interactions? There are three reasons for first presenting the scenarios as if the three components were independent:

1. In the short to medium term it is unclear whether any connection between, for example, fertility and mortality or fertility and migration exists. If such an interaction exists, it may be specific to certain regions.
2. There are an infinite number of possible types and intensities of dependence in different parts of the world; no set of interaction scenarios can be exhaustive.

3. The scenarios presented in Section 15.2 provide details on the
   extreme cases. Any assumed interaction that keeps each component within the bounds defined by the high and low extremes
   – for example, a positive correlation between fertility and mortality – results in more moderate population trends than those
   presented in the extreme scenarios. In this sense users are on the
   safe side when they look at the range of uncertainty as described
   by the scenarios that assume the components are independent
   of one another.

But clearly not all of the possible interactions can be derived
from the scenario results provided above, especially if the objective
is to focus on paths that change over time. To illustrate what types
of scenarios may be defined, the following three sections provide
a small sample of possible future "stories" in selected parts of the
world.

15.3.1   Can migrants to Western Europe and North America stop the aging process?

This question is often directed to demographers when the issue of immigration into industrialized countries is under discussion. Clearly,
a one-time wave of young migrants can improve the old-age dependency ratio temporarily because the working-age population is increased while that above age 60 remains unchanged. But over time
these immigrants age, and ultimately increase the dependency ratio
when they pass age 60. If retiring immigrants are replaced by the
same number of young immigrants there will be no additional deterioration in the dependency ratio but also no long-term improvement
(assuming that the migrant population has the same fertility as the
native population). Only if the absolute number of immigrants continuously increases, can the otherwise increasing dependency ratio
be kept down in a sustainable way.

To determine the growth rate of the immigrating population to
Western Europe and North America necessary to reduce the proportion of the population above age 60 – or more precisely, to have it
increase more slowly – we have defined a number of specific scenarios with different growth rates. The annual net migration under the
central scenario was taken as the basis for comparison. This means

a constant annual net inflow of 500,000 to Western Europe and 1 million to North America. Each number was assumed to increase by 0.5 percent, 1 percent, or 2 percent per year until 2080–2085 under three additional scenarios.

In summary, the results show that, even with a 2 percent annual increase, immigration has a very low impact on the proportion elderly. Under constant net migration (central scenario) the proportion age 60+ in Western Europe increases from today's 18.6 percent to 35 percent in 2050. This percentage is only 1.9 percentage points lower (33.1 percent) under the assumption of a 2 percent annual increase. Until 2100 further improvements are even more moderate. But this scenario also results in a total population that is 7 percent higher in 2050 and even 39 percent higher by 2100 than today's. The pattern for North America is not much different from Western Europe's, although at somewhat lower levels of old-age dependency. By 2100 under a 2 percent annual increase the proportion above age 60 is only 27 percent instead of 31 percent but the total population is higher by 66 percent; in other words, the population of North America is about 775 million with the migration factor instead of 467 million as shown in the central scenario.

From this exercise we conclude that even immigration rates that significantly increase the total population size have only a minuscule effect in counteracting long-term increases in the proportion above age 60 if fertility remains low.

15.3.2 Overshooting carrying capacity in sub-Saharan Africa

The popular literature, as well as parts of the scientific literature in ecology, frequently mentions the scenario of overshooting carrying capacity – namely, the possibility of a collapse resulting from a population size so large that it hits the growth ceiling beyond which adequate food supplies cannot be secured. Usually nothing specific is said about the type of collapse. To illustrate a demographic scenario that reflects this situation, we simply assumed that the collapse shows itself in the form of an increase in mortality. But mortality can increase in many different ways and, in turn, can result in very different demographic consequences. In the following we briefly look at alternative ways such a collapse might happen.

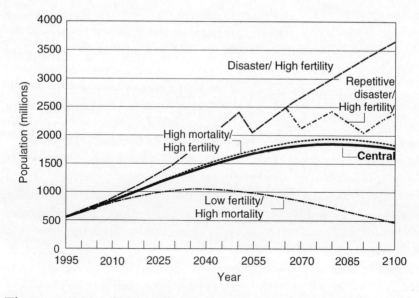

Figure 15.6. Projected population size (in millions) in sub-Saharan Africa, with and without feedbacks on mortality.

Sub-Saharan Africa is chosen for this example because it is the region most likely to experience the fastest population growth in coming decades. It is also a region that might surpass the critical point of population size that was derived from a joint FAO/UNFPA/IIASA (1984) land-carrying capacity study. In this study, an agricultural carrying capacity of 4 billion people was given for sub-Saharan Africa, assuming medium agricultural inputs. The low-input scenario resulted in sufficient agricultural production for less than 1 billion people.[5] For this study we look at a hypothetical intermediate case in which the carrying capacity is fixed at 2.5 billion.

Figure 15.6 gives future population sizes in sub-Saharan Africa projected until 2100, including feedback and disaster scenarios. The solid line gives the evolution derived from the central scenario, with a gradual increase in population size over the next 80 years and a stabilization at some 1.8 billion people over the extended long term. All other lines reflect disastrous developments. Both the dotted line and the short dashed line assume gradually increasing mortality (high-mortality or *unspectacular disaster* scenarios) as defined under the high-mortality assumptions for the region. Life expectancy decreases by two years per decade until 2030–2035 and then remains constant. This situation reflects the possibility of a slowly spreading mortality crisis which could be due to AIDS, deteriorating health systems, local famines, and regional conflicts. Fertility rates in both scenarios reflect the high- and low-fertility assumptions. Both cases have undesirably high mortality. Combined with high fertility, the trend is very close to the central scenario and almost reaches the 2 billion mark. Combined with low fertility, population increases to slightly over 1 billion and then declines.

The remaining scenario projects initially more fortunate developments in mortality: life expectancy increases four years per decade until 2030–2035, when it reaches a level of 66 years for men and 69 years for women, and continues to grow more slowly thereafter (low-mortality scenario). Fertility, on the other hand, does not decline as rapidly. The TFR declines as in the high-fertility scenario reaching a level of 4.0 in 2030–2035 and 2.4 by 2080–2085. By 2055 this scenario passes the assumed critical level of 2.5 billion. At this point, *something* must happen along the lines of a Malthusian "positive check." Under this assumed collapse, 20 percent of the population (more children than adults) die from war, starvation, disease, or some other cause. Because fertility is not assumed to change, only 10–15 years later, however, the magic 2.5 billion threshold is again exceeded (dashed line in *Figure 15.6*). Assuming that no further improvements are made in agricultural production and fertility and mortality remain unchanged (except for years of collapse), catastrophes occur in 10- to 15-year cycles.

The purpose of this highly speculative exercise of defining a collapse through an overshooting carrying capacity has been twofold: first, to show that the complaint of some ecologists that population projections simply do not consider the possibility of such feedbacks is not justified; second, to illustrate that the high-fertility/high-mortality scenario (labeled the *unspectacular disaster* scenario), under which the population size stays below the limits of carrying capacity, is not really more desirable than the high-fertility/low-mortality path checked by 20 percent collapses. In both cases there are large numbers of premature deaths. The exercise also shows that ecologists must provide more details about the kinds of collapse they have in mind if demographers should incorporate them into their projections.

15.3.3   Fertility responses to rapid aging in China & CPA and the Pacific OECD regions

Unprecedented aging of populations might also cause reactions. If the mean age of the population or the proportion of elderly exceeds a certain threshold, a feedback to the migration or fertility components seems possible. Extremely high levels of aging could be disadvantageous for economic and/or social reasons. Economic handicaps might result in increased immigration, which would only have minor long-term impacts on the proportions above age 60 as demonstrated earlier. It is conceivable that reproductive behavior in such societies changes through a combination of individual reorientation and strong public incentives. In the following discussion it is assumed that such a response occurs. China (and CPA) and the Pacific OECD region are used as examples because they are particularly interesting as far as the speed of the fertility transition (China) and the level of life expectancy already reached (Japan) are concerned. The central scenario has been modified for these calculations.

The underlying assumption is simple: when a certain level of aging is reached, the TFR is assumed to increase by 0.3. When the aging level exceeds a somewhat higher threshold, fertility is assumed to increase further by another 0.3 – a total of 0.6 children per woman. The aging levels at which fertility responses are simulated are 20 and 25 percent above age 60 in China and CPA (reached in 2025–2030 and 2045–2050 under the central scenario) and 25 and 33 percent in the Pacific OECD (reached in 2005–2010 and 2030–2035). Results of such fertility feedbacks are given in *Table 15.7*, which contrasts total population sizes and proportions of elderly under three scenarios: the central scenario without responses, the central scenario with only the one response, and the central scenario with two responses.

The effects of the first response become visible by 2050. By 2100, the proportion of elderly in China and CPA is lowered by 4

Table 15.7. Proportion above age 60 (in %) and population size (in millions) in China and CPA and Pacific OECD under the population-aging/fertility-feedback scenarios.

Year	China & CPA			Pacific OECD		
	No response	One response	Two responses	No response	One response	Two responses
Proportion elderly						
1995	9.2	–	–	19.4	–	–
2050	26.7	25.5	25.3	38.4	34.7	33.6
2100	28.7	24.3	21.0	38.2	33.0	28.5
Population size						
1995	1,362	–	–	147	–	–
2050	1,837	1,946	1,964	148	164	169
2100	1,796	2,339	2,711	125	177	214

and 8 percentage points, depending on whether one or two fertility responses are assumed. The respective figures for the Pacific OECD region are 5 and 10 percentage points. Effects on population size, however, are even more pronounced. In the China and CPA region two fertility responses increase the population by 900 million (or 50 percent) to 2.7 billion by 2100. In the Pacific OECD countries two fertility responses increase the total population size by 90 million or 70 percent.

This example shows that impacts of feedbacks on fertility become effective only very slowly. But in the long run the effect on the proportion above age 60 is clearly more significant than that of increasing migration discussed above. The scenario assuming 2 percent annual growth of net migration in the USA results in a 66 percent larger population and a four percentage point decline in the proportion above age 60. The two fertility increases in the Pacific OECD region result in a decline of 10 percentage points with a 70 percent increase in the population.

There is no reduction in population aging without a substantial increase in population size. Only the undesirable case of higher mortality could bring down both. In this sense the laws of population dynamics are merciless.

15.4 Comparison with Other World Population Projections

In Chapter 2 we argue that there is a need for additional world population projections that supplement those prepared by the United Nations, World Bank, and others. Because the differences in results often lie in the approach taken by the organization – such as how to deal with uncertainty, whether to vary mortality assumptions in addition to fertility assumptions, whether to consider dependencies between the regions and between the components – it is difficult to directly compare our results with those of the other agencies. But all sets of projections have one common feature: they include one projection that is presented as the most likely one, called the medium variant by the UN and the central scenario by us. *Table 15.8* summarizes the most likely projections of the UN, the World Bank, the US Bureau of the Census, and IIASA.

However, even when a comparison is restricted to the most likely case, it is impeded by the fact that different projections have different time horizons and different forms of spatial aggregation. For this reason the information presented in *Table 15.8* refers only to two points in time (2025 and 2100) and to the total world population. While the degree of increase between the two points in time gives a fair representation of the total path resulting from the assumptions made by each agency, the global aggregation clearly hides some important regional differences. For example, the UN 1994 medium variant and the IIASA 1996 central scenario yield almost exactly the same total world population size for 2025 but have different population figures for specific world regions and different proportions above age 60. One reason for this is that the UN assumes lower mortality improvements in industrialized countries and higher improvement in Africa than we do.

Naturally the differences between the projections are larger in 2100 than in 2025. The UN long-range projections produce the highest population size and the lowest proportion above age 60. This is mostly due to higher fertility assumptions and, to a certain extent, to lower life-expectancy assumptions. But these projections already date back to 1992 when most agencies were still assuming higher fertility. In fact, the recent projections of population size

Table 15.8. Most likely projections produced by the United Nations, the US Bureau of the Census, the World Bank, and IIASA.

	Total population size (in million)		Proportion above age 60	
	2025	2100	2025	2100
UN 1992 (long range)	8,504	11,186	13%[b]	26%[b]
UN 1994	8,279[a]	–	14%[a]	–
US Bureau of the Census	7,944	–	15%	–
World Bank 1994	8,121	10,958	14%	28%
IIASA 1996	8,276	10,350	15%	27%

[a]Mean of values given for 2020 and 2030.
[b]Estimated from information for age groups 65–79 and 80+.

of all the agencies are lower than their previous forecasts. This reflects the fact that over the past five years fertility has declined in all world regions and AIDS and other infectious diseases have cast serious doubts on further mortality improvements in several developing regions.

As to the treatment of uncertainty, the World Bank 1994 published only one projection to the year 2150 without any uncertainty variants. The UN 1994 assessment published three variants (high, medium, and low) up to the year 2050, which are only distinguished by different fertility assumptions – mortality and migration assumptions remain constant. The UN 1992 long-range projections provide five fertility variants up to the year 2150. UN 1994 and UN 1992 both present an additional "Constant-Fertility Scenario," which can only be intended for illustrative purposes because the resulting population size of more than 100 billion by the end of next century belongs in the category of "impossible scenarios." Aside from this outlier, the UN 1992 uncertainty variants for 2100 range between 6 and 19 billion. The IIASA 1996 scenarios presented in this chapter show population sizes ranging between 4 and 23 billion. This broader range is entirely due to the fact that our scenarios consider mortality uncertainty in addition to the fertility uncertainty. When limited to the scenarios assuming central mortality, the IIASA range is very close to the UN range.

For all projections discussed above it remains somewhat unclear what is meant by uncertainty variants or alternative scenarios: Do they mark the bounds within which population sizes may grow or are they just randomly chosen sample paths? However, even in the latter case, they may serve a useful purpose by providing extreme sample paths to be used for sensitivity analysis. A more rigorous treatment of the uncertainty issue in population projection, however, requires that specific probabilities of alternative paths be defined. These definitions are provided in Chapter 16.

Notes

[1] In all regions, 1990 age patterns of fertility were kept unchanged and scaled down (or up) according to the specification of the total fertility rate.

[2] UN model life tables (UN, 1982) corresponding to the respective region were used as input for 1995 to obtain age-specific mortality rates for today's developing regions. For the remaining regions, observed mortality rates were used. For regions with assumed high AIDS mortality special sets of age-specific mortality were used.

[3] Future age-specific mortality patterns were derived from model life tables (UN, 1982; Coale and Guo, 1989). Coale-Guo "west tables" were extended up to life expectancies of 100 to provide mortality schedules for very high life expectancies.

[4] Some very preliminary cross-sectional analyses suggest that such a relationship may indeed exist among societies that have fully passed through the demographic transition. It would also correspond to an ecological approach which typically thinks in terms of "carrying capacity" and "crowdedness." But clearly much more research is needed on this issue. Here the rationale is assumed simply to present an alternative to the ubiquitous replacement-level assumption which also lacks sound scientific foundations.

[5] This study has frequently been criticized for overestimating the agricultural potential of rain forests. Hence, without improvements in agricultural production and with no massive imports of food it is feasible to assume a limit of 4 billion people for this region.

Chapter 16

Probabilistic Population Projections Based on Expert Opinion

Wolfgang Lutz, Warren Sanderson, Sergei Scherbov

One thing that we know with certainty about the future population sizes is that they are uncertain. The nature of this uncertainty and ways to deal with it are highly controversial and still scientifically unresolved issues. Can we speak meaningfully about a distribution of possible future population sizes? Can mean, median, and modal future population sizes be determined? Can confidence intervals for future population sizes be derived? The literature on projections contains three views, none of which we find completely satisfactory (see discussion in Chapter 2). In this chapter, we provide a fourth perspective.

Most national and international agencies that produce population projections avoid addressing the issue of uncertainty explicitly. Typically they provide one main variant that is generally considered the most likely case. Sometimes high, low, and other variants are added, but these are virtually never given a probabilistic interpretation. If anything is said explicitly, it is that the high and low variants should not be considered to define confidence intervals. Supplementing variants with presentations of extreme case scenarios can be useful for sensitivity analysis, but it does not help in quantifying the extent of uncertainty.

In contrast, many methods of producing fully probabilistic population projections have been proposed and implemented, although so far only at the national level (see, for example, Alho, 1990; Carter and Lee, 1986; Lee and Tuljapurkar, 1994; McNown *et al.*, 1995; and Pflaumer, 1992). These approaches, which are almost exclusively based on time-series models, produce distributions of future population sizes and, thus, seem to be able to tell us, quite precisely, how much uncertainty there is in the results of population projections. A third possibility of forecasting the uncertainty of future population sizes is to make an assessment of the likely error in future projections; this is done by evaluating the errors made in past projections. This tack has been suggested in Keyfitz (1981) and Stoto (1983).

In this chapter, we propose and implement a new method for dealing with the uncertainty of future population sizes. We call our projections "probabilistic population projections based on expert opinion." Our method is distinguished from other methods by its use of expert opinion both on the future courses of fertility, mortality, and migration, and on the extent of their uncertainty. To our knowledge, this is the first time that probabilistic population projections have been made in this manner (aside from discussions in Muhsam, 1956, and Keyfitz, 1977), and the first time that a probabilistic model has been applied to all world regions. Therefore, our results should be treated with caution because these new ideas have not yet been thoroughly tested. More systematic sensitivity analysis of the Delphi method in this context is needed. Nathan Keyfitz (personal communication) points out that there is the danger of a downward bias in the range of uncertainty assumed by experts. Nevertheless, we think that the use of expert opinion could have significant advantages over the use of time-series models or past projection performance.

In Section 16.1, we briefly discuss our motivation for developing this approach to probabilistic population projections. Section 16.2 provides a discussion of the interpretation of confidence intervals in the present context. Section 16.3 contains a description of how we combined the opinions of the experts presented in the first 14 chapters of this book to produce the assumptions for our probabilistic population projections. In Section 16.4, we present the information we have obtained on population size and age structure for the 13 world regions. In Section 16.5, we present similar data for the world as a whole. We conclude in Section 16.6 with a discussion of the implications of the expert-based probabilistic projections for the interpretation of the projections in Chapter 15, as well as for projections produced by others.

16.1 The Motivation for New Probabilistic Population Projections

The usefulness of a population projection is enhanced by knowing its range of uncertainty. Indeed, the uncertainty, as well as the mean of a projection, could influence the actions of policy makers. Currently, there are two methods of quantitatively assessing the likely error of a population projection: time-series analysis and *ex post* error analysis. In time-series analysis, parameters are estimated from past data on certain demographic variables. These parameters, along with estimates of their uncertainty, are used to produce the information needed for population projections. In *ex post error* analysis, data are collected on the errors in past projections. On the assumption that similar errors may occur again in future projections, we can tell policy makers and others the expected range of errors.

Time-series analysis is an approach, not a specific recipe. Different researchers using time-series analysis on the same data have produced different projections along with different error estimates.[1] Most of the assumptions in the time-series approach are statistical in nature. Thus, in the evaluation of a set of different time-series-based projections, we must consider concepts such as stationarity, linearity, transformations of variables, orders of autoregressive and moving-average processes, autocorrelation, error-term correlations, as well as other elements that have no easy translation into the birth rates, death rates, and migration rates that we need to produce a population projection. It is easy to use statistical assumptions that, although individually seem plausible, produce implications for future demographic changes that would be regarded as highly unlikely by experts in the field. The problem may not be with any particular assumption, but rather may be with a complex interaction of assumptions that is difficult to diagnose. In addition, time-series analysis typically derives only short-term information from a historical data set. Demographic variables are often only related to their own values over the previous few years. This application is appropriate for making relatively short-run projections. However, long-run projections require a procedure that focuses on the determinants of longer-term changes. Because of the indirect connection between assumptions and implications, it is difficult for policy makers and others untrained in statistics to assess the error bounds produced by time-series analysis.

Ex post error analysis is more comprehensive than time-series analysis, but it also has a problem when used in multiple projections of the same population over the same period. Suppose one projection estimates the population at some future date at 10 million people and another estimates it at 20 million. If the mean error of past projections were plus or minus 15 percent, we would tell policy makers that the population would be 10 million plus or minus 15 percent or 20 million plus or minus 15 percent. Thus it is possible that the average of past errors is small compared to the variation in the projections. In such cases, policy makers may ignore the average past errors and use the range of population projections as an indicator of uncertainty. Also the application of *ex post* errors to future projections involves the important assumption that today's forecasters make the same mistakes or neglect the same structural discontinuities as did the forecasters of the past.

All population projections are based on judgment. In our judgment, the best way to produce projections is to base them explicitly on the synthesized opinions of a group of experts.[2] We have already discussed some of the advantages of using expert opinion as a foundation for making population projections in Chapters 2 and 15. In the case of probabilistic projections, we obtain information from the experts not only on fertility, mortality, and migration trends, but also on the uncertainty of the trends. This information is provided in a clear and easy-to-assess form. By bringing together information from experts who are specialists in different fields, we believe that we can capture the best information currently available. This is reflected in the subtitle of this volume, "What can we assume today?"

16.2 The Concept of Confidence Intervals for Population Projections

In making a projection, we must focus on only a few elements from an extremely complex reality. There are an infinite number of ways of making these abstractions, and it is natural that different projections would embody different assumptions. At any future date, differences in assumptions generally imply different distributions of population sizes, in particular, different mean populations and different 95 percent confidence intervals.

Table 16.1 contains data on probabilistic projections of the population of the United States around 2065; most of these projections were made in the early 1990s. The figures in the table are adapted from Lee and Tuljapurkar (1994) and are ordered according to the lower bound of the 95 percent confidence interval. The first column identifies the forecaster. The second column lists the mean population size and the third and fourth columns show the lower and upper bounds, respectively, of the 95 percent confidence interval. In the table, the mean population of the USA around 2065 ranges from 296 million to 680 million. The lower bound of the 95 percent confidence interval ranges from 207 million to 551 million people. The upper bound ranges between 349 million and 836 million.

The inconsistencies in this table are clear. Pflaumer (1992), using a time-series approach with the logarithm of population as the variable to be explained, is 95 percent confident that the US population around 2065 would lie between 551 and 836 million people. The US Bureau of the Census (1989) is 95 percent confident that the US population at that time would lie between 207 and 456 million people. Clearly, both cannot be correct at the same time. For example, we cannot simultaneously believe that the probability of the population being 551 million or less is 2.5 percent and the probability of the population being 456 million or less is 97.5 percent.

The nine projections in *Table 16.1* all produce different confidence intervals. How should we interpret this? First, it is vital to realize that there is no "correct" 95 percent confidence interval in that table. Given that there are a large number of ways to forecast a future that will be clearly different from our current understanding of the world today, it is to be expected that different projections would

Table 16.1. Forecasts and 95 percent confidence intervals (CI) for the population (in million) of the USA around 2065.

Forecaster	Population around 2065	Lower bound of 95% CI	Upper bound of 95% CI
US Bureau of the Census, 1989	296	207	456
Pflaumer, 1988	301	253	349
Lee and Tuljapurkar, 1994	398	259	609
US Census Bureau, 1992	413	268	599
Pflaumer, 1992			
(ARIMA with dep.var.POP)	443	270	611
Social security, 1989	324	272	389
Social security, 1991	351	291	435
Pflaumer, 1992			
[ARIMA with dep.var.log(POP)]	680	551	836
Logarithmic estimate	620	552	701

Estimates are ordered in ascending order of the lower bound of the 95 percent confidence interval.
Source: Adapted from Lee and Tuljapurkar, 1994:Table 1, which includes detailed explanatory notes that are not reproduced here.

embody different assumptions and produce different confidence intervals. Thus, it is never correct to say that the future population will certainly lie within a particular 95 percent confidence interval. These confidence intervals are dependent on the assumptions made in the projections and, as can be seen from *Table 16.1*, can vary dramatically from one projection to another.

Second, the problem of multiple inconsistent confidence intervals is not just a problem with the projections in *Table 16.1*. It is a generic phenomenon that afflicts all probabilistic population projections regardless of the methodology used. Time-series analysis and the projections based on the expert opinion presented in this book produce different confidence intervals whenever their underlying assumptions change.

Thus, it is just as impossible to tell policy makers and others what the future confidence interval for a population would be, as it is to tell them what the future population size would be. We can produce projections of population distributions with associated means, medians, and confidence intervals, but all these statistics depend on the assumptions that are used. Our procedure uses clear assumptions, but no procedure can free us from our assumptions and provide us with true future population distributions. We can provide policy makers and others with possible mean future population sizes and confidence intervals, given the set of assumptions that we use. The assumptions we use are the best assessments that we can make about future trends and their uncertainties. Tomorrow, however, we may be able to make even better assessments, which, in turn, will result in more accurate projected mean population sizes and confidence intervals.

16.3   The Methodology

In Chapter 15, we discuss how the opinions of the experts were translated into the high and low values that constituted 90 percent confidence intervals for total fertility rate, life expectancy, and migration level in the period 2030–2035 and extended to 2100. These assumptions, however, are not sufficient to produce the probabilistic projections. To complete them, we must first explore the additional assumptions that are needed.

16.3.1   Fertility

Our fertility assumptions are based on the data in *Table 15.1* and the Appendix Tables. *Table 15.1* gives four numbers for each region: the 1995 total fertility rate (TFR) and low, central, and high values for the interval 2030–2035. The Appendix Tables define in more detail the three paths from 1995 to 2100. Clearly, there are many ways to use these data to generate random TFR paths into the future. We have chosen a simple procedure of random lines (or piecewise linear paths).[3] Normal distributions are used to specify random lines that conform to the 90 percent confidence intervals in the Appendix Tables.

In the procedure, we use only one random draw from the normal distribution to determine the full fertility path from 1995 to 2100. We do not think that all paths of the total fertility rate will be random lines. An alternative view would be that the TFRs would behave like a random walk within predefined bounds. Each bounded random walk would produce a population total (see Goldstein *et al.*, 1994, for a discussion of this sort of model) and in the aggregate a population distribution would be generated for each projection period. These bounded random walks produce distributions of population sizes that are concentrated on a central value, and which are similar to those obtained using the assumptions described above.

The prime advantage of this combination of assuming normality and linear trends over time (random lines instead of random walks) is that it provides a simple and reasonably robust way of generating population distributions. Its main disadvantage is that it is inappropriate for predicting short-term population dynamics. Those dynamics can be much more volatile than would be predicted using the combination of the normality and linearity assumptions.

16.3.2   Mortality

The procedure selected to produce mortality paths is analogous to that described for fertility. Because the mortality scenarios had been defined in terms of improvements over 10-year periods, the low, central, and high values must be converted into values of life expectancy. This conversion provides us with three points of the 2030–2035 life-expectancy distribution, which are the exact analog of the three points of the 2030–2035 TFR distribution given by the experts. As in the case of fertility, random points are determined for life expectancies in 2030–2035 and 2080–2085.

Next, the time path of the life expectancy is linearly interpolated from the 1995 level to the randomly but jointly chosen 2030–2035 and 2080–2085 levels. After 2080–2085, all life expectancies are assumed to remain constant. After the path of change in life expectancy at birth is selected, age-specific mortality rates are derived using the model life tables as described in Chapter 15.

16.3.3   Migration

Expert opinion guided the production of a table of interregional migration flows (see *Table 15.3* for the annual levels of net migration). These flows are assumed to remain constant over time. The data in *Table 15.3* represent the high values of those flows. The central value is assumed to be half of the high value, and the low value is assumed to be zero.[4] Again a normal distribution is assumed with 90 percent of all cases falling between the high and low values.[5]

We apply the same age-specific interregional migration rates that were used in Chapter 15. These rates are derived from age-specific schedules in Rogers and Castro (1981).

16.3.4 Interrelationships between the components

Population projections typically do not assume that the trends in the three components of population change are related to one another. In this chapter, we consider migration to be independent of the other two components and of the age structure and size of the population, but we also consider the possibility of a correlation between fertility and mortality. In Sections 16.4 and 16.5, we provide population projections of perfectly (positively) correlated fertility and mortality and of uncorrelated fertility and mortality.

16.3.5 Interrelationships between regions

Most international population projections assume that all countries and regions simultaneously have higher than expected fertility in their high variants and lower than expected fertility in their low variant. However, fertility and mortality may not follow parallel trends across regions. The interdependencies between the two demographic variables can be quite complex. For example, across the regions in which the majority of inhabitants are Muslim fertility may be correlated, but the fertility level may be uncorrelated in Europe and Latin America.

In dealing with interrelations between regions, we considered the situations in which fertility and mortality are either perfectly correlated across regions or uncorrelated. Fertility and mortality levels may be correlated across regions, but within regions, fertility and mortality may still be either correlated or uncorrelated with each other. Similarly, fertility and mortality may be uncorrelated with fertility and mortality, respectively, across regions, but correlated with one another within each specific region.

In the case of both interrelationships between components and interrelationships between regions, we are dealing with long-term dependencies. To address the relationships in both cases we use procedures that link the entire time paths of fertility and mortality together within regions and across regions.

16.4 Regional Results

16.4.1 Regional population sizes

Table 16.2 shows the populations of the 13 world regions in 1995. In addition, it gives the mean and median projected populations in 2020, 2050, and 2100, as well as the upper and lower bounds of the 95 percent confidence interval for each year. These numbers were produced on the assumption that there is no long-run correlation between fertility and mortality within regions. In Section 16.4.3, we provide an example of the impact that such a correlation could have.

The table contains two indicators of asymmetric population size distributions: the difference between the mean and median populations, and the difference between the average of lower and upper bounds of the 95 percent confidence interval and the median. When the mean is greater than the median and the difference between the average and the bounds is positive, then the distribution of the population size is asymmetric and points in the direction of higher population sizes.

Consider first, the data for China and Centrally Planned Asia (CPA). In 1995, the region had a population of 1.36 billion people. Look at what happens to the lower bounds of the 95 percent confidence interval. By 2020 according to our population distribution, there is a 2.5 percent chance that the population will be below 1.53 billion. Thirty years later, there is a 2.5 percent chance that the population will be below 1.35 billion, and by the end of the 21st century there is a 2.5 percent chance that the population will be below 0.71 billion. The table tells us that between 2050 and 2100, China's population may decline by almost half. At the high end of the spectrum, the table shows that in 2100 China has a 2.5 percent chance of having a population above 4.43 billion. The population distribution for China in 2100 is very skewed, with relatively high probabilities of relatively high population sizes. The future population distributions of China behave in this way because we assume that the lower end of its TFR range is below replacement level, while its upper end is above replacement.

The time paths of the populations of North America and the European part of the former Soviet Union (predominantly Russia)

Table 16.2. Population (in millions) by regions, independent case. Mean, median, and 95 percent confidence intervals: 2020, 2050, 2100.

Region	1995	2020 Mean[b]	2020 Med.[c]	2020 2.5%[d]	2020 97.5%[d]	2050 Mean[b]	2050 Med.[c]	2050 2.5%[d]	2050 97.5%[d]	2100 Mean[b]	2100 Med.[c]	2100 2.5%[d]	2100 97.5%[d]
North Africa	162	277	277	254	300	440	439	309	583	630	598	228	1202
Sub-Saharan Africa	558	1059	1058	965	1159	1625	1605	1085	2316	1909	1738	578	4345
China & CPA	1362	1670	1670	1526	1826	1888	1865	1351	2574	2051	1873	709	4428
Pacific Asia	447	629	629	576	678	802	796	579	1047	876	829	322	1696
Pacific OECD	147	155	155	145	167	146	146	117	182	125	120	59	221
Central Asia	54	87	87	76	100	139	137	88	206	212	194	65	477
Middle East	151	300	300	279	324	520	515	380	692	786	738	320	1516
South Asia	1240	1845	1845	1737	1949	2380	2368	1833	2970	2365	2246	1014	4327
Eastern Europe	122	124	124	116	133	111	110	86	141	83	78	31	168
European FSU[a]	238	224	224	209	240	189	188	144	241	147	138	53	290
Western Europe	447	479	479	446	512	472	471	370	584	430	416	196	769
Latin America	477	697	696	646	746	930	925	707	1177	1163	1106	489	2142
North America	297	356	356	320	400	405	403	303	534	482	467	229	865

[a]European part of the former Soviet Union.
[b]Columns labeled Mean give data on the mean population size.
[c]Columns labeled Med. give data on the median population size.
[d]Columns labeled 2.5% and 97.5% provide data on the lower and upper bounds, respectively, of the 95 percent confidence interval; 2.5 percent of all observations lie below the lower bound and 97.5 percent of all observations lie below the upper bound. All figures are based on 1,000 simulations and were produced using DIALOG, the multistate population projection model. Fertility and mortality are assumed to be uncorrelated within regions.

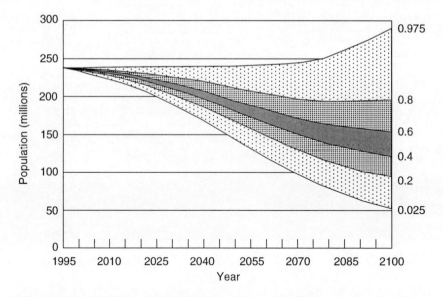

Figure 16.1. Future population size in the European part of the former Soviet Union, uncorrelated random variations in fertility and mortality paths. The figures on the right-hand side refer to the probability that population size will lie below the line indicated.

are interesting to compare. The population of the European part of the former Soviet Union was 238 million in 1995 (this total includes the Russian Federation with a population of 147 million). *Figure 16.1* shows the region's population distribution changes from 1995 to 2100 under the assumption that the random variations in fertility, mortality, and migration are uncorrelated with one another. Each line is labeled with the probability that the population size would lie below it. According to the assumptions, there is a 2.5 percent chance that the population will be below the bottom line and a 2.5 percent chance that it will lie above the top line. Thus, the interval between the bottom and top lines gives the 95 percent confidence interval. There is a 20 percent chance that the population will lie between the two middle lines and a 60 percent change that the population will lie between the second and fifth lines.

Over the course of the 21st century, population change in the region is likely to be negative. By 2020, the mean population falls

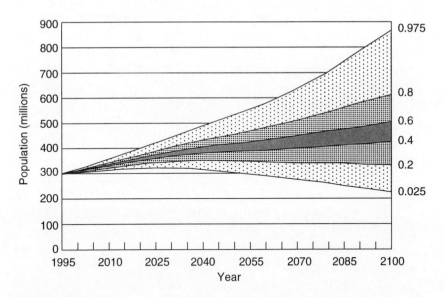

Figure 16.2. Future population size in North America, uncorrelated random variations in fertility and mortality paths. The figures on the right-hand side refer to the probability that population size will lie below the line indicated.

from 238 million in 1995 to 224 million. By 2050, the mean population falls to 189 million and by 2100 to 147 million. At the midpoint of the century, there is a 2.5 percent chance that the population will be below 144 million and a 2.5 percent chance that it will be above 241 million. This means that, according to the assumptions used here, there is slightly over a 2.5 percent chance that the population of the region will not decline between 1995 and 2050.

The causes of the decline in the population of the European part of the FSU are below replacement fertility, relatively high mortality, especially for males, and net out-migration. After 2030, there is a possibility of above replacement fertility and significantly improved mortality rates. This accounts for the possible population growth in the second half of the century that we see from the top two lines in *Figure 16.1*.

Figure 16.2 shows population distribution changes in North America under the assumption that random variations in fertility and mortality paths are uncorrelated. The population of North

America in 1995 was 297 million. The mean population distribution increases to 356 million in 2020, 405 million in 2050, and 482 million in 2100. There is a possibility that the population of North America will be smaller in 2100 than it was in 1995 but, given the assumptions used here, the chances of this are less than 20 percent. The continued growth of the US population is largely fueled by continuing migration. The population will shrink only if migration is greatly restricted and the USA had a long period of below replacement fertility.

It is interesting to compare our 95 percent confidence intervals for North America in 2065 with those for the USA shown in *Table 16.1*. The lower bound of our 95 percent confidence interval for North America is around 280 million and our upper bound is around 610 million (*Figure 16.2*). Taking into consideration the larger population of North America (which includes Canada, Mexico, and the USA), our 95 percent confidence intervals are roughly similar to those in Lee and Tuljapurkar (1994) and the US Bureau of the Census (1992) and only slightly lower than the Pflaumer (1992) time-series model with the population size as the dependent variable.

16.4.2   Regional age structures

Tables 16.3 and *16.4* are arranged like *Table 16.2* except that they refer to the percentage of the population in the 0–14 age group and the percentage in the 60 and above age group, respectively. It is interesting to note that while the percentage of children 14 and under will likely decrease during the 21st century in all regions, the percentage 60 and above will grow. For example, in North Africa, 38.8 percent of the population were age 14 and below in 1995. In 2050, given the assumptions used here, the mean percentage falls to 27.0 percent, with the 95 percent confidence interval lying between 18.6 and 34.2 percent. By 2100, the mean is 18.7 percent and the 95 percent confidence interval lies between 11.5 and 25.1 percent. On the other hand, the proportion of the North African population age 60 and above was 5.9 percent in 1995. In 2100, the mean percentage is 24.0 percent, with the 95 percent confidence interval between 15.2 and 37.4 percent. The phenomenon of population aging will occur on a worldwide scale during the 21st century. In our next examples, we look again at the case of China and CPA and at the comparison between the European part of the FSU and North America.

In China and CPA, 27.3 percent of the population in 1995 were between ages 0 and 14. By 2020, given the assumptions used here, the mean percentage falls to 21.2, with a 95 percent confidence interval stretching from 16.5 to 25.6 percent. This means that the probability of a fall in the percentage of the 0–14 age group is over 97.5 percent. The decrease in the percentage of this group continues over the century, with the mean at 17.1 percent in 2100 and a 95 percent confidence interval between 9.8 and 24.1 percent. It is interesting to note that the skewness in the distribution of population sizes that emerges in the region between 2050 and 2100 is not mirrored in the distribution of the percentage of younger people, which remains quite symmetric. Indeed, the percentage distribution of younger people in the population remains quite symmetric throughout the 21st century for all regions in *Table 16.3*.

With this decrease in the percentage of the 0–14 age group in the China and CPA region there is an increase in the percentage of the population age 60 and above (*Table 16.4*). In 1995, 9.2 percent of the population was 60 and above; by 2050 the mean is 25.3 percent, and by 2100 it increases to 28.3 percent. Most of the increase in the older population takes place in the first half of the 21st century. We are quite confident of this, because the 95 percent confidence interval for 2050 lies between 17.8 and 34.1 percent. Even at the lower bound, the percentage of the population 60 and above almost doubles between 1995 and 2050.

The comparison between the age structure changes in the European part of the former Soviet Union and those in North America is especially interesting in view of the differences in their population growth trends. *Figures 16.3a* and *16.3b* show the comparisons of the 0–14 populations and *Figures 16.4a* and *16.4b* provide a comparison of the 60 and above populations. In the European part of the FSU and in North America, the percentages of the 0–14 populations were almost identical in 1995, 21.6 and 22.0 percent, respectively. In 2100, the mean percentages are even closer, 17.6 and 17.5 percent, respectively.

There is slightly more uncertainty about the percentage of this age group in the European part of the FSU than in North America

Table 16.3. Percentage of the population in the 0–14 age group, by regions, independent case. Mean, median, and 95 percent confidence intervals: 2020, 2050, 2100.

Region	1995	2020				2050				2100			
		Mean[b]	Med.[c]	2.5%[d]	97.5%[d]	Mean[b]	Med.[c]	2.5%[d]	97.5%[d]	Mean[b]	Med.[c]	2.5%[d]	97.5%[d]
North Africa	38.8	33.9	34.0	30.0	37.5	27.0	27.3	18.6	34.2	18.7	19.0	11.5	25.1
Sub-Saharan Africa	45.4	39.7	39.8	36.1	42.9	28.0	28.3	19.2	35.2	18.1	18.3	11.0	24.5
China & CPA	27.3	21.2	21.3	16.5	25.6	19.9	20.0	12.3	27.3	17.1	17.2	9.8	24.1
Pacific Asia	33.2	26.5	26.6	22.6	29.9	21.8	21.9	15.0	27.8	16.4	16.5	9.0	23.1
Pacific OECD	17.1	13.9	13.9	10.8	16.7	13.0	13.0	8.1	17.8	13.1	13.1	7.0	19.4
Central Asia	36.3	31.5	31.7	25.0	37.0	26.5	26.8	16.8	34.7	18.7	18.9	11.4	25.7
Middle East	42.8	37.0	37.0	33.4	40.3	27.1	27.3	18.8	34.3	18.2	18.3	11.2	24.5
South Asia	36.6	30.1	30.1	27.4	32.7	22.5	22.6	16.4	28.1	15.3	15.4	8.7	21.8
Eastern Europe	21.3	16.5	16.6	13.3	19.6	14.1	14.1	8.9	19.4	15.0	17.3	7.8	15.6
European FSU[a]	21.6	16.0	16.0	12.3	19.2	14.5	14.5	8.8	19.8	17.6	17.7	9.5	24.7
Western Europe	19.9	15.8	15.9	12.8	18.8	14.2	14.3	9.3	19.3	15.2	15.3	8.7	21.6
Latin America	33.7	27.0	27.1	23.5	30.4	22.2	22.3	16.0	28.2	18.7	18.7	11.8	25.2
North America	22.0	17.9	17.9	14.6	21.1	16.7	16.7	11.8	21.3	17.5	17.6	11.6	23.3

[a]European part of the former Soviet Union.
[b]Columns labeled Mean give data on the mean population size.
[c]Columns labeled Med. give data on the median population size.
[d]Columns labeled 2.5% and 97.5% provide data on the lower and upper bounds, respectively, of the 95 percent confidence interval; 2.5 percent of all observations lie below the lower bound and 97.5 percent of all observations lie below the upper bound. All figures are based on 1,000 simulations and were produced using DIALOG, the multistate population projection model. Fertility and mortality are assumed to be uncorrelated within regions.

Table 16.4. Percentage of the population in the 60+ age group, by regions, independent case. Mean, median, and 95 percent confidence intervals: 2020, 2050, 2100.

Region	1995	2020				2050				2100			
		Mean[b]	Med.[c]	2.5%[d]	97.5%[d]	Mean[b]	Med.[c]	2.5%[d]	97.5%[d]	Mean[b]	Med.[c]	2.5%[d]	97.5%[d]
North Africa	5.9	7.9	7.9	7.2	8.7	13.6	13.3	9.4	19.2	24.0	23.0	15.2	37.4
Sub-Saharan Africa	4.7	5.4	5.4	5.1	5.9	9.3	9.2	6.9	12.8	22.5	21.7	15.0	34.3
China & CPA	9.2	15.4	15.4	14.0	16.8	25.3	24.9	17.8	34.1	28.3	27.6	18.0	41.2
Pacific Asia	6.8	11.2	11.2	10.2	12.3	19.7	19.4	14.4	26.5	28.0	27.3	18.0	42.6
Pacific OECD	19.4	31.2	31.2	29.0	33.4	39.6	39.5	31.5	48.7	40.2	40.0	28.4	53.8
Central Asia	7.8	9.7	9.7	8.5	11.2	15.9	15.4	10.2	24.0	24.7	23.7	15.5	38.0
Middle East	5.4	6.8	6.8	6.2	7.4	12.6	12.5	9.1	17.3	25.5	24.9	16.5	38.4
South Asia	6.7	10.1	10.1	9.5	10.7	16.7	16.6	13.4	20.8	28.7	28.1	19.9	40.7
Eastern Europe	16.7	24.0	23.9	22.3	25.8	34.4	34.0	26.7	43.4	35.7	34.4	23.3	52.7
European FSU[a]	16.9	23.7	23.6	21.8	25.6	34.5	34.1	26.3	44.5	30.7	29.9	18.9	48.0
Western Europe	18.6	25.2	25.2	23.3	27.1	35.1	35.0	27.5	43.9	35.7	35.4	24.3	49.9
Latin America	7.6	11.9	11.9	11.0	12.8	20.6	20.4	15.8	26.4	27.4	26.8	18.6	39.3
North America	16.4	24.0	24.0	21.8	26.4	30.5	30.2	24.0	38.6	31.4	30.9	22.3	43.1

[a]European part of the former Soviet Union.
[b]Columns labeled Mean give data on the mean population size.
[c]Columns labeled Med. give data on the median population size.
[d]Columns labeled 2.5% and 97.5% provide data on the lower and upper bounds, respectively, of the 95 percent confidence interval; 2.5 percent of all observations lie below the lower bound and 97.5 percent of all observations lie below the upper bound. All figures are based on 1,000 simulations and were produced using DIALOG, the multistate population projection model. Fertility and mortality are assumed to be uncorrelated within regions.

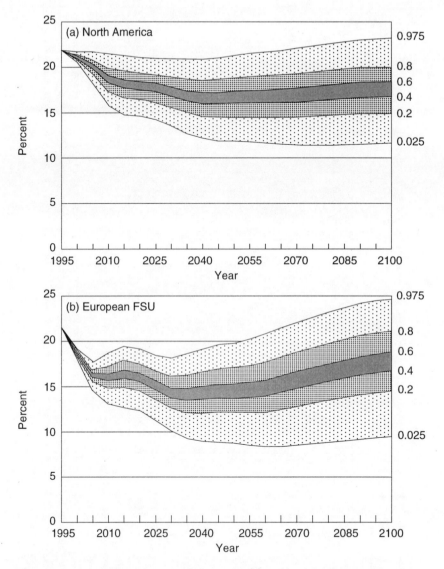

Figure 16.3. Percentage of the population in the 0–14 age group; random variations in fertility and mortality paths: (a) North America and (b) European FSU. The figures on the right-hand side show the proportion of cases in which the percentages fall below the line indicated.

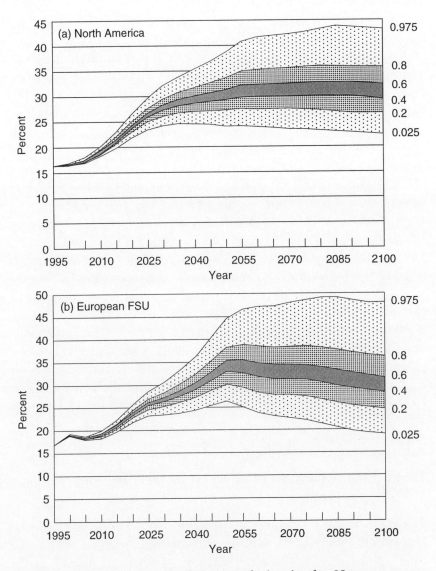

Figure 16.4. Percentage of the population in the 60+ age group; random variations in fertility and mortality paths: (a) North America and (b) European FSU. The figures on the right-hand side show the proportion of cases in which the percentages fall below the line indicated.

in 2100. The 95 percent confidence interval for the European part of the FSU is between 9.5 and 24.7 percent, while for North America it is between 11.6 percent and 23.3 percent. Most of the difference between the 95 percent confidence intervals is in the lower bounds. The large gap between the two bottom lines in *Figure 16.3b* for the European part of the FSU indicates that the distribution is slightly skewed in the direction of the smaller percentages. We can see the same trend in *Table 16.3* because the mean percentage of the 0–14 population is less than the median percentage. Indeed, in all regions it is generally the case that the mean percentage of the 0–14 age group is less than the median.

The percentages of the 60 and above population were very close in the two regions in 1995. In the European part of the FSU it was 16.9 percent and in North America it was 16.4 percent. According to the assumptions, by 2050 the two mean percentages are 34.5 and 30.5 percent, respectively. The four percentage point difference is small compared with the 95 percent confidence intervals. In the case of the European part of the FSU we are 95 percent confident that the percentage would lie somewhere between 26.3 and 44.5 percent in 2050. For North America, the 95 percent confidence interval is bounded by 24.0 and 38.6 percent in 2050. Clearly, we cannot be sure in which region the percentage will rise more rapidly. In both cases, the percentage for the 0–14 age group and the percentage for the 60 and over age group, the differences between the two regions are relatively minor. This is the case even though the trends in population growth are very different.

16.4.3　An example of correlated fertility and mortality

The regional data presented above were computed on the assumption that there would be no future long-run relationship between the random variations in the time paths of fertility and mortality. To see the effect of such a correlation, *Table 16.5* compares two cases in sub-Saharan Africa in 2100: in one case the time paths of fertility and mortality are independent (uncorrelated) over time and in the other they are perfectly correlated.[6] Sub-Saharan Africa currently has a high fertility rate, but we assume that it will experience its demographic transition during the period of our projection. Given the knowledge that we have on the experience of other countries that have passed through fertility transitions, it is reasonable to assume that the speeds of mortality and fertility decline will be positively correlated over time. Correlated fertility and mortality means that if, in the future, sub-Saharan Africa has a relatively fast decline in mortality, it would also have a relatively rapid decline in fertility, but if the decline in mortality were slow, the fall in fertility would also be slow.[7]

Table 16.2 shows that sub-Saharan Africa is the region of the world with the greatest uncertainty about future population size. In 1995, the population in the region was 558 million people. By 2100, the mean population size is estimated at 1.909 billion; the median is 1.738 billion; and the 95 percent confidence interval encompasses almost 4 billion people, with a lower bound of 578 million and an upper bound of 4.345 billion. This gigantic confidence interval is the result of unusually large uncertainty about both fertility and mortality in the region, and the assumption that the speeds of the decline in fertility and mortality are unrelated to each other.

Table 16.5 shows that under correlated and uncorrelated assumptions, the median population size is about the same: 1.738 billion when the paths of fertility and mortality are independent and 1.728 billion when they are perfectly correlated. However, the population size distributions vary considerably. If fertility and mortality trends are considered unrelated, then the mean population size will be 1.909 billion in 2100; if the trends are assumed to be correlated, the mean will be 1.663 billion. The greatest difference is in the extent of uncertainty. In the case of uncorrelated trends the 95 percent confidence interval lies between 578 million and 4.345 billion people; in the case of perfectly correlated trends the 95 percent confidence interval lies between 1.174 and 1.859 billion people. Thus, in the future the mean population size and especially the 95 percent confidence intervals of Sub-Saharan Africa depend, to a great extent, on whether or not future fertility and mortality trends are assumed to be correlated.

Although uncertainty about population size shrinks dramatically when future trends in fertility and mortality are perfectly correlated, uncertainty about age structure does not necessarily lessen.

Table 16.5. Mean, median, and 95 percent confidence intervals for sub-Saharan Africa: 2100.

	1995	Independent random mortality and fertility paths				Correlated random mortality and fertility paths			
		Mean	Median	2.5%	97.5%	Mean	Median	2.5%	97.5%
Population (in millions)	558.0	1,909.4	1,738.0	578.4	4,345.0	1,662.7	1,728.0	1,174.0	1,859.0
0–14 age group (in %)	45.4	18.1	18.3	11.0	24.5	17.8	18.4	10.2	22.9
60+ age group (in %)	4.7	22.5	21.7	15.0	34.3	23.1	21.4	14.7	40.0

Each distribution is based on 1,000 simulations.

Table 16.6. Summary of world population projections (in millions) with different assumptions of the correlation between fertility and mortality both within and between regions: 2020, 2050, 2100.

Correlation		1995	2020				2050				2100			
Between regions	Between f&m within regions[a]		Mean	Med.	2.5%[b]	97.5%[b]	Mean	Med.	2.5%[b]	97.5%[b]	Mean	Med.	2.5%[b]	97.5%[b]
0	0	5,702	7,902	7,900	7,671	8,144	10,047	10,040	8,965	11,260	11,259	11,190	8,200	15,490
1	0	5,702	7,900	7,902	7,315	8,464	10,035	10,000	7,361	12,950	11,212	10,600	4,374	21,370
0	1	5,702	7,890	7,893	7,736	8,045	9,948	9,947	9,343	10,590	10,644	10,620	8,869	12,640
1	1	5,702	7,880	7,881	7,488	8,239	9,906	9,891	8,285	11,490	10,521	10,330	5,945	15,710
Merged		5,702	7,893	7,895	7,474	8,290	9,984	9,963	8,108	11,950	10,909	10,710	5,715	17,330

[a] Between fertility and mortality within regions.
[b] Columns labeled 2.5% and 97.5% provide data on the lower and upper bounds, respectively, of the 95 percent confidence interval.
Each of the four rows is based on 1,000 projections to the year 2100. Each is based on 13 regional projections. The merged case combines those simulations and therefore is based on 4,000 observations.

The 95 percent confidence interval for the percentage of the population in the 0–14 age group is slightly smaller when we assume a perfect correlation, but the confidence interval for the percentage of the population age 60 and above is larger.

16.5 World Projections

In this section, we project world population sizes by combining the regional projections presented in Section 16.4. The process of aggregation adds one more complication, because we cannot simply add the regional figures together. We must also take into account the possibility that fertility and mortality paths could be correlated across regions.

Table 16.6 shows five world population projections. In the first, fertility and mortality paths are uncorrelated both across regions and within regions. These data are derived by aggregating the regional data presented in Section 16.3. In *Table 16.6*, the mean population size of the world at a future date can be derived by adding together the means for each region. The median and particularly the bounds on the 95 percent confidence interval, however, are not derived from addition. They must be simulated. In the second projection, fertility and mortality paths are each correlated across regions, but not within regions (i.e., high fertility in one region goes along with high fertility in all other regions). In theory, the mean populations in this projection are the same as those in the first case. In practice, they are slightly different from each other because the random samples are different.

To illustrate the difference between these two assumptions, *Figures 16.5a* and *16.5b* show the resulting distributions of total population size for all world regions together in the case of perfect correlation between regions (*Figure 16.5a*) and in the case of independence (*Figure 16.5b*). The X axis is given on a relative scale with 1.0 corresponding to the mean. One thousand simulations were conducted for each distribution. It is clearly visible that, in the case of independence, the distribution is more concentrated. This is because under the independence assumption regions may compensate for one another; for example, an unusually low fertility level in one region may partly be offset by high fertility in another region. In the case of

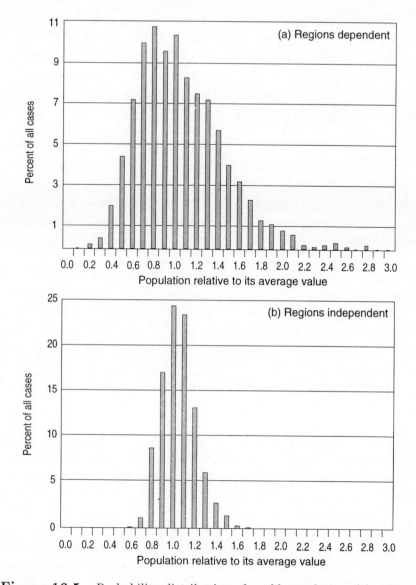

Figure 16.5. Probability distribution of world population, (a) regions dependent and (b) regions independent; fertility and mortality independent: 2100. Each graph is based on 1,000 projections. The mean population is 11.212 billion. The results are plotted to that mean. For example, a population of 12 billion in 2100 would be plotted as 1.07 (12 divided by 11.212) on the horizontal axis. Each figure represents the right endpoint of an interval of width 0.1. For example, the tick mark labeled 1.0 is the right endpoint of the interval 0.9 to 1.0. The height of each bar indicates the percentage of the 1,000 populations in 2100 that fall within each interval.

perfect correlation such compensations are not possible, thus many more extreme cases result.

The third and fourth projections in *Table 16.6* are based on the assumption that fertility and mortality are perfectly correlated within regions. This situation is most plausible in regions that are still undergoing demographic transitions. The third projection assumes no correlation of fertility and mortality across regions, while the fourth assumes a perfect positive correlation across regions. Again, in theory the mean populations should be identical, but are not because of random sampling.

We call the fifth projection the "merged" case because it is computed by merging the outcomes of the other four. Each of the first four projections is based on a sample size of 1,000 observations. The merged projection is based on 4,000 observations. The experts were not asked about correlations of fertility and mortality within and between regions; nevertheless, to produce world population projections, information on these correlations is required. In particular, we must know both the correlations themselves and the uncertainty associated with each one. In the absence of expert opinion, we introduce uncertainties into the correlations by giving equal weight to, or merging, the four extreme case projections.[8]

The range of the 95 percent confidence intervals depends on which projection is chosen. On the one hand, if we were certain that future time paths of fertility and mortality were uncorrelated within and across regions, then according to the assumptions, the mean population of the world in 2050 would be 10.0 billion people, with the range of the 95 percent confidence interval between 9.0 and 11.3 billion. On the other hand, if we were certain that future fertility and mortality trends were perfectly correlated across regions, but not within regions, the mean population of the world in 2050 would also be 10.0 billion, but the range of the 95 percent confidence interval would be wider, between 7.4 and 13.0 billion.

It is useless to try to determine which 95 percent confidence interval is the "correct" one. There is no "correct" 95 percent confidence interval. Each projection embodies different assumptions about the correlations and their uncertainties and, therefore, produces different confidence intervals. We prefer the merged projection because it is the only one of the five that incorporates uncertainty

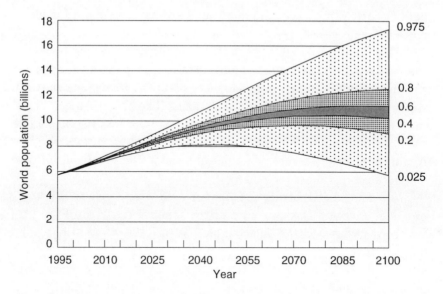

Figure 16.6. Merged distribution of the size of the world's population (in billions): 1995–2100.

about the correlations in addition to fertility and mortality uncertainties. For this reason, in the remainder of this section we focus on the merged projection.

Figure 16.6 shows the distributions of future population sizes derived from the merged projection at five-year intervals to the year 2100. The top and bottom lines bound the 95 percent confidence interval. The top line indicates that there is an unlikely possibility of almost linear population growth between 1995 and 2100. The bottom line shows that there is an equally unlikely possibility that population would peak in the mid-21st century and fall thereafter to below 6 billion by 2100. The range covering 60 percent of all cases (between the 0.2 and 0.8 fractiles) is remarkably small. By 2050 this uncertainty range is less than 1.5 billion people and by 2100 it doubles to about 3 billion people.

The figure also shows that in more than 60 percent of all cases the growth of the world population would level off during the second half of next century or even start to decline. Given that the world population in early 1996 was estimated at 5.75 billion, we can determine the probability of when or if it will double – that is, hit the

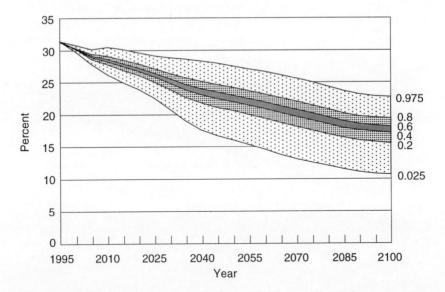

Figure 16.7. Merged distribution of the population of the world in the 0–14 age group (in percent). The figures on the right-hand side refer to the proportion of cases, out of 4,000 projections, in which the percentage of the 0–14 age group falls below the line indicated.

11.5 billion mark – in the next century. Roughly two-thirds of our simulated cases do not reach 11.5 billion during the 21st century; the remaining one-third surpasses that mark. Because those paths that do not reach 11.5 billion level off by the end of the century, we project that they will also not surpass that level during the 22nd century. From this we conclude that, given the assumptions used here, there is a 66 percent probability that the population of the world will never again double.

Figure 16.7 shows the distribution of the percentage of the population in the 0–14 age group. In 1995, 31.4 percent of the population was in this group. The percentage will clearly fall over time, the only question is how fast. In 2100, its 95 percent confidence interval lies between 10.6 and 22.7 percent. It is interesting to note that the uncertainty about the percentage of younger people in the population does not considerably increase in the second half of the next century, even though there is a substantial increase in the uncertainty about population size.

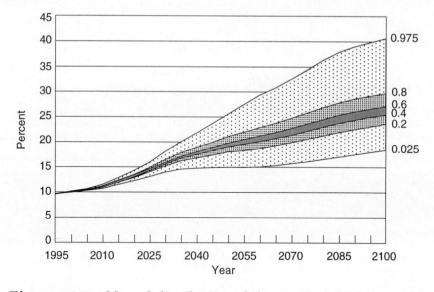

Figure 16.8. Merged distribution of the population of the world in the 60+ age group (in percent).

The percentage of the population at age 60 and above is shown in *Figure 16.8*. All the lines ascend, indicating that we are quite confident that the percentage of older people in the population will increase over time. In 2050, the mean percentage is 19.7 compared with 9.5 in 1995; the 95 percent confidence interval for 2050 is between 15.1 and 25.7 percent. By 2100, the mean increases to 27.1 percent, with a 95 percent confidence interval between 18.6 and 40.6 percent. Hence, given the assumptions used here, there is a 97.5 percent chance that the proportion of elderly will at least double by 2100; in the most likely case it will almost triple; and it may even more than quadruple. The uncertainty with respect to the percentage above age 60 grows significantly during the second half of the 21st century; this clearly contrasts with the uncertainty surrounding the percentage of the population age 14 and below. The uncertainty in the older age group increases particularly at the upper end due to the uncertainty about future old-age mortality when combined with low fertility. According to the assumptions used here, by 2100 there is a 20 percent chance that 30 percent or more of the population of the world will be age 60 or above.

16.6   Discussion

To generate population projections, we must make assumptions about an unknown future. There are many ways of making these assumptions and, in general, different assumptions will result in different future population sizes and different confidence intervals. There is no way around this problem. One tempting shortcut is to assume that the processes which generated fertility, mortality, and migration in the past will continue unchanged in the future. Unfortunately, this assumption does not get us very far, because there are a large number structures that could have generated the same past data (see Sanderson, 1995). We must first specify the equations for past processes before we estimate their parameters. Therefore, in making projections, and in particular probabilistic ones, there is no substitute for judgment. The main question is, What is the best way to incorporate judgment into projections?

In this chapter we have proposed a methodology for using judgment in making probabilistic projections. We suggest that experts be asked about: (1) the time paths of fertility, mortality, and migration; (2) the perceived uncertainty of these time paths; (3) the correlations between the time paths both within and between regions; and (4) the assessment of the uncertainty of those correlations. We have also implemented the methodology by using information obtained from experts on future fertility, mortality, and migration paths and on their uncertainty about those paths. In contrast to the conventional Delphi model we were concerned with the synthesized judgment of a group of experts on the extent of uncertainty in fertility and mortality rather than in deriving probability distributions from what the experts thought to be the most likely occurrences. This is an important aspect for the choice of the normal distribution because in usual Delphi studies where experts give just one value the symmetry assumption is problematic because of the dependence of experts. As to the shape of these intuitive (subjective) uncertainty distributions in the mind of the expert, the normal distribution seems to be a natural choice. The calculations have also been made assuming a uniform distribution resulting in a somewhat wider uncertainty range of future populations. Since the uniform distribution is less appealing in that it gives equal weight to the central value and to the high and low values and does not allow any cases to be outside the range of the high and low values, the presentation in this chapter is based on the normal distribution. In our case, the experts were not asked about correlations and so we assumed that there was a wide range of uncertainty.

Asking experts about future trends and uncertainties is one way to obtain the information needed to make population projections. Another is to use statistical analyses of various sorts to determine the parameters that are assumed to characterize the past. These parameters and the estimated randomness of past time-series data can be used to make projections of the future. We use expert opinion because it makes the inputs into the projections very clear. Statistical assumptions, such as whether to use some transformation of the dependent variable or the untransformed variable, can have important implications for the outcome of a projection, but their exact meaning is often unclear. Since our proposal on how to use expert opinion to make probabilistic projections is a new one in the field of population projections, it will take time to assess whether it has significant advantages over the alternative ways of making probabilistic projections.

The variation in the confidence intervals based on different assumptions about correlations is not just of theoretical interest. The United Nations regularly publishes its population projections with low, medium, and high variants for each country. Low, medium, and high variants for the world are derived by adding together the respective variants for each country. By doing so the UN implicitly assumes that fertility trends in all countries of the world are perfectly correlated. In the more likely case that trends are divergent, the uncertainty range for the population of the world becomes smaller because diverging country trends partly compensate for one another.

Finally, it is important to stress, even at the risk of being repetitive, that the confidence intervals that we produced are not *true* confidence intervals in the sense that we definitely know that the future population, at a specific future date, has a 95 percent probability of being within some interval. Our probabilistic projections are our best estimates of expected future population sizes at future dates combined with our best estimates of the associated confidence intervals. The population sizes and confidence intervals are based on expert opinion on both the components of population growth and the uncertainty about those components. Expert opinion can be wrong and often is wrong. But there is no better alternative. Expert opinion – especially when derived from an interactive group process – incorporates the relevant knowledge that has been accumulated over years of experience and study into a wide range of disciplines. It also accommodates human intuition and nonquantitative judgment and is therefore more comprehensive than any specific formal model. It is far from perfect, but until we develop a true model that generates future fertility, mortality, and migration trends, expert opinion is the best guide that we have.

Acknowledgments

We would like to thank Nathan Keyfitz and Gustav Feichtinger for valuable comments on this chapter.

Notes

[1] This can be seen in *Table 16.1* below. Sanderson (1995) also shows this phenomenon using a simulation approach.
[2] The procedure that we used to elicit the expert opinion required that the experts reach a consensus and thus synthesize their opinions. Those who have studied a particular issue in detail can influence the opinions of those who have not. We believe that synthesized opinions provide a better measure of the extent of uncertainty than the individual opinions of the experts. (More details about the process from which the assumptions were derived can be found in Lutz, 1995.)
[3] Let x_i be the ith draw from a standard normal distribution. We use x_i to choose three TFRs: one for 2000, one for the period 2030–2035, and the third for the interval 2080–2085. We denote these TFRs by $\text{TFR}_{i,j}$, where $j = 1,2,$ or 3 depending on the date of the TFR. To complete our notation, we call the central value at time $j, \mu_j,$ and the difference between the high and low value at time j, Δ_j. We can express the ith random TFR at time j as

$$\text{TFR}_{i,j} = \mu_j + x_i \cdot \frac{\Delta_j}{3.29} \quad ,$$

where 3.29 is the difference between the upper and lower bounds of the 90 percent confidence interval for the standard normal distribution. The same x_i term appears in the expression for each TFR date. This means that we are assuming persistence in fertility patterns. If fertility starts out lower than the average in 2000, it will be lower than average in 2100. TFRs at other dates are computed from linear interpolation between two adjacent dates. TFRs after 2080–2085 are assumed to remain at their 2080–2085 values.

[4] Let $M_{i,r,j}$ be the migration flow in the ith random draw for cell r in *Table 15.3*, at time j. We can write:

$$M_{i,r,j} = \mu_r + x_i \cdot \frac{\Delta_r}{3.29} \ ,$$

where μ_r is the central migration level for region r, x_i is the value of the ith random draw from a standard normal distribution, Δ_r is the difference between the high and low values for region r, and the constant 3.29 is the difference between the upper and lower bounds of the 90 percent confidence interval of the standard normal distribution. The subscript j does not appear on the right-hand side of the equation, indicating that the migration flow is constant over time.

[5] If a random migration flow is less than zero, the migration flow in the projection is assumed to be zero.

[6] A different scenario which can be derived from the data given in Chapter 15 would be to assume that increasing mortality caused by AIDS is associated with a rapid fertility decline due to the increase of condom use and a higher awareness of reproductive health.

[7] In the future, experts should address these correlations.

[8] An alternative is to introduce the two correlations that are uniformly distributed over a unit square. This procedure would have been consistent with our emphasis on distributions, but it would have been computationally more burdensome.

Chapter 17

Epilogue: Dilemmas in Population Stabilization

Wolfgang Lutz

There is no doubt that population growth will come to an end at some point in the future. Infinite physical growth on a finite planet is impossible. Even if technological progress makes advances that are unimaginable today, there is a limit to growth in the number of people. Current understanding of our natural, social, and economic environs indicates that the sooner population growth stabilizes the better-off humankind will be. Hence population stabilization has become a major goal of international politics. This goal was recently emphasized at the 1994 International Population Conference in Cairo. In this epilogue I take a look at some of the trade-offs encountered in efforts to stabilize population growth that result from the nature of population dynamics as described in this book.

17.1 Possible, Likely, and Desirable Population Trends

This book tries to give the best possible answer we can give today to the question, What will be the size, regional distribution, and age and sex structure of the future world population? It also tries to answer a related question, What is the range of uncertainty of this population projection? The book describes possibilities and

429

likelihoods. But to ask which of the projected alternatives is desirable is an altogether different question. This question intentionally was not discussed before because the book does not take a normative approach. This latter issue is, however, addressed in this epilogue because discussions of future world population growth often mix together these different questions, and the end result tends to be confusion.

One area where the combination of these questions tends to lead to confusion is in the discussion of the world's carrying capacity. Chapter 10 reviewed a large number of alternative estimates of how many people can live and be fed on earth; these estimates range from less than 1 billion to 1 trillion. In recent years a number of estimates have been published that give figures which are below or only slightly above the present world population (e.g., Ehrlich *et al.*, 1993; Resources for the Future, 1984). These estimates are clearly wrong because evidently the earth can support a larger population (at least for the present and most likely also in the future). To infer from such estimates that the quality of life will deteriorate after a certain threshold, transcends the original ecological meaning of carrying capacity (How many people can be alive?) and introduces living standards that are clearly part of the second question, namely, What is the desirable quality of life? This question is far beyond the scope of this book. In fact, it may never be possible to answer this question. Great inequalities exist among people and are not likely to disappear soon. Therefore, it is impossible to apply a universal standard for quality of life, let alone define such a standard in the face of differing views on what is good.

In this context one must be cautious. Ecologists may demand, in the name of sustainable development, a drastic reduction in population size that can only be reached through increased mortality. The projections described in Chapters 15 and 16 clearly show that even with the most rapid fertility decline that can reasonably be assumed the world population will increase to more than 7 billion by the middle of the 21st century. Lower growth means higher mortality which is associated with immense human suffering. This must be taken into account when considering the benefits of a smaller population size.

17.2 The Low-Mortality/ Rapid-Stabilization Dilemma

Future population growth cannot simply be switched off through population policies for two reasons: the reproductive behavior of large populations does not change radically overnight and due to past high fertility ever-increasing numbers of young women are entering the reproductive ages (i.e., the so-called momentum of population growth). These two basic facts are slowly being recognized outside the demographic community. Of course, catastrophically high mortality levels or declines in birth rates to less than one-third of today's level could always stop population growth, but these situations are extremely unlikely. In sub-Saharan Africa, for example, simulations show that fertility would have to decline to less than one child per woman overnight to prevent further population growth; this is an absurd scenario. This book gives estimates of what is possible in the real world based on our current understanding of human behavior.

Within the limits of what is possible, alternatives exist. These alternatives have been numerically demonstrated in Chapters 15 and 16. One can interpret the minimum population growth resulting from the low-fertility scenarios as realistically unavoidable further population growth, which is due to the combination of the age-structural momentum and the inertia of fertility rates. *Figure 17.1* gives this unavoidable population growth until 2050 as the shaded area in the context of the five scenarios (disregarding migration) defined in Chapter 15. The figure shows that this realistically unavoidable growth adds 2.4 to 3.8 billion people (depending on the choice of mortality assumptions) to the world population.[1]

Figure 17.1 also shows that low fertility combined with high mortality would result in the lowest population growth (only 7.1 billion by 2050). Although this scenario is possible, it is by no means desirable because the higher mortality would be associated with tremendous human suffering (for example, under this scenario male life expectancy in sub-Saharan Africa declines from today's 52 years to only 44 years in 2030–2035). Hence, it can be assumed that any policy intending to increase the quality of life by averting avoidable

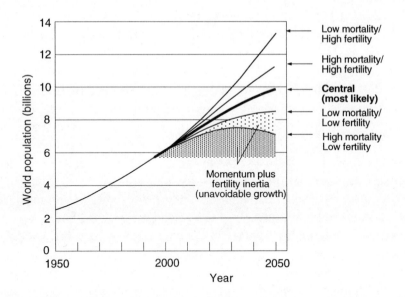

Figure 17.1. Unavoidable and possibly avoidable world population growth to 2050.

population growth also aims at decreasing mortality. For this reason the scenario in *Figure 17.1* that combines low fertility with low mortality is chosen as the borderline between possibly avoidable and unavoidable growth.[2]

This clearly illustrates the dilemma that arises in the context of population stabilization: lower mortality results in slower population stabilization and higher mortality results in faster stabilization. The international community (WHO, UNFPA, UNICEF, etc.) wants to achieve both rapidly declining mortality and rapid stabilization simultaneously and the documents produced do not always seem to take into account the merciless laws of population dynamics that make these two goals contradictory. Put simply: lower mortality means more people on earth.

This low-mortality/rapid-stabilization dilemma became apparent during discussions on the preamble to the Programme of Action at the 1994 Cairo Conference (see Lutz, 1995b). At the conference proposals were made that the low variant of the UN population projections should be considered a likely trend if the Programme of Action were to be successfully implemented. The UN, however, uses identical mortality assumptions for all three variants, whereas an important and widely praised aspect of the Cairo Programme of Action was to embed family planning into reproductive health efforts, maternal mortality, child mortality, and health improvements in general. Hence, successful implementation of the Programme would result in not only lower fertility, but also lower mortality – that is, more survivors – which contradicts the unchanged mortality assumptions of the UN low variant. Therefore, when producing future population projections, variants that combine low fertility with low mortality must be taken into account if the Cairo Programme of Action is to be given serious consideration; this, however, will inevitably result in higher population growth.

17.3   The Population-Growth/ Population-Aging Dilemma

Growth of total population size – which receives a great deal of attention in the discussion of future world population trends – is only one side of the coin. The other side is population aging. If population growth follows the central scenario, the percentage of the world population above age 60 increases from 9.5 percent currently to 13.2 percent in 2020, 19.6 percent in 2050, and 26.8 percent in 2100. The low-fertility/low-mortality scenario would bring the proportion above age 60 to an incredible 42.5 percent in 2100. For comparison, in the region with the oldest population today, Western Europe, less than 20 percent of the population is above age 60. And today's developing countries are hardly prepared to cope with the social challenges of massive aging.

The figures on projected population aging under different scenarios clearly show that when discussing possible and desired future population trends both sides of the coin – population growth and population aging – must be taken into consideration. The issue of population aging is sometimes consciously disregarded with the argument that, for an eventual stable situation of low fertility and low mortality, the laws of population dynamics imply that at some point a certain high mean age of the population would be reached in any case whereas the ultimate population size would depend on the speed of fertility decline. This is certainly true in the very long run;

however, in the coming decades the speed of aging will have a big impact. A mean age of 36 years, which under a high-growth scenario will only be reached in 2100, will already be reached around 2030 under the low-growth scenario. Hence the low-growth scenario will certainly put more stress on society to adapt to rapid and massive aging and develop support networks for the aged that can no longer count on traditional family support.

Mentioning the aging associated with a rapid curbing of population growth is not to say that the problems associated with aging cancel the benefits of rapid stabilization. A science-based weighting of the socioeconomic and environmental consequences of both population aging and rapid decrease in population growth is beyond the focus of this book and requires very different considerations. Without in-depth analyses I would guess that the benefits of rapidly declining fertility, such as a lower child dependency ratio, less stress on infrastructure and life support systems, better educational opportunities for women, and a likely boost to productivity, would more than compensate the problems of aging, if sufficient attention is given to timely social policies.[3]

17.4   Conclusion

This book attempts to assemble the most relevant knowledge about past and future trends in fertility, mortality, and migration in different parts of the world, translate this knowledge into alternative population projections, and give a quantitative assessment about the degree of uncertainty involved. In doing so it also tries to include in the uncertainty assumptions the possible impacts of future environmental, economic, political, and cultural changes as far as they can be foreseen today as (even low-probability) possibilities of the future.

All of the chapters have made contributions to answer the question in the subtitle of this book: What can we assume today? As trends evolve and more knowledge is acquired about the interacting processes that shape our future, tomorrow's assumptions will probably look different from today's.

Notes

[1] This decomposition into avoidable and unavoidable growth follows a somewhat different logic than the analysis by Bongaarts (1994) which estimates that, of the likely 5.7 billion additional people in the developing world by 2100 (based on the World Bank projections), 2.8 billion are due to population momentum, 1.0 billion to high desired family size, and 1.9 billion to unwanted pregnancies. Aside from the issue of wanted and unwanted pregnancies, which is part of the assumptions of our scenarios but not a defining criterion, Bongaarts' decomposition is different from ours in that it takes stable replacement-level fertility – a convenient but problematic concept as discussed in previous chapters – as the point of reference. All births below replacement fertility are considered momentum, all births above that level are considered avoidable through reductions in unwanted pregnancies and reductions in demand for large families. Alternative mortality trends are not considered in these calculations.

[2] Alternatively the low-fertility/high-mortality scenario may be chosen as a reference if one prefers to consider high mortality as part of a strategy to avoid growth.

[3] This was found to be the case in a recent in-depth study on Mauritius (see Lutz, 1994).

Appendix Table 1. Definition of World Regions

Thirteen World Regions

I. North Africa

Algeria	Morocco
Egypt	Sudan
Libya	Tunisia

II. Sub-Saharan Africa

Angola	Madagascar
Benin	Malawi
Botswana	Mali
British Indian Ocean Territory	Mauritania
Burkina Faso	Mauritius
Burundi	Mozambique
Cameroon	Namibia
Cape Verde	Niger
Central African Republic	Nigeria
Chad	Réunion
Comoros	Rwanda
Congo	St. Helena
Côte d'Ivoire	Sao Tomé and Príncipe
Djibouti	Senegal
Equatorial Guinea	Sierra Leone
Eritrea	Seychelles
Ethiopia	Somalia
Gabon	South Africa
Gambia	Swaziland
Ghana	Tanzania
Guinea	Togo
Guinea-Bissau	Uganda
Kenya	Zaire
Lesotho	Zambia
Liberia	Zimbabwe

III. China & CPA

Cambodia	Mongolia
China	North Korea
Hong Kong	Taiwan
Laos	Vietnam

Thirteen World Regions Continued

IV. Pacific Asia

American Samoa	Papua New Guinea
Brunei	Philippines
East Timor	Singapore
Fiji	Solomon Islands
French Polynesia	South Korea
Indonesia	Thailand
Kiribati (Gilbert Islands)	Tonga
Malaysia	Vanuatu
Myanmar	Western Samoa
New Caledonia	

V. Pacific OECD

Australia	New Zealand
Japan	

VI. Central Asia

Kazakhstan	Turkmenistan
Kyrgyzstan	Uzbekistan
Tajikistan	

VII. Middle East

Bahrain	Oman
Iran	Qatar
Iraq	Saudi Arabia
Israel	Syria
Jordan	United Arab Emirates
Kuwait	Yemen
Lebanon	

VIII. South Asia

Afghanistan	Maldives
Bangladesh	Nepal
Bhutan	Pakistan
India	Sri Lanka

IX. Eastern Europe

Albania	Macedonia
Bosnia–Herzegovina	Poland
Bulgaria	Romania
Croatia	Slovak Republic
Czech Republic	Slovenia
Hungary	Yugoslavia

X. European FSU

Armenia	Latvia
Azerbaijan	Lithuania
Belarus	Moldova
Estonia	Russian Federation
Georgia	Ukraine

Thirteen World Regions Continued

XI. Western Europe

Andorra	Ireland
Austria	Isle of Man
Azores	Italy
Belgium	Liechtenstein
Canary Islands	Luxembourg
Channel Islands	Madeira
Cyprus	Malta
Denmark	Monaco
Faeroe Islands	Netherlands
Finland	Norway
France	Portugal
Germany	Spain
Gibraltar	Sweden
Greece	Switzerland
Greenland	Turkey
Iceland	United Kingdom

XII. Latin America

Antigua & Barbuda	Guatemala
Argentina	Guyana
Bahamas	Haiti
Barbados	Honduras
Belize	Jamaica
Bermuda	Martinique
Bolivia	Mexico
Brazil	Netherlands Antilles
Chile	Nicaragua
Colombia	Panama
Costa Rica	Paraguay
Cuba	Peru
Dominica	St. Kitts & Nevis
Dominican Republic	St. Lucia
Ecuador	St. Vincent
El Salvador	Surinam
French Guiana	Trinidad & Tobago
Grenada	Uruguay
Guadeloupe	Venezuela

XIII. North America

Canada	Virgin Islands
Guam	USA
Puerto Rico	

Six Aggregated World Regions

Africa
   North Africa
   Sub-Saharan Africa

Asia–East
   China & CPA
   Pacific Asia
   Pacific OECD

Asia–West
   Central Asia
   Middle East
   South Asia

Europe
   Eastern Europe
   European FSU
   Western Europe

Latin America

North America

Two Economic Regions

Industrialized region
   North America
   Western Europe
   Eastern Europe
   European FSU
   Pacific OECD

Developing region
   Latin America
   Central Asia
   Middle East
   North Africa
   Sub-Saharan Africa
   China & CPA
   South Asia
   Pacific Asia

Appendix Table 2. Alternative Assumptions for Life Expectancy at Birth in 13 World Regions: 1995, 2000, 2030–2035, 2080–2085

Region	1995	2000 L	C	H	2030–2035 L	C	H	2080–2085 L	C	H
Male										
North Africa	62.7	63.0	63.8	64.7	64.6	71.1	77.7	64.6	74.9	85.2
Sub-Saharan Africa	50.6	49.6	51.1	52.6	43.1	54.4	65.6	43.1	58.1	73.1
China & CPA	66.4	66.9	67.2	67.4	70.2	72.0	73.9	70.2	75.8	81.4
Pacific Asia	63.1	63.1	64.1	65.1	63.1	70.6	78.1	63.1	74.4	85.6
Pacific OECD	76.1	76.6	77.1	77.6	79.9	83.6	87.4	79.9	87.4	94.9
Central Asia	65.1	65.6	66.1	66.6	68.9	72.6	76.4	68.9	76.4	83.9
Middle East	65.6	65.9	66.7	67.6	67.5	74.0	80.6	67.5	77.8	88.1
South Asia	59.7	59.7	60.5	61.2	59.7	65.3	71.0	59.7	69.1	78.5
Eastern Europe	67.3	67.8	68.3	68.8	71.1	74.8	78.6	71.1	78.6	86.1
European FSU	61.1	61.1	62.1	63.1	61.1	68.6	76.1	61.1	72.4	83.6
Western Europe	72.1	72.6	73.1	73.6	75.9	79.6	83.4	75.9	83.4	90.9
Latin America	66.3	66.8	67.3	67.8	70.1	73.8	77.6	70.1	77.6	85.1
North America	72.3	72.8	73.3	73.8	76.1	79.8	83.6	76.1	83.6	91.1
Female										
North Africa	65.3	65.6	66.4	67.3	67.2	73.7	80.3	67.2	78.7	90.3
Sub-Saharan Africa	53.9	52.9	54.4	55.9	46.4	57.7	68.9	46.4	62.7	78.9
China & CPA	70.1	70.6	71.1	71.6	73.9	77.6	81.4	73.9	82.6	91.4
Pacific Asia	67.4	67.4	68.4	69.4	67.4	74.9	82.4	67.4	79.9	92.4
Pacific OECD	82.2	82.7	83.2	83.7	86.0	89.7	93.5	86.0	94.7	103.5
Central Asia	72.5	73.0	73.5	74.0	76.3	80.0	83.8	76.3	85.0	93.8
Middle East	68.0	68.3	69.1	70.0	69.9	76.4	83.0	69.9	81.4	93.0
South Asia	59.7	59.7	60.7	61.7	59.7	67.2	74.7	59.7	72.2	84.7
Eastern Europe	75.0	75.5	76.0	76.5	78.8	82.5	86.3	78.8	87.5	96.3
European FSU	72.8	73.3	73.8	74.3	76.6	80.3	84.1	76.6	85.3	94.1
Western Europe	78.6	79.1	79.6	80.1	82.4	86.1	89.9	82.4	91.1	99.9
Latin America	71.5	72.0	72.5	73.0	75.3	79.0	82.8	75.3	84.0	92.8
North America	79.1	79.6	80.1	80.6	82.9	86.6	90.4	82.9	91.6	100.4

L = low, C = central, H = high.

Appendix Table 3. Alternative Assumptions for Total Fertility Rates in 13 World Regions: 1995, 2000, 2030–2035, 2080–2085

Region	1995	2000			2030–2035			2080–2085		
		L	C	H	L	C	H	L	C	H
North Africa	4.35	3.92	4.13	4.35	2.00	3.00	4.00	1.54	2.04	2.54
Sub-Saharan Africa	6.18	5.56	5.87	6.18	2.00	3.00	4.00	1.44	1.94	2.44
China & CPA	2.00	1.60	2.00	2.40	1.50	2.25	3.00	1.37	1.87	2.37
Pacific Asia	2.88	2.30	2.65	3.00	1.70	2.35	3.00	1.29	1.79	2.29
Pacific OECD	1.53	1.22	1.53	1.84	1.30	1.70	2.10	1.24	1.74	2.24
Central Asia	3.35	2.68	3.34	4.00	2.00	3.00	4.00	1.45	1.95	2.45
Middle East	5.47	4.92	5.20	5.47	2.00	3.00	4.00	1.45	1.95	2.45
South Asia	3.77	3.39	3.58	3.77	1.70	2.35	3.00	1.20	1.70	2.20
Eastern Europe	1.66	1.33	1.66	2.00	1.30	1.70	2.10	1.39	1.89	2.39
European FSU	1.50	1.20	1.50	1.80	1.30	1.70	2.10	1.55	2.05	2.55
Western Europe	1.67	1.34	1.67	2.00	1.30	1.70	2.10	1.39	1.89	2.39
Latin America	3.10	2.48	2.79	3.10	1.70	2.35	3.00	1.60	2.10	2.60
North America	1.97	1.58	1.94	2.30	1.40	1.85	2.30	1.59	2.09	2.59

L = low, C = central, H = high.

Appendix Table 4. Summary Results to 2100.

North Africa

Fertility	C	L	C	H	L	H	L	C	H
Mortality	C	H	H	H	C	C	L	L	L
Migration	C	C	C	C	C	C	C	C	C
Total population size (in millions)									
1995	162	162	162	162	162	162	162	162	162
2010	228	220	226	232	222	233	223	229	235
2020	277	256	272	288	261	294	266	282	299
2050	439	311	407	519	337	558	362	468	593
2100	607	227	489	912	290	1117	357	716	1288
Mean age (in years)									
1995	24.6	24.6	24.6	24.6	24.6	24.6	24.6	24.6	24.6
2010	26.0	26.5	25.9	25.4	26.5	25.5	26.6	26.0	25.5
2020	27.4	28.4	27.3	26.2	28.6	26.3	28.8	27.6	26.5
2050	32.1	35.9	31.5	28.1	36.7	28.6	37.8	33.0	29.4
2100	39.5	43.5	37.7	33.7	46.0	34.9	49.8	42.2	36.9
Percentage of population aged 60+									
1995	5.9	5.9	5.9	5.9	5.9	5.9	5.9	5.9	5.9
2010	6.3	6.4	6.2	6.0	6.5	6.2	6.6	6.4	6.3
2020	7.9	8.0	7.5	7.1	8.4	7.4	8.7	8.2	7.8
2050	13.2	15.3	11.7	9.2	17.2	10.4	19.4	15.0	11.8
2100	22.7	27.2	19.1	14.1	32.3	16.8	39.2	27.6	20.4
Percentage of population aged 0–14 years									
1995	38.8	38.8	38.8	38.8	38.8	38.8	38.8	38.8	38.8
2010	36.8	35.1	36.7	38.3	35.2	38.3	35.2	36.8	38.4
2020	34.1	30.9	34.0	36.9	30.9	36.9	30.9	34.1	36.9
2050	27.3	20.3	27.5	33.4	20.1	33.3	19.7	26.9	33.0
2100	19.4	14.2	20.0	25.0	13.4	24.6	12.1	18.2	23.6
Annual number of births (in thousands)									
1995–2000	5,543	5,405	5,542	5,686	5,406	5,687	5,407	5,544	5,688
2010–2015	6,681	5,724	6,657	7,603	5,745	7,631	5,764	6,704	7,656
2020–2025	7,250	5,416	7,169	9,014	5,476	9,116	5,530	7,321	9,207
2050–2055	8,566	4,095	8,095	13,700	4,330	14,500	4,512	8,929	15,120
2095–2100	7,907	1,997	6,674	16,790	2,372	19,890	2,615	8,704	21,880
Assumed total fertility rates									
1995–2000	4.24	4.14	4.24	4.35	4.14	4.35	4.14	4.24	4.35
2010–2015	3.70	3.18	3.70	4.22	3.18	4.22	3.18	3.70	4.22
2020–2025	3.35	2.59	3.35	4.11	2.59	4.11	2.59	3.35	4.11
2050–2055	2.62	1.82	2.62	3.42	1.82	3.42	1.82	2.62	3.42
2095–2100	2.04	1.54	2.04	2.54	1.54	2.54	1.54	2.04	2.54
Assumed life expectancies for both sexes combined (in years)									
1995–2000	64.8	64.4	64.4	64.4	64.8	64.8	65.2	65.2	65.2
2010–2015	67.9	64.9	64.9	64.9	67.9	67.9	71.0	71.0	71.0
2020–2025	70.2	65.4	65.4	65.4	70.2	70.2	75.0	75.0	75.0
2050–2055	74.1	65.9	65.9	65.9	74.1	74.1	82.5	82.5	82.5
2095–2100	76.8	65.9	65.9	65.9	76.8	76.8	87.7	87.7	87.7

The nine scenarios combine low (L), central (C), and high (H) fertility and mortality assumptions with central migration assumptions (and low and high migration in the cases of Western Europe and North America).

Sub-Saharan Africa

Fertility	C	L	C	H	L	H	L	C	H
Mortality	C	H	H	H	C	C	L	L	L
Migration	C	C	C	C	C	C	C	C	C

Total population size (in millions)

1995	558	558	558	558	558	558	558	558	558
2010	842	805	827	849	819	865	833	856	880
2020	1,055	945	1,006	1,067	991	1,120	1,032	1,099	1,168
2050	1,601	1,001	1,303	1,654	1,225	2,041	1,437	1,876	2,390
2100	1,759	479	996	1,827	849	3,232	1,305	2,632	4,770

Mean age (in years)

1995	22.1	22.1	22.1	22.1	22.1	22.1	22.1	22.1	22.1
2010	22.7	23.2	22.8	22.3	23.2	22.2	23.2	22.7	22.2
2020	23.8	24.9	23.9	23.0	24.9	22.9	24.9	23.8	22.9
2050	30.0	34.3	30.2	27.1	34.1	26.8	34.5	30.3	27.0
2100	39.0	45.0	39.0	34.7	45.2	34.5	47.6	40.7	35.8

Percentage of population aged 60+

1995	4.7	4.7	4.7	4.7	4.7	4.7	4.7	4.7	4.7
2010	5.2	5.3	5.1	5.0	5.3	5.0	5.4	5.2	5.1
2020	5.4	5.7	5.4	5.1	5.8	5.1	6.0	5.6	5.3
2050	9.1	11.6	8.9	7.0	11.9	7.2	13.1	10.0	7.8
2100	21.1	29.2	20.5	15.1	30.2	15.5	34.9	24.5	18.0

Percentage of population aged 0–14 years

1995	45.4	45.4	45.4	45.4	45.4	45.4	45.4	45.4	45.4
2010	43.3	41.3	42.9	44.4	41.7	44.8	42.0	43.6	45.1
2020	39.7	36.1	39.0	41.6	36.8	42.3	37.2	40.1	42.7
2050	28.3	20.1	27.2	32.9	21.1	34.2	21.3	28.6	34.6
2100	18.8	12.3	17.8	22.8	12.9	23.9	12.3	18.3	23.7

Annual number of births (in thousands)

1995–2000	26,010	25,330	25,990	26,660	25,340	26,680	25,350	26,020	26,690
2010–2015	32,500	28,170	32,120	36,090	28,500	36,510	28,810	32,840	36,900
2020–2025	34,540	25,780	33,310	41,230	26,720	42,760	27,560	35,630	44,120
2050–2055	33,590	14,150	27,690	46,550	17,130	56,580	19,680	38,620	65,110
2095–2100	22,630	3,885	12,950	32,780	6,786	57,390	9,607	32,020	81,240

Assumed total fertility rates

1995–2000	6.03	5.87	6.03	6.18	5.87	6.18	5.87	6.03	6.18
2010–2015	4.77	4.19	4.77	5.34	4.19	5.34	4.19	4.77	5.34
2020–2025	3.88	3.10	3.88	4.67	3.10	4.67	3.10	3.88	4.67
2050–2055	2.58	1.78	2.58	3.38	1.78	3.38	1.78	2.58	3.38
2095–2100	1.94	1.44	1.94	2.44	1.44	2.44	1.44	1.94	2.44

Assumed life expectancies for both sexes combined (in years)

1995–2000	52.7	51.9	51.9	51.9	52.7	52.7	53.4	53.4	53.4
2010–2015	54.0	48.7	48.7	48.7	54.0	54.0	59.2	59.2	59.2
2020–2025	55.0	46.7	46.7	46.7	55.0	55.0	63.2	63.2	63.2
2050–2055	57.7	44.7	44.7	44.7	57.7	57.7	70.7	70.7	70.7
2095–2100	60.3	44.7	44.7	44.7	60.3	60.3	75.9	75.9	75.9

China & CPA

Fertility	C	L	C	H	L	H	L	C	H
Mortality	C	H	H	H	C	C	L	L	L
Migration	C	C	C	C	C	C	C	C	C

Total population size (in millions)

1995	1,362	1,362	1,362	1,362	1,362	1,362	1,362	1,362	1,362
2010	1,554	1,487	1,549	1,612	1,492	1,617	1,497	1,559	1,622
2020	1,665	1,524	1,650	1,778	1,538	1,793	1,551	1,679	1,808
2050	1,837	1,311	1,759	2,321	1,378	2,412	1,449	1,916	2,503
2100	1,796	640	1,587	3,331	745	3,715	862	2,000	4,055

Mean age (in years)

1995	29.7	29.7	29.7	29.7	29.7	29.7	29.7	29.7	29.7
2010	34.0	35.1	33.9	32.9	35.1	32.9	35.2	34.0	33.0
2020	36.3	38.3	36.1	34.3	38.4	34.4	38.6	36.4	34.6
2050	40.2	45.8	39.4	34.5	46.7	35.2	47.8	41.2	36.0
2100	42.8	48.3	41.1	35.9	50.7	37.1	53.9	45.1	38.8

Percentage of population aged 60+

1995	9.2	9.2	9.2	9.2	9.2	9.2	9.2	9.2	9.2
2010	11.7	12.1	11.6	11.1	12.2	11.2	12.3	11.8	11.3
2020	15.5	16.4	15.1	14.1	16.7	14.3	17.1	15.8	14.6
2050	25.3	31.7	23.7	17.9	33.7	19.2	35.8	27.1	20.7
2100	28.1	35.7	24.7	17.9	40.3	20.3	45.8	32.1	23.2

Percentage of population aged 0–14 years

1995	27.3	27.3	27.3	27.3	27.3	27.3	27.3	27.3	27.3
2010	22.1	18.9	22.1	25.1	18.8	25.1	18.8	22.1	25.1
2020	21.1	16.9	21.1	24.8	16.8	24.8	16.8	21.0	24.7
2050	19.6	12.7	19.9	26.3	12.4	26.0	12.1	19.2	25.6
2100	16.8	11.0	17.4	23.1	10.3	22.7	9.4	15.9	21.9

Annual number of births (in thousands)

1995–2000	24,710	22,230	24,710	27,180	22,240	27,180	22,240	24,710	27,180
2010–2015	24,560	18,240	24,520	30,840	18,260	30,880	18,280	24,590	30,920
2020–2025	24,480	15,670	24,370	34,330	15,730	34,490	15,800	24,580	34,640
2050–2055	24,080	9,713	23,510	45,820	9,946	46,950	10,130	24,550	47,860
2095–2100	19,550	4,105	18,010	54,980	4,454	59,680	4,677	20,520	62,680

Assumed total fertility rates

1995–2000	2.00	1.80	2.00	2.20	1.80	2.20	1.80	2.00	2.20
2010–2015	2.10	1.56	2.10	2.63	1.56	2.63	1.56	2.10	2.63
2020–2025	2.17	1.53	2.17	2.82	1.53	2.82	1.53	2.17	2.82
2050–2055	2.10	1.45	2.10	2.75	1.45	2.75	1.45	2.10	2.75
2095–2100	1.87	1.37	1.87	2.37	1.37	2.37	1.37	1.87	2.37

Assumed life expectancies for both sexes combined (in years)

1995–2000	69.0	68.8	68.8	68.8	69.0	69.0	69.2	69.2	69.2
2010–2015	71.2	69.9	69.9	69.9	71.2	71.2	72.5	72.5	72.5
2020–2025	73.0	70.9	70.9	70.9	73.0	73.0	75.0	75.0	75.0
2050–2055	76.4	71.9	71.9	71.9	76.4	76.4	81.0	81.0	81.0
2095–2100	79.1	71.9	71.9	71.9	79.1	79.1	86.3	86.3	86.3

Pacific Asia

Fertility	C	L	C	H	L	H	L	C	H
Mortality	C	H	H	H	C	C	L	L	L
Migration	C	C	C	C	C	C	C	C	C

Total population size (in millions)

1995	447	447	447	447	447	447	447	447	447
2010	554	530	550	569	535	574	539	559	579
2020	623	568	609	650	581	665	594	636	679
2050	776	550	703	884	611	970	673	845	1049
2100	783	289	609	1136	385	1433	492	951	1688

Mean age (in years)

1995	26.7	26.7	26.7	26.7	26.7	26.7	26.7	26.7	26.7
2010	30.0	30.8	29.9	29.1	30.9	29.2	31.0	30.1	29.3
2020	32.1	33.4	31.8	30.5	33.7	30.7	34.0	32.4	31.0
2050	37.2	40.5	36.0	32.5	41.9	33.5	43.7	38.9	34.9
2100	42.7	46.5	40.4	35.8	49.6	37.7	54.4	46.5	40.6

Percentage of population aged 60+

1995	6.8	6.8	6.8	6.8	6.8	6.8	6.8	6.8	6.8
2010	8.7	8.8	8.5	8.2	9.0	8.4	9.2	8.9	8.6
2020	11.3	11.5	10.7	10.0	12.1	10.6	12.7	11.9	11.1
2050	19.8	22.2	17.3	13.8	25.2	15.9	28.9	23.0	18.5
2100	27.6	31.7	22.7	17.0	38.1	20.7	46.5	34.2	25.8

Percentage of population aged 0–14 years

1995	33.2	33.2	33.2	33.2	33.2	33.2	33.2	33.2	33.2
2010	28.2	25.6	28.2	30.6	25.6	30.7	25.6	28.3	30.7
2020	26.2	22.7	26.2	29.3	22.7	29.3	22.6	26.1	29.2
2050	21.5	16.0	21.9	27.1	15.6	26.8	14.9	20.8	26.1
2100	16.3	11.3	17.2	22.4	10.4	21.7	9.0	14.9	20.4

Annual number of births (in thousands)

1995–2000	10,930	10,240	10,930	11,620	10,240	11,620	10,240	10,930	11,620
2010–2015	11,500	9,324	11,450	13,590	9,359	13,640	9,390	11,530	13,690
2020–2025	11,590	8,402	11,460	14,780	8,499	14,950	8,580	11,710	15,100
2050–2055	11,200	5,393	10,540	17,890	5,728	19,020	5,968	11,680	19,830
2095–2100	8,214	1,906	6,853	18,200	2,294	21,810	2,521	9,010	23,910

Assumed total fertility rates

1995–2000	2.77	2.59	2.77	2.94	2.59	2.94	2.59	2.77	2.94
2010–2015	2.54	2.07	2.54	3.00	2.07	3.00	2.07	2.54	3.00
2020–2025	2.44	1.89	2.44	3.00	1.89	3.00	1.89	2.44	3.00
2050–2055	2.13	1.54	2.13	2.72	1.54	2.72	1.54	2.13	2.72
2095–2100	1.79	1.29	1.79	2.29	1.29	2.29	1.29	1.79	2.29

Assumed life expectancies for both sexes combined (in years)

1995–2000	66.0	65.5	65.5	65.5	66.0	66.0	66.5	66.5	66.5
2010–2015	68.8	65.2	65.2	65.2	68.8	68.8	72.3	72.3	72.3
2020–2025	70.7	65.2	65.2	65.2	70.7	70.7	76.2	76.2	76.2
2050–2055	74.4	65.2	65.2	65.2	74.4	74.4	83.7	83.7	83.7
2095–2100	77.1	65.2	65.2	65.2	77.1	77.1	88.9	88.9	88.9

Pacific OECD

Fertility	C	L	C	H	L	H	L	C	H
Mortality	C	H	H	H	C	C	L	L	L
Migration	C	C	C	C	C	C	C	C	C
Total population size (in millions)									
1995	147	147	147	147	147	147	147	147	147
2010	155	150	154	158	151	159	152	156	160
2020	156	146	154	161	149	163	151	159	166
2050	148	118	139	164	126	172	135	157	181
2100	125	65	112	183	75	200	87	139	217
Mean age (in years)									
1995	38.6	38.6	38.6	38.6	38.6	38.6	38.6	38.6	38.6
2010	42.9	43.7	42.7	41.8	43.9	42.0	44.1	43.1	42.2
2020	45.3	46.4	44.8	43.3	46.9	43.8	47.4	45.8	44.3
2050	49.2	51.6	47.3	43.5	53.5	45.3	55.7	51.2	47.2
2100	49.6	51.7	45.9	41.0	55.9	44.0	60.7	53.7	47.4
Percentage of population aged 60+									
1995	19.4	19.4	19.4	19.4	19.4	19.4	19.4	19.4	19.4
2010	27.6	27.9	27.2	26.5	28.3	26.9	28.7	27.9	27.2
2020	31.1	31.6	30.1	28.8	32.6	29.7	33.5	32.0	30.6
2050	38.9	42.1	35.7	30.4	45.5	33.4	48.8	42.1	36.4
2100	39.1	41.7	33.3	26.5	48.5	31.4	54.9	44.8	36.1
Percentage of population aged 0–14 years									
1995	17.1	17.1	17.1	17.1	17.1	17.1	17.1	17.1	17.1
2010	15.5	13.3	15.6	17.7	13.2	17.7	13.1	15.4	17.6
2020	14.1	11.8	14.3	16.6	11.6	16.4	11.5	13.9	16.2
2050	13.2	9.9	13.9	17.8	9.3	17.1	8.8	12.5	16.3
2100	13.6	9.9	14.9	19.9	8.7	18.6	7.7	12.3	17.3
Annual number of births (in thousands)									
1995–2000	1,608	1,445	1,608	1,771	1,445	1,771	1,446	1,608	1,771
2010–2015	1,449	1,134	1,448	1,763	1,135	1,763	1,135	1,449	1,763
2020–2025	1,356	998	1,355	1,742	999	1,743	1,000	1,357	1,744
2050–2055	1,229	671	1,222	1,985	674	1,995	677	1,233	2,002
2095–2100	1,073	371	1,057	2,504	376	2,544	378	1,080	2,562
Assumed total fertility rates									
1995–2000	1.53	1.38	1.53	1.69	1.38	1.69	1.38	1.53	1.69
2010–2015	1.60	1.25	1.60	1.94	1.25	1.94	1.25	1.60	1.94
2020–2025	1.65	1.28	1.65	2.02	1.28	2.02	1.28	1.65	2.02
2050–2055	1.72	1.28	1.72	2.16	1.28	2.16	1.28	1.72	2.16
2095–2100	1.74	1.24	1.74	2.24	1.24	2.24	1.24	1.74	2.24
Assumed life expectancies for both sexes combined (in years)									
1995–2000	79.7	79.5	79.5	79.5	79.7	79.7	80.0	80.0	80.0
2010–2015	82.6	80.9	80.9	80.9	82.6	82.6	84.4	84.4	84.4
2020–2025	84.7	81.9	81.9	81.9	84.7	84.7	87.4	87.4	87.4
2050–2055	88.3	82.8	82.8	82.8	88.3	88.3	93.9	93.9	93.9
2095–2100	91.0	82.8	82.8	82.8	91.0	91.0	99.0	99.0	99.0

Central Asia

Fertility	C	L	C	H	L	H	L	C	H
Mortality	C	H	H	H	C	C	L	L	L
Migration	C	C	C	C	C	C	C	C	C
Total population size (in millions)									
1995	54	54	54	54	54	54	54	54	54
2010	73	68	73	77	69	77	69	73	78
2020	88	78	87	97	78	98	79	89	98
2050	138	92	133	184	96	191	101	143	197
2100	195	70	173	361	81	402	93	216	435
Mean age (in years)									
1995	26.3	26.3	26.3	26.3	26.3	26.3	26.3	26.3	26.3
2010	28.0	29.3	27.9	26.7	29.4	26.7	29.4	28.0	26.8
2020	29.2	31.4	29.0	27.1	31.5	27.3	31.7	29.4	27.4
2050	33.1	38.2	32.4	28.2	39.1	28.8	40.1	33.9	29.4
2100	40.5	45.1	38.6	34.1	47.7	35.4	51.0	42.8	37.1
Percentage of population aged 60+									
1995	7.8	7.8	7.8	7.8	7.8	7.8	7.8	7.8	7.8
2010	7.6	7.9	7.5	7.0	8.1	7.2	8.2	7.7	7.3
2020	9.6	10.5	9.3	8.4	10.8	8.7	11.2	10.0	9.0
2050	15.3	20.1	13.9	10.0	21.9	11.1	23.9	16.8	12.2
2100	24.2	29.8	20.6	15.0	35.0	17.6	40.7	28.2	20.5
Percentage of population aged 0–14 years									
1995	36.3	36.3	36.3	36.3	36.3	36.3	36.3	36.3	36.3
2010	33.0	28.7	33.0	36.8	28.7	36.8	28.7	33.0	36.8
2020	31.9	26.7	31.9	36.3	26.6	36.2	26.5	31.8	36.1
2050	26.9	19.1	27.2	33.8	18.7	33.6	18.3	26.5	33.2
2100	18.5	13.0	19.2	24.6	12.2	24.1	11.1	17.6	23.3
Annual number of births (in thousands)									
1995–2000	1,515	1,365	1,515	1,664	1,366	1,664	1,366	1,515	1,664
2010–2015	1,947	1,463	1,946	2,432	1,464	2,434	1,465	1,949	2,435
2020–2025	2,100	1,366	2,092	2,917	1,371	2,928	1,376	2,107	2,939
2050–2055	2,622	1,094	2,566	4,897	1,117	5,007	1,136	2,668	5,095
2095–2100	2,369	541	2,199	6,375	583	6,875	609	2,475	7,184
Assumed total fertility rates									
1995–2000	3.35	3.02	3.35	3.68	3.02	3.68	3.02	3.35	3.68
2010–2015	3.21	2.42	3.21	4.00	2.42	4.00	2.42	3.21	4.00
2020–2025	3.11	2.21	3.11	4.00	2.21	4.00	2.21	3.11	4.00
2050–2055	2.58	1.78	2.58	3.38	1.78	3.38	1.78	2.58	3.38
2095–2100	1.95	1.45	1.95	2.45	1.45	2.45	1.45	1.95	2.45
Assumed life expectancies for both sexes combined (in years)									
1995–2000	69.7	69.5	69.5	69.5	69.7	69.7	69.9	69.9	69.9
2010–2015	72.4	70.5	70.5	70.5	72.4	72.4	74.1	74.1	74.1
2020–2025	74.4	71.6	71.6	71.6	74.4	74.4	77.2	77.2	77.2
2050–2055	78.0	72.5	72.5	72.5	78.0	78.0	83.6	83.6	83.6
2095–2100	80.5	72.5	72.5	72.5	80.5	80.5	88.6	88.6	88.6

Middle East

Fertility	C	L	C	H	L	H	L	C	H
Mortality	C	H	H	H	C	C	L	L	L
Migration	C	C	C	C	C	C	C	C	C

Total population size (in millions)

1995	151	151	151	151	151	151	151	151	151
2010	234	226	232	238	228	240	229	235	241
2020	301	278	296	313	283	318	287	305	323
2050	517	375	484	610	402	651	426	546	685
2100	738	299	606	1,088	373	1,309	453	859	1,491

Mean age (in years)

1995	23.1	23.1	23.1	23.1	23.1	23.1	23.1	23.1	23.1
2010	24.3	24.8	24.3	23.8	24.8	23.8	24.8	24.3	23.8
2020	25.7	26.8	25.7	24.7	26.8	24.8	27.0	25.9	24.9
2050	31.8	35.6	31.4	28.1	36.2	28.5	37.1	32.6	29.1
2100	41.0	45.1	39.3	35.1	47.7	36.3	51.6	43.9	38.3

Percentage of population aged 60+

1995	5.4	5.4	5.4	5.4	5.4	5.4	5.4	5.4	5.4
2010	5.6	5.6	5.5	5.3	5.7	5.4	5.8	5.7	5.5
2020	6.8	6.9	6.5	6.1	7.2	6.4	7.5	7.1	6.7
2050	12.4	14.4	11.2	8.9	16.0	9.9	17.8	13.9	11.1
2100	25.0	29.7	21.3	16.0	34.9	18.7	41.7	29.9	22.2

Percentage of population aged 0–14 years

1995	42.8	42.8	42.8	42.8	42.8	42.8	42.8	42.8	42.8
2010	40.3	38.6	40.2	41.7	38.7	41.8	38.8	40.4	41.9
2020	37.0	33.9	36.9	39.5	34.1	39.7	34.2	37.1	39.8
2050	27.3	20.3	27.3	33.1	20.3	33.2	20.0	27.1	33.0
2100	18.1	12.9	18.5	23.4	12.3	23.2	11.1	17.0	22.4

Annual number of births (in thousands)

1995–2000	6,035	5,877	6,035	6,188	5,877	6,188	5,878	6,036	6,189
2010–2015	7,885	6,850	7,867	8,875	6,866	8,895	6,880	7,901	8,914
2020–2025	8,657	6,604	8,584	10,640	6,659	10,730	6,710	8,724	10,810
2050–2055	10,090	4,984	9,610	15,940	5,228	16,760	5,415	10,460	17,380
2095–2100	8,886	2,386	7,639	18,740	2,768	21,850	3,002	9,651	23,750

Assumed total fertility rates

1995–2000	5.34	5.20	5.34	5.47	5.20	5.47	5.20	5.34	5.47
2010–2015	4.35	3.80	4.35	4.91	3.80	4.91	3.80	4.35	4.91
2020–2025	3.68	2.90	3.68	4.45	2.90	4.45	2.90	3.68	4.45
2050–2055	2.58	1.78	2.58	3.38	1.78	3.38	1.78	2.58	3.38
2095–2100	1.95	1.45	1.95	2.45	1.45	2.45	1.45	1.95	2.45

Assumed life expectancies for both sexes combined (in years)

1995–2000	67.7	67.2	67.2	67.2	67.7	67.7	68.1	68.1	68.1
2010–2015	70.7	67.7	67.7	67.7	70.7	70.7	73.8	73.8	73.8
2020–2025	72.9	68.2	68.2	68.2	72.9	72.9	77.7	77.7	77.7
2050–2055	77.0	68.7	68.7	68.7	77.0	77.0	85.3	85.3	85.3
2095–2100	79.6	68.7	68.7	68.7	79.6	79.6	90.5	90.5	90.5

South Asia

Fertility	C	L	C	H	L	H	L	C	H
Mortality	C	H	H	H	C	C	L	L	L
Migration	C	C	C	C	C	C	C	C	C

Total population size (in millions)

1995	1,240	1,240	1,240	1,240	1,240	1,240	1,240	1,240	1,240
2010	1,604	1,559	1,590	1,622	1,572	1,636	1,584	1,617	1,649
2020	1,839	1,717	1,798	1,880	1,756	1,922	1,792	1,876	1,962
2050	2,340	1,743	2,124	2,558	1,923	2,817	2,098	2,545	3,056
2100	2,202	872	1,653	2,872	1,180	3,797	1,528	2,772	4,701

Mean age (in years)

1995	25.8	25.8	25.8	25.8	25.8	25.8	25.8	25.8	25.8
2010	28.1	28.5	28.1	27.6	28.6	27.7	28.6	28.1	27.7
2020	29.7	30.7	29.7	28.8	30.7	28.8	30.9	29.9	28.9
2050	35.6	39.0	35.2	32.1	39.4	32.4	40.1	36.2	32.9
2100	43.3	48.8	42.3	37.4	50.2	38.1	52.8	45.3	39.7

Percentage of population aged 60+

1995	6.7	6.7	6.7	6.7	6.7	6.7	6.7	6.7	6.7
2010	8.6	8.7	8.5	8.3	8.8	8.4	8.8	8.7	8.5
2020	10.1	10.4	9.9	9.5	10.6	9.7	10.8	10.3	9.9
2050	16.8	19.3	15.9	13.2	20.4	14.0	21.9	18.1	15.1
2100	28.2	35.9	26.0	19.5	38.7	21.1	43.6	31.9	24.0

Percentage of population aged 0–14 years

1995	36.6	36.6	36.6	36.6	36.6	36.6	36.6	36.6	36.6
2010	32.5	31.0	32.4	33.7	31.1	33.8	31.2	32.6	33.9
2020	29.9	27.3	29.8	32.0	27.5	32.2	27.6	30.0	32.3
2050	22.3	16.6	22.1	27.1	16.7	27.3	16.6	22.2	27.2
2100	15.4	9.8	15.5	20.8	9.6	20.9	9.0	14.8	20.4

Annual number of births (in thousands)

1995–2000	36,870	35,910	36,860	37,810	35,920	37,830	35,930	36,880	37,840
2010–2015	40,300	35,280	40,060	44,860	35,490	45,130	35,690	40,520	45,370
2020–2025	39,820	31,010	39,120	47,590	31,570	48,450	32,070	40,450	49,230
2050–2055	35,170	17,630	32,150	51,770	19,270	56,650	20,650	37,690	60,710
2095–2100	21,690	4,900	16,610	42,420	6,409	55,420	7,642	25,850	66,010

Assumed total fertility rates

1995–2000	3.68	3.58	3.68	3.77	3.58	3.77	3.58	3.68	3.77
2010–2015	3.11	2.74	3.11	3.47	2.74	3.47	2.74	3.11	3.47
2020–2025	2.73	2.22	2.73	3.24	2.22	3.24	2.22	2.73	3.24
2050–2055	2.09	1.50	2.09	2.68	1.50	2.68	1.50	2.09	2.68
2095–2100	1.70	1.20	1.70	2.20	1.20	2.20	1.20	1.70	2.20

Assumed life expectancies for both sexes combined (in years)

1995–2000	60.5	60.0	60.0	60.0	60.5	60.5	60.9	60.9	60.9
2010–2015	62.8	59.7	59.7	59.7	62.8	62.8	65.8	65.8	65.8
2020–2025	64.5	59.7	59.7	59.7	64.5	64.5	69.3	69.3	69.3
2050–2055	68.0	59.7	59.7	59.7	68.0	68.0	76.2	76.2	76.2
2095–2100	70.6	59.7	59.7	59.7	70.6	70.6	81.5	81.5	81.5

Eastern Europe

Fertility	C	L	C	H	L	H	L	C	H
Mortality	C	H	H	H	C	C	L	L	L
Migration	C	C	C	C	C	C	C	C	C
Total population size (in millions)									
1995	122	122	122	122	122	122	122	122	122
2010	124	120	124	127	121	128	121	125	129
2020	123	115	121	128	116	130	118	125	132
2050	109	84	103	125	90	133	97	116	140
2100	77	30	66	128	37	144	45	88	160
Mean age (in years)									
1995	35.6	35.6	35.6	35.6	35.6	35.6	35.6	35.6	35.6
2010	39.0	39.9	38.9	37.9	40.0	38.0	40.1	39.1	38.2
2020	41.1	42.5	40.8	39.2	42.8	39.5	43.2	41.5	39.9
2050	46.2	49.5	44.7	40.6	51.1	41.9	52.8	47.9	43.5
2100	46.5	51.2	43.5	38.0	54.9	40.4	59.7	50.5	43.5
Percentage of population aged 60+									
1995	16.7	16.7	16.7	16.7	16.7	16.7	16.7	16.7	16.7
2010	19.6	19.9	19.3	18.8	20.2	19.0	20.5	19.9	19.3
2020	24.1	24.7	23.3	22.1	25.5	22.8	26.3	24.9	23.5
2050	34.5	38.8	31.6	25.9	41.9	28.5	45.2	37.6	31.3
2100	34.9	41.3	29.4	21.8	48.1	26.1	55.4	41.1	31.0
Percentage of population aged 0–14 years									
1995	21.3	21.3	21.3	21.3	21.3	21.3	21.3	21.3	21.3
2010	17.5	15.0	17.6	20.0	15.0	20.0	14.9	17.5	19.9
2020	16.4	13.6	16.5	19.3	13.5	19.1	13.3	16.2	19.0
2050	14.1	10.0	14.6	19.2	9.5	18.6	9.0	13.4	17.9
2100	15.0	9.8	16.2	22.0	8.7	20.9	7.5	13.6	19.6
Annual number of births (in thousands)									
1995–2000	1,499	1,350	1,499	1,652	1,350	1,652	1,350	1,499	1,652
2010–2015	1,394	1,091	1,393	1,703	1,092	1,704	1,092	1,395	1,705
2020–2025	1,208	846	1,204	1,619	849	1,625	852	1,212	1,630
2050–2055	971	472	953	1,679	481	1,711	488	985	1,736
2095–2100	741	169	694	1,994	182	2,127	189	768	2,203
Assumed total fertility rates									
1995–2000	1.66	1.50	1.66	1.83	1.50	1.83	1.50	1.66	1.83
2010–2015	1.68	1.32	1.68	2.04	1.32	2.04	1.32	1.68	2.04
2020–2025	1.69	1.31	1.69	2.07	1.31	2.07	1.31	1.69	2.07
2050–2055	1.78	1.34	1.78	2.22	1.34	2.22	1.34	1.78	2.22
2095–2100	1.89	1.39	1.89	2.39	1.39	2.39	1.39	1.89	2.39
Assumed life expectancies for both sexes combined (in years)									
1995–2000	72.0	71.8	71.8	71.8	72.0	72.0	72.3	72.3	72.3
2010–2015	74.7	72.9	72.9	72.9	74.7	74.7	76.5	76.5	76.5
2020–2025	76.7	73.9	73.9	73.9	76.7	76.7	79.5	79.5	79.5
2050–2055	80.3	74.8	74.8	74.8	80.3	80.3	85.9	85.9	85.9
2095–2100	82.8	74.8	74.8	74.8	82.8	82.8	91.0	91.0	91.0

European FSU

Fertility	C	L	C	H	L	H	L	C	H
Mortality	C	H	H	H	C	C	L	L	L
Migration	C	C	C	C	C	C	C	C	C

Total population size (in millions)									
1995	238	238	238	238	238	238	238	238	238
2010	231	223	229	235	225	238	227	233	240
2020	224	207	219	230	212	236	217	229	241
2050	187	139	171	209	154	227	171	206	246
2100	135	51	112	217	64	254	79	158	289
Mean age (in years)									
1995	36.0	36.0	36.0	36.0	36.0	36.0	36.0	36.0	36.0
2010	39.4	40.2	39.2	38.3	40.3	38.5	40.5	39.6	38.7
2020	41.2	42.5	40.8	39.3	42.9	39.7	43.4	41.7	40.2
2050	45.5	48.6	43.8	39.8	50.3	41.3	52.5	47.7	43.4
2100	43.4	47.3	40.4	35.4	51.1	37.8	56.2	47.6	41.2
Percentage of population aged 60+									
1995	16.9	16.9	16.9	16.9	16.9	16.9	16.9	16.9	16.9
2010	19.1	19.3	18.7	18.2	19.6	18.6	20.0	19.4	18.9
2020	23.6	24.0	22.7	21.6	24.9	22.4	25.9	24.6	23.3
2050	34.0	37.7	30.6	25.0	41.3	28.0	45.6	38.0	31.7
2100	30.0	34.7	24.5	18.1	41.7	22.4	50.2	37.1	27.9
Percentage of population aged 0–14 years									
1995	21.6	21.6	21.6	21.6	21.6	21.6	21.6	21.6	21.6
2010	16.1	13.7	16.1	18.4	13.7	18.4	13.6	16.0	18.3
2020	16.0	13.3	16.2	18.9	13.1	18.7	12.9	15.8	18.5
2050	14.6	10.6	15.4	19.9	10.0	19.1	9.2	13.6	18.0
2100	17.4	12.5	18.9	24.6	11.1	23.2	9.4	15.6	21.5
Annual number of births (in thousands)									
1995–2000	2,529	2,276	2,529	2,782	2,276	2,782	2,276	2,529	2,782
2010–2015	2,549	1,992	2,547	3,106	1,994	3,109	1,995	2,551	3,111
2020–2025	2,084	1,460	2,076	2,778	1,465	2,789	1,470	2,091	2,800
2050–2055	1,748	854	1,709	2,982	874	3,052	890	1,780	3,108
2095–2100	1,568	385	1,445	3,972	420	4,304	441	1,643	4,506
Assumed total fertility rates									
1995–2000	1.50	1.35	1.50	1.65	1.35	1.65	1.35	1.50	1.65
2010–2015	1.58	1.24	1.58	1.92	1.24	1.92	1.24	1.58	1.92
2020–2025	1.64	1.27	1.64	2.01	1.27	2.01	1.27	1.64	2.01
2050–2055	1.84	1.40	1.84	2.28	1.40	2.28	1.40	1.84	2.28
2095–2100	2.05	1.55	2.05	2.55	1.55	2.55	1.55	2.05	2.55
Assumed life expectancies for both sexes combined (in years)									
1995–2000	67.8	67.3	67.3	67.3	67.8	67.8	68.2	68.2	68.2
2010–2015	70.5	67.6	67.6	67.6	70.5	70.5	73.2	73.2	73.2
2020–2025	72.5	68.0	68.0	68.0	72.5	72.5	76.9	76.9	76.9
2050–2055	76.1	68.6	68.6	68.6	76.1	76.1	83.7	83.7	83.7
2095–2100	78.7	68.6	68.6	68.6	78.7	78.7	88.6	88.6	88.6

Western Europe (High Migration)

Fertility	C	L	C	H	L	H	L	C	H
Mortality	C	H	H	H	C	C	L	L	L
Migration	H	H	H	H	H	H	H	H	H
Total population size (in millions)									
1995	447	447	447	447	447	447	447	447	447
2010	478	462	476	489	465	492	467	481	494
2020	492	461	486	510	468	517	474	499	524
2050	505	402	477	564	429	592	457	534	622
2100	484	260	434	702	297	769	338	536	834
Mean age (in years)									
1995	37.0	37.0	37.0	37.0	37.0	37.0	37.0	37.0	37.0
2010	40.1	40.9	40.0	39.0	41.1	39.2	41.2	40.3	39.3
2020	42.0	43.2	41.6	40.1	43.6	40.5	44.0	42.4	40.9
2050	46.3	48.8	44.7	41.1	50.5	42.6	52.4	48.1	44.3
2100	46.2	48.1	43.1	38.7	51.8	41.3	56.1	49.9	44.3
Percentage of population aged 60+									
1995	18.6	18.6	18.6	18.6	18.6	18.6	18.6	18.6	18.6
2010	21.6	22.0	21.3	20.8	22.3	21.0	22.6	21.9	21.3
2020	24.7	25.2	24.0	22.8	26.0	23.5	26.8	25.5	24.3
2050	34.0	36.8	31.0	26.3	40.0	28.9	43.2	37.0	31.7
2100	34.1	35.8	28.8	23.0	42.1	27.3	48.3	39.5	31.8
Percentage of population aged 0–14 years									
1995	19.9	19.9	19.9	19.9	19.9	19.9	19.9	19.9	19.9
2010	17.1	14.8	17.1	19.4	14.7	19.4	14.6	17.0	19.3
2020	16.0	13.4	16.2	18.7	13.3	18.5	13.1	15.8	18.3
2050	14.6	11.1	15.2	19.2	10.5	18.5	9.9	13.9	17.8
2100	15.6	11.9	16.8	21.7	10.8	20.5	9.6	14.3	19.2
Annual number of births (in thousands)									
1995–2000	5,599	5,045	5,599	6,152	5,045	6,152	5,046	5,599	6,152
2010–2015	5,203	4,087	5,201	6,320	4,089	6,323	4,091	5,206	6,326
2020–2025	5,075	3,710	5,067	6,552	3,716	6,563	3,722	5,083	6,573
2050–2055	4,796	2,656	4,754	7,653	2,679	7,723	2,694	4,826	7,772
2095–2100	4,974	1,872	4,845	10,910	1,915	11,230	1,935	5,036	11,380
Assumed total fertility rates									
1995–2000	1.67	1.51	1.67	1.84	1.51	1.84	1.51	1.67	1.84
2010–2015	1.68	1.33	1.68	2.04	1.33	2.04	1.33	1.68	2.04
2020–2025	1.69	1.31	1.69	2.07	1.31	2.07	1.31	1.69	2.07
2050–2055	1.78	1.34	1.78	2.22	1.34	2.22	1.34	1.78	2.22
2095–2100	1.89	1.39	1.89	2.39	1.39	2.39	1.39	1.89	2.39
Assumed life expectancies for both sexes combined (in years)									
1995–2000	75.8	75.6	75.6	75.6	75.8	75.8	76.1	76.1	76.1
2010–2015	78.8	77.0	77.0	77.0	78.8	78.8	80.6	80.6	80.6
2020–2025	80.8	78.0	78.0	78.0	80.8	80.8	83.6	83.6	83.6
2050–2055	84.5	79.0	79.0	79.0	84.5	84.5	90.0	90.0	90.0
2095–2100	87.1	79.0	79.0	79.0	87.1	87.1	95.2	95.2	95.2

Western Europe (Low Migration)

Fertility	C	L	C	H	L	H	L	C	H
Mortality	C	H	H	H	C	C	L	L	L
Migration	L	L	L	L	L	L	L	L	L

Total population size (in millions)

1995	447	447	447	447	447	447	447	447	447
2010	462	446	459	472	449	475	451	464	477
2020	463	433	457	480	440	487	446	470	494
2050	433	340	408	487	364	513	391	460	541
2100	341	159	302	530	186	585	217	383	639

Mean age (in years)

1995	37.0	37.0	37.0	37.0	37.0	37.0	37.0	37.0	37.0
2010	40.4	41.3	40.3	39.4	41.4	39.5	41.6	40.6	39.7
2020	42.6	43.8	42.2	40.6	44.2	41.0	44.6	43.0	41.4
2050	47.5	50.4	45.8	41.9	52.1	43.5	54.1	49.4	45.3
2100	47.6	50.8	44.3	39.2	54.8	41.9	59.6	51.6	45.1

Percentage of population aged 60+

1995	18.6	18.6	18.6	18.6	18.6	18.6	18.6	18.6	18.6
2010	22.1	22.4	21.8	21.2	22.7	21.5	23.1	22.4	21.8
2020	25.7	26.3	24.9	23.7	27.1	24.4	27.9	26.5	25.2
2050	36.1	39.7	33.0	27.7	43.0	30.5	46.3	39.3	33.4
2100	36.5	40.7	30.9	23.9	47.5	28.4	54.2	42.3	33.2

Percentage of population aged 0–14 years

1995	19.9	19.9	19.9	19.9	19.9	19.9	19.9	19.9	19.9
2010	16.8	14.5	16.9	19.1	14.4	19.1	14.4	16.8	19.0
2020	15.6	13.0	15.8	18.3	12.9	18.1	12.7	15.4	17.9
2050	13.9	10.2	14.6	18.7	9.7	18.0	9.1	13.2	17.3
2100	14.8	10.6	16.1	21.4	9.4	20.1	8.2	13.5	18.8

Annual number of births (in thousands)

1995–2000	5,544	4,996	5,544	6,092	4,997	6,092	4,997	5,544	6,092
2010–2015	4,888	3,839	4,885	5,937	3,841	5,940	3,842	4,890	5,943
2020–2025	4,613	3,357	4,606	5,979	3,363	5,990	3,368	4,621	6,000
2050–2055	3,880	2,048	3,843	6,381	2,068	6,443	2,082	3,907	6,488
2095–2100	3,293	986	3,191	8,056	1,017	8,316	1,033	3,343	8,444

Assumed total fertility rates

1995–2000	1.67	1.51	1.67	1.84	1.51	1.84	1.51	1.67	1.84
2010–2015	1.68	1.33	1.68	2.04	1.33	2.04	1.33	1.68	2.04
2020–2025	1.69	1.31	1.69	2.07	1.31	2.07	1.31	1.69	2.07
2050–2055	1.78	1.34	1.78	2.22	1.34	2.22	1.34	1.78	2.22
2095–2100	1.89	1.39	1.89	2.39	1.39	2.39	1.39	1.89	2.39

Assumed life expectancies for both sexes combined (in years)

1995–2000	75.8	75.6	75.6	75.6	75.8	75.8	76.1	76.1	76.1
2010–2015	78.8	77.1	77.1	77.1	78.8	78.8	80.6	80.6	80.6
2020–2025	80.8	78.0	78.0	78.0	80.8	80.8	83.6	83.6	83.6
2050–2055	84.5	79.0	79.0	79.0	84.5	84.5	90.1	90.1	90.1
2095–2100	87.1	79.0	79.0	79.0	87.1	87.1	95.2	95.2	95.2

Western Europe (Central Migration)

Fertility	C	L	C	H	L	H	L	C	H
Mortality	C	H	H	H	C	C	L	L	L
Migration	C	C	C	C	C	C	C	C	C
Total population size (in millions)									
1995	447	447	447	447	447	447	447	447	447
2010	470	454	467	480	457	483	459	473	486
2020	478	447	471	495	454	502	460	485	509
2050	469	371	442	525	397	553	424	497	582
2100	413	209	368	616	241	677	278	459	736
Mean age (in years)									
1995	37.0	37.0	37.0	37.0	37.0	37.0	37.0	37.0	37.0
2010	40.3	41.1	40.1	39.2	41.2	39.4	41.4	40.4	39.5
2020	42.3	43.5	41.9	40.4	43.9	40.8	44.3	42.7	41.2
2050	46.9	49.5	45.2	41.5	51.3	43.0	53.2	48.7	44.8
2100	46.8	49.2	43.6	38.9	52.9	41.5	57.4	50.6	44.7
Percentage of population aged 60+									
1995	18.6	18.6	18.6	18.6	18.6	18.6	18.6	18.6	18.6
2010	21.9	22.2	21.6	21.0	22.5	21.3	22.8	22.2	21.6
2020	25.2	25.7	24.4	23.2	26.5	24.0	27.3	26.0	24.7
2050	35.0	38.1	32.0	26.9	41.3	29.7	44.6	38.1	32.5
2100	35.1	37.7	29.6	23.4	44.1	27.8	50.6	40.7	32.4
Percentage of population aged 0–14 years									
1995	19.9	19.9	19.9	19.9	19.9	19.9	19.9	19.9	19.9
2010	17.0	14.6	17.0	19.3	14.6	19.2	14.5	16.9	19.2
2020	15.8	13.2	16.0	18.5	13.1	18.3	12.9	15.6	18.1
2050	14.3	10.7	14.9	19.0	10.1	18.3	9.6	13.6	17.6
2100	15.3	11.4	16.5	21.6	10.2	20.3	9.0	13.9	19.0
Annual number of births (in thousands)									
1995–2000	5,571	5,021	5,571	6,122	5,021	6,122	5,021	5,572	6,122
2010–2015	5,046	3,963	5,043	6,128	3,965	6,131	3,967	5,048	6,134
2020–2025	4,844	3,534	4,836	6,266	3,539	6,277	3,545	4,852	6,286
2050–2055	4,338	2,352	4,298	7,017	2,373	7,083	2,388	4,366	7,130
2095–2100	4,134	1,429	4,018	9,484	1,466	9,771	1,484	4,189	9,910
Assumed total fertility rates									
1995–2000	1.67	1.51	1.67	1.84	1.51	1.84	1.51	1.67	1.84
2010–2015	1.68	1.33	1.68	2.04	1.33	2.04	1.33	1.68	2.04
2020–2025	1.69	1.31	1.69	2.07	1.31	2.07	1.31	1.69	2.07
2050–2055	1.78	1.34	1.78	2.22	1.34	2.22	1.34	1.78	2.22
2095–2100	1.89	1.39	1.89	2.39	1.39	2.39	1.39	1.89	2.39
Assumed life expectancies for both sexes combined (in years)									
1995–2000	75.8	75.6	75.6	75.6	75.8	75.8	76.1	76.1	76.1
2010–2015	78.8	77.1	77.1	77.1	78.8	78.8	80.6	80.6	80.6
2020–2025	80.8	78.0	78.0	78.0	80.8	80.8	83.6	83.6	83.6
2050–2055	84.5	79.0	79.0	79.0	84.5	84.5	90.0	90.0	90.0
2095–2100	87.1	79.0	79.0	79.0	87.1	87.1	95.2	95.2	95.2

Latin America

Fertility	C	L	C	H	L	H	L	C	H
Mortality	C	H	H	H	C	C	L	L	L
Migration	C	C	C	C	C	C	C	C	C

Total population size (in millions)

1995	477	477	477	477	477	477	477	477	477
2010	607	586	605	624	588	627	590	610	629
2020	693	644	686	729	650	737	656	700	743
2050	906	687	867	1,080	722	1,125	756	945	1,169
2100	1,056	454	927	1,700	530	1,910	612	1,180	2,096

Mean age (in years)

1995	26.9	26.9	26.9	26.9	26.9	26.9	26.9	26.9	26.9
2010	29.9	30.7	29.9	29.2	30.7	29.2	30.8	30.0	29.2
2020	32.0	33.4	31.9	30.6	33.5	30.7	33.6	32.2	30.8
2050	37.5	41.4	36.8	33.1	42.2	33.7	43.1	38.3	34.4
2100	41.7	46.3	40.0	35.3	48.7	36.6	51.9	44.1	38.4

Percentage of population aged 60+

1995	7.6	7.6	7.6	7.6	7.6	7.6	7.6	7.6	7.6
2010	9.4	9.6	9.3	9.0	9.7	9.1	9.8	9.5	9.2
2020	11.9	12.4	11.6	10.9	12.7	11.2	13.0	12.2	11.5
2050	20.7	24.4	19.4	15.5	26.0	16.7	27.8	22.3	18.0
2100	27.1	33.1	23.8	17.8	37.5	20.3	42.8	31.1	23.2

Percentage of population aged 0–14 years

1995	33.7	33.7	33.7	33.7	33.7	33.7	33.7	33.7	33.7
2010	29.3	27.0	29.3	31.4	27.0	31.4	27.0	29.3	31.5
2020	26.8	23.6	26.9	29.8	23.6	29.8	23.5	26.8	29.8
2050	21.9	16.2	22.1	27.5	15.9	27.2	15.6	21.5	26.9
2100	18.6	13.3	19.3	24.6	12.6	24.1	11.6	17.7	23.2

Annual number of births (in thousands)

1995–2000	12,370	11,720	12,370	13,020	11,720	13,020	11,720	12,370	13,020
2010–2015	13,050	10,800	13,030	15,280	10,810	15,300	10,820	13,060	15,320
2020–2025	13,290	9,792	13,230	16,960	9,835	17,040	9,875	13,340	17,110
2050–2055	13,730	6,990	13,400	22,530	7,158	23,090	7,295	13,990	23,540
2095–2100	13,350	3,765	12,280	31,030	4,097	33,720	4,314	14,040	35,460

Assumed total fertility rates

1995–2000	2.95	2.79	2.95	3.10	2.79	3.10	2.79	2.95	3.10
2010–2015	2.62	2.18	2.62	3.06	2.18	3.06	2.18	2.62	3.06
2020–2025	2.49	1.94	2.49	3.03	1.94	3.03	1.94	2.49	3.03
2050–2055	2.25	1.66	2.25	2.84	1.66	2.84	1.66	2.25	2.84
2095–2100	2.10	1.60	2.10	2.60	1.60	2.60	1.60	2.10	2.60

Assumed life expectancies for both sexes combined (in years)

1995–2000	69.8	69.6	69.6	69.6	69.8	69.8	70.1	70.1	70.1
2010–2015	72.4	70.6	70.6	70.6	72.4	72.4	74.1	74.1	74.1
2020–2025	74.4	71.6	71.6	71.6	74.4	74.4	77.1	77.1	77.1
2050–2055	78.1	72.6	72.6	72.6	78.1	78.1	83.6	83.6	83.6
2095–2100	80.7	72.6	72.6	72.6	80.7	80.7	88.8	88.8	88.8

North America (High Migration)

Fertility	C	L	C	H	L	H	L	C	H
Mortality	C	H	H	H	C	C	L	L	L
Migration	H	H	H	H	H	H	H	H	H

Total population size (in millions)

1995	297	297	297	297	297	297	297	297	297
2010	351	340	350	360	341	362	343	353	363
2020	388	363	384	404	368	409	372	393	414
2050	480	386	458	543	407	566	429	503	589
2100	623	360	568	890	402	964	447	678	1,031

Mean age (in years)

1995	35.6	35.6	35.6	35.6	35.6	35.6	35.6	35.6	35.6
2010	38.1	39.0	38.0	37.1	39.1	37.2	39.2	38.3	37.4
2020	39.7	41.0	39.4	37.9	41.3	38.2	41.7	40.0	38.5
2050	43.2	45.6	41.7	38.3	47.1	39.6	48.8	44.7	41.1
2100	43.6	45.3	40.8	36.7	48.6	38.9	52.3	46.7	41.5

Percentage of population aged 60+

1995	16.4	16.4	16.4	16.4	16.4	16.4	16.4	16.4	16.4
2010	18.5	18.8	18.3	17.8	19.1	18.0	19.4	18.8	18.3
2020	22.7	23.3	22.0	20.9	24.0	21.5	24.6	23.4	22.2
2050	28.6	30.9	26.0	22.0	33.7	24.2	36.6	31.2	26.6
2100	30.1	31.3	25.4	20.3	36.9	24.1	42.5	34.8	27.9

Percentage of population aged 0–14 years

1995	22.0	22.0	22.0	22.0	22.0	22.0	22.0	22.0	22.0
2010	19.2	16.9	19.3	21.6	16.8	21.5	16.8	19.2	21.5
2020	18.5	15.7	18.6	21.4	15.5	21.2	15.4	18.4	21.1
2050	17.0	13.2	17.6	22.0	12.6	21.3	12.1	16.4	20.7
2100	17.9	14.2	19.1	24.0	13.0	22.9	11.9	16.7	21.7

Annual number of births (in thousands)

1995–2000	4,283	3,888	4,283	4,677	3,888	4,677	3,888	4,283	4,677
2010–2015	4,624	3,644	4,621	5,610	3,645	5,613	3,647	4,626	5,615
2020–2025	4,818	3,487	4,811	6,275	3,492	6,286	3,497	4,825	6,295
2050–2055	5,546	3,141	5,503	8,774	3,164	8,847	3,180	5,577	8,899
2095–2100	7,671	3,235	7,493	15,890	3,298	16,320	3,326	7,752	16,510

Assumed total fertility rates

1995–2000	1.96	1.78	1.96	2.14	1.78	2.14	1.78	1.96	2.14
2010–2015	1.91	1.51	1.91	2.30	1.51	2.30	1.51	1.91	2.30
2020–2025	1.88	1.46	1.88	2.30	1.46	2.30	1.46	1.88	2.30
2050–2055	1.95	1.48	1.95	2.42	1.48	2.42	1.48	1.95	2.42
2095–2100	2.09	1.59	2.09	2.59	1.59	2.59	1.59	2.09	2.59

Assumed life expectancies for both sexes combined (in years)

1995–2000	76.2	76.0	76.0	76.0	76.2	76.2	76.5	76.5	76.5
2010–2015	79.2	77.4	77.4	77.4	79.2	79.2	81.0	81.0	81.0
2020–2025	81.2	78.4	78.4	78.4	81.2	81.2	84.0	84.0	84.0
2050–2055	84.8	79.4	79.4	79.4	84.8	84.8	90.4	90.4	90.4
2095–2100	87.5	79.4	79.4	79.4	87.5	87.5	95.5	95.5	95.5

North America (Low Migration)

Fertility	C	L	C	H	L	H	L	C	H
Mortality	C	H	H	H	C	C	L	L	L
Migration	L	L	L	L	L	L	L	L	L
Total population size (in millions)									
1995	297	297	297	297	297	297	297	297	297
2010	318	307	316	326	309	327	310	320	329
2020	329	307	325	343	311	348	315	333	352
2050	332	257	314	382	274	401	292	351	421
2100	311	141	278	503	164	550	189	344	594
Mean age (in years)									
1995	35.6	35.6	35.6	35.6	35.6	35.6	35.6	35.6	35.6
2010	38.9	39.8	38.8	37.9	39.9	38.0	40.1	39.1	38.1
2020	41.0	42.4	40.6	39.0	42.7	39.4	43.1	41.3	39.7
2050	45.3	48.4	43.6	39.5	50.2	41.0	52.1	47.1	42.7
2100	45.4	48.9	42.3	37.2	52.7	39.7	57.4	49.1	42.5
Percentage of population aged 60+									
1995	16.4	16.4	16.4	16.4	16.4	16.4	16.4	16.4	16.4
2010	19.6	19.9	19.3	18.8	20.2	19.0	20.5	19.9	19.3
2020	25.1	25.9	24.4	23.1	26.6	23.8	27.3	25.8	24.5
2050	32.2	35.9	29.3	24.1	39.1	26.7	42.4	35.3	29.4
2100	33.3	37.8	28.1	21.3	44.3	25.4	50.9	38.7	29.6
Percentage of population aged 0–14 years									
1995	22.0	22.0	22.0	22.0	22.0	22.0	22.0	22.0	22.0
2010	18.6	16.1	18.6	20.9	16.1	20.9	16.0	18.5	20.8
2020	17.6	14.7	17.8	20.5	14.6	20.4	14.4	17.4	20.2
2050	15.9	11.6	16.5	21.2	11.1	20.5	10.5	15.1	19.8
2100	16.9	12.3	18.2	23.7	11.0	22.5	9.7	15.5	21.2
Annual number of births (in thousands)									
1995–2000	4,162	3,779	4,162	4,545	3,779	4,545	3,779	4,162	4,545
2010–2015	3,940	3,102	3,938	4,785	3,104	4,787	3,105	3,942	4,789
2020–2025	3,806	2,720	3,799	5,009	2,724	5,019	2,728	3,812	5,027
2050–2055	3,485	1,796	3,452	5,860	1,813	5,916	1,825	3,509	5,957
2095–2100	3,544	1,070	3,437	8,758	1,103	9,036	1,119	3,596	9,169
Assumed total fertility rates									
1995–2000	1.96	1.78	1.96	2.14	1.78	2.14	1.78	1.96	2.14
2010–2015	1.91	1.51	1.91	2.30	1.51	2.30	1.51	1.91	2.30
2020–2025	1.88	1.46	1.88	2.30	1.46	2.30	1.46	1.88	2.30
2050–2055	1.95	1.48	1.95	2.42	1.48	2.42	1.48	1.95	2.42
2095–2100	2.09	1.59	2.09	2.59	1.59	2.59	1.59	2.09	2.59
Assumed life expectancies for both sexes combined (in years)									
1995–2000	76.2	76.0	76.0	76.0	76.2	76.2	76.5	76.5	76.5
2010–2015	79.2	77.4	77.4	77.4	79.2	79.2	81.0	81.0	81.0
2020–2025	81.2	78.4	78.4	78.4	81.2	81.2	84.0	84.0	84.0
2050–2055	84.9	79.4	79.4	79.4	84.9	84.9	90.4	90.4	90.4
2095–2100	87.5	79.4	79.4	79.4	87.5	87.5	95.5	95.5	95.5

North America (Central Migration)

Fertility	C	L	C	H	L	H	L	C	H
Mortality	C	H	H	H	C	C	L	L	L
Migration	C	C	C	C	C	C	C	C	C
Total population size (in millions)									
1995	297	297	297	297	297	297	297	297	297
2010	335	323	333	343	325	345	327	336	346
2020	359	335	354	374	339	378	344	363	383
2050	406	321	386	463	340	483	360	427	505
2100	467	251 ·	423	697	283	757	318	511	812
Mean age (in years)									
1995	35.6	35.6	35.6	35.6	35.6	35.6	35.6	35.6	35.6
2010	38.5	39.3	38.4	37.5	39.5	37.6	39.6	38.6	37.7
2020	40.3	41.6	39.9	38.4	42.0	38.7	42.3	40.6	39.1
2050	44.0	46.7	42.5	38.8	48.4	40.2	50.2	45.7	41.8
2100	44.2	46.3	41.3	36.9	49.8	39.2	53.8	47.5	41.9
Percentage of population aged 60+									
1995	16.4	16.4	16.4	16.4	16.4	16.4	16.4	16.4	16.4
2010	19.0	19.4	18.8	18.2	19.6	18.5	19.9	19.3	18.8
2020	23.8	24.5	23.1	21.9	25.2	22.6	25.9	24.5	23.2
2050	30.0	32.9	27.4	22.8	35.9	25.2	38.9	32.9	27.8
2100	31.2	33.2	26.3	20.6	39.1	24.6	45.0	36.1	28.5
Percentage of population aged 0–14 years									
1995	22.0	22.0	22.0	22.0	22.0	22.0	22.0	22.0	22.0
2010	18.9	16.5	19.0	21.3	16.5	21.2	16.4	18.9	21.2
2020	18.1	15.2	18.2	21.0	15.1	20.8	15.0	17.9	20.7
2050	16.6	12.5	17.2	21.7	12.0	21.0	11.4	15.9	20.3
2100	17.6	13.7	18.8	23.9	12.5	22.7	11.2	16.3	21.5
Annual number of births (in thousands)									
1995–2000	4,222	3,833	4,222	4,611	3,834	4,611	3,834	4,222	4,611
2010–2015	4,282	3,373	4,280	5,197	3,375	5,200	3,376	4,284	5,202
2020–2025	4,312	3,103	4,305	5,642	3,108	5,652	3,113	4,319	5,661
2050–2055	4,516	2,468	4,477	7,317	2,488	7,382	2,502	4,543	7,428
2095–2100	5,608	2,152	5,465	12,330	2,201	12,680	2,223	5,674	12,840
Assumed total fertility rates									
1995–2000	1.96	1.78	1.96	2.14	1.78	2.14	1.78	1.96	2.14
2010–2015	1.91	1.51	1.91	2.30	1.51	2.30	1.51	1.91	2.30
2020–2025	1.88	1.46	1.88	2.30	1.46	2.30	1.46	1.88	2.30
2050–2055	1.95	1.48	1.95	2.42	1.48	2.42	1.48	1.95	2.42
2095–2100	2.09	1.59	2.09	2.59	1.59	2.59	1.59	2.09	2.59
Assumed life expectancies for both sexes combined (in years)									
1995–2000	76.2	76.0	76.0	76.0	76.2	76.2	76.5	76.5	76.5
2010–2015	79.2	77.4	77.4	77.4	79.2	79.2	81.0	81.0	81.0
2020–2025	81.2	78.4	78.4	78.4	81.2	81.2	84.0	84.0	84.0
2050–2055	84.8	79.4	79.4	79.4	84.8	84.8	90.4	90.4	90.4
2095–2100	87.5	79.4	79.4	79.4	87.5	87.5	95.5	95.5	95.5

Industrialized Region

Fertility	C	L	C	H	L	H	L	C	H
Mortality	C	H	H	H	C	C	L	L	L
Migration	C	C	C	C	C	C	C	C	C

Total population size (in millions)									
1995	1,251	1,251	1,251	1,251	1,251	1,251	1,251	1,251	1,251
2010	1,315	1,270	1,307	1,344	1,278	1,353	1,286	1,323	1,361
2020	1,340	1,250	1,319	1,388	1,270	1,410	1,291	1,360	1,431
2050	1,319	1,032	1,241	1,486	1,107	1,568	1,188	1,402	1,654
2100	1,216	607	1,081	1,841	700	2,033	806	1,355	2,214

Mean age (in years)									
1995	36.5	36.5	36.5	36.5	36.5	36.5	36.5	36.5	36.5
2010	39.9	40.7	39.7	38.8	40.8	38.9	41.0	40.0	39.1
2020	41.8	43.1	41.4	39.9	43.5	40.3	43.9	42.2	40.7
2050	46.0	48.8	44.4	40.5	50.5	42.1	52.4	47.9	43.8
2100	45.7	48.2	42.6	37.9	51.9	40.4	56.4	49.4	43.4

Percentage of population aged 60+									
1995	17.7	17.7	17.7	17.7	17.7	17.7	17.7	17.7	17.7
2010	21.1	21.4	20.8	20.2	21.7	20.5	22.0	21.4	20.8
2020	25.1	25.7	24.4	23.1	26.5	23.9	27.3	25.9	24.7
2050	33.7	36.9	30.7	25.7	40.2	28.4	43.6	36.9	31.3
2100	33.4	36.2	28.1	21.9	42.5	26.1	49.1	39.0	30.7

Percentage of population aged 0–14 years									
1995	20.5	20.5	20.5	20.5	20.5	20.5	20.5	20.5	20.5
2010	17.2	14.8	17.2	19.5	14.8	19.5	14.7	17.1	19.4
2020	16.3	13.6	16.5	19.1	13.5	18.9	13.3	16.1	18.7
2050	14.9	11.1	15.5	19.8	10.5	19.1	9.9	14.2	18.3
2100	16.2	12.2	17.5	22.7	11.0	21.5	9.7	14.8	20.1

Annual number of births (in thousands)									
1995–2000	15,429	13,925	15,429	16,938	13,926	16,938	13,927	15,430	16,938
2010–2015	14,720	11,553	14,711	17,897	11,561	17,907	11,565	14,727	17,915
2020–2025	13,804	9,941	13,776	18,047	9,960	18,086	9,979	13,831	18,121
2050–2055	12,802	6,817	12,659	20,980	6,890	21,223	6,944	12,907	21,404
2095–2100	13,124	4,506	12,679	30,284	4,644	31,426	4,716	13,354	32,021

Assumed total fertility rates									
1995–2000	1.69	1.52	1.69	1.85	1.52	1.85	1.52	1.69	1.85
2010–2015	1.71	1.35	1.71	2.07	1.35	2.07	1.35	1.71	2.07
2020–2025	1.73	1.34	1.73	2.12	1.34	2.12	1.34	1.73	2.11
2050–2055	1.83	1.38	1.83	2.28	1.38	2.28	1.38	1.83	2.28
2095–2100	1.97	1.47	1.97	2.47	1.47	2.47	1.47	1.97	2.47

Assumed life expectancies for both sexes combined (in years)									
1995–2000	74.5	74.2	74.2	74.2	74.5	74.5	74.8	74.8	74.8
2010–2015	77.5	75.6	75.5	75.5	77.5	77.5	79.5	79.5	79.5
2020–2025	79.6	76.5	76.5	76.5	79.6	79.6	82.7	82.6	82.6
2050–2055	83.5	77.8	77.8	77.7	83.5	83.5	89.3	89.3	89.3
2095–2100	86.5	78.5	78.2	78.0	86.7	86.3	94.8	94.7	94.5

Developing Region

Fertility	C	L	C	H	L	H	L	C	H
Mortality	C	H	H	H	C	C	L	L	L
Migration	C	C	C	C	C	C	C	C	C

Total population size (in millions)

1995	4,451	4,451	4,451	4,451	4,451	4,451	4,451	4,451	4,451
2010	5,696	5,482	5,652	5,823	5,524	5,869	5,564	5,738	5,912
2020	6,541	6,011	6,404	6,802	6,138	6,946	6,257	6,665	7,080
2050	8,554	6,071	7,780	9,810	6,694	10,765	7,301	9,285	11,643
2100	9,137	3,330	7,040	13,228	4,433	16,915	5,701	11,325	20,524

Mean age (in years)

1995	26.6	26.6	26.6	26.6	26.6	26.6	26.6	26.6	26.6
2010	29.0	29.7	29.0	28.3	29.8	28.4	29.8	29.1	28.4
2020	30.6	32.0	30.6	29.3	32.0	29.4	32.1	30.7	29.5
2050	35.4	39.7	35.1	31.4	40.1	31.7	40.9	36.1	32.2
2100	41.6	46.8	40.4	35.7	48.5	36.6	51.5	43.8	38.2

Percentage of population aged 60+

1995	7.2	7.2	7.2	7.2	7.2	7.2	7.2	7.2	7.2
2010	8.8	9.0	8.7	8.5	9.1	8.5	9.2	8.9	8.6
2020	10.8	11.2	10.5	9.9	11.5	10.1	11.7	11.0	10.4
2050	17.4	21.1	16.4	13.0	22.2	13.8	23.8	18.8	15.0
2100	25.9	32.9	23.3	17.3	36.4	19.2	41.6	29.8	22.1

Percentage of population aged 0–14 years

1995	34.5	34.5	34.5	34.5	34.5	34.5	34.5	34.5	34.5
2010	31.0	28.7	30.9	32.9	28.8	33.0	28.9	31.1	33.1
2020	29.1	25.7	28.9	31.7	25.9	32.0	26.0	29.2	32.1
2050	23.3	16.7	23.1	28.7	16.8	29.0	16.7	23.3	29.0
2100	17.3	11.6	17.5	22.9	11.3	22.8	10.5	16.5	22.1

Annual number of births (in thousands)

1995–2000	123,983	118,077	123,952	129,828	118,109	129,869	118,131	124,005	129,891
2010–2015	138,423	115,851	137,650	159,570	116,494	160,420	117,099	139,094	161,205
2020–2025	141,727	104,040	139,335	177,461	105,860	180,464	107,501	143,862	183,156
2050–2055	139,048	64,049	127,561	219,097	69,907	238,557	74,786	148,587	254,645
2095–2100	104,596	23,485	83,215	221,315	29,763	276,635	34,987	122,270	322,114

Assumed total fertility rates

1995–2000	3.36	3.21	3.36	3.51	3.21	3.51	3.21	3.36	3.51
2010–2015	3.04	2.57	3.04	3.52	2.57	3.52	2.57	3.05	3.53
2020–2025	2.80	2.17	2.79	3.41	2.17	3.42	2.18	2.80	3.42
2050–2055	2.27	1.59	2.26	2.93	1.60	2.94	1.60	2.27	2.95
2095–2100	1.88	1.38	1.88	2.39	1.38	2.38	1.38	1.88	2.38

Assumed life expectancies for both sexes combined (in years)

1995–2000	64.2	63.8	63.8	63.8	64.2	64.2	64.6	64.6	64.6
2010–2015	66.0	63.2	63.3	63.3	66.0	66.1	68.8	68.8	68.8
2020–2025	67.5	63.1	63.1	63.2	67.5	67.6	71.9	71.9	72.0
2050–2055	70.5	62.9	63.0	63.1	70.5	70.6	78.5	78.5	78.5
2095–2100	73.3	63.6	64.0	64.3	73.2	73.5	83.6	83.6	83.7

World

Fertility	C	L	C	H	L	H	L	C	H
Mortality	C	H	H	H	C	C	L	L	L
Migration	C	C	C	C	C	C	C	C	C

Total population size (in millions)

1995	5,702	5,702	5,702	5,702	5,702	5,702	5,702	5,702	5,702
2010	7,012	6,752	6,960	7,168	6,802	7,221	6,850	7,061	7,272
2020	7,879	7,261	7,723	8,191	7,408	8,356	7,547	8,026	8,510
2050	9,874	7,103	9,021	11,300	7,802	12,330	8,488	10,690	13,300
2100	10,350	3,937	8,120	15,070	5,134	18,950	6,507	12,680	22,740

Mean age (in years)

1995	28.8	28.8	28.8	28.8	28.8	28.8	28.8	28.8	28.8
2010	31.1	31.8	31.0	30.3	31.8	30.3	31.9	31.1	30.4
2020	32.5	33.9	32.4	31.1	34.0	31.2	34.1	32.7	31.3
2050	36.9	41.0	36.4	32.6	41.6	33.0	42.5	37.6	33.7
2100	42.1	47.1	40.7	36.0	49.0	37.0	52.1	44.4	38.7

Percentage of population aged 60+

1995	9.5	9.5	9.5	9.5	9.5	9.5	9.5	9.5	9.5
2010	11.1	11.3	11.0	10.7	11.5	10.8	11.6	11.2	10.9
2020	13.2	13.7	12.9	12.2	14.0	12.5	14.4	13.6	12.8
2050	19.6	23.4	18.4	14.7	24.8	15.7	26.6	21.1	17.0
2100	26.8	33.4	24.0	17.8	37.2	19.9	42.5	30.8	22.9

Percentage of population aged 0–14 years

1995	31.4	31.4	31.4	31.4	31.4	31.4	31.4	31.4	31.4
2010	28.4	26.1	28.3	30.4	26.2	30.5	26.3	28.5	30.6
2020	26.9	23.6	26.8	29.6	23.8	29.8	23.9	27.0	29.9
2050	22.2	15.9	22.1	27.6	16.0	27.8	15.8	22.1	27.7
2100	17.2	11.7	17.5	22.9	11.3	22.6	10.4	16.4	22.0

Annual number of births (in thousands)

1995–2000	139,400	132,000	139,400	146,800	132,000	146,800	132,000	139,400	146,800
2010–2015	153,100	127,400	152,400	177,500	128,100	178,300	128,700	153,800	179,100
2020–2025	155,500	114,000	153,100	195,500	115,800	198,500	117,500	157,700	201,300
2050–2055	151,900	70,860	140,200	240,100	76,800	259,800	81,730	161,500	276,100
2095–2100	117,700	27,990	95,910	251,600	34,410	308,000	39,700	135,600	354,100

Assumed total fertility rates

1995–2000	2.96	2.81	2.96	3.12	2.81	3.12	2.81	2.96	3.12
2010–2015	2.81	2.36	2.81	3.26	2.36	3.27	2.36	2.82	3.27
2020–2025	2.65	2.07	2.64	3.22	2.07	3.23	2.08	2.66	3.23
2050–2055	2.23	1.58	2.22	2.86	1.58	2.87	1.59	2.23	2.88
2095–2100	1.90	1.40	1.90	2.40	1.40	2.40	1.39	1.89	2.39

Assumed life expectancies for both sexes combined (in years)

1995–2000	65.0	64.5	64.6	64.6	65.0	65.0	65.4	65.4	65.5
2010–2015	67.3	64.0	64.2	64.4	67.1	67.4	70.1	70.3	70.4
2020–2025	68.7	63.5	63.7	63.9	68.5	68.8	73.3	73.4	73.5
2050–2055	71.4	62.8	63.1	63.4	71.2	71.6	79.7	79.8	79.9
2095–2100	74.0	64.7	64.8	64.9	74.0	74.2	84.3	84.4	84.5

References

Ackefors, H., and Enell, M., 1990, Discharge of nutrients from Swedish fish farming to adjacent sea areas, *Ambio* **19**(1):28–35.

Ahlburg, D.A., and Land, K.C., 1992, Population forecasting: Guest editors' introduction, *International Journal of Forecasting* **8**(3):289–299.

Ahlburg, D.A., and Vaupel, J., 1990, Alternative projections of the US population, *Demography* **27**:639–652.

Alexandratos, N., ed., 1995, *World Agriculture: Towards 2010*, FAO, Rome, Italy.

Alho, J.M., 1990, Stochastic methods in population forecasting, *International Journal of Forecasting* **6**:521–530.

Allan, J.A., 1976, The Kufrah agricultural schemes, *The Geographical Journal* **142**(1):48–56.

Allman, J., Vu, Q.N., Nguyen, M.T., Pham, B.S., and Vu, D.M., 1991, Fertility and family planning in Vietnam, *Studies in Family Planning* **22**(5):308–317.

Alonso, W., 1974, Policy-Oriented Interregional Demographic Accounting and Generalization of Population Flow Models, Working Paper 247, University of California, Institute of Urban and Regional Development, Berkeley, CA, USA.

Andersen, O., 1991, Occupational impacts on mortality declines in the Nordic countries, in W. Lutz, ed., *Future Demographic Trends in Europe and North America: What Can We Assume Today?* Academic Press, London, UK.

Anderson, R.M., 1991, AIDS and its demographic impact, in R. Feachem and D. Jamison, eds., *Disease and Mortality in Sub-Saharan Africa*, World Bank/Oxford University Press, New York, NY, USA.

Anderson, R.M., and May, R.M., 1988, Epidemiological parameters of HIV transmission, *Nature* **333**:514–522.

Anderson, R.M., and May, R.M., 1992, *Infectious Diseases of Humans: Dynamics and Control*, Oxford University Press, New York, NY, USA.

Anderson, R.M., May, R.M., Boily, M.C., Garnett, G.P., and Rowley, J.T., 1991, The spread of HIV-1 in Africa: Sexual contact patterns and the predicted demographic impact of AIDS, *Nature* **352**:581–589.

Arnold, F., 1989, Revised Estimates and Projections of International Migration 1980–2000, Policy, Planning, and Research Working Papers, World Bank, Washington, DC, USA.

Arshat, H., Tan, B.A., Tey, N.P., and Subbiah, M., 1988, *Marriage and Family Formation in Peninsular Malaysia: Analytic Report on the 1984/85 Malaysian Population and Family Survey*, National Population and Family Development Board, Kuala Lumpur, Malaysia.

Ascher, W., 1978, *Forecasting: An Appraisal for Policy Makers and Planners*, Johns Hopkins University Press, Baltimore, MD, USA.

Atoh, M., 1989, Trends and differentials in fertility, Reprinted from *Country Monograph Series No. 11, Population of Japan*, UN ESCAP, 1984, Reprint Series No. 9, Institute of Population Problems, Ministry of Health and Welfare, Tokyo, Japan.

Baade, F., 1960, *Der Wettlauf zum Jahre 2000*, Oldenburg, Munich, Germany.

Bale, M.D., 1981, Price distortions in agriculture and their effects: An international comparison, *American Journal of Agricultural Economics* **63**(1):8–22.

Bandyopadhyay, J., 1989, Riskful confusion of drought and man-induced water scarcity, *Ambio* **18**(5):284–292.

Banister, J., 1987, *China's Changing Population,* Stanford University Press, Stanford, CA, USA.

Banister, J., 1989, Vietnam's evolving population policies, *International Population Conference* **1**:155–168.

Bariloche Group, 1976, The Latin American world model, in G. Bruckmann, ed., *Proceedings of the Second IIASA Conference on Global Modeling,* CP-76-8, International Institute for Applied Systems Analysis, Laxenburg, Austria.

Barnett, A., Kiernan, B., and Boua, C., 1980, The bureaucracy of death: Documents from inside Pol Pot's torture machine, *New Statesman,* May 2.

Bartiaux, F., and van Ypersele, J.-F., 1993, The role of population growth in global warming, in *IUSSP International Population Conference: Montreal,* Vol. 4, International Union for the Scientific Study of Population, Liège, Belgium.

Bates, R.H., 1981, *Markets and States in Tropical Africa: The Political Basis of Agricultural Politics,* University of California Press, Berkeley, CA, USA.

Baumgartner, A., and Reichel, E., 1975, *The World Water Balance,* Elsevier Scientific Publishers, Amsterdam, Netherlands.

Becker, E., 1986, *When the War Was Over: The Voices of Cambodia's Revolution and Its People,* Simon & Schuster, New York, NY, USA.

Becker, C., and Collignon, R., 1989, *Santé et Population en Sénégambie des origines à 1960,* INED, Paris, France.

Becker, C., and Martin, V., 1983, *Les premiers recensements au Sénégal, et l'évolution démographique,* ORSTOM, Dakar, Senegal.

Behn, R.D., and Vaupel, J.W., 1982, *Quick Analysis for Busy Decision Makers,* Basic Books, New York, NY, USA.

Benamrane, D., 1983, *L'Emigration Algerienne en France,* Société Nationale d'Edition et de Diffusion, Algiers, Algeria.

Berkley, S.F., 1994, Public health measures to prevent HIV spread in Africa, in M. Essex, S. Mboup, P.J. Kanki, and M.R. Kalengayi, eds., *AIDS in Africa,* Raven Press, New York, NY, USA.

Bernstein, T.P., 1984, Stalinism, famine, and the Chinese peasants: Grain procurements during the Great Leap Forward, *Theory and Society* **13**:339–377.

Bhat, P.N.M., 1989, Mortality and fertility in India, 1881–1961: A reassessment, in T. Dyson, ed., *India's Historical Demography,* Curzon Press, London, UK.

Birdsall, N., 1992, Another Look at Population and Global Warming, Policy Research Working Paper WPS 1020, November, World Bank, Washington, DC, USA.

Birg, H., 1995, *World Population Projections for the 21st Century: Theoretical Interpretations and Quantitative Simulations,* Campus Verlag, Frankfurt and New York.

Biswas, A.K., 1993, Water for agricultural development: Opportunities and constraints, *Water Resources Development* **9**(1):3–12.

Biswas, A.K., and Arar, A., 1988, *Treatment and Reuse of Wastewater,* Butterworths, London, UK.

Blacker, J.G.C., 1991, Infant and child mortality: Development, environment, and custom, in R.G. Feachem and D.T. Jamison, eds., *Disease and Mortality in Sub-Saharan Africa,* World Bank/Oxford University Press, New York, NY, USA.

Blanchard, O., Layard, R., Dornbusch, R., and Krugman, P., 1991, East-West Migration: The Alternatives – A Report of the Wider World Economy Group, Working Paper No. 101, Centre for Economic Performance, London, UK.

Bogue, D.J., and Tsui, A.O., 1979, Zero world population growth? *The Public Interest* **55**(Spring):99–113.

Böhning, W.R., 1981, Elements of a theory of international migration to industrial nations, in M. Kritz, C. Keely, and S. Tomasi, eds., *Global Trends in Migration: Theory and Research on International Population Movements,* Center for Migration Studies, Staten Island, NY, USA.

Bongaarts, J., 1992, Population growth and global warming, *Population and Development Review* **18**(2):299–319.

Bongaarts, J., 1994, Population policy options in the developing world, *Science* **263**(February 11):771–776.

Bongaarts, J., Reining, P., Way, P., and Conant, F., 1989, The relationship between male circumcision and HIV infection in African populations, *AIDS* **3**:373–377.

Bongaarts, J., Mauldin, W.P., and Phillips, J.E., 1990, The demographic impact of family planning programs, *Studies in Family Planning* **21**(6):299–310.

Bos, E., Vu, M.T., Levin, A., and Bulatao, R.A., 1992, *World Population Projections 1992–1993 Edition: Estimates and Projections with Related Demographic Statistics,* World Bank/Johns Hopkins University Press, Baltimore, MD, USA.

Boserup, E., 1965, *The Conditions of Agricultural Growth,* Aldine, Chicago, IL, USA.

Boserup, E., 1981, *Population and Technological Change,* University of Chicago Press, Chicago, IL, USA.

Bourgeois-Pichat, J., 1952, Essai sur la mortalité "biologique" de l'homme, *Population* **7**:381–394.

Bourgeois-Pichat, J., 1978, Future outlook for mortality declines in the World, *Population Bulletin of the United Nations,* No. 11, United Nations, New York, NY, USA.

Bradley, D.J., 1991, Malaria, in R. Feachem and D. Jamison, eds., *Disease and Mortality in Sub-Saharan Africa,* World Bank/Oxford University Press, New York, NY, USA.

Brass, W., Coale, A.J., Demeny, P., Heisel, D.F., Lorimer, F., Romaniuk, A., and van de Walle, E., eds., 1968, *The Demography of Tropical Africa,* Princeton University Press, Princeton, NJ, USA.

Brillinger, D.R., 1986, The natural variability of vital rates and associated statistics, *Biometrics* **42**(4):693–734.

Bulatao, R.A., 1991, The Bulatao approach: Projecting the demographic impact of the HIV epidemic using standard parameters, in *The AIDS Epidemic and Its Demographic Consequences,* United Nations, New York, NY, USA.

Bulatao, R.A., and Bos, E. (with P.W. Stephens and M.T. Vu), 1989, Projecting Mortality for All Countries, Policy, Planning, and Population Research Working Paper Series 337, World Bank, Washington, DC, USA.

Bulatao, R.A., Bos, E., Stephens, P.W., and Vu, M.T., 1990, *World Population Projections 1989–1990 Edition: Short- and Long-Term Estimates,* World Bank/Johns Hopkins University Press, Baltimore, MD, USA.

Bundesministerium für Raumordnung, Bauwesen und Städtebau, eds., 1991, *Raumordnungsbericht 1991,* Bonn, Germany.

Buringh, P., and Van Heemst, H.D.J., 1977, *An Estimation of World Food Production Based on Labour-oriented Agriculture,* Centre for World Food Market Research, Agricultural Press, Wageningen, Netherlands.

Buringh, P., Van Heemst, H.D.J., and Staring, G.J., 1975, *Computation of the Absolute Maximum Food Production of the World,* Centre for World Food Market Research, Wageningen, Netherlands.

Büttner, T., and Lutz, W., 1990a, Estimating fertility responses to policy measures in the German Democratic Republic, *Population and Development Review* 16(3):539–555.

Büttner, T., and Lutz, W., 1990b, Vergleichende Analyse der Fertilitätsentwicklungen in der BRD, DDR und Österreich, *Acta Demographica* 1:27–45, Physica-Verlag, Heidelberg, Germany.

Caldwell, J.G.C., 1986, Routes to low mortality in poor countries, *Population and Development Review* 12(2):171–220.

Caldwell, J.C., and Caldwell, P., 1983, The demographic evidence for the incidence and cause of abnormally low fertility in tropical Africa, *World Health Statistics Quarterly* 36:221.

Caldwell, J.C., and Caldwell, P., 1990, High fertility in sub-Saharan Africa, *Scientific American* May:118–125.

Caldwell, J.C., and Caldwell, P., 1993, The nature and limits of the sub-Saharan African AIDS epidemic: Evidence from geographic and other patterns, *Population and Development Review* 19:817–848.

Caldwell, J.C., and Caldwell, P., 1994, The neglect of an epidemiological explanation for the distribution of HIV/AIDS in sub-Saharan Africa: Exploring the male circumcision hypothesis, in J. Cleland and P. Way, eds., *AIDS Impact and Prevention in the Developing World: Demographic and Social Science Perspectives,* Supplement to *Health Transition Review* 4:23–46, Health Transition Centre, Australian National University, Canberra, Australia.

Caldwell, J.C., Caldwell, P., and Quiggin, P., 1989, The social context of AIDS in sub-Saharan Africa, *Population and Development Review* 15:185–234.

Cameron, D.W., Simonsen, J.N., D'Costa, L.J., Ronald, A.R., Maitha, G.M., Gakinya, M.N., Cheang, M., Ndinya-Achola, J.O., Piot, P., Brunham, R.C., *et al.,* 1989, Female to male transmission of Human Immunodeficiency Virus Type 1: Risk factors for seroconversion in men, *The Lancet* (19 August):403–407.

Cantrelle, P., Diop, I.L., Garenne, M., Gueye, M., and Sadio, A., 1986, The profile of mortality and its determinants in Senegal, 1960–1980, in *Determinants of Mortality Change and Differentials in Developing Countries: The Five-Country Case Study Project,* Population Studies, No. 94, United Nations, New York, NY, USA.

Caraël, M., Cleland, J., Deheneffe, J.-C., and Adeokun, L., 1992, Research on sexual behaviour that transmits HIV: The GPA/WHO collaborative surveys, Preliminary findings, in T. Dyson, ed., *Sexual Behaviour and Networking: Anthropological and Socio-Cultural Studies on the Transmission of HIV*, Derouaux-Ordina Editions, Liège, Belgium.

Carter, L.R., and Lee, R.D., 1986, Joint forecasts of US marital fertility, nuptiality, births and marriages using time series models, *Journal of the American Statistical Association* 81(396):902–911.

Casterline, J., 1994, Fertility transition in Asia, in T. Locoh and V. Hertrich, eds., *The Onset of Fertility Transition in Sub-Saharan Africa*, Ordina, Liège, Belgium.

Centers for Disease Control and Prevention, 1991, Patterns of behavior change among homosexual/bisexual men: Selected US sites, 1987–1990, *Morbidity and Mortality Weekly Report* 40:792–794.

Centers for Disease Control and Prevention, 1994, *National HIV Serosurveillance Summary: Results through 1992*, Vol. 3, US Department of Health and Human Services, Atlanta, GA, USA.

Chastanet, M., 1982, Les crises de subsistances dans les villages Soninke du cercle de Bakel de 1858 à 1945, *Problèmes méthodologiques et perspectives de recherches,* ORSTOM, Dakar, Senegal.

Chaudhry, M.D., 1989, Fertility behavior in India, 1961–1986: The stalled decline in the crude birth rate, in S.N. Singh, M.K. Premi, P.S. Bhatia, and A. Bose, eds., *Population Transition in India*, Vol. 2, B.R. Publishing Corp., Delhi, India.

Chen, R.S., 1990, Global agriculture, environment, and hunger: Past, present, and the future, *Environmental Impact Assessment Review* 10:335–358.

Chen, P., and Kols, A., 1982, Population and birth planning in the People's Republic of China, *Population Reports,* Series J, Number 25, Family Planning Programs, Population Information Program, Johns Hopkins University, Baltimore, MD, USA.

Chesnais, J.-C., 1985, Les conditions d'efficacité d'une politique nataliste: examen theoretique et exemples historiques (The conditions of efficiency of a pronatalist policy: Theoretical considerations and some historical examples), *International Population Conference, Florence 1985* 3:413–425, International Union for the Scientific Study of Population, Liège, Belgium.

Chin, J., 1990, Current and future dimensions of the HIV/AIDS pandemic in women and children, *The Lancet* 336:221–224.

Chin, J., and Lwanga, S.K., 1991a, Estimation and projection of adult AIDS cases: A simple epidemiological model, *Bulletin of the World Health Organization* 69:399–406.

Chin, J., and Lwanga, S.K., 1991b, The World Health Organization approach: Projections of non-paediatric HIV infection and AIDS in pattern II areas, in *The AIDS Epidemic and Its Demographic Consequences,* United Nations, New York, NY, USA.

China Population Information Center, 1984, *Analysis on China's National One-per-Thousand Population Fertility Sampling Survey,* China Population Information Center, Beijing, China.

Cho, L.-J., Retherford, R.D., and Choe, M.K., 1986, *The Own-Children Method of Fertility Estimation,* East–West Center, University of Hawaii Press, Honolulu, HI, USA.

Clark, C., 1967, Population and food, in *Population Growth and Land Use,* Macmillan, London, UK.

Clark, C., and Haswell, M., 1964, *The Economics of Subsistence Agriculture,* Macmillan, London, UK.

Clarke, R.D., 1950, A bio-actuarial approach to forecasting rates of mortality, *Proceedings of the Centenary Assembly of the Institute of Actuaries,* University Press, Cambridge, UK.

Cleland, J., and Wilson, C., 1987, Demand theories of the fertility transition: An iconoclastic view, *Population Studies* 41(1):5–30 (March).

Cleland, J., Onuoha, N., and Timæus, I., 1994, Fertility change in sub-Saharan Africa: A review of the evidence, in T. Locoh and V. Hertrich, eds., *The Onset of Fertility Transition in Sub-Saharan Africa,* Ordina, Liège, Belgium.

Cliquet, R., ed., 1993, *The Future of Europe's Population: A Scenario Approach,* Council of Europe, European Population Committee, Strasbourg, France.

Coale, A.J., 1984, *Rapid Population Change in China, 1952–1982,* Committee on Population and Demography, Report No. 27, National Academy Press, Washington, DC, USA.

Coale, A.J., and Chen, S.L., 1987, *Basic Data on Fertility in the Provinces of China, 1940–1982,*

Coale, A.J., and Demeny, P., 1966, *Regional Model Life Tables and Stable Populations,* Princeton University Press, Princeton, NJ, USA.

Coale, A.J., and Demeny, P. (with B. Vaughan), 1983, *Regional Model Life Tables and Stable Populations,* 2nd Edition, Academic Press, New York, NY, USA.

Coale, A.J., and Freedman, R., 1993, Similarities in the fertility transition in China and three other East Asian populations, in R. Leete and I. Alam, eds., *The Revolution in Asian Fertility,* Oxford University Press, Oxford, UK.

Coale, A.J., and Guo, G., 1989, Revised regional model life tables at very low levels of mortality, *Population Index* 55(4):613–643.

Coale, A.J., and Watkins, S.C., eds., 1986, *The Decline of Fertility in Europe,* Princeton University Press, Princeton, NJ, USA.

Coale, J.A., and Kisker, E.E., 1986, Morality crossovers: Reality or bad data? *Population Studies* 40:389–401.

Coale, J.A., and Kisker, E.E., 1990, *Asian and Pacific Population Forum* 4(1):1–36. Papers of the East–West Population Institute, Number 104, East–West Center, Honolulu, HI, USA.

Cohen, J., 1992, How many people can earth hold? *Discover,* November:114–119.

Cohen, J., 1994a, Are researchers racing toward success, or crawling? *Science* **265**:1373–1375.

Cohen, J., 1994b, The epidemic in Thailand, *Science* **266**:1647.

Cohen, J.E., 1995, *How Many People Can the Earth Support?* Norton, New York, NY, USA.

Comfort, A., 1964 [1979], *The Biology of Senescence*, 3rd Edition, Elsevier, New York, NY, USA.

Constant, K.M., and Sheldrick, W.F., 1992, *World Nitrogen Survey*, Technical Paper No. 174, World Bank, Washington, DC, USA.

Council of Europe, 1991, *Recent Demographic Developments in Europe*, Council of Europe Press, Strasbourg, France.

Council of Europe, 1995, *Recent Demographic Developments in Europe*, Council of Europe Press, Strasbourg, France.

Country Report, 1992, Population and Sustainable Development: The Challenges of Vietnam, Paper circulated during the 4th Asian and Pacific Population Conference, Bali, Indonesia, 19–27 August.

Country Report: Indonesia, 1992, Paper circulated during the 4th Asian and Pacific Population Conference, Bali, Indonesia, 19–27 August.

Country Report: Malaysia, 1992, Paper circulated during the 4th Asian and Pacific Population Conference, Bali, Indonesia, 19–27 August.

Country Report: Philippines, 1992, Paper circulated during the 4th Asian and Pacific Population Conference, Bali, Indonesia, 19–27 August.

Country Statement: Thailand, 1992, Paper circulated during the 4th Asian and Pacific Population Conference, Bali, Indonesia, 19–27 August.

Critchley, W., Reij, C., and Seznec, A., 1992, *Water Harvesting for Plant Production, Volume 2: Case Studies and Conclusions for Sub-Saharan Africa*, World Bank, Washington, DC, USA.

Davis, K., 1951, *The Population of India and Pakistan*, Princeton University Press, Princeton, NJ, USA.

De Almeida e Silva, M., 1991, Persian Gulf exodus stretched resources, *Refugees* **87**(October):12–15 (Geneva).

Demeny, P., 1984, A perspective on long-term population growth, *Population and Development Review* **10**:103–126.

De Vincenzi, I., and Mertens, T., 1994, Male circumcision: A role in HIV prevention? *AIDS* **8**:153–160.

Diop, I.L., 1990, Etude de la mortalité à Saint-Louis du Sénégal à partir des données d'état civil, Thèse de doctorat de 3ème cycle, Université de Paris I, Panthéon-Sorbonne, Paris, France.

Dréze, J., and Sen, A., 1989, *Hunger and Public Action*, Clarendon Press, Oxford, UK.

Durkheim, E., 1902, *De la Division du Travail social*, Felix Alcan, Paris, France.

Durning, A., 1989, *World Poverty*, Worldwatch Institute, Washington, DC, USA.

Dyson, T., and Moore, M., 1983, Kinship structure, female autonomy and demographic behavior in India, *Population and Development Review* **9**:35–60.

Dyson, T., and Murphy, M., 1985, The onset of the fertility transition, *Population and Development Review* **11**:399–440.

Easterlin, R.A., 1980, *Birth and Fortune: The Impact of Numbers on Personal Welfare*, Basic Books, New York, NY, USA.

Eaton, J.W., and Mayer, A.J., 1954, *Man's Capacity to Reproduce: The Demography of a Unique Population*, The Free Press, New York, NY, USA.

Economist Intelligence Unit, 1990, *Saudi Arabia: Country Report*, No. 2.

Ehrlich, P., Ehrlich, A., and Daily, G.C., 1993, Food security, population, and environment, *Population and Development Review* **19**(1):1–32.

Elias, Ch.J., and Heise, L.L., 1994, Challenges for the development of female-controlled vaginal microbicides, *AIDS* **8**:19.

ENHR Report, 1990, *Volume 1, Health Research: Essential Link to Equity in Development*, Report from the Commission on Health Research for Development, Oxford University Press, New York, NY, USA.

ENHR Report, 1991, *Volume 2, Essential National Health Research: A Strategy for Action in Health and Human Development*, Report from the Task Force on Health Research for Development, UNDO, Geneva, Switzerland.

Eurobarometer, 1991, Desire for children, *Eurobarometer* **32**.

EUROSTAT, 1991, Two Long-Term Population Scenarios for the European Community, Scenarios prepared for the International Conference on Human Resources in Europe at the Dawn of the 21st Century, November 27–29, Luxembourg.

FAIR (Federation for American Immigration Reform), 1992, Chinese student amnesty legislation passes, *FAIR Immigration Report* **12**(8):3.

Falkenmark, M., 1989, The massive water scarcity now threatening Africa: Why isn't it being addressed? *Ambio* **18**(2):112–118.

Falkenmark, M., 1991, Water, energy, and development, Rapid population growth and water scarcity: The predicament of tomorrow's Africa, in K. Davis and M.S. Bernstam, eds., *Resources, Environment, and Population: Present Knowledge, Future Options*, A Supplement to Volume 16, 1990, Oxford University Press, New York, NY, USA.

Family Planning and Maternal and Child Health Project, 1987, *Nepal Fertility and Family Planning Survey Report 1986*, Central Bureau of Statistics, Kathmandu, Nepal.

FAO, 1978a, *Report on the Agro-Ecological Zones Project, Volume 1: Methodology and Results for Africa*, World Soil Resources Report 48/1, Food and Agriculture Organization, Rome, Italy.

FAO, 1978b, *Report on the Agro-Ecological Zones Project, Volume 2: Results for Southwest Asia*, World Soil Resources Report 48/2, Food and Agriculture Organization, Rome, Italy.

FAO, 1981a, *Report on the Agro-Ecological Zones Project, Volume 3: Methodology and Results for South and Central America*, World Soil Resources Report 48/3, Food and Agriculture Organization, Rome, Italy.

FAO, 1981b, *Report on the Agro-Ecological Zones Project, Volume 4: Results for Southeast Asia*, World Soil Resources Report 48/4, Food and Agriculture Organization, Rome, Italy.

FAO, 1988, *World Agriculture: Towards 2000: An FAO Study*, New York University Press, New York, NY, USA.

FAO, 1992, *Fertilizer Yearbook*, Food and Agriculture Organization, Rome, Italy.

FAO, 1994, PC-AGROSTAT, Food and Agriculture Organization, Rome, Italy.

FAO/UNDP/IIASA, 1982, *Potential Population Supporting Capacities of Lands in the Developing World,* Technical Report of the Project, FPA/INT/513, Food and Agriculture Organization, Rome, Italy.

FAO/UNFPA/IIASA, 1984, *Potential Population Carrying Capacities in the Developing Countries,* Technical information to the project INT/75/P13, Food and Agriculture Organization, Rome, Italy.

Farid, S., 1993, Family Planning, Health and Family Well-Being in the Arab World, Paper presented at the Arab Population Conference, Ammon.

Feachem, R., and Jamison, D., eds., 1991, *Disease and Mortality in Sub-Saharan Africa,* World Bank/Oxford University Press, New York, NY, USA.

Feeney, G., 1986, *Period Parity Progression Ratios of Fertility in Japan,* NUPRI Research Paper Series No. 35 (December), Nihon University Population Research Institute, Tokyo, Japan.

Feeney, G., 1988a, Comparative Structure of Low Fertility in Japan and the United States, Paper presented to the Conference on Future Changes in Population Age Structure, Sopron, Hungary, 18–21 October 1988, organized by the International Institute for Applied Systems Analysis, Laxenburg, Austria.

Feeney, G., 1988b, The use of parity progression ratios in evaluating family planning programs, in *Proceedings of African Population Conference, Dakar,* International Union for the Scientific Study of Population, Liège, Belgium.

Feeney, G., 1990, *The Demography of Aging in Japan: 1950–2025,* NUPRI Research Paper Series No. 55, Nihon University Population Research Institute, Tokyo, Japan.

Feeney, G., 1991, Fertility decline in Taiwan: A study using parity progression ratios, *Demography* **28**:467–480.

Feeney, G., and Lutz, W., 1991, Distributional analysis of period fertility, in W. Lutz, ed., *Future Demographic Trends in Europe and North America: What Can We Assume Today?* Academic Press, London, UK.

Feeney, G., and Wang, F., 1993, Parity progression and birth intervals in China: The influence of policy in hastening fertility decline, *Population and Development Review* **19**(1):61–101.

Feeney, G., and Yu, J., 1987, Period parity progression measures of fertility in China, *Population Studies* **41**(1):77–102.

Feeney, G., and Yuan, J., 1994, Below replacement fertility in China? A close look at recent evidence, *Population Studies* **48**:381–394.

Feeney, G., Wang, F., Zhou, M., and Xiao, B., 1989, Recent fertility decline in China: Results from the 1987 one percent population survey, *Population and Development Review* **15**(2):297–322.

Feeney, G., Luther, N.Y., Meng, Q.P., and Sun, Y., 1993, Recent fertility trends in China: Results from the 1990 census, in *China 1990 Population Census,* State Statistical Bureau, Beijing, China.

Ferreira de Paiva, A., 1983, Portuguese migration: A critical survey of Portuguese studies on the economic aspects of the phenomenon since 1973, *International Migration Review* **17**(1):138–147.

Fielding, A., 1993, Migrations, institutions and politics: The evolution of European migration policies, in R. King, ed., *Mass Migration in Europe: The Legacy and the Future*, Belhaven Press, London, UK.

Forrester, J.W., 1971, *World Dynamics*, Wright-Allen Press, Cambridge, MA, USA.

Freedman, R., Khoo, S., and Supraptilah, D., 1981, *Modern Contraceptive Use in Indonesia: A Challenge to Conventional Wisdom*, WFS Scientific Report No. 20, International Statistical Institute, Voorburg, Netherlands.

Frejka, T., 1968, Reflections on the demographic conditions needed to establish a US stationary population growth, *Population Studies* **22**(3):379–397.

Frejka, T., 1973a, *The Future of Population Growth: Alternative Paths to Equilibrium*, John Wiley & Sons, New York, NY, USA.

Frejka, T., 1973b, The prospects for a stationary world population, *Scientific American* **228**(3):15–23.

Frejka, T., 1981a, World population projections: A concise history, in *International Population Conference*, Vol. 3, IUSSP, Manila, Philippines.

Frejka, T., 1981b, Long-term prospects for world population growth, *Population and Development Review* **7**(3):489–511.

Fries, J.F., 1980, Aging, natural death, and the compression of morbidity, *New England Journal of Medicine* **303**:130–135.

Fries, J.F., 1983, The compression of morbidity, *Milbank Memorial Fund Quarterly/Health and Society* **61**:397–419.

Fries, J.F., 1984, The compression of morbidity: Miscellaneous comments about a theme, *The Gerontologist* **24**:354–359.

Fries, J.F., and Crapo, I.M., 1981, *Vitality and Aging*, W.H. Freeman, San Francisco, CA, USA.

Fries, J.F., Green, L.W., and Levine, S., 1989, Health promotion and the compression of morbidity, *The Lancet* **I**:481–483.

Garcia, R., 1981, *Drought and Man: The 1972 Case History, Volume 1: Nature Pleads Not Guilty*, Pergamon Press, New York, NY, USA.

Gardner, B., 1990, European Agriculture's Environmental Problems, Paper presented at the First Annual Conference of the Hudson Institute, Indianapolis, IN, USA.

Garenne, M., Cantrelle, P., and Diop, I.L., 1985, Senegal, in J. Vallin and A. Lopez, eds., *Health Policy, Social Policy and Mortality Prospects*, Ordina, Liège, Belgium.

Garenne, M., Leroy, O., Beau, J.P., Sene, I., Whittle, H., and Sow, A.R., 1991, *Efficacy, Safety and Immunogenicity of Two High Titer Measles Vaccines: A Study in Niakhar*, Final Report, ORSTOM, Dakar, Senegal.

Garenne, M., Cantrelle, P., Sarr, I., Diop, I.L., and Becker, C., 1993, Estimation of Mortality Trends in Urban and Rural Senegal, Working Paper Series, Harvard Center for Population and Development Studies, Cambridge, MA, USA.

Garenne, M., Madison, M., Tarantola, D., *et al.*, 1995, *Conséquences démographiques du Sida en Abidjan: 1986–1992*, Etudes du CEPED, Paris, France.

Garenne, M., Coninx, R., and Dupuy, C., 1996, *Survie de l'enfant dans le district de Maringué au Mozambique et évaluation d'une intervention*, Dossiers du CEPED, No. 38, CEPED, Paris, France (forthcoming).

Gasser, C.S., and Fraley, R.T., 1989, Genetically engineering plants for crop improvement, *Science* **244**(16 June):1293–1299.

Gavrilov, L.A., and Gavrilova, N.S., 1991, *The Biology of Life Span*, Harwood Academic Publishers, Chur, Switzerland.

GDA, 1967, *Manuel de démographie africaine*, Groupe de Démographie Africaine, Paris, France.

Geertz, C., 1963, *Agricultural Involution: The Process of Ecological Change in Indonesia*, University of California Press, Berkeley, CA, USA.

Gibb, D., and Wara, D., 1994, Paediatric HIV infection, *AIDS* **8** (Suppl. 1) S275–S284.

Gilland, B., 1983, Considerations on world population and food supply, *Population and Development Review* **9**(2):203–211.

Gisser, R., *et al.*, 1985, Kinderwunsch und Kinderzahl, in R. Münz, ed., *Leben mit Kindern: Wunsch und Wirklichkeit*, Deuticke, Vienna, Austria.

Goldstein, J.R., Lutz, W., Pflug, G., 1994, Constant Variance Forecasting, unpublished manuscript, International Institute for Applied Systems Analysis, Laxenburg, Austria.

Golini, A., Gerano, G., and Heins, F., 1991, South–North migration with special reference to Europe, in W.A. Dumon, ed., *Ninth IOM Seminar on Migration, South–North Migration*, International Organization for Migration, Geneva, Switzerland.

Gompertz, B., 1825, On the nature of the function expressive of the law of human mortality, and on a new mode of determining the value of life contingencies, *Philosophical Transactions of the Royal Society of London,* Series A 115:513–585, Abstract in *Abstracts of Philosophical Transactions of the Royal Society of London* 252–253.

Gonnot, J.-P., Keilman, N., and Prinz, C., eds., 1994, *Social Security, Household and Family Dynamics in Aging Societies*, Swets & Zeitlinger, Amsterdam, Netherlands.

Gouse, S.W., Gray, D., Tomlinson, G.C., and Morrison, D.L., 1992, Potential world development through 2100: The impacts on energy demand, resources, and the environment, *World Energy Council Journal* December: 18–32.

Green, A.G., 1976, *Immigration and the Post-War Canadian Economy*, Macmillan, New York, NY, USA.

Greenhalgh, S., 1986, Shifts in China's population policy, 1984–1986: Views from the central, provincial, and local levels, *Population and Development Review* **12**(3):491–515.

Greenhalgh, S., 1990, The Peasantization of Population Policy in Shaanxi: Cadre Mediation of State-Society Conflict, Working Paper No. 21, The Population Council, New York, NY, USA.

Greenhalgh, S., 1993, The peasantization of the one-child policy in Shaanxi, in D. Davis and S. Harrell, eds., *Chinese Family in the Post-Mao Era*, Harvard University Press, Cambridge, MA, USA.

Greenwood, M.J., and McDowell, J.M., 1992, The Macrodeterminants of International Migration, Paper presented at the Conference on Mass Migration in Europe, 5–7 March, Laxenburg, Austria.

Greenwood, M.J., and Trabka, E., 1991, Temporal and spatial patterns of geographically indirect immigration to the United States, *International Migration Review* **25**(1) (Spring).

Gregson, S., Garnett, G.P., and Anderson, R.M., 1994, Is HIV-1 likely to become a leading cause of adult mortality in sub-Saharan Africa? *Journal of Acquired Immune Deficiency Syndromes* **7**:839–852.

Griffiths, I.L., 1988, Famine and war in Africa, *Geography* **73**(1):59–61.

Griffiths, I.L., and Binns, J.A., 1988, Hunger, help and hypocrisy: Crisis and response to crisis in Africa, *Geography* **73**(1):48–54.

Guralnik, J.M., Yanagishita, M., and Schneider, E.L., 1988, Projecting the older population of the United States: Lessons from the past and prospects for the future, *Milbank Memorial Fund Quarterly* **66**:283–308.

Guzman, J.M., 1994, The onset of fertility decline in Latin America, in T. Locoh and V. Hertrich, eds., *The Onset of Fertility Transition in Sub-Saharan Africa*, Ordina, Liège, Belgium.

Hallberg, G.R., 1989, Pesticides pollution of groundwater in the humid United States, *Agriculture, Ecosystems and Environment* **26**:299–367.

Hanenberg, R.S., Rojanapithayakorn, W., Kunasol, P., and Sokal, D.C., 1994, Impact of Thailand's HIV-control programme as indicated by the decline of sexually transmitted diseases, *The Lancet* **344**:243–245.

Hardee-Cleaveland, K., and Banister, J., 1988, Fertility policy and implementation in China, 1986–1988, *Population and Development Review* **14**(2): 245–286.

Harman, D., 1991, The aging process: Major risk factor for disease and death, *Proceedings of National Academy of Sciences USA* **88**:5360–5363.

Haskey, J., Shaw, C., Grebenik, E., Coleman, D., Balajaran, R., and Bulusu, L., 1989, Country Report: Great Britain, Paper prepared for the Working Group on Immigrant Populations.

Hayflick, L., 1977, The cellular basis for biological aging, in C.E. Finch and L. Hayflick, eds., *Handbook of the Biology of Aging*, Van Nostrand Reinhold, New York, NY, USA.

Hayflick, L., 1980, The cell biology of human aging, *Scientific American* **242**:58–65.

Haynes, B.F., 1993, Scientific and social issues of human immunodeficiency virus vaccine development, *Science* **260**:1279–1286.

Heilig, G.K., 1993, Food, lifestyles, and energy, in D.G. van der Heij, ed., *Food and Nutrition Policy*, Proceedings of the Second European Conference on Food and Nutrition Policy, The Hague, Netherlands, 21–24 April 1992, Pydoc, Wageningen, Netherlands.

Heilig, G.K., 1994a, Neglected dimensions of global land-use change: Reflections and data, *Population and Development Review*, September.

Heilig, G.K., 1994b, The greenhouse gas methane: Sources, sinks and possible interventions, *Population and Environment* **16**(2):109–137.

Heisel, D.F., 1968, The demography of the Portuguese territories: Angola, Mozambique, and Portuguese Guinea, in W. Brass, A.J. Coale, P. Demeny, D.F. Heisel, F. Lorimer, A. Romaniuk, and E. van de Walle, eds., 1968, eds., *The Demography of Tropical Africa*, Princeton University Press, Princeton, NY, USA.

Herrera, A.D., Scolnik, H.D. *et al.*, 1976, *Catastrophe or New Society? A Latin American World Model*, International Development Research Centre, Ottawa, Canada.

Heyden, H., 1991, South–North migration, in W.A. Dumon, ed., *Ninth IOM Seminar on Migration, South–North Migration*, International Organization for Migration, Geneva, Switzerland.

Higgins, G.M., Kassam, A.H., Naiken, L., Fischer, G., and Shah, M.M., 1982, *Potential Population Supporting Capacities of Lands in the Developing World*, Technical Report FPA/INT/513 of Project Land Resources for Population of the Future, Food and Agriculture Organization, Rome, Italy.

Hill, A., 1989, La mortalité des enfants: niveau actuel et évolution depuis 1945, in *Mortalité et société en Afrique: Cahier de l'INED,* No. 124.

Hill, A., 1991, Infant and child mortality: Levels, trends and data deficiencies, in R. Feachem and D. Jamison, eds., *Disease and Mortality in Sub-Saharan Africa*, World Bank/Oxford University Press, New York, NY, USA.

Hill, A., 1992, Trends in Childhood Mortality in Sub-Saharan Africa in the 1970s and 1980s, Draft paper, World Bank, Washington, DC, USA.

Hill, A., and Hill, K., 1988, Mortality in Africa: Levels, trends, differentials and prospects, in E. van de Walle, P.O. Ohadike, and M.D. Sala-Diakanda, eds., *The State of African Demography*, IUSSP-Derouaux, Liège, Belgium.

Hoem, J.M., 1990, Social policy and recent fertility change in Sweden, *Population and Development Review* **16**(4):735–748.

Hoffman-Nowotny, J., 1981, A sociological approach toward a general theory of migration, in M. Kritz, C. Keely, and S. Tomasi, eds., *Global Trends in Migration: Theory and Research on International Population Movements*, Center for Migration Studies, Staten Island, NY, USA.

Hoffmann-Nowotny, H.-J., 1987, The future of the family, in *Plenaries. European Population Conference 1987: Issues and Prospects,* Central Statistical Office of Finland, Helsinki, Finnland.

Höhn, Ch., 1991, Policies relevant to fertility, in W. Lutz, ed., *Future Demographic Trends in Europe and North America: What Can We Assume Today?* Academic Press, London, UK.

Holló, J., 1986, Foreseeable developments in food production and processing, United Nations, Economic Commission for Europe: Biotechnology and Economic Development, *Economic Bulletin for Europe* **38**(1).

Hong Kong, 1988, *Hong Kong 1986 By-Census: Main Report,* Volume 1, Census and Statistics Department, Government Printer, Hong Kong.

Hopes dry up for food security, 1989, *Middle East Economic Digest* **33**(40).

Horiuchi, S., and Coale, A.J., 1983, Age Patterns of Mortality for Older Women: Analysis Using the Age-Specific Rate of Mortality Change with Age, Paper presented at the 1983 Annual Meeting of the Population Society of America.

Huang, S., 1989, *The Spiral Road: Change in a Chinese Village Through the Eyes of a Communist Party Leader*, Westview Press, Boulder, CO, USA.

IIASA (International Institute for Applied Systems Analysis) and WEC (World Energy Council), 1995, *Global Energy Perspectives to 2050 and Beyond*, WEC, London, UK.

ILO, 1990, Informal Report on Migrant Workers Affected by the Gulf Crisis, International Labour Orgnization, Geneva, Switzerland.

Israel, 1990, *Monthly Bulletin of Statistics*, Central Bureau of Statistics, Jerusalem, Israel.

Japan, 1990, *Statistics on Immigration Control*, Tokyo, Japan.

Jasso, G., and Rosenzweig, M.R., 1986, Family reunification and the immigration multiplier: US immigration law, origin, country conditions, and the reproduction of immigrants, *Demography* **23**(3) (August).

Johnston, M.I., and Hoth, D.F., 1993, Present status and future prospects for HIV therapies, *Science* **260**:1286–1293.

Kahn, H., 1982, *The Coming Boom*, Simon and Schuster, New York, NY, USA.

Kannisto, V., 1988, On the survival of centenarians and the span of life, *Population Studies* **42**:389–406.

Kaufman, J., Zhang, Z., Qiao, S., and Zhang, Y., 1989, Family planning policy and practice in China: A study of four rural counties, *Population and Development Review* **15**(4):707–729.

Keilman, N.W., 1990, *Uncertainty in National Population Forecasting: Issues, Backgrounds, Analyses, Recommendations,* Swets & Zeitlinger, Amsterdam, Netherlands.

Kelley, A.C., and Schmidt, R.M., 1979, Modeling the role of government policy in post-war Australian immigration, *Economic Record* **55**(2).

Kelly, M.J., 1991, Education in a declining economy: The case of Zambia, 1975–1985, *EDI Development Case Series, Analytical Case Studies No. 8*, The World Bank, Washington, DC, USA.

Kenya, 1989, *Kenya Demographic and Health Survey, 1989,* Ministry of Home Affairs and National Heritage, National Council for Population and Development, Nairobi, Kenya; and Institute for Resource Development/Macro Systems, Inc., Columbia, MD, USA.

Keyfitz, N., 1977, *Applied Mathematical Demography*, John Wiley & Sons, New York, NY, USA.

Keyfitz, N., 1978, Improving life expectancy: An uphill road ahead, *American Journal of Public Health* **68**:954–956.

Keyfitz, N., 1981, The limits of population forecasting, *Population and Development Review* **7**(4):579–593.

Keyfitz, N., 1985, A probability representation of future population, *Zeitschrift für Bevölkerungswissenschaft* **11**:179–191.

Keyfitz, N., 1989, Measuring in Advance the Accuracy of Population Forecasts, WP-89-72, International Institute for Applied Systems Analysis, Laxenburg, Austria.

Keyfitz, N., 1991, Subreplacement fertility: The third level of explanation, in W. Lutz, ed., *Future Demographic Trends in Europe and North America: What Can We Assume Today?* Academic Press, London, UK.

Kiernan, K., 1991, *The Respective Roles of Men and Women in Tomorrow's Europe,* Human Resources in Europe at the Dawn of the 21st Century, Eurostat, International Conference, 27–29 November, Luxembourg.

Kiernan, K., 1992, The impact of family disruption in childhood on transitions made in young adult life, *Population Studies* **46**.

Kiernan, K., 1993, The future of partnership and fertility, in R. Cliquet, ed., *The Future of Europe's Population,* Population Studies 26, Council of Europe Press, Strasbourg, France.

King, G., 1696 [1973], 17th Century Manuscript Book of Gregory King, *The Earliest Classics: Graunt and King,* Gregg International, Germany.

Kiros, F.G., 1991, Economic consequences of drought, crop failure and famine in Ethiopia, 1973–1986, *Ambio* **20**(5):183–188.

Klinger, A., 1985, Population policy measures: Effects on reproductive behavior in Hungary, *Population Bulletin of the United Nations* **17**:64–79.

Knibbs, G.H., 1928 [1976], *The Shadow of the World's Future,* Reprint Edition, Arno Press, New York, NY, USA.

Kohn, R.R., 1982, Cause of death in very old people, *Journal of American Medical Association* **247**:2793–2797.

Kryger, J.F., 1764, Svar på den af Kongl. Vetenskaps Academien för sistledit ar 1963, framstälde frågan: Hvad kan vara orsaken, at sådan myckenhet Svensk folk årligen flytter ur Landet? Och genom hvilka författningar kan det bäst före-kommas?

Lamb, H.H., 1982, *Climate, History and the Modern World,* Methuen, London, UK.

Lamb, W.H., Foord, F.A., Lamb, C.M.B., and Whitehead, R.G., 1984, Changes in maternal and child mortality rates in three isolated Gambian villages over ten years, *The Lancet* 8408 (October 20):912–913.

Lamptey, P.R., and Coates, T.J., 1994, Community-based AIDS interventions in Africa, in M. Essex, S. Mboup, P.J. Kanki, and M.R. Kalengayi, eds., *AIDS in Africa,* Raven Press, New York, NY, USA.

Larson, A., 1989, Social context of Human Immunodeficiency Virus transmission in Africa: Historical and cultural bases of East and Central African sexual relations, *Reviews of Infectious Diseases* **2**:716–731.

Laumann, E.O., Gagnon, J.H., Michael, R.T., and Michaels, S., 1994, *The Social Organization of Sexuality: Sexual Practices in the United States,* University of Chicago Press, Chicago, IL, USA.

Lavasseur, E., 1885, Emigration in the nineteenth century, *Journal of the Statistical Society.*

Lavely, W.R., 1991, China unveils its monumental Two-per-Thousand Fertility Survey, *Asian and Pacific Population Forum* **5**(4):89–92, 116.

Le Bras, H., 1991, *Marianne et les lapins: l'obsession démographique,* Olivier Orban, Paris, France.

Lee, E., 1966, A theory of migration, *Demography* **3**.

Lee, R.D., 1974, Forecasting births in post-transitional populations: Stochastic renewal with serially correlated fertility, *Journal of the American Statistical Association* **69**(247):607–617.

Lee, R.D., 1991, Long-run global population forecasts: A critical appraisal, in K. Davis and M.S. Bernstam, eds., *Resources, Environment, and Population: Present Knowledge, Future Options,* Oxford University Press, New York, NY, USA.

Lee, R.D., 1992, Stochastic demographic forecasting, *International Journal of Forecasting* **8**:315–328.

Lee, R.D., and Carter, L., 1992, Modeling and forecasting the time series of US mortality, *Journal of the American Statistical Association* **87**(September):659–675.

Lee, R.D., and Tuljapurkar, S., 1994, Stochastic population forecasts for the United States: Beyond high, medium, and low, *Journal of the American Statistical Association* **89**(428):1175–1189.

Leete, R., and Tan Boon An, 1993, Contrasting fertility trends among ethnic groups in Malaysia, in R. Leete and I. Alam, eds., *The Revolution in Asian Fertility,* Oxford University Press, Oxford, UK.

Leistra, M., and Boesten, J., 1989, Pesticides contamination of groundwater in Western Europe, *Agriculture, Ecosystems and Environment* **26**:369–389.

Leontief, W., and Sohn, I., 1984, Population, food, and energy: The prospects for worldwide economic growth to the year 2030, in B.N. Kursunoglu *et al.*, eds., *Global Energy Assessment and Outlook: Proceedings of the International Scientific Forum on Changes in Energy,* November 9–13, Mexico City, Harwood, London, UK.

Lesetedi, L.T., Mompati, G.D., Khulumani, P., Lesetedi, G.N., and Rutenberg, N., 1989, *Botswana Family Health Survey II, 1988,* Ministry of Finance and Development Planning, Gaborone, Botswana; and Institute for Resource Development/Macro Systems, Inc., Columbia, MD, USA.

Leslie, P.H., 1945, On the use of matrices in certain population mathematics, *Biometrika* **33**:183–212.

Lestaeghe, R., 1983, A century of demographic and cultural change in Western Europe: An exploration of underlying dimensions, *Population and Development Review* **9**(3):411–435.

Littman, G., and Keyfitz, N., 1977, The Next Hundred Years, Working Paper No. 101, Harvard University Center for Population Studies, Cambridge, MA, USA.

Livi Bacci, M., 1991, *Population and Nutrition: Essay on the Demographic History of Europe,* Cambridge University Press, Cambridge, UK.

Lohman, P.H.M., Sankaranarayanan, K., and Ashby, J., 1992, Choosing the limits to life, *Nature* **357**:185–186.

Lucas, R.E.B., 1981, International migration: Economic causes, consequences and evaluation, in M. Kritz, C. Keely, and S. Tomasi, eds., *Global Trends in Migration: Theory and Research on International Population Movements,* Center for Migration Studies, Staten Island, NY, USA.

Luther, N.Y., and Cho, L.-J., 1988, Reconstruction of birth histories from census and household survey data, *Population Studies* **42**(3):451–472.

Luther, N.Y., and Pejaranondam, C., 1991, The parity structure of fertility decline in Thailand, 1953–1979, *Genus* **47**(1–2):63–88.

Luther, N.Y., Feeney, G., and Zhang, W., 1990, One-child families of a baby-boom? Evidence from China's 1987 one-per-hundred survey, *Population Studies* **44**(2):341–357.

Lutz, W., 1985, Realisation und Veränderung von Kinderwünschen: der dynamische Aspect, in R. Münz, ed., *Leben mit Kindern: Wunsch und Wirklichkeit*, Deuticke, Vienna, Austria.

Lutz, W., 1989, *Distributional Aspects of Human Fertility: A Global Comparative Study*, Academic Press, London, UK.

Lutz, W., ed., 1991, *Future Demographic Trends in Europe and North America: What Can We Assume Today?* Academic Press, London, UK.

Lutz, W., 1993a, Effects of children on divorce probabilities and of divorce on fertility: The case of Finland 1984, *Yearbook of Population Research in Finland* **31**:72–80.

Lutz, W., 1993b, Population and environment, what do we need more urgently: Better data, better models, or better questions? in J. Clarke and B. Zaba, eds., *Environment and Population Change,* Ordina, Liège, Belgium.

Lutz, W., ed., 1994a, *Population–Development–Environment: Understanding Interactions in Mauritius*, Springer-Verlag, Berlin, Germany.

Lutz, W., ed., 1994b, *The Future Population of the World: What Can We Assume Today?* 1st Edition, Earthscan Publications Ltd, London, UK.

Lutz, W., 1995a, Scenario Analysis in Population Projection, WP-95-57, International Institute for Applied Systems Analysis, Laxenburg, Austria (forthcoming in *Journal of Official Statistics*).

Lutz, W., 1995b, Dilemmas of a demographic delegate, or the death of the wrong "Cairo Target," *POPNET* **26**, International Institute for Applied Systems Analysis, Laxenburg, Austria.

Lutz, W., and Prinz, Ch., 1991, Scenarios for the World Population in the Next Century: Excessive Growth or Extreme Aging, WP-91-22, International Institute for Applied Systems Analysis, Laxenburg, Austria.

Lutz, W., and Prinz, Ch., 1992, What Difference Do Alternative Immigration and Integration Levels Make to Western Europe, WP-92-29, International Institute for Applied Systems Analysis, Laxenburg, Austria.

Lutz, W., and Prinz, Ch., 1993, Modeling future immigration and integration in Western Europe, in R. King, ed., *The New Geography of European Migrations*, Belhaven Press, London, UK.

Lutz, W., and Scherbov, S., 1989, Modellrechnungen zum Einfluß regional unterschiedlicher Fertilitätsniveaus auf die zukünftige Bevölkerungsverteilung in der Sowjetunion, *Zeitschrift für Bevölkerungswissenschaft* **15**(3):271–292.

Lutz, W., and Vaupel, J., 1987, The division of labor for society's reproduction: On the concentration of childbearing and rearing in Austria, *Österreichische Zeitschrift für Statistik und Informatik* **17**:81–96.

Lutz, W., Scherbov, S., and Volkov, A., eds., 1994a, *Demographic Trends and Patterns in the Soviet Union Before 1991,* Routledge, London, UK.

Lutz, W., Prinz, Ch., and Langgassner, J., 1994b, The IIASA world population scenarios to 2030, in W. Lutz, ed., *The Future Population of the World: What Can We Assume Today?* 1st Edition, Earthscan Publications Ltd, London, UK.

Lutz, W., Goldstein, J.R., and Prinz, Ch., 1994c, Alternative approaches to population projection, in W. Lutz, ed., *The Future Population of the World: What Can We Assume Today?* 1st Edition, Earthscan Publications Ltd, London, UK.

Lutz, W., Sanderson, W., and Scherbov, S., 1995, Probabilistic Population Projections Based on Expert Opinion, WP-95-123, International Institute for Applied Systems Analysis, Laxenburg, Austria.

MacPhee, C.R., and Hassan, M.K., 1990, Some economic determinants of Third World professional immigration to the United States: 1972–1987, *World Development* **18**(8) (August).

Malthus, R., 1967 [1798], *Essay on the Principle of Population,* 7th Edition, Dent, London, UK.

Mandjale, A.E., 1985, *Mortalité infantile et juvénile en Afrique: niveaux et caractérisitiques, causes et déterminants,* CIACO, Louvain la Neuve, Belgium.

Mann, D.W., 1981, Fewer people for a better world: A plea for negative population growth, *Environmental Conservation* **8**(40):260–261.

Mann, J.M., Tarantola, D.J.M., and Netter, T.W., eds., 1992, *AIDS in the World,* Harvard University Press, Cambridge, MA, USA.

Manton, K.G., 1982, Changing concepts of mortality and morbidity in the elderly population, *Milbank Memorial Fund Quarterly* **60**:183–244.

Manton, K.G., 1991, New biotechnologies and the limits to life expectancy, in W. Lutz, ed., *Future Demographic Trends in Europe and North America: What Can We Assume Today?* Academic Press, London, UK.

Manton, K.G., and Soldo, B.J., 1985, Dynamics of health changes in the oldest old: New perspectives and evidence, *Milbank Memorial Fund Quarterly* **63**:177–451.

Manton, K.G., and Woodbury, M.A., 1987, Biological Models of Human Mortality and the Limits to Life Expectancy, Paper presented at the Annual Meeting of the Population Association of America, 29 April–2 May, Chicago, IL, USA.

Manton, K.G., Stallard, E., and Tolley, H.D., 1991, Limits to human life expectancy: Evidence, prospects, and implications, *Population and Development Review* **17**(4):603–637.

Marchetti, C., 1978, *On 10^{12}: A Check on Earth Carrying Capacity for Man,* RR-78-7, International Institute for Applied Systems Analysis, Laxenburg, Austria.

Mauldin, W.P., and Berelson, B., 1978, Conditions of fertility decline in developing countries, 1964–1975, *Studies in Family Planning* **9**(5).

Mauldin, W.P., and Ross, J., 1991, Family planning programs: Efforts and results, 1982–1989, *Studies in Family Planning* **22**:350–367.

Mauldin, W.P., and Segal, S.J., 1988, Prevalence of contraceptive use: Trends and issues, *Studies in Family Planning* **19**:335–353.

Mazess, R.B., and Forman, S.H., 1979, Longevity and age exaggeration in Vilcabamba, Ecuador, *Journal of Gerontology* **34**:94–98.

McNown, R., and Rogers, A., 1989, Forecasting mortality: A parameterized time series approach, *Demography* **26**:645–660.

McNown, R., Rogers, A., and Little, J., 1995, Simplicity and complexity in extrapolative population forecasting models, *Mathematical Population Studies* **5**(3).

Meadows, D.L., and Meadows, D.H., eds., 1973, *Toward Global Equilibrium: Collected Papers,* MIT Press, Cambridge, MA, USA.

Meadows, D.H., Meadows, D.L., Randers, J., and Behrens III, W.W., 1972, *The Limits to Growth,* Universe Books, New York, NY, USA.

Meadows, D.L., Behrens III, W.W., Meadows, D.H., Naill, R.F., Randers, J., and Zahn, E.K.O., 1974, *Dynamics of Growth in a Finite World,* MIT Press, Cambridge, MA, USA.

Meadows, D.H., Meadows, D.L., and Randers, J., 1992a, *Beyond the Limits: Global Collapse or a Sustainable Future,* Earthscan, London, UK.

Meadows, D.H., Meadows, D.L., and Randers, J., 1992b, *Beyond the Limits: Confronting Global Collapse, Envisioning a Sustainable Future,* Chelsea Green Publishing Company, Post Mills, VT, USA.

Melamed, A., 1989, Commentary on Gerald Stanhill's Paper, in S.F. Singer, ed., *Global Climate Change: Human and Natural Influences,* Paragon House, New York, NY, USA.

Mellor, J.W., and Paulino, L., 1986, Food production needs in a consumption perspective, in M.S. Swaminathan and S.K. Sinha, eds., *Global Aspects of Food Production,* Tycooly International, Oxford, UK.

Mertens, T.E., *et al.,* 1994, Global estimates and epidemiology of HIV infections and AIDS, *AIDS* **8** (Suppl. 1)S361–S372.

Mesarovic, M., and Pestel, E., 1974, *Mankind at the Turning Point,* E.P. Dutton, New York, NY, USA.

Mesle, F., 1993, The future of mortality, in R. Cliquet, ed., *The Future of Europe's Population: A Scenario Approach,* The Council of Europe, European Population Committee, Strasbourg, France.

Meybeck, M., Chapman, D., and Helmer, R., 1990, *Global Environment Monitoring System: Global Freshwater Quality: A First Assessment,* Blackwell Reference for WHO/UNEP, Cambridge, MA, USA.

Ministry of Health, 1992, Population and Development in Singapore, Country Report circulated during the 4th Asian and Pacific Population Conference, Bali, Indonesia, 19–27 August.

Montanari, A., and Cortese, A., 1993, Third World immigrants in Italy, in R. King, ed., *Mass Migration in Europe, the Legacy and the Future,* Belhaven Press, London, UK.

Morris, M., and Dean, L., 1994, Effect of sexual behavior change on long-term human immunodeficiency virus prevalence among homosexual men, *American Journal of Epidemiology* **140**:217–232.

Moser, S.W., 1983, *Broken Earth: The Rural Chinese,* The Free Press, New York, NY, USA.

Moses, S., Bradley, J.E., Nagelkerke, N.J.D., Ronald, A.R., Ndinya-Achola, J.O., and Plummer, F.A., 1990, Geographical patterns of male circumcision practices in Africa: Association with HIV prevalence, *International Journal of Epidemiology* **19**:693–697.

Mostert, W., 1991, Recent fertility trends in South Africa, in W. Mostert and J. Lötter, eds., *South African Demographic Future,* Human Science Research Council, Pretoria, South Africa.

Mückenhausen, E., 1973, Die Produktionskapazität der Böden der Erde, Vorträge N234, Rheinisch-Westfälische Akademie der Wissenschaften, Germany.

Muhsam, H.V., 1956, The utilization of alternative population forecasts in planning, *Bulletin of the Research Council of Israel* 5:133–146.

Murray, C.J.L., Styblo, K., and Rouillon, A., 1990, Tuberculosis in developing countries: Burden, intervention and cost, *Bulletin of the International Union Against Tuberculosis and Lung Disease* 65(1):2–20.

Myers, G.C., and Manton, K.G., 1984, Compression of mortality: Myth or reality? *The Gerontologist* 24:346–353.

Nilsson, A., 1990, A Comparison of the Statistics on the Migration Flows between Sweden and the Other Nordic Countries: 1945–1988, Paper presented at the Conference of European Statisticians, 9–11 April, Geneva, Switzerland,

Norse, D., 1991, Socioeconomic Impact of AIDS on Food Production in East Africa, Paper prepared for the Seventh International Conference on AIDS, 16–21 June, Florence, Italy.

Norse, D., 1992, A new strategy for feeding a crowded planet, *Environment* 34(5):6–39.

Notestein, F.W., 1945, Population: The long view, in T.W. Schultz, ed., *Food for the World,* University of Chicago Press, Chicago, IL, USA.

Notestein, F.W., Taeuber, I.B., Kirk, D., Coale, A.J., and Kiser, L.K., 1944, *The Future Population of Europe and the Soviet Union: Population Projections 1940–1970,* League of Nations, Geneva, Switzerland.

Nzilambi, N., De Cock, K.M., Forthal, D.N., Francis, H., Ryder, R.W., Malebe, I., Getchell, J., Laga, M., Piot, P., and McCormick, J.B., 1988, The prevalence of infection with human immunodeficiency virus over a 10-year period in rural Zaire, *New England Journal of Medicine* 318:276–279.

Öberg, S., and Boubnova, H., 1993, Poverty, ethnicity and migration potentials in Eastern Europe, in R. King, ed., *Mass Migration in Europe, the Legacy and the Future,* Belhaven Press, London, UK.

Öberg, S., and Wils, A.B., 1992, East-West migration in Europe, *POPNET* 22, International Institute for Applied Systems Analysis, Laxenburg, Austria.

Odell, P.R., and Rosing, K.E., 1980, *The Future of Oil: A Simulation Study of the Inter-Relationships of Resources, Reserves and Use, 1980–2080,* Kogan Page, London, UK.

OECD, 1990, *SOPEMI: Continuous Reporting System on Migration 1989,* Organisation for Economic Co-operation and Development, Paris, France.

OECD, 1991, *SOPEMI: Continuous Reporting System on Migration 1990,* Organisation for Economic Co-operation and Development, Paris, France.

OECD, 1992, *SOPEMI: Trends in International Migration,* Organisation for Economic Co-operation and Development, Paris, France.

Oldemann, L.R., Hakkeling, R.T.A., and Sombroek, W.G., 1990, *World Map of the Status of Human Induced Soil Degradation: An Exploratory Note,* International Soil Reference and Information Centre, Wageningen, Netherlands.

Olshansky, S.J., Carnes, B.A., and Cassel, C., 1990, In search of Methuselah: Estimating the upper limits of human longevity, *Science* **250**: 634–640.

Onuoha, N., and Timæus, I., 1995, Has a fertility transition begun in West Africa? *Journal of Development Studies* **7**:93–116.

Ortiz, V., 1986, Changes in the characteristics of Puerto Rican migrants from 1955 to 1980, *International Migration Review* **20**(3):612–628.

Over, M., and Piot, P., 1993, HIV infection and sexually transmitted diseases, in D.T. Jamison, W.H. Mosley, A.R. Measham, and J.L. Bobadilla, *Disease Control Priorities in Developing Countries*, Oxford University Press for the World Bank, New York, NY, USA.

Pagnini, D.L., and Rindfuss, R.R., 1993, The divorce of marriage and childbearing: Changing attitudes and behavior in the United States, *Population and Development Review* **19**(2):331–348.

Parikh, K.S., Fischer, G., Frohberg, K., and Gulbrandsen, O., 1988, *Towards Free Trade in Agriculture*, Nijhoff, Dordrecht, Netherlands.

Park, C.B., 1992, Family building in the Republic of Korea: Recent trends, in *Impact of Fertility Decline on Population Policies and Program Strategies*, Korean Institute for Health and Social Affairs, Seoul, South Korea.

Parry, M.L., and Carter, T.R., 1988, The assessment of effects of climatic variations on agriculture: Aims, methods and summary of results, in M.L. Parry, T.R. Carter, and N.T. Konijn, eds., *The Impact of Climate Variations on Agriculture*, Volume 1, Kluwer, Dordrecht, Netherlands.

Parry, M.L., Carter, T.R., and Konijn, N.T., eds., 1988, *The Impact of Climate Variations on Agriculture*, Volumes 1 and 2, Kluwer, Dordrecht, Netherlands.

Pearce, F., 1991, Africa at a watershed, *New Scientist*, March 23:34–40.

Pearl, R., 1923, *The Rate of Living*, Alfred Knopf, New York, NY, USA.

Pearl, R., 1924, *Studies in Human Biology*, Williams and Wilkins, Baltimore, MD, USA.

Pearl, R., and Gould, S., 1936, World population growth, *Human Biology* **8**(3):399–419.

Pearson, K., 1897 [1923], *The Chances of Death, and Other Studies in Evolution*, Arnold, London, UK.

Pearson, F.A., and Harper, F.A., 1945, *The World's Hunger*, Cornell University Press, New York, NY, USA.

Penck, A., 1925, Das Hauptproblem der physischen Anthropogeographie, *Zeitschrift für Geopolitik* **2**.

Peng, X., 1981, *Demographic Transition in China*, Oxford University Press, Oxford, UK.

Penhale, B., 1984, The Course of Fertility in France, Italy and England and Wales since 1955, Msc. Thesis, Centre for Population Studies, London School of Hygiene and Tropical Medicine, London, UK.

Peoples, J., and Bailey, G., 1991, *Humanity*, West Publishing Company, St. Paul, MN, USA.

Peto, R., Parish, S.E., and Gray, R.G., 1986, There is no such thing as aging, and cancer is not related to it, in A. Likhachev *et al.*, eds., *Age-Related*

Factors in Carcinogenesis, International Agency for Research on Cancer, Lyon, France.

Pflaumer, P., 1988, Confidence intervals for population projections based on Monte Carlo methods, *International Journal of Forecasting* 4:135–142.

Pflaumer, P., 1992, Forecasting US population totals with the Box–Jenkins approach, *International Journal of Forecasting* 8(3):329–338.

Philipson, T., and Posner, R.A., 1995, The microeconomics of the AIDS epidemic in Africa, *Population and Development Review* 21:835–848.

Pimentel, D., 1984, Energy flow in the food system, in D. Pimentel and C.W. Hall, eds., *Food and Energy Resources,* Academic Press, Orlando, FL, USA.

Piot, P., and Caraël, M., 1988, Epidemiological and sociological aspects of HIV-infection in developing countries, *British Medical Bulletin* 44:68–88.

Piot, P., Plummer, F., Mhalu, F., Lamboray, J., Chin, J., and Mann, J., 1988, AIDS: An international perspective, *Science* 239:573–579.

Piot, P., Goeman, J., and Laga, M., 1994, The epidemiology of HIV and AIDS in Africa, in M. Essex, S. Mboup, P.J. Kanki, and M.R. Kalengayi, eds., *AIDS in Africa,* Raven Press, New York, NY, USA.

Plummer, F.A., Simonsen, J.N., Cameron, D.W., Ndinya-Achola, J.O., Kreiss, J.K., Galeinya, M.N., Waiyaki, P., Cheang, M., Piot, P., Ronald, A.R., and Ngugi, E.N., 1991, Cofactors in male–female sexual transmission of Human Immunodeficiency Virus Type 1, *Journal of Infectious Diseases* 163:233–239.

Plummer, F.A., Tyndall, M.W., Ndinya-Achola, J.O., and Moses, S., 1994, Sexual transmission of HIVs and the role of sexually transmitted diseases, in M. Essex, S. Mboup, P.J. Kanki, and M.R. Kalengayi, eds., *AIDS in Africa,* Raven Press, New York, NY, USA.

Poston, D.L., and Yu, M.Y., 1990, The distribution of the overseas Chinese in the contemporary world, *International Migration Review* 24(3):480–508.

Poterba, J.M., and Summers, L.H., 1987, Public policy implications of declining old-age mortality, in G. Burtless, ed., *Work, Health, and Income among the Elderly,* Brookings, Washington, DC, USA.

Potter, S.H., and Potter, H.M., 1990, *China's Peasants: The Anthropology of a Revolution,* Cambridge University Press, Cambridge, UK.

Potts, M., Anderson, R., and Boily, M.-C., 1991, Slowing the spread of human immunodeficiency virus in developing countries, *The Lancet* 338:608–613.

Prinz, Ch., 1994, Patterns of marriage and cohabitation in Europe, with emphasis on Sweden, *POPNET* 24, International Institute for Applied Systems Analysis, Laxenburg, Austria.

Prinz, Ch., 1995, *Cohabiting, Married, or Single: Portraying, Analyzing and Modeling New Living Arrangements in the Changing Societies of Europe,* Avebury, Aldershot, UK.

Prinz, Ch., and Lutz, W., 1993, Alternative demographic scenarios for 20 large member states of the Council of Europe 1990–2050, in R. Cliquet, ed., *The Future of Europe's Population: A Scenario Approach,* The Council of Europe, European Population Committee, Strasbourg, France.

Pursel, V.G., Pinkert, C.A., Miller, K.F., Bolt, D.J., Campbell, R.G., Palmiter, R.D., Brinster, R.L., and Jammer, R.E., 1989, Genetic engineering of livestock, *Science* **244**(16 June):1281–1288.

Quigley, J.M., 1972, An economic model of Swedish emigration, *Quarterly Journal of Economics* (February).

Rauchberg, H., 1893, Innere Wanderungen in Österreich, *Allgemeines Statistisches Archiv* **3**:183–208.

Ravenstein, E.G., 1885, The laws of migration, *Journal of the Statistical Society* **48**(2):167–227.

Ravenstein, G., 1891, Lands of the globe still available for European settlement, *Proceedings of the Royal Geographic Society* **13**(27).

Reij, C., Mulder, P., and Begemann, L., 1988, *Water Harvesting for Plant Production,* Technical Paper No. 91, World Bank, Washington, DC, USA.

Reinans, S.A., and Hammar, T., 1993, *New Citizens by Birth and Naturalization,* CEIFO, Stockholm, Sweden.

Resources for the Future, 1984, Feeding a hungry world, *Resources* **76**:1–20.

Revelle, R., 1967, The resources available for agriculture, *Scientific American* **235**(3):165–178.

Ricardo, D., 1964, *The Principles of Political Economy and Taxation,* Dent, London, UK.

Ridker, R.G., 1973, To grow or not to grow: That is not the relevant question, *Science* **128**(December):1315–1318.

Rivière, J.W.M., 1989, Threats to the world's water, *Scientific American,* Special Issue: Managing Planet Earth **261**(3):48–55.

Rodriguez, G., and Aravena, R., 1991, Socio-economic factors and the transition to low fertility in less developed countries: A comparative analysis, in *Proceedings of the Demographic and Health Surveys World Conference,* Vol. 1, IRD/Marco International Inc., Washington, DC, USA.

Rodriguez, G., and Hobcraft, J.N., 1984, *Illustrative Analysis: Life Table Analysis of Birth Intervals in Colombia,* WFS Scientific Report No. 16, International Statistical Institute, Voorburg, Netherlands.

Rogers, A., 1975, *Introduction to Multiregional Mathematical Demography,* John Wiley & Sons, New York, NY, USA.

Rogers, A., and Castro, L., 1981, *Model Migration Schedules,* RR-81-30, International Institute for Applied Systems Analysis, Laxenburg, Austria.

Rogge, J.R., 1992, Refugee Migration: Changing Characteristics and Prospects, Working Paper ESD/P/ICPD.1994/EG.VI/19, United Nations, New York, NY, USA.

Rosenfeld, A., 1976 [1985], *Prolongevity,* 2nd Edition, Knopf, New York, NY, USA.

Rosenwaike, I., 1981, A note on new estimates of the mortality of the extremely aged, *Demography* **18**:257–266.

Rowe, J.W., and Kahn, R.L., 1987, Human aging: Usual and successful, *Science* **237**:143–149.

Rubenson, S., 1991, Environmental stress and conflict in Ethiopian history: Looking for correlations, *Ambio* **20**(5):179–182.

Russell, S.S., 1990, Policy Dimensions of Female Migration to the Arab Countries of Western Asia, Paper presented at the Meeting on International Migration Policies and the Status of Female Migrants, 26–31 March, San Miniato, Italy.

Ryder, N.B., 1975, Notes on stationary populations, *Population Index* **41**(1): 3–28.

Ryder, N.B., 1983, Cohort and period measures of changing fertility, in R.A. Buletao and R.D. Lee, eds., *Determinants of Fertility in Developing Countries*, Vol. 2, Academic Press, New York, NY, USA.

Sabatello, E., 1992, Migrants from the USSR to Israel in the 1990s: Socio-Demographic Background and First-year Occupational Trends, Paper presented at the Conference on Mass Migration in Europe – Implications in East and West, 5–7 March, Laxenburg, Austria.

Sacher, G.A., 1977, Life table modification and life prolongation, in C.E. Finch and L. Hayflick, eds., *Handbook of the Biology of Aging,* Van Nostrand Reinhold, New York, NY, USA.

Sanches, P.A., Couto, W., and Buol, S.W., 1982, The fertility capability soil classification system: Interpretation, applicability and modification, *Geoderma* **27**:283–309.

Sanderson, W., 1995, Predictability, complexity, and catastrophe in a collapsible model of population, development, and environmental interactions, *Mathematical Population Studies* **5**(3):259–279.

Schatzkin, A., 1980, How long can we live? A more optimistic view of potential gains in life expectancy, *American Journal of Public Health* **70**:1199–1200.

Schneider, E.L., and Brody, J.A., 1983, Aging, natural death, and the compression of morbidity: Another view, *New England Journal of Medicine* **309**:854–856.

Schneider, E.L., and Guralnik, J., 1987, The compression of morbidity: A dream which comes true someday! *Gerontologica Perspecta* **1**:8–13.

Schoorl, J.J., and Voets, S.Y., 1990, Country Report: The Netherlands, Paper prepared for the Working Group on Immigrant Populations.

Seaman, J., 1987, Famine mortality in Ethiopia and Sudan, in *Proceedings of the IUSSP Seminar on Comparative Mortality Changes,* Younde, Cameroon, 19–23 October, Oxford University Press, London, UK.

Seed, J., Allen, S., Mertens, T., Hudes, E., Serufilira, A., Caraël, M., Karita, E., Van De Perre, P., and Nsengumuremyi, F., 1995, Male circumcision, sexually transmitted disease, and risk of HIV, *Journal of Acquired Immune Deficiency Syndromes and Human Retrovirology* **8**:83–90.

Sen, A., 1993, The economics of life and death, *Scientific American* (May).

Serwadda, D., Mhalu, F.S., Karita, E., and Moses, S., 1994, HIVs and AIDS in East Africa, in M. Essex, S. Mboup, P.J. Kanki, and M.R. Kalengayi, eds., *AIDS in Africa,* Raven Press, New York, NY, USA.

Sewankambo, N.K., *et al.*, 1994, Demographic impact of HIV infection in rural Rakai District, Uganda: Results of a population-based cohort study, *AIDS* **8**:1707–1713.

Shah, N.M., 1992, Migration Between Asian Countries and Its Likely Future, Working Paper ESD/P/ICPD.1994/EG, VI/114, United Nations, New York, NY, USA.

Shah, M.M., Fischer, G., Higgins, G.M., Kassam, A.H., and Naiken, L., 1985, Estimates of arable land: Past studies, in *People, Land, and Food Production*, CP-85-11, International Institute for Applied Systems Analysis, Laxenburg, Austria.

Shorter, E., 1990, What can two historical examples of sexually-transmitted diseases teach us about AIDS? in *Proceedings of the IUSSP Seminar on Anthropological Studies Relevant to the Sexual Transmission of HIV*, 19–22 November, Sonderborg, Denmark.

Shryock, H.S., and Siegel, J.S., 1976, *The Methods and Materials of Demography*, Academic Press, New York, NY, USA.

Simon, J., 1981, *The Ultimate Resource*, Princeton University Press, Princeton, NJ, USA.

Simon, J., 1993, The economic effect of immigration, *European Review* 1(1).

Sindermann, C.J., 1982, Aquatic animal protein food resources: Actual and potential, in R.G. Woods, ed., *Future Dimensions of World Food and Population*, A Winrock International Study, Westview Press, Boulder, CO, USA.

Skeldon, R., 1986, Hong Kong and its hinterland: A case of international rural-to-urban migration? *Asian Geographer* 5(1):1–24.

Smil, V., 1987, *Energy, Food, Environment: Realities, Myths, Options*, Clarendon Press, Oxford, UK.

Spain, 1991, *Anuario Estadístico*, Instituto Nacional de Estadística, Madrid, Spain.

Spencer, G., 1986, The First-Ever Examination of the Characteristics of Centenarians in the 1980 Census, Paper presented at the 1986 Annual Meeting of the Population Association of America.

Spencer, G., 1989, *Current Population Reports, Series P-25, No. 1018, Projections of the Population of the United States, by Age, Sex, and Race*, US Bureau of the Census, US Government Printing Office, Washington, DC, USA.

Srikantan, K.S., and Balasubramanian, K., 1989, Stalling of fertility decline in India, in S.N. Singh, M.K. Premi, P.S. Bhatia, and A. Bose, eds., *Population Transition in India*, Vol. 2, B.R. Publishing Corp., Delhi, India.

Srinivasan, K., 1989, Natural fertility and nuptiality patterns in India: Historical levels and recent changes, in S.N. Singh, M.K. Premi, P.S. Bhatia, and A. Bose, eds., *Population Transition in India*, Vol. 1, B.R. Publishing Corp., Delhi, India.

Stanhill, G., 1983, The distribution of global solar radiation over the land surfaces on earth, *Solar Energy* 31:95–104

Stanhill, G., 1986, Water use efficiency, *Advances with Agromanagement* 39:53–85.

Stanhill, G., 1989, World water problems: Desertification, in S.F. Singer, ed., *Global Climate Change: Human and Natural Influences*, Paragon House, New York, NY, USA.

State Statistical Bureau of China, 1995, *A Statistical Survey of China: 1995*, China Statistical Press, Beijing, China.

Stoto, M., 1983, The accuracy of population projections, *Journal of the American Statistical Association* **78**(381):13–20.

Suhrke, A., 1993, *Pressure Points: Environmental Degradation, Migration and Conflict*, Number 3 of the Occasional Paper Series of the Project on Environmental Change and Acute Conflict, University of Toronto and the American Academy of Arts and Sciences (March), Washington, DC, USA.

Tapinos, G., 1975, *L'Immigration Etrangère en France: 1946–1973*, Presses Universitaires de France, Paris, France.

Thomas, D.S., 1941, *Social and Economic Aspects of Swedish Population Movements*, Macmillan, New York, NY, USA.

Timæus, I.M., 1991, Adult mortality: Levels, trends, and data sources, in R. Feachem and D. Jamison, eds., *Disease and Mortality in Sub-Saharan Africa*, World Bank/Oxford University Press, New York, NY, USA.

Tönnies, F., 1887, *Gemeinschaft und Gesellschaft: Grundbegriffe der reinen Soziologie*, Wissenschaftliche Buchgesellschaft, Darmstadt, Germany.

Torrealba, R., 1982, *La migración internacional hacia Venezuela en la década de 1970: Características socio-demográficas*, Consejo Nacional de Recursos Humanos, Caracas, Venezuela.

Torrealba, R., 1985, *El trabajador migrante en situación irregular y su legalización en Venezuela*, International Migration for Employment Programme, International Labour Organization, Geneva, Switzerland.

Trani, J.F., 1992, *Mémoire de DEA*, Institut des Etudes Politiques de Paris, Paris, France.

Tribalat, M., and Muñoz-Pérez, F., 1989, Rapport Français, Groupe de Travail sur les Migrations Internationales de l'Association Européenne pour l'Etude de la Population, The Hague, Netherlands.

Tuan, Chi-hsien, 1982, China's population in perspective, in H. Brown, ed., *China Among the Nations of the Pacific*, Westview Press, Boulder, CO, USA.

Tuljapurkar, S., 1992, Stochastic population forecasts and their uses, *International Journal of Forecasting* **8**:385–392.

UN, 1955, Age and sex patterns of mortality: Model life tables for underdeveloped countries, *Population Studies* **2**.

UN, 1958, The future growth of world population, *Population Studies* **28**.

UN, 1973, *World Population Prospects as Assessed in 1968*, Population Studies, No. 53, United Nations, New York, NY, USA.

UN, 1975, *Concise Report on the World Population Situation in 1970–1975 and its Long-range Implications*, Population Studies, No. 56, United Nations, NY, USA.

UN, 1977a, *A Modified Method Estimating Age-Specific Survival Ratios*, ESA/P/WP.61, United Nations, New York, NY, USA.

UN, 1977b, *World Population Prospects as Assessed in 1973*, Population Studies, No. 60, United Nations, New York, NY, USA.

UN, 1978, *Demographic Yearbook 1977*, Statistical Office, United Nations, New York, NY, USA.

UN, 1979, *World Population Trends and Prospects by Country, 1950–2000: Summary Report of the 1978 Assessment,* ST/ESA/SER.R/33, United Nations, New York, NY, USA.

UN, 1981a, *World Population Prospects as Assessed in 1980,* Population Studies, No. 78, United Nations, New York, NY, USA.

UN, 1981b, *Long-range Global Population Projections, Based on Data As Assessed in 1978,* Population Division Working Paper, ESA/P/ WP.75, United Nations, New York, NY, USA.

UN, 1982a, *Model Life Tables for Developing Countries,* Population Studies, No. 77, United Nations, New York, NY, USA.

UN, 1982b, Long-range global population projections, as assessed in 1980, *Population Bulletin of the United Nations,* **14.**

UN, 1985a, *World Population Trends, Population and Development Interrelations and Population Policies: 1983 Monitoring Report,* Volume 1, United Nations, New York, NY, USA.

UN, 1985b, *World Population Prospects, Estimates and Projections as Assessed in 1982,* Population Studies, No. 86, United Nations, New York, NY, USA.

UN, 1986, *World Population Prospects, Estimates and Projections as Assessed in 1984,* Population Studies, No. 98, United Nations, New York, NY, USA.

UN, 1988, *Ground Water in North and West Africa,* Natural Resources/Water Series No. 18, Department of Technical Co-operation for Development and Economic Commission for Africa, United Nations, New York, NY, USA.

UN, 1989a, *Levels and Trends of Contraceptive Use as Assessed in 1988,* United Nations, New York, NY, USA.

UN, 1989b, *World Population Prospects 1988,* Population Studies, No. 106, United Nations, New York, NY, USA.

UN, 1991a, *World Population Prospects: 1990,* Population Studies, No. 120, Publication No. ST/ESA/SER.A/120, Department of International Economic and Social Affairs, United Nations, New York, NY, USA.

UN, 1991b, *1990 Assessment of the World Population,* United Nations, New York, NY, USA.

UN, 1992a, *World Population Monitoring, 1991,* Population Studies, No. 126, United Nations, New York, NY, USA.

UN, 1992b, *Child Mortality Since the 1960s: A Database for Developing Countries,* United Nations, New York, NY, USA.

UN, 1992c, *Long-Range World Population Projections: Two Centuries of Population Growth 1950–2150,* ST/ESA/SER.A/125, United Nations, New York, NY, USA.

UN, 1993a, *World Population Prospects: The 1992 Revision,* Department for Economic and Social Information and Policy Analysis, United Nations, New York, NY, USA.

UN, 1993b, *Population Distribution and Migration: The Emerging Issues,* United Nations, New York, NY, USA.

UN, 1994a, *AIDS and the Demography of Africa,* United Nations, New York, NY, USA.

UN, 1994b, *World Population Monitoring, 1993,* ESA/P/WP.121, United Nations, New York, NY, USA.

UN, 1995, *World Population Prospects: The 1994 Revision*, United Nations, New York, NY, USA.

UNEP and UNDP, 1992, *World Resources*, Oxford University Press, Oxford, UK.

UNICEF, 1989, *The State of the World's Children 1989*, United Nations Children's Fund/Oxford University Press, New York, NY, USA.

UNICEF, 1992, *The State of the World's Children 1992*, United Nations Children's Fund/Oxford University Press, New York, NY, USA.

UNO/FAO, 1976, *Report of the FAO Technical Conference on Aquaculture*, Kyoto 1976, FAO Fishery Report No. 188, Food and Agriculture Organization, Rome, Italy.

US, 1967, *The World Food Problem*, A Report of the President's Science of Advisory Committee, Volume 11, Washington, DC, USA.

US Bureau of the Census, 1979, Illustrative projections of world populations to the 21st century, *Current Population Reports: Special Studies*, Series P-23, No. 79, Washington, DC, USA.

US Bureau of the Census, 1989, *Projections of the Population of the United States, by Age, Sex, and Race: 1988 to 2080*, Current Population Reports, Series P-25, No. 1018, Washington, DC, USA.

US Bureau of the Census, 1992, *Statistical Abstract of the United States 1992*, Washington, DC, USA.

US Bureau of the Census, 1993a, Trends and patterns of HIV/AIDS infection in selected developing countries: Country profiles, Research Note No. 10 (June), US Bureau of the Census, Center for International Research, Washington, DC, USA.

US Bureau of the Census, 1993b, Trends and patterns of HIV/AIDS infection in selected developing countries: Country profiles, Research Note No. 12 (December), US Bureau of the Census, Center for International Research, Washington, DC, USA.

US Bureau of the Census, 1994a, Recent HIV seroprevalence levels by country: December 1994, Research Note No. 15 (December), US Bureau of the Census, Center for International Research, Washington, DC, USA.

US Bureau of the Census, 1994b, Trends and patterns of HIV/AIDS infection in selected developing countries: Country profiles, Research Note No. 14 (June), US Bureau of the Census, Center for International Research, Washington, DC, USA.

US Immigration and Naturalization Service, 1991, *1990 Statistical Yearbook of the Immigration and Naturalization Service*, Government Printing Office, Washington, DC, USA.

Uthoff, D., 1978, Endogene und exogene Hemmnisse in der Nutzung des Ernährungspotentials der Meere, 41, Deutscher Geographentag Mainz 1977, Tagungsberichte und Wissenschaftliche Abhandlungen, pp. 347–361, Wiesbaden, Germany.

Valkonen, T., 1991, Assumptions about mortality trends in industrialized countries: A survey, in W. Lutz, ed., *Future Demographic Trends in Europe and North America: What Can We Assume Today?* Academic Press, London, UK.

van de Kaa, D., 1987, Europe's second demographic transition, *Population Bulletin* **42**(1), Population Reference Bureau.

Vandermotten, C., and Vanlaer, J., 1993, Immigrants and the extreme-right vote in Europe and in Belgium, in R. King, ed., *Mass Migration in Europe, the Legacy and the Future*, Belhaven Press, London, UK.

van de Walle, E., Ohadike, P.O., and Sala-Diakanda, M.D., eds., 1988, *The State of African Demography*, IUSSP-Derouaux, Liège, Belgium.

Vaupel, J.W., 1986, How change in age-specific mortality affects life expectancy, *Population Studies* **40**:147–157.

Vaupel, J.W., and Gowan, A.E., 1986, Passage to Methuselah: Some demographic consequences of continued progress against mortality, *American Journal of Public Health* **76**:430–422.

Vaupel, J.W., and Owen, J.M., 1986, Anna's life expectancy, *Journal of Policy Analysis and Management* **5**:383–389.

Vaupel, J.W., and Yashin, A.I., 1983, *The Deviant Dynamics of Death in Heterogeneous Populations*, RR-83-1, International Institute for Applied Systems Analysis, Laxenburg, Austria.

Vaupel, J.W., Manton, K.G., and Stallard, E., 1979, The impact of heterogeneity in individual frailty on the dynamics of mortality, *Demography* **16**:439–454.

Vaupel, J.W., Gambill, B.A., and Yashin, A.I., 1987, *Thousands of Data at a Glance: Shaded Contour Maps of Demographic Surfaces*, RR-87-16, International Institute for Applied Systems Analysis, Laxenburg, Austria.

Verhoef, R., 1986, The Netherlands population registers as a source of international migration statistics, in *National Data Sources and Programmes for Implementing the United Nations Recommendations on Statistics of International Migration*, Department of International Economic and Social Affairs, United Nations, New York, NY, USA.

Vietnam, 1989, Vietnam's new fertility policy, *Population and Development Review* **15**(1):169–172.

Vining, D.R., Jr., 1984, Family salaries and the East German birth rate: A comment, *Population and Development Review* **10**(4):693–696.

Vishnevsky, A., 1991, Demographic revolution and the future of fertility: A systems approach, in W. Lutz, ed., *Future Demographic Trends in Europe and North America: What Can We Assume Today?* Academic Press, London, UK.

Vu, M.T., 1984, *World Population Projections 1984: Short- and Long-Term Estimates by Age and Sex with Related Demographic Statistics*, World Bank, Washington, DC, USA.

Vu, M.T., 1985, *World Population Projections 1985: Short- and Long-Term Estimates by Age and Sex with Related Demographic Statistics*, World Bank/Johns Hopkins University Press, Baltimore, MD, USA.

Wangnick, K., 1990, *IDA Worldwide Desalting Plants Inventory*, Report No. 11, Prepared for the International Desalination Association (Wangnick Consulting), Gnarrenburg, Germany.

Wawer, M.J., Sewankambo, N.K., and Gray, R.H., 1994, Trends in crude prevalence may not reflect incidence in communities with mature epidemics, Paper presented at the Tenth International Conference on AIDS – International Conference on STD, 7–12 August, Yokohama, Japan.

Way, P.O., and Stanecki, K.A., 1994, *The Impact of HIV/AIDS on World Population*, US Government Printing Office, Washington, DC, USA.

Webster's New Collegiate Dictionary, 1974, Merriam-Webster, Springfield, MA, USA.

WECCC (World Energy Conference Conservation Commission), 1983, *Energy 2000–2020: World Prospects and Regional Stresses*, J.R. Frisch, ed., Graham and Trotman, London, UK.

Weintraub, S., and Díaz-Briquets, S., 1992, The Use of Foreign Aid to Reduce Incentives to Emigrate from Central America, Working Paper, Work Employment Programme Research, International Labour Organization, Geneva, Switzerland.

Westing, A.H., 1981, A world in balance, *Environmental Conservation* 8(3): 177–183.

Westoff, Ch.F., 1990, Reproductive intentions and fertility rates, *International Family Planning Perspectives* 16(3):84–89 (September).

Westoff, Ch.F., 1991a, The return to replacement fertility: A magnetic force? in W. Lutz, ed., *Future Demographic Trends in Europe and North America: What Can We Assume Today?* Academic Press, London, UK.

Westoff, Ch.F., 1991b, Reproductive preferences: A comparative view, *Comparative Studies* 3:19–20, Institute for Resources Development, Columbia, MD, USA.

Westoff, Ch.F., and Ochoa, L.H., 1991, *Unmet Need and the Demand for Family Planning*, DHS Comparative Studies No. 5, Institute for Resource Development, Columbia, MD, USA.

Westoff, Ch.F., and Rodríguez, G., forthcoming, *Mass Media and Reproductive Behavior in Kenya: An Illustrative Analysis*.

Westoff, Ch.F., Hammerslough, R., and Paul, L., 1987, The potential impact of improvements in contraception on fertility and abortion in western countries, *European Journal of Population* 3:7–32.

Whelpton, P.K., 1936, An empirical method of calculating future population, *Journal of the American Statistical Association* 31:457–473.

WHO, 1994, The HIV/AIDS pandemic: 1994 overview, Document WHO/GPA/TCO/SEF/94.4, World Health Organization, Geneva, Switzerland.

WHO, 1995a, The current global situation of the HIV/AIDS pandemic, Global Programme on AIDS memo, 3 July, World Health Organization, Geneva, Switzerland.

WHO, 1995b, Unpublished data compiled by the Global Programme on AIDS, World Health Organization, Geneva, Switzerland.

Widgren, J., 1992, *Report for the Intergovernmental Consultations on Asylum, Refugees, and Migration Policies in Europe, North America, and Australia*, IC, Geneva, Switzerland.

Wilkinson, M., 1967, Evidence of long swings in the growth of Swedish population and related economic variables, 1860–1965, *Journal of Economic History* **27** (March).

Woodrow, K.A., and Passel, J.S., 1990, Post-IRCA undocumented immigration to the United States: An assessment based on the June 1988 CPS, in F.D. Bean, B. Edmonston, and J.S. Passel, eds., *Undocumented Migration to the United States: IRCA and the Experience of the 1980s,* Urban Institute Press, Washington, DC, USA.

World Bank, 1978, *World Development Report 1978,* Washington, DC, USA.

World Bank, 1992a, *World Development Report 1992,* World Bank/Oxford University Press, New York, NY, USA.

World Bank, 1992b, *World Population Projections: 1992–1993 Edition,* Johns Hopkins University Press, Baltimore, MD, USA.

World Resources Institute/United Nations Environment Programme/ United Nations Development Programme, 1990, *World Resources, 1990–1991,* Oxford University Press, New York, NY, USA.

World Resources Institute/United Nations Environment Programme/ United Nations Development Programme, 1992, *World Resources, 1992–1993,* Oxford University Press, New York, NY, USA.

Xie, M., Küffner, U., and LeMoigne, G., 1983, *Using Water Efficiently: Technological Options,* Technical Paper No. 205, World Bank, Washington, DC, USA.

Yousif, H., Goujon, A., and Lutz, W., 1996, Future Population Trends and Education in the Countries of Northern Africa, Research Report, International Institute for Applied Systems Analysis, Laxenburg, Austria (forthcoming).

Yuan, J., 1995, Population Projections for China: Part 1, in J. Yu and E. Zhang, eds., *Population Projections for China,* Monograph on the 1990 Population Census of the People's Republic of China, China Statistical Press, Beijing, China.

Zachariah, K.C., and Vu, M.T., 1978, *Population Projections: 1975–2000,* World Bank, Washington, DC, USA.

Zachariah, K.C., and Vu, M.T., 1980, *Population Projections, 1980–2000 and Long-Term (Stationary Population),* World Bank, Washington, DC, USA.

Zachariah, K.C., and Vu, M.T., 1988, *World Population Projections 1987–1988 Edition: Short- and Long-Term Estimates,* World Bank/Johns Hopkins University Press, Baltimore, MD, USA.

Zelinsky, W., 1971, The hypothesis of the mobility transition, *Geographical Review* **61**:219–249.

Zeng, Y., 1989, Is the Chinese family planning program "tightening up"? *Population and Development Review* **15**(2):333–337.

Zimbabwe, 1989, *Zimbabwe Demographic and Health Survey, 1988,* Ministry of Finance, Economic Planning, and Development, Central Statistical Office, Harare, Zimbabwe; and Institute for Resource Development/Macro Systems, Inc., Columbia, MD, USA.

Zlotnik, H., 1987, The concept of international migration as reflected in data collection systems, *International Migration Review* **21**(4):925–946.

Index

Africa
  carrying capacity 389–392
  fertility 69, 73–86
    in sub-Saharan Africa 37,
      63–67, 416–419
    impact of AIDS in 143, 144, 158,
      162, 170–195, 239, 240
    HIV seroprevalence/AIDS
      mortality 164,174
    past trends 176–182
    projection of mortality for the
      continent 182–194
    summary of projection model
      182–188
    trends in HIV infections/AIDS
      worldwide 170–176
  migration flows
    North Africa 317–319
    sub-Saharan Africa 312–317
  mortality in sub-Saharan Africa
    149–169
    colonial period (1920–59)
      150–154
    prospects 160–169
    since independence 155–160
  probabilistic projections 397–428
  summary results 441–444
aging, population 27, 28, 382–386,
  388, 389, 392–394
  population growth *versus* aging
    social crisis/fertility increase 386,
    387, 433–434
AIDS 143, 144, 148, 162
  epidemological factors 167, 168
  global trends in mortality 170–194
    impact on population growth
      189–193
    past trends 176–182
    projections 182–194
alternative approaches to population
  projections 14–43, 397–428
  customers/clients for 15–18
  expected output parameters 24–29
    age/sex composition 27, 28
    multistate models 28, 29

  total population size 25–27
  interactions among components/
    feedback from results 38–40
  non-probabilistic approaches
    32–34
  past experience/assumptions for
    the future 29–32
    future as continuation of past
      trend 29
    structure/understanding from
      history 30
    uncertainty 34–38
    variance from history 30
  population aging
    growth *versus* aging 386, 387,
      433–434
  population size by region 406–410
  probabilistic approaches 34–38,
    397–428
  spatial resolution/heterogeneity
    22–24
  time horizon 18–22
Arab States, fertility in 61–63
Asia 88–101
  4th Asian and Pacific Population
    Conference (APPC) 89, 90
  fertility in
    East and Southeast Asia 49–53,
      88–101
    South Asia 53–57
  land-carrying capacity 204
  migration flows
    East and Southeast Asia
      326–328
    South Asia 324–326
    West Asia 317–319
  mortality in 137–138
  population policies/
    family-planning Southeast
      Asia 99–113
    demographic situation 89–90
    policies and programs 90–99
    program effectiveness 99–101
  probabilistic projections 397–428

495

summary results 441, 442,
    445–448, 450
    water resources 219
asylum seekers 310–312

baby boom/echoes of 19, 21, 69, 269,
    386, 387
Bali Declaration 90
Bangladesh, fertility rates in 53, 54,
    55
Bariloche Model 40
Beyond the Limits (Meadows) 196
bioengineering 229–230
Bogue, D J 10, 13
Bongaarts, J 170–195
breeding programs, animal 224–230
Bucht, B 133–148

Caribbean
    migration flows 329–331
    mortality rates in 134, 138, 139
    summary results 441, 442, 456
    water resources 219
Carter, T 237
Central America
    migration flows 329–331
    mortality rates in 139–144
    summary results 441, 442
    see also Latin America
Central Asia, summary results 441,
    442, 448
child survival programs 148
childlessness 262–266
China
    fertility in 49–52, 102–130,
        385–387, 392, 393, 406–416
    migration flows 328, 329
    population aging 392–394
    summary results 441, 442, 445
circumcision and susceptibility to
    HIV infection 175–176
Clark, C 197
Cleland, J 47–72
climate, effect of 222–224, 233–237
Club of Rome 10, 11
Cohen, J 197, 246–248
cohort fertility 258–262
Concepcion, M B 88–101
confidence interval 400–428
consumerism and fertility 273, 274
contraceptives 274, 275
correlated variables 399–428

Demographic and Health Survey
    (DHS) 55, 60, 65, 73, 74, 80, 81,
        83, 136, 155, 160–164
developing countries

fertility in 45–130
    China 49–52, 102–130, 385–387,
        392, 393, 406–416
    population policies/
        family-planning Southeast
        Asia 88–101
    regional review 49–72
future mortality in 131–249
    impact of AIDS in Africa 143,
        144, 162, 164, 167, 169,
        170–195
    population carrying capacity
        196–249
    sub-Saharan Africa 149–169
    trends: a survey 133–148
    summary results 461
    see also migration,
        intercontinental
DIALOG 372

Eastern Europe, summary results
    441, 442, 451
ecological constraints
    mechanisms 203
ecological limits 233–237
Economic and Social Commission for
    Asia and the Pacific (ESCAP)
    88, 89
economic barriers 202, 203
education factor 40, 156–159
Ehrlich, P 198
energy demand models 16
environmental factors 15–16, 203,
    222–238
    catastrophes 348, 349
ethnic rivalry and fertility 270
European part of former Soviet
    Union, summary results 441,
    442, 452
EUROSTAT 233

Falkenmark, M 213
family-planning policies/programs
    18, 90–101
    demographic situation 89, 90
    effectiveness 99–101
    Indonesia 90–92
    Malaysia 92, 93
    the Philippines 93–95
    Singapore 95, 96
    Thailand 96, 97
    Vietnam 97–99
family size/childlessness 262–266
feedbacks 38–40, 199, 387–393
Feeney, G 102–130, 253–277, 362–366
fertility, future 45–130, 253–277,
    362–366

in China 102–130
  decline: international
      perspective on 103–109
  decline: single-year time series
      109–114
  period parity progression
      measures (PPPRs)
      114–121
  scenarios for future change
      121–125
in developing countries 47–130
  fertility forecasts 77–80
  reproductive preferences 73–87
  trends: 1930–1995 47–72
IIASA scenario assumptions
      361–428
  consumerism/use of time 273,
      274
  desired family size/
      childlessness 39, 262–266
  economic independence of
      women 272
  fertility assumptions/
      population heterogeneity
      266–277
  fertility cycles 267–269
  homeostatis 266, 267
  improving contraception 274,
      275
  individualism, trend to 271, 272
  in industrialized countries
      253–277
  methodology in scenarios 403,
      404
  national identity/ethnic rivalry
      270
  partnership formation/dissolution
      254–258
  partnership instability 273
  period/cohort fertility 258–262
  pronatalistic policies 269, 270
  population policies/
      family-planning Southeast
      Asia 88–101
    demographic situation 89, 90
    policies/programs 90–99
    program effectiveness 99–101
  regional review 47–72
    the Arab States 61–63
    East and Southeast Asia 49–53
    Island states 67
    Latin America 57–61
    South Asia 53–57
    sub-Saharan Africa 63–67
    synthesis/implications for the
      future 68–72
fertilizer application 226, 227

Food and Agriculture Organization
      (FAO) forecasts 16
food processing 230–232
Forrester–Meadows Group 40
fossil energy 224, 225
'Frankenfood' *see* synthetic food
      production
Frejka, T 3–13

Garenne, M 149–169
global warming 16, 203
Goldstein, J R 14–43
Goujon, A 361-396

Heilig, G H 196–249
Herrera, A D *et al.*
heterogeneity, population 275–277,
      339
  spatial resolution and 22–24
HIV/AIDS in Africa 143, 144, 162,
      164, 167–195
  global patterns 172–176
  past trends 176–182
  projections 182–195
homeostatis 266, 267

India, fertility rates in 56, 57
individualism, trend to 271, 272
Indonesia, family-planning
      policies/programs 90–92
industrialized countries
  future fertility in 253–277
  future mortality in 278–295
  summary results 460
International Institute for Applied
      Systems Analysis (IIASA)
  special scenarios to 2100 361–428
    and other projections 401
    compared with UN/World Bank
      projections 394–396
    confidence interval 400–428
    interaction scenarios for selected
      regions 387–394
    motivation 399, 400
    probabilistic projections
      397–428
international migration theories
      339–345
International Passenger Survey 303
irrigation 227–229
Island states, fertility in 67
Israel, migration flows 319, 320

Keyfitz, N 14, 274

land-carrying capacity 196–212,
      234–236, 389–392

Latin America, fertility in 57–61
   summary results 441, 442, 456
Lexis maps of mortality 288–290
life expectancy 291, 292
Lundström, H 278–295
Lutz, W 14–43, 253–277, 361–396,
   397–428, 429–435

Malaysia family-planning
      policies/programs 92, 93
   fertility rates 52
Middle East, summary results 441,
   442, 449
migration, intercontinental 297–357,
   369–372
   asylum seekers 310–312
   data classification 304–310
   future South–North migration
      361, 362, 369–375
      definitions 337–339
      international migration theories
         339–345
      policies 353–357
      pull factors 350–353
      push factors 345–344
   IIASA scenario assumptions
      369–372
   methodology in scenarios 404
   past trends: a review 299–335
      Central America/Caribbean
         329–331
      China 328, 329
      East and Southeast Asia
         326–328
      Israel 319, 320
      North Africa/West Asia
         317–319
      oil-rich countries 320–324
      South America 331–333
      South Asia 324–326
      sub-Saharan Africa 312–317
   statistics 300–312
Monte Carlo simulation methods 36
mortality 20, 37, 133–195, 278–295,
   366–369
   IIASA scenario assumptions
      366–369
   methodology in 404
   impact of AIDS in Africa 170–195
      global patterns 172–176
      past trends 176–182
      projections 182–195
   in developing countries 131–195
      comparison of projections 145,
         146
      pace of decline 147, 148
      projections 140–145
      trends since 1950 134–140

   in industrialized countries 278–295
      85 or 100+ 280–284
      force of mortality: at 85, 90,
         and 95 284–286
      force of mortality: Lexis maps
         288–290
      reduction in mortality rates
         286–288
      remaining life expectancy
         291–293
   population carrying capacity
      196–249, 382–392
      dimensions of 199–205
      ecological limits 233–237
      natural resources 205–225
      social, economic, and political
         dimensions 238–241
      technical limitations/chances
         225–233
   sub-Saharan Africa 149–169
      assumptions about future
         trends 140–144, 160–168
      changes in pace of decline 147,
         148
      past assumptions/actual
         performance compared
         145, 146
      since 1950 134–140
      trends 133–148

national identity and fertility 270
Nepal, fertility rates in 53–55
net primary production (NPP),
   earth's 199, 200
North Africa
   migration flows 317–319
   summary results 441–443
North America, summary results
   441, 442, 457–459
Notestein, F 6, 7

Öberg, S 336–357
oil-rich countries, migration flows
   320–324
old-age dependency ratio 17
   see also industrialized countries,
      future mortality in

Pacific Asia, summary results 441,
   442, 446
Pacific OECD, summary results 441,
   442, 447
Pakistan, fertility rates in 54, 55
Parry, M L 237
partnership formation/dissolution
      trends 254–258
   partnership instability 273

Pearl, R 4
period fertility 258–262
period parity progression measures
    (PPPRs) 114–117
  in China 117–120
persecution, fertility and 347
Philippines family-planning
    policies/programs 93–95
  fertility rates 52, 53
population aging 382–386, 388, 389
  in China 392, 393
  versus population growth 386,
    387, 433, 434
population carrying capacity, global
    4, 196–249, 389–392
  dimensions of
    ecological constraints/feedback
      mechanisms 199–205
    economic barriers 202, 203
    hypothetical maximum capacity
      199
    social, cultural, and political
      conditions 204, 205
    technical/logistic restrictions
      and chances 201
  ecological limits 233–237
    climate change 236, 237
    genetic engineering/advanced
      breeding practices 236
    shrinking systems 234
    soil degradation/water pollution
      234
  natural resources 205–225
    climate 222–224
    fossil energy input 224, 225
    land 205–212
    water 213–222
  social, economic, and political
    dimensions 238–241
  technical limitations/chances
    225–233
    breeding/bioengineering 229,
      230
    fertilizer application 226, 227
    food processing 230
    irrigation 227–229
    limitations 232, 233
    synthetic food production 230,
      231
population heterogeneity 275–277
population policies/family-planning
  in developing countries 64, 65, 71,
    73–87
    determinants of reproductive
      preferences 80, 81
    fertility forecasts 77–80
    individual-level analysis 83–86
    regional-level analysis 81–83

reproductive preferences
  in industrialized countries 258–277
    arguments assuming higher
      fertility 266–270
    arguments assuming lower
      fertility 271–275
    desired family size/
      childlessness 262–266
    fertility assumptions/
      population heterogeneity
      275–277
    partnership formation/
      dissolution trends 254–258
    period/cohort fertility trends
      258–262
  in Southeast Asia 88–101
    demographic situation 89, 90
    family-planning
      policies/programs 90–99
    program effectiveness 99–101
population projections 3–13, 359–428
  alternative approaches 14–43
    age–sex composition 27, 28
    spatial resolution 22–24
    time horizon 18–22
  confidence interval 400–428
  lessons learned 3–13
    contemporary long-range
      projections 8–11
    early global projections:
      extrapolations 4
    modern global component
      projections 4–7
    recent critical review 11, 12
  unavoidable *versus* avoidable
    growth 432
population projection scenarios
    361–396
  comparison with other projections
    394–396
  scenarios with independent trends
    372–387
    model assumptions 372–375
    population size 375–382
    population aging 382–384,
      392–394
    population aging *versus*
      population growth 386, 387
  special scenarios 357–394
    migration and aging process
      385–389
    carrying capacity in
      sub-Saharan Africa
      389–392
    population aging in China
      392–394
  synthesis of expert views
    fertility 361–366

migration 369–372
mortality 366–369
world projection 419–427
population stabilization 429–435
dilemmas 429–435
trends 429–431
versus low mortality 431–433
probabilistic population projections
397–428
confidence intervals 400–428
methodology 403–406
fertility 403, 404
interrelationships 405
migration 404
mortality 404
motivation 399, 400
results
correlated fertility and
mortality 416–419
regional population sizes
406–410
regional age structure 410–416
world projections 419–428
poverty 347
Prinz, C 14–43
pronatalistic policies 269, 270

regional definitions 437–440
reproductive behavior/preferences
see population policies/family
planning

Sanderson W 361–428
Scherbov S 361–428
Singapore, family-planning
policies/programs 95, 96, 99,
100
social loneliness 349
South America
migration flows 331–333
mortality rates in 140–144
see also Latin America
Southeast Asia *see* Asia
South–North migration 336–357
definitions 337–339
IIASA scenario assumptions
369–372
international migration theories
339–345
policies 353–357
pull factors 350–353
push factors 345–349
spatial resolution/heterogeneity
22–24
starvation 347
sub-Saharan Africa
carrying capacity 389–392

fertility in 63–67
migration flows 312–317
mortality in 131–195
adults 156
colonial period 150–154
epidemiological factors 167–169
public health/primary health
care 157–160
recent evolution 160–164
socioeconomic correlates
152–154, 156, 157
sociopolitical factors 164–167
summary results 441, 442, 444
synthetic food production 230–232

Thailand, family-planning
policies/programs 96, 97, 100
Tsui, A O 10

Ultimate Resource (Simon) 196
United Nations projections 7, 9, 13,
23, 24, 33, 41, 133, 394–396
*Ground Water in North and West
Africa* 213

Vaupel, J W 278–295
Vietnam
family-planning policies/
programs 97–99

water, global availability 213–222
Western Europe, summary results
441, 442, 453–455
Westoff, C F 73–87
women, economic independence of
272
World3 model 40
World Bank projections 23, 41,
394–396
World Development Report (World
Bank) 143, 144
World Fertility Survey (WFS) 60,
63, 74, 136, 138, 155
World Population Monitoring (UN)
133
World Population Projections
(World Bank) 143, 394–396
World Population Prospects (UN) 7,
9, 13, 24, 48, 394–396
World Resources Institute (WRI)
205–213
world summary results 462

Xie, N *et al.* 227

Zlotnik, H 299–335